PHOTO
JOURNALISM

THE PROFESSIONALS' APPROACH

Kenneth Kobré
Editing & Design by Betsy Brill
SIXTH EDITION

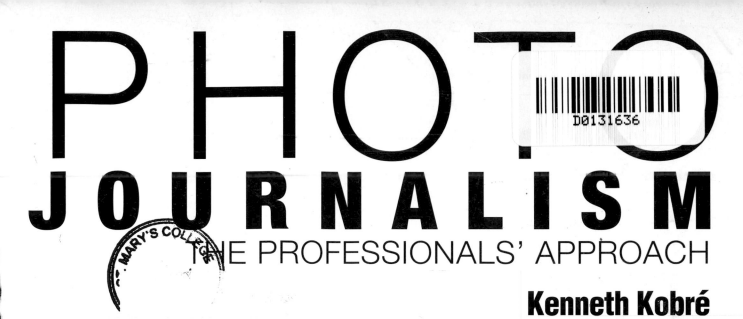

Firefighters snuff an electrical fire aboard an airplane parked on a Boston runway. George Rizer, *Boston Globe*

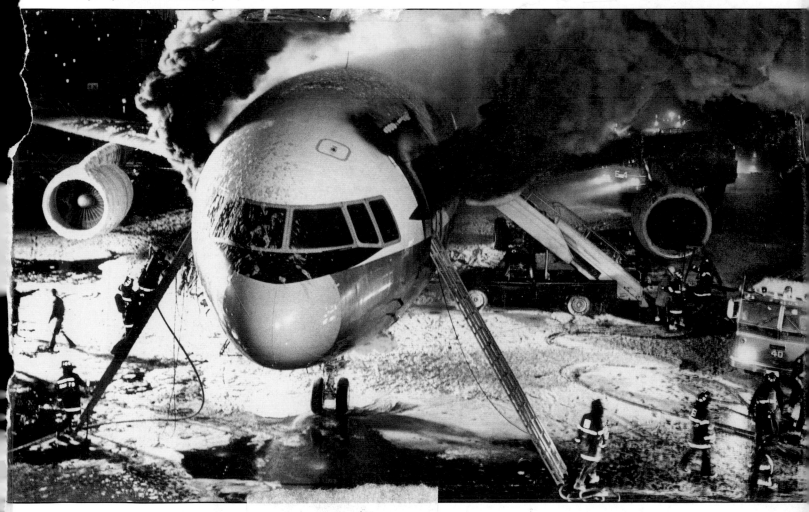

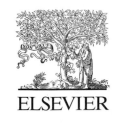

AMSTERDAM • BOSTON • HEIDELBERG • LONDON
NEW YORK • OXFORD • PARIS • SAN DIEGO
SAN FRANCISCO • SINGAPORE • SYDNEY • TOKYO

Focal Press is an imprint of Elsevier

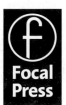

ELSEVIER

Focal Press

Publisher: Marie Hooper
Acquisitions Editor: Cara Anderson
Publishing Services Manager: George Morrison
Senior Project Manager: Dawnmarie Simpson
Associate Acquisitions Editor: Asma Palmerio
Assistant Editor: Katy Stencer
Marketing Manager: Christine Degon Veroulis
Cover Design: Eric DeCicco

Focal Press is an imprint of Elsevier
30 Corporate Drive, Suite 400, Burlington, MA 01803, USA
Linacre House, Jordan Hill, Oxford OX2 8DP, UK

Cover design and interior design: Betsy Brill, San Francisco
Line art illustration and design of Digital Darkroom special section: Ben Barbante, San Francisco

Cover photograph: Oded Balilty, Associated Press/Wide World Photos
*A Jewish settler struggles with an Israeli security officer during clashes that erupted as authorities evacuated the West
Bank settlement outpost of Amona, east of the Palestinian town of Ramallah.*

Library of Congress Cataloging-in-Publication Data
Kobré, Kenneth, 1946-
    Photojournalism : the professionals approach / Kenneth Kobré. – 6th ed.
        p. cm.
    Includes bibliographical references and index.
    ISBN 978-0-7506-8593-1 (pbk. : alk. paper) 1. Photojournalism. I. Brill, Betsy. II. Title.
    TR820.K75 2008
    070.4'9–dc22

                                2007039440

British Library Cataloguing-in-Publication Data
A catalogue record for this book is available from the British Library.

ISBN: 978-0-7506-8593-1

For information on all Focal Press publications
visit our website at www.books.elsevier.com

08 09 10 11 5 4 3 2 1

Printed in China.

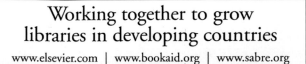

**Working together to grow
libraries in developing countries**

www.elsevier.com | www.bookaid.org | www.sabre.org

ELSEVIER   BOOK AID
            International   Sabre Foundation

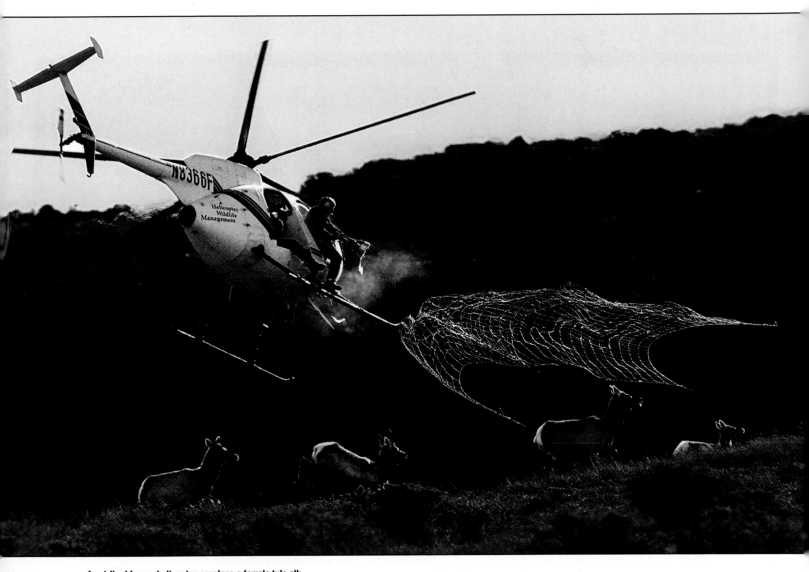

A net fired from a helicopter envelops a female tule elk. Scientists take specimens and measurements from the elk and attach a radio collar to track the movement and habits of the 270 animals in the area. John Burgess, *Santa Rosa Press Democrat*

Dedication

This book is dedicated
to my parents, Reva and Sidney Kobre.

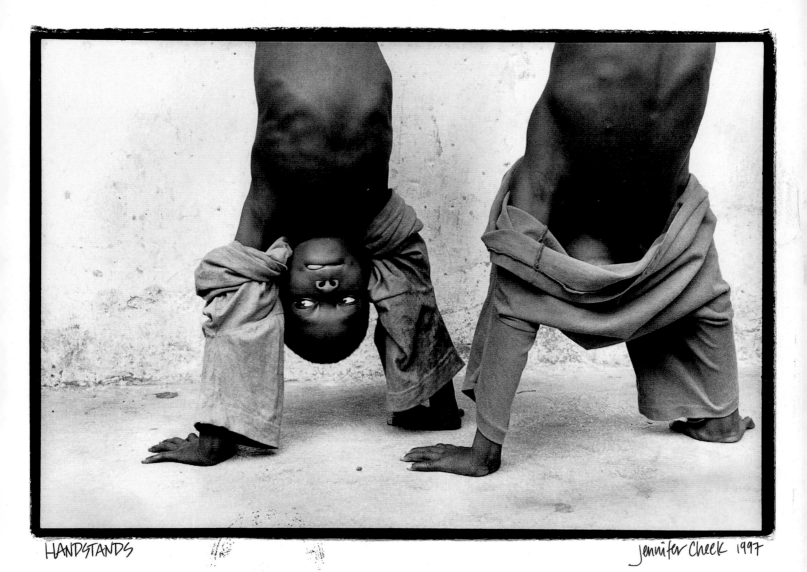

HANDSTANDS   Jennifer Cheek 1997

Children perform handstands at the Lafanmi Selavi, a home for 350 street kids in Haiti. Jennifer Cheek Pantaléon, Pacifica, California

Contents

Dedication   iii
Preface   vi
Acknowledgments   vii

CHAPTER

ONE ■ Assignment 2   **ELEVEN** ■ Photo Story 228

TWO ■ Spot News 26   **TWELVE** ■ Multimedia 268

THREE ■ General News 48   **THIRTEEN** ■ Video 306

FOUR ■ Features 64   **FOURTEEN** ■ Illustration 334

FIVE ■ Portraits 80   **FIFTEEN** ■ Ethics 352

SIX ■ Sports 96   **SIXTEEN** ■ Law 390

SEVEN ■ Photo Editing 124   **SEVENTEEN** ■ History 414

EIGHT ■ Camera Bag 154   **EIGHTEEN** ■ Turning Pro 454

NINE ■ Strobe 178   **Special Section** ■ Digital Darkroom 468

         Selected Bibliography 482
         Index 495

TEN ■ Covering the Issues 202

Preface

The Internet and its increasing capacity for broadband distribution of the news are changing print and broadcast journalism, as is the availability of digital equipment from still cameras and audio recorders to video cameras and editing software.

As new media technologies converge toward news distribution on the Internet, journalistic skills and job descriptions are merging rapidly, too.

This morning's newspaper photojournalist is likely to be this afternoon's multimedia producer or tomorrow's videographer. The picture taker may be called on to record sound, to write, narrate, and edit stories.

Will the story be told in a single image on paper, or will it spill forward on the Internet as a multimedia piece containing dozens of still images supported by audio interviews, and video? Will video documentaries distributed on the Internet become the primary vehicle for journalistic storytelling?

As the sixth edition of this book goes to press, answers to these questions are playing out in news organizations around the world. How does this new reality change the role of the photojournalist—and the education and preparation of that photojournalist?

Technologies change. Media change. The need to recognize news and convey it clearly has not. Visual storytelling skills are more vital than they have ever been.

For more than 27 years this book's goal has remained the same—to prepare journalists with cameras. From the first edition of *Photojournalism*:

A first-time bull rider takes a spill at the annual rodeo at the Howard County Fairgrounds.
Rich Riggins, Patuxent [Maryland] Publishing Co.

Photojournalists report with cameras; their job is to search out news, recording it in visual form.... Today's news photographers must combine the skills of an investigative reporter and the determination of a beat reporter with the flair of a feature writer. The resulting pictures do not merely supplement the news stories of the day as tangential illustrations or serve as ornaments to break up the gray type on the page. Today's photos represent the best means available to report human events concisely and effectively.

Preface, ***Photojournalism: The Professionals' Approach***, 1980

Yes, new media are changing the necessary technical skills a photojournalist must bring to the job, but today, more crucial than ever, is the JOURNALISM in photojournalism. ∎

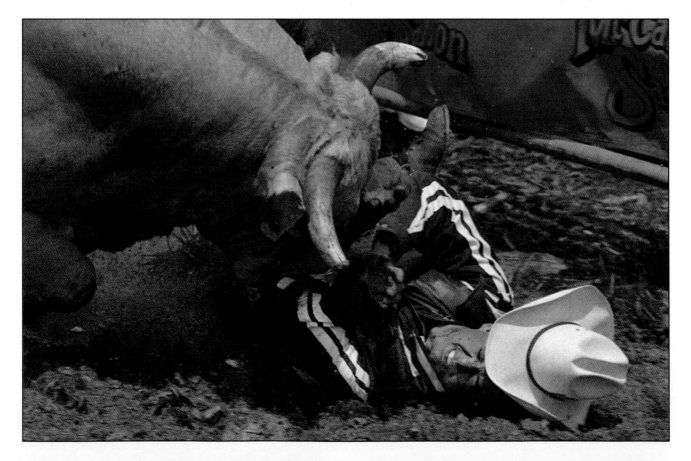

Acknowledgments

As always, my thanks go to my parents, Dr. and Mrs. Sidney Kobré. Without their advice and guidance, I would never have written the first edition of this book. My father, who was a reporter, editor, and professor of journalism, helped give the book its clear journalistic focus. His specialty was the history of journalism. My mother, also a writer, suggested many ways to improve the prose of the original manuscript.

This edition of the book would have never obtained its look nor even been completed without the devotion, love, and expertise of Betsy Brill, my wife. For nearly a year and a half, through many rewrites, she guided the revision from initial idea to the final design of the printed page. Her experience as a professional photojournalist, writer, editor, and designer helped bring my abstract ideas into reality. Our daughter, Daria, says that the completion of each new edition is like a renewal of our marriage vows.

For some books, the author goes to the mountaintop and writes. That has never been the case with this book. This book has always been based on interviews—both formal and informal—with working pros on newspapers, magazines, wire services, and now web sites. I have mentioned their names in the text whenever possible. Without their expertise and time, this book would not be complete.

Numerous photographers, photo editors, academics, students, and lawyers have read parts of this and previous editions. Their thoughtful suggestions improve each revision. I greatly appreciate their time and effort. Profound thanks to this edition's reviewers: Rich Beckman, Bo Bogatin, Keith Birmingham, Hal Buell, John Burgess, Sean Connelley, Travis Fox, Jesse Garnier, Bruce Gilbert, Jack Gruber, David Guralnick, John Hewitt, John Kaplan, Tom Kennedy, John Knowlton, Kim Komenich, David Leeson, John Long, Jim MacMillan, Brad Mangin, John McDonough, Jim McNay, Peter Menzel, Josh Meltzer, Kent Porter, Pete Souza, Brian Smale, Brian Smith, Brian Storm, Kathy Strauss, Cammie Toloui, James Wagstaffe, David Weintraub, and Hal Wells.

Jimmy Colton, Steve Fine, and Porter Binks at *Sports Illustrated* welcomed me into their offices to document their work for "Inside *Sports Illustrated*," on the enclosed DVD. Rudy Winston and Jim Rose at Canon reviewed technical material, as did Nikon's Lindsay Silverman and Scott Frier. Nikon made a vital extended loan of its equipment. Santiago Lyon, Colin Crawford, and Ellen Erwitt helped me obtain critical images.

Almost all the photos have been lent to me by photographers, some of whom I know and others I've not had the honor to meet; some former students and some current ones. Their credits appear next to each of their pictures. I thank them all for their generous contribution to this project. A book of this scope and quality would be impossible without their collaboration.

I also am grateful to the news organizations large and small that generously allow their photographers' work to appear here.

I am proud and honored that many photographers who share images tell me they used the book when they were students or were just starting out. I also hear from contributers who used an earlier edition as students and who now are teaching and assigning it to their own students. They and their images reach a new generation.

Liz Forst edited the manuscript. Rhoda Feldman and, especially, Barbara Oleksiw applied eagle eyes to proofing. Paolo Vescia shot many demo pictures. Michele Kackovic helped prepare pictures. Ben Barbante's skill in explaining technical material with clear drawings is formidable.

Diane Heppner at Focal Press encouraged me to undertake this revision. I taxed all my Focal Press editors' patience with requests for more pages and the need to push deadlines to fill them. Cara Anderson, who took Diane's place, went the extra mile in accommodating those requests.

My department chairman at San Francisco State University, Erna Smith, was supportive of my work, as was our dean, Paul Sherwin. My associate, Scot Tucker, helped me hold the pieces of the puzzle together at school.

Finally, like a chemist's research lab, my classes at SFSU continue to allow me the opportunity to experiment on new approaches to photojournalism, particularly the picture story, the portrait, and now, new media. I thank my students for undergoing the trials and tribulations of exploring new ways to tell stories photographically. These experiments have resulted in several extensive photo and writing projects, parts of which appear in this book. ∎

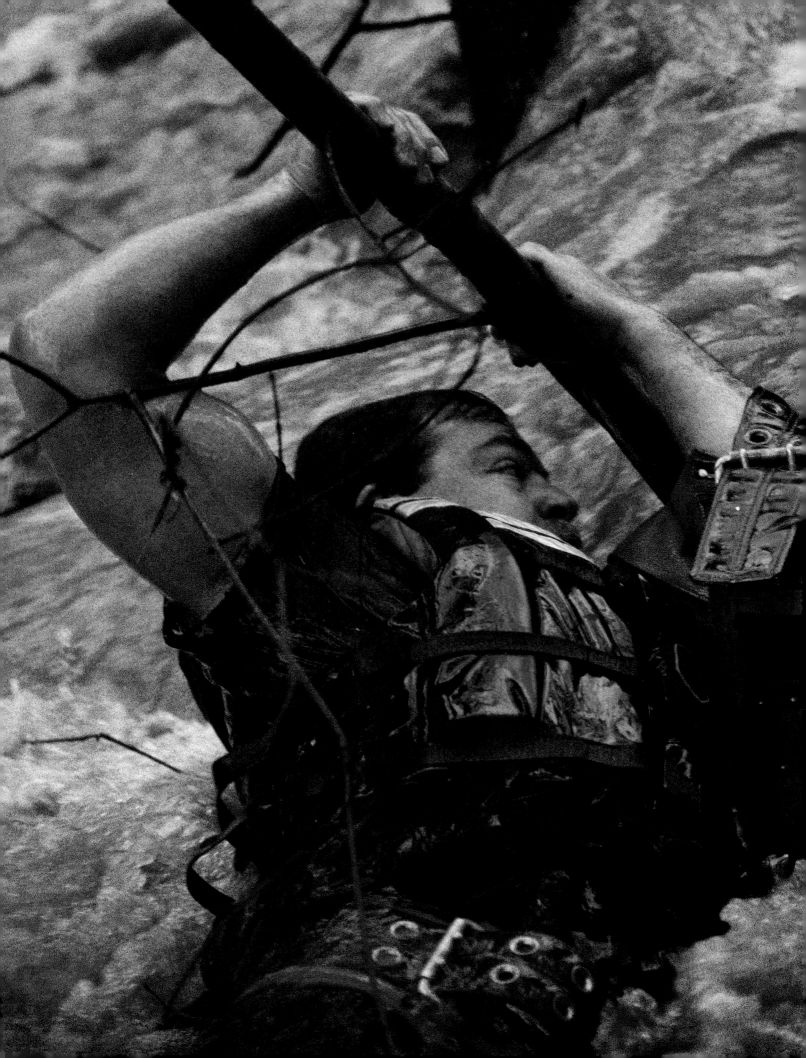

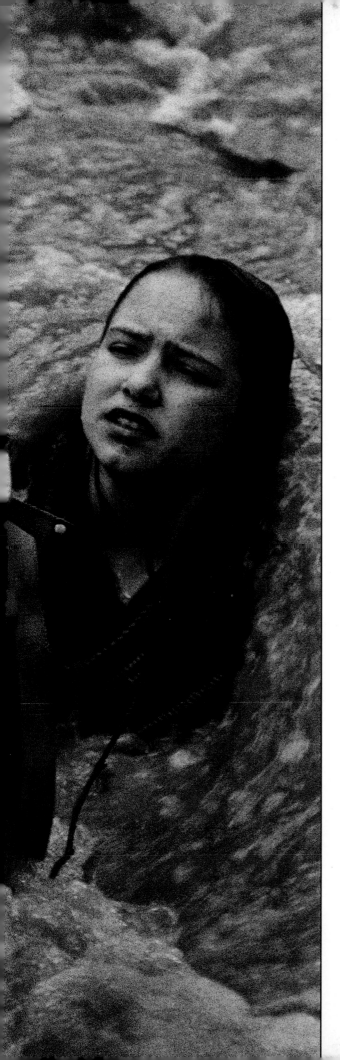

PHOTO
JOURNALISM
THE PROFESSIONALS' APPROACH

The exhausted rescuer was making his third and final attempt to save the girl. The rescue was successful.
Annie Wells, for the *Santa Rosa Press Democrat*

.1

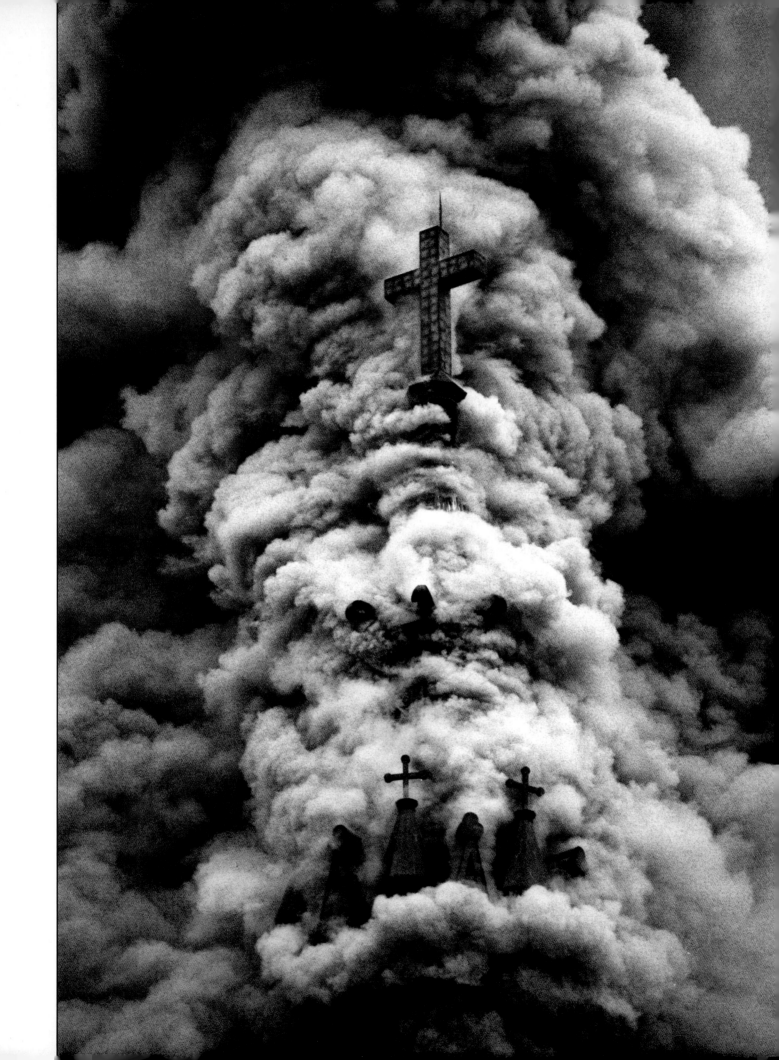

Assignment

WHERE TO FIND NEWS

Steve Linsenmayer, of the *Fort Wayne* (Indiana) *News-Sentinel*, heard the newsroom's emergency band scanner cackle, "Structure fire." Looking out the window of the newsroom, he saw black rain clouds covering a sky broken by distant lightning.

Linsenmayer hesitated to race out into the storm until his boss, Keith Hitchens, came running down the hall yelling, "Church fire."

Hitchens had heard the second call on the radio asking for more fire companies and identifying the burning structure as St. Mary's Church.

"Oh shit," Linsenmayer gasped as he grabbed his camera bag on the way to his car.

The photographer heard about this out-of-control fire at a nearby church by monitoring the emergency scanner radio. Steve Linsenmayer, *Fort Wayne News-Sentinel*

When he got to St. Mary's, the lightning storm that had started the blaze was still in full glory. Within minutes of starting to shoot, Linsenmayer's umbrella blew out, so he radioed back to the office to send more photographers—and dry towels.

About an hour later, heavy smoke started to billow out of the rear steeple. Linsenmayer kept shooting as he captured the shot of the church's crosses enveloped by smoke. The photo filled nearly the entire front page of the next day's edition (see page 2).

NEWS HAPPENS
SCANNER RADIO SIGNALS FIRES AND ACCIDENTS

Most dramatic news photographs result not from city desk assignments but from vigilant photographers who monitor scanner radios to learn about breaking news situations. Police, fire, and other emergency agencies communicate with cops and firefighters in the field via low frequency, very high frequency (VHF), and ultra-high frequency (UHF) radio wave bands. Each agency—the police, the highway patrol, Coast Guard—broadcasts on a different frequency. A scanner radio automatically switches from one frequency to another, stopping whenever a transmission is occurring. The scanner continually rotates through the frequencies it is programmed to listen for. By monitoring a scanner radio, a photographer

can listen to transmissions from all the emergency agencies in an area. If a warehouse fire takes place, the dispatcher will call for fire engines and give a location. By noting the number of the alarms (indicating the size of the fire), the number of engines called, and the location, a photographer can determine the magnitude of a blaze, its news value, and whether it will be burning by the time the photojournalist arrives on the scene.

Jim MacMillan, a winner of the Pulitzer Prize who has covered spot news for the *Philadelphia Daily News* for years, says 90 percent of his tips come from listening to the scanner radio—make that four scanners, all of which he monitors simultaneously. He recommends keeping one scanner tuned to the citywide police, one to local police, one to the fire department, and one to pick up transmissions from the local TV news desk, as well as the Coast Guard and airport.

Sam Costanza, on contract with the *New York Post*, spends six nights a week parked near the intersection of three main highways that lead to New York's boroughs—all the while monitoring the transmissions of the New York Police Department's special operations section. "I'm a listener," he says. "There aren't many listeners. Other photographers respond to assignments. By the time they arrive, I'm already leaving the scene."

Political groups like this one demonstrating in front of an abortion clinic in Wichita, Kansas, often tip off the media about the time and place of their protests. Kim Johnson, for the *Wichita* [Kansas] *Eagle*

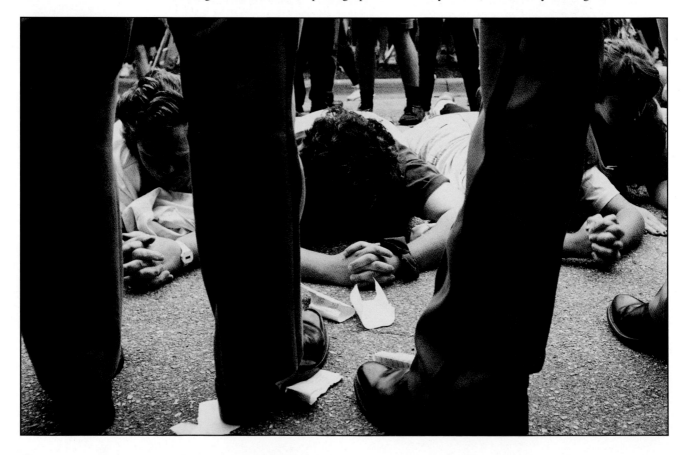

Kent Porter of the *Santa Rosa Press Democrat* covers spot news—news that occurs without warning—in rural Northern California. He tracks the action with four antennae on his Toyota Tacoma as well as a scanner inside his house. He monitors scanner transmissions, carries a cell phone, and stays tuned to local news radio. He says the antennae make his truck look like a centipede.

Different agencies use their own special codes when talking on the air. Porter knows he is heading out for a strong-arm robbery or assault with a weapon when he hears "211." He also knows to "be on the lookout" when he hears "B-O-L," and that "code 20" means an officer needs immediate assistance. In New York Costanza knows that a "1045, code one," means a fire-related death.

Although there are no uniform codes from one city to another, stores that sell scanner radios usually have printed copies of local codes available.

The codes tell photographers what is taking place, but they do not always indicate the importance of the action. Every photographer interviewed for this chapter said that the tension in a dispatcher's voice reveals an emergency's significance. "I listen for the voices

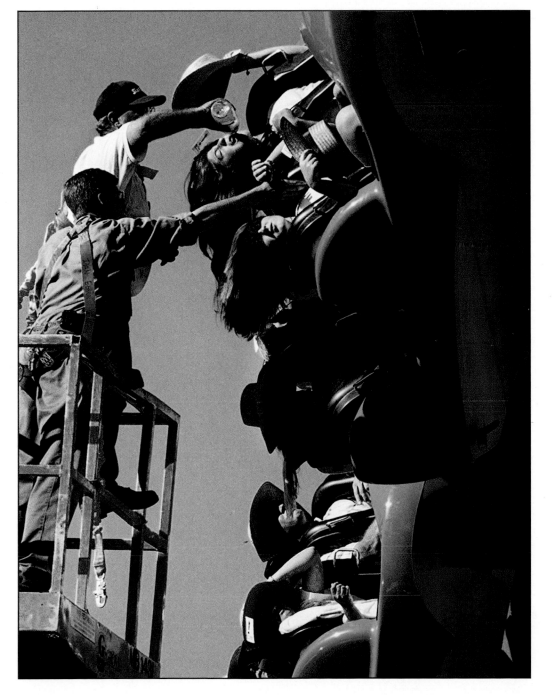

In near-100-degree heat at Marine World, staff members distribute hats and water to stranded riders after a cable broke on the thrill ride Boomerang. The photographer heard the tip on an all-news-radio station while driving home. Dean Coppola, *Contra Costa* [California] *Times*

on the scanner," says Santa Rosa's Porter. "The stress in their voices will tell you so much." The *Post*'s Costanza puts it this way: "The dispatchers have distinctive voices— you can tell when they are alarmed. Listen hard and quick. You might only get one shot at it."

STAY TUNED TO ALL-NEWS RADIO, TELEVISION, AND WEB SITES

Alternatives include all-news radio stations, television stations that provide frequently updated news reports, and web sites that post the latest information as soon as it comes across the wires. MacMillan in Philadelphia begins each day by checking all the local newspaper, TV, and radio news sites as well as wire service date books, and activist calendars.

An all-news radio station or a cable network like Cable News Network (CNN) interrupts in-progress programming immediately if an emergency arises. These stations monitor several scanner channels, including the fire and police departments, and will announce when a major fire alarm or multicar accident occurs. Radio alerted Dean Coppola to riders trapped on a stalled roller coaster at a local theme park. He was the first still shooter on the scene. With temperatures nearing 100 degrees, park workers started distributing water and hats to the people on the ride. Shooting with a 400mm lens, Coppola took a page-one picture based on a tip from the all-news-radio station.

The all-news channel's weather forecaster monitors natural disasters such as hurricanes or tornadoes. The information provided by all-news stations is not as immediate as what you will learn on a scanner, but their reports often will suffice. See if your community has a local Internet site that provides up-to-the-minute news tips. Sites like these feed data directly from all the emergency services in the area. You may even be able to download these feeds onto your cell phone.

For magazine and freelance photographers working overseas, CNN as well as the BBC and MSNBC provide around-the-clock news updates. Even photographers covering huge, breaking, international stories turn to one of the 24-hour outlets to get news in English and see how the rest of the world is receiving the story. Cell phones with Internet access also can provide nearly instant access to developing news.

Today, many photojournalists on foreign assignments carry laptop computers with modems that allow them to track developing stories on the web and, of course, transmit pictures and stay in touch with editors.

USE CONTACTS

Michael Meinhardt of the *Chicago Tribune* has developed his own system of finding out about local spot news as it happens. Using a system of pagers, two-way radios, cellular phones, and a network of sources and contacts, he stays abreast of news as it breaks in the Chicago and greater-Chicago area.

Firefighters, police officers, dispatchers, and even air-traffic controllers at surrounding airports notify Meinhardt of news events via a voice-message pager that he carries 24 hours a day. He has befriended these contacts at other news events, where he introduced himself, left a business card, and followed up by giving them photographs of themselves at work.

"You'd be surprised how many of them remember me when the news breaks," he says.

"Additionally," he explains, "I belong to a network of contacts led by a local radio news reporter who is considered the dean of spot news. . . . We all have two-way radios on our own frequency that we monitor around the clock. . . . Once the closest person arrives on the scene, I can usually ascertain whether it's worth traveling to shoot pictures. They can also let me know how urgently I need to get there before the scene clears up."

Not surprisingly, Meinhardt is considered a great source of information by his colleagues in the newsroom and also by the newspaper's city desk.

Bruce Chambers of the *Orange County Register*, who has been nominated for the Pulitzer six times, recommends talking to the police and to firefighters. He goes even further and recommends giving them pictures you have taken of them if your news organization allows. To find stories, Chambers reads the events calendar at City Hall. Of course he reads his own paper, but he does not stop there. He reads every news outlet in the area.

Chambers may have an edge when it comes to story ideas, though—a secret and proprietary source. "My mom is my favorite source for ideas," he reveals.

TIPS HELP

News organizations often get leads on top news stories when people call or write with tips. In fact, some newspapers, web sites, and a few magazines offer monetary rewards for tips. The desk editor sizes up the event; then, if the decision is to respond, the editor or an assistant may send out a reporter and photographer or call a local freelancer.

Special-interest groups also notify news outlets if group members think publicity will do them some good. If minorities, mothers on

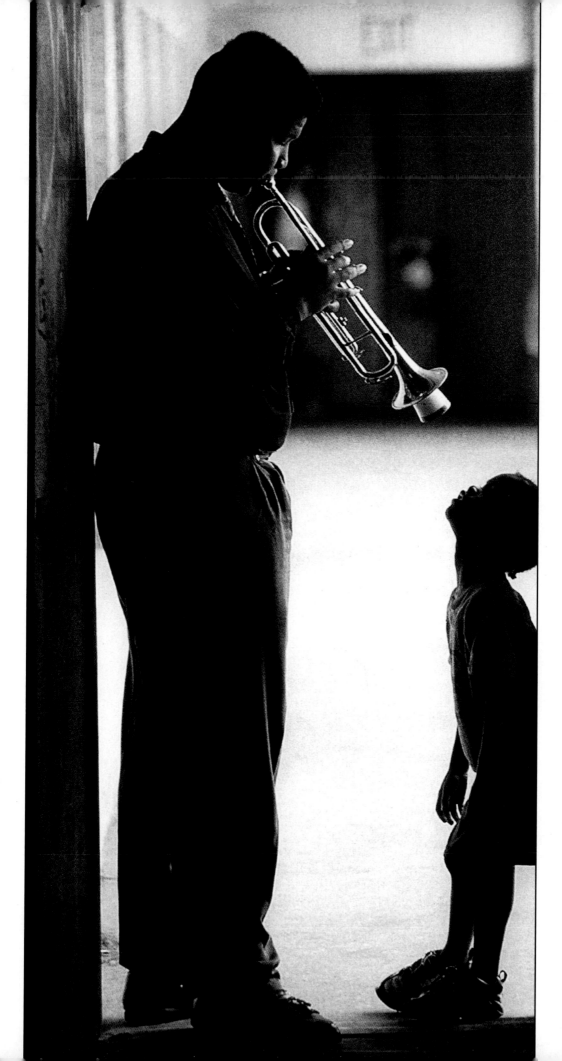

.7

MAKING THE MOST OF AN ASSIGNMENT
PHILADELPHIA'S HOMELESS: HOW THEY SURVIVE

Tom Gralish of the *Philadelphia Inquirer* recalls that when he received an assignment to photograph the homeless, editors suggested he "might do portraits of the street people, each standing in front of their grates or cardboard boxes or whatever else they called home. At that point, I wasn't sure what I would do, but I decided then and there that whatever it was, it would be the most honest photography I'd ever done. I was determined to do something as true as possible to the traditional ideals of documentary photojournalism."

Consequently, Gralish did not set up portraits. Instead, he followed street people with names like Hammerman, Spoon, and Redbeard through the ups and downs of their barren, subsistence lives. He photographed them staying warm atop steam grates on a frozen street, drinking wine, and panhandling. He showed them sleeping in boxes. Rather than a series of formulated, posed portraits, Gralish photographed the nitty gritty of these men's lives. For his efforts, he won both the Pulitzer Prize and the Robert F. Kennedy Memorial Prize. ■

Photos by Tom Gralish, *Philadelphia Inquirer*

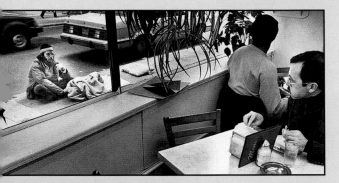

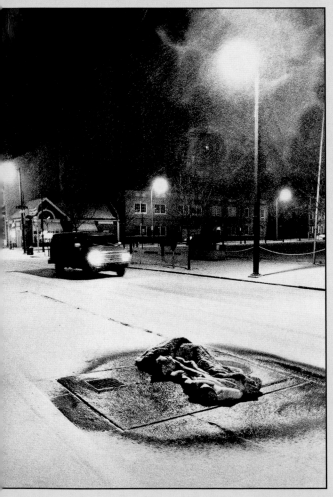

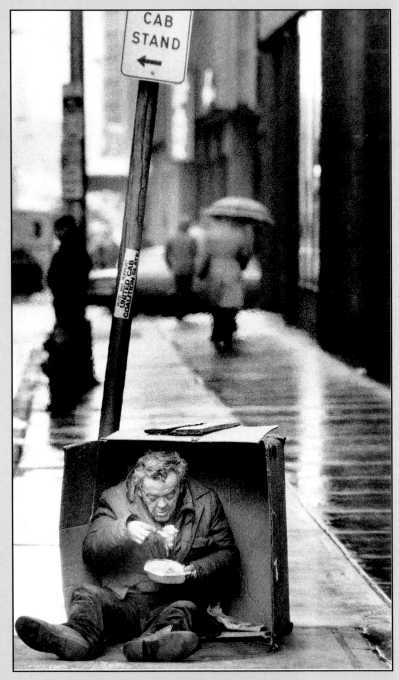

welfare, gays, or antinuclear groups, for example, are going to stage a protest for which they want coverage, they might contact local and national outlets with the time and place of their planned demonstration.

BEAT REPORTER KNOWS THE TERRITORY

Most news outlets assign reporters to cover a certain beat: city hall, hospitals, or police headquarters for a city newspaper or web site, or the White House, education, or medicine for a national magazine or 24-hour cable station. These specialists keep up with the news and events in their area; consequently, they know when to expect a major story to break. The city hall reporter may call in to the city desk to say, "The mayor is greeting some astronauts today. It will be worth a good picture." The editor will probably assign a photographer. A magazine writer working on a story about education in America may need pictures of a school for the gifted. The magazine's photo editor, often in New York or Washington, will assign a photographer who is under contract with the publication or will call a local freelancer.

PR OFFICE IS THERE TO AID YOU

The senator will arrive at her office at 9:00 A.M. She leaves for the airport at 10:15 A.M. to dedicate a new runway. She will be at the Golden Age Senior Citizens' Home from 11:30 A.M. until 12:30 P.M. During a 1:00 P.M. lunch at Parker House, the senator will address the State Beautification Committee.

If you want to know the whereabouts of the senator at practically any minute of the day, just consult the politician's schedule. The senator's itinerary is planned weeks in advance. From the mayor to the president of the United States, politicians have carefully planned schedules, usually handled by media relations officers.

Companies, schools, hospitals, prisons, and governmental departments also have press or public relations offices. Sometimes called public affairs or public information departments, they generate a steady stream of news releases announcing the opening of a new college campus, the invention of a long-lasting light bulb, or the start of a new special-education program. Many of these PR releases suggest good picture possibilities.

When Bruce Chambers of the *Orange County Register* set out to do a story about a multigenerational fire-fighting family for the anniversary of the September 11 attacks, the public affairs officer for the fire department provided Chambers with contact information. (See Chapter 4, "Features," for more on working with PR professionals.)

SCHEDULES IN PRINT OR ONLINE

Another source for upcoming news events comes daily to your doorstep rolled and held with a rubber band. The daily newspaper and its web site carry birth, wedding, and death announcements. Here is where you will find schedules of local theaters, sports events, parades, and festivals. When the circus arrives in your town, start with your local media outlets to find the time and place.

Web sites also offer lists of upcoming events. Many organizations and sports facilities list activities on their own sites. Surf the Internet for updated schedules.

UNUSUAL LEADS IN TRADE MAGAZINES AND ON SPECIALIZED WEB SITES

For more unusual activities check special-interest newspapers, magazines, and special-interest groups on the web. Dog and cat lovers, cyclists, plumbers, skateboarders, mental health professionals, and environmental groups all publish magazines or newsletters, and most have web sites that announce special events.

To track upcoming happenings with visual possibilities, newspapers, wire services, web sites and magazines maintain log books listing the times, places, and dates of activities that might turn into stories. The notation in the book includes a telephone number for the sponsoring organization in case the photographer needs more information. Freelancers can adapt this idea to track events for themselves.

WORKING WITH REPORTERS: CLICKERS MEET SCRIBBLERS
PHOTO REQUEST STARTS THE PROCESS

Whether it's *Time* magazine, *The New York Times*, or *MSNBC.com*, most news organizations have many more staff reporters than photographers. From their sources, these newshounds generate potential stories. When an editor approves a story proposal, the reporter makes out a photo request.

For the photographer, the key to great photo coverage depends on the information and arrangements on the photo request. Typical assignment requests include the name of the person or event to be photographed, as well as the time, date, and place. The editor usually assigns a slug—a one- or two-word designation for the story that serves as the story's name until the copy desk writes a final headline. The assignment sheet often includes a brief description of the proposed article, as well as a telephone number with which to contact the key subject if anything needs to be changed.

PHOTOGRAPHER AND REPORTER MEET IN ADVANCE

Under the best of circumstances, the reporter, photographer, and assigning editors meet or talk on the telephone or by email at this point in the story's development to discuss the team's approach or define the story's thrust. Here, the photojournalist can suggest visual ways to tell the story that correspond to the reporter's written approach. The photographer can recommend candids, a portrait, or a photo illustration—and also can estimate the amount of time needed for the shoot, or identify props and necessary clearances.

At some outlets, unfortunately, the photographer never meets with the reporter and assigning editor. Instead, the shooter receives the information from an intermediary editor, or is briefed by notes on the assignment sheet. In these circumstances the photographer plays a reduced role in determining the story's final outcome. Located at the end of the assignment chain, the photographer has little say in determining the best approach to the story.

DETERMINING THE BEST TIME TO SHOOT

At many news outlets, the reporter calls the subject and makes shooting arrangements. Sometimes this saves the photographer time. In most cases, though, the reporter will probably overlook great picture opportunities.

The reporter, for example, may decide to do a story about the controversial principal at Lincoln High School.

The writer asks when the principal is free for an interview and pictures. The principal responds: "Well, I'm busy all day. I greet the kids as they get off the bus. Then I meet with parents and teachers. Next I observe classes and eat lunch with the kids. Then I usually work with student discipline problems in the afternoon. All the teachers and students are gone by four. How about meeting me in my office after four?"

From the reporter's point of view, four o'clock is fine. The principal is free to answer questions and chat in a quiet environment in her office.

From the photojournalist's perspective, four o'clock is okay if formal portraits or headshots are satisfactory. But four o'clock is a disaster if the goal is to produce revealing candid pictures.

Shooting at a writer's appointed hour is more likely to result in a portrait in front of the school or inside a classroom. The environmental portrait can show what a principal looks like but can hardly reveal her character.

PHOTOGRAPHERS MAKE THEIR OWN ARRANGEMENTS

Although reporters can hold a telephone interview or call back later for more facts, photographers need to be present when the subject is engaged in work. Photographers and photo editors need to educate those who report, or assign reporting, about this need if pictures are ever to go beyond the routine.

Photographers usually find that they can make better arrangements than a reporter or editor because they know the kinds of pictures they are looking for. Photographers are mindful of both the subject's activities and the quality of light at different times of the day. High noon outside rarely provides attractive light for an outdoors portrait, for example. Ideally, photographers would get names and phone numbers of subjects and then make the appointment, or decide what other pictures might go with the story. The reporter might tape the interview at four o'clock, and the photographer might arrange to shoot the subject from dawn until dusk on a different day.

When scheduling a shoot with a subject it's always good to ask, "What is your typical day like?" As the subject, like the principal mentioned earlier, describes a normal day's activities, you can note which hours the person is sitting behind a desk talking and which hours he or she is doing something active and therefore photogenic. You also should find out if anything unusual is coming up that would lend itself to revealing photos.

ON THE SCENE: WORKING IN TANDEM

For some types of news, the photojournalist and reporter must cover the event together. Sometimes it's the reporter who knows the important players. Sometimes the photographer needs a second set of eyes to help provide protection, such as at a violent street protest. "You be my extra ears," says Ellie Brecher, a photographer-friendly reporter for the *Miami Herald*, "and I'll be your extra eyes." (See Chapter 3, "General News," page 52, for special situations where photographers must not share information.)

Even at dangerous breaking-news events like street riots, when the situation calls for all available eyes and ears, the photographer and reporter should not become joined at the hip. Each has different needs. One is following the action as it flows down a street, while the other is checking a quote and making sure the name is spelled correctly. However, while the photographer and reporter each need independence, the two also need to reconnect every once in a while to confirm they are developing the story in parallel ways.

Although the photographer and writer may not shoot and interview at the same moment, they should coordinate the message of their words and pictures. Photographers should pass on their observations about the subject or event to the writers. Writers can explain how their story might lead.

In the end, the reader will be looking at both the picture and the accompanying story. If the writer describes the subject as drab, yet the picture shows a smiling person wearing a peacock-colored shirt, the reader is left to resolve the conflict. Writers and photographers should resolve conflicts between words and pictures before the story goes to press.

PICTURE POLITICS

With good planning, editors avoid poor use of photo resources. However, many news outlets continue to operate in a traditional structure long unfriendly to the effective use of photography.

Traditionally, news organizations have been organized to handle assignments proposed by either reporters or editors. Photographers rarely originated story ideas. And even if they did, the photo-reporters received little in the way of picture play for their efforts.

While some of this is changing as print outlets shift toward distribution of content on the visually friendly Internet (see Chapter 12, "Multimedia," and Chapter 13, "Video"), the process in many publications continues to work like this: once the reporter gets the green light, research begins. The reporter might interview subjects, check the publication's library for related articles, do a web search, call authorities, and, finally, write the copy over a period of days or even weeks. Only when the story is nearly completed and ready for publication does the reporter fill out a photo request. Finally, the photo department becomes aware of the issue.

With the story written and the publication date set, the shooter has little flexibility. While the reporter took days and weeks to develop the story, the photographer may have only hours to produce photos. While juggling three or four other assignments for the day, the photojournalist is unlikely to be able to shoot in the best light, have time to wait for a candid moment, or to reshoot.

THE BUDGET MEETING

At most news organizations, the decision about how much space or how much time to allocate to a story as well as where it will play takes place at a daily, weekly, or monthly conference often known as a budget meeting. Representing each section of a

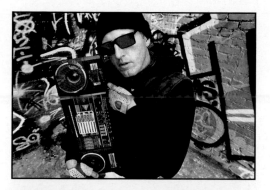

To avoid being attacked during his forays into San Francisco's Tenderloin neighborhood, Fred Larson dressed unobtrusively and hid his camera inside a portable stereo. Scott Sommerdorf, *San Francisco Chronicle*

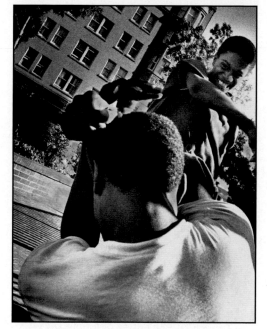

Street fighters continued their battle while an unobtrusive Larson moved in close with his camera-in-a-boombox. Frederic Larson, *San Francisco Chronicle*

media outlet, different editors pitch their best stories to the managing editor, who ultimately decides which stories get cover display and which will run inside. While the photo editor speaks up for pictures at this meeting, word editors always outnumber the lonely representative from the photography department. (See Chapter 7, "Photo Editing." Also see the documentary "Inside *Sports Illustrated*," on the DVD enclosed with this book.)

At the budget meeting, editors defend their turf. At a large news outlet, the sports editor, fashion editor, city editor, and foreign desk editor might each have an entire section. On a news magazine, the national editor, political editor, and music editor each might have a minimum number of pages to cover the most important topics in a specific area. Too often, the photo editor has no designated turf: there is no space assigned solely to photo stories. Though seated at the table with other decision makers, the picture editor has no formally reserved space.

Furthermore, the picture editor is up against colleagues who think that their sections cover the most important news, contain the best writers, and ought to have the most space. And, because more and bigger photos mean fewer words, few print editors see the advantages of storytelling pictures that eclipse longer stories. Furthermore, managing editors, most of whom have moved up from the writing rather than the visual side, make the final decisions about the use of space. The upshot in most organizations: even a very outspoken photo editor can rarely counterbalance these inherent structural biases toward words.

On the other hand, the Internet's capacity to deliver unlimited numbers of pictures and video without incurring additional cost provides inherent advantages over print publications. On web sites, you might think, having space for pictures should not be an issue.

Think again.

The "splash" or "home" page is a news outlet's guide to its web site. The demand for space by section editors means that pictures on the home page are often run the size of postage stamps. In addition, because of download-speed considerations, web designers often reduce the number of pictures on the opening page as well as their size so the pages will load quickly. Just when photographers thought they had found a photo-friendly medium on the web, they discovered their work squeezed again—at least on the opening page.

Fortunately, many news organizations are now recognizing the draw of telling stories with photography on the Internet and are assigning photojournalists to shoot and often report and produce in-depth photo stories that include audio. While words may still reign in print, photojournalism is finding its place in powerful multimedia projects that include still images, sound, words, and, increasingly, stand-alone video projects.

See Chapters 12, "Multimedia," and 13, "Video," for more on taking advantage of these new opportunities when approaching assignments.

TAKE A REPORTER TO LUNCH

To avoid the trap of being the last one to know about important stories—and having your pictures played poorly—try this: If you are a new staffer, ask the managing editor which reporter stands out in the newsroom. If you have been on staff for a while, you already know the names of the best writers.

Start by introducing yourself to one reporter and asking what he or she is working on. If the story sounds interesting, discuss picture possibilities. If you know that an event is coming up that would help explain the story,

suggest to your photo editor or managing editor an assignment that will help illustrate the story. On your own, start reading about the issue. If you notice a picture that might support the story, shoot it. Look for as many ways as you can to photograph the writer's story even before the wordsmith has finished the masterpiece.

When the story results in a formal photo request, your editor will likely assign the job to you because you already have started on the photos. By now you have a clear idea of the possible pictures that would expand the story. Also, a story written by a top writer will probably receive prominent play.

If you continue to look for good writers, anticipate photo requests, and build alliances with the word side, you will likely find writers agreeable to listening to your story ideas. A writing/photography partnership is likely to claim more space than your proposal alone.

GENERATE YOUR OWN ASSIGNMENT

Sometimes a photographer pulls over next to an overturned car, jumps out, and shoots. No written assignment at all. Usually, a photographer receives a verbal or written assignment from an editor. But many shooters report that their best assignments are those they proposed themselves. Self-generated assignments allow the photographer to pick exciting topics that lend themselves to visuals.

When a photographer has researched a good story, the next step is to request a reporter to provide the needed text. The more stories photographers propose, the more control they will have over their work. Fred Larson of the *San Francisco Chronicle* spent weeks photographing the city's tough neighborhood known as the Tenderloin (see page 11). The *Chronicle*'s Kim Komenich leapt from the world of stills into video journalism when he assigned himself to follow a Bay Area Santa Claus nearly all the way to the North Pole. (See pages 307–308, Chapter 13, "Video." Chapter 10, "Covering the Issues," and Chapter 11, "Photo Story," feature other successful self-generated assignments.)

INTERNATIONAL ASSIGNMENTS

Many news outlets have expanded their beats to include the world. From covering earthquakes in India to uprisings in Rwanda, photojournalists are literally on the move. Photographers who covered high school football on Friday night may find themselves boarding a plane for Iraq on Sunday morning. Never has the mastery of foreign languages or knowledge of international affairs been more important to photojournalists.

Michael Kodas, who has covered international news for the *Hartford Courant*, reads voraciously: *The Wall Street Journal*, the *Christian Science Monitor*, and *The New York Times*, among others. National Public Radio (NPR) is a good source of international news for car-bound photojournalists. If an intensive language course is out of your budget, try substituting language tapes for your favorite rock groups when you are stuck in traffic.

And do not forget the most basic preparations of all, as recommended by freelancer Keith Philpott, who shoots for *Time* and *People*. Keep a current passport in your camera bag, and make sure your inoculations are current for travel in developing countries.

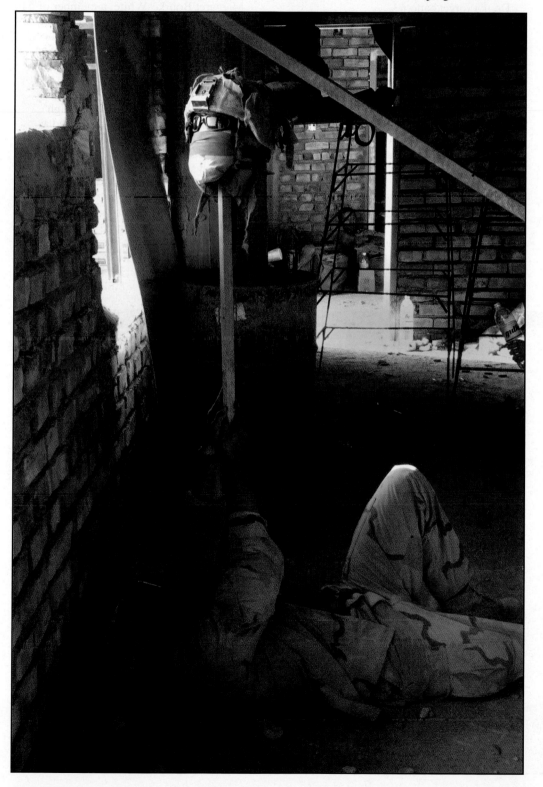

The photographer was on the front with the U.S. military during an incursion into Najaf, Iraq. Their temporary outpost was taking constant sophisticated sniper fire through windows and down corridors. American soldiers used the sniper dummy to draw the enemy into sight and return fire.

A sniper was spotted about 450 yards away in an abandoned hotel. U.S. forces called in an air strike, and a fighter jet soon dropped two aerial bombs onto the hotel, shattering the building and probably killing the sniper, although incoming sniper fire resumed just a day later.
Jim MacMillan, Associated Press

Carol Guzy, who covered the Ethiopian famine for the *Miami Herald* and the tumbling of the Berlin Wall for the *Washington Post*, says to pack light for international assignments. She carries as little photo gear as she feels she can get away with, she says, but does bring an extra camera body—and memory cards, lots of memory cards.

Do not forget batteries.

VISUAL VARIETY
OVERALL SHOT SETS THE SCENE

If readers themselves were at a news event, they would stand in the crowd and move their eyes from side to side to survey the panorama. The overall photo gives readers at home the same perspective. A good overall allows viewers to orient themselves to the scene. The overall shot is one that will serve you well in video as well as in stills (see Chapter 13, "Video").

For some stories, an overall might include just a long shot of a room. For others, the overall might cover a city block, a neighborhood, or even a whole town. The scope of the shot depends on the size of the event. The overall shows where the event took place: inside, outside, country, city, land, sea, day,

night, and so on. The shot defines the relative position of the participants. In a confrontation, for example, the overall angle would show whether the demonstrators and police were a block apart, or across the street from one another. The overall shot also allows the reader, by judging crowd size, to evaluate the magnitude of the event.

Margaret Bourke-White, a member of the original *Life* magazine staff, always shot overalls on each assignment, even if she thought they would not be published. She explained that she wanted her editor to see the shooting location so that he could interpret the rest of the pictures she had taken.

Generally the overall requires a high angle. Knowing this, Gene Pepi rented a 12-foot-tall ladder and stationed it right in the middle of San Francisco's Market Street to photograph a peace demonstration. His ladder and position provided the best location to capture the historic size of the crowd.

When you arrive at a news event, quickly survey the scene to determine what is happening. Then search for a way to elevate yourself above the crowd. In a room, a chair will suffice. But outside, a telephone pole, a leafless tree, or a nearby building will give

GET HIGH

Gene Pepi knew the shot he wanted at a peace march in San Francisco could not be taken from ground level. He rented a 12-foot-tall ladder so he could photograph over the heads of the marchers for an overall shot of demonstrators filling the length of Market Street, with the city's Ferry Building in the background. A telephoto lens appears to compress the space between the banners down Market Street, making them seem closer together than they really are.
Gene Pepi, *Frontlines*

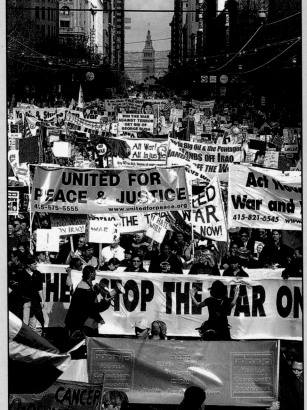

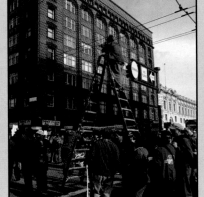

Gene Pepi gets the picture from atop a ladder he rented for the occasion. © Ken Kobré

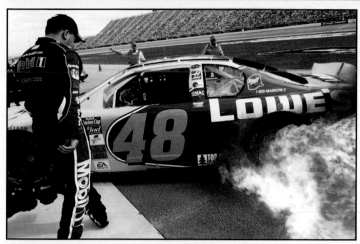

MEDIUM
When published alone, a medium shot must tell a complete story. Ryan Newman (left) jumps back as the last challenger's car erupts into fire while heading into the garage at the NASCAR Winston Cup Tropicana 400 at Chicagoland Speedway. Scott Strazzante, *Chicago Tribune*

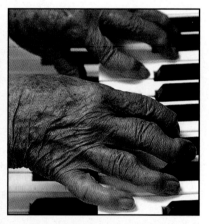

CLOSE-UP
A musician's hands resting on her church's organ keys shows the reader the curvature of the woman's fingers and the texture of her skin. The 92-year-old organist had played at her church since 1927.
Rich Abrahamson, *Fort Collins Coloradoan*

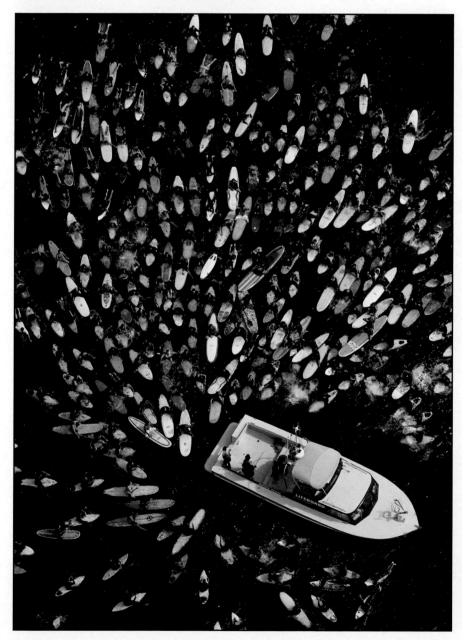

OVERALL
Shot from a helicopter, this high vantage point best conveys how many people paddled out to attend this memorial for a young professional surfer who had died. With the door removed from the chopper, the photographer was harnessed in and able to lean out safely to get a clean shot.
K.C. Alfred,
The San Diego Union-Tribune

you the high angle you need for an effective overall. When in a flat area, even the roof of your car will add some height to your view.

The wider angle lens you have, obviously, the less distance from the scene you will need. However, on a major news story that encompasses a vast area, such as a flood, hurricane, or conflagration, you may need to work with your editors to rent a helicopter or small airplane to get high enough to capture the dimensions of the destruction.

MEDIUM SHOT TELLS THE STORY

The medium shot should "tell the story" in one photograph. Shoot the picture close enough to see the participants' action, yet far enough away to show their relationship to one another and to the environment. The medium shot contains all the storytelling elements in the scene. Like a news story lead, the photo must tell the whole story quickly by compressing the important elements into one image. This is another shot video shooters share with still photographers (see Chapter 13, "Video").

An accident photo might show the victims in the foreground, the wrecked car in the background. Without the car, the photo would omit an essential detail—the cause of the victims' injuries. With only the crumpled car,

the reader would wonder if anyone had been hurt. The combination of elements—car plus victims—briefly tells the basic story.

A medium shot gains dramatic impact when the photograph captures action. Although the camera can catch fast action, you may still have difficulty: action often happens so quickly that you have no time to prepare. Shooting action is like shooting sports (see Chapter 6, "Sports"). For both, you must anticipate when and where the action will take place.

If a man starts a heated argument with a police officer, you might predict that fists will fly and an arrest will follow. Aim your camera when the argument starts; do not wait until a punch is thrown. If you hesitate, the quarrel might end while you are still fiddling with your equipment.

For the medium shot, a wide-angle lens such as a 24mm or 28mm works well on a full-frame camera. On a digital camera with a small chip, you need at least a 17mm or 18mm to shoot comfortably.

CLOSE-UP ADDS DRAMA

Nothing beats a close-up for drama when shooting stills or video. The close-up slams the reader into eyeball-to-eyeball contact with the subject. At this intimate distance, a

High angles such as this shot of a hurdler and a competing shadow give the reader a fresh perspective on the race. The photographer shot from the roof of the press box for this early morning competition.
Jeremy Portje, *Telegraph Herald* [Dubuque, Iowa]

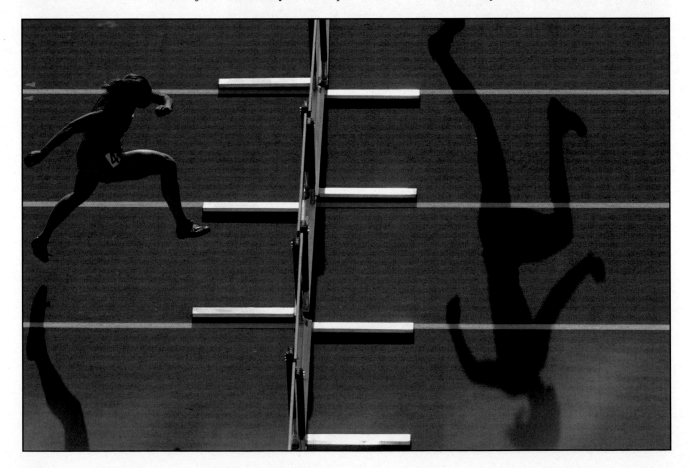

subject's face, contorted in pain or beaming happily, elicits empathy in readers.

How close is close?

A close-up should isolate and emphasize one element. And not all close-ups include a person's face. Rich Abrahamson photographed only the hands of a 92-year-old organist who had played the organ at her church for more than three-quarters of a century. The aged hands tell the woman's story without showing her face (see page 15).

Sometimes objects can tell the story even when the story involves tragedy. A close-up of a child's doll covered with mud might tell the story of a flood better than an aerial view of the disaster.

Longer lenses enable shooters to be less conspicuous when shooting close-ups. With a lens zoomed to 200mm, you can stand ten feet away and still get a tight facial close-up.

The telephoto lens decreases the depth-of-field and thus blurs the foreground and background. This effect isolates the subject from unwanted distractions.

In addition to using a telephoto for close-up work, some photographers employ a macro lens or a standard lens with an extension tube if the subject is tiny—and stationary. With either of these lenses, the camera can take a picture of a small object such as a contact lens and enlarge it until it is easily seen (see page 144).

HIGH/LOW ANGLES BRING NEW PERSPECTIVES

Since most people see the world from a sitting or standing perspective, a photojournalist shooting stills or video can add instant interest to pictures simply by shooting from a unique elevation. Shoot down from a 30-story building or up from a manhole cover. Either way, the viewer will get a new, sometimes jarring, but almost always refreshing look at a subject. Even when covering a meeting in a standard-sized room, standing on a chair or taking pictures while sitting on the floor can add interest to your pictures.

Avoid the "5'7" syndrome." On every assignment, avoid taking all your pictures at eye level. When you start shooting, look around for ways to take the high ground. Whether going out on a catwalk or shooting from the balcony, find some way to look down on the scene you are shooting.

"Get down. Get dirty. Get your camera where the action is," says Bruce Chambers, the outstanding feature photographer for the *Orange County Register*. Digital cameras and video cameras with flip-up LCD screens allow shooting from (literally) ground level. Even without a flip-up screen, use a

A low angle provided additional power to this commemoration of the second anniversary of the September 11 attacks.
Bruce Chambers,
Orange County Register

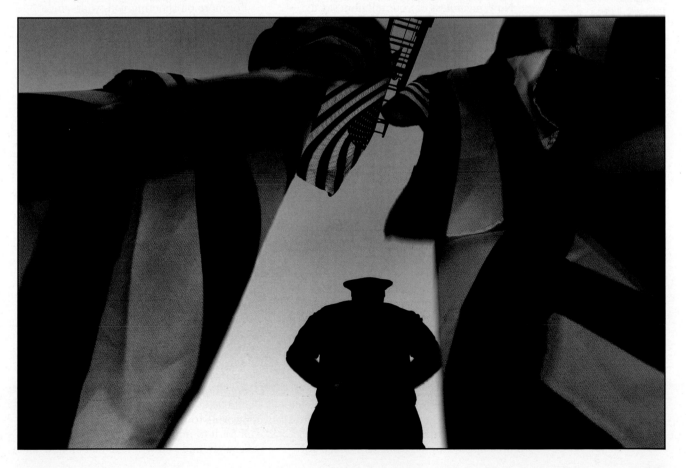

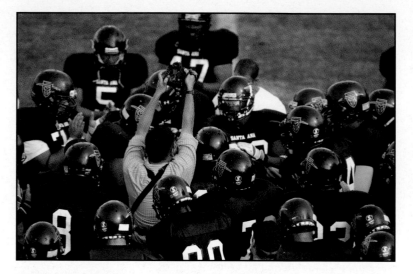

When more height is called for, like the situation at this Santa Ana College football game, the photojournalist can try holding the camera overhead, aiming and shooting without looking in the viewfinder. Photographers call this shot a "Hail Mary" because they hope and pray for a good image when they cannot see what they are shooting. A wide-angle lens usually works best in these situations.
David Pardo, freelance

wide-angle lens to place your camera as low as you like, even on your toes. Aim. Then shoot without looking. It's easy to check the results with the LCD screen on digital cameras. Try pointing a wide-angle lens in the approximate direction of your target, take a picture, and then check it on the screen. If you miss, just bend down and shoot again.

Using a wide-angle lens, hold your camera as high as you can stretch your arms, aiming the lens in the direction of your target. Do not worry about looking through the viewfinder.

Now, regardless of your religion, say a "Hail Mary" and pray your picture was framed well. Then check the image on the LCD screen in case your prayers were not answered. Then shoot again if necessary. Photographers call this shot a "Hail Mary."

The "Hail Mary" often provides an unusual view and works especially well when battling other photographers for a shot of the winning athlete after a game. Some photographers even extend the "Hail Mary" by attaching their cameras to a monopod and triggering the shutter with a hard-wired cable release or a remote control radio slave like the PocketWizard.

The over-the-head "Hail Mary" is also effective for shooting at a dance or street fair. These crowded circumstances often make it hard to get a clean shot without a distracting background. Coming up close to your subject, holding your camera high, and pointing down will clean up the background nicely.

Shooting at shoe level or rising above the crowd with a "Hail Mary" will greatly expand the visual variety of all your assignments.

GOING WIDE
Walter Green, who worked for the Associated Press for many years, noted that he took most medium shots with a 24mm lens (equal to a 16mm on some digital cameras). Green got

extremely close to his subjects and filled the entire frame. The resulting pictures, he said, tended to project a more intimate feeling between the subject and the viewer.

Because shooters like Green work close to a subject, few distracting elements appear in their images This proximity also emphasizes the subject. Finally, a wide-angle lens takes in a large area of the background, thus establishing the relationship of the subject to his or her surroundings.

Eugene Richards, a photographer who has won numerous awards, is master of the wide-angle lens. His lens is like a mother spreading her arms to include all her children in an embrace. Richards's wide-angle lens encompasses his subjects, often bringing together two elements into one picture to tell a more comprehensive story in a single image. His topics, which also have appeared in books, have ranged from drug addicts (***Cocaine True, Cocaine Blue***) to emergency room personnel (***The Knife and Gun Club***). One of his award-winning pictures includes, to the right of the frame, a tiny coffin in the front seat of a hearse; in the middle, open car doors; and, at the extreme left, a young child. Richards brought together the widely separated elements of the child-sized coffin and the youngster in one visual whole.

For more on shooting with wide-angle lenses, see Chapter 8, "Camera Bag."

Multi-layered Images
The wide-angle lens is the perfect tool for "layering" images. Here a photographer tries to frame the main subject occupying the middle ground of the image with something else of interest on the edge. The inclusion of this additional element produces a more complex image, causing the viewer to study both the dominant subject and its relationship to the framing elements. The guitarist on the opposite page is the obvious subject of the picture, but the other musicians in the foreground and background add layers of interest.

PERSISTENCE PAYS OFF
Photographers stay on site until they get the best picture possible within their time limits. Amateurs take a few snaps and hope for the best. Still photojournalists search for the decisive moment and know when they get it. A pro might take 100 or even 1000 shots to get the perfect moment.

Former *New York Times* photographer George Tames said, "If you see a picture, you should take it—period. It is difficult if not impossible to recreate a picture, so do not wait for it to improve. Sometimes the action gets better, and you will take that picture also, but if you hesitate, you've lost the moment, and you can't go back."

Chambers of the *Orange Country Register* echoes that advice, "Don't always wait for the perfect moment. It never comes. Start and make a picture. Make the next picture better."

Sometimes, staying with a situation yields a series that has more impact than any single image (see pages 20–21). While the video shooter isn't looking for a particular moment, both Chambers' and Tames's words ring true for another reason. If the action is interesting, keep the camera rolling. If you turn it off too soon, you'll miss the entire sequence.

An unedited set of still pictures straight from a novice's camera, or "take" as it is often called, usually shows a few shots of many different scenes throughout. All might be taken from exactly the same position. Professionals, however, visually explore each scene, taking a number of pictures of essentially the same thing but at different moments or from different angles. (See a variety of one pro's images on page 124.)

Usually this means that they will take a few shots, then move to a different position, and shoot the same thing from a fresh vantage. They might shoot six frames from one location and then walk around the subject and shoot six more. By watching the subject as well as the background, photographers are trying to find the perfect balance of a picture's elements while capturing a revealing expression or telling body position.

The video shooter will also explore a scene from a variety of angles and locations for a different reason—the need to have sufficient footage to edit cuts into seamless scenes. (See Chapter 13, "Video," for more on shooting for video.)

MAGNUM PHOTOGRAPHERS' SHOOTING APPROACHES

Each photographer's shooting style differs, though. In his book, ***Magnum: Fifty Years at the Front Line of History***, Russell Miller described a wide range of shooting styles practiced by the diverse members of the Magnum picture agency, which was founded after World War II.

Ernst Haas. A Magnum photographer known for exquisite color work, Haas always began shooting before the action occurred,

With the bass fiddle close up, the banjo in the rear, and the guitarist as the central subject, each member of the Roanoke Valley Pickers is on a different plane in the photograph. The photographer moved in tight with a wide-angle lens.
Josh Meltzer, *The Roanoke Times*

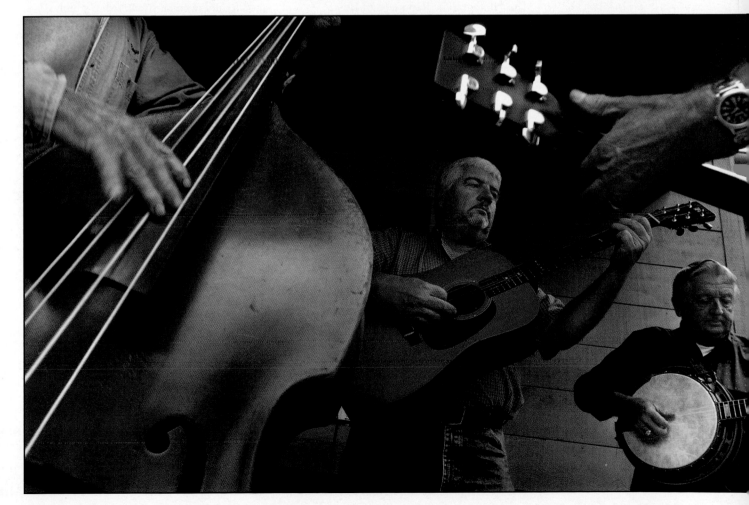

according to Eve Arnold, another Magnum shooter. Haas, she said, followed through to the peak of the action, and then tapered off.

Henri Cartier-Bresson. Magnum's Henri Cartier-Bresson is famous for capturing one decisive moment in an image. In fact, his 1952 book was published in the United States under the title ***The Decisive Moment***, which suggests perfect shutter timing to freeze action at its peak. But Cartier-Bresson also looked for balanced composition.

He wrote: "To me, photography is the simultaneous recognition, in a fraction of a second, of the significance of an event as well as of a precise organization of forms which give that event its proper expression. . . . Inside movement, there is one moment at which the elements in motion are in balance. Photography must seize upon this moment and hold immobile the equilibrium of it."

For Cartier-Bresson, a photograph must not only freeze an instant of time, but must capture that instant within a well-designed composition. Cartier-Bresson did shoot some 15,000 rolls of film during his active career—not all of which caught decisive moments—according to Claude Cookman's dissertation, "The Photographic Reportage of Henri Cartier-Bresson, 1933–1973." (See pages 441–443 for more about Cartier-Bresson).

Robert Capa. Capa, whose real name was André Friedmann, was perhaps the world's greatest war photographer and the founder of Magnum, the picture agency cooperative (see pages 440–443). He had a yet different approach to shooting.

According to Magnum colleague Eve Arnold, Capa's contact sheets did not show Haas's persistence in pursuing a sequence. Nor were Capa's individual pictures as well designed as Cartier-Bresson's.

Yet Capa took some of history's most memorable images. During the Spanish Civil War, he photographed a soldier, arms flung wide, falling backward at the moment of death (see page 442). Capa also took the classic World War II D-day landing pictures. He was killed while covering the war in Vietnam. When Eve Arnold told *New Yorker* writer Janet Flanner that Capa's pictures were not well designed, Flanner shot back, "History doesn't design well, either."

After that, Arnold said, "I began to understand that the strength of Capa's work was that just by being there, where the action was, he was opening new areas of vision.

"He was aware that it is the essence of a picture, not necessarily its form, which is important."

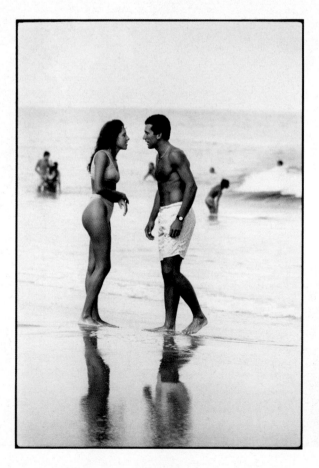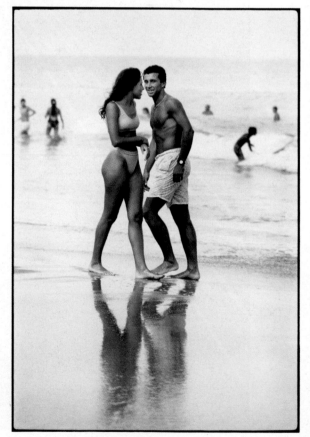

CATCHING CANDIDS

What sets photojournalistic pictures apart from other types of photography? The photojournalistic style depends on catching candid moments. Good photojournalists have developed the instinct to be at the right place, at the right time, with the right lens and camera. Often, they can steal images like a pickpocket, without anyone ever knowing that photographic sleight-of-hand has taken place.

Photojournalists must catch their subjects as unaware as possible to record real emotions. Rather than stage-managing pictures, photographers observe but do not direct. The results depend on their ability to record intimate moments without interrupting. In good candid pictures, subjects never gaze at the camera. Eye contact tips off the reader that the picture is not candid and suggests that the subject was at least aware of the photographer and might even be performing for the lens.

TECHNICAL STRATEGIES

Preset Your Camera. Prepare your camera before you point it. If you are fiddling with the camera's dials, you might catch the subject's attention instead of a candid moment. Make sure you have set your ISO, shutter speed, aperture, focus mode, selection area, and continuous shooting mode.

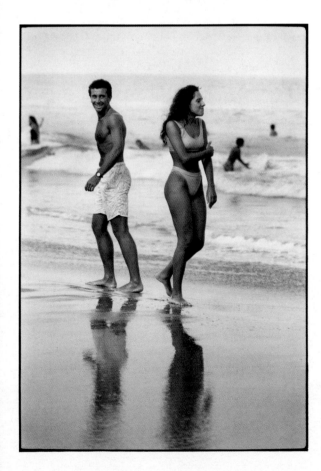

Some encounters play out like a short story. The photographer anticipated the encounter, kept shooting, and caught the final glance on this Brazilian beach. As is often the case, some stories are told best in more than one image.
Elliott Erwitt, Magnum

About 95 percent of the time, you will get a correctly exposed picture with the camera on either Aperture Priority or Shutter Speed Priority. These are not bad odds. (See page 157 for exceptions.)

Photojournalists often use Aperture Priority for catching candids since this option allows control of depth of field by selection of the lens aperture, while leaving shutter speed selection to the camera. The photographer is free to shoot quickly without readjusting the lens as the subject moves from the deep shadows under an oak tree into the brilliant sunlight of a grassy field.

This semi-automatic exposure mode reduces the number of under- or overexposed shots while increasing chances for catching the decisive moment. All photographers still must keep an eye on the camera-determined shutter speed so that the speed will be fast enough to stop any subject or camera movement.

Photojournalists covering sports with long lenses often use Shutter Priority, selecting a fast shutter speed to stop the action. With the camera set on shutter speed priority, a lightning fast tennis player will be properly exposed whether serving from the shadows or guarding the net in bright light.

Decide ahead of time how you might want to frame the picture. Before pointing your lens toward your intended subject, select your autofocus "hot zone." Do you plan to frame the subject in the middle of the photo or off to the side? Adjust the hot zone accordingly. Then, with the designated hot zone focus area in the viewfinder over your subject, let the camera itself focus the lens as you press the shutter. (For more on autofocus, see pages 106–108, 158 and 160.)

Use autofocus on continuous mode. On "autofocus continuous," the camera is focusing as long as you keep the shutter pressed halfway down. If the subject moves forward or backward, the lens will stay focused. Camera manufacturers offer other ways to hold focus if the subject is likely to move to the right or left.

Select the appropriate lens before you bring the camera to your eye. Of course you might have to zoom in or out to frame your subject most advantageously.

Watch your subject. You have preset your camera and now you must concentrate on your subject's expression.

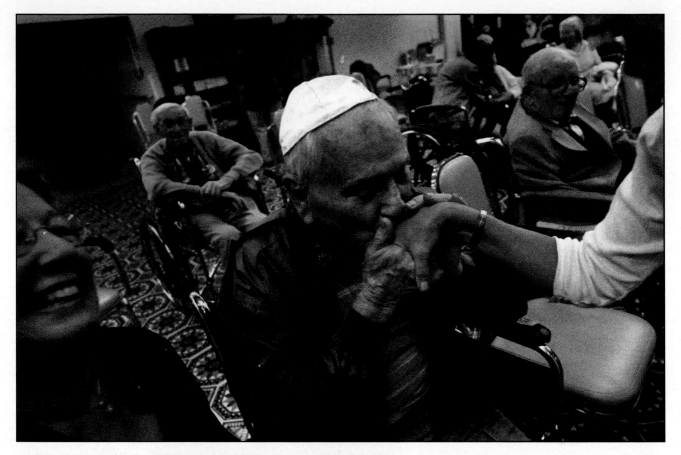

Everyone was aware of the photographer's presence during a Yom Kippur service at a retirement home. The subject was more involved in kissing the hand of the female rabbi than in the photographer. Robert Cohen, *St. Louis Post-Dispatch*

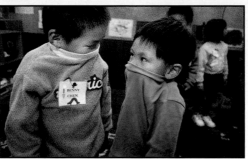

The photographer moved in quickly with a wide-angle lens for this candid shot. The moment was over in one frame. Julie Stupsker, *San Francisco Examiner*

With all your camera control choices set ahead of time, you can swing the camera up, frame, and press the shutter at the same time to freeze a meaningful moment. The lens will almost instantly focus and expose automatically to catch a natural scene. (See pages 106–108, 158 and 160 for more about using autofocus.)

Anticipation and Timing
Candid photography requires the skill of a weather forecaster. Photographers must guess what is going to happen based on how they see a situation developing. If two kids have their fists up, they are likely to fight. A couple holding hands might kiss. Sometimes the photographer, like the meteorologist, judges the evidence correctly and is prepared with the right lens, shutter speed, ISO, and f-stop. At other times, like the weather person, the photographer misinterprets the obvious.

Timing to release the shutter at the optimum moment is as important as anticipation. Even with continuous shooting mode and autofocus, photographers must get into the flow of the action. Most action builds to a peak and then settles down again. Almost every event has a crucial moment.

FOUR APPROACHES TO CANDID PHOTOGRAPHY
Out in the Open
An out-in-the-open approach works when subjects, engaged in an engrossing activity, forget that a photographer is present.

Robert Cohen arrived at a Jewish nursing home early for the high holy days of Yom Kippur.

He introduced himself to everyone and asked whether anyone in the room either did not want to be photographed or could not be photographed for legal reasons.

"With elderly people I tend to stick with those who are with their family members or those who I am convinced are lucid enough to make decisions on their own," he says.

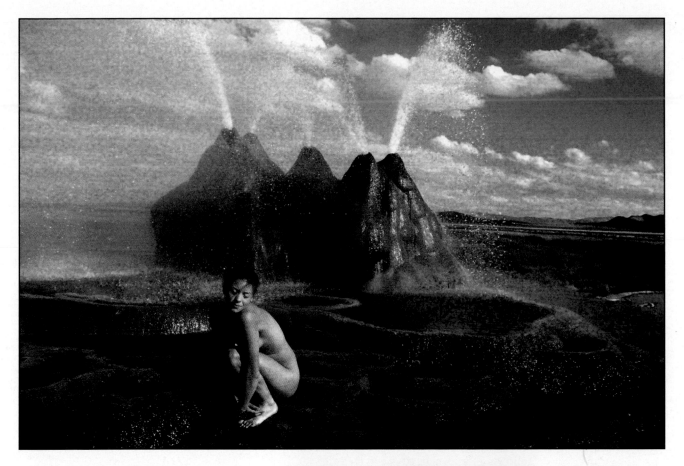

As the service proceeded, the female rabbi visited with residents. Cohen anticipated that a special spark might take place between the rabbi and one of the congregants.

Just as an elderly man reached out and kissed the rabbi's hand, Cohen moved in close and grabbed a candid with his wide-angle zoom lens. The man was far more engaged in his act of courtliness than the photographer. After taking the picture, Cohen slipped away so as not to interfere with the event's natural flow (see opposite page).

Click and Run

Some photographers use a click-and-run approach rather than try to work unobserved. They catch candid images by walking past the subject, shooting quickly with a wide-angle lens, and then moving on.

According to observers, Henri Cartier-Bresson would pause in front of his subject and, with one fluid motion, raise his Leica, focus, and click several frames. By the time the subject turned toward the photographer, Cartier-Bresson had gone his way.

Julie Stupsker saw two children at a day-care center about to duck into their sweat-shirts. She moved in close with a wide-angle lens and bounce flash just in time to grab one

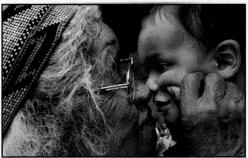

With his telephoto lens, the photographer could shoot unob-served from a distance when the 101-year-old grandmother gave a kiss and a pinch to her great-great grandson. Bryan Patrick, *Sacramento Bee*

A woman enjoying a hot spring in the California desert was aware of the photographer who, by the way, also was naked. The subject returned to her own reverie after the photographer told her to ignore the camera. Julie Stupsker, *San Francisco Examiner*

frame as they partially disappeared into their clothing. With the flash ready and the camera preset, Stupsker shot quickly and caught the candid moment (see opposite page).

Big Game Hunter

Like a hunter stalking prey, a photojournalist studies his or her subject. Sighting through a rifle-like telephoto lens, the photographer stands across the room or across the street—watching, waiting, and trying to anticipate what might happen next.

Patience, if this is your approach, is not only a virtue but a necessity.

Bryan Patrick had been covering the "Gathering of Honored Elders" at the Indian Museum for two hours when he noticed an elderly woman playing with a young child. Using a medium-telephoto zoom lens, he focused on the pair and watched from afar as the woman held up the child.

Just as she pinched the child's cheek and rubbed his nose, the *Sacramento Bee* photographer snapped the shutter. Only after he approached her for caption information did the centenarian realize she and her great-great grandson had been photographed (see page 23).

When hunting features, many photographers carry a medium-long zoom lens and an even longer fixed telephoto lens.

Introduce Yourself

Even when someone is engaged in another activity, the sight of a photographer loaded with gear can bring all action to a stop. The advantage of stealth is gone. The simplest solution is to ask the person to continue, "Go on about your business and ignore me." If the person returns to work or fun, you may be forgotten altogether in the moments that pass.

Spotting a woman bathing in a hot spring in the California desert, Stupsker climbed a fence to get closer for the scenic shot. Then, following the ancient advice to do as the Romans when in Rome, the photographer stripped and joined the woman in the water.

Having watched the photographer climb the fence with her gear and then take off her clothes, the woman was curious, of course. When Stupsker explained she was taking pictures for the *San Francisco Examiner*, the woman resumed her respite and ignored the photographer. Stupsker was able to capture a natural moment before the arrival of a group of teenage boys quickly brought the shooting session to an end (see page 23).

Diana Walker, who shoots behind-the-scene photos at the White House for *Time* magazine, must catch candid images in private areas almost every day. She says she tries to avoid conversation with her subjects so they will forget she is there. (For more on Walker's technique, see pages 50–51, Chapter 3, "General News.")

SAVE ROOM ON YOUR FLASH CARD

By changing memory cards before the last megabyte is filled, photographers build in some insurance. Having extra capacity at the end of an assignment is like having money in the bank. You may never need it, but it might save you in an emergency—and reduce your own anxiety, as well. ∎

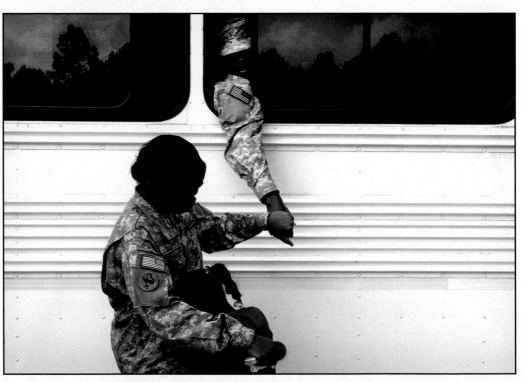

A captain comforts her daughter and says good-bye to her husband, one of about 250 paratroopers departing for a deployment to Iraq. Even at the end of your assignment, save some room on your memory card in the event a moment like this occurs.
Andrew Craft,
The Fayetteville Observer

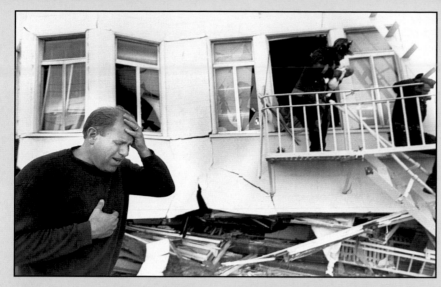

A few minutes after the 1989 San Francisco earthquake, a father reacts as his dead baby is removed from a collapsed apartment building. The photographer sold the picture to *Life* magazine.
Kaia Means
Oslo, Norway

When the Loma Prieta earthquake rocked San Francisco in 1989, journalism student Kaia Means was one of thousands who initially thought the quake was "just another" shaker. Visiting friends atop Russian Hill, however, the San Francisco State University student noted a huge cloud of dust rising above the Marina District. She said her good-byes and left for a 5:30 P.M. meeting, thinking she'd drive by the Marina first to see what the dust was all about.

"I knew I had to turn in a spot news assignment sometime during the semester," recalls Means, who was a news-editorial major taking her second semester of photography. "So I thought I'd drive by to see if there was anything to take a picture of." Means found more than fallen bricks and broken glass. The first photographer on the scene, the 22-year-old student from Norway photographed a distraught father awaiting the rescue of his wife and baby.

In addition to the father in the crowd, Means photographed firefighters carrying the baby from the building, its father grieving in the foreground. Later, in tears upon realizing that the baby was dead, Means photographed the mother's rescue and reunion with her husband.

Although Means was "shaking all over" by the time she finished shooting the tragedy, the young photojournalist's real-life midterm exam was just beginning.

DETERMINING POSSIBLE OUTLETS
The photo student's pictures certainly had wide local and national interest. And Means was in a good bargaining position because

she had exclusive images. However, the earthquake had shaken local news outlets as well as buildings and bridges.

Means took the film to the *San Francisco Examiner*, which had lost all electricity and phone capabilities, and was conducting its photo operation out of a van in the paper's parking lot. Having told the photo chief about the pictures, she helped out for a while and then left the film, marked "DEAD BABY" on the canister.

In less chaotic circumstances, Means could have bargained for the sale of the pictures. Having gotten a bid from the *Examiner*, she could have contacted local TV stations to see how much they would offer for rights to the photos. With the story's national impact, she could have offered the film to the wire services, either the Associated Press (AP), Agence France-Presse (AFP), or Reuters— all of which depend a great deal on stringers and freelancers.

None of the services maintains a large enough photo staff to cover the country—or the world—thoroughly. Many photos appearing in print and carrying the AP, AFP, or Reuters credit line are taken by independent photographers.

Alternatively, Means could have called other large dailies around the country. Today, newspapers want their own photos of a major story to augment those supplied by the wires, and many send staff photographers. However, none would have had this series of pictures.

But with phone lines down and chaos around her, Means left the film with the *Examiner*. Naturally, she was surprised when she opened the paper the following day and

did not see her dramatic pictures. She called to see what had happened and learned that, in the confusion, the film had never even been processed.

Following more confusion at the newspaper, the young photojournalist finally got her film back—still unprocessed two days after the event. Under normal circumstances, this series of faux pas would have spelled photographic disaster for the fledgling photojournalist. The pictures' timeliness would have dissipated.

However, once the film was processed, it was easy to see that these were no ordinary pictures. It was time to seek a national market. The news magazines were already closing by the time the film had been processed, and they rarely buy anything but color. Her photo teacher, this author, gave her the number of Peter Howe, picture editor at *Life* magazine at the time. Means took over from there. Howe was out of town, but editors at *Life* wanted to see the prints.

A REAL *LIFE* ASSIGNMENT
After viewing the pictures, *Life* editors purchased first North American rights for six months and sent a reporter to San Francisco to interview Means and the parents she had photographed. When an order for a follow-up story came in, the second-semester photo student received the five-day *Life* assignment.

In the year-end issue of the magazine, Means' photo of the distraught father, in addition to two of the follow-up pictures she shot on assignment, ran as a two-page spread. ∎

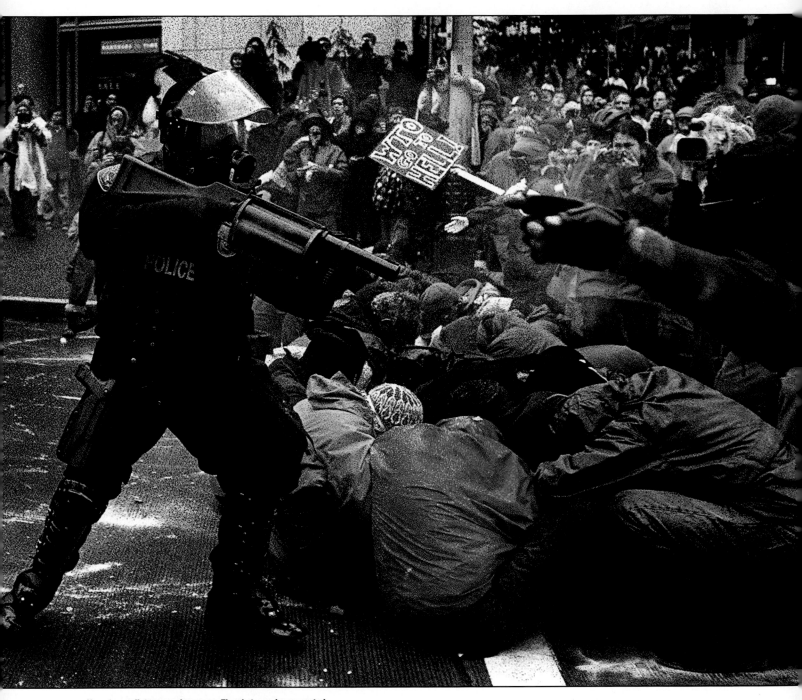

You can predict some crime news. The photographer expected violence on the first day of World Trade Organization meetings in Seattle. Paul Joseph Brown, *Seattle Post-Intelligencer*

2

News

MAKING HEADLINES

Crime, whether it's a riot in Seattle or a hostage situation in Arlington, Texas, is costly to society. Crime can be a deep human tragedy for criminals and their families, as well as for victims and theirs. Almost any kind of crime makes a printable story in newsrooms across the country. The cub reporter soon learns that whether it's an atrocious murder or a $100 hold-up of a gas station, the event is considered news in city rooms from coast to coast. Depending upon a crime's violence, its cost, the prominence of people involved, or the crime's humorous or unusual aspects, the news receives varying amounts of emphasis.

ARMING FOR ACTION

Most spot news photographers have worked out the exact combination of cameras, lenses, and strobes that they need to work in the particular area they cover. Those who mainly shoot mayhem at night carry different hardware than those on the day shift. Photographers covering murder in the big city pack differently than those covering wildfires in the countryside.

DAYTIME ARSENALS

When covering spot news for the *Philadelphia Daily News*, Jim MacMillan never left home without three cameras, including one mounted to a 500mm f/4 lens and connected to a monopod—plus a 1.4X and a 2X tele-extender. "In Philly, the police keep us far away from the crime scene," explains MacMillan. "I've gotten some of my best pictures from a block away."

To carry all three cameras and lenses at one time, he would hang his wide-angle zoom around his neck, sling a telephoto zoom over his right shoulder, and haul an extreme telephoto, pointing backwards, over his left shoulder. "I could put two hands on any one of the cameras at any time," he points out. (See Chapter 13, "Video," for more on MacMillan's work.)

On the fire watch for most of the dry season in Northern California, Kent Porter of the *Santa Rosa Press Democrat*, uses the full complement of lenses. "At a working fire I try to get pictures of the weary firemen. I also use an extreme wide angle so I can get close to my subjects and incorporate the area the people are working in. I use a long telephoto quite a bit," he says.

NIGHT ON THE STREETS

Sam Costanza, shooting mostly at night for the *New York Post*, rarely gets to use a long lens. He sets up his camera and strobe like a point-and-shoot so that he can concentrate on the scene and not worry about technical details. Usually working around a hostile crowd, anxious police, or upset relatives, the New York newshound often gets off just one shot with his strobe. No need for a continuous shooting mode, either, he says. It's got to be right. No second chances here.

Porter in California, though, warns against using the strobe in some night news situations. The strobe light can be dangerous in a hostage situation, he cautions, especially when a confrontation involves guns. "You can also blind the police with the strobe," he says. During a tense hostage situation, Porter sticks to shooting available light with his long lenses—even at night.

Police Sergeant Carl Yates, who works with the media in Louisville, Kentucky, agrees. "Never underestimate the potential impact of a sudden flash of bright light at a night scene. It can anger officers; in some cases, escalate the incident; or worse, light up officers and others, making them potential targets."

GETTING ALONG WITH THE COPS

When Costanza approaches a crime scene at night, the first thing he does is shout "*New York Post* photographer." But he does not wait to begin taking pictures. "By the time the 'New York' comes out, I've fired the first picture," he says. On the nighttime crime beat, Costanza must be within 15 to 30 feet of his subject to get a well-exposed picture. Otherwise, the light from his strobe just will not be bright enough.

When faced with police at a crime scene, Costanza advances confidently but will walk away instead of confronting police if they are hostile. Bruce Chambers, a six-time Pulitzer nominee who shoots for the *Orange County Register* says, "Don't ask cops. They will say, 'stand behind the yellow line. Firefighters don't care where you are. They are so busy doing their job."

Jim MacMillan, who at one time covered at least 30 murders a year for the *Philadelphia Daily News*, says that he goes in with confidence. "If I am going to get in a dispute with them over my rights, I have already lost," he says. Like Costanza, MacMillan will try to find the path of least resistance, but he has still faced everything from special treatment to harassment. The cops are especially protective of the scene if children are involved or if a cop has been hurt, he says. Under those circumstances, "I know I am going to run into problems," he notes. "Whatever happens, my advice to photographers is to leave the baggage of any dispute when approaching your next scene. One cop may have been abusive one day, while another may lay out the red carpet the next."

WHEN THE POLICE SAY NO PICTURES

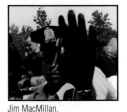

Jim MacMillan,
Philadelphia Daily News

The police cite a number of reasons for pushing the media away from crime, accident, or disaster scenes. They sometimes feel (mistakenly) that they must protect the privacy of citizens from the press, says Donald Middlebrooks, who has written about police

HOSTAGE SITUATION: A CASE STUDY

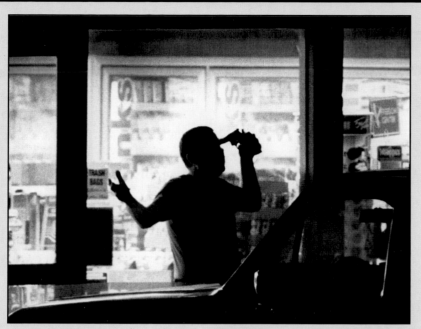

At home early one morning, *Fort Worth Star-Telegram* staffer Joyce Marshall received a call from her paper's city desk. A man was holding his wife hostage at a 7–Eleven convenience store in nearby Arlington, Texas. Joyce threw on her clothes and, without brushing her teeth or combing her hair, jumped into her car.

"This is probably a false alarm," she was thinking. "Most of them are." With her cameras already in the trunk, she sped the five miles to the store in her two-door Subaru. As soon as she got to the store's parking lot, she got out of her car, grabbed her gear, and checked with the police officer in charge for an update. After determining that this standoff was for real, she called her office for backup equipment, including a 600mm lens and a two-way portable radio.

She knew the man had already shot and possibly killed someone inside the store. Later, she learned that the gunman's name was Thomas Stephens. His wife had left him because of his continued physical abuse during their 17-year marriage. When the divorce papers had arrived the day before, he snapped. He left the drug treatment center he was in and tracked down his wife, at work in the store. In taking her hostage, he killed several of her coworkers.

Aware there had been gunfire at the store, Marshall used a car in a nearby driveway as protection. She had a clear view of the store window. Her telephoto lens and radio arrived via another staffer who took up a position behind the store.

"I was inside the police barrier," she recalls.

"That area was cordoned off. The time dragged on interminably. I had not eaten; I could not get a drink of water. I had not brushed my teeth or my hair, and there was no bathroom."

Marshall knew that if she left she would not be allowed to get across the police barrier again. "I had to stay."

As the sun was setting directly into Marshall's lens, police went in to remove the victims. Marshall constructed a homemade sunshade on her lens barrel with some cardboard she found nearby and tape she kept wrapped around one leg of her tripod.

When removing the victims, the officers left the front door open. With her eye glued to her viewfinder, Marshall noticed Stephens coming to the front of the store while holding a gun to his wife's head. Marshall snapped off several frames.

By this time, a crowd had gathered behind the police lines. The neighborhood audience drank pop and beer and watched the situation in the 7–Eleven unfold like a movie playing in a theater. When the SWAT team arrived, the crowd started to yell, "Shoot them, shoot them. Hurry up and get this thing over with."

Marshall began switching to more sensitive ISOs. She went from ISO 200 to 400 then to 800 and then to 1600. Only the lights in the store illuminated the site. Just then, Marshall could make out movement at the front of the store—a shadowy figure so low to the ground she could not photograph it. It was Stephens's wife.

Marshall later learned that when the gunman allowed his wife to go to the bathroom, she slipped outside. Within minutes, Stephens, holding a gun to his head, walked out of the store. He said he would shoot himself at the count of 30.

"Surely they will do something about it," Marshall thought. In the silhouette against the store's window she could see that the gun's hammer was pulled back, ready to fire. When he got to 30, Stephens paused a few seconds. Marshall quickly took a few frames.

Then the gunman fired a bullet into his own head and slumped to the ground. The crowd rushed forward.

"I'm not sure I shot a photo of the body," Marshall says now. "My mind was on getting back to the paper."

Marshall quickly selected the frame of Stephens pointing the gun to his own head.

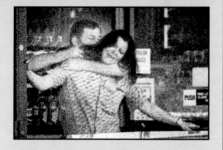

From daylight until dark, Joyce Marshall waited seven hours while a tense hostage situation played itself out. The stand-off finally ended (ABOVE, TOP) when the man took his own life. His wife, whom he had been holding hostage, escaped (ABOVE, BOTTOM). Joyce Marshall, *Fort Worth Star-Telegram*

She then found the frame of Stephens holding his wife hostage, which was difficult to print because of the sun's flare. Also, because the subjects occupied only a small part of the image, she had to enlarge it extensively. The paper's editors felt the suicide picture was too graphic for the front page and ran it inside, but they played the hostage photo as the lead picture on page one for the following day. ■

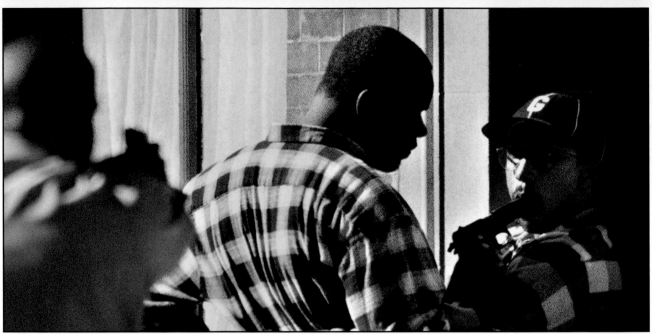

After a high-speed chase into the center of Philadelphia, a triple-murder suspect bailed out of his car and led police on a brief foot-chase. As officers closed in, guns drawn, the suspect took a hostage (the man in the checkered shirt), and placed the barrel of his gun into his own mouth. Jim MacMillan shot this part of the sequence with a 500mm lens plus a 1.4X tele-extender, giving him an effective 700mm telephoto. The long lens allowed him to stay back and avoid the possibility of taking a bullet himself. All photos, Jim MacMillan, *Philadelphia Daily News*

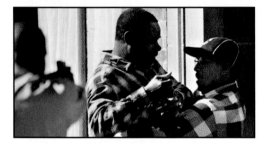

The hostage wrestles away the suspect's gun.

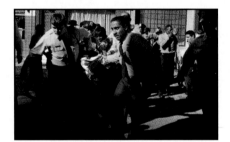

Police carry the wounded suspect to the paddy wagon. After the hostage pulled the gun away, police opened fire and hit the suspect twice. Using a second camera body, MacMillan rushed in and shot this photo with a wide-angle lens.

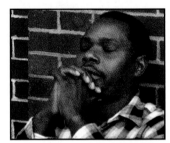

The relieved hostage gives thanks while police arrest the gunman. The hostage was unharmed, and hailed as a hero by police for his cool demeanor under pressure. MacMillan, using a 80–200mm zoom on his third camera body, took this candid portrait. The entire incident lasted 30 seconds.

and photojournalistic access. Sometimes police claim to be pushing the media away to prevent interference with rescue efforts or to avoid pretrial problems that will prevent them from successfully prosecuting their case.

Too often, these reasons are an easy dodge for getting reporters and photographers out of law enforcement's hair at a time when the police are excited and sometimes overwhelmed by a disaster or a crime scene at which they are working. But that does not mean you can ignore the police when they do not want you around.

KNOW YOUR BOUNDS

Many police agencies today use a two-perimeter system to deal with the media, says Sergeant Yates of the Louisville, Kentucky, police department. They first establish an outer perimeter as a barrier for the general public. Once the scene has been secured, they create an inner perimeter for the news media.

One way to avoid some problems is to be aware of the crime-scene perimeter. If you get there before the police put up the yellow tape, you do not want to contaminate the scene—by stepping on a bullet, for example. Kent Porter recounts the time he arrived before police when a man had been bludgeoned with

The hour was sneaking up on midnight in Manhattan. Sam Costanza was sitting behind the wheel of his 1976 Ford Maverick, casually listening to the crackling sound of his scanner radio. So far, the evening was business as usual for the veteran contract photographer for the *New York Post*. Then he heard the New York City Police Department's special operations dispatcher: "10-10 shots fired on Wheeler Avenue in the Bronx."

Costanza did not move, but he continued listening. A shooting on Wheeler Avenue was not news. Just another of many weekly shootings in that rough section of the Bronx—definitely not page-one news for the next day's *Post*. There was no payoff for Costanza, a contract photographer, to cover "another routine shooting."

But, the next transmission from the special operations dispatcher alerted Costanza that a "newsworthy condition" was shaping up.

The disembodied voice on the radio said, "Three men to Jacobi Hospital for trauma."

From years of listening to the police department, Costanza knew that the second transmission meant that three officers were involved in a situation involving the death of a civilian but that no officers had been injured. According to police procedure, a New York officer always goes to a city hospital following situations involving the death of a civilian—"trauma." Putting the first and second transmissions together, Costanza figured that police had been involved with the "10-10 shots fired."

"Now my wheels are turning," Costanza recalls. "I head for the Bronx from my current position on the upper West Side of Manhattan."

Pushing his powder-blue Maverick at 80 miles per hour down the Sheridan Expressway, the photographer heard the crucial third transmission by the Special Operations Division, but by now the dispatcher's voice was tense. "Perp down. DOA, 1157 Wheeler Avenue, Bronx."

Costanza's experienced ears translated. At least three officers had been involved in shooting another person. That person was now dead at 1157 Wheeler Avenue, Bronx.

The photographer arrived at Wheeler Avenue, parked, jumped out of his car, and

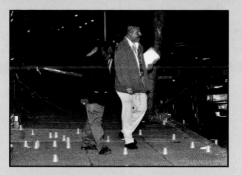

Costanza could fire only three quick frames before the police hustled him away from the scene where they had shot an unarmed man. Sam Costanza, Sipa Press

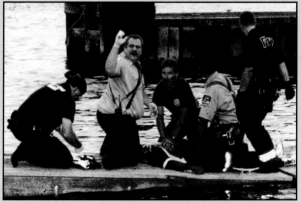

Medics frantically try to revive one of two drowning victims. To arrive in time to cover this kind of spot news, Sam Costanza carefully monitors two scanners in his car and as well as a portable scanner that he carries with him. Sam Costanza, *New York Post*

slung his two Nikons, mounted with Vivitar 283s, over his shoulder. Starting toward the crime scene, which was halfway down the block, he was accosted by no fewer than four officers who, seeing the cameras, told him he could proceed no further because an active crime scene had been set up.

Faced with tough, big-city cops attempting to block his access to crime scenes nearly every night of his working life, Costanza was not discouraged. Rather than waste time, he returned to his car, and drove around the block. This time, he knew he'd need a ruse to get near.

Now, wearing a black military fatigue jacket, he left the car and headed out with just one Nikon and flash unit tucked under his arm and out of view of the officers. He placed his hand radio, cranked up to full volume, in his upper jacket pocket. Perhaps, he hoped, the uniformed cops on this end of Wheeler would mistake him for a detective.

The ruse worked. The uniformed cops, he recalls, "neglected to accost me." Costanza got to within 25 feet of the crime scene, where

he noticed Styrofoam cups, at least 30 at first count, placed upside down on the sidewalk. From past experience, he knew that the police use the cups to mark the location of spent bullet rounds or bullet casings. The number of cups indicated that an incredible orgy of gunfire had taken place. He had never seen so many cups at a crime scene.

"As soon as I spotted the cups, I knew this was the picture," Costanza says. "The cups would immediately show that multiple rounds had been fired in this area no larger than 40 square feet."

Costanza also knew that once he pulled out his camera and shot, the cops would shut him down. He knew he could get off one—and only one—shot before he was out. Costanza picked up the camera and flash. He had prefocused the camera on infinity, set the f-stop at 5.6 on his 35mm lens, the shutter speed at 1/60 sec., and the strobe on auto. Just as a pair of plainclothes investigators walked by the overturned cups, he fired off three frames.

"All hell broke loose," he says. The police surrounded him and "escorted" him away. The first thing Costanza did when he got back to his Maverick was to call the city desk of the *New York Post*. "At least 30 shots appear to have been fired by N.Y.P.D., and there's a dead perp in the vestibule at 1157 Washington Avenue," he reported.

The editor responded, "I'm only interested if it's a cop that gets shot, not a perp."

Despite the editor's bad call, Costanza had left the scene with incredibly important pictures. Four members of N.Y.P.D.'s elite Street Crimes Unit had fired 41—not just 30—bullets at Amadou Diallo, an unarmed immigrant from Guinea, West Africa.

Nineteen bullets riddled the man's body. Diallo's death set off an intense racial conflict in New York and a review of New York police policies. When the four officers were found not guilty of second-degree murder, a new round of protests erupted—not just in New York but also around the country.

While the *Post* never ran Costanza's picture, his agency, Sipa Press, sold the image to publications around the world. For Costanza, it was just another night in the life of a spot news photographer. ■

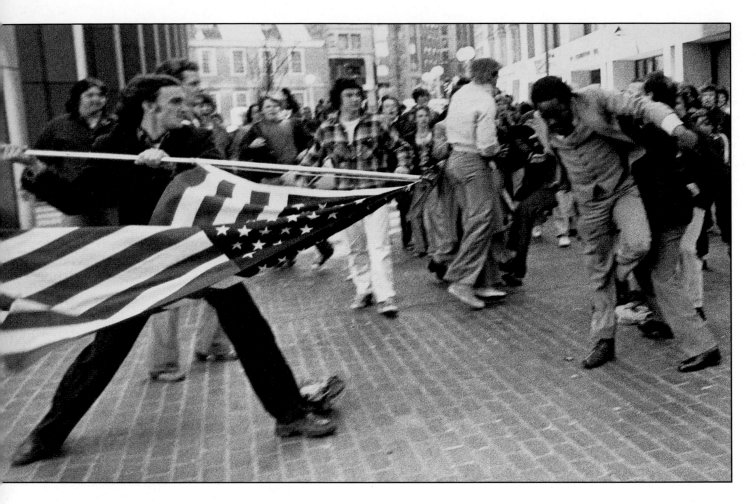

a tire iron 27 times. "My shoe prints got all over the crime scene," he recalls. "I had blood on my shoes. 'We have to make sure you are not the murderer,' the cops said. And then they took my shoes. The only thing I had to wear were my spiked baseball shoes."

The outer perimeter is designed to keep away curiosity-seekers. Photographers with media credentials should be able to cross the outer perimeter but not the inner perimeter. Inside the yellow tape is where the crime scene is located.

Sergeant Yates suggests that photographers look for an officer (preferably a commanding officer), identify themselves, and then ask, "Could you direct me to where you want the news media?" If this fails, ask if there is anyone on the scene in charge of public information.

Do not violate the inner perimeter. You have no more legal right of access than the general public. What you do have, and what you hope the police will know, is a more significant reason to be there than the general public does. (See Chapter 16, "Law.")

Yates recommends that, unless an immediate photo is necessary, you take time to talk to officers before shooting. Try to get a feel

for the mood of the scene. Police are particularly on edge when a fellow officer has been injured or killed and may overreact. "These are times to ask first and shoot later," Yates points out. "Express regrets and ease into the situation."

In the rare instances when you arrive at the scene of a crime in progress, the police do not have the right to evict you even for your own safety. Of course, do not get in their way. They definitely have enough problems without trying to protect you.

Finally, Yates observes, do not argue with a police officer. "You can argue until you're blue in the face," he says, "and all you will usually be left with is a blue face."

ON THE SCENE
Once the police have set up their perimeter, you often have to shoot with a long lens and even add the tele-extender. Jim MacMillan's 500mm lens and extenders come in handy at times like this.

Sometimes the problem is not the length of lens but of time. You just have to wait.

Sam Costanza has done a lot of waiting in his time. He puts it this way: "Wait for the chief medical examiner to get there. Wait for the crime scene detectives to arrive. Wait for the medical examiner to check the wounds. Wait for the police photographer to photograph the body. And, finally, wait for the crime scene detectives to look to see if there are any weapons on the ground." While shooting spot news can produce an adrenaline rush, it can also result in fallen arches and tired legs.

Kent Porter in Santa Rosa says he tries to be as thorough as the detectives themselves. "I check to see if I have all the evidence," he says. "Do I have all the names I need? If it is a shooting, do I have a picture of the gun? Do I have the picture of the main investigator? Do I have all the players the reporter has talked to? Do I have a photo of the surrounding scene? Did I get low and shoot the tape?" To ensure complete coverage, Porter says he always shoots the crime scene like it was a picture story with a beginning, a middle, and an end.

PHOTOGRAPHING A CRIME IN PROGRESS
Unlike reporters who can reconstruct the details of a mugging from police reports and eyewitness accounts, the photographer must be at the crime scene to get action pictures. Robbers, kidnappers, rapists, and murderers tend to shy away from the harsh glare of public exposure.

Predicting Violence
A photographer with a good news sense, however, can learn to predict some situations that might erupt into violence. For instance,

tension was running high during the National Basketball Association Playoffs in Los Angeles. Stan Lim of the *Inland Valley Daily Bulletin* knew, based on fans' behavior after previous tight games, to expect rowdiness after the sixth game of the series.

Lim's news sense led him to stick around after the game rather than going straight back to the newsroom.

When the final horn signaled a win by the Lakers, Lim headed for the streets. The crowd went wild, even torching a media truck parked outside the coliseum. Using a strobe and slow shutter speed, Lim photographed one of the rioters carrying a cardboard cut-out of the Lakers's Shaquille O'Neal as fire consumed the truck in the background. Anticipating what was about to happen had put Lim in the right place at the right time.

Be aware that demonstrations and marches can also become crime scenes. Even the police can overreact. Paul Brown was covering protests against the World Trade Organization for the *Seattle Post-Intelligencer* when police began firing rubber bullets at point-blank range into a group of demonstrators (see page 26). Seattle police initially denied doing so, but Brown's photos clearly showed police bearing down on the crowd with the menacing weapons. The photographer himself was hit by one of the bullets. After one of Brown's photos appeared on the newspaper's front page, the police were forced to admit that they had been firing

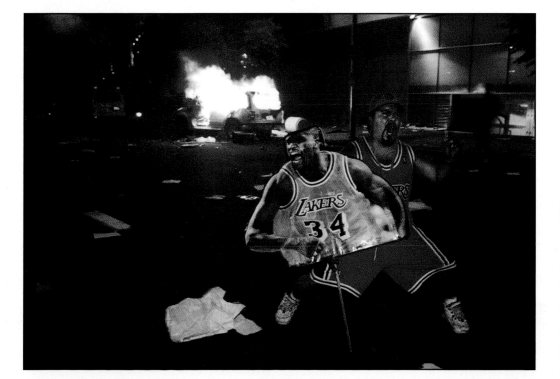

A fan hoists a life-size cutout of the LA Lakers's Shaquille O'Neal outside the Staples Center in Los Angeles. The team had just defeated the Indiana Pacers in the NBA Finals. In the background is a burning news media truck, set ablaze by out-of-control fans. The photographer combined flash and a slow shutter to get both the rioter and the burning truck.
Stan Lim, *Inland Valley* [California] *Daily Bulletin*

the weapons. The picture eventually ran on the cover of *Time* magazine.

STAYING ALIVE: A CASE STUDY

Whether anticipating violence or racing into it on assignment, photographers must stay mentally alert to protect themselves while covering the story.

With the acquittal of white police officers who had been videotaped beating Rodney King, an African-American man, Los Angeles erupted into riots. By the second day of the riots, the Associated Press had called in John Gaps III, at the time one of the photographers the AP flies in when the agency needs an extra shooter to hit the ground running. They call this breed of photojournalist a photographic "fireman." Gaps was on the AP's photographic emergency squad.

"They told me to get to L.A.," Gaps recalls of receiving the assignment as the riots started to unfold. He landed at LAX, rented a car, and, after picking up another AP staffer (who had never covered a riot), headed for 18th and Broadway—the heart of the violence.

The photographers drove up to a blazing electronics warehouse, where looters were still hauling out the expensive goods. "It didn't seem like a violent crowd," Gaps recalls. "I told the other photographer that I was going to park the car. If I could get on the ground, we wouldn't look like a drive-by." Gaps knew that by taking pictures from the car, he could be mistaken for an undercover policeman.

Gaps's less experienced partner, however, started photographing through the windshield. Almost immediately, a young Latino came to the driver's side of the car and aimed a gun at Gaps. Gaps picks up the story:

"I put my hands up, opened the car door, and said 'Here.' I showed him the camera, a Nikon with a medium zoom and strobe on it, and held it out the car door.

"Here, take the camera," Gaps told the man. "He lowered the gun, reached across, and took the camera from me.

"He had the camera in his hand, and I began to pull out. He raised the gun and aimed at me through the (closed) window," Gaps recalls. "Then he pulled the trigger right by my head. The car window just exploded.

"Fortunately, the glass deflected the bullet. He was standing right beside me when he pulled the trigger. He tried to blow my head off.

"Then I looked up, and traffic had cleared in front of the car. I hit the accelerator and drove like a bat out of hell down the street with my head down.

"I got about two blocks away before I stopped to see if anyone was hit. The bullet was lodged in the back seat.

"I guess we looked like cops taking pictures from the car. That set people off. We're just lucky we got out alive."

Of course, no flak jacket or bulletproof vest would have saved Gaps had the shooter's aim been slightly more accurate.

The moral to the story is this: take care when covering news. Even an automobile provides no real protection.

WHY SHOOT FIRES?

Reporting fires is an important part of the photojournalist's job. More than 500,000 homes catch fire each year. Fires also destroy apartment houses, stores, office buildings, and factories. Fires sweep through schools where children are having classes. Autos and trucks burn up, and fires devour forests in all parts of the country.

Altogether, 2 million fires are reported annually, costing more than $12 billion in property damage, according to the National Board of Fire Underwriters. Still more serious than monetary loss, thousands of people die in fires each year.

A photo can show not only the emotion of the participants but also the size of the fire better than words can. If a fire breaks out on the 23rd story of a building from which an occupant might jump, a photo can indicate just how high 23 stories really is. The reader can quickly grasp the danger of jumping. If a wooden warehouse catches fire, requiring four companies to halt the spread of the flames, a photo can give the reader an idea of the vastness of the blaze.

After the fire has been extinguished, a photo of the charred aftermath carries impact beyond a mere statistical description of the loss. A photo of a house burning or an office worker trapped in a building ignites an empathetic reaction in the viewer, who thinks, "that could be my house . . . that could be me in that building."

FINDING AND FLEEING FIRES

Scanner radios, of course, provide one key means of learning about fires, but you can also develop a sense for when fires might occur. Kent Porter of Santa Rosa, California, has become an amateur meteorologist. By watching for low humidity and high winds, he is aware of the kinds of days when Northern California will be susceptible to wildfires.

These fires might start in a field of dry grass, a grove of trees, or in someone's backyard. When conditions are right, such fires

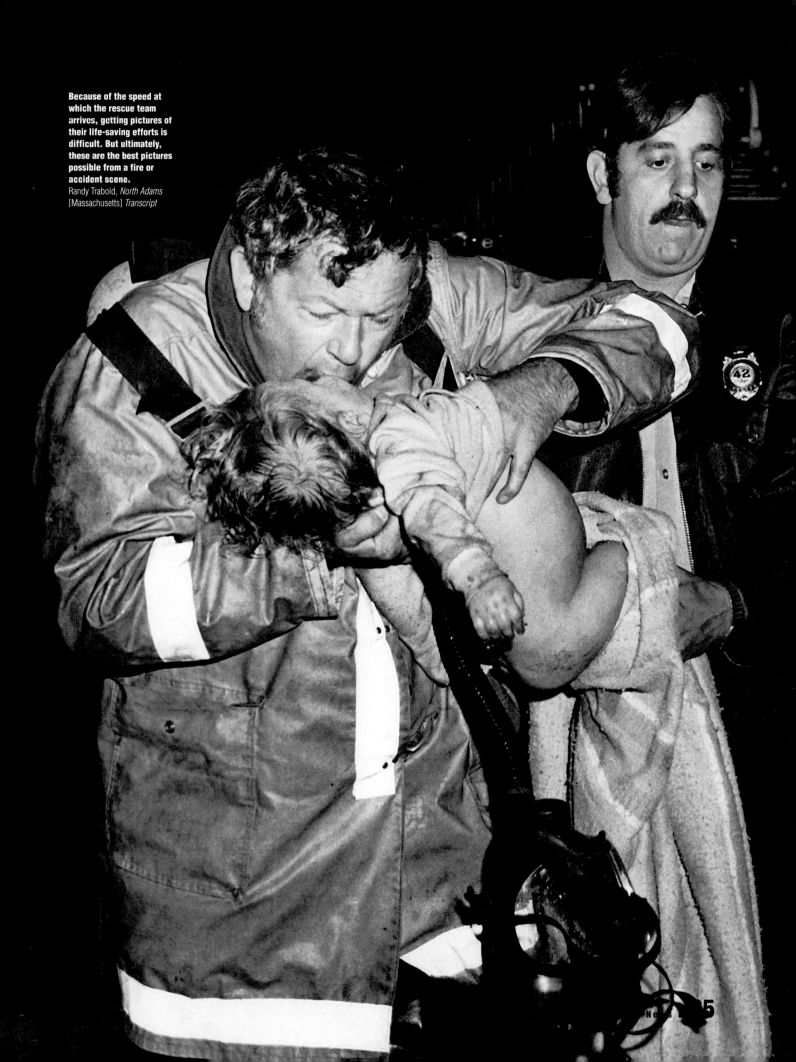

Because of the speed at which the rescue team arrives, getting pictures of their life-saving efforts is difficult. But ultimately, these are the best pictures possible from a fire or accident scene.
Randy Trabold, *North Adams* [Massachusetts] *Transcript*

LEAP FOR LIFE
A FIRE IN BOSTON

Stanley Forman, three-time Pulitzer Prize-winning photographer, knows Boston like the back of his hand. In this instance, he was cruising when he actually smelled smoke and pulled up to the burning house along with police. Trapped on the roof, the man in the pictures first tossed down the child. When the woman froze, the man pushed her off before he jumped. The woman suffered minor injuries, but everyone else was okay. Forman approached the fire as if shooting a picture story. He takes the reader through the danger to the trapped residents on the roof, follows up with pictures of the rescue, and comes in tight to end with a close-up of the officer holding the child. ■

Photos by Stanley Forman

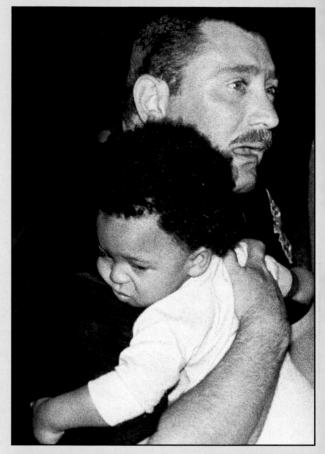

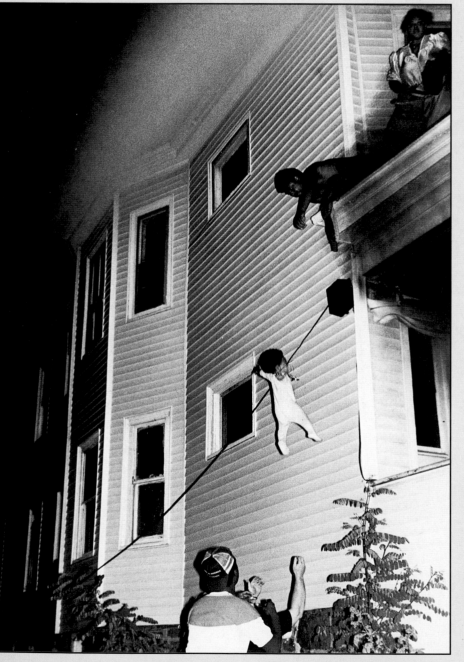

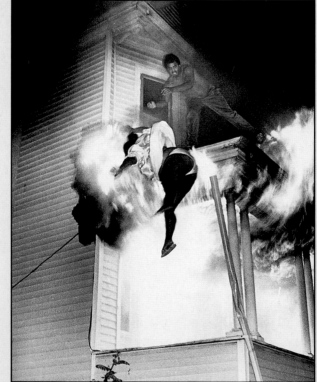

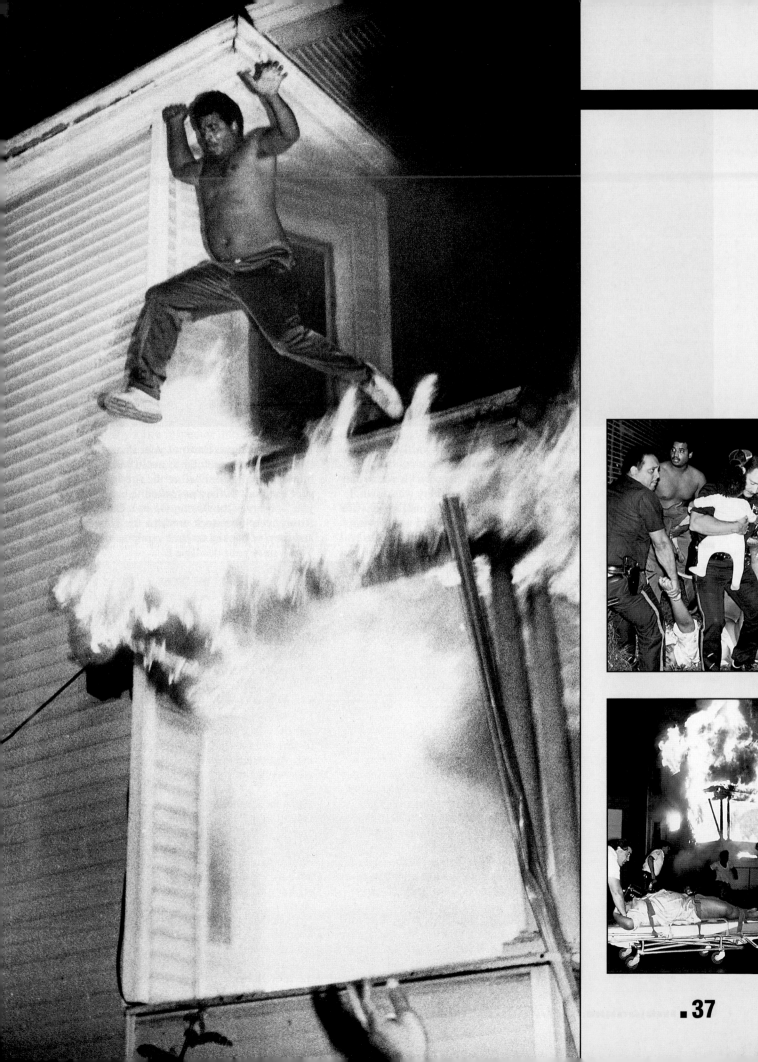

both the fire and police chiefs for cutline information: the exact location of the fire, the number of alarms sounded, the companies that responded, an estimate about the extent of the damage, and the names of the injured and what hospitals they were taken to.

NIGHT FIRES ARE DIFFICULT

Night fires tend to flare up between midnight and 6:00 A.M., when people are sleeping and smoke goes unnoticed. Arsonists choose nighttime for this reason. Because nighttime fires are not reported quickly, they tend to be larger and more frequent.

Photographically, night fires pose difficulties. The *Boston Globe*'s George Rizer, for example, does not take a reflected light-meter reading at nighttime fires.

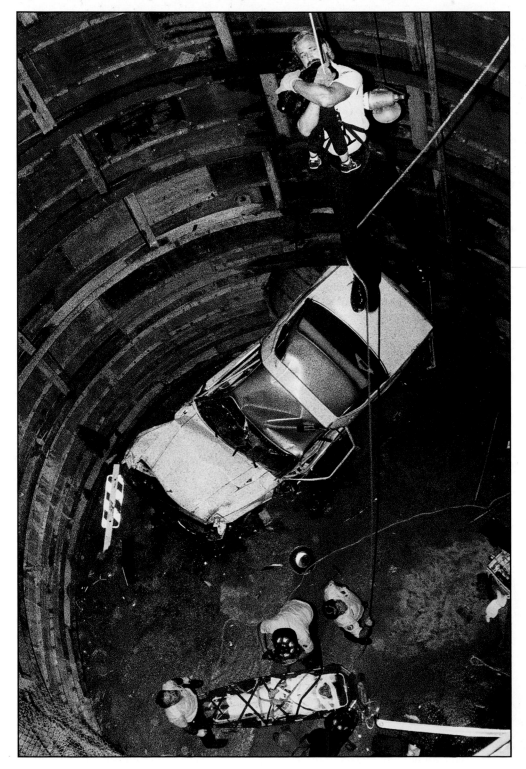

Remarkably, no one was hurt in this freak accident. Often a report on the scanner radio will provide the first tip of a news event.
Craig Hartley, *Houston Post*

"Why bother?" he asks. "A meter will be misled by the light from the flames and will not accurately measure the amount of light reflected off the sides of the building."

For night fires, Rizer puts his camera on manual, uses a slow shutter speed, and adds flash. At faster shutter speeds, the flames still appear in the image, but the building goes black. Rizer is balancing the light from the strobe with the available light from the fire, the streetlights, and the portable working lights set up by the fire department. Within 50 feet, the flash also helps light up the building.

Kent Porter uses the same basic technique. Porter puts the flash on 1/8 power. Using a 20mm or 24mm lens, he shoots at f/5.6, usually at a 1/30 sec. He warns against using this technique with a long lens, lest the flash give subjects "red eye."

Besides lighting up the foreground, the strobe has an additional benefit. If the fire-fighters have brought in portable lights, the spots will give off an orange color. The light from the strobe helps to counterbalance this orange cast from the tungsten lights. (See Chapter 9, "Strobe.")

With the slow shutter speed, you must avoid even slight camera movement during the exposure. Rizer recommends resting the camera on a car, a fire hydrant, or holding the camera tightly and leaning against a lamppost to reduce camera movement.

Philadelphia's Jim MacMillan finds he can even use his longer lenses at night if he braces himself carefully. He can shoot at 1/15 or 1/8 sec. with a 200mm lens when he is leaning securely against a car or utility pole. He tries to wedge the camera lens against a stationary object and then "hammer off a number of frames to try to get one that's sharp." But he puts away the strobe when flames start shooting out of every window in the building. "If it looks like a Christmas tree," he says, "you can shoot in available light, and you'll get great, action-packed fire pictures."

COVERING ACCIDENTS AND DISASTERS: GRIM BUT NECESSARY

(Dateline Baltimore)
One Dead, 21 Hurt in Bethlehem Steel Blast
(Dateline Houston) Fatal Pileup on I45
So read the daily headlines, as accidents take

A bicycle accident might not merit photographic coverage–except when Sidewalk Santas come to the aid of the cyclist. This minor accident takes on the properties of a feature photo. Marty Lederhandler, Associated Press

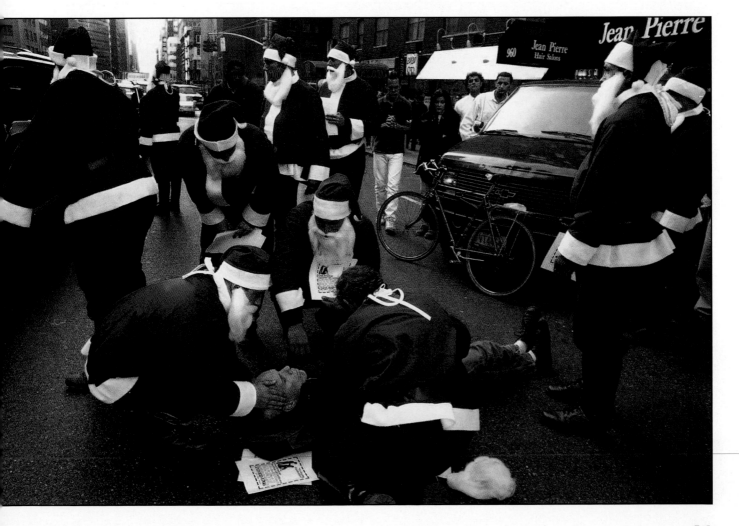

their toll of more than 100,000 lives and 10 million injuries each year (according to the National Safety Council). Almost half the accidents in the United States involve cars. But people also die from falls, burns, drownings, gunshot wounds, poisonings, and work-related accidents.

Accidents make news. If one million Bay Area residents drive home safely on the freeway Friday night, that's not news. But if two people die in an auto crash on the Golden Gate Bridge, readers want to read a story and see a picture of the accident.

PHOTO POSSIBILITIES: FROM TRAGIC TO BIZARRE
If 100 accidents take place daily in a typical city, no two will be identical. However, all accidents have certain points in common for the photographer.

Check Human Tragedy First
Concentrate on the human element of any tragedy. Readers relate to people pictures. Rick Roach of the *Vacaville Reporter* knew this when he came in close to photograph an emergency worker attempting to comfort a woman trapped beneath her car (see page 39).

Make a record
Make a straightforward record of what happened. The viewer, who does not know how the cars hit or where they landed, wants to see the cars' relationship to one another and to the highway.

Symbolic pictures imply rather than tell
In some situations, an accident story is better told with a symbolic rather than a literal picture. A bent wagon lying in the street carries its own silent message. There is no need to show the body of the dead child.

Photograph the cause
In news events such as riots or murders, there is no way to photograph the cause. At an accident, however, you can sometimes show clearly what caused the collision. If a car failed to stop on a slippery street, you might show the wet pavement in the foreground and the damaged vehicle in the background.

Weather is a constant news topic, and photographers are often assigned to find "weather art." The photographer captured this brilliant rainbow at sunset as fast-moving showers were leaving the area.
John Tlumacki, *Boston Globe*

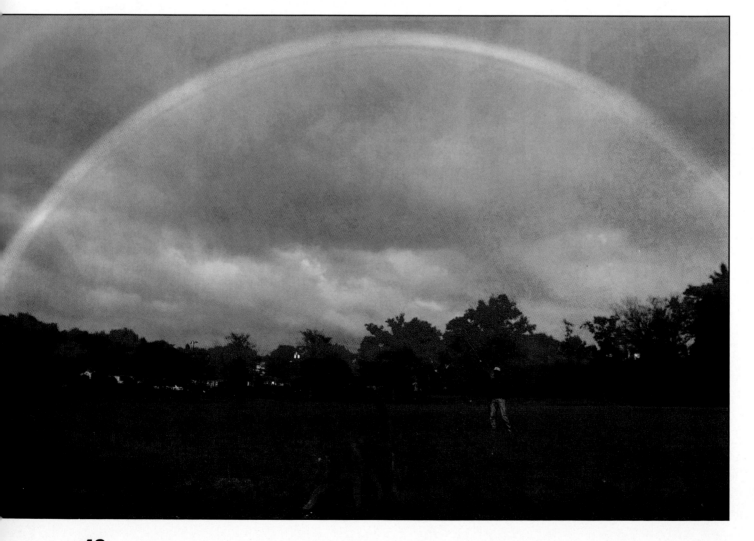

On a dry day, you might photograph skid marks left by the car as it screeched to a halt. Perhaps the accident was caused by the poor visibility of street signs. In that situation, a picture that showed the confusing array of flashing lights and fluorescent billboards that distracted the driver would be effective.

Show the impact
Accidents affect more than the drivers of the involved vehicles. Look in both directions for long lines of blocked traffic and drivers slowing down to gaze as they pass the site.

Feature one aspect
Notice how people adapt to their misfortune. Record the kinds of items people save from their wrecked vehicles. Note whether they act angry, sad, or frustrated.

Catch the distress on the face of an owner of a new Mini Cooper as she views for the first time her crumpled fender. See if an owner of a 13-year-old Saturn reacts the same way when he sees the damage to his clunker.

Do not become hardened, however. No matter the size of the mishap, the accident usually is still a tragedy, or at least a traumatic experience, to the people involved. Even a bicycle accident can result in a telling picture, especially if several Santas stop to aid the victim (see page 41).

Follow up
If accidents keep occurring at one particular intersection, you might follow up to see if the highway department does anything to correct the hazard. A time exposure showing the traffic congestion might help to spur the highway department into action.

WEATHER:
NEWS EVERYBODY TALKS ABOUT
Photographers do cover blinding snowstorms or raging hurricanes on every shift. However, even the slightest change in weather, from sunny and hot to cloudy and cool, interests and affects readers. The weather forecast is one of the most highly read sections of a web site or newspaper.

Just one month before a tornado ripped the roof from this home, it had been featured in an architectural magazine. Using the magazine spread in the photograph helps tell the before as well as the after of this disaster. Robert Cohen, for the *Memphis* [Tennessee] *Commercial Appeal*

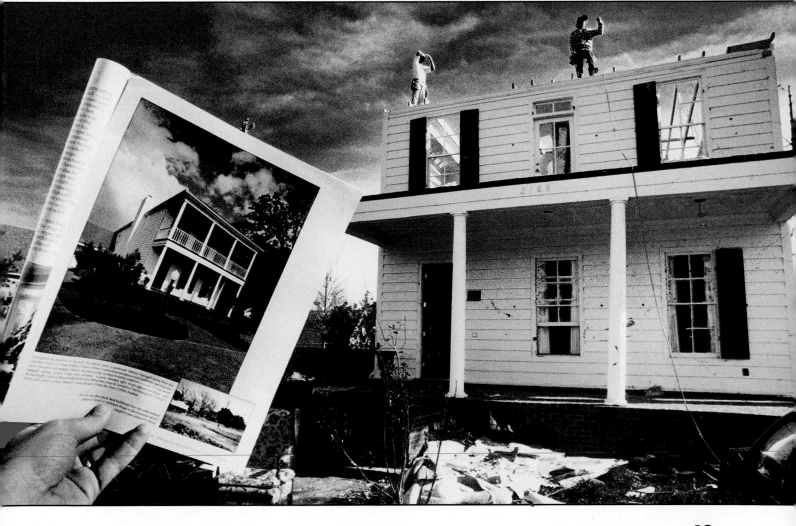

On a slow news day, editors often call for "weather art"—regardless of the forecast.

GETTING THERE MAY BE THE BIGGEST CHALLENGE

Taking pictures at the scene of a spot-news event requires a photographer with a cool head, someone who can work under pressure and adverse conditions. You need no unusual equipment or techniques—just nerves of steel and an unruffled disposition. However, before you arrive at the accident scene, you must be prepared. Load your camera and charge up your electronic flash so you will be ready to start clicking the minute you get out of the car.

In fact, getting to an accident in time is often the biggest challenge for the spot-news photographer. If you are stuck on the North Loop when two cars crash on the South Loop, you might find only a few glass shards from a broken windshield by the time you get

to the scene. The ambulance has come and gone. Removed by the wrecker, even the smashed vehicles are already on their way to the garage.

Consequently, a news photographer's three most important pieces of equipment—after camera gear and a car, of course—are a scanner radio, a cell phone, and a Thomas Brothers map or GPS device. The radio provides the first report of the accident, the cell phone allows the photographer to check the location, and the detailed map or GPS shows the quickest way to get to the scene.

However, Stanley Forman attributes his success in winning three Pulitzer Prizes to old-fashioned, low-tech brainpower—knowing his city like the back of his hand. (See Forman's dramatic fire coverage on pages 36–37 and on page 377.)

Bruce Chambers of the *Orange County Register* keeps it simple. If two news events

The oil tanker Argo Merchant went aground and broke up off the coast of Nantucket. Thousands of gallons of heavy fuel oil soiled the water. The Coast Guard provided journalists transportation by helicopter to the wreck site. Ken Kobré, for the *Boston Phoenix*

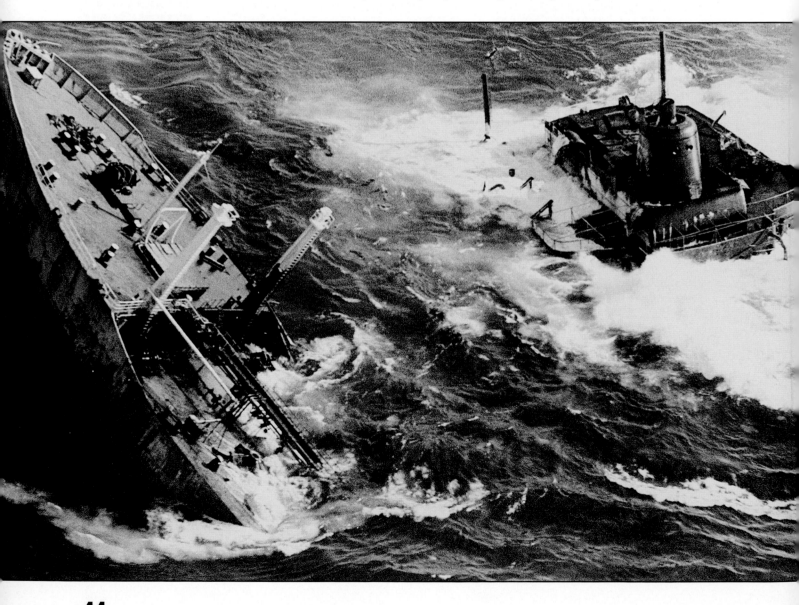

happen at the same time, he points out, "the best choice is the one closest at hand."

A spot-news photographer finds hardest to cover the story in which all forms of transportation are down. During a flood, hurricane, tornado, or blizzard, you often cannot drive a car or take public transportation.

Faced with a major natural disaster, you can sometimes get assistance from one of the public agencies such as the police department, fire department, Red Cross, civil defense headquarters, or the National Guard. In case of disasters at sea, you can telephone the Coast Guard. Each of these agencies has a public information officer who handles problems and requests from the media. When a major disaster occurs, many of these agencies provide not only facts and figures but transportation, as well, for the photojournalist.

When the oil tanker Argo Merchant ran aground, cracked in half, sank off Nantucket Island, and leaked thousands of barrels of oil into the sea, this author contacted the U.S. Coast Guard on Cape Cod in Massachusetts. The Coast Guard arranged for this author to fly in one of its planes to take pictures over the site (see opposite page).

In another case, when all of New England was buried under four-foot drifts during a major blizzard, this author contacted the National Guard, which provided a four-wheeled-drive vehicle and driver so he could photograph outlying areas.

As Dave Wurzel, a former New England photo bureau chief for United Press International, said, "When a big storm breaks and everyone else heads for home, that's when the spot news photographer goes to work."

DON'T SHOOT THE LAST FRAME
News photographers use multiple camera bodies so that they do not have to change

In hurricane-ravaged New Orleans, a man watches as a helicopter tries futilely to extinguish an out-of-control house fire. Because of the extensive flooding caused by the city's broken levies, fire trucks were unable to reach burning homes. In some cases whole blocks burned to the ground in the days following Hurricane Katrina.
Craig Warga, *Daily News* (New York)

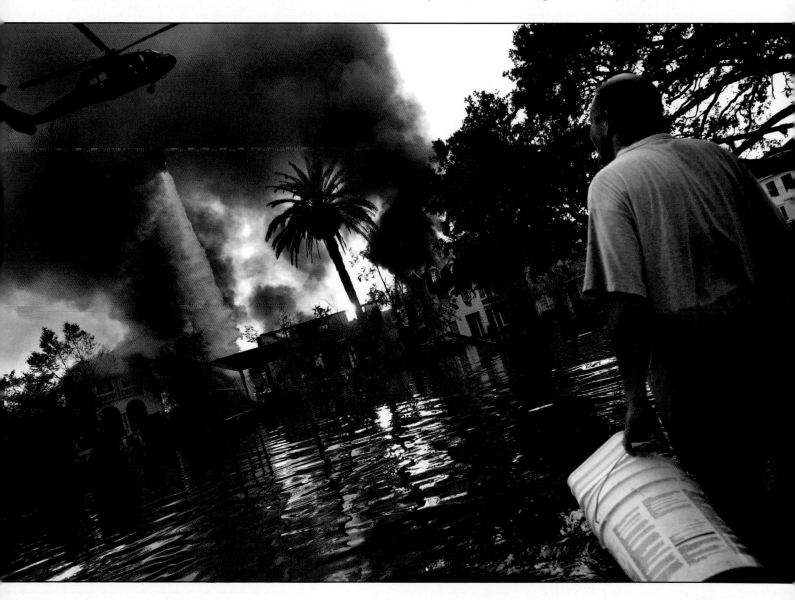

memory cards when the action is coming down. Some carry two or three bodies. Sam Costanza even carries a point-and-shoot automatic camera just in case he needs a backup.

One piece of advice worth repeating: do not shoot to the last megabyte. Memory cards' seemingly endless capacity can still come up short at a critical moment, especially when you are shooting RAW (see pages 158–159).

Annie Wells, now with the *Los Angeles Times*, attributes her Pulitzer Prize to conservative shooting while photographing the heroic rescue of a young woman in a flooded river (see page 1). Although she was shooting film at the time, the same strategy would apply today. (Wells shot the picture while at the *Santa Rosa Press Democrat*.) The last thing you want is to have to replace memory cards at the most dramatic moment. ∎

THE IMPACT OF COVERING TRAGEDY

Photojournalists have always worked on the front lines of tragedy—from covering the loss of life in local fires and accidents to recording the sweeping devastation of natural disasters and the bloody reality of international conflicts. In 2005, the American Psychological Association identified journalists as "first responders," people who rush in toward a disaster at personal risk when all other are rushing away.

Psychiatrist Anthony Feinstein, who has researched and written extensively on the subject of journalists and trauma, has concluded that photojournalists are the most affected by traumatic experiences.

The camera is no shield to the emotional trauma of bearing witness to horror.

The Dart Center for Journalism & Trauma, based at the University of Washington, together with the International Society for Traumatic Stress Studies, has published *Tragedies and Journalists: a guide for more effective coverage*, reproduced in part on the opposite page. The full report is available for download at *www.dartcenter.org*.

"We are working within a new age of war, terrorism, and coincidental natural disasters that no longer affect just spot news specialists like myself—who may be somewhat more prepared—but also the newspaper photographers who happened to be in New York for Fashion Week and found themselves covering the 9/11 attack, those who returned to find their own homes destroyed after covering Katrina, any parent who covers a school shooting, and all of us who learn that war and death don't cease—and that our new acquaintances will continue to die—after the completion of a combat assignment."

— Jim MacMillan, *Philadelphia Daily News*
Pulitzer Prize
Associated Press Team Coverage, Iraq War

NATIONAL PRESS PHOTOGRAPHERS ASSOCIATION CRITICAL INCIDENT RESPONSE TEAM (CIRT)
CIRT is a group of volunteers trained in peer support and sponsored by the National Press Photographers Association.

All team members are working photojournalists with extensive experience covering hard-news situations. The team has been trained to listen, to give information on emotional responses to traumatic incidents, and to find and give referrals (if necessary) to specialists in trauma therapy around the world through Newscoverage Unlimited and the International Society of Traumatic Stress Studies.

The services are free. Your identity, if you want to give it, and what you share with any member of the team will be held in the strictest confidence.
info@nppa.org
919/383-7246 phone
919/383-7261 fax

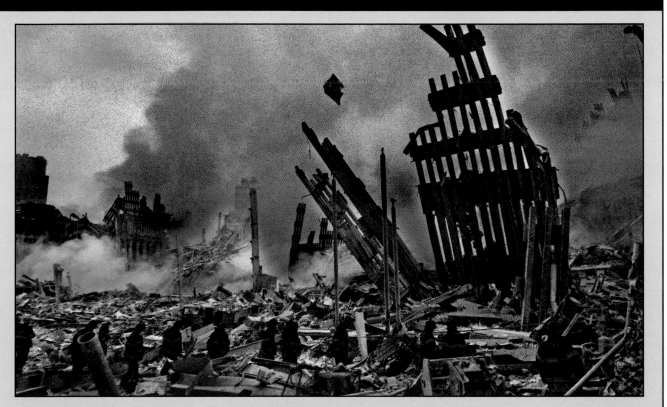

Covering any tragedy, from terrorist attacks like those on the World Trade Center on September 11, 2001 (ABOVE), to fatal car accidents, can take a psychological toll on photojournalists. Photojournalists, considered first responders in times of disaster and tragedy, need to recognize their potential vulnerability and not be fearful of seeking help. Jim MacMillan, *Philadelphia Daily News*

TRAGEDIES AND JOURNALISTS

TIPS FOR PHOTOJOURNALISTS WHO RESPOND TO TRAGEDIES

1. Understand that you may be the first to arrive at any scene. You may face dangerous situations and harsh reactions from law enforcement and the public. Stay calm and focused throughout. Be aware that a camera cannot prevent you from being injured. Do not hesitate to leave a scene if it becomes too dangerous. Any supervisor or editor should understand that a person's life is more important than a photo.
2. Treat every victim that you approach at a tragedy with sensitivity, dignity and respect. Do not react harshly to anyone's response to you. Politely identify yourself before requesting information.
3. You will record many bloody images during a tragedy. Ask yourself whether these are important enough for historical purposes or too graphic for your readers or viewers.
4. Do everything possible to avoid violating someone's private grieving. That doesn't mean that you shouldn't record photos of emotion at public scenes. However, do not intrude upon someone's private property or disturb victims during their grieving process.

5. Realize that you are a human being who must take care of your mind. Admit your emotions. Talk about what you witnessed to a trusted peer, friend or spouse. Write about it. Replace horrible images with positive ones. Establish a daily routine of healthful habits. Dr. Elana Newman, a licensed clinical psychologist who conducted a survey of 800 photojournalists, told a National Press Photographers Association convention: "Witnessing death and injury takes its toll, a toll that increases with exposure. The more such assignments photojournalists undertake, the more likely they are to experience psychological consequences." If your problems become overwhelming, do not hesitate to seek professional counseling.

TIPS FOR TAKING CARE OF YOURSELF

1. Know your limits. If you've been given a troublesome assignment that you feel you cannot perform, politely express your concerns to your supervisor. Tell the supervisor that you may not be the best person for the assignment. Explain why.

Excerpt from the Dart Center report *Tragedies and Journalists: a guide for more effective coverage*

2. Take breaks. A few minutes or a few hours away from the situation may help relieve your stress.
3. Find someone who is a sensitive listener. It can be an editor or a peer, but you must trust that the listener will not pass judgment on you. Perhaps it is someone who has faced a similar experience.
4. Learn how to deal with your stress. Find a hobby, exercise, attend a house of worship or, most important, spend time with your family, a significant other or friends — or all four. Try deep-breathing. The Eastern Connecticut Health Network recommends that you "take a long, slow, deep breath to the count of five, then exhale slowly to the count of five. Imagine breathing out excess tension and breathing in relaxation." All of these can be effective for your mental and physical well-being.
5. Understand that your problems may become overwhelming. Before he died in April 1945, war correspondent Ernie Pyle wrote, "I've been immersed in it too long. My spirit is wobbly and my mind is confused. The hurt has become too great." If this happens to you, seek counseling from a professional.

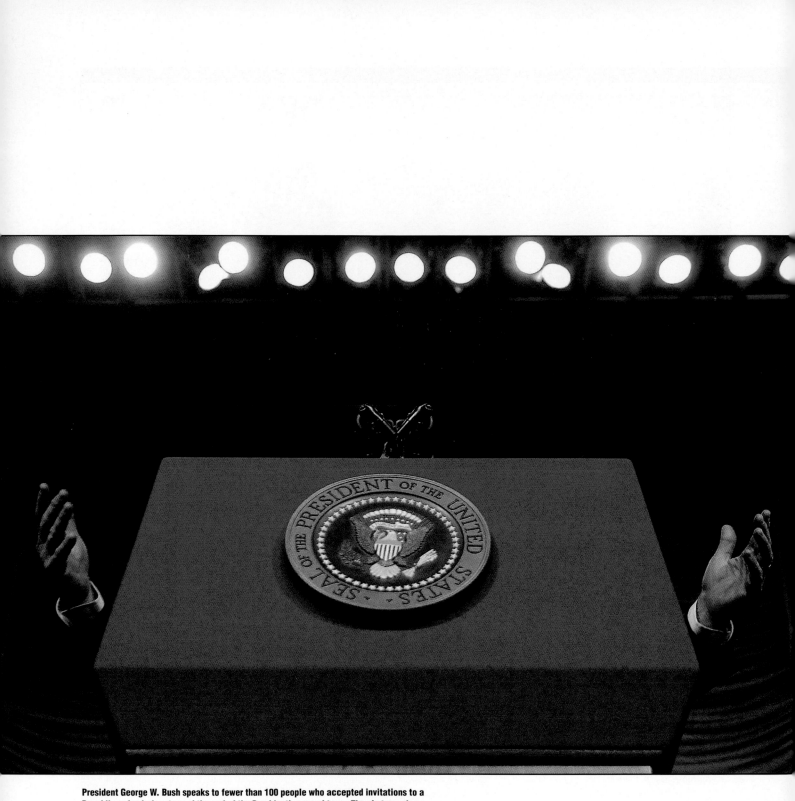

President George W. Bush speaks to fewer than 100 people who accepted invitations to a Republican fundraiser toward the end of the President's second term. The photographer looked for a picture that said "disappearing president."
Olivier Douliery, Abaca Press

General News

3

BEYOND THE PHOTO OP

Olivier Douliery had been assigned to cover President George W. Bush speaking at a Republican Party fundraiser. Shooting for the French agency Abaca Press, he found himself among 20 other photographers covering a planned event that attracted fewer than 100 attendees. The president's popularity in his final year in office was in a downward spiral, even among his former supporters.

As the photographers moved about the room, shooting from one position and then another, Douliery knew he did not want another routine picture of the president lecturing and gesturing.

A thinking person's photographer, he decided to go for an interpretive shot that would visually express the downward trend in the president's popularity.

First, though, he got his safe picture of the president speaking. Then he noticed that if he stood exactly beneath the podium that the President seemed to disappear behind the podium and the microphones.

Douliery waited in the same spot for 25 minutes. From his position beneath the podium, the presidential seal framed in the middle of his viewfinder, Douliery first got a shot of one presidential arm extending from the side of the podium. Then the other arm. Finally, and in only two frames, Douliery found the shot he was looking for.

Douliery's wide-angle lens captured President Bush hidden behind the microphones, both arms outstretched on either side of the podium. The president had faded away, leaving only his arms to wave up and down, the presidential seal standing in for his head.

The picture was an instant success. It was picked up by Getty Images, Polaris, United Press International, and Black Star picture agency, and then reproduced in many newspapers and magazines around the world.

Politicians plan media events that attract the camera, even if the events themselves have little news value. Called "photo opportunities or photo ops" these non-events, often filled with balloons and confetti, have been designed for the camera journalist.

If a senator puts on a stupid hat for a photo, editors can't resist the picture. Politicians and photographers manipulate each other, to their mutual benefit. Politicians look for free publicity and photographers want visual events. The picture of the senator wearing a cowboy hat is not wrong. It is simply not good journalism.

The challenge—and one that is not easy for photojournalists to meet when assigned to cover these orchestrated situations—is to look beyond what the politicos have planned and focus instead on the reality behind the staging. Douliery met the challenge.

GOING BEHIND THE SCENES

Politicians come alive at election time. The old "pol" leaves the desk in his plush office and starts pressing the flesh at ward meetings, cultural parades, and organizations for the elderly. The young challenger, by contrast, walks the streets of the ghetto with her suit jacket thrown over her shoulder. Both candidates plaster stickers on cars, erect billboards, appear in "I promise" TV ads, and attend massive rallies.

A photographer can take two sets of campaign pictures. One would show the candidate's public life—shaking hands, giving speeches, and greeting party workers. The other would reveal the candidate's private life—grabbing a few minutes alone with the family, planning strategy behind closed doors, pepping up the staff, and collapsing at the end of a 14-hour day.

All too often, news outlets present their readers with a one-sided visual portrait of the candidate—the public side, planned and orchestrated by the candidate's campaign directors. Editors tend to publish only upbeat, never downbeat, pictures; only happy, never sad, moments. Photographers continue to churn out photos of the candidate shaking hands and smiling—photos that reveal little about the person who wants to run the city, state, or federal government.

The major U.S. news magazines have done a much better job of behind-the-scenes coverage than most of the country's newspapers and web sites. To capture insightful pictures of politicians, some magazine photographers and their news organizations have developed special access to high-level officials. While these photojournalists have uncommon access, their techniques are still useful for photographing people whose lives seem to be one long photo op.

Diana Walker, contract photographer for *Time* magazine, has been covering the White House since the last year of the Jimmy Carter administration. Presidents come and go at the White House. Walker remains. Walker says she is afforded access behind the scenes at the White House to show readers what the president is about when he is offstage. "I can show you relationships and atmosphere," she says, "how these people look when they are not in front of the lights and microphones."

Walker tries to act like a "fly on the wall" when photographing private moments in a president's life. "My whole approach is for the president not to know I am there. I try not to engage with him—ever. I don't talk unless he talks to me," she says.

By becoming as familiar—and as unobtrusive—as the wallpaper in the Oval Office, Walker quietly records intimate moments inside the White House. The night before President Clinton's impeachment trial began, she recalls, "The president turned to his wife, suddenly put his arms around her neck and held on to her just for a quick second." That photograph, she says, captures a personal moment and an emotion that the president would not necessarily reveal in public.

While the president knows that Walker is in the room, neither he nor his staff can control how the people in the Oval Office will behave, she points out. "The scene is set, but the characters are themselves."

Walker, by the way, shoots only black-and-white when photographing inside the White House. *Time* signals its behind-the-scenes access by publishing these kinds of stories in black and white.

P.F. Bentley has covered every presidential election since 1980. Shooting solely in black-and-white all these years, Bentley has followed the campaigns of George H. W. Bush, Bill Clinton, Robert Dole, and Newt Gingrich for up to a year at a time. As Bentley says, the campaign stops are just the tip of the iceberg. "In the hotel room is your picture."

At the 1992 Democratic convention, Bentley's picture of Bill Clinton warming up his vocal cords in the steam room before going onstage was more revealing than any picture of the candidate at the podium.

STRATEGIES FROM THE PROS

Not every photographer has the chance to shadow presidential candidates for months at a time or to document the president of the United States on a daily basis. However, the experiences of shooters like Bentley, Walker, and other magazine professionals provide insights into how to cover any official—from governor to mayor to local supervisor.

WATCH BUT DON'T TALK

Diana Walker has developed several techniques for avoiding conversation with her subjects. If someone looks at her, she immediately breaks eye contact by looking at her watch. If they try to start a conversation, she adjusts her camera.

"Of course, if the president begins to talk to me," she admits, "I have no choice but to answer back." She describes her working manner as "trying to be as discreet, quiet, out-of-the-way, and unobtrusive" as she can. "Of course, he knows I am in the room," she continues, "but it is the closest I can get to the way people really are."

Covering politicians on the campaign trail has taught Bentley to be flexible. The observer should remain unobserved, he says. "You have to become a chameleon," he explains. "You have to adjust to who (the politicians) are and to their routine. After awhile, you kind of know their moods. You know when to go in tight, when to back off, and, finally,

Senator Barack Obama campaigns for president at the University of Chicago. The photographer had unusual access since he had been traveling with the candidate for many months.
Pete Souza, *Chicago Tribune*

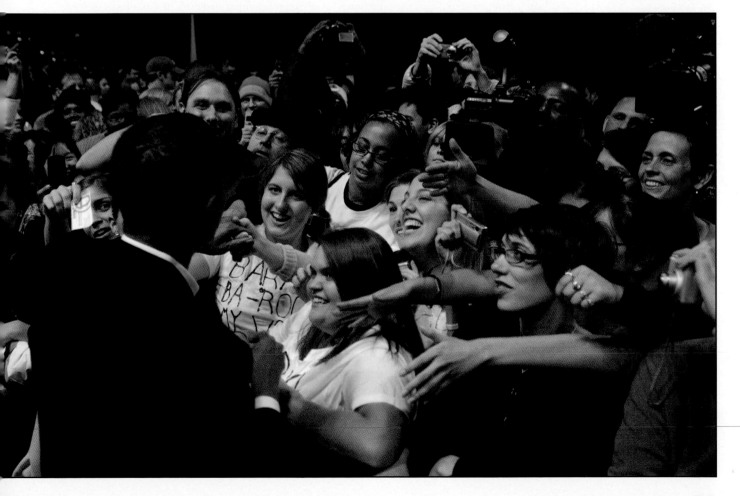

when to lay low." If things aren't going on, for example, he will usually walk out of a room and check in later. "I don't hover all the time," he notes.

Newsweek photographer David Hume Kennerly is a well-known raconteur when he is not working, but he finds it advantageous not to chat when he is trying to catch candids. "Usually I am in a place where there is no reason for me to talk," he observes.

ZIP YOUR LIPS
All the photographers interviewed for this book who work behind the scenes have made tacit agreements with their subjects not to reveal what they overhear. "I don't talk about what I hear, and my writers never ask me," says *Time*'s Walker. Bentley agrees: "Of course, there is a trust that I won't ever talk about anything I hear."

Kennerly points out that still photographers have a real advantage over their television counterparts. Politicians can be themselves and say what is on their minds with still photographers in the room. They know their comments will stay off the record. With video cameras rolling, he says, politicians are unlikely to be their usual loquacious selves.

"If you introduce sound into the situation, politicians will not talk naturally," he says.

NO GEAR YOU CAN HEAR
To carry out this unobtrusive approach, photographers rely on fast lenses and a high ISO to avoid using flash. Bentley's mantra is "No gear that you can hear."

Walker, too, prefers to shoot with rangefinder cameras but carries a single lens reflex with a longer lens—"just in case." In each frame, she says, she tries to include the president and other players who are in the Oval Office. "I am not doing tight head shots," she explains. Walker looks for relationships not portraits. But if a portrait is appropriate, the longer lens is in her bag.

SELL YOURSELF
You can have the right approach, the right ISO, and the best cameras, but without access to politicians, you can't make revealing pictures. Bentley talks to politicians ahead of time about recording their entire campaigns from the inside. "I tell them about the type of pictures I will take and the type I won't take. They know they are part of history."

Bentley assures politicians that he is not out to ridicule them by taking "cheap-shot" pictures. No photos of scratching or adjusting, no images of people eating, he assures potential subjects. "I have been in the hotel room where the candidate is in

Diana Walker, who covers the White House for *Time* magazine, had behind-the-scenes access to Bill and Hillary Clinton during a trip to Africa. Walker was able to catch this rare, unguarded moment of President Clinton and his wife joking together.
Diana Walker, *Time* magazine

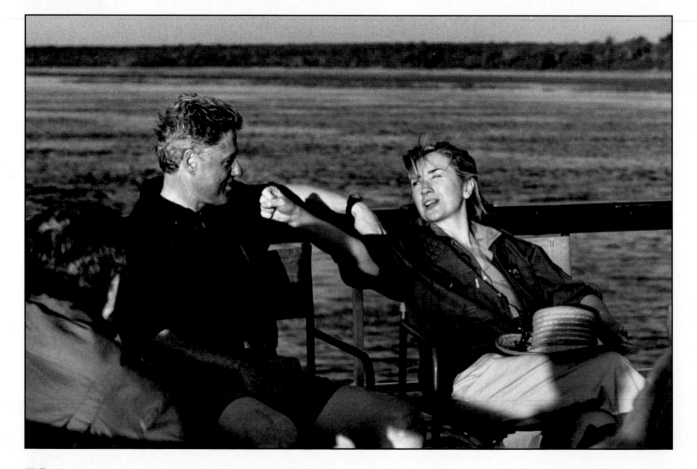

his underwear," he says. "That is not the kind of picture I care to take. It is not a picture that has any meaning."

Kennerly, who has been on the inside as the White House photographer for President Ford and on the outside as the *Newsweek* photographer covering Clinton, has learned about getting access under difficult conditions. "The picture is only a small part of what I do. I am a salesman first and foremost. I have to sell myself to people to come into their lives."

Members of the House and the Senate are, for the most part, easy to deal with, he says. They have to be re-elected and they have to get along. "Photographers are not considered to be the enemy," he says. "Reporters fall into that category."

Having worked in Washington on and off since the Ford administration, Kennerly has excellent connections. "I actually know a lot of senators," he says. "I would count 10 senators that I am well acquainted with and could call on a moment's notice."

During President Clinton's impeachment trial, photographers were denied access to the Senate chambers during the proceedings. Kennerly likens the situation to covering a bullfight when you can't see the bull or the matador. He wanted to take exclusive photographs at a high-level meeting of the representatives who were bringing the ominous charges against the President. He called on an old friend for whom he had done a favor 20 years ago. The friend was now a representative—and one of the managers of the impeachment trial. The 20-year-old favor paid off, and Kennerly got exclusive access for *Newsweek*.

MEETINGS GENERATE NEWS

In large cities and small towns, journalists cover the news of governmental meetings because the results of those meetings are important to readers. Meetings possess the same news value as fires and accidents. Often, the results of a governmental meeting—those involving changes in the tax rate, for instance—directly bear on readers' lives even more than yesterday's fender-bender.

Meetings and press conferences carry a challenge. They test the photographer's creativity. Unfortunately, a critical meeting of the Senate Armed Services Committee looks very much like an ordinary meeting of the local zoning board. If the pictures remained uncaptioned, readers could easily be confused. Press conferences as well as awards ceremonies all tend to look identical after a while. Sometimes, through the creative application of framing techniques, catching the

moment, and using long lenses and light, the photographer can help portray the excitement, the tension, the opposition, and the resolution of the meeting.

FACE AND HANDS REVEAL EMOTION

Ray Lustig of the *Washington Post* has covered some of the most momentous as well as some of the most trivial political moments in the country's recent history. Capitol Hill is his beat as the *Post*'s chief political photographer. When Lustig raises his 70–210mm f/2.8 zoom lens at a committee hearing or press conference, he looks for expressive faces. "A wrinkled brow, a grin, or a curled lip can add life to a routine meeting picture," Lustig says. "Hands, too, reveal a speaker's emotion." Readers, of course, understand the meaning of a clenched fist or a jabbing finger.

REVEALING VERSUS ACCIDENTAL PHOTOS

A speaker's facial expressions and hand gestures can be accidental and misleading. They might have nothing to do with the personality of the individual or the thrust of the message. Suppose that during a luncheon the governor is discussing closing the border to illegal immigrants. You take 100 to 200 frames. You might catch a shot while he is eating—showing him with his mouth screwed into a knot. This picture, although an actual moment, reflects nothing about the nature of the topic or even the speaker's character. The misleading picture, in fact, tends to distort the news rather than reveal it.

As *Time*'s Bentley says, "I don't care who it is, eating pictures are ugly. Once people start to eat, it is not a picture I care to have."

WHO'S WHO IS IMPORTANT

Meetings, speeches, or press conferences in a town take on news value based on the personalities involved and on the importance of the subject debated. The photographer must know or be able to recognize the players in the game without a scorecard. If you are not familiar with the participants in a meeting, ask someone for information about the speakers. What are their names? Which ones are elected officials? Who is best known? With this information, you can zero in on the most newsworthy individuals.

Here is how Ray Lustig prepares for a day on Capitol Hill. "When I am preparing to go to the Hill, I first review the Reuters daybook. (The daybook lists all upcoming activities, including Congressional caucuses, press conferences, speeches, etc.) If I have questions, I try to meet with the appropriate editors—national or defense, for example. When I get to the Hill in the morning, I check the web

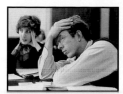
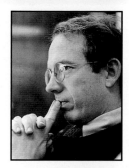
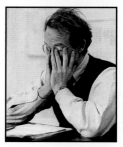
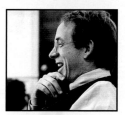

The hands of former Massachusetts Secretary of Human Services Jerald Stevens reveal the pressure, the pleasure, the tension, and the ease of this powerful state official.
Bill Collins

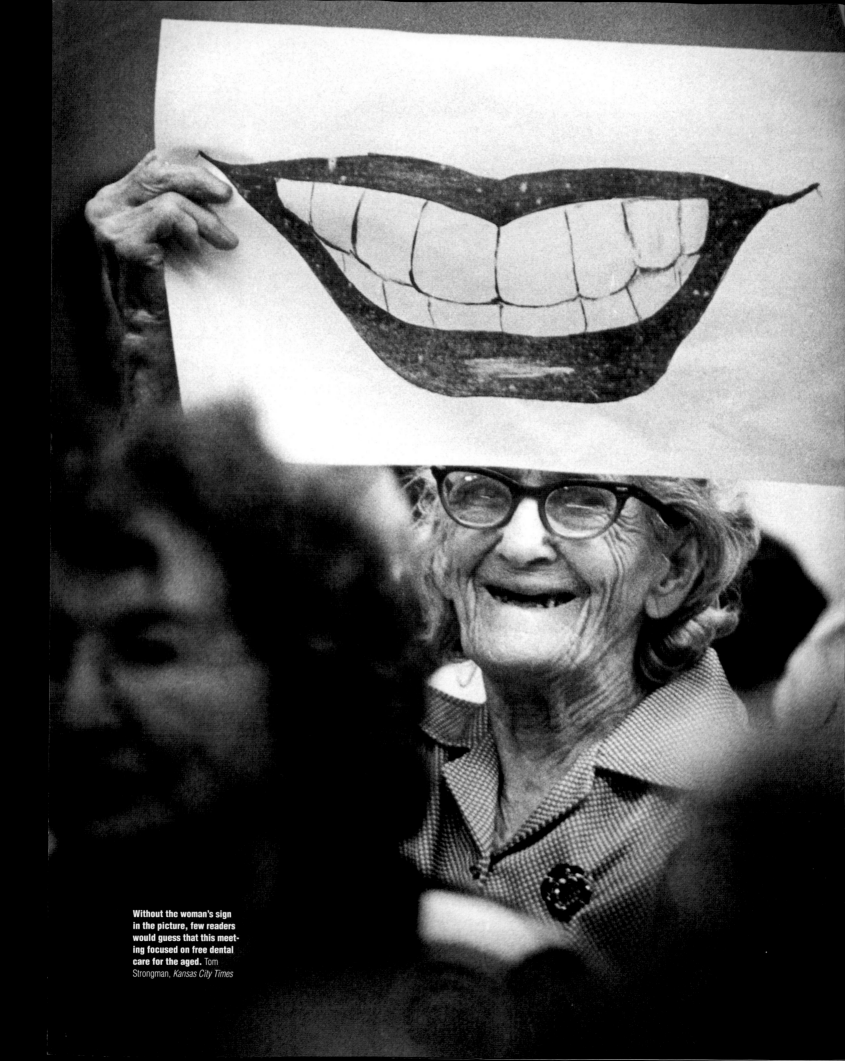

Without the woman's sign in the picture, few readers would guess that this meeting focused on free dental care for the aged. Tom Strongman, *Kansas City Times*

for committee schedules. I read the *Washington Post* thoroughly before I arrive, and when I get to the pressroom I take a look at *The New York Times* and the *Washington Times*. I also will do a quick scan of our newspaper's web sites. I also carry a pager that gives me information from both Houses' radio/TV gallery of events. I am doing my homework. I've got to know what is going on. That's my business."

The advantage of all this reading and preparation is that Lustig has a broad grasp of all the day's planned news. This allows him to select the most visual or most newsworthy events to cover.

Fully briefed on the day's events, he is the first to arrive at a packed hearing or overcrowded press conference. He gets there early and stakes out a spot. His meticulous forethought gives Lustig the edge on his competition.

PROPS ADD MEANING

Props can add meaning to a routine meeting photo. If someone holds up a prop, the reader will have an easier time understanding the point of the photo. If the speaker who denounces the lack of gun control laws brings to the meeting a few "Saturday Night Specials," the photographer can photograph the person examining or displaying the guns. A photo of an elderly woman, minus a few teeth yet holding aloft a poster of a toothy smile, helped summarize a meeting on free dental care for the aged (facing page).

SURVIVAL TACTICS

When Lustig covers an important committee meeting on Capitol Hill for the *Washington Post*, his gear bag contains two strobes and two SLR camera bodies: one with a 28–70mm (18–50mm digital) zoom lens and the other with a 70–210mm (50–140mm digital) zoom lens. He uses the short zoom for overalls of the conference room but saves the telephoto zoom for close-up portraits. The close-up brings the viewer and the subject nearer than they normally would meet in public.

Lustig also carries a small aluminum stool, which allows him to sit rather than kneel while waiting for a picture. "You need it," he says, "because it saves wear and tear on your body." He also carries a monopod and cable release.

Seated on his stool, his camera mounted on the monopod, and his cable release at the ready, Lustig can shoot at slower shutter speeds when necessary and also keep his lens aimed at his subject during those long, drawn-out meetings. Without tiring his arm

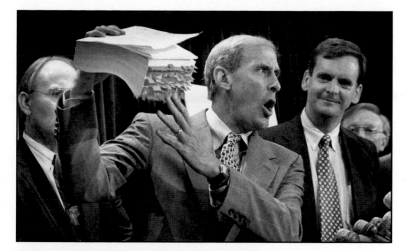

Republican Senator Dan Coates (Indiana) holds legislation that would create a comprehensive health care package. Republicans critical of the plan claimed it was too big, complicated, and bureaucratic. Both the Senator and the photographer know that props help visualize the story behind a meeting or press conference. Ray Lustig, *Washington Post*

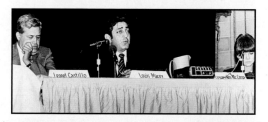

Avoid shooting perpendicular to the line of speakers. The perspective results in a picture with large blank spaces between each person, and each face appears quite small.
Jan Ragland

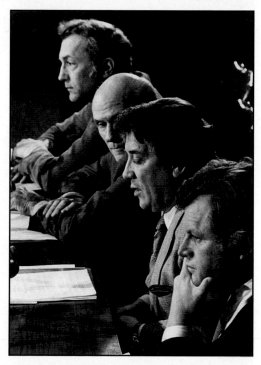

Shooting these dignitaries from the side eliminated dead space between the subjects. Photographing with a telephoto lens appears to bring the individuals closer together.
James K.W. Atherton, *Washington Post*

or having to keep his eye glued to the viewfinder, Lustig can train the lens on his target and look for gestures, mannerisms, and expressions—all the way through each politician's speech.

PHOTOGRAPH THE ISSUES

Most political issues can be translated into pictures. If the mayor says city education is poor and should be improved, the photographer must search for supporting evidence of the claim. Are schools overcrowded? Do students hang around in the halls with nothing to do after class? If racial tension exists between white and African-American students, can the journalist photograph the situation?

A set of realistic photos will transform rhetoric into observable issues.

More than a million immigrants enter the United States illegally each year to join the millions of others already living here.

Politicians debate what to do, activists hold protests, and Congress appropriates millions of dollars to staunch the flow.

These pictures go beyond the numbers and the staged events to see where some of the money spent on immigration control goes.

Two thousand three hundred three federal agents of the U.S. Department of Homeland Security are assigned to "detect, detain, and deport" the illegal immigrants.

(TOP) Immigration Enforcement Agents Paul Kouame and Greg Dews prepare shackles for the people they will transport to San Diego for that evening's flight to a detention center in Arizona. Illegal aliens are processed in Arizona and then flown to the Los Angeles field office of the Department of Homeland Security. They will then be returned to Mexico and Central America. Most will attempt to return. (See pages 302–304 for a story about the dangerous journey many of these immigrants undertake.)

(BOTTOM) A female detainee sits on her cot in a women's pod at a detention facility in Florence, Arizona. Criminal detainees must wear red jumpsuits.

Mary Calvert, *Washington Times*

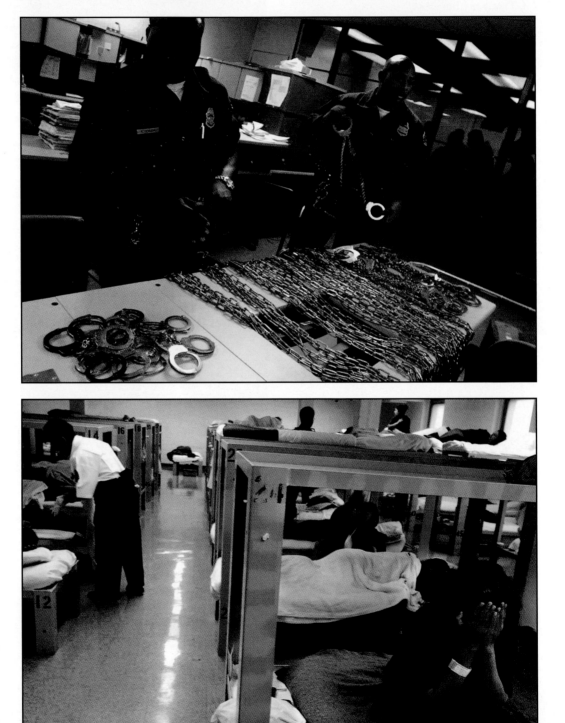

Photographers spend too much time shooting political mug shots and too little time digging up visuals that either confirm or deny the claims of politicians.

When covering a campaign, election, or any other contested issue, photographers have the same responsibility to objectivity as reporters. Like reporters, photographers can directly distort a scene.

An ultra-wide-angle lens can make a small room look large. Strong lighting and harsh shadows can transform, in Jekyll-and-Hyde fashion, a mild-mannered speaker into a tyrannical orator. Even more damaging, photographers, like writers, can report one side of an issue and, intentionally or not, leave the other side uncovered.

Because papers often run only one or two pictures, such biased photo reporting can creep into publications easily.

Honest photographers, however, try to select the lens, light, and camera angle as well as a representative moment or scene to present a balanced view of a complicated topic.

Unfortunately, few photojournalists receive adequate time for investigative political photography. Editors find it easy to send a staffer to cover a press conference. They know the time and place of the gathering and can guarantee that some usable "art" will result. But readers do not want to see another "mayor talking" picture. They already know what the mayor looks like. They want to determine if the mayor is telling the truth about the school system. Pictures can help substantiate or negate the mayor's assertions.

STEER CLEAR OF THE PACK

Even if you are conducting photographic political investigations, your editor in all likelihood will continue to assign you to rallies, speeches, and photo opportunities.

Cover these events if you must, but resist the PR-packaged photos politicians hope to see in tomorrow's paper. At the most, look for where the packaging has peeled away—but do not be surprised if you cannot find reality. At the least, turn your camera toward the crowd to find unusual political boosters.

Rather than taking a dull meeting picture of Congressional debates on the merits of allowing snow mobiles in national parks, the photographer recorded the confrontation between four mechanized human intruders and one of the few remaining buffalo in Yellowstone National Park.
Pete Souza, *Chicago Tribune*

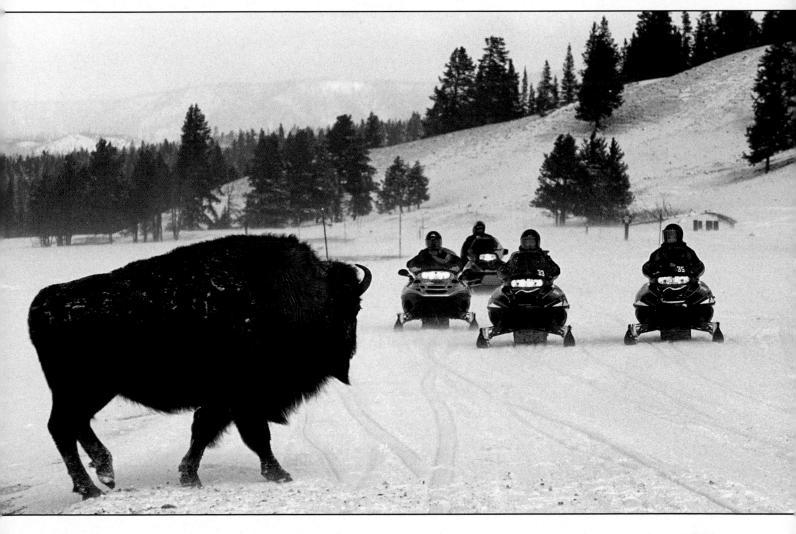

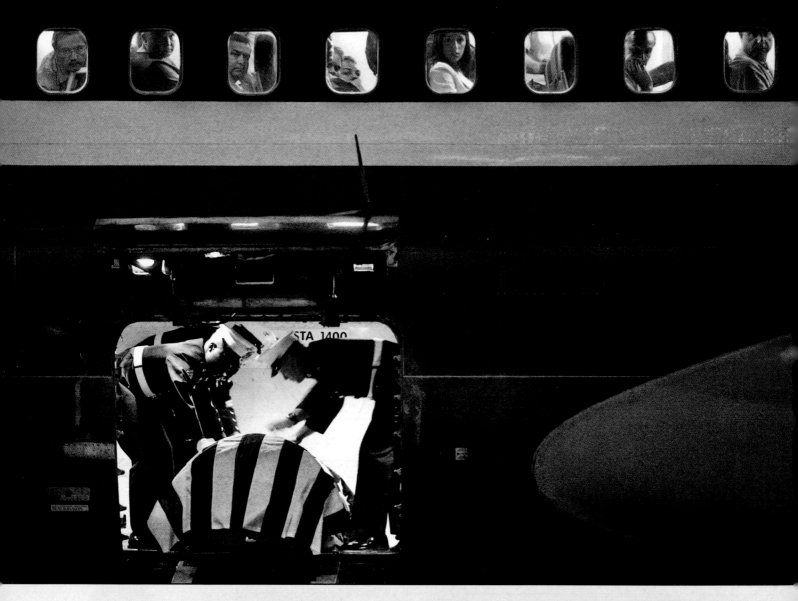

Photos by
Todd Heisler,
Rocky Mountain News

Photographer Todd Heisler and reporter Jim Sheeler of the *Rocky Mountain News* spent a year with the Marines stationed at Colorado's Buckley Air Force Base who are assigned to notify families of the deaths of their sons in Iraq. The families agreed to let the journalists chronicle their loss and their grief.

"They wanted people to know their sons, the men and women who brought them home, and the bond of traditions more than 200 years old that unite them. Though readers are led through the story by the white-gloved hand of Major Steve Beck, he remains a reluctant hero. He is, he insists, only a small part of the massive mosaic that is the Marine Corps." — *Rocky Mountain News*

This story powerfully demonstrates that photographers do not need to go into battle to document the ravages of war. The pictures on this spread cover Major Beck's vigil with just one young widow, Katherine Cathey, and are but a small part of the project.

▲ Upon the arrival of 2nd Lieutenant James Cathey's body at the Reno Airport, Marines climb into the cargo hold of the plane to drape the flag over his casket as passengers watch the family gather on the tarmac.

During the arrival of another Marine's casket at Denver International Airport, Major Steve Beck described the scene as one of the most powerful in the process:

"See the people in the windows? They'll sit right there in the plane, watching those Marines. You gotta wonder what's going through their minds, knowing that they're on the plane that brought him home," he said. "They're going to remember being on that plane for the rest of their lives. They're going to remember bringing that Marine home. And they should."

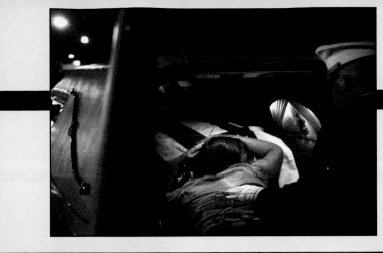

◄ Minutes after her husband's casket arrives at the Reno airport, Katherine Cathey falls onto the flag. When 2nd Lt. James Cathey left for Iraq, he wrote a letter to Katherine that read, in part, "there are no words to describe how much I love you, and will miss you. I will also promise you one thing: I will be home. I have a wife and a new baby to take care of, and you guys are my world."

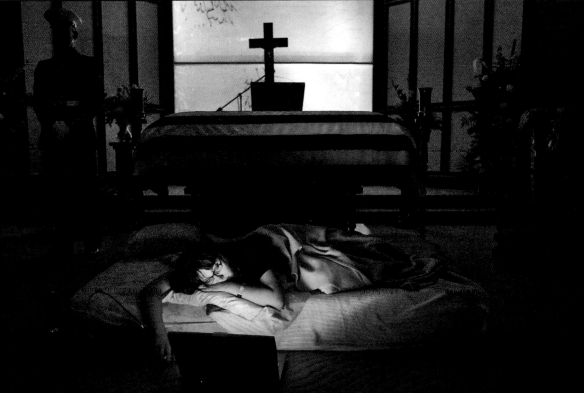

◄ The night before the burial of her husband's body, Katherine Cathey refuses to leave the casket, asking to sleep next to his body for the last time. The Marines make a bed for her, tucking in the sheets below the flag. Before she falls asleep, she opens her laptop computer and plays songs that reminds her of "Cat." One of the Marines asks if she would like them to continue standing watch as she sleeps. "I think it would be kind of nice if you kept doing it," she says. "I think that's what he would have wanted."

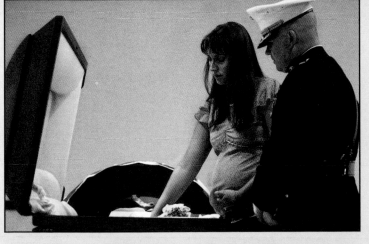

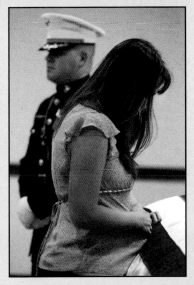

◄ Katherine Cathey presses her pregnant belly to her husband's casket, moaning softly. The baby will be named James Jeffrey Cathey.

▲ Since James Cathey was killed in a massive explosion, his body is delicately wrapped in a shroud by military morticians, then his Marine uniform laid atop his body. Katherine Cathey decides not to view her husband's body, so Major Beck has pressed her hand down on the uniform. "He's here," Major Beck says quietly. "Feel right here."

And, photographically, struggle to avoid the cliché of simply recording the routine picture.

Sometimes you will have to shoot next to other photographers. The *Washington Post*'s Lustig, who sometimes has to vie for position among 20 other still and video shooters, warns against using an extreme wide-angle lens in this situation. To get close enough to your subject with an extreme wide-angle lens, you will have to walk in front of all your fellow shooters—and block their shots. The best solution to herd journalism, he points out, is to avoid the pack and find another angle for the shot.

Without doubt, all political events start to look alike. But, by angling for a new view, like Olivier Douliery's shot of Supreme Court Justice John Roberts, perhaps you can at least bring back a photo you and your readers have not seen thousands of times before.

COME EARLY—STAY LATE

Alex Burrows, director of photography at the *Norfolk Virginian Pilot*, tells this story about several of his photographers who were assigned to cover a funeral. "One of our young photographers was assigned the grave site. He thought his work was over after the service, but one of our pros stayed really late and got a shot of one of the funeral directors putting a final flower on the covered grave site. It was a great ending photo for the two-page spread. The younger photographer learned a lesson."

The advice "come early and stay late" will serve you well whether you are covering a funeral or other events like rallies, parades, or fairs. The best parade pictures often occur when the performers are waiting to begin. They are loose, natural, and relaxed. They often are kidding one another and joking around. You are more likely to get candid moments at this point than after the parade begins and the participants go into perform-ing mode. Likewise, at the parade's end, the tuba player might be feeling goofy enough to put his head in the horn, or the majorette might be energized enough to turn flips.

Do not leave even after the principals have gone home. The leftover signs and banners forlornly festooning a trash barrel might tell more about the event than the staged moments earlier in the day. Julie Stupsker, shooting for the *San Francisco Examiner*, hung around long after the lead competitors had passed to make her funny picture of a

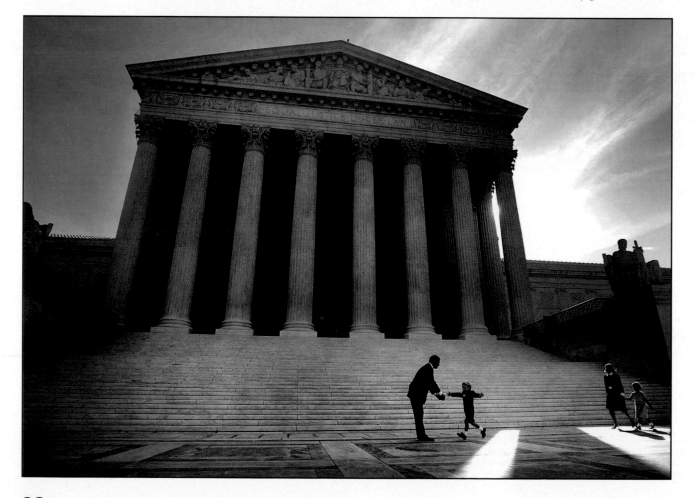

While other photographers used long telephoto lenses to record newly appointed Chief Justice John Roberts greeting his child on the steps of the Supreme Court, this photographer used a wide-angle lens to encom-pass the court building itself in the frame.
Olivier Douliery, Abaca Press

nude runner in the infamous Bay to Breakers footrace in San Francisco.

Photographers cover many prearranged events, from an annual Founders' Day parade to the bicentennial celebrations. Statues are unveiled. Old-timers wear costumes. Politicians give speeches. A photographer's real assignment is to look beyond the stage-managed elements for something surprising, revealing, or out of place. Robert Cohen, of the *St. Louis Post Dispatch*, found just such a situation when he noticed a veteran wheeling his own oxygen tank and positioned between two well-built young soldiers at a war memorial dedication (see page 62).

When covering events like street fairs, isolating your subject within the crowd is difficult. You cannot use a long lens and let a wide aperture blur the background because foreground elements will interfere with your picture. You can dramatize your main target if you can get near enough with a wide-angle lens, but you will still have to contend with a bothersome busy background. Of course, you can use a low angle with the sky as your background, or perhaps shoot with a telephoto from a high perch and let the ground serve as a nondistracting background. You can also try

working the edges of the crowd. Here you will find most of the same characters you were targeting before, but you can more easily—with any length lens—visually isolate them from the distracting crowd.

IN-DEPTH PHOTOJOURNALISM
PHOTOGRAPH THE TOPIC, NOT THE TALKER

Even with the best lens technique and a keen sensitivity to light, photographers still have trouble distinguishing for readers the difference between a city council meeting called to increase taxes and a meeting convened to decrease the number of district schools. The difference between these meetings lies in what the council members said verbally, not what they did visually. The photojournalist must translate speakers' words into pictures that portray the underlying controversy.

Arthur Perfal, a former associate editor of *Newsday*, gave his view of the problem at a conference of editors. "Remember that people talking often supply material for good stories," Perfal said, "but they seldom supply material for good pictures. Particularly when the same officials or the same chairmen are doing the talking. Let the photographer go

When you cover a parade or other event like the San Francisco Bay to Breakers footrace, it pays to stay to the end. Sometimes the funniest pictures occur after the main affair is over.
Julie Stupsker,
San Francisco Examiner

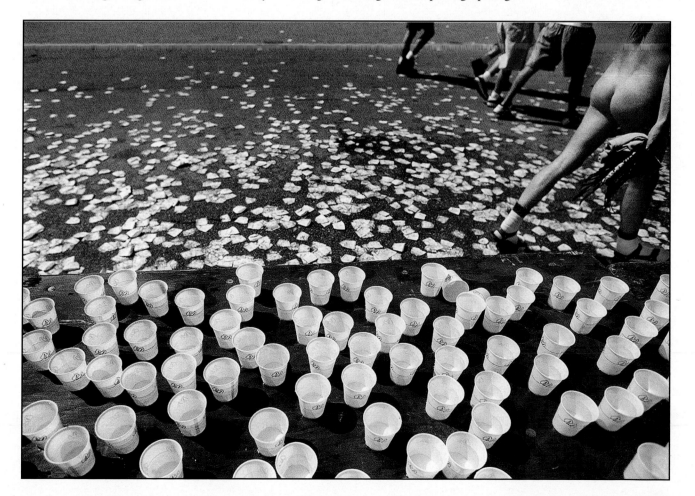

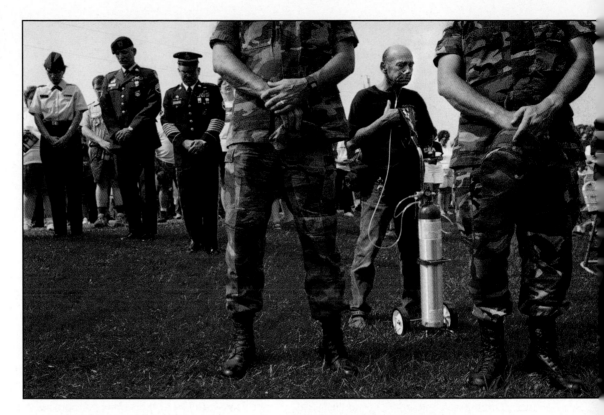

where the action is—shoot what they are talking about."

Although studies and news releases announced the decline of the small farm, Scott Strazzante actually documented how cattle farmers Harlow Cagwin and his wife confronted age and suburban sprawl. Because Strazzante had followed the story over several years, he was there on the day the couple moved out of their house and saw it demolished by a land developer (facing page).

One of the rare instances where a ground-breaking photo op produced an unusual picture. It did not run.
Philip Wartena, *The Columbus Ledger-Enquirer*

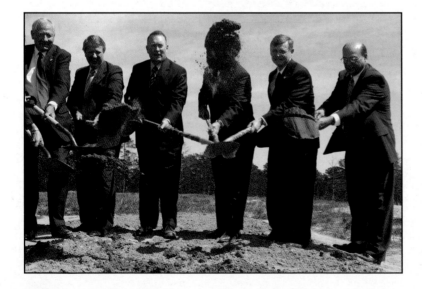

MEDIA EVENTS AND PHOTO OPS

After news conferences, meetings, and public events, the awards ceremony ranks as one of the most common of planned news events. Some photographers argue that pictures of staged situations like awards ceremonies and news conferences simply should not run.

Greg Mironchuk, a photographer in Revere, Massachusetts, spoke for many colleagues in his comments to the National Press Photographers Association online discussion list, NPPA-L. "It doesn't matter if (a press conference) was set up by the president, the World Health Organization, your local police department, Demi Moore's press agent, or the Maharishi Mahesh Yogi," he wrote. "It's still a set-up and still something that wouldn't exist without a press presence . . . . We (the press) are in tacit collusion with every flack, hack, and terrorist that calls a press conference. If we didn't come, there'd be no reason to do it."

Many news outlets, however, especially in smaller communities, continue to publish such pictures. In a column for *News Photographer* magazine, Bryan Grigsby, photo editor at the *Philadelphia Inquirer*, discussed his strategy for dealing with such assignments. "Whenever I get an assignment to cover something that is obviously being staged for the media, I ask the photographer to step back and record the staged quality of that event rather than go along with the intended charade of the event's sponsors."

If you polled professional photojournalists, they would vote overwhelmingly to eliminate awards pictures. Some news outlets, in fact, have policies forbidding awards photos except for special circumstances. Most editors, nevertheless, continue to assign hand-shaking, check-passing pictures.

THE STORY BEHIND THE AWARD

As with meeting pictures and political pictures, the real secret to covering press conferences and awards lies in searching out the reason for the event and bringing out this fact in your picture. Sometimes you only have to arrange a portrait to point out the meaning of an event. If a woman wins an award for most valuable player on the softball team, her uniform and equipment in the portrait cues the reader to the nature of the award.

In some cases, an award might even be a peg for a picture story. For example, the ceremony at which Annemarie Madison received an award for her work with people dying from AIDS was, as most of these stiff ceremonies are, a visual zero. However, her dedication and compassion became the subject of a moving photo story that was part of a photo project that won awards of its own—"Helpers in the War on AIDS." (See pages 212–218, "Developing a Feature Beat" in Chapter 10, "Covering the Issues.") ■

A former cattle farmer cannot bear to watch as his house is demolished. The cleared land will be transformed into a subdivision. The photographer was present at this emotional moment because he had followed the plight of the family over a period of several years.
© Scott Strazzante

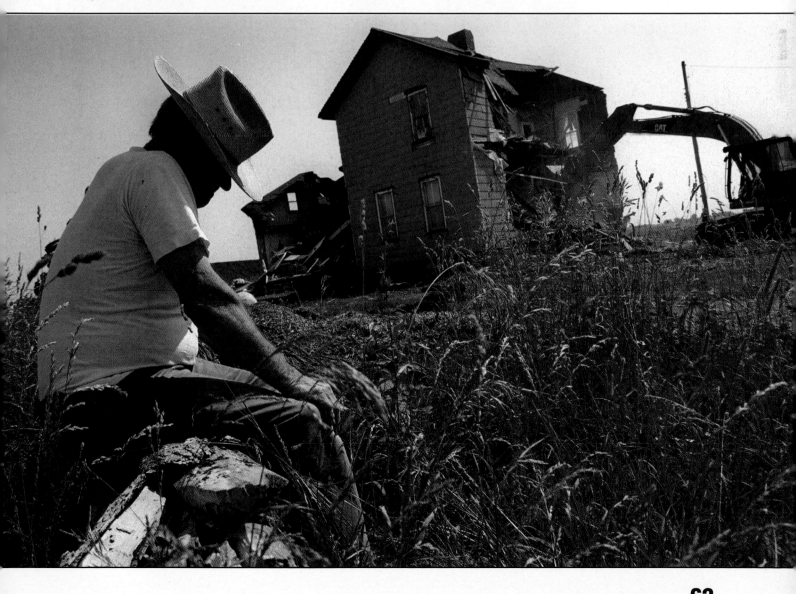

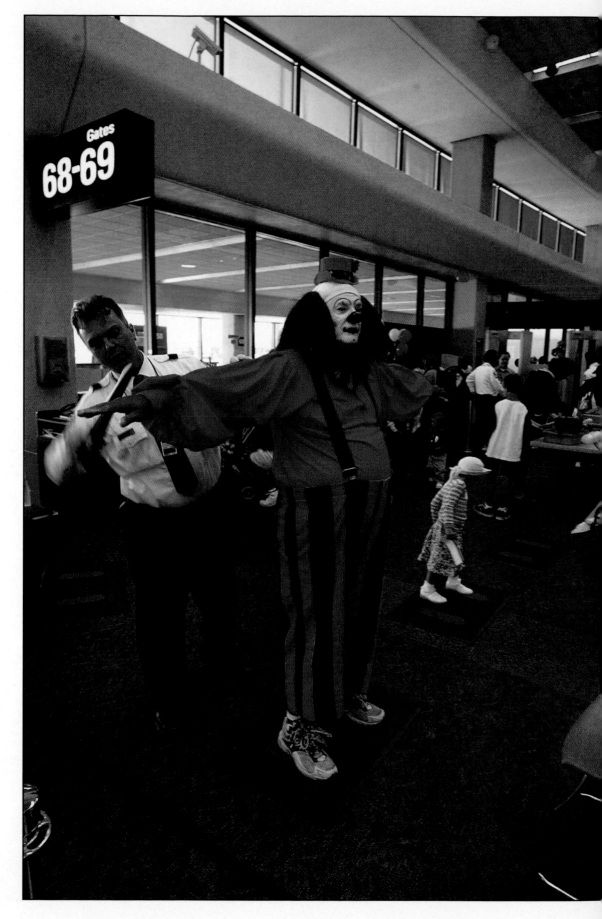

"Buttons" the Clown undergoes a security check
before boarding a free
United Airlines "Fantasy
Flight" for dozens of children with special needs and
their families.
Michael Macor, San Francisco

4

Features

Feature photos provide a visual dessert to subscribers who digest a daily diet of accident, fire, political, and economic news. Many editors argue that because readers receive so much depressing news in the gray columns of type, subscribers deserve a break when they look at pictures.

For some publications, feature pictures provide a diversion from the news and have even become the mainstay of the front page. Surveys consistently show that readers respond favorably to feature pictures. (See pages 134–137, Chapter 7, "Photo Editing," for more on reader preferences.)

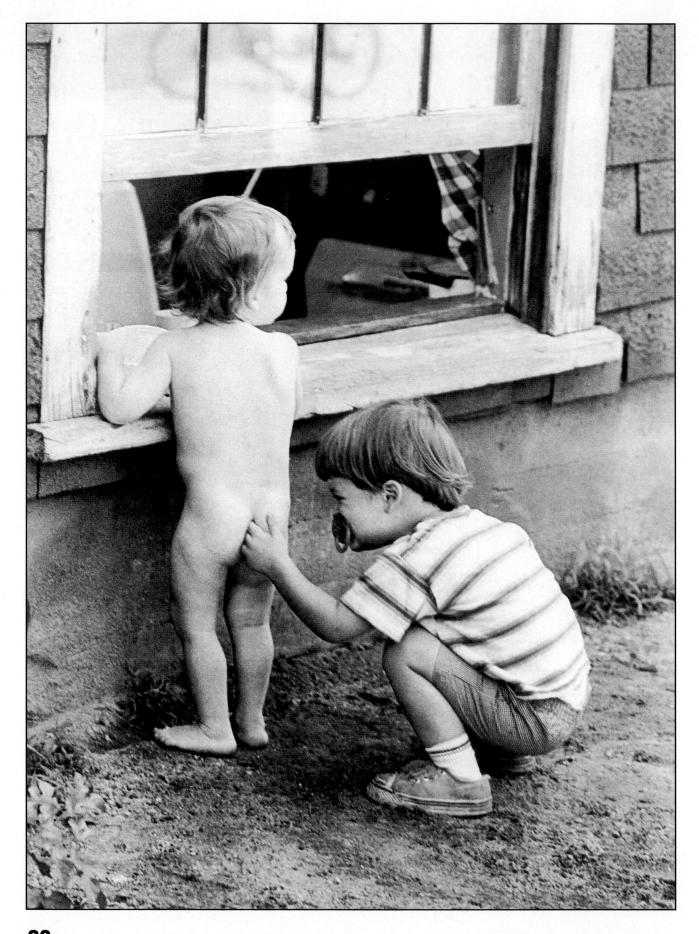

Cammie Toloui, an online photo editor for the *San Francisco Chronicle*'s *SFGate.com*, scouts the wire services every day for fresh and funny features. Her gallery on the site, which contains lots of feature pictures, attracts more than 100,000 hits a day. (See an interview with Toloui on page 129.)

Features allow newspapers and web sites to play up average citizens in circumstances other than accidents and other tragedies. Mark Johnson, a Massachusetts freelancer, argues that most feature pictures are interesting only to the people in the pictures. By contrast, Charlie Riedel, who shot for many years at the *Daily News* in Hays, Kansas, says feature pictures "freeze experiences in time so others can scrutinize them." Gordon Converse, who worked for the *Christian Science Monitor* for more than 20 years, described feature photography as the "search for moments in time that are worth preserving forever."

For Mark Hertzberg, director of photography at the *Journal Times* in Racine, Wisconsin, "the measure of a newspaper's success is how many of these moments are in clippings held onto readers' refrigerator doors with magnets." These days such moments may find themselves bookmarked in a web browser, forwarded as emails, or posted as screen savers on computer monitors.

HOW FEATURES AND NEWS DIFFER
TIMELESSNESS
Feature photos differ from news photos in several respects. Because news is timely, news pictures get stale quickly. Many feature pictures, on the other hand, are timeless. Feature pictures do not improve with time, as good wine does, but neither do they turn sour. Some editors, in fact, refer to features as evergreens. Like evergreen trees, feature photos never turn brown. Wire service photos showing President Bush giving his inaugural speech carry little interest today. Yet feature pictures like those in this chapter will long retain their holding power.

SLICE OF LIFE
A news picture accrues value when its subject is famous, the event is of large magnitude, or the outcome is tragic. A feature picture, by contrast, records the commonplace, the everyday, the slice of life.

The feature photograph, sometimes called "wild art," "standalone art," or "evergreen," tells an old story in a new way, with a

new slant. Two children playing games at a day-care center will not change the state of world politics, but the photo might capture a funny moment and provide a feature picture. And while flattened armadillos are commonplace in some parts of the country, a highway stripe painted over the poor thing adds an ironic twist to what otherwise is an ordinary roadside fixture.

With hard news, the event controls the photographer. Photojournalists jump into action when their editor assigns them to cover a plane crash or a train wreck. When they reach the scene, they limit their involvement to recording the tragedy.

As a feature photographer, on the other hand, you often can generate your own assignments. In fact, many newspapers and web sites call features "enterprise pictures."

What kind of enterprise might you employ to find great features? You might arrange to spend the day shooting photos of a man who

◄ A feature picture records the commonplace, an everyday happening, or a slice of life. A child's curiosity at the Harvard day-care center is a natural feature subject. Ken Kobré, for *Boston Phoenix*

A flattened armadillo with a white stripe down its back elicits a chuckle from most viewers. Features provide a break from the daily dose of bleak news.
Philip Wartena, *The Columbus Ledger-Enquirer*

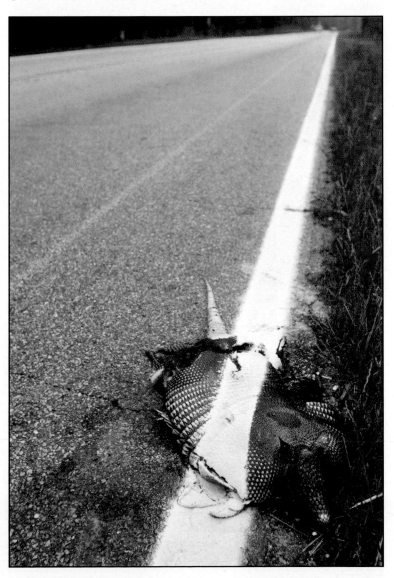

makes artificial arms and legs. Or you might head to a school for dog groomers to find a student learning how to clip a poodle.

"FEATURIZING" THE NEWS

News does not stop with fires and accidents, and features do not begin with parks and kids. The division between these two types of pictures is not that clear-cut. The sensitive photographer, for instance, could uncover features even at a major catastrophe. This is called "featurizing the news." The main story might describe a fire's damage to an apartment house, and give a list of the injured and dead. The news photo might show the firefighter rescuing the victims with the building burning in the background.

For a news feature, the photographer might take a photo of a firefighter being kind to a dog. This, along with a caption about the canine rescue, might run as a sidebar alongside the main story and photos, which would concentrate on the residents' injuries and the general damage to the building. Likewise, a picture of a driving school student in a wrecked car bearing the school's name straddles the line between news and features.

UNIVERSAL EMOTIONS

Great feature pictures, and there are few, evoke a reaction in the viewer. When viewers look at a powerful feature photo they might laugh, cry, stand back in amazement, or peer more closely for another inspection. If so, the photo has succeeded.

Some features are even universal in their appeal. They will get a response no matter in which country they are shown. When individuals in Europe, Asia, and Africa respond to the same photo, then the photographer has tapped into the universally understood language of feature pictures.

The term feature picture tends to serve as a catchall category. In fact, some writers call features "anything that's not news." Yet many pictures are neither news nor feature. Snapshots from a family album, for example, do not really belong in either pigeonhole.

GOOD FEATURE SUBJECTS

Years back, each time a new photographer was hired by Florida's *St. Petersburg Times and Independent*, a veteran staffer would draw the newcomer aside to explain the secret ingredients of the feature picture.

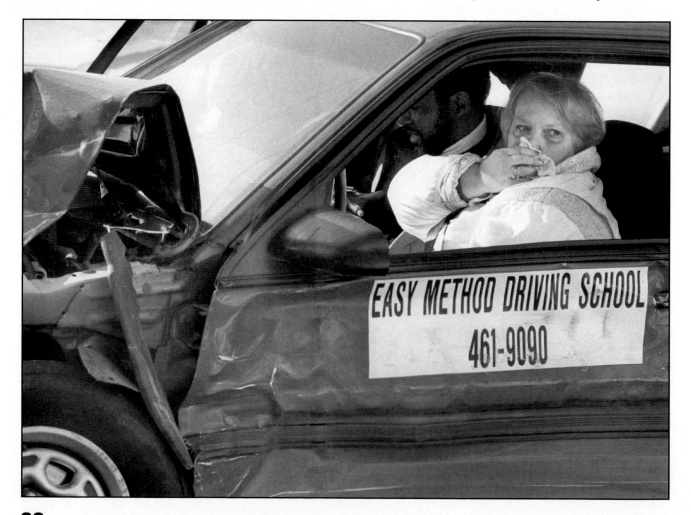

Few fender benders merit photographic coverage—except when the driver is a trainee at the Easy Method Driving School. While serious to the student driver, this minor accident takes on the properties of a funny feature photo. J.M. Eddins, Jr., Patuxent [Maryland] Publishing Co.

"Friend," he would say, "if you need a feature picture for today's edition, you can't go wrong by taking photos of kids, animals, or nuns wearing habits." These were not bad words of advice because a large percentage of published feature pictures includes kids, animals, and, sometimes, even nuns.

KIDS IMITATING ADULTS

Photographers find children to be relatively easy and willing subjects because they act in natural ways, play spontaneously, and look cute. "Kids are good subjects for features because they are uninhibited," says Charlie Riedel in Kansas. "They tend to be themselves. They don't have anything to prove to anyone." To grownups, children seem particularly funny when they imitate adult behavior. The child often acts as a mirror, showing the adult how grown-up behavior appears to the younger generation.

Ulrike Welsch, a specialist in photographing children when she worked for the *Boston Globe*, always asked permission of parents before photographing youngsters. "That way the parent does not become suspicious and does not interrupt the shooting," she explains.

If a parent is not around, Welsch would ask the child to lead the way to the adult, giving Welsch the opportunity to secure the permission. Although asking permission interrupts the child's activity, Welsch notes, once the parent gives the go-ahead, a child almost always quickly resumes playing

Given today's unhappy reality of child molestation and kidnapping, this advice has never been more on target. If parents are not around, Josh Meltzer of *The Roanoke Times* leaves his card with children he has photographed. "That way," he says, "When they tell their parents 'some guy took my pictures in the park' and the parents understandably freak out, the kid can hand the card to mom or dad. Then the parents can call to confirm, but usually the card is enough to ease their minds.

THE INCONGRUOUS

A picture of a technician appearing to be peering into the posterior of a prehistoric predator will always provoke a chuckle. And a photo of a masked Venetian reveler apparently stepping through the centuries to take a picture with a point-and-shot digital

A technician readies a robotic dinosaur for a tail connection. Even extinct animals make for fun features. Robert Cohen, for the *Memphis Commercial Appeal*

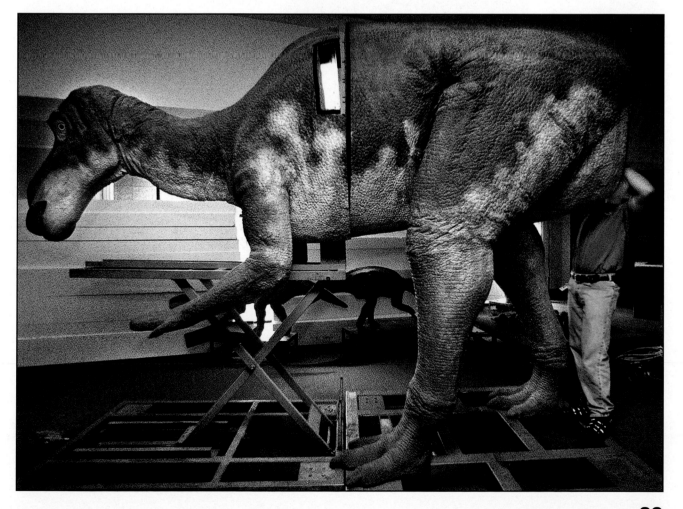

camera looks incongruous. The 21st-century technology seems out of place. Images like these often have an ironic twist and provide eye-catching features.

PEOPLE LIKE PEOPLE
Clearly, the feature does not restrict photographers to picturing only kids, animals, and nuns, although whenever you can include these elements in a picture, the photo has a greater chance for publication. People of any age prove fascinating when they labor or learn, play or pray.

ANIMALS ACTING LIKE PEOPLE
People commonly attribute human traits to animals. People respond to pictures in which

pigs seem to smile or chimps look bored—and camels kiss cute little girls. Pet lovers often believe their animals exhibit human emotions and treat their animals as if they were little human beings. Dog fanciers feed their pooches at the dinner table, dress them in sweaters for walks, and at night tuck them in velvet beds. Such idiosyncrasies supply the material for good features.

FIRST AND LAST EVENTS
"First time and last time events may be small happenings, but they are important moments in most people's lives and usually laden with emotion," notes Dave LaBelle in his outstanding book *The Great Picture Hunt 2*.

Whether it's a child's first haircut or a beloved coach's final game, these moments elicit a nostalgic feeling in a viewer's mind. Besides these classic moments, search for people daring enough to try something they have never tried before. The first day a new teacher attempts to hold the attention of a class can be as scary as the first time a person rappels down the side of a mountain. You might put yourself mentally in the shoes of someone else and ask, "How would I feel about trying this?"

DISCOVERING FEATURES
KEEP A FRESH EYE
To keep a fresh eye for features, Ulrike Welsch drives to an area she's never seen before. The experience is similar to traveling to a new country, even though the place might be only a few miles away. Whenever you live in the same place for a while and see the same things daily, you grow accustomed to your surroundings.

Psychologists call this phenomena "habituation." Feature photographers face the same problem. They come to accept as commonplace the unique aspects of the areas they live in and cover.

"Whenever I go to a new place, even if it's just a little way down the road, everything is novel," Welsch points out. She notices and photographs the differences between the new environment and her familiar territory. When she first arrives, her eye is sharpest.

Those first impressions usually lead to her best photos. "I take pictures I might have overlooked if the subjects were in my backyard," she says.

When called on for a feature picture by 5:00 P.M. for the next day's metro-section cover, many photographers jump in their cars and head to their favorite neighborhoods.

Like a fisherman returning to a fondly remembered fishing hole, they go back, hoping for one more catch of the day.

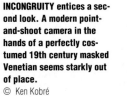

INCONGRUITY entices a second look. A modern point-and-shoot camera in the hands of a perfectly costumed 19th century masked Venetian seems starkly out of place.
© Ken Kobré

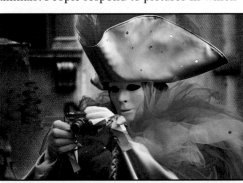

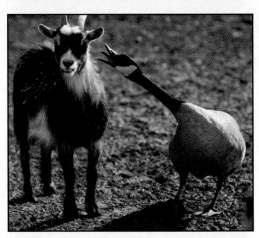

ANIMALS often provide great feature subjects. This goose seems to be giving the goat an earful. The goose actually had adopted the female goat and has not left her side since making her acquaintance.
Andrea Roth, *Napa Valley Register*

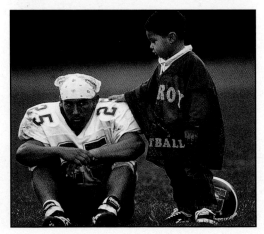

CHILDREN ACTING LIKE ADULTS, like this 4-year-old boy comforting his uncle during a losing football game, prove to be appealing feature subjects.
Terry Pierson, *Gilroy* [California] *Dispatch*

Other photographers start cruising. Charlie Riedel, who spent most of his life photographing in the small town of Hays, Kansas, says that he finds 95 percent of his features by driving around.

Alan Berner of the *Seattle Times* says to stop your car and shoot if you see a feature while driving. "In general, you can't go back and get it again." Doug Kapustin of the *Baltimore Sun* agrees: "If you think you should, stop. If you don't, you will regret it later."

Some photographers, however, shun the car altogether. Even if they are on their way to an assignment, they prefer to walk if they have the time. They point out that if you are in a car whizzing through a neighborhood, you miss seeing how the residents respond to one another. This interchange provides the basis for good features.

As Greg Locke, chairman of the Photojournalism Caucus of the Canadian Association of Journalists, told *News Photographer* magazine, "Talk to people you meet. Sometimes keeping moving means you are never in one place long enough to see what's going on."

Think of yourself as a visual anthropologist. Like Margaret Mead observing the coming-of-age rituals of adolescents in Samoa, study your community as if it were a remote, recently discovered island. What are its traditions? What is left of the old ways of doing things? And, of course, what is changing?

TAKE A CANDID

Constantine Manos, an outstanding freelance feature photographer for Magnum picture agency, looked for candid features during the year he spent shooting 500 rolls of black-and-white and color film for a 40-projector slide show called "Where's Boston?"

He says that he never posed or arranged any of the pictures contained in the show. Manos explored each area of the city on foot, introducing himself to the residents. "If you sneak up on people," he explains, "they have a right to resent you. Instead, if you say 'Hello,' and talk a bit about what you are doing, people will let you continue with your work. All my subjects are aware of me."

Henri Cartier-Bresson, a founding member of Magnum who is often referred to as the father of candid photography, used a different approach for taking street pictures. According to Russell Miller in his book ***Magnum: The Story of the Legendary Photo***

The photographer captured this candid "decisive moment" of fans checking out the action off the field at the Chicago Cubs' Wrigley Field.
Aristide Economopoulos, *State Journal-Register*

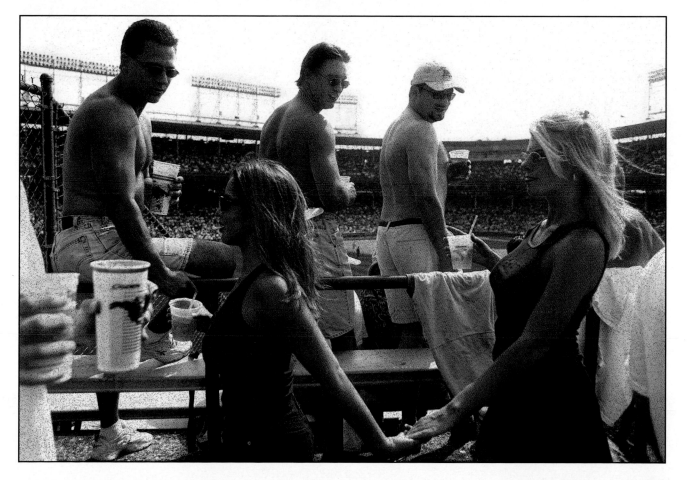

Agency, Cartier-Bresson liked to pop up, as if out of nowhere, take a picture, and then innocently walk on as if nothing had happened.

Many photographers are fearful of photographing strangers on the street. Going up to someone you do not know and sticking a camera in his or her face is not a natural act for everyone.

Emily Nottingham studied the brief relationship formed between feature photographers and their subjects in her doctoral dissertation, "From Both Sides of the Lens: Street Photojournalism and Personal Space." While it might last only a few seconds or minutes, the relationship greatly affects the outcome of the picture, as well as how subject and shooter feel about the encounter.

Nottingham found that 86 percent of people approached by photographers on the streets of Bloomington, Indiana, agreed to be photographed, cooperated with the photographer, and even gave their names and addresses. The high percentage of cooperative—and satisfied—subjects reported in the study should put at ease those photographers

fearful of street photography.

Nottingham also found that photographers who emphasized forming a relationship with the subjects as people rather than simply as subjects received a more favorable response from the individuals they were photographing. "Those photographers tended to take more time with the subjects than the other photographers, spent a larger percentage of that time in conversation, and exchanged more personal information with the subjects," she observed.

While the photographer/subject bond does not indicate the quality of the final image, the study clearly shows that sensitive, caring photographers will find their subjects more receptive.

Keep in mind, however, the differences between what Nottingham observed in

► A call to the highway department's public affairs office gained the photographer access atop San Francisco's Bay Bridge along with a painter applying primer to one of its cables. The high-angle perspective adds drama to this feature picture. Ken James, for the *Examiner* [San Francisco]

Just as the photographer made this shot, the "Lineman's Rodeo," a competition for electrical workers, ended for the morning. The "unusual," like this surprising scene, always makes good feature material. Terry Barner, *Independence* [Missouri] *Examiner*

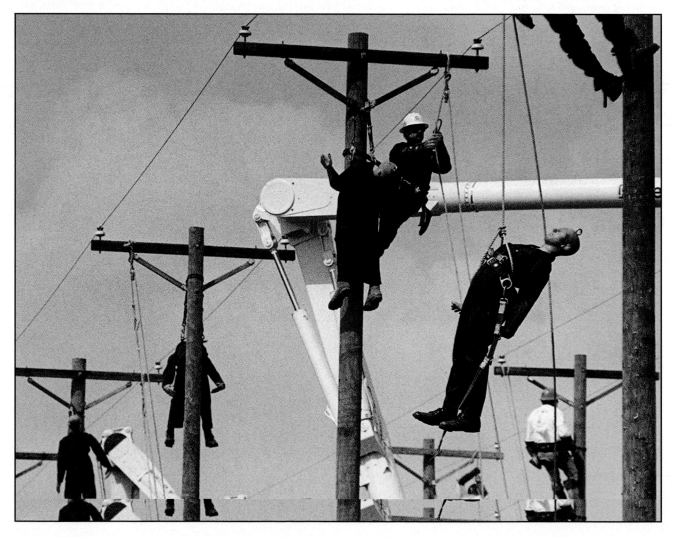

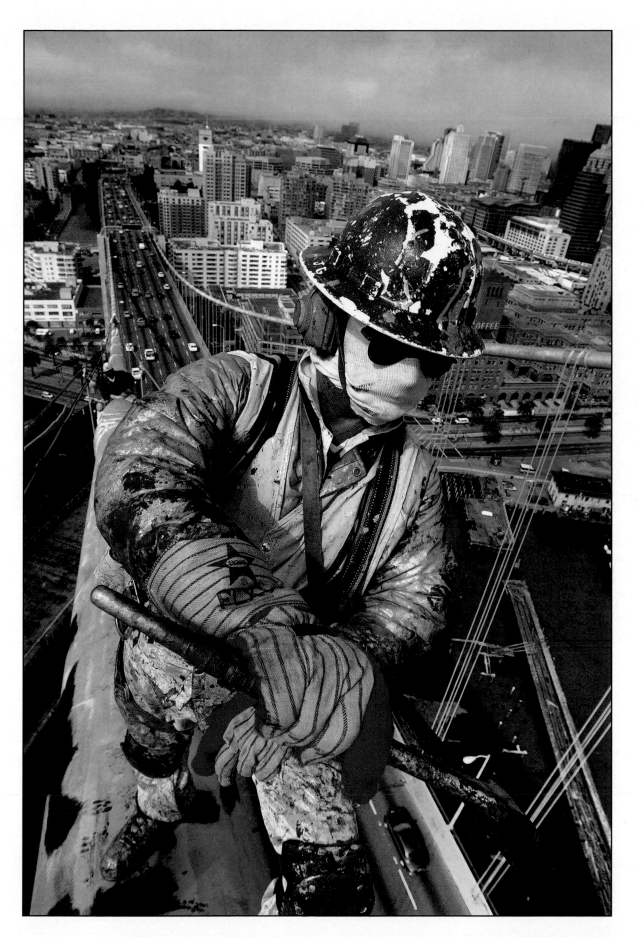

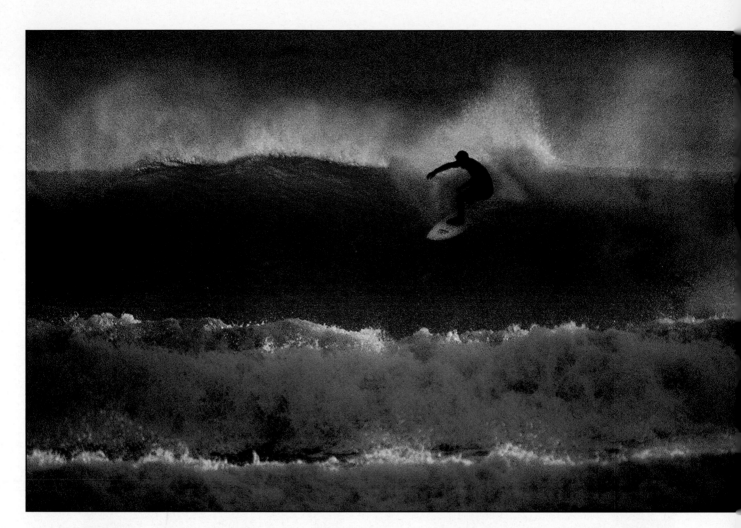

The photographer shot this feature as part of an essay about surfing. The waves were big that day, but it was overcast and drizzly, Tehan recalls. "I almost gave up because the light was so dull, and I was cold and tired. But I noticed that there was a break in the clouds near the horizon, and I figured if I waited long enough I might get some sun." The setting sun broke through the clouds, acted as a backlight, and helped isolate the surfer and rim the waves. Pat Tehan, *San Jose Mercury News*

Indiana and Cartier-Bresson's approach to street photography. The Indiana approach involves an introduction by the photographer before taking a picture. The Cartier-Bresson approach depends on a photographer taking pictures without engaging the subject. In fact, Cartier-Bresson's method, when executed in the style of the master himself, means that the photographer will shoot so fast that subjects may not realize they have been photographed at all.

Of course, photographers must decide which approach will work best and be most comfortable for them.

CALL A PR PERSON

Almost any city has more PR pros than journalists. While these professionals have many roles, one of their important functions is helping their organizations get coverage in the media. They are there, in part, to help photographers. In fact, they love photographers. The relationship can be mutual.

Ken James, a freelancer in San Francisco, was producing a weekly picture page for the *Examiner*, and so needed a continuous supply of story leads. With a call to Pier 39's

Aquarium by the Bay, he discovered that divers would be cleaning the tank's underside on the day he needed to shoot. "Perfect," he said to himself.

Next, he called the public affairs office of the Post Office. He learned that a mail carrier would be testing the then-new single-person people mover, the Segway, at a specific location the following Thursday. James would never have known about this test if he had not called the Post Office's public affairs department. The chance of happening upon the right spot at the right time would have been slim to none.

With these successes behind him, James began contacting all sorts of PR people. He wanted to take a picture from the Bay Bridge. Three calls later, he had permission to shoot high above the bay while standing on one of the cables that holds up the span between Oakland and San Francisco. Going down the cable was his most frightening moment, he says.

James advises calling for feature pictures long in advance. He says PR pros prefer to make media arrangements several weeks before a shoot. Patience pays off. "Once you

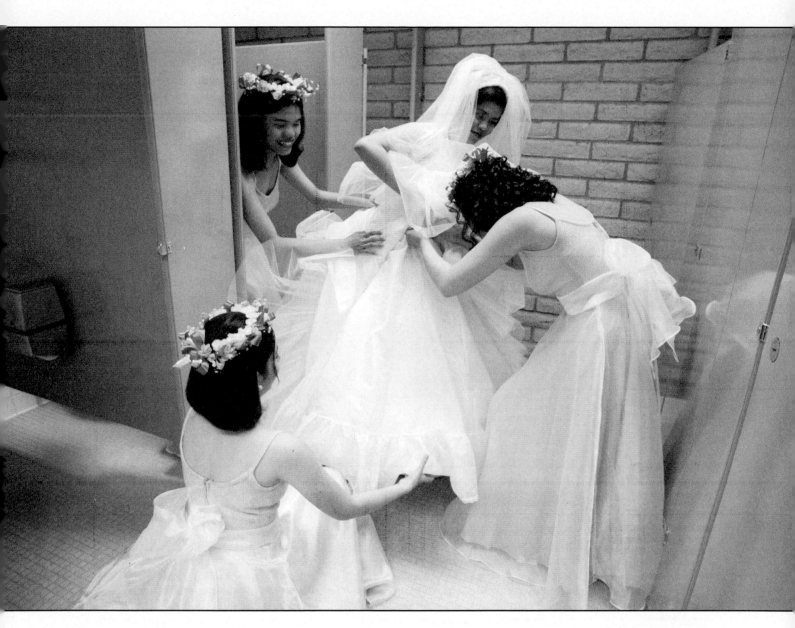

start making the calls, they self-generate. One story leads to another," he says.

FIND A UNIQUE ANGLE
Sometimes the key to the feature photo is not a candid moment found on the street but rather taking the viewer to see a common event from a unique vantage point. "I try to show people what they would not normally see," says Charlie Riedel, who climbed a radio tower to show someone changing a light bulb atop it. Such an ordinary act seen at ground level certainly was not interesting, but from the tower, where few people ever get to go, readers saw an everyday activity from a fresh perspective.

Riedel—who exhibits no symptoms of vertigo—has climbed radio towers, mounted his cameras on bikes, airplanes, parachutes, and Gyrocopters. Not only does he go up but

he also climbs down manholes and even under trampolines to bring the readers in his small town a unique perspective. More commonly, he climbs a tree or takes the prism off his camera and lies flat on the ground to give his readers a new view of their world.

Pat Tehan of the *San Jose Mercury News* used a combination of a long lens, the right light, perfect time of day, and favorable weather conditions to take a dramatic surfing picture. He had been shooting a series on surfing on the northern coast of California, so he already knew the location of the best waves and the lenses he would need. He waited for the kind of weather conditions that would produce giant rollers, and then waited even longer for the dramatic light of late afternoon.

To find a rich source of photo-perfect possibilities, recommends Dave LaBelle, ask

Photo-driven columns often allow photographers to cover subjects overlooked on routine news assignments. For her *Mercury News* column, Luci Williams Houston regularly covered weddings in search of moments unlikely to appear in a typical wedding album.
Luci S. Williams Houston,
San Jose Mercury News

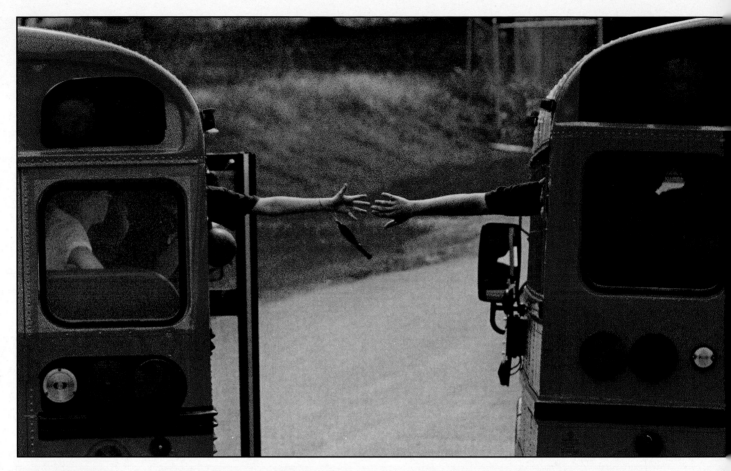

yourself, "Where would I be and what would
I be doing right now if I were 10 years old?
Or 70?'

He encourages photographers to go where
people gather—like malls, parks, swimming
pools, concerts, fairs, or anywhere people
congregate to work or play. For the photographer who has covered the same annual street
fair or county fair, he suggests that the shooter set up a personal challenge to come up
with something surprising.

"Don't shoot the same picture you shot
last year," he emphasizes. Perhaps his best
advice is to leave your comfort zone by
shooting subjects you despise. If you special-
ize in shooting sports, try your hand at covering ballet. If you are the go-to person for
planned events, start listening to the scanner
for breaking news.

THE PHOTO-DRIVEN COLUMN

A photo-driven feature column allows the
photographer latitude to take pictures as well
as to write. These regularly appearing
columns often explore an overlooked area of
a town or city or an aspect of city life.
Originated in 1975 by Charlie Nye at *The
Columbia Missourian*, the idea has been
emulated in different incarnations by a number of photographers at newspapers and web

sites from San Jose, California, to Concord,
New Hampshire. Some columns have a
consistent theme—running from marriage to
mayhem.

Luci S. Houston of the *San Jose Mercury
News* called her weekly look at weddings in
the San Francisco Bay Area "From This Day
Forward." After nine months of memos and
meetings, the police allowed the *Boston
Globe*'s Susan Kreiter to ride along with
them during patrols. Her column was
called "Cops."

Some columns, like those of Tom Burton
of the *Orlando Sentinel*, seek quiet moments
that typically do not earn news coverage.
Tom Gralish of the *Philadelphia Inquirer* initially used his photographic platform to focus
attention on each of one hundred neighborhoods in his city.

A few columns consist strictly of photos
with a brief headline or short caption. Sylvia
Plachy's weekly column in the *Village Voice*
ran with just the title "Unguided Tour."
Typically, photo columns include a short text
block, usually written by the photographer.

David Reese, now head of the photojournalism program at the University of Missouri,
was an early photo columnist. He outlined
several tips for getting started in *News
Photographer* magazine.

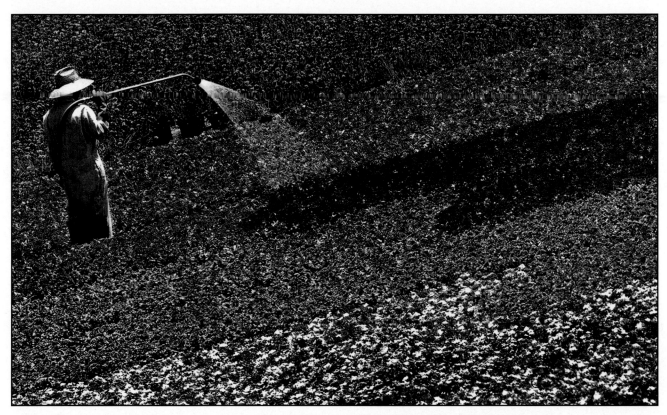

Feature pictures can simply capture the beauty of an area. A gardener watering ornamental flowers adds a center of interest to this picture. Bruce Chambers, *Orange County Register*

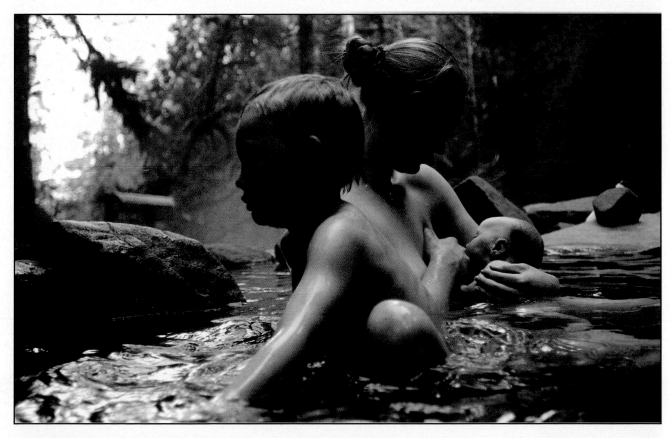

A quiet moment can become a timeless feature to give readers a respite from the news of the day. Sol Neelman, *Oregonian*

- Identify a niche in your paper that might be receptive to photo-driven columns—perhaps in the style or the metro section.
- Shoot a prototype before proposing the idea to the section editor.
- Emphasize the importance of building reader anticipation by featuring the column in the same position on a regular basis.
- Maintain photos as the column's priority.

AVOID THE TRITE

The bread-and-butter feature in today's newspaper or web site is still the pretty child playing in the park or the chimp clowning at the zoo. Photographers take pictures of kids and animals so often, however, that these topics can become trite.

Robert Garvin, writing in *Journalism Quarterly*, explained the genesis of the unsubstantial feature picture.

"I have known picture editors (including myself up until ten years ago) who, on a dull afternoon, assign a photographer to walk around town and photograph anything he sees. What does he see? On an August day, he sees a small boy in the spray of a fire hydrant, or a group of tenement dwellers sitting on a fire escape.

"These are so obvious that every passerby has seen them in the newspaper for the last 40 years. If there is no thought and preparation, one cannot expect striking pictures with more lasting merit."

When Arthur Goldsmith, an editor for *Popular Photography* magazine, judged the Pictures of the Year Contest, he concluded that pictures in the feature category tended to be hackneyed that year. He wrote, "Feature pictures often mean space fillers for a slow news day. Here are the visual puns, the cornball, the humorous, the sentimental, the offbeat. (Greased pigs and belly dancers were especially big during this year's competition.)"

Goldsmith said editors divide the photo world into two camps. "Either an event is hard news, which usually means violence, death, horror, confrontation, etc., or the event is a 'feature,' meaning something that appeals to our warm, furry sentimentality. But between the two extremes—the agony of the spot-news disaster and the ecstasy of the feature picture—lies that great amorphous zone that is most of our life." ∎

Sometimes seeing the world from another person's point of view yields a surprising picture. The photographer shoots weddings, pregnancies, and portraits of children. Angela Lang

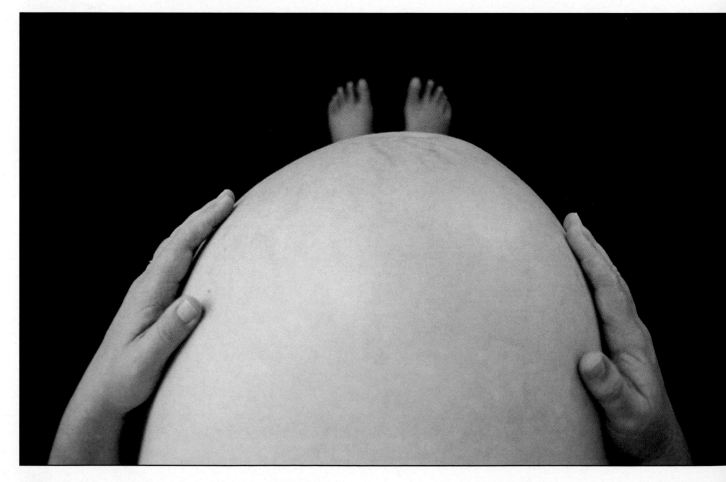

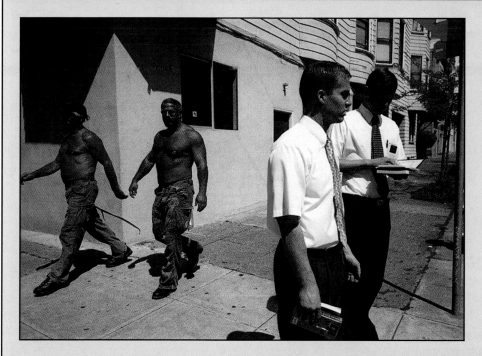

Contrasts in lifestyles make interesting features. Here, neatly attired Mormon missionaries waiting for a bus in San Francisco draw the attention of two locals wearing nipple rings and little else. The photographer was doing a story about the missionary life when this contrasting moment took place.
© Martin Jimenez

You can make the most of the amorphous—and possibly have your image displayed on your readers' refrigerators or computer monitors—by having an organized approach to looking for features. Here are some suggestions to send you on your search.

1 **Head for a good cruising location** such as the old part of town or a special neighborhood like Chinatown or Little Italy, where people are out and about.

2 **Keep an idea book** containing pictures you admire as reminders to yourself of places or people that can make good subjects.

3 **Watch the calendar** for upcoming topical days like the first day of summer, Flag Day, Secretaries Day, Martin Luther King Day.

4 **Shoot from a unique vantage** such as the top of City Hall's dome, underwater at the town's pool, or beneath a trampoline.

5 **Collect news releases** about upcoming events and activities that individuals or organizations are trying to promote.

6 **Give out your business cards** and ask people to fax, call, or email you with story suggestions or picture possibilities.

7 **Check the classified ads** for people who are trying to sell belongings. You will find everything from trained chimpanzees to antique art collections.

8 **Peruse events calendars** for listings ranging from the opening of a science fair to the Gay Pride Parade.

9 **Get on the mailing lists of organizations**—the more obscure the better. Ask them to send newsletters and press releases.

10 **Localize a national story or trend.** If swing dancing is the rage in New York and San Francisco, is it happening on your campus or in your hometown?

11 **Explore a new neighborhood.**

12 **Weatherize.** Whether it is Hades hot or just chilly cold, the weather can provide great feature subjects. While the rain, wind, or ice can be interesting in itself, look for ways that people and animals adapt to uncomfortable conditions.

13 **Select a word** like "love" to capture in a picture. Then look for examples that reflect the word. A couple holding hands might come to mind, but see what other examples of this emotion you can find. Other words to try: contrast (see page 88), youth and age, friendship.

14 **Examine extremes.** The best and the worst. The largest and the smallest. The highest and the lowest. Readers gravitate to these stories to learn about what make others exceptional.

15 **Seek out striking scenics.** From Ansel Adams's "Moonrise Over Hernandez" to *National Geographic*'s sunsets in Saudi Arabia, scenics can be scintillating.

16 **Dig out dangerous professions** like high-wire walkers, test pilots, or lion tamers. You should also check out unusual if not dangerous professions: tea tasters or flagpole painters come to mind.

17 **Study the students** at vocational schools. What's in the curricula at the mortuary academy, the hairdressing school, or the clown college, all listed in the yellow pages?

18 **Simplify the world** by looking for graphic photos like silhouettes, patterns, or shadows.

19 **Take the time to stop** if you see a situation that lends itself to a feature.

20 **View the world with unusual lenses** like a fish-eye, 600mm telephoto, or close-up macro lens.

21 **Develop a feature beat.** (See Chapter 10, "Covering the Issues.")

22 **Leave your subjects with a good memory—and your business card.** If you promise to give a photograph to your subject, deliver. If you fail to come through with a print, or email an image, subjects will have a bad taste left in their mouths and not be cooperative when the next photojournalist asks to take their picture. If you leave them with a good memory and your card, they may even let you know when another opportunity for photos arises.

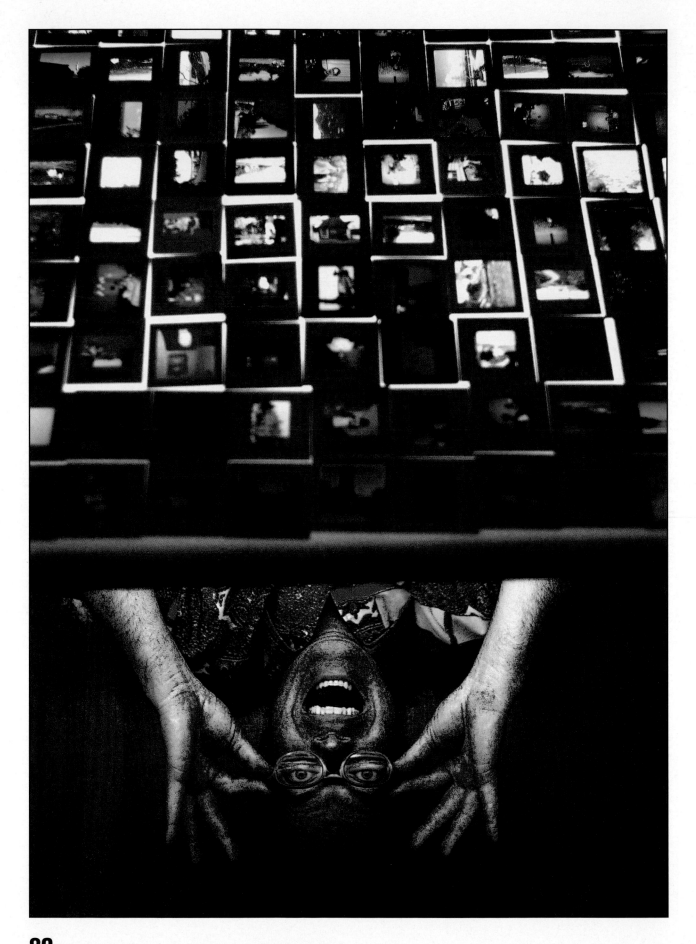

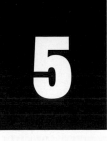

Portraits

5

THE JOURNALISTIC PORTRAIT

The journalistic portrait of a scientist should not look like that of a steelworker. An aggressive personality deserves a different portrait from the shy and retiring type. To tell each person's story, photojournalists shoot both posed and candid portraits. Candid photography can produce honest, believable portraits without a lot of elaborate prompting, staging, or lighting, says Steve Raymer, the longtime staff photographer for *National Geographic* who now teaches at Indiana University. "It's a matter of knowing the subject, using the light, and waiting for the moment," he observes.

Charles Phoenix uses old slides in his theatrical productions. By photographing the artist under his slide table, the photographer conveys the artist's outgoing personality as well as an aspect of his profession. Genaro Molina, *Los Angeles Times*

Even when they arrange elements for a portrait, photojournalists look for honest, candid moments. Nicole Bengiveno, who shoots for *The New York Times*, expresses the sentiment of many of her colleagues. "My favorite pictures are real moments when the subjects have forgotten you are there," she says. Indeed, shooting posed portraits is not a natural activity for many news photographers, whose instincts are to observe—not control.

However, photojournalists often are assigned to shoot posed portraits that reveal both why the person is in the news and something about the person's personality.

PUTTING YOUR SUBJECT AT EASE

If someone does not feel comfortable in front of the camera, the best photojournalistic techniques in the world will not produce a revealing portrait. When a photographer disappears behind the camera, even if it is a relatively small single-lens-reflex, the shooter loses eye contact with the subject, who is left alone to respond to a piece of coated glass and a black mechanical box—not exactly a situation conducive to stimulating conversation.

Bengiveno of *The New York Times* can relate to people who freeze when faced down by a camera. "All photographers should have a camera pointed at them," she says. "It is a scary feeling."

To understand the mindset of "the subject," Richard Koci Hernandez of the *San Jose Mercury News* photographed himself. "I took a lot of self-portraits so that I would know how uncomfortable it is to have your picture taken," he says.

Photographers develop different techniques to loosen up and relax their subjects. Keep in mind that an approach that works for one photographer might not work for you. Here are some choices to consider.

TALK IT OVER

One of the most enjoyable aspects of photojournalism is meeting different kinds of people. The most successful photojournalists research why their portrait subjects are in the headlines. During a shooting session, the talk usually turns to the person's involvement in the story. When people become engrossed in conversation, they often forget about the camera, which allows those candid moments in otherwise controlled situations.

"Ideally, I will talk to the subjects for 15 to 20 minutes to find out what in their life might relate to the picture assignment," Koci Hernandez says.

He asks subjects where they feel most comfortable. "I take advice if people are willing to give it."

Smiley Pool of the *Houston Chronicle* enlists his subjects as collaborators. "How do you want to have your picture made?" he asks. "It's your picture."

The best ideas often come from his subjects, Pool says. "Other times, you have to dream something up."

LOOK 'EM IN THE EYE

"When we put the camera to our eye it blocks our face," says David Leeson of *The Dallas Morning News*. "It's like staring down a gun barrel. I find it unnerving."

Rather than using the viewfinder for portraits, many photographers use the camera's LCD monitor to frame the picture while still maintaining eye contact.

Alfred Eisenstaedt, an original *Life* magazine staffer, avoided the disruption of picking up and putting down the camera by using a tripod and cable release. He put his camera on a tripod and focused, which freed him to talk directly and keep eye contact with his

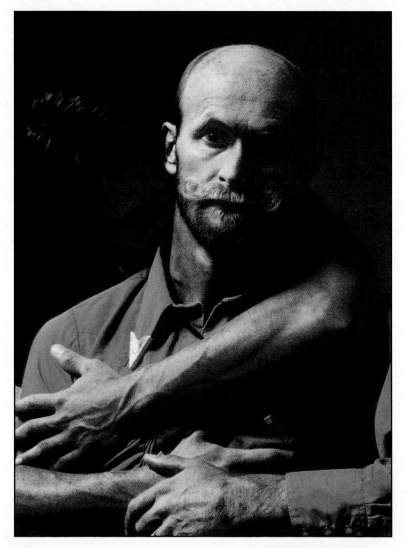

A real moment that developed during the shooting session gives intimacy to this portrait of a person with AIDs. Nicole Bengiveno, for *Newsweek*

subject while taking pictures with the cable release. "For me," he said, "this method often gives the most relaxed pictures."

LET PEOPLE BE THEMSELVES

The secret to posing is to study your subjects, says Sibylla Herbrich. As photographer and photo editor of the *San Francisco Daily Journal*, her job for more than five years was to cajole 15 minutes or so of billable hours from busy attorneys to take their portraits for the legal newspaper.

"From the time you initially meet them and while you are setting up the lights or arranging the background, watch for the subject's natural body language," she says.

How do they hold themselves, erect or relaxed? Do they point with their fingers or make a fist? Which way do they tip their head? When they are relaxed, do they use one hand or two to hold up their head?

"Look to see how comfortable they are with their own body," Herbrich says. "Start by shooting the way they are naturally standing. Then, if they are frozen, hands rigidly at their sides and face pointed straight ahead, remind them of a gesture that you had seen them use earlier." Although you are directing the person, the body position you suggest will be natural, not something you have imagined.

BE A BORE (BUT NOT A BOOR)

When you have time, the boredom technique works well; if you wait long enough, the subject often gets tired of posing, and you can shoot natural-looking photos that result in casual, relaxed portraits.

Arthur Grace, who has been a staffer for both *Time* and *Newsweek* and photographer for the book **The Comedians**, says, "Once you put people in a location, you just wait, and they will get lost in their own thoughts." Grace just sits there. "Maybe I'll take one frame to make them think that I've started, but I haven't." Eventually, the subjects get so bored they forget they are having their picture taken and they relax. That's when Grace goes to work.

As the photo shoot seems to be coming to an end, the thoughtful photojournalist often looks for one more frame. The *New York Times*'s Bengiveno says that sometimes when people think the picture session is over they let their guard down. "They might put their hand over their head," she says. "Then the real shooting session begins."

LET SOMEONE ELSE DO THE TALKING

Because it's often difficult to work the camera and carry on a meaningful conversation simultaneously, some photographers shoot

This swimmer's career had been damaged because of doping allegations, even though he took a vitamin supplement company to court and won. The photographer used a Nikonos with a 16mm lens and a flash. He had the subject remove the goggles so his eyes would be visible.

Al Schaben, *Los Angeles Times*

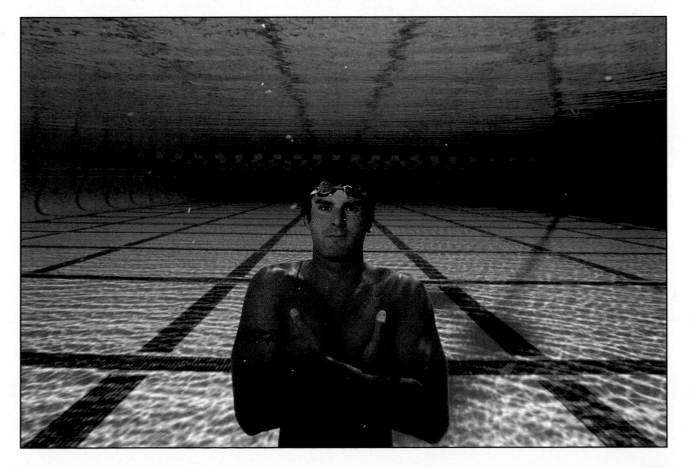

while the subject is being interviewed. If an interviewer does not accompany you on an assignment, take a friend along. When no outsider is available, look for someone on location, like the subject's colleague, to whom he or she might enjoy talking. Involved in conversation, the subject thaws and becomes animated—and the resulting photograph is natural and not contrived.

LIGHT AS A STORYTELLING ELEMENT

Whether soft from the side or streaming in from above, light in all its various incarnations usually determines the picture's mood. When photographers shoot a picture that is lit brightly yet has only a few shadows, the photo is called "high key." They often employ high-key lighting for pictures of brides, for example, because they want the photo to have an upbeat mood.

When a more moody effect is desired, however, photographers often choose lighting that will leave large areas of the picture in shadow. The photo's dominant tones are dark gray and black. At night, a tough police chief might be photographed with the available light of a street lamp. The moody lighting called "low key" will support the story's thrust. For many photographers, the atmosphere created by light in a portrait is more important than any other element.

UNDERSTAND LIGHT

To add depth to a subject's face, arrange the person so that the main light, whether it is from flood, flash, or window, falls toward the side of his or her face. Unlike direct frontal light, side light adds a roundness and three-dimensionality to the portrait. Side light also emphasizes the textural details of the face—a technique especially suited for bringing out the character lines in a person's features.

Saw the hot shoe off your camera was the advice the *Miami Herald*'s Jeffrey Salter gave to *Sporting News* staffer Robert Seale when he was starting out. Portraits are almost always more interesting when the light comes from any angle other than head on.

Alternatively, glamour photographers often light people with a large, flat light located near the camera's lens to eliminate shadows. Shadowless light, sometimes called "butterfly" lighting, tends to eliminate wrinkles, giving a youthful look to the portrait sitter. (See more on lighting in Chapter 9, "Strobe.")

Not all light has to come from a strobe or even a window. Jeff Vendsel, working for the *Marin* [California] *Independent Journal* used the light of an overhead projector to illuminate his portrait of two members of a multimedia association (see page 89).

LOOK FOR LIGHT

"I arrive 15 minutes early to a portrait session," says Koci Hernandez of the *San Jose Mercury News*. "I look for a beautiful shaft of light in the hallway. Then I put the subject in it, and hope and pray for a candid moment."

The San Jose photographer goes on to point out, "You can have everything working against you—background, uptight person. But if you have great light, everything will work out."

Like Koci Hernandez, Nicole Bengiveno will use any light she can find. "There have been times I have used the headlight of a car, street lamps, or a table lamp," she says.

To find the right light and to catch her subjects in a more relaxed atmosphere, Bengiveno often will take people for a walk in the streets of New York. This allows her to spend some time with them and watch how they move. "When I walk with someone, I try to keep the session flowing," she says. "All of a sudden I will turn a corner and see some great light."

Bengiveno was assigned to photograph a person who claimed to have memories of being abducted by aliens. She walked the subject around the South of Houston (SoHo) section of New York looking for anything that suggested "otherworldliness."

"We found a loft building with a fire escape," Bengiveno recalls. "The sun was shining down, casting a shadow through the fire escape. The light gave the feeling of something emanating from above."

While the shadows did not prove the existence of aliens, they did help shift the sense

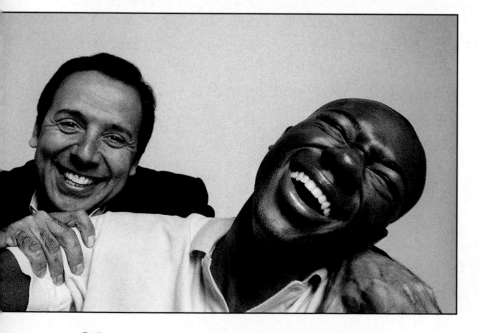

A writer (left) and his subject were on a book tour together. The photographer took the pair to the newspaper's studio and managed to get this lively reaction by kidding around with the subjects during the photo and interview sessions. The portrait's lighting and light background give it a "high-key" feel. Julie Stupsker, *San Francisco Examiner*

Actor Laurence Fishburne's image, dramatically lit, is captured in a mirror. "I told him that I wanted to photograph him holding a mirror in his hand as a symbol that he was taking control of his own fate by directing his first feature film," explains the photographer. Genaro Molina, *Los Angeles Times*

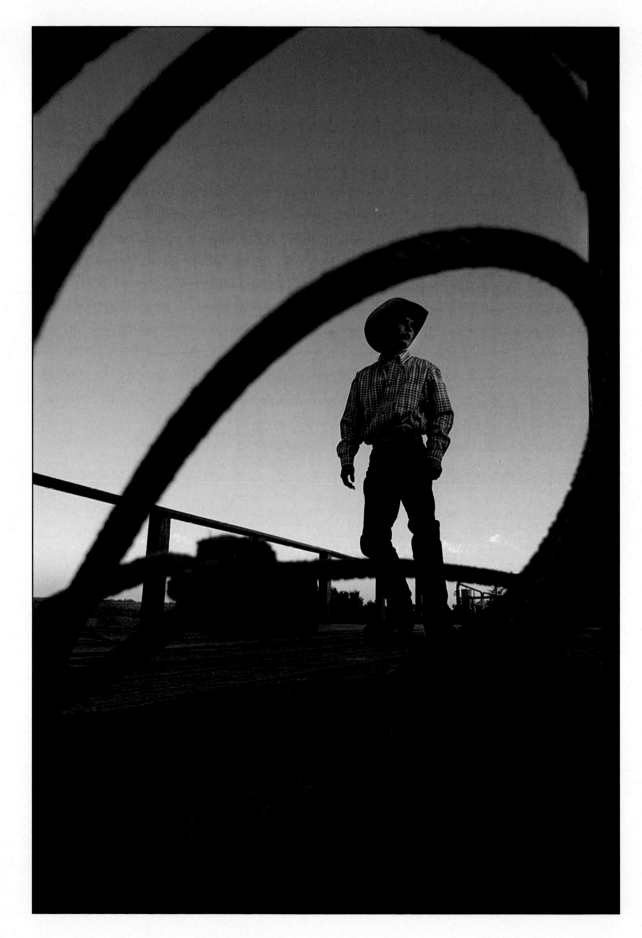

of reality and added a haunting mood to the final picture.

"I love discovering and finding things, being spontaneous," Bengiveno says.

COMPOSITIONAL ELEMENTS ADD IMPACT

Suppose your editor assigns you to photograph a banker. You size up the situation and decide to show "The Banker as a Stable Person in the Community." You might want to position the person in the middle of the frame, lending balance and therefore dignity to the picture. You have used composition to help tell your story, conveying to the reader the point you wish to make about the banker.

Suppose, on another day, you must photograph the director of the Little Theater, an offbeat dramatic group. You want your picture of the director to be as exciting and tension-producing as a good Stephen King thriller. By placing the theater director on the edge of the frame and leaving the remaining area black, you can produce an off-balanced picture that suggests added visual suspense.

CLOSE-UP VERSUS SCENE-SETTER

The effect of the final picture changes, depending on whether the photographer fills the frame with the sitter's face or stands back for a full-length portrait. An extreme close-up, for instance, appears to bring the subject so near that the viewer is allowed an unusual intimacy with the sitter, such as in the intense close-up of actor/director Laurence Fishburne on page 85.

On the other hand, because body language and clothing help to reveal a sitter's personality characteristics, the photographer sometimes must take a step backward to include in the composition the full length of the subject. Sometimes an overall photo can reveal more than a close-up showing only the face. Genaro Molina's picture of a theatrical artist under his light table explains more than what a simple head shot might reveal (see page 80).

AVOID BUSY BACKGROUNDS

A busy background can easily distract readers from the subject of the photo. You do not want the background to compete with your main subject for the viewer's attention.

Light as well as tone, color, and sharpness help define and separate the subject from the background. The background affects the "readability" of a photograph.

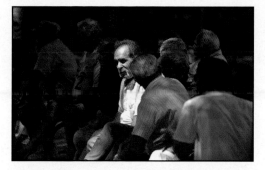

A shaft of light helps isolate the subject from a busy, distracting background.
© Ken Kobré

Readability requires that the subject not get lost in the details of the environment.

Dave Kittering of Dubuque, Iowa, found a simple, plain background by shooting a cowboy against a clear sky (opposite). Other shooters find an unadorned wall or bring their own paper or fabric background to the shoot. Josh Meltzer of *The Roanoke Times* also used the sky as a background while directing a strobe to the side of a ball player's face to make a graphic image of the young pitcher and his teammates (see page 186).

Directing some light to the back of a subject's dark hair or using available light can create a highlight that helps visually separate the subject from a dark wall. Alternatively, a shaft of light late in the afternoon can isolate a subject from the crowd, as in the portrait above of a Frenchman watching a game of pétanque (above).

Many still and video journalists use telephoto lenses to shoot portraits. These lenses, when used at wide apertures, help blur the background behind a subject. To achieve this effect, keep the subject as far away from the background as possible. The background will still show up, but it will be soft and partially indistinct. With a blurry background, the viewer's attention will remain on your primary subject.

PROPS HELP TELL THE STORY

Often an object a person is holding or the uniform he or she is wearing supports the thrust of the story. These props add visual information and help the reader go beyond just the contours of the subject's face. These props often cue the reader to a portrait's news peg. The location of the picture and the props in it tell the viewer something about a subject's profession, hobbies, and interests. A portrait taken in a dark factory, with the worker holding a wrench, says something different about the sitter than a portrait taken in a pristine office with the accountant seated at a computer.

In Rob Goebel's portrait of "Bones" Kah and his son, Harley, big, burly Bones wears his biker outfit, including sunglasses,

For a background clear of distractions, the photographer shot this rodeo contestant against the plain blue sky. The foreground rope that frames the cowboy helps tell his story.
Dave Kettering,
Telegraph Herald [Dubuque, Iowa]

sleeveless jacket, and skull-and-crossbones tattoos. He holds up his infant son, Harley. The visual contrast between the huge, rough-looking biker and vulnerable child gives the picture power. The biker details also add storytelling information to the image.

Sometimes photographers ask subjects to hold pictures of a relative who is missing or dead. These pictures often seem artificial or staged without revealing new information.

They merely serve as a way to combine two images into one, saving space yet adding little new information. In such cases, the photographer is often wiser to make a strong portrait of the subject using interesting light. A snapshot of the missing or deceased family member could run separately.

Shooting for the *Marin Independent Journal*, Jeff Vendsel used a projected image of a woman looking at a computer to light his

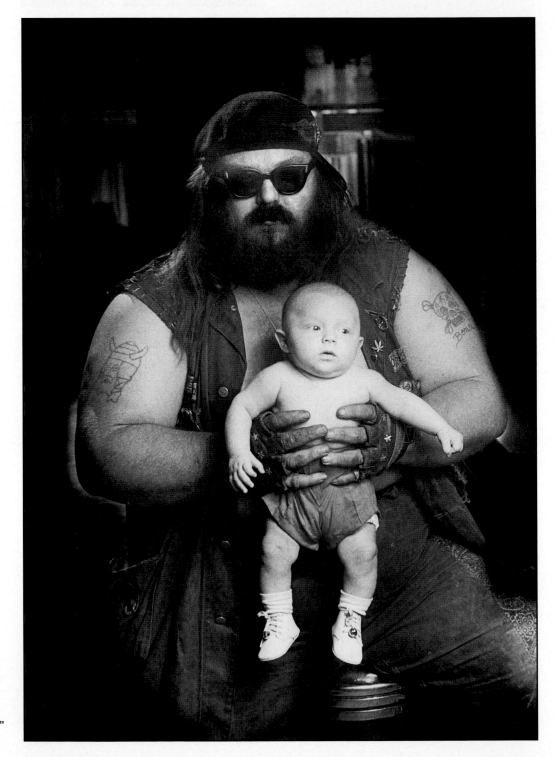

The father-son portrait of "Bones" Kah and his young offspring, Harley Davidson, resulted from a series of self-assignments created by the photographer. This personal assignment was to illustrate the word "contrast."
Rob Goebel, *Indianapolis Star*

subjects, members of a multimedia association. The projected image helped to explain the subjects' relationship to the news event. Of course, the projection also added interest to the final portrait.

In Arnold Newman's portrait of Piet Mondrian, an easel establishes that Mondrian was an artist (see page 92).

In each of these situations, props or clothing suggest why the subject was in the news.

PROVIDE CLUES
TO THE "INNER PERSON"

Besides quality of the light, composition, and props, other elements add to the storytelling nature of a portrait.

A subject's face, hands, and body position reflect the psychological state of the sitter. Is the subject smiling or showing a grim face? Are his hands pulling at his beard or resting at his side? Is he standing confidently or shifting awkwardly?

FACE

Of all the elements in a photo, the face still carries a disproportionate amount of psychological weight. Studies show that children, almost from birth, recognize the basic elements of a face, including the eyes, nose, and mouth. Whether true or not, people assume that the face is the "mirror of the soul,"

If the face is the soul's reflection, then the soul is multidimensional. Even the most sedate face reflects a surprising number of variations. Shoot 20 pictures of one person's face as she talks about her favorite topic. Note the number of distinctly different expressions the person exhibits. Is one frame of those 20 true to the nature of the person? Have the others missed the essence of the person's underlying character?

The great portraitist Arnold Newman says in his book *One Mind's Eye*, "I'm convinced that any photographic attempt to show the complete man is nonsense. We can only show what the man reveals."

The photojournalist usually selects an image of the subject talking, laughing, or frowning, an action coinciding with the thrust of the news story. When a recently appointed city manager expresses fear about his new job, the photo might show him with his hand massaging his wrinkled brow.

A year later, a story in which the city manager talks about his accomplishments might show him talking and smiling. The photojournalist's portrait does not reveal a person's "true inner nature" as much as it reflects the subject's immediate response to the current situation.

The respected magazine portrait photographer Mary Ellen Mark never asks her

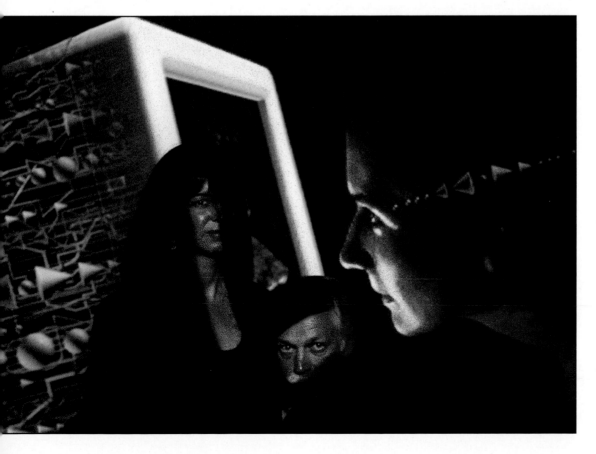

By placing his subjects carefully, the photographer highlighted two members of a multimedia association with a strip of white light from a digitally projected image. In a darkened room, the exposure was 1/15 sec.
Jeff Vendsel, *Marin* [California] *Independent Journal*

subjects to smile for the camera. A smile, she says, can be a person's defense mechanism against the discomfort of being the focus of a camera's lens. On the other hand, she does not hesitate to photograph a person's spontaneous laughter or glee.

EYES

Where should the subject look? Early journalism portraits taken around the turn of the century showed the sitter staring into the camera's lens during the prolonged time exposures.

During the Depression, Farm Security Administration subjects seemed always to gaze into space (see page 440). Portraits taken during the 1960s and 1970s often showed subjects looking as if they were in action, never noticing the camera's presence. Later, portraits tended to return to the direct gaze.

Photographers often feel that the viewer will be most involved with a portrait's subject when the two make eye contact. David Leeson of the *Dallas Morning News* continues to ask the subject to look into the camera. "I don't want any doubt in the reader's mind that this is a portrait," he says, echoing the sentiment of many photojournalists.

This convention—subject looking directly into the lens—is in the process of yielding to

another. Confronted with so many subjects staring into the lens, some photographers in the late 1990s began returning to the Depression-era approach in which the subject looks away from the camera into the distance. "Sometimes I have the subjects looking away," says Bengiveno of the *New York Times*. "Sometimes I have them looking over their shoulder. It depends on what feeling I want."

Like other stylistic variables that contribute to this kind of picture, this new convention is likely to change as well.

BODY LANGUAGE

Hands help tell a story in a nonverbal way. A news photographer covering a speech will not even bother to click the shutter until the lecturer raises a hand to make a point. When shooting a portrait, watch the individual's hands as she toys with her hair, touches her chin, or pushes up her cheek. A person chewing his fingernails reveals a certain tension about the situation in which he finds himself.

Desmond Morris's excellent book, *Manwatching: A Field Guide to Human Behavior,* is a terrific guide for improving your observational skills. Morris documented various types of gestures and signals that people use to express inner feelings. The way an individual stands, whether as straight as a

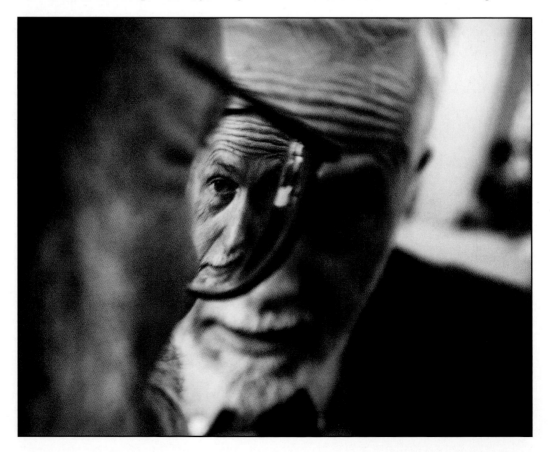

While you cannot really see the world through someone else's eyes, this picture allows you to see it through one person's glasses. The photographer used the glasses as a compositional device to direct the viewer's attention. John Burgess, [Santa Rosa, California] *Press Democrat*

West Point cadet or as bowlegged as a cowboy, provides clues about the subject's mood, way of life, or even upbringing. Studying ways people communicate nonverbally can sensitize you to good picture possibilities in portrait sessions and beyond.

PRECONCEIVING THE PHOTO

When assigned to shoot a portrait, many photojournalists go to great lengths to imagine how a picture might look before they ever arrive on the scene.

Koci Hernandez of the *Mercury News* says he almost always has some kind of preconceived notion when he approaches a portrait. "Sometimes you have to illustrate a point," he says. "If a scientist has invented a new baseball bat, I know I am going to need the bat in the picture."

To stay fresh, Koci Hernandez maintains an idea book. "I clip out portraits from magazine and newspapers," he explains. "I keep the pictures in a binder and flip through the book before I go into a portrait session."

Paolo Vescia's assignment was to take a portrait of Moshe Cohen, a member of "Clowns Without Borders." The group aims to bring comic relief to war-ravaged and underdeveloped countries.

Cohen arrived with the humor, but Vescia came up with the idea of integrating clown and world in one photo. Vescia bought several blowup plastic globes and after setting up the lights, asked his subject to juggle. The preconceived picture captures the spirit of clowning while differentiating this jester's story from any other.

The *Los Angeles Times* assigned Genaro Molina to photograph Laurence Fishburne after the actor directed his first movie.

Molina preconceived a picture. "I told him that I wanted to photograph him holding a mirror in his hand as a symbol that he was taking control of his own fate by directing his first feature film," Molina says.

The portrait of the actor goes past a record of his face and implies something about why Fishburne was in the news at the time (see page 85).

Even if you have a great idea for a picture, do not hesitate to throw it away if something better comes along. Be flexible. Your preconceived idea/location/pose for a shoot may be great, but it helps to be open to new ideas presented by the subject or the setting.

"You might get to a location and find a great window, or a great architectural detail, or a great colored wall, or sky that you can build a great photo out of. Do not be afraid to chuck your original idea and go with something that your environment provides," advises Robert Seale, who spends

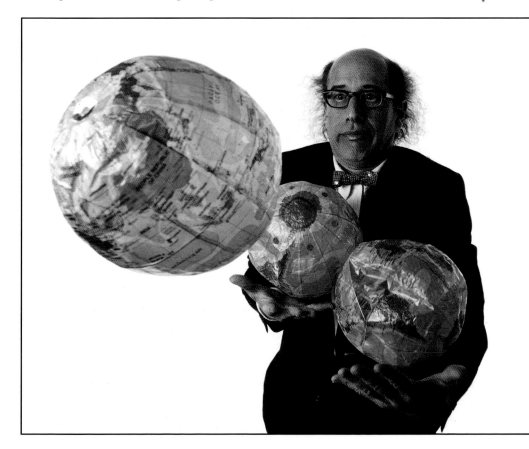

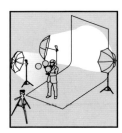

The mission of "Clowns Without Borders" is to bring comic relief to war-ravaged and developing countries. The photographer conceived the idea of the performer juggling the world and brought the inflatable globes to the photo session. The photographer "blew out" the background with two strobes bounced into umbrellas that he aimed at the white seamless paper. A third strobe/umbrella lit the juggler and also caught all three balls in the air. For more on lighting, see Chapter 9, "Strobe."
Paolo Vescia, *SF Weekly* [San Francisco]

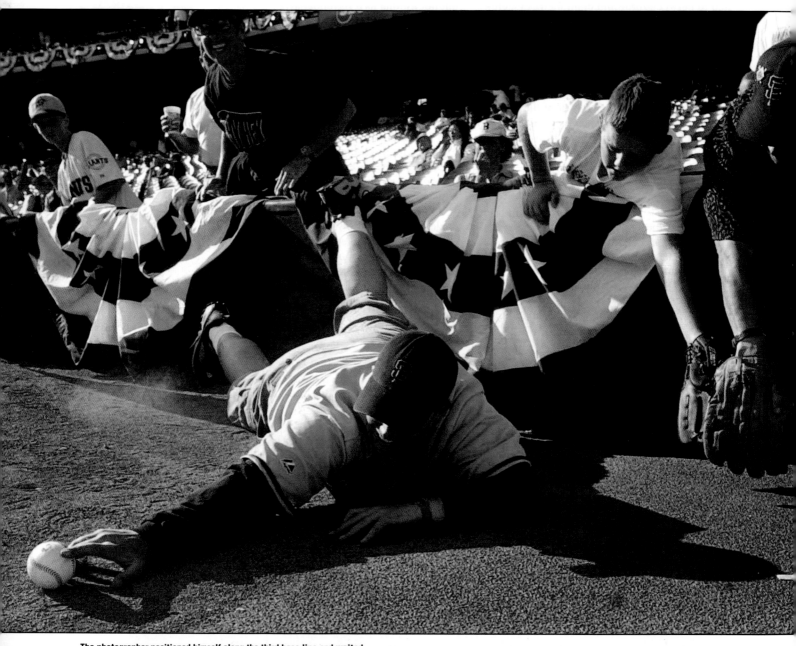

The photographer positioned himself along the third base line and waited for fans to catch foul balls during batting practice at the National League Championships. By keeping his eye on the fans as well as the batters, the photographer captured this over-eager future star spilling out of the bleachers in pursuit of a ball. Jeff Vendsel, *Marin* [California] *Independent Journal*

6

Sports

SPORTS AS NEWS

Sports photographers are like athletes. They need the aim of a major league pitcher, the reflexes of a basketball guard, and the concentration of a tennis player. Sports shooters talk about getting in slumps, just as baseball players having trouble at the plate get into ruts. "At the beginning of the season I'm rusty," says Brad Mangin, a freelance sports specialist whose clients include *Sports Illustrated* and Major League Baseball. "After a few games I get into the groove."

shoot from this position during part of the game. This vantage point is ideal for pictures of the tip-off with all the players looking straight up into your lens. "It's very important to safely secure all overhead equipment with cables," advises Guralnick on shooting from this position, "and don't expect to have access to your camera until after the game."

BEHIND THE BACKBOARD

Photographers sometimes mount remote cameras behind clear backboards.

Using sturdy clamps, they attach the camera behind the backboard, prefocus the distance, set the aperture, and fire the camera with a remote trigger attached to the camera. To avoid reflections from the backboard, they create a surround of black tinfoil around the camera. Equally important, they always attach a safety line to the camera lest it shake loose from the clamp during the game. Once the game begins, these cameras must stay in place.

THE "ARMPIT" SHOT

The bread-and-butter basketball photo, nicknamed the "armpit" shot, shows a leaping player with arms extended over his head, pumping the ball toward the basket. Pro players use the jump shot so often that conscientious photographers actually have to work hard to avoid taking this predictable basketball photo.

Skipping the Cliché

Loose basketballs on the court are your opportunity to take unique pictures. "You can bet when a ball's free, there will be a scramble for it, and then a fight to gain possession of it," the AP's Schuyler explains. "Players fouling one another always look funny in pictures, and these seem to be the pictures people remember longest. When a ball bounces loose or a foul is committed, the rhythm of the game is broken. A mistake was made. The game gets interesting, and so do the pictures."

For this photo of James Lebron coming in to dunk the ball, the *Sports Illustrated* photographer remotely fired a camera he had installed behind the glass backboard. When the photographer triggered the camera, a radio transmitter fired four strobes located in the rafters of the basketball arena. There's no such thing as a routine "armpit" shot from this angle.

John McDonough,
Sports Illustrated

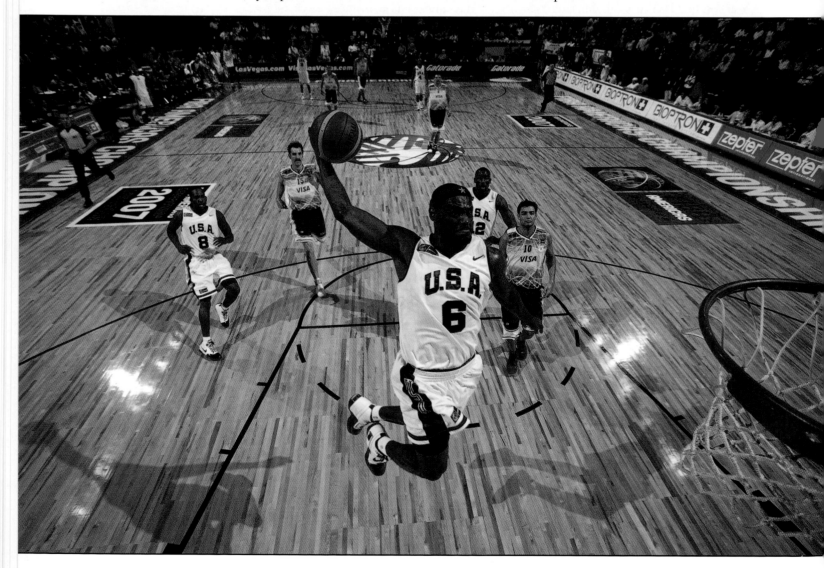

When you cannot attend practice sessions, or when you do not have time to learn the team's basic patterns, concentrate your coverage on the player with the star reputation. Stars tend to score the most points and snag the majority of rebounds.

Also, stars do not sink baskets like regular folk; they exhibit individual styles and almost choreographed moves. Michael Jordan, for example, would seem to counteract gravity as he floated through the air, passed the basket, and, as if it were an afterthought, changed direction in mid-flight to make a basket. A good sports photographer tries to capture in pictures the style of the star. ■

HOW *SPORTS ILLUSTRATED* COVERS A BASKETBALL GAME

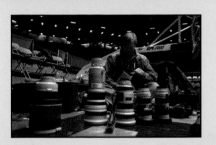

To cover a basketball game, *Sports Illustrated*'s John McDonough and an assistant arrive at least a day before the game to set up overhead strobe lights and install up to eight remote cameras in the arena.

Sports Illustrated strobes are already in place at many professional arenas. Otherwise the magazine rents their use for the game. At college gyms, the *SI* crew sets up its own strobes in a catwalk above the court for each game.

McDonough and his assistant confirm that the hard wire running from the gym's ceiling to the floor and/or a radio slave will connect to the primary camera or remote trigger. The strobe system must fire the overhead strobes consistently and reliably. They check and double-check the exposure.

McDonough attaches cameras to each clear glass backboard, places one or more overhead cameras in the rafters, and positions cameras in various sections of the stands by clamping them to metal hand railings. Each remote camera is wirelessly connected to a master switch and then to a separate remote switch taped to the camera. Each remote camera is prefocused to a spot in the lane about the height of a player, its exposure set. McDonough tapes everything down so the settings will not be jarred loose during the game.

Once the game begins, the *SI* shooter is often poised on a small camp stool at the end of the court, behind the basket and just outside the court boundary. He sometimes positions himself just to the side of the escape lane or, at other times, toward the corner of the court.

A camera with a 20mm wide-angle lens is on the floor and ready. McDonough picks up his hand-held camera, usually with a 70–200mm zoom or 24–105mm zoom lens for near-court action. Using autofocus, he follows the action. When he presses the camera's shutter, the overhead strobes fire. He also has a trigger taped to the side of his camera and connected to the master radio slave. Pressing this button fires the four remote cameras on the near side of the gym fire as well as the camera in his hands. The ceiling strobes blast their light at the same instant.

For down-court three-pointers or lost-ball action McDonough has prepared a second camera with a monopod-mounted 300mm lens coordinated with the overhead strobes. In addition, he has a radio-activated trigger taped to his camera that activates just the remote cameras down court that are aimed at the lane. Shooting pictures of the far court means he often is shooting action that is out of direct view, making it necessary for him to know and keep in mind the location and angle of view of every remote camera.

As soon as the game is over, it is time to photograph the teams' reactions — jubilation or dejection. The goal is two-fold: a clean shot of the winners celebrating as well as the losers' sense of failure... or anything else like the coach, fans, or cheerleaders that might help tell the story of that particular contest.

Immediately after the teams go to the locker room, McDonough's assistant collects all the memory cards and downloads them through a computer onto an external hard drive. The drive is shipped to New York on the next available flight. As soon as possible, the assistant uploads pictures to *Sports Illustrated*'s web site. If the game takes place on the magazine's deadline, McDonough transmits a few pictures directly to the photo editors back in New York.

Only after all the images have been sent, does McDonough have the time to relax and enjoy the great shots he has taken, and, perhaps, analyze how to adjust techniques for the next game and the next arena.

To learn about picture editing at *Sports Illustrated* and to view some of photo editor James Colton's favorite shots, see "Inside *Sports Illustrated*," on the DVD enclosed in this book. ■

(ABOVE) John McDonough prepares eight remote cameras to cover a basketball game. (BELOW) McDonough covers one of the March Madness play-offs in Albuquerque, New Mexico.
© Ken Kobré

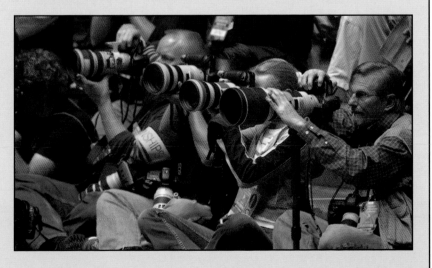

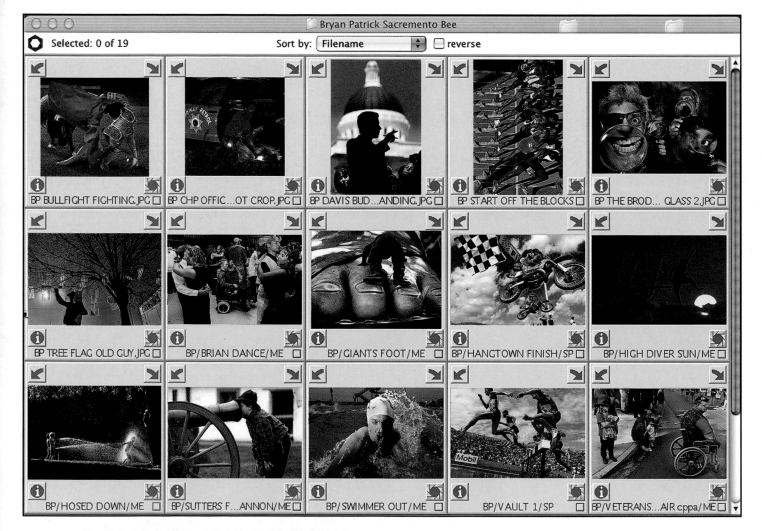

Choosing the right photo is an art. Surprisingly, some of the best photo editors were never photographers. All by Bryan Patrick, *The Sacramento Bee*

7

Photo Editing

THE ROLE OF THE PICTURE EDITOR

Are you ready for reality? You have less than three-quarters of a second to capture a reader's attention with a photograph. Using an innovative research tool, Sheree Josephson followed readers' eye movements as they looked at a variety of published pictures. The device she used, developed by Eye-Trac Research Systems, consists of two tiny video cameras mounted on the subject's head that record where, how long, and in which order the person looks at photos in a newspaper, a magazine, or on a web site. The startling result, revealed in her doctoral dissertation, was that readers spend less

Eye-Trac research follows a person's eyes as they travel across a newspaper page or web site. Recent studies suggest that in print, readers' eyes first go to photographs. On the Internet, however, they look at headlines and text before photos.

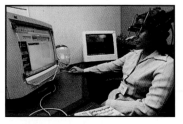

than three-quarters of a second looking at a photograph.

Now that is a challenge for any photo editor! How do you assign photographers and then select pictures that will communicate to the reader in less than a second?

Not surprisingly, photo editing takes strong eyes, a steady hand on the computer mouse, and the psychological strength to reject thousands of pictures while seeking the one frame or part of a frame that tells the story and has visual impact that will—literally—engage a viewer in an instant.

START WITH IMAGINATIVE ASSIGNMENTS

Striking pictures result from solid assignments. Picture editors at magazines, newspapers, agencies, or web sites peruse lists of news stories to determine which lend themselves to pictorial reporting, which need an illustration or computer graphic, and which need no accompanying artwork at all. With limited staff and resources—and most newspapers, magazines, and web sites fall into this category—editors must choose to cover articles or front-page stories with a certain amount of intrinsic visual interest.

When Bruce Baumann was assistant managing editor of graphics for the *Pittsburgh Press*, he warned that a photo department should not become a "service station." He pointed out that a photographer's job is not just to provide the service of illustrating a writer's story.

The enlightened photo editor, therefore, not only assigns the news stories of the day, but also generates pictorial story ideas. For example, a news conference announces a $4 million grant for nursing homes.

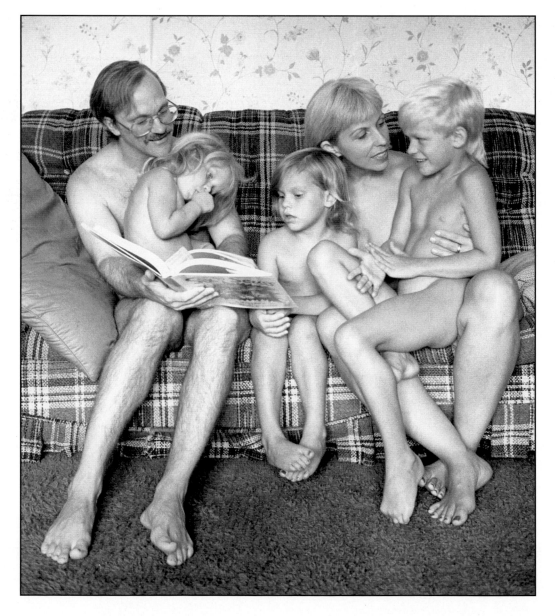

Good photos like this one start with good assignments. The members of this family, who wear no clothes at home, had been featured on "The Donahue Show." When the photographer's newspaper followed up the family's TV debut with a local story, he exposed carefully without revealing too much. Doug Kapustin, Patuxent [Maryland] Publishing Co.

Although a picture of the press conference may be necessary, it has little chance of producing exciting photos and less opportunity for providing valuable information about aging or the crisis in care for the elderly. The story is about statistics—the percentage increase in care costs—and about the number of dollars spent on nursing home facilities.

A photo editor, on the other hand, might try to interpret these statistics visually by instructing the photographer to spend several days in a nursing home. These kinds of photos would help translate the dull, itemized costs into more human terms.

Readers would see the conditions of the facility and the regressive effects of aging on the home's clientele. Finally, photos showing an elderly patient slumped in a wheelchair in an empty hallway can bring the dollars-and-cents issue home to the reader. (See Chapter 10, "Covering the Issues.")

SELECT THE PHOTOGRAPHER

A perceptive photo editor realizes the strengths and weaknesses of staff and freelance photographers. Not all photographers like sports; only a few take funny pictures. Some photographers notice subtle shadings of light and shade, whereas others have an eye for action. Some photographers have a lot of experience traveling overseas, speak different languages, and can figure out how to transmit their pictures from any phone jack in the developing world. Matching the correct photographer with the appropriate assignment can be a complex task.

Picture editors look at photographers' portfolios each week, searching for fresh work that represents new trends in photography.

Pairing the right photographer with the right assignment is a crucial job for the photo editor. In this case, the story required someone who could handle portable strobes. The photographer set up strobes with umbrellas on either side of an aquarium exhibit at the Alaska Department of Fish and Game.

The strobes froze the moment the large Pike opened its mouth and swallowed the unsuspecting Rainbow fingerling.
Jim Lavrakas,
Anchorage Daily News

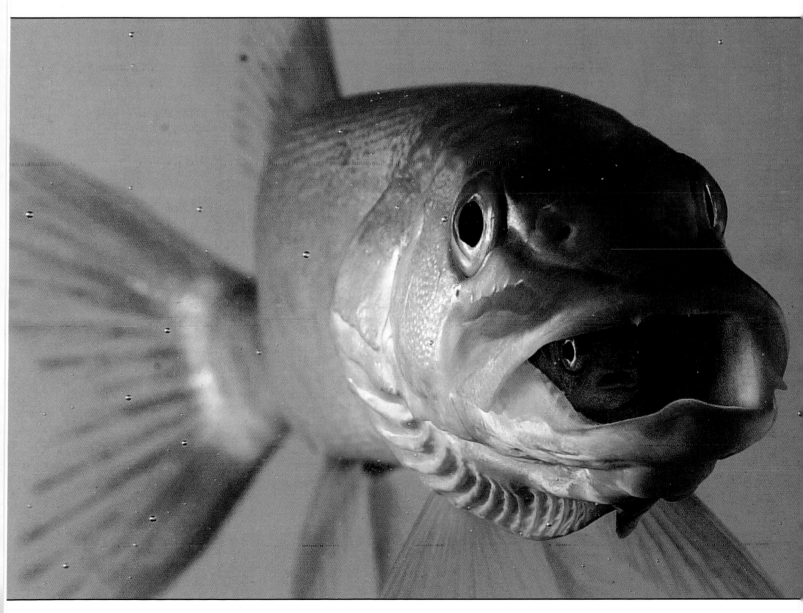

supports findings that readers prefer features to news. Whereas older studies asked readers what they liked or remembered about pictures, the equipment actually recorded the amount of time people gazed at each image.

Sharon H. Polansky, vice president of Gallup Applied Science Partnership (Princeton, New Jersey), says that the majority of subjects reading newspapers gravitate to feature images rather than to news photos, although she qualifies her statement by restricting her conclusions to "some newspapers and audiences." She says feature photos have a slightly higher "attention" factor.

CAN PROFESSIONAL EDITORS PREDICT READERS' PREFERENCES?

Who knows what kinds of pictures people like? Logically, you might assume that photo editors know their audiences, but another study by MacLean and Kao, published in *Journalism Quarterly*, suggests that editors are just guessing when they predict readers' responses to pictures.

The researchers asked average newspaper readers to sort through pictures and to arrange them in order—from most favorite to least favorite photos.

Then the researchers gave a group of experienced photo editors and a group of untrained students statistical information about the readers. Armed with this data, the group of editors and the group of students sorted through the same images to predict how they thought the readers had ordered their preferences.

MacLean and Kao hypothesized that the more information (such as age, gender, and occupation) the editors and students had, the more accurately they could predict the likes and dislikes of readers.

The researchers' hypothesis was wrong. Professional photo editors performed little better than even chance when given detailed information about their readers. Furthermore, photo editors did no better at their predictions than did the students.

However, once the professionals had seen how their readers had sorted one set of photos, the editors could anticipate how the readers would sort a second set. These predictions were even better if the editors knew more about the reader, including the person's age, hobbies, and lifestyle.

Until the editors had seen the readers' selections, however, they could not predict an individual's preferences. Clearly, more editors should find out what pictures their readers are actually looking at, rather than make editorial decisions on their own biases.

Do Readers and Editors Agree?

To discover if editors and readers agree on what constitutes interesting and newsworthy photos, an Associated Press Managing Editors photo survey was designed to determine which kinds of pictures readers liked, as well as which type editors preferred, and whether readers and editors shared the same taste.

The results indicated a surprisingly close agreement between readers and editors.

Both selected the same photos in the sports, general news, and feature categories.

Editors' and readers' opinions, however, differed radically on the use of dramatic news pictures. Editors were twice as likely as readers to choose action-packed, often violent, and sometimes gruesome news pictures. A majority of the readers not only disliked such pictures, but also thought that violent pictures should never be published.

As the pictures became successively more gruesome, fewer readers voted for photos in this category.

The AP's former director of photography, Hal Buell, tried to draw some conclusions from the survey. Newspapers and magazines have to be all things to a lot of different people, he said. Editors must balance what people want and also what the editors think is significant.

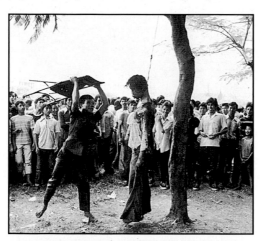

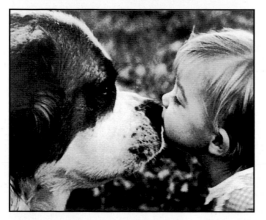

Which picture do you prefer? In an Associated Press survey, editors selected the hard news shot of a rightist striking the lifeless body of a hanged student in Bangkok, Thailand. Readers preferred the feature picture of a Saint Bernard and child.
© Wide World Photos

In the end, a publication has to print some of both to present a complete picture of the world: pictures of dogs kissing kids as well as pictures of political violence.

See Chapter 15, "Ethics," for more discussion on gruesome images.

HOW READERS REACT TO COLOR

Although many photographers still prefer black-and-white, readers prefer color photos, according to different studies by J.W. Click and G.H. Stempel, and by the Poynter Institute Color Project, conducted by Drs. Mario Garcia and Robert Bohle.

Overall, readers prefer color photos and think they are more realistic. Readers seem to remember color photos better than black-and-white ones.

Black-and-White but Read All Over?

In a colorful world, black-and-white images sometimes stand out. Even though publications today can easily run color, some choose to publish black-and-white images instead. Black-and-white images convey an air of dignity and seriousness. Shades of gray connote the traditional, respected, documentary style. Black-and-white journalistic photos stand out against competing, colorful advertisements.

Critic Susan Sontag wrote in *On Photography* that monochrome, black-and-white pictures give an image a sense of age, historical distance, and aura.

While both *Time* and *Newsweek* magazines run mostly color photos, each frequently publishes behind-the-scenes political stories as black-and-white photo essays.

Time had dropped the traditional black-and-white photo essay when it went all-color, so bringing it back wasn't easy, recalls P.F. Bentley, a former *Time* contract shooter.

"The hardest part was to get the managing editor to understand the impact black-and-white can have," he says. "Once he looked at the first take and once they printed it, the essays got rave reviews. They have not questioned it at all since. Now it is being done not only by me but also by Diana Walker, Jim Nachtwey, Chris Morris, and others."

Time's former picture editor Michele Stephenson assigned black-and-white images to give a story a certain mood, to signal "documentary," she said. In "*Time*'s Past in the Present: Nostalgia and the Black-and-White Image," she told researcher Paul Grainge that breaking news will almost certainly run in color, while black-and-white is used to give a story qualities of introspection and poignancy.

Carol Guzy, a two-time Pulitzer Prize winner for the *Washington Post*, says, "I love

black-and-white, and I've been with black-and-white all my life. Color can be distracting." She points out that her photograph of two nomad women carrying a baby between them (see page 494) would not have worked in color because of the colors of the women's garments. "They were horrible colors that clashed really badly," she explains. "You lost the baby."

While editors should not use photos just because they are as multi-hued as Joseph's proverbial coat, neither should they forget

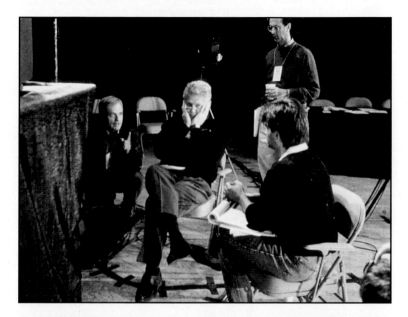

News magazines often use black-and-white images to alert the reader to documentary moments taken behind the scenes. Here, President Clinton is practicing for a debate during his reelection campaign. Diana Walker, *Time*

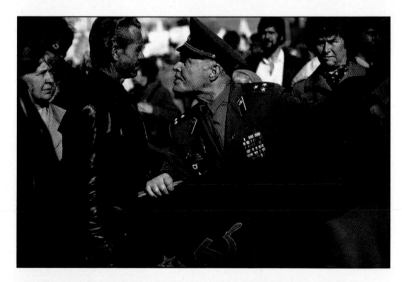

While on assignment for *National Geographic*, the photographer caught this retired Russian colonel arguing with anti-Communist demonstrators during the May Day celebration in Red Square. The picture captured the country's old and new attitudes and provided a visual synopsis for his story "Mother Russia on a New Course." The red flag adds to both the visual and storytelling power of the picture. Steve Raymer, for *National Geographic*

CROP THE EXCESS

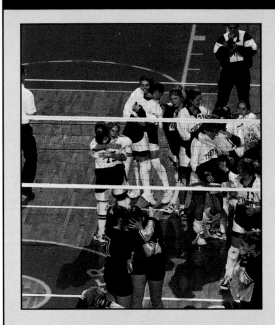

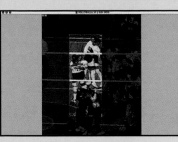

Careful cropping transformed this chaotic scene into a strong, easy-to-read image of victory and defeat. John Martin, *Cedar Rapids* [Iowa] *Gazette*

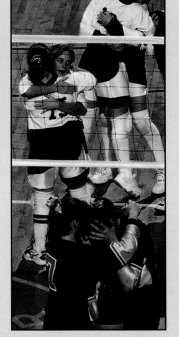

BUT PLEASE, DON'T AMPUTATE AT THE JOINTS

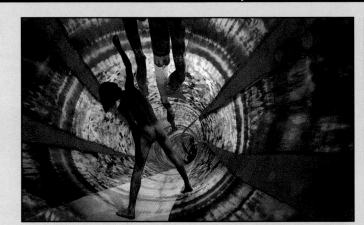

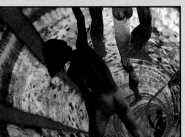

A man dances inside a giant windsock at Burning Man Festival, which takes place each year in California's Mojavi Desert.
Julie Stupsker
San Francisco Examiner

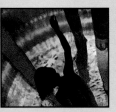

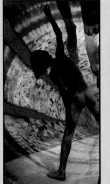

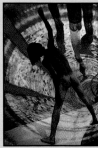

The editor's most perceptive skills come into play when cropping a picture containing a person. Parts of the body can be cropped, but usually the crop should not fall on a joint like an elbow or knee. If it's necessary to sever a head from a body in a photo, some of the shoulder should be left so that the head will have a platform on which to sit. It also can work to crop into the face of a person as long as the cut doesn't leave just half of an eye, for example, or just part of a mouth. Look at the pictures of the dancer here and decide which crops seem natural and which seem arbitrary or absurd.

that color carries information that can be lost in a black-and-white image. Journalists are in the information business. Additional information usually adds to readers' understanding of a story. However, black-and-white can add authority to that story.

WORKING WITH IMAGES
CROPPING: CUTTING OUT THE FAT

Regardless of how good the original is, if a photo is butchered during editing or reduced to the size of a postage stamp on the web, no one will see the picture. Newspapers do this every day. Says Roy Paul Nelson, author of **Publication Design**, "The typical daily or weekly newspaper is not designed, really; its parts are merely fitted together to fill all the available space, sort of like a jigsaw puzzle." To save their photographs, many camera journalists are getting involved in design, at least on newspapers and online. These photographers want a say in how their pictures are cropped and sized.

Perfect Framing is Rare

When you take a picture, you must decide what to include and what to leave out. The impact of a picture often depends on this decision. By including too much, you risk distracting the viewer from the main subject. By framing too tightly, you might leave out important storytelling elements.

While photographers carry a variety of lenses to enable them to zoom in or draw back to include only the important pictorial elements, not every subject does not fit neatly into a 35mm format. For that matter, all subjects do not fit naturally into a 2¼"x2¼" square or a 4"x5" rectangle, despite tight in-camera framing. Some subjects are low and wide, like the deck of an aircraft carrier (see pages 142–143), whereas other subjects are tall and skinny, like the Washington Monument.

No matter how carefully you compose the picture in a camera's viewfinder, the image from the real world may not completely fill the frame. In these situations, all you can do is shoot and then crop the image later.

REDUCED QUALITY: THE PRICE OF CROPPING

A perceptive editor can improve a photo's impact with thoughtful cropping, but often at a price. Enlarging a small portion of the original shot magnifies defects in the image.

If the original photograph lacked perfect sharpness, then the published picture will look soft. Even if the original is sharp, enlarging a portion of the image emphasizes each pixel, thereby decreasing the photo's clarity. Digital images enlarged beyond their ideal resolution are likely to appear pixelated. (See pages 169–170 for more about digital resolution and picture quality.)

While the technical quality of a picture decreases when the image is drastically cropped and enlarged, its visual impact often is improved.

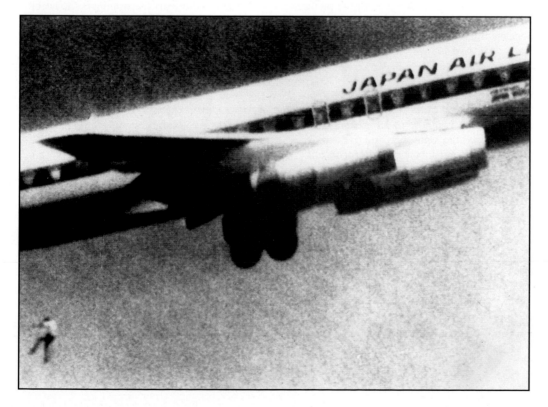

The price of extreme enlargement is increased grain and decreased quality. Only for news as unusual as this airplane stowaway falling to his death should poor quality photos be enlarged to this extent. John Gilpin, Wide World Photos

Cropping, therefore, involves a trade-off between possibly poorer quality and better composition. Taking a one-inch-square segment of an 8"x10" photo and publishing it as a half-page spread in the newspaper or magazine might produce a perfectly composed picture that is too pixelated to appreciate.

While few situations merit an extreme blow-up from such a tiny portion of a picture, a good photo editor generally will opt for a dramatic image at the expense of some sharpness and pixelation. The editor reasons that it is better to catch readers' attention with an exciting photo than lose them with a technically perfect but otherwise dull image.

CROP THE EXCESS

Like a writer editing copy, the picture editor, designer, or photographer should emphasize significant elements in the picture by eliminating extraneous material that carries little meaning. If a person's expression gives the picture sparkle, zero in on the face and cut out the peripheral material.

Light, bright areas of the picture, like windows and lights, tend to attract the eye. If these windows and lights are extraneous to the main subject, they will pull the reader's attention away. Avoid a competing area that might distract a reader's interest from the photo's primary subject. Crop out these irritating sidelights from the picture. If the action occurs in one corner of the picture, focus on that area. There should be a good reason for leaving in each area of the picture. No corner of the picture should remain just because it happened to be in the original frame. The rule is save the meat of the photo by cutting out the fat.

CROP RUTHLESSLY

"Crop ruthlessly," advises Edmond Arnold, a pioneer of modern newspaper design. "Cut out anything that's not essential to the picture, so that the reader's attention won't be distracted or wasted. Ruthless cropping leads to stronger images."

Research supports the notion that eliminating extraneous details helps a picture's readability. Gallup's Sharon Polansky, recording readers' eye movements as they perused printed material, found that the simpler a picture's background, the more attention the photograph received.

BUT PRESERVE THE MOOD

Cropping can improve a picture by eliminating irritating details. But mindless cropping can ruin a picture's intent by slicing off areas that deliver its mood. The sensitive slicer preserves the ingredients that give a

photograph its arresting look by leaving the brooding gray sky in a scenic or including the cluttered bookshelves in a college professor's portrait.

Sometimes a blank area in the picture balances an active area. Leaving a little room on the print in front of a runner helps create the illusion that the athlete is moving across the picture. Similarly, some blank space in front of a profile portrait keeps the subject from looking as if he or she is peering off the edge of the print. Insensitive cropping can rip away parts of a picture that give it context. Sometimes it's important to know that a riot occurred in the ornate foyer of city hall or in a barren, dusty field. Overzealous cropping could eliminate such telling details.

WHEN CROPPING CAN CHANGE THE MESSAGE

Editors turned to cropping to handle an extremely gory picture. The photo, taken by *El Pais* photographer Pablo Torres Guerrero, showed stunned and injured victims being helped by rescue workers and bystanders along the tracks outside of a Madrid subway station after 13 bomb-loaded backpacks exploded and killed 190 people and injured about 1800. In the lower left foreground of Guerrero's picture is a body part that medical experts identified as a femur.

Guerrero's picture, distributed around the world by Reuters, was subject to intense scrutiny and was the topic of much discussion prior to publication—and after.

"Around the world, cropping is the accepted form of alteration or editing—the photographic equivalent of paraphrasing or ellipsis within the photographic narrative of a picture," wrote Kenny Irby, Visual Journalism Group Leader of the Poynter Institute, in "Beyond Taste: Editing Truth," published in *Poynter Online*. Media outlets around the world chose to crop the image and thus emphasize the material damage over the human toll. (See Chapter 15, "Ethics," for more on how editors handle gory images.)

Of course photographers in the field always choose to frame one part of the scene they are photographing and leave out the rest. They effectively are cropping before the picture is even taken.

However, once the photographer has snapped the photo, the editor should be cautious about changing its impact and meaning by slicing off an edge. Leaving out a storytelling element like the femur of the victim of a terrorist attack could sap the power of an otherwise strong image.

A photo editor at the *Washington Post*, the only major U.S. news outlet to publish the uncropped image, told the Poynter Institute's

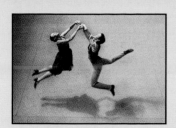

Be careful when you crop not to cut out storytelling, environmentally important elements that give the picture its impact. The beautiful hall would be lost with a tight crop that only included the performing ballet students. Cloe Poisson, *Hartford* [Connecticut] *Courant*

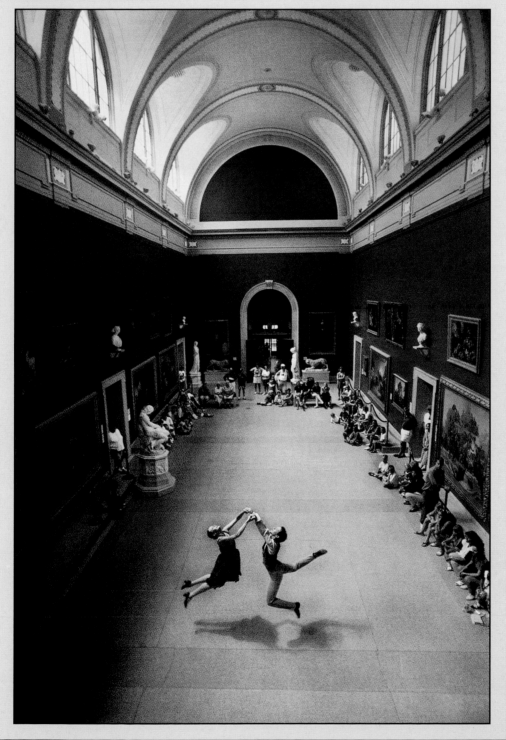

Irby that the bombing was "so huge to the world that people needed to see its reality."

SIZING UP FOR IMPACT

A battle between writers and photographers rages daily on many publications. Its outcome determines the size of the pictures in the next edition.

SPACE: THE FINAL FRONTIER

Wordsmiths, backed up by the copy and managing editors, fight for small pictures to leave room for plenty of type. Reinforced by the photo editor, the photographer demands that the pictures be printed large enough so that readers will not miss them.

The camera contingent argues that the larger the picture, the more powerful its impact. And, in fact, ample evidence supports this claim. According to a study by Burt Woodburn, the average story is read by only 12 percent of a publication's readers while an average one-column picture attracts 42 percent of the readers.

Writing for *Journalism Quarterly*, Woodburn concluded in "Reader Interest in Newspaper Pictures" that as the size of a photo increases, so does the number of readers it attracts. The 42 percent drawn to the story, for example, grew to 55 percent when the photo ran two columns. A four-column-wide picture caught the attention of about 70 percent of the readers.

Both Seith Spaulding, in "Research on Pictorial Illustration," and Hyun-Joo Lee Huh, in "The Effect of Newspaper Picture Size on Readers' Attention, Recall and Comprehension of Stories," confirmed Woodburn's findings. And when all other factors were equal, Gallup's Sharon Polansky came to the same conclusion using Eye-Trac research.

Her research confirmed that increasing the size of an image also increases attention to it. Polansky found that one reason "mug shots" receive little attention is because editors play these portraits so small. The research demonstrated that 44 percent of the subjects looked at a one-column mug shot whereas the rate increased to 92 percent when readers viewed the same photo at three columns wide.

Even this axiom—bigger size gets more attention—has a corollary: if the subject

The USS Boxer, a multipurpose amphibious assault ship, sails into San Francisco Bay for Fleet Week. Cropping this picture into a slim horizontal and running it across two pages gives it added impact.
Ken James, *Examiner* [San Francisco]

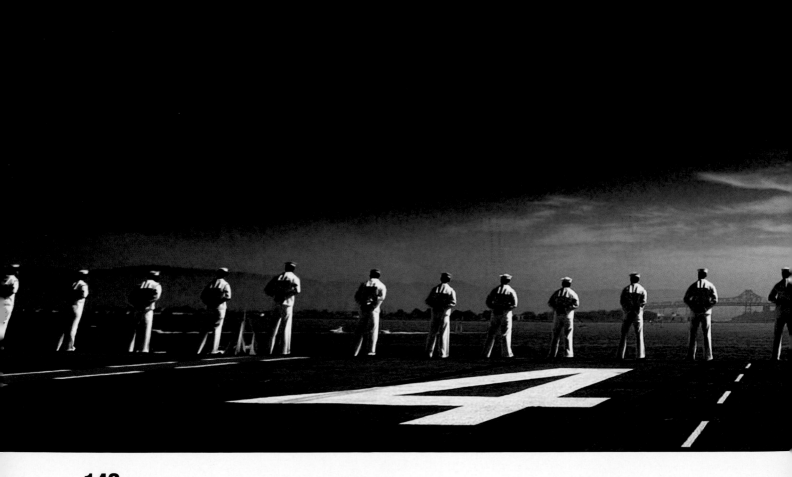

matter is exceptionally galvanizing, even small pictures will be noticed.

Polansky noted during one of her studies that a tiny ad showing a female mud wrestler (with lots of torso showing)—played on the inside of a sports section—got much more attention than its size would have predicted. When it comes to sex, at least, picture size is not the only determinant for reader attention.

Bigger pictures also draw readers into stories and aid them in recalling the material. A study by William Baxter, Rebecca Quarles, and Hermann Kosak found that although a small, two-column picture accompanying an article does not help the reader remember the story's details, a large picture, six columns wide, measurably improves readers' recall of details in the piece.

Hyun-Joo Lee Huh replicated those findings in a study at Syracuse University but went on to show that a larger photo also improves readers' comprehension of the story. Only 13 percent of readers correctly answered questions about a story's content when it had no accompanying picture. Well over 75 percent of those reading the same story accompanied by a large photograph correctly understood the text and could explain the story's significance. Further, increasing the picture's size induced readers to finish reading the article and helped them understand its implications.

According to the Syracuse researchers, the presence of a larger picture probably causes readers to read more of an accompanying story, which then results in greater recall and better comprehension.

Reporters should be begging editors to run large pictures with their stories if they want readers to notice their writing, understand its implications, and recall the information later. Large pictures don't just decorate the page.

Reporters, editors, educators, and almost anyone else involved in communications constantly complain that the MTV generation does not read. Even for people more familiar with changing channels than with turning pages, editors have at their disposal a tool that influences reading. Like a magnet, big pictures draw in readers of all ages to the story associated with it.

In the most recent Eye-Trac data available, "The Best of Eyetrack III: What We

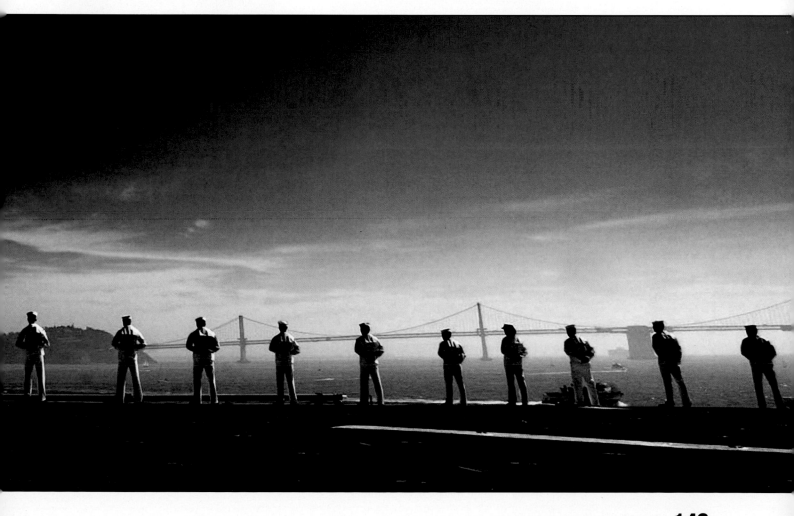

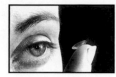

Pictures must be displayed large enough to see the detail in a close-up shot like this one of a woman replacing a contact lens.

Ken Kobré, for *Boston Phoenix*

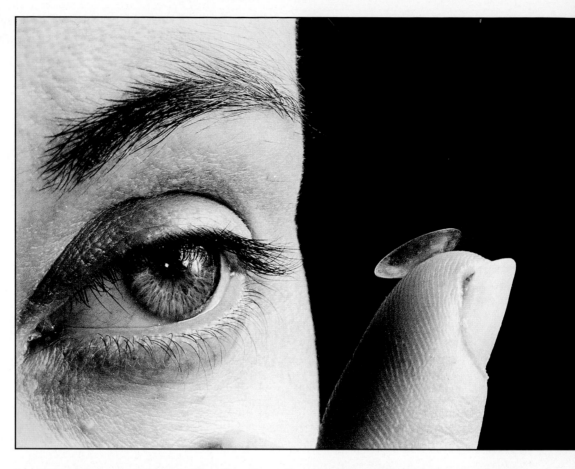

Saw When We Looked Through Their Eyes," Steve Outing and Laura Ruel found that even on the Internet, bigger is better. Larger images on the Internet held readers' attention for longer periods of time.

Increasing a picture's size gives an editor more bang for the buck, even if sacrificing story length is necessary. Subscribers will read, remember, and understand words that remain rather than overlook them altogether.

The never-ending battle between the word and visual camps continues, but the photographer can gain space if he or she is willing to sacrifice a few weaker pictures so that stronger ones can be printed larger.

Photographers must fight for space when their images are striking. Bad photos, of course, should not appear at all, but if they must, play them small. Oversizing a technically poor photo calls attention to its deficiencies. On the other hand, underplaying an exciting, technically good photo does a disservice to photographer and reader alike.

WHEN SIZE IS IMPORTANT
DRAMA
Armed with research and Arnold's axioms, the photographer fights for larger photos so that the audience can easily see the textural detail of the original image. A one-column

"head shot" is so small that it communicates almost nothing. The person is barely recognizable. With a four-column portrait, the reader can examine the two-day-old whiskers on the mayor's face, or the size of a contact lens on a woman's finger.

DETAIL
A long shot, such as an overall of a church interior or an aerial shot from a plane, also demands space. Compressed into one column, all the details blend together and lose the bits of information that give the picture meaning.

"Exquisite," says the reader who sees a larger-than-life photo. A common object, like a pencil or pen, a contact lens, or even a media-worn face, becomes fresh and exciting when magnified beyond its natural size.

Pictures of large crowds also need considerable reproduction size, according to Tom Ang, author of *Picture Editing: An Introduction*. Ang says, "The richness and intricacy of detail can make a fascinating pattern when the picture is used small, but when used large, another layer of detail and meaning can be made out. A crowd scene that's an abstraction of color and pattern when seen small becomes full of individual human beings when enlarged."

CONTRAST IN A PAGE LAYOUT

Publishing some pictures small and others big heightens contrast between them and adds interest to a page. Running them all in a 3"x5" size or shape produces a deadening effect. No photo dominates. Just as a reporter or copy editor emphasizes certain points of an article by placing them in the lead, the photo editor or page designer spotlights certain pictures by playing them larger than others on a page.

SIZE AND THE INTERNET

A number of studies, such as "Eyes on the News" by Pegie Stark and Mario Garcia, have shown that a reader's first glance at the front page of a newspaper goes to photos and graphics. Only later does the reader turn to a story.

Researchers call these graphic-and-photo elements entry points onto the page. The larger the photo, the more people look it. The photo also appears to motivate them to read the accompanying story.

Preliminary research by Marion Lewenstein, Andrew DeVigal, Greg Edwards, and Deborah Tatat indicates that readers may respond differently to visuals on the Internet than they do to pictures in print. Conducted with Eye-Trac equipment, the Stanford-Poynter study found web viewers to have a strong preference for text over graphics. Study subjects looked at 92 percent of all the articles on the screen but only 64 percent of the pictures. When the web pages first came up, the subjects' attention was drawn to brief stories and captions, rather than to images.

To account for this strange reversal in behavior, researchers postulate that photos appear on the Internet more slowly than the text and thus may lose their draw. Others suggest that photos on the web are not large enough to attract viewers' attention.

If future research confirms the original findings, photos in print may have a different magnetic hold on viewers than those on the web. Even the study's authors, however, do not suggest that web pages contain only text. The study does conclude that because web users typically are busy and distracted, photos should be simple so as to encourage readers to spend more time looking before they start reading.

In a more recent study, researchers Outing and Ruel found that most test participants did not look at images first, although images received a significant number of eye fixations. Of most import, they found, not surprisingly, that "the bigger the image, the more time people took to look at it."

Good page layout usually involves playing pictures so that one image dominates. Dominance is achieved through size. The dominant picture seems large especially when it is played alongside considerably smaller images. If the dominant and subordinate images are too close in size, they compete for the reader's attention.

Yuki Saito, San Francisco

ACHIEVING CONTRAST WITH SIZE IN A LAYOUT

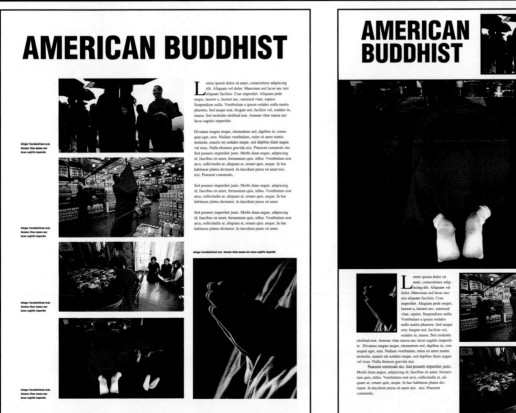

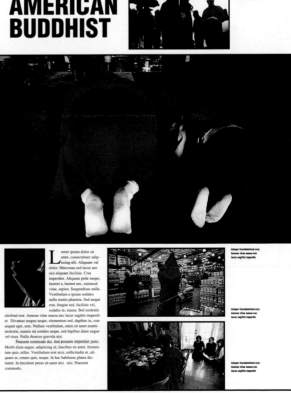

Despite these findings, web designers continue to use small images on their sites.

MULTIPLE IMAGES
PAIRING PICTURES FOR THE THIRD EFFECT

Sometimes one picture can sum up an event. The flag raising at Iwo Jima or the explosion of the Hindenburg needed only one photo to tell the story. Other situations require several. Pairing photos, according to Wilson Hicks in his landmark book *Words and Pictures*, causes a third effect. The reader looks at the two pictures separately and then mentally combines them. The effect is different from what any picture alone can produce.

UNRELATED PICTURE PAIRING

Pairing pictures can create what is called "the third effect"—the two conveying information that neither can relate alone. The photographs of the Naval Academy graduates each tell stand-alone stories but when seen next to one another they send a more complicated message.

Sometimes an editor can pair pictures taken at the same event by the same photographer and sometimes the pairing comes from pictures taken by two different photographers at completely different events.

"The danger in third-effect pairing is that while each photo may be valid alone, together they may tell a lie," according to Angus

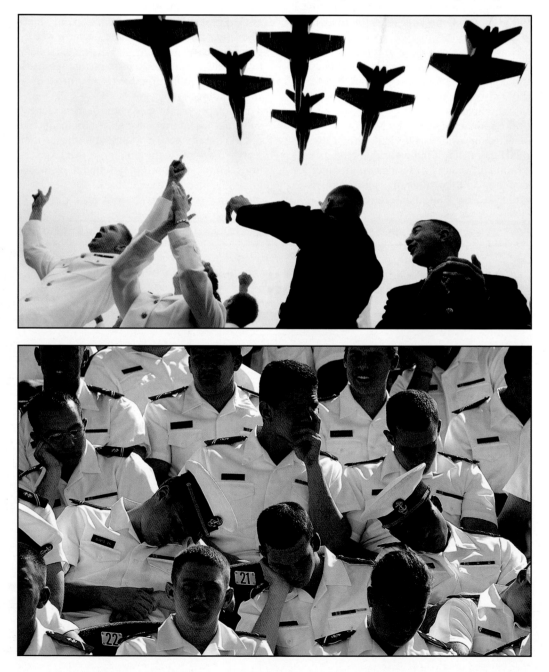

Joyous midshipmen cheer a Blue Angel flyover at the Naval Academy graduation in the top photo, while the graduates' responses at another time is in stark contrast, bottom photo. Does placing the pictures together tell a more insightful story of graduation at the Naval Academy, or does their juxtaposition result in a confusing message?
TOP
Mary Calvert,
Washington Times
BOTTOM
Olivier Douliery,
Abaca Press

McDougall in his book *Picture Editing and Layout*. Do the two pictures from the Naval Academy reveal a deeper truth than each picture alone can tell, or does the artificial pairing mislead in any way?

Visual Homonyms

Some words—like "to," "two," and "too"—sound the same but carry completely different meanings. These are called homonyms. Likewise, some pictures look superficially similar but carry dissimilar information.

For example, a picture of an Egyptian pyramid and a photo of a pile of oranges might look similar—both are triangle-shaped. Some pairs may be entertaining, but, because the pictures share no editorial relationship, a reader trying to find a common thread may be confused. The pictures share no real journalistic commonality.

Be careful, then, of visual homonyms, photos unrelated except by looks. Pairing such pictures can lead to editorial abuse, intended or not. Pairing pictures that are not intrinsically connected editorially can lead to silly or, in even worse situations, offensive results.

Consider a collection of unrelated pictures of overweight people—shot by different photographers for different purposes—published together on a page in an actual photo book. The editor may have thought it clever to assemble these editorially unrelated pictures because they shared a common visual element: overweight people. What was the message of this insensitive pairing?

Picture Sequences and Series

Sometimes a story takes place over time, even if only in minutes. One picture cannot record this change. Two can provide a comparison, but with three or more, the event unfolds. For example, a couple's brief encounter on a Brazilian beach plays out like a mini-story when three pictures run instead of just one or two (see pages 20–21.)

Packaging Pictures

Some situations are multifaceted. One or two photos just will not explain many elements.

John Burgess of the *Santa Rosa Press Democrat* documented an unusual animal hospice called Brighthaven. Although the facilities are simple, the atmosphere is caring and family-like, to the point that animals' meals are prepared in the owners' kitchen.

A picture of one animal alone would not tell Burgess's story. Nor would a single picture of one person helping an injured critter. Packaged together, though, pictures of 21 of 68 cats being fed, a dog running about on wheels, and a three-legged cat nuzzling a deaf and blind dog all begin to show the range of care and after-care provided at Brighthaven (see pages 148–149).

THE CAPTION: STEPCHILD OF THE BUSINESS

Some pictures—such as Norman Rockwell's cover illustrations for the *Saturday Evening Post*—need no words. The idea portrayed is so simple or its emotional content so powerful that the illustration tells the story clearly and immediately without any captions.

But most photos do need words. An old proverb relates that "a picture is worth a thousand words," but the modern corollary is that a picture without words is worth little.

A picture raises as many questions as answers. Look at the pictures on these two pages and ask yourself if, without captions, you would know who is in the pictures, what is happening, when the events took place, and why the action occurred. Pictures usually answer these questions only partially. A picture that can stand alone is rare. The point is not whether photographs can survive without words or words without photos, but whether pictures and words will perform better when combined.

WORDS INFLUENCE PICTURE MEANING

While assistant professor of journalism at the University of California, Berkeley, Jean Kerrick conducted research to determine the influence of captions on readers' interpretations of pictures. Captions, she found, can at least modify and sometimes change the meaning of a picture, especially when the picture itself is ambiguous. A caption can change the viewer's interpretation of the same picture from one extreme to another.

Kerrick presented a profile shot of a well-dressed man sitting on a park bench to two groups of subjects. She asked each group to rate the picture on several subjective scales. The scales ranged from "good to bad," "happy to sad," "pleasant to unpleasant," and so forth.

Then the first group was shown the same picture with this caption: *"A quiet minute alone is grabbed by Governor-elect Star. After a landslide victory, there is much work to be done before taking office."*

The second group was shown the same picture with a different caption: *"Exiled communist recently deported by the U.S. broods in the Tuilleries Garden alone in Paris on his way back to Yugoslavia."* Both groups were again asked to evaluate the picture.

After the first group read the positive caption, they rated the picture "happier,"

NOT JUST ANY ANIMAL SHELTER

Photos by John Burgess
Santa Rosa Press Democrat

John Burgess's story about a holistic home shelter for infirm animals has a consistent theme. Every image shows an animal that has suffered some form of trauma. An injured dog whisks around in a special harness. A cat is administered an IV. A high-angle overall taken at feeding time that shows just some of the 68 cats living at Brighthaven gives the reader a sense of how many felines would be homeless without this retreat.

Each photograph adds another building block to the story—from a three-legged cat snuggling up to a deaf and blind dog to an attendant bathing a raven.

The photos isolate the most visually interesting, distinctive aspects of the place while building a visual overview with the package.

This isn't a "how-to" story. The pictures don't try to tell how to run a hospital of this sort. They don't document every aspect of the place. The pictures don't show the owner buying the food or cleaning the floors, for instance.

Burgess did not shoot a "day in the life" of Brighthaven. The photographer felt no requirement to record the activities of the home from morning until night. The photographer does

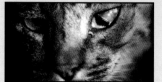

▲ Eighteen-year-old Joey came to Brighthaven with 10 BB pellets imbedded in his body. Later, a tumor was removed from his eye.

not try to tell a narrative of one animal's course of recovery from the time of arrival until its eventual return to health. Nor did the photographer tell the hospital's story through the eyes or actions of one person such as the pet owner or hospice founder.

Instead, the project reveals the most interesting and exceptional aspects of this unusual animal clinic.

Since the story is not a narrative, the pictures do not have to be presented according to a time-line, starting with the first pictures and ending with the last. The layout relies on a dominant image with which to draw in the reader. This image must both captivate the reader's attention and summarize the exceptional aspects of the animal respite. Which picture would you have selected for this role? ■

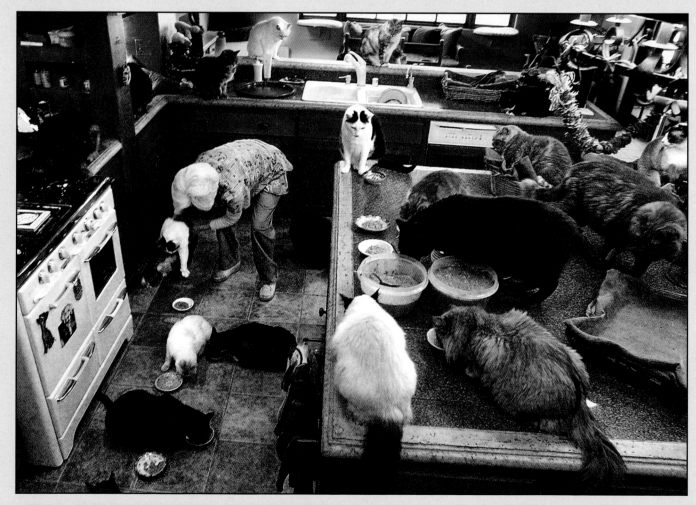

▲ Twice a day, Gail Pope mixes up fresh turkey meat, vegetables, and supplements for the cats at Brighthaven. First she feeds the kitchen cats, of which only 21 are shown, then on to the living room and bedroom for the rest of the 68 cats in their house.

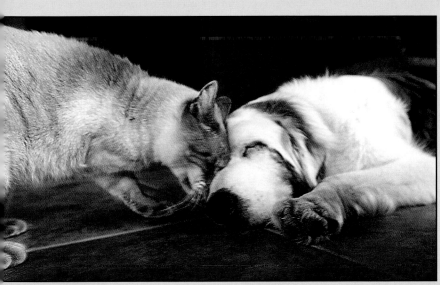

◄ Oliver, the three-legged cat, left, snuggles up to his best friend, Sgt. Pepper, a deaf and blind dog who suffers from a brain disorder.

▼ Ted the Toad arrived at Brighthaven with gangrenous back feet but now enjoys life with a female toad rescued after being crushed by a concrete slab. She was too shy to be photographed.

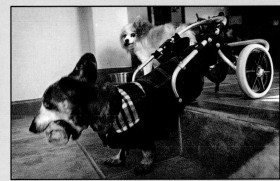

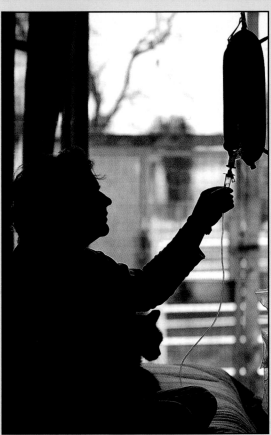

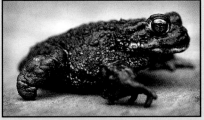

◄ In a wheelchair following back surgery, Ollie the Dachshund navigates the steps on his way to the garden to bury his bone.

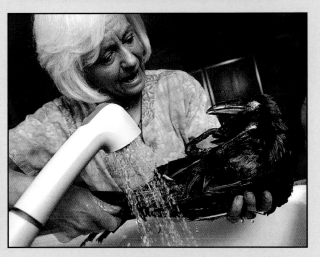

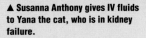
▲ Susanna Anthony gives IV fluids to Yana the cat, who is in kidney failure.

▲ Gail Pope gives Brighthaven's resident raven, Colin, his daily bath in the kitchen sink. Run over by a car, Colin was nursed back to health but was still eyeless, had deformed legs, and suffered from selzures. Pope was later forced to euthanize the bird.

"better," and "more pleasant" than they had originally judged it.

The second group, who saw the caption about the brooding exiled communist, rated the photo "sad" and "unpleasant." In this instance, the caption completely reversed the impression initially given by the picture alone.

In a similar study, Fred Fedler, Tim Counts, and Paul Hightower used high-impact news photos and varied just one or two words in their captions. They did not find striking changes when they varied just a few words with this particular set of pictures.

Perhaps changing captions influences how viewers interpret neutral images but not how they read more clear, dramatic photographs like the ones in the news-oriented study.

Photographs appear to serve as a primitive means of communication that carry out their task instantly. Words function as a sophisticated means of communication, but lack the impact of the visual message. Pictures transmit the message immediately, but words shape and give focus to that message.

WRITING CLEAR CAPTIONS

The need for clear and concise caption-writing is obvious. Readers often determine whether they are going to read an entire article based on what they gleaned from a picture and caption. If you glance through some newspapers and magazines, however, you may get the impression that the first person to

walk into the room wrote the captions in the paper or magazine that day. Writers polish their story leads, and photographers polish their lenses, but no one shines up the captions. Writers claim that caption-writing is beneath them, while photographers often seem to find an important blazing fire to cover when the time comes to compose captions. The caption—stepchild of the media business—is the most read but least carefully written text in most publications.

Poor captions sometimes result when photographers fail to get adequate information at the time they take the pictures or forget to include the information when they write the captions. Howard Chapnick, who ran Black Star picture agency for many years, said, "One cannot err on the side of providing too much caption information. The editor who finds a photographer who understands the importance of detailed captioning will figuratively embrace him bodily and professionally."

One photographer even lost his job because of writing poor captions. The *St. Petersburg Times* released Victor Junco because of caption errors after he had shot for the paper for 10 years.

Former *People* magazine photo editor John Dominis once told the story of holding up the magazine's production because a photographer did not send in one critical identification. Lights in the New York headquarters burned past midnight as the editors carried out a desperate search by telephone

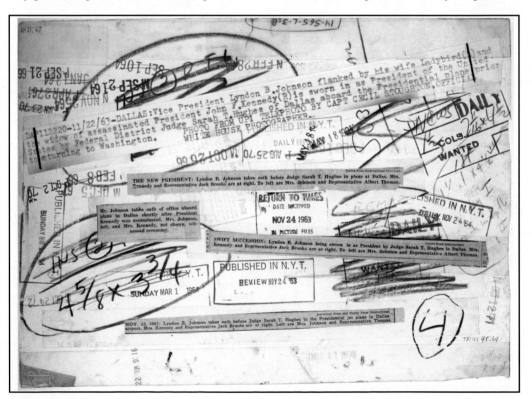

The back of a photograph from *The New York Times* picture archive. Each time the picture ran, a new caption was pasted on back of the print.

for the forgetful photographer. Editors, writers, layout artists, designers, and production staff all waited hour after hour for the missing caption, costing *People* magazine thousands of dollars in overtime.

PUTTING THE FIVE 'W'S AND AN 'H' IN A CAPTION

"A caption is a verbal finger pointing at the picture," wrote John Whiting in his book ***Photography is a Language***. Captions, like fingers, come in many sizes and shapes. The opening words of a caption must capture the reader's attention just as do the lead words of a news story or feature.

The caption writer starts off the sentence with the most newsworthy, interesting, or unusual facts. Copy desks have developed different kinds of captions, each emphasizing a different element of the story.

What?

The reader wants an explanation of what is happening in the picture; hence, the first words of the caption, also called a cutline in the newspaper business, should explain the action. Unless the situation in the picture is obvious, the cutline must describe what is going on. *"After two years of drought, it rained yesterday in the southern part of the state. . . ."* Further down in the cutline, the writer can fill in the other details of the story by giving the remaining four Ws.

Who?

The who may be emphasized in the caption when the person in the news is featured in the photo: *"President Bush said yesterday that he will spend the weekend at Camp David."*

In this situation, the newsworthy aspect of the picture is the person, President George Bush. The fact that the president was speaking outweighed what he had to say or where he said it.

A person's name should lead the caption only when that person is well known to readers. Do not start the caption "John Doe said yesterday that the budget should be slashed." No one knows John Doe, so placing his name prominently in the cutline neither adds to the picture's interest nor explains its news value.

However, if John Doe's face is recognizable in the photo, he should be mentioned somewhere in the caption. People's names are always included in the caption even if they are not famous. Someone—spouse, parents, or friends—certainly will recognize them.

Also, readers can misidentify the person in the photo if the name is left out of the caption. Often you may hear, "That woman in the picture in the paper looks just like. . . ."

Many editors will not run a picture unless the caption includes the names of all recognizable people. The wire services, whose pictures go around the world, include the person's first and last names, as well as middle initial, regardless of the individual's prominence in the community or in the world.

The name and the age of any youngster in the picture are essential. This information often adds additional human interest: *"The collie pup would have drowned if the Selleck girls (left to right) Debbie, 3, Heidi, 5, and Becky, 7, had not pulled their dog, Sam, from the stream in time."*

Note that the phrase "left to right" clearly identifies each girl. Sometimes the words "top row," "wearing the tie," or other identifying features will help readers match the faces in the photo with the names in the captions. Indicate to the copy editor that you are not sure about the spelling of names you have not double-checked.

When and Where?

Photos rarely tell readers exactly when or where a picture was taken. If this information helps readers understand the picture, supply the location and the time of the news event. Use the day of the week, not the calendar date; *"Barry Bonds hit the home run yesterday that gave the Giants their win over the A's." (Not "Bonds hit the home run July 6.")*

The writer should begin the cutline with time or place only when that fact is significant or unusual: "At 3 A.M. Mayor Ted Stanton finally signed the zoning bill."

Or: "Standing in the massive waterworks, Edna Lee, the water commissioner, explained the new drainage system."

ASSOCIATED PRESS CAPTION STYLE

Nearly all AP captions follow a simple formula.

- The first sentence describes what the photo shows, in the present tense, and states where and when the photo was made. It must ALWAYS include the day and date the photo was made (e.g., Friday, Jan. 29, 2009).
- The second sentence gives background on the news event or describes why the photo is significant.
- Whenever possible, try to keep captions to no more than two concise sentences, while including the relevant information. Try to anticipate what information a newspaper editor or reader will need.

EXAMPLE

The Mississippi River flows through a hole in the Snay Island, Ill., levee, flooding farmland and homes 10 miles south of Quincy, Ill., Sunday, July 25, 1993. About 2,000 people were evacuated from the 44,000 acres that flooded. (AP Photo/Bill Waugh) ∎

Why?

Some caption writers claim that explaining why the action occurred in a picture takes away the reason for reading the story and thus causes readers to skip the adjoining article. Other news photographers and editors argue that extensive captions pique reader interest for the main body of the story. *"Because of the transit strike, highways leading into the city were jammed at the early morning rush hour today."* Without answering the "why," this photo and caption do not tell the full story.

How?

The caption is the place to tell readers if the subject in the picture was posed. If the photographer took the picture with a special lens or manipulated the print in the computer, this should be noted. The caption should explain anything about the picture that differs significantly from the actual event and thus might distort the facts.

Small Detail. Casually glancing at a photo, readers might miss an important but small detail. Cutlines can focus attention on various parts of the picture and emphasize the elements the photographer thinks are important.

Cutlines can supply details about the four senses that the picture does not convey. How something tastes or feels might explain a subject's reaction in a picture. Without an explanatory phrase in the caption, the picture might not make sense: *"David Krathwohl, 10, struggles to climb an oil-coated plastic pole."*

Quote. Sometimes this purpose can be accomplished by telling what the subject said with a catchy quote: *"Some days I wish I had never left Kansas," said rock star Dorothy Oz on the eve of her 34th record-breaking performance.*

Before and After. A camera shutter, open for 1/500 sec., results in a photo that accurately describes what happened in that brief span of time. But the photo does not inform readers about what happened before or after that split second. The cause of the event and its effect are absent. Captions must supply the befores and afters.

Color. Even though black-and-white photos record the world in almost infinite detail, one visual element is omitted: color. When color is an important aspect of the scene, the caption must supply this missing dimension: *"Members of the Franklin High football team, wearing their new bright pink and purple uniforms, yellow shoes, and lime-green helmets, performed practice drills yesterday before defending their 15th title in the state championships."*

Special Camera or Computer Effects. Whenever your picture's overall look is the result of a special photographic effect, your caption should let the reader know how you accomplished this.

When Marshall Spurrier was assigned to photograph the farmers who grew a large watermelon, he placed the fruit on the ground, attached an ultra-wide lens to the camera and positioned the man and his wife on either side of the frame, several feet back. The resulting picture (below) made the plant look as if it were almost as big as an SUV. Spurrier used the picture's caption to explain how he achieved the effect.

Special effects such as the close placement of the wide-angle lens (28mm) used in this picture should always be explained in a caption. Marshall Spurrier, *Chanute* [Kansas] *Tribune*

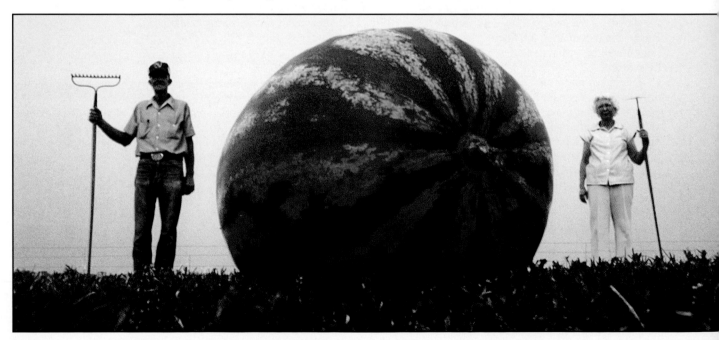

As well as the exaggerating effects of the wide-angle lens, you may also need to point out the compression effect of an extra-long telephoto, color shifts produced when shooting in mixed lighting, or elements changed with digital manipulation.

(For a full discussion of ethical issues regarding computer-manipulated photos, see Chapter 15, "Ethics.")

CAPTION-WRITING STYLES

Write short, declarative sentences with as few words as possible. Avoid complex sentences. Do not put unrelated facts in the same sentence. Keep facts separated with periods, not commas or other punctuation.

The AP's Hal Buell says, "Skip the adjectives and adverbs in a caption. Let the picture speak for itself."

Two schools of thought differ on the question of the tense of verbs in captions. The first group advises putting everything in the present tense, because the words in the caption are describing a photo immediately in front of the reader. The present tense also involves the reader more than does the past tense. Says Karen Cater of the *Seattle Times*, "Present-tense captions give a sense of action, immediacy, and life to a photo."

The opposing view advocates using the past tense because all the action in the picture has already taken place: *"John Brown tags (tagged) the runner to make the last out in yesterday's game."*

Be careful not to mix tenses. Writing coach Paula Larocque points out in *Quill* magazine that the most common problem with captions is pairing a present-tense verb with a past-tense time element. She points out that we would not say, *"A new mayor is (present tense) sworn in last (past tense) week."* Avoid the same problem with captions. Do not write: *"Kelly holds her son Wednesday while he undergoes dialysis."* The event has already taken place. Larocque calls this mistake a sequence-of-tense hash. Use the present tense or the past but not both in the same sentence.

Avoid the obvious. Phrases like "firefighter fighting blaze" or "basketball player going for hoop" are unnecessary because readers can see that, in the first picture, the people are firefighters, and, in the second, the athlete is a basketball player.

Phrases like "pictured above" also add no new information when accompanying a single image. Captions should avoid telling readers what they can find out for themselves by looking at the picture.

Avoid speculation about what a subject might be thinking. Such guessing can be inaccurate and give the wrong impression: *"Claire Katz smiles with happiness as she receives a check from the president."* Perhaps she thinks the check is far too small for her efforts. No one can look into someone's mind.

And no one, even a photographer, can read an animal's mind. Do not fall into this trap: *"These pigs seem to be wondering. . . ."*

Write simply. Also, do not forget to identify old morgue photos as "file photos." Otherwise readers might think they were taken yesterday.

THE LAST WORD

Caption writers—both neophytes and old hands—must always remember to start with the picture. The writer who looks at the picture at least will avoid the mistake that one caption writer made. The caption read: "Police seized a quantity of opium." But in the picture, there were no police, and there was no opium.

Joseph Kastner, who was the head copy editor and caption writer for *Life* magazine, said that the discipline of caption writing is of an order that no other kind of journalism requires. "And when this discipline is exerted, it produces writing that is as taut, as spare, as evocative, and as cogent as any writing in journalism today." ■

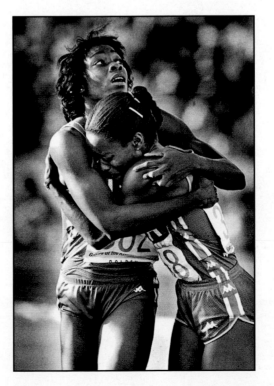

Sometimes pictures capture great emotion but, without a caption (which in this case the photographer supplied), readers may be unable to determine just what emotion they are seeing. Are these women happy or sad? Did they win or lose the competition? Paul Chinn, for *Herald Examiner* [Los Angeles, California]

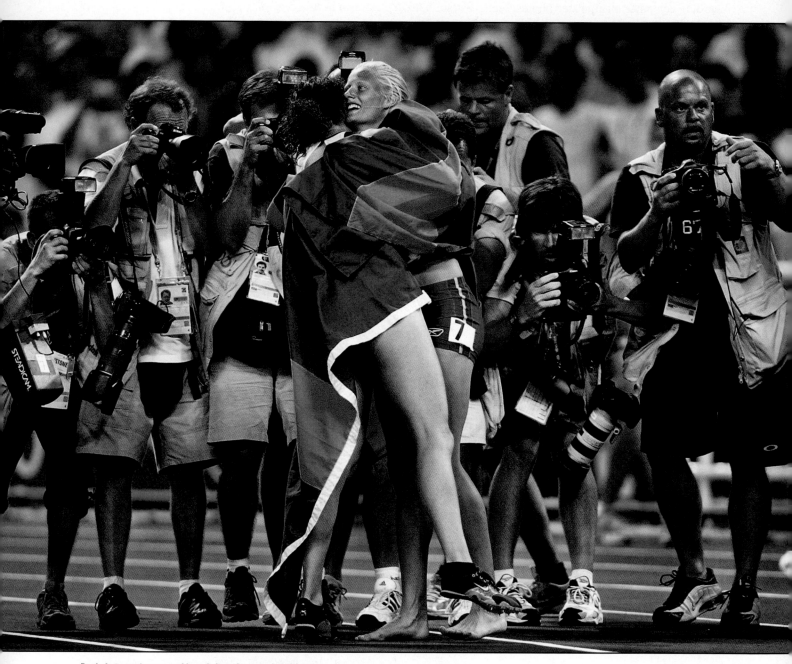

Pool photographers scramble and shove for a good position to shoot the women's track and field medalists at the Athens Olympics.

Jack Gruber, *USA Today*

Camera Bag

8

OUTFITTING THE PHOTOJOURNALIST

A photojournalist's bag is like a physician's—each contains the essentials for handling any emergency the professional might face. Like each doctor, each photographer carries different equipment, depending on professional needs and personal taste. Some photographers are partial to extra-long lenses, whereas others like wide-angle lenses. Yet all news photographers pack enough gear to handle any assignment, whether the event they cover takes place in the brilliant light of day or the pitch black of night. A news photographer must have a sturdy camera, a variety of lenses, a strobe, plenty of batteries, and, of course, lots of memory cards. The digital photojournalist also packs a cell phone, and, often, a laptop as well. The most expensive purchase a photojournalist will make will be a camera system. Cameras and lenses can cost from hundreds to thousands of dollars, especially digital equipment. Working photojournalists want a camera sturdy enough to take the bashes of the business yet light enough so that the photographer can carry at least two bodies at the same time. Photojournalists need a camera that can be subjected to freezing weather one day and melting temperatures the next. Yet, they want that camera to continue to function perfectly, frame after frame.

No perfect camera system exists. Each photographer weighs the trade-off of weight, ruggedness, and, of course, cost when outfitting a camera bag of photographic tools.

CAMERA FEATURES
AUTO-EXPOSURE

In-camera auto-exposure light meters can be amazingly accurate. However, they can be fooled in certain situations. These measure the light reflected off a subject. Most cameras provide different metering options depending on how you want to take your light meter reading. With the spot-meter option, the camera reads the brightness of a tiny pinpoint in a scene; an option called evaluative or matrix metering reads the whole vista contained in the viewfinder and tries to determine the best average exposure for the scene. A third option is called "center weighted," which primarily measures the exposure of the center of the image and ignores the edges of the frame. These center-weighted meters are generally accurate except when most of the subject matter is either extremely light—like a bride wearing a white gown in front of a white church—or extremely dark—like the groom wearing a black tux in front of the church's dark brown doors.

Remember that a light meter sees the world as neutral gray, whether the scene is an igloo in a blizzard or a black cat in a coal bin. Joel Draut, who shot for the *Houston Post*, exposed manually when he shot a funny face carved in the snow (opposite). Knowing that his automatic light meter would read the snow as neutral gray, Draut opened the aperture about two stops above the reading to compensate.

Richard Koci Hernandez, who shoots for the *Mercury News* in San Jose, California, took a careful reading of Carolivia Herron (opposite), the author of the controversial children's book *Nappy Hair*. The writer was wrapped in a dark cape in front of a dark,

unlit wall. On automatic, the camera's light meter would have seen the dark scene as neutral gray and overexposed the picture. Backlit situations, such as a window or the sun behind the subject, also present a challenge to automatic center-weighted exposure meters.

Avoid incorrect exposures by taking a reflected-light reading of the subject's face or of your own hand in situations like this. (For light skin, open up half a stop; for dark skin, close down a stop.)

A camera's spot meter is particularly good for a light subject against a dark background, like a rocker spotlighted on a stage.

When setting up auto-exposure, some photographers prefer to select the aperture (aperture priority) and let the camera select the appropriate shutter speed. This choice is good for the photographer who wants to have the minimum or maximum depth of field for a series of pictures. Selecting the shutter speed (shutter speed priority) allows the camera to select the corresponding aperture. This approach allows you to select a shutter speed that can freeze a subject's action, such as that of an athlete in motion, and avoids blurry surprises from routine camera movement.

The Digital Camera's Unique Exposure Tool

Most single-lens-reflex (SLR) digital cameras allow you to confirm a photograph's tonality while shooting. Taking advantage of the histogram feature allows you to adjust your lighting setup or make other exposure decisions so highlights and shadows in the image are not lost.

An in-camera histogram is a graph that displays the distribution of a photograph's tones, from highlights to shadows (see opposite page). The graph shows how many times any of the 256 tones that make up a photograph occur. The height of the bars in the graph indicates the number of pixels, anywhere in the picture, at each brightness level.

A photograph with an average exposure, for example, will have tones distributed throughout the whole graph, with most bunched in the middle. An overexposed image will have most bars located on the right—an indication to adjust the exposure and take another shot if possible. If all the pixels are skewed to the left, the photo has no detail in its shadows, signaling you to adjust the next exposure to give it more light. Of course the histogram of a picture of an igloo in a snowy landscape will look different than that of a group portrait of the black-shirted Oakland Raiders football team. However, regardless of the shape of the curve, the histogram will indicate whether there is detail at the two ends of the brightness spectrum.

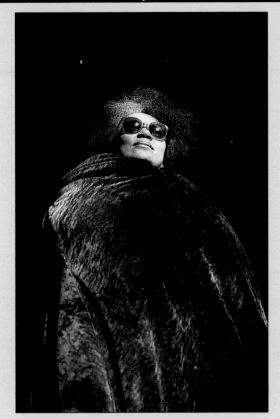

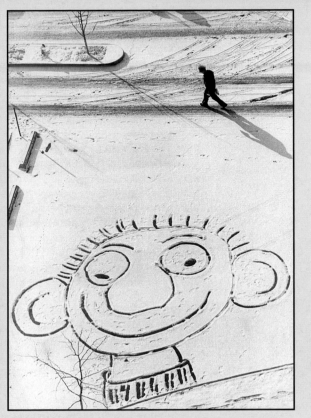

In a predominantly dark scene like this one, the camera's automatic light meter would be fooled into overexposing the final picture. In this situation, take a meter reading off the subject's face. Richard Koci Hernandez, *San Jose Mercury News*

A camera's automatic exposure meter would see this predominantly white scene as 18 percent neutral gray and underexpose the final picture. For proper exposure in similar situations, increase your exposure about two stops or take a reading off something in the same light that reflects a neutral gray. Joel Draut, *Houston Post*

DIGITAL EXPOSURE CONFIRMATION: THE HISTOGRAM

Bring up the histogram for each picture on the camera's LCD screen for precise information about the exposure.

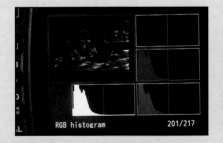

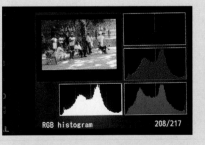

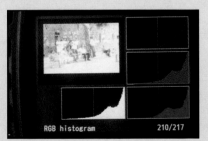

The graph of an underexposed photo displays bars grouped to the left. Because the bars are off to the left side, you can tell that the digital exposure will not capture the full range of possible tones. The darker tones represented by the bars at the extreme left will be pure black, with no available detail.

With the bars spread from one end of the graph almost to the other, the picture will capture a full tonal range and be correctly exposed.

Bars clustered on the right edge indicate that the photo is probably overexposed. The brightest tones represented by the bars on the extreme right will print as "paper white," with no detail at all.

Typically, you can elect to view the histogram of an image you have just taken in the camera's LCD monitor.

The histogram is an ideal light meter. Without prayers or multiple light meter readings, you can determine with one test shot if your picture has detail in its highlights as well as its shadows. Then you can decide with confidence whether or not to adjust the exposure for the next snap.

RAW: The Exposure Advantage

What happens if, by accident, you have underexposed a crucial image—an attempt on the president's life, for example? Just to complicate things, perhaps your camera was still color balanced for "incandescent" although you had just followed the entourage into broad daylight.

You will have a much better chance of brightening and color correcting the final picture in the computer if you are shooting in RAW format rather than JPEG.

Here's why. Standard JPEG files squeeze all the technical information in an image into a small file size (see page 169). This compression process, performed on the fly each time you click the shutter, means the camera's software program throws away pixel information it determines is redundant. It dumps some information at the two extremes of the exposure—the top of the highlights and the bottom of the shadows.

RAW files, however, are not processed in the camera. They contain exactly the information collected by the camera's sensor, regardless of any preset color balance settings.

RAW files provide great latitude for in-camera adjustments to brightness and color balance—even with underexposed or improperly color-balanced images. Your underexposed and ill-hued picture of the president's assailant may have enough pixel information to produce a publishable, valuable image.

Photographers compare shooting in RAW mode to using the original negative from a film-based camera. You are working with what the camera captured not what the camera's software reinterpreted after you took the picture. Besides helping you recover from embarrassing mistakes, shooting RAW can improve images shot in conditions of high contrast. If you are shooting a groom wearing all black sitting in the shadow of the reception hall while the bride wearing white cavorts on the dance floor a few feet away under a bright spotlight, a JPEG file might not hold the entire brightness range. Switching to RAW for a shot like this can help hold detail in both the groom's handsome tux and the bride's lace dress.

The obvious question is why not shoot RAW format all the time? Many photographers, including all those shooting for the *National Geographic* and *Sports Illustrated*, shoot everything in RAW.

But, like most other things in life, there are trade offs when using RAW. This format is a memory hog. RAW files are typically two to six times larger than JPEG files and are much slower to download from the camera's buffer and memory card than their lighter, smaller JPEG cousins.

Shooting beefed up RAW files means you must wait longer before you can view each image on the camera's LCD screen. Of course, fewer pictures will fit on each memory card. And because the memory card cannot hold as many images, you must wait for the images to transfer to your computer—where they take up much more space on the hard drive than JPEGs. Finally, using special software, you must convert RAW images into usable files before you can evaluate the pictures.

While each camera manufacturer has a unique system for converting its own RAW images into viewable files, some have adopted a more universal system, created by Adobe software, called digital negative (DNG). Photo editing programs like Adobe's Lightroom and Apple's Aperture will read and convert RAW files.

Some photographers swear by RAW. Globetrotting Keith Philpott says he would not expose a digital frame with any other format. Yet, photojournalists working on tight news deadlines often prefer a JPEG image. They cannot afford to wait for their RAW images to download.

Some photographers who want the maximum flexibility, or who just cannot make a decision, opt for a setting called RAW+JPEG. With this option, the camera not only saves all the data as a RAW file but also saves a second copy compressed into JPEG format, ready for editing.

Research indicates (see examples) that under circumstances where subjects are properly exposed and color-balanced in relatively even lighting, you will not see a lot of difference between RAW and JPEG. However, when shooting in a situation of high contrast, such as one including bright skies and deep shadows, you will find RAW just right.

AUTOFOCUS

Most photojournalists use autofocus cameras. Because autofocus cameras can adjust faster than the human eye-hand combination can

For this series of pictures the camera setting for "Quality" was set on RAW + JPEG Fine. At each shutter release the camera made two identical files, one a JPEG file containing a compressed version of the image and the other a RAW file containing an uncompressed version of the same image.

The f/stop and shutter-speed combination was bracketed over a 10-stop range from extremely overexposed to considerably underexposed.

These examples of overexposed and underexposed JPEG and RAW photos were corrected in Photoshop to produce the best possible image.

As you can see, the RAW images that were extremely over or underexposed were salvageable with adjustment in Photoshop. The same cannot be said for the JPEG images.

Conclusion: RAW is a good choice when working in extreme brightness-range conditions or situations where your meter reading may be inaccurate. The JPEG option works fine under most normal conditions when the camera's controls, including exposure and white balance, are set correctly.

JPEG **RAW**

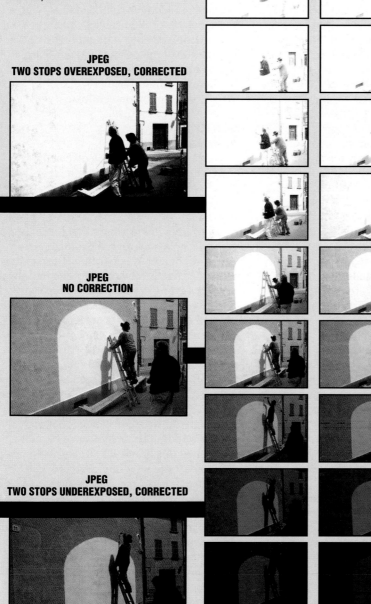

**JPEG
TWO STOPS OVEREXPOSED, CORRECTED**

**RAW
TWO STOPS OVEREXPOSED, CORRECTED**

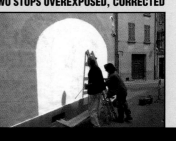

**JPEG
NO CORRECTION**

**RAW
NO CORRECTION**

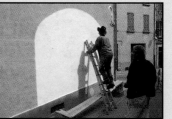

**JPEG
TWO STOPS UNDEREXPOSED, CORRECTED**

**RAW
TWO STOPS UNDEREXPOSED, CORRECTED**

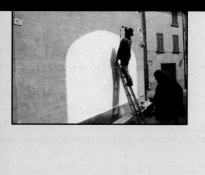

twist the lens barrel, novice shooters using autofocus often can hold their own with pros.

The technique works well when you are tracking an isolated tight end running down the sidelines. You'll get the highest number of sharp pictures in sports like track and field, where the focusing mechanism can lock onto a single runner and follow that person to the finish line. (See Chapter 6, "Sports.")

Using autofocus, the photographer selects an area of the viewfinder by pressing the shutter release halfway down or by using a back focus button. (See below for more on the back focus button.) Provided the focus is locked in, the picture should be sharp as long as the subject is in the autofocus "hot zone."

Yet autofocus is not a cure-all for producing sharp pictures under all circumstances on every frame. Because contrast is what guides the autofocus mechanism, the camera can be fooled, especially in low-light situations. Also, the bars of a cage, the wires in a fence, or even a window's surface can confuse autofocus. The mechanism is not smart enough to know to focus on the subject beyond the bars, the fence, or the window. Strong background light or a light source in the background also can throw off autofocus.

Personalizing Autofocus Controls

Autofocus shooting actually requires as much attention, concentration, and dexterity as manual focusing, yet often results in a higher percentage of sharp images when following a moving target.

Not all important action happens in the middle of the frame. Sometimes the primary subject should be sharp on the edge of the picture. Autofocus cameras allow photographers to select the quadrant where they want to activate autofocus. A wheel on the back of some cameras allows selection from among an array of target areas in the viewfinder. When the target is framed in red, for example, the autofocus feature will operate in the hot zone.

Some cameras allow customization of the autofocus setup. You can set autofocus to operate when you press lightly on the shutter release, for example. Or you can have it go into action using an alternative button on the camera back. Using a second button to activate the autofocus can be challenging at first, says David Guralnick of the *Detroit News*, but will offer more flexibility when composing your image. These options help you customize the camera to your shooting style. (See page 108, Chapter 6, "Sports," for more on using the back focus button.)

You can set up the camera to autofocus continuously as long as the shutter is held halfway down (AF-C Nikon or Artificial Intelligence servo Canon). This option works best with moving subjects like athletes.

With certain cameras you can use autofocus to shoot even in extremely low light or total darkness. These cameras use the built-in flash, a built-in focusing light or an external dedicated strobe that emits near-infrared light that the camera can sense. The built-in autofocus-assist lights are fairly weak so they only work when the subject is relatively close. This autofocus-assist technology allows the camera to focus the lens accurately and automatically in total darkness, within a certain distance. You can take pictures even in a pitch-black alley without focusing the camera. Just point, shoot, and get sharply focused photos as long as the subject is not too far away. (See Chapter 6, "Sports," pages 107–109, for more on autofocus.)

SHUTTER SPEED
Digital Reaction Time

All cameras have a delay between the moment you press the shutter release and the shutter opens to take the picture. This delay is relatively short with high-end digital SLR cameras.

Depending on the make and model of their cameras, however, digital photographers report slight delays between the instant they press the shutter release and when the camera actually records a picture. Less expensive as well as older professional cameras can have a marked delay time that hampers shooting candid photos. A digital camera might delay as much as 80 milliseconds. This digital hesitation can throw off your timing if you are shooting sports—and can mean the difference between getting the peak action or not, warns Deanne Fitzmaurice of the *San Francisco Chronicle*. More sophisticated (but more expensive) digital cameras have virtually eliminated this drawback. Rapidly changing technology suggests further improvements with time.

Shutter speeds range from 1/8000 sec. or higher to 30 minutes or even longer.

Longer exposures require setting the camera for time exposure—bulb, as it is called. The shutter will remain open for minutes or hours as long as the shutter button is pressed.

Tip: Some manufacturers' representatives recommend turning off your digital camera when changing lenses. When "on," the camera creates an electrical field that attracts dust to sensors. When the inside of the camera is exposed during a lens change, dust particles can become attracted to the chip and result in unsightly spots on future images.

Turning off the camera when exchanging lenses can reduce this problem. (See "Keeping the Sensor Clean," page 170.)

Potential Digital Delays

Digital cameras can take a burst of pictures, but at some point must store the images—transferring them from temporary memory (a buffer) to the storage card. While sending the digital bits and bytes, some models require waiting for the buffer to empty before more photos can be shot. This lag time can provide another frustration for photojournalists shooting in fast-moving situations.

Naturally, more expensive cameras have buffers with higher capacities. A sufficiently large buffer is mandatory for a photojournalist, who cannot ask a fleeing rioter to wait while the camera's memory buffer clears itself. Some cameras can fire 110 10.1-megapixel images in one burst—10 frames per second; some memory cards have write speeds that are faster than others and will help speed up the process.

Tip: When a digital camera is downloading pictures from its temporary buffer to a storage card, a small, usually green "access" light comes on. Do not turn the camera off, remove the memory card, or remove or disconnect the power source until the light has gone out. The picture that is downloading at the time could be lost, as may others waiting in the queue. You can run into longer delays when shooting the images on the "RAW" setting. This option requires the camera to download a file averaging three times the size of a JPEG file.

LCD MONITOR

Most digital cameras have an LCD monitor on the back. One of its great advantages is being able to see a picture almost as soon as you have taken it. Note that a single image at

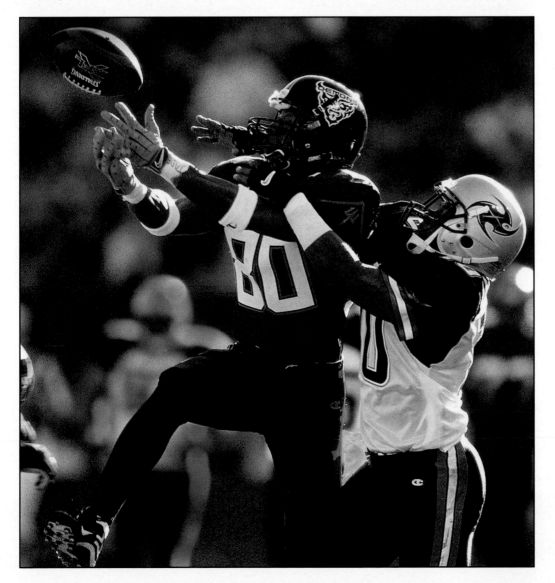

Most sports shooters use autofocus lenses to follow the action. The lenses respond so quickly that the photographer can swing from a quarterback to his receiver and still get a sharp picture of the play. Brad Mangin, for *Sports Illustrated*

full display on the LCD monitor is relatively small. It is possible to enlarge the image on the LCD screen for a close examination of sharpness and expression.

Some SLR models allow the option of viewing the scene through the optical viewfinder or using the LCD screen on the back of the camera. The LCD option allows the photographer to frame the scene exactly the way the lens and sensor will record the picture. It also simplifies taking high and low shots since you can frame from the back of the camera without the viewfinder pressed to your face. Perhaps its most valuable use is checking exposure with the histogram (see pages 156–158).

Also, most professional cameras have a custom option to cause any overexposed part of the image to blink. This is an easy way to quickly see if the exposure is off.

Tip: Viewing the camera's LCD monitor drains the battery more quickly. Some photojournalists call the act of looking at the screen "chimping," probably in reference to chimpanzees' fascination with their own image in a mirror. The term might also have derived from photographers scrolling through their images after a good football play, saying, "ooh, ooh, ooh" when the good frames appear. Do not "chimp" too much, photographers warn, unless you are packing extra batteries or only plan to take a limited number of pictures.

Of course, no artist would undertake a painting without standing back to look at the canvas. The same urge is true for photojournalists in the digital age. The trick is not to spend too much time "chimping" and miss the next play on or off the field.

LENSES
Zoom Lenses Offer Versatility
Today's camera engineers have developed an array of fast, sharp zoom lenses that cover the range of focal lengths most photographers regularly carry in their bags. These fast, wide-aperture zoom lenses also will snare a significant portion of your salary, though. Of course, using a single zoom lens does save the cost of owning two or three individual lenses.

Buyer beware, however.

First, some zoom lenses change apertures as you zoom through the focal-length range. For instance, an 18–135mm zoom lens might have a maximum aperture of f/3.5 at 18mm—but at 135mm, the maximum aperture may decrease to f/5.6. In general, you will find variable-aperture telephoto zooms too slow for practical work when shooting indoors or outside in low light. For low-light photography without a vibration reduction/ stabilization lens (see pages 163–164), you usually need at least an f/2.8 zoom lens that maintains the same aperture at all focal lengths. These lenses tend to be expensive.

Second, zoom lenses are internally complicated and more prone to alignment errors when the lenses are knocked around at a football game or in a riot. Treat zoom lenses with care, and confirm their sharpness often.

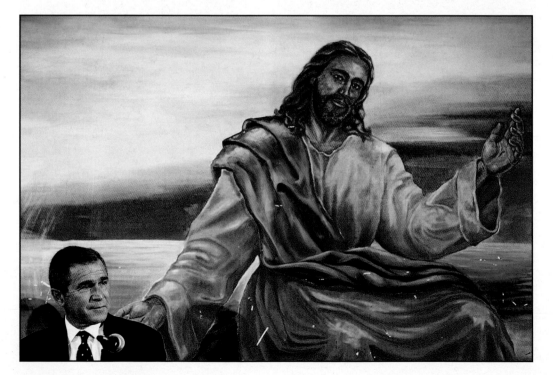

While on the road covering presidential candidates, the photographer could verify the quality of each image while shooting with a digital camera. Tom Gralish, *Philadelphia Inquirer*

Third, fast, wide-aperture zoom lenses are often very heavy. A number of professionals report back and arm strain after using these lenses over long periods. Holding an f/2.8 80–200mm zoom lens to your eye for the entire length of a press conference can lead to hours at the chiropractor's office. Use a monopod in these situations lest you face the fate of photographers who have had to leave the field because of this workplace hazard.

See Chapter 6, "Sports," page 110 for more on zoom lenses.

Telephoto Lenses Bring Action Nearer

A telephoto lens can be a photojournalist's best friend when a subject is far away. The obvious example is a sport such as football, in which the key player scampers down the field while the photographer is restricted to the sidelines. Photographers deploy their telephotos when they are forced behind a police barricade during a standoff between the cops and a criminal holding a hostage.

Besides filling a photograph's frame with the subject, telephoto lenses have another characteristic especially valuable to photojournalists when used at wide apertures. Suppose the photographer is taking feature pictures of young wrestlers at a meet, but the crowd behind the youngsters is distracting. Focusing a telephoto lens on the little athletes with the aperture at f/2.8 will likely cause the busy background to become blurry and indistinct. Many photojournalists carry long lenses just to achieve this strong visual effect.

In some digital cameras, the proportionate size of the CCD (charge-coupled device) or CMOS sensor is smaller than traditional 35mm film.

This has led to a few differences that photographers must consider when using digital equipment. The smaller chip size on some cameras means that standard lenses will produce a magnifying effect. (Not all camera models use the same size sensor chips, so magnification factors vary.) On one model SLR digital camera with a reduced size chip, for example, a classic 50mm lens will provide the coverage of a 75mm; a 200mm effectively becomes a 300mm. Achieving the wide-angle effect of a 21mm lens requires using a 14mm lens.

On the other hand, while the effective reach of the lens increases on a digital camera, a lens retains the same depth-of-field as when it is used on a film camera. However, the digital camera is not magnifying the image with the lens. Because of its relatively smaller chip size, the camera uses only the center segment of the image. The camera is cropping the image captured by the lens, not

magnifying it. For example, a 300mm lens provides the equivalent reach of a 450mm lens but with the same depth of field as the original 300mm lens.

Stabilization/Vibration-Reduction Telephoto Lenses

Generally, hand-holding a 300mm lens requires a shutter speed of at least 1/500 sec. or faster to avoid "soft" (not sharp) pictures caused by routine camera movement. Everyone's hands shake just a bit and this slight trembling can translate to blurry images. Stabilization (Canon) and vibration reduction (Nikon) lenses automatically counterbalance the small movements that can occur when a lens is handheld.

With a 300mm stabilization lens you can hand hold the lens at 1/125 sec. or possibly even slower yet still get crisp images. These lenses may have relatively small maximum

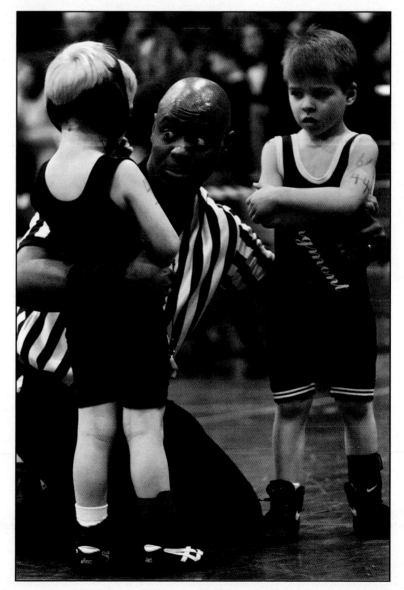

Used at a wide aperture like f/2.8, a telephoto lens helps blur the distracting background behind these 6-year-old wrestlers. The out-of-focus background keeps the readers' attention on the 44-pound grapplers and the referee between them.
Rich Abrahamson, [Fort Collins] *Coloradoan*

apertures like f/4 or f/5.6, which require shooting at slower shutter speeds. However, the stabilization/vibration-reduction feature reduces the impact of camera movement. These lenses tend to be lighter in weight than faster lenses, another advantage for the shooter.

The technology is also available in fast, wide-aperture lenses. These versatile lenses permit shooting in extremely low light without the aid of a tripod or flash.

While stabilization/vibration-reduction technology dramatically cuts down blurry pictures due to hand tremors, it does not eliminate blur caused by subject movement.

You will be able to photograph a speaker in a dimly lit room at a relatively slow shutter speed and still get a sharp image of the orator, for example, as long as he does not gesture too much with his hands. As he finishes his speech and begins to walk rapidly into the audience, the slow shutter speed may not freeze his high-fives to the crowd.

See Chapter 6, "Sports," for more on lenses and teleconverters.

Wide-Angle Lenses for Intimacy

Most photojournalists who do not shoot sports exclusively take most of their daily pictures with a wide-angle lens. Cartier-Bresson, the French photographer famous for his candid images, used a 35mm lens for many of his classic photos. James Nachtwey, the outstanding war photographer, shoots primarily with a wide-angle 17–35mm zoom lens. (See Chapter 1, "Assignment," for more on using a wide-angle lens).

Wide-angle lenses allow photographers to work very near to their subjects, which provides an intimate feel to pictures. Often, a photographer's lens is only inches away from the subject's face or body. Shooting from almost ground level, Pat Tehan of the *San Jose Mercury News* was only inches away from a toreador dressing for the ring (see opposite page). The viewer looking at the picture can almost reach out and help the bullfighter adjust his sash.

For news photographers elbowing for a shot in a crowd, the wide-angle lens offers another advantage—great depth of field. This feature allows shooting quickly without critically focusing the lens. Of course, the increased depth of field makes it more difficult to blur distracting backgrounds.

The 20mm or 24mm lens allows close focusing. By getting close to a subject like a political candidate, photographers can avoid having their lenses blocked by the politician's handlers, competing members of the media, or enthusiastic supporters crowding the political hopeful as she glad-hands her way through the crowd.

Wide-angle lenses also allow photographers to shoot in low light and still hand-hold the camera at relatively slow shutter speeds. Most photographers can comfortably shoot at 1/30 sec. with a 28mm lens and produce sharp pictures without blur from routine camera movement. Photographers report sharp images at 1/8 sec., sometimes even slower, when using 20mm lenses to photograph relatively stable subjects.

Keep in mind that a camera held two feet away from the action might disrupt the spontaneity. On the other hand, sometimes subjects just ignore the close-in camera because their own activities are so compelling.

Tip: When using a digital camera with a sensor smaller than standard 35mm film, extremely wide lenses in the 14mm to 17mm range are necessary to achieve the look and feel of typical images shot with wide-angle lenses.

Keys to Working Wide

A wide-angle lens is not a photographer's cure-all. The wider the angle of the lens, the greater the chance for apparent distortion caused by exaggerated perspective. This is because you can focus very close to a subject with a wide-angle lens. But the closer any part of a subject is to the lens, the bigger it will appear in the picture. This effect is particularly noticeable when the subject's face is at the edge of the frame.

Standing relatively close to and above a person and tilting the camera with a wide-angle lens down to include the subject's full length will cause the person's head to appear to be the size of a basketball and the feet small enough to fit into baby shoes.

KEEPING YOUR CAMERA DRY

Marty Forscher, who spent more than 50 years in the camera-repair business, always warned photographers, "Keep your camera dry." His advice has never been truer, given the sensitive electronics in digital cameras. Electrical contacts can corrode on exposure to moisture, especially salty moisture at the beach. Forscher always told the story of how well-known war photographer David Douglas Duncan shot great pictures in Korea under the worst rain and mud conditions possible by using a simple underwater camera.

Today, various commercial "rain hoods" that fit over photographer and camera help keep both reasonably dry.

Forscher suggests that if you are caught in the rain without a raincoat for your camera and have neither an underwater camera nor waterproof housing, wrap your regular lens and camera body in a plastic bag sealed with a rubber band. Cut one hole in the front of the bag to let the lens stick out, and another in the back of the bag to enable you to see through the viewfinder. Put the lens and eye-piece through the holes and secure them with rubber bands. Now you can operate the camera through the bag, but you can shoot and view through a clear area. Remember to keep the front element of the lens dry because drops of water here will distort the final image.

(See this effect used deliberately on page 348.)

The careful shooter can reduce these exaggerations by standing slightly farther back. Be careful not to make the mistake of many novice shooters, though. Standing too far away with the wide-angle lens can cause subjects to appear too small in the frame.

Pointing a wide-angle lens up to include a building's full height causes the structure to look as if it is falling over. This happens with any lens, but particularly so with a wide-angle lens. To avoid apparent distortion with the wide-angle lens, keep the back of the camera parallel to the subject. With a building, either get far enough away or high enough that the back of the camera is perpendicular to the ground and so parallel to the structure.

Use a wide-angle lens successfully by working in tight and keeping the lens parallel to the subject if possible. You may have to trade off some technical imperfections for the impact this lens can provide.

Packing a Lens for Every Occasion

While specific assignments often require specialized lenses—like 400mm "big glass" for sports action at a baseball game or a macro lens for shooting close-ups of insects at a science museum—news photographers with daily deadlines typically try to be prepared to cover any event that pops up. Some photographers cover six or more different assignments a day. From a shootout in the morning to a playoff at night, a photojournalist's motto is "be prepared."

For that reason, most photojournalists carry an array of lenses in their camera bags. These usually include a wide-angle-to-medium telephoto zoom and a medium-to-long telephoto zoom. Photojournalists may tote as many as three zoom lenses. For wide-angle shots, they carry a 10–17mm. For the medium range, some carry an f/2.8 17–55mm or an f/2.8 24–70mm zoom. And for the telephoto, a number carry an f/2.8 stabilization (Canon)/vibration reduction (Nikon) that covers the 70–200mm range. Then there are those with exceptionally strong backs who, in addition to their standard kits, regularly haul lenses in the 300mm or 400mm range.

A wide-angle lens allows the photographer to work up close and personal with a toreador dressing for his upcoming confrontation with the bull. Pat Tehan, *San Jose Mercury News*

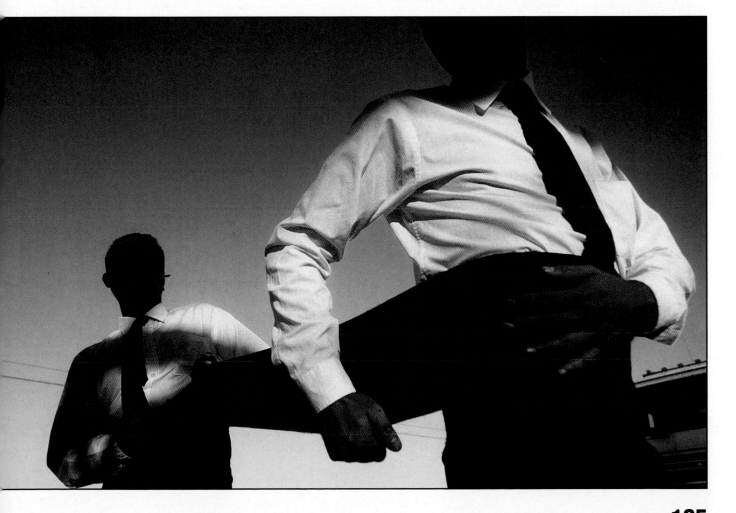

Jack Gruber has been a staff photographer at *USA TODAY* since 2000. Based in San Francisco, he must be ready to leave on assignment at a moment's notice for any destination in the world. To stay organized, Gruber has created what he calls a "Load Out Sheet" that lists all his gear, including serial numbers. Above are items he considers essential for international travel.

A Canon 70-200/2.8 lens. This telephoto is pretty much my standard lens in a two-camera system along with a 16-35/2.8 lens.

B Canon 300/4 lens. Lightweight long glass which fits into backpack or case without taking up a great deal of space and weight.

C & D Canon 1D Mark III. I carry at least two bodies and a possible third depending on the assignment or if the risk of the cameras going down is high in extreme conditions.

E Canon 16-35/2.8 lens is my standard lens when using a two-camera setup along with the 70-200/2.8 lens.

F Canon Extender EF 1.4x will extend either the 70-200 or 300/f4 when needing the longer glass.

G & H Canon 1D Mark III LP-E4 batteries. Extra batteries for the digital cameras. The new batteries are lighter and longer lasting then previous 1D versions.

I Canon Digital Battery Charger. I keep another charger as a backup in case of damage in another bag.

J Compact Flash Cards. I carry at least ten 2GB SanDisk compact flash cards in a ThinkTankPhoto Pixel Pocket Rocket and another set of 1GB compact flash cards in another card holder kept in different location in case I misplace or lose one set of cards.

K Edirol R-09 MP3 Recorder. A great lightweight audio recorder. The unit saves the files onto 2GB SD cards and runs on AA batteries.

L Canon Speedlite 580EX II

M Canon Video Camera. Tape camera for capturing video for the web.

N. Canon Wireless ST-E2. A great tool allows for off-camera and easy multiple strobe setups using Canon Speedlites.

O Reporter's Notebook

P USA TODAY official company ID. I keep the ID in a lanyard around my neck in a holder with business cards.

Q Apple Powerbook 12-inch computer Small and lightweight computer.

R USA Passport Primary. Good for ten years.

S USA Passport Secondary. This is valid for only two years but good to have in order to visit countries that frown upon passports with stamps from countries such as Israel.

T Cash—US, Euro, and local

U Medical record documenting inoculations, allergies, and other medical conditions.

V Passport type personal photos of varying sizes visa applications or other ID requirements.

W Tylenol

X Sharpee pen

Y Point-and-shoot Canon camera. A camera you can carry that does not draw attention.

Z Hard drive, external. Any good external Firewire hard drive to back up digital files from assignments.

AA Bgan Satellite Device allows for Internet access anywhere in the world but at a price of between $8–$12 per megabyte of data transfer. Fast transfer times allow for transmitting of pictures.

BB. Thuraya Satellite Phone works off SIMM cards either prepaid or on an open account, and allows for communications from remote areas with no cell service.

CC. Dual time watch allows for two different time zones to be displayed at once—home time and local time—in order to remember and make international deadlines

DD. Analog phone handset for Bgan satellite device

EE. US cell phone

FF. GSM cell phone with SIMM cards for local area With multiple country-specific SIM cards, allows less expensive local calling, less expensive cell phone calls and provides a local call-back phone number for people locally to get in touch with you.

GG. Handheld GPS can track trips in order not to get lost

HH International electric plug adapter has multiple settings for adapting to most of the world's power outlets

II. Three-way plug to plug multiple chargers into one outlet

JJ. Ipod

KK. Power inverter car adapter. A great backup in case you have no access to electricity but still have a vehicle in which you can charge cameras and computers.

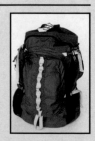

In order to walk off a plane with everything I need to work and transmit images, I use a Kelty Redwing 3100 front-loading backpack that contains all the above items. I pack a small Domke bag with most of my basic camera kit, two see-through Columbia mesh pouches containing the mess of chargers, adapters, and other stuff, and another mesh pouch containing the satellite unit.

TOOLS FOR STABILITY

While a tripod is three times as stable as a monopod, it also takes up three times the space. Both pieces of hardware are necessary for the photojournalist. Many photographers use the tripod for portraits (see pages 82–83). A tripod allows shooting under low light unencumbered by strobe lights. It also provides solid support that eliminates blurry pictures due to camera movement.

While a monopod can also stabilize the camera many photographers also use it on the baseball and football field to help hold extremely long and usually very heavy telephoto lenses. Without a monopod, carrying a 400mm lens for two hours at a football game can send even the fittest photojournalist on a trip to the chiropractor.

MEMORY CARDS

All digital cameras require a removable memory card, compact disk, or hard drive to store images before they are transferred to a computer or printer. They vary in the amount of data they can hold as well as in format.

The amount of memory you need depends on the resolution necessary for reproduction. Resolution is the number of pixels in an image, a key factor in determining quality. You will need at least three million pixels (three megapixels) to produce an 8"x10" image for a newspaper. An uncompressed three-megapixel image creates a 9.4 megabyte file.

You will not need such a big file for a photo intended for the Internet. But generally, the more pixels, the better the quality will be if the photograph is going to be printed or reproduced at a large size (see page 168.)

CompactFlash (CF) and their more petite cousins Secure Digital (SD) memory cards have no moving parts. They come in standard physical sizes but vary in how much information they hold. Also, some memory cards can download information from the camera faster than others. (See Rob

---

BUYING A PHOTOJOURNALIST'S DIGITAL CAMERA

No company has yet built the perfect digital camera for journalists—one that will hold up to hard knocks, rain, sleet, hail, sand, heat, cold, humidity, etc., and continue to perform. With that caveat in mind, here are a few things to keep in mind when buying a digital camera for shooting news, sports, features, and portraits.

1) **Cost.** Although prices are decreasing, digital cameras are still expensive. The most expensive camera is not necessarily the best one for your particular needs, body size, hand size, or pocketbook.

2) **Weight.** Lugging a heavy camera and compatible lenses can send a photographer to the chiropractor. Sometimes a lighter camera with fewer features will allow you to shoot all day and into the night.

3) **Size of the sensor chip.** Is the chip full-frame, the size of a traditional 35mm film, or smaller? A full size chip means pre-digital lenses will operate normally. A smaller chip means the camera and its corresponding lenses could be smaller and lighter.

4) **Number of megapixels.** The more the merrier although for most reproduction in a newspaper, magazine or online you will not see any improvement in quality in images having more than 10 megapixels.

5) **Burst rate.** How many frames per second do you really need? Serious sports photographers prefer frame rates of nine per second or higher. For most shooting situations this high speed capability is not essential or useful.

6) **ISO range.** The real question is image quality in semidarkness. While a wide range of ISOs is good, confirm at the high end whether the pictures are "clean" without a lot of undesirable random noise.

7) **Focusing system.** Some systems are faster and more accurate than others. Check the speed and sharpness under flat, low-contrast, dark-lighting conditions and see which camera works best for you.

8) **Compatibility.** Will the new digital camera work with your old lenses? Will you need a super wide-angle lens (17mm or greater) to compensate for

the difference in format size? Does the flash you use now work with a digital camera you are going to buy?

9) **Handling ease.** People's hands come in different sizes, but manufacturers build camera bodies that must fit all.

10) **Live view from the image sensor.** This feature allows you to hold the camera away from your body and still frame the picture.

11) **Wireless connectivity.** You can shoot and send your pictures directly to your laptop, but do you need this feature?

12) **Image stabilization.** To reduce blur due to camera movement, the mechanism is in the lens in some systems, in the camera body in others. Which system is best is still an open debate.

13) **Frequently used controls.** Make sure that the control buttons and dials you need are on the camera body itself and not buried as a menu item.

14) **Obsolescence.** Digital cameras fall behind the technological curve quickly. You will need/want a new camera sooner than you think.

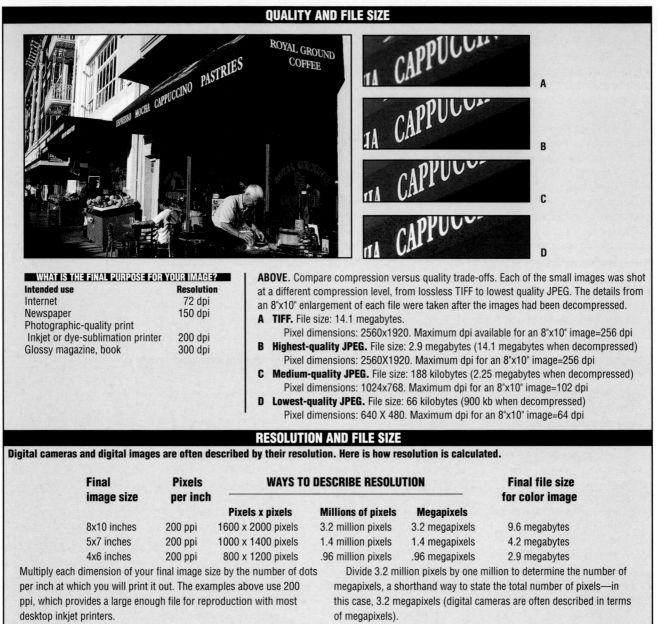

QUALITY AND FILE SIZE

WHAT IS THE FINAL PURPOSE FOR YOUR IMAGE?

Intended use	Resolution
Internet	72 dpi
Newspaper	150 dpi
Photographic-quality print	
Inkjet or dye-sublimation printer	200 dpi
Glossy magazine, book	300 dpi

ABOVE. Compare compression versus quality trade-offs. Each of the small images was shot at a different compression level, from lossless TIFF to lowest quality JPEG. The details from an 8"x10" enlargement of each file were taken after the images had been decompressed.

A   TIFF. File size: 14.1 megabytes.
Pixel dimensions: 2560x1920. Maximum dpi available for an 8"x10" image=256 dpi

B   Highest-quality JPEG. File size: 2.9 megabytes (14.1 megabytes when decompressed)
Pixel dimensions: 2560X1920. Maximum dpi for an 8"x10" image=256 dpi

C   Medium-quality JPEG. File size: 188 kilobytes (2.25 megabytes when decompressed)
Pixel dimensions: 1024x768. Maximum dpi for an 8"x10" image=102 dpi

D   Lowest-quality JPEG. File size: 66 kilobytes (900 kb when decompressed)
Pixel dimensions: 640 X 480. Maximum dpi for an 8"x10" image=64 dpi

RESOLUTION AND FILE SIZE

Digital cameras and digital images are often described by their resolution. Here is how resolution is calculated.

Final image size	Pixels per inch	WAYS TO DESCRIBE RESOLUTION			Final file size for color image
		Pixels x pixels	Millions of pixels	Megapixels	
8x10 inches	200 ppi	1600 x 2000 pixels	3.2 million pixels	3.2 megapixels	9.6 megabytes
5x7 inches	200 ppi	1000 x 1400 pixels	1.4 million pixels	1.4 megapixels	4.2 megabytes
4x6 inches	200 ppi	800 x 1200 pixels	.96 million pixels	.96 megapixels	2.9 megabytes

Multiply each dimension of your final image size by the number of dots per inch at which you will print it out. The examples above use 200 ppi, which provides a large enough file for reproduction with most desktop inkjet printers.

In the first row, for example, 8 inches times 200 equals 1600, 10 inches times 200 equals 2000. Pixel by Pixel dimension equals 1600 x 2000. This is one way to describe resolution. Now, multiply 1600 times 2000. The answer is 3.2 million pixels. Millions of pixels also describes resolution.

Divide 3.2 million pixels by one million to determine the number of megapixels, a shorthand way to state the total number of pixels—in this case, 3.2 megapixels (digital cameras are often described in terms of megapixels).

Now, because each pixel consists of three color values—red, green, and blue—multiply the number of megapixels times 3 to determine the final file size of the image.

An 8"x10" color inkjet print requires a file size of at least 9.6 megabytes. A 4"x6" snapshot needs only 2.9 megabytes.

FILE SIZE AND STORAGE CAPACITY

DIGITAL CAMERA MEMORY CARDS

Capacity	Number of 10 MB files (8x10, 200 dpi inkjet prints)
32 MB	3
64 MB	6
128 MB	12
256 MB	25
1 GB	100
2 GB	200
Etcetera	

COMPUTER STORAGE

	Capacity	Number of 10 MB files (8x10, 200dpi inkjet prints)
200MB Zip Disk	196+ MB	19
Compact Disk	600+ MB	60
1GB Jazz cartridge	1 GB	100
3.9GB DVD	3.9 GB	380+
5.2GB DVD	5.2 GB	500+
100 GB hard drive	100 GB	10,000

Galbraith's web site, *www.robgalbraith.com*, for more information.)

The greatest amount of memory with the fastest download time is the ideal choice when selecting a memory card. Bigger for storing more pictures, faster so that less time is required between shots as the photos actually travel from the camera to the card. Note that the various brands of memory cards are not always interchangeable. Check your camera's manual to identify compatible cards.

Because the capacity of memory cards is increasing even as their prices are decreasing, some pros recommend carrying several. This allows them to continue shooting while downloading a full card into a laptop or other storage device. Allocating shots to different cards also ensures that an entire assignment is not in one place if a card is damaged or lost.

Other shooters prefer one large-capacity memory card. The larger capacity permits fewer download sessions, an advantage when shooting in poor weather conditions or when covering a fast-breaking story.

The Memory/Quality Trade-Off

Photojournalists want great image quality, but they also must pack the maximum number of images possible on a storage card. The size and quality of a digital image determine how much storage space the file requires—on a storage card or on a hard drive.

High-quality images require high-quality digital files, which consume the most memory and storage space, especially those shot in the RAW format. If print quality is your goal, bigger is almost always better. A small file size is ideal when it comes to storage space, transmission over the Internet, or ease of working with an image.

A memory card may hold just a few pictures at top quality but many at low quality. If you are traveling without a laptop to which you can transfer the images, your memory cards will quickly run out of space if you shoot all your pictures at top quality. Even a computer's hard drive can fill up quickly if you are shooting uncompressed RAW files.

Resolution & Compression

To achieve smaller digital files, a camera uses either fewer pixels to record pictures, compresses the files, or does both. Low-quality settings use the fewest pixels to take a picture initially and/or compress an image the most. High quality uses the most pixels and/or compresses the least.

Because of this trade-off between image quality and memory, most cameras provide a way to preselect quality for each or all pictures. Some models record and save the

HOW THE COMPUTER TRANSLATES PICTURES INTO NUMBERS

Do you remember paint-by-number canvases from your childhood? So that you could paint a picture of the Eiffel Tower, the canvas would indicate a specific number for each color of paint. When a segment of the picture needed a blue sky, the canvas would call for a number five (blue). When a section of the tower needed to be red, the canvas would call for a number three (red). On the original canvas, the area representing the sky was covered with number fives, and the Eiffel Tower itself was filled with number threes. All you had to do was match the paint color on the little jar with the number printed on the canvas. Even if you did not know what the canvas was supposed to look like, you would eventually produce a painting of the Eiffel Tower if you painted in all the numbers correctly.

Now, imagine a paint-by-number canvas in which sections are of equal size, like graph paper, but smaller than a pinpoint. These tiny squares are called picture cells—or pixels. Each pixel is assigned a number indicating its location and it brightness. Now imagine if, instead of a few jars in your paint set, your canvas called for 16.7 million jars, each a different shade, level of brightness, or saturation. Each square (pixel) on your canvas could be any one of these 16 million plus colors. If the squares (pixels) are small enough and if you have enough paints, you can accurately represent in the computer any picture you might take. Now you can appreciate how many numbers the computer is crunching whenever it deals with a color image. Basically, a computer is selecting from millions of jars of colors to paint by number millions of tiny, evenly spaced squares.

HOW DOES COMPRESSION WORK?

How do you squeeze a large picture file into a smaller space? By eliminating redundant information. Let's say you have a picture with a large blue sky. To represent the blue, the computer stores hundreds of individual identical numbers, each representing the color blue. To compress the information, software counts up the number of blue pixels that are the same and stores the total count rather than a number for each individual pixel.

If x stands for blue, the original file might be xxxxxxxxxxxxxxxxxxxxxxxxxx xxxxxxxxxxxxxxxxxxxxxxxx, while the new file would be (x50) and take up a much smaller space. When you decompress the image, the program lays out the original number of blue pixels representing the sky.

The method of compression called "lossless" throws away no data. The reconstituted picture is exactly the same as the original. The file size still remains relatively large, however.

The method known as "lossy" throws out some of those identical blue pixels, which can degrade quality. Depending on the degree of compression, though, the loss can be so slight that the degradation is not noticeable.

The commonly used JPEG format is a lossy method of compression. JPEG files can be saved in different quality modes—high, medium, low. You might also run across choices such as fine, normal, or low. High compresses a little but leaves the image looking almost perfect. Low, on the other hand, compresses a lot, and the loss will be obvious if the image is reproduced in a magazine but not when posted to a web site. (Keep in mind that repeated editing and saving an image in JPEG format will eventually degrade its quality noticeably.)

After you have transferred an image to the computer and want to work with it, make a copy and work with that. This will preserve the original at its highest quality in case you need to start over again. ∎

images RAW—uncompressed, exactly as they were taken, with all information saved—resulting in a very large file (see page 158). You can usually opt to save a corresponding JPEG file simultaneously. You may find numerical settings for compression and resolution, choices such as high, medium, or low, or a system of stars or numbers. Your camera manual describes these choices.

How good is good enough? Your quality choice will depend on how the photo will be used. A low-quality image will look fine on the web. But if you print out the same image at a large size, you probably will not like the results. High quality is the choice for images intended for display or reproduction in books or magazines. Medium quality works well for some newspaper reproduction. Your news outlet will be able to tell you the optimum file size for the best reproduction.

Tip: You can downsize a high-quality file for the web, but you cannot expand a low-quality file to create a double-page spread.

For the best quality—and thus the largest file size—select the highest resolution possible and do not compress the image at all. This choice makes sense for a photographer with lots of high-capacity storage and who plans to use the pictures for a glossy magazine or book or as prints in exhibitions.

To create the smallest possible file, select the lowest resolution and highest compression ratio. This option is best for someone shooting only images for the web.

Since manufacturers do not use the same terminology to describe resolution and compression, review your camera's manual.

Oops!

Have a favorite image shot at too low a resolution to be reproduced in a magazine or enlarged for the wall? There may be hope depending on the final size required. While upsampling in Photoshop and programs like Genuine Fractals does not increase the detail in a picture, they do help avoid obvious pixelation. Many photographers report excellent results with software solutions like these.

DIGITAL NOISE

Digital cameras allow the use of different ISOs for shooting under almost any lighting conditions—even from one shot to the next. On some cameras, ISO ratings range between 100 and 3200 or even higher. Increased "noise" can appear in pictures shot at the higher digital ISO ratings. Depending on the camera model, noticeable noise starts to show up above ISO 800. The noise looks like an unnatural pattern or tiny brightly colored pixels in the darker areas of the picture. Photographers often find noise more objectionable to the eye than old-fashioned film grain.

In low-light situations, some photographers recommend using on- or off-camera flash rather than increasing the ISO. Others shoot at ISO 800 with good results. Some people report better results by turning off "image-sharpening" mode in their cameras when shooting at a high ISO. This mode tends to exaggerate noise levels in some photographs.

Photo editing software can help seek out and eliminate offending noisy pixels and thus improve the picture's overall appearance. Check out Rob Galbraith's web site, *www.robgalbraith.com*, for information about noise-reduction filters and other issues regarding digital photojournalism.

COLOR CONSIDERATIONS

Color is a special language, says Steve Raymer, a former *National Geographic* staffer. "I pass up pictures when the color gets in the way. It's a matter of learning to read color, light, and subject in a new way."New photographers often make pictures filled with bold primary colors that can detract from a photograph's editorial content.

Red, for example, is a color that produces strong emotions. Like the bull attracted to the

---

KEEPING THE SENSOR CLEAN

Only if you shoot in a dust-free microchip manufacturing facility can you hope to avoid getting dust particles on your sensor when changing lenses. You will face this problem when shooting in the sand storms of Iraq or the windy streets of Chicago. Each time you change lenses, the sensor is left exposed for a few minutes—just enough time for a tiny piece of dust to settle on the sensor and leave a speck on every following picture.

"Never leave a digital camera open without a lens or lens cap for more than just a few seconds," warns David Guralnick of the *Detroit News*.

To save hours of Photoshop retouching work, keep your sensor clean. Never stick any object into the camera unless it's a tool specifically designed to clean the sensor. If you are not comfortable or familiar with sensor-cleaning kits, leave the job to a professional.

Do NOT use compressed air to clean the inside of a camera.

Nikon manuals recommend using a manual air blower to clean the low-pass filter that resides in front of the camera's sensor. They do not recommend compressed air or a brush.

Rob Galbraith, on the other hand, says, "The Sensor Brush and its companion Sensor Clean liquid/swab combo, from Canadian company Visible Dust, are the first products of their type we've used that can remove dust, dirt, and other particles effectively with little chance of either streaking or scratching the cover glass over the image sensor."

Photographers and manufacturers are coming up with many more alternatives. Check out this site for more information on keeping your sensors clean: *http://www.cleaningdigitalcameras.com /methods.html.* ∎

matador's red cape, photographers are equally drawn to bright red in the scene they are photographing. The color, unfortunately, tends to dominate a visual message so much that you must be extremely careful in how much red you include in a picture.

If your assignment is an environmental portrait of a racecar driver, for example, be careful that the driver's red Ferrari does not take over the picture. On the other hand, if you are in Red Square, as Raymer was in Russia, including the country's red flag in a picture makes both visual and editorial sense (see page 137).

Raymer recommends searching out colors that complement one another and create a mood. "Start with the concept of harmony," he says. "Before moving to dominant primary colors like red and blue, learn that when it comes to color less is usually more."

TIME OF DAY IS CRITICAL

Editors often disregard the hour of the assignment when they set up a photographer's

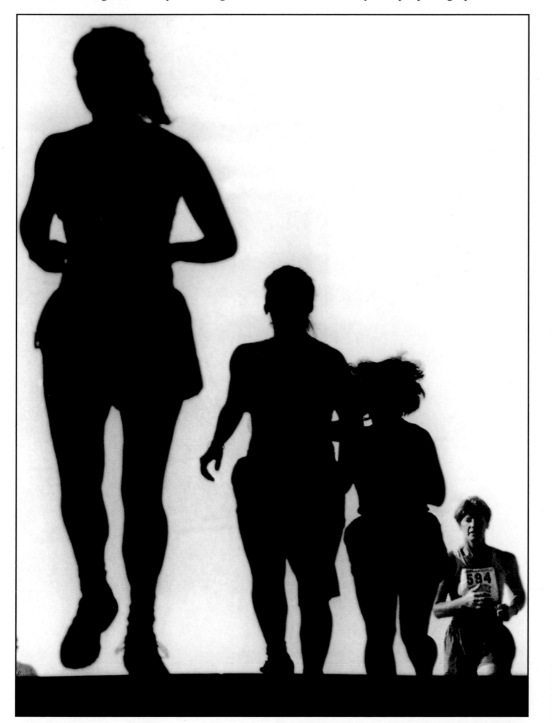

Rich Abrahamson, the *Coloradoan*

A muted color palette adds impact to this photo. As the runners arrived on the scene, the stadium shadowed the first three runners and left the third lit by the sun.

schedule. They ignore the angle and the color of the light.

For an indoor job, time of day might be less crucial, but when shooting outdoors, timing is everything. From 5 A.M. to 5 P.M., color changes, intensity changes, and mood changes. A routine shot of a building taken at noon becomes an *Architectural Digest* photo at 6 P.M. A common mug shot photographed at 10 A.M. becomes a gallery portrait taken at sunset. The selection of time to photograph is as important as the choice of lens or film.

A painter picks oils from a palette to create mauves and maroons. Likewise, a photographer picks the time of day to capture delicate morning pink or late afternoon red.

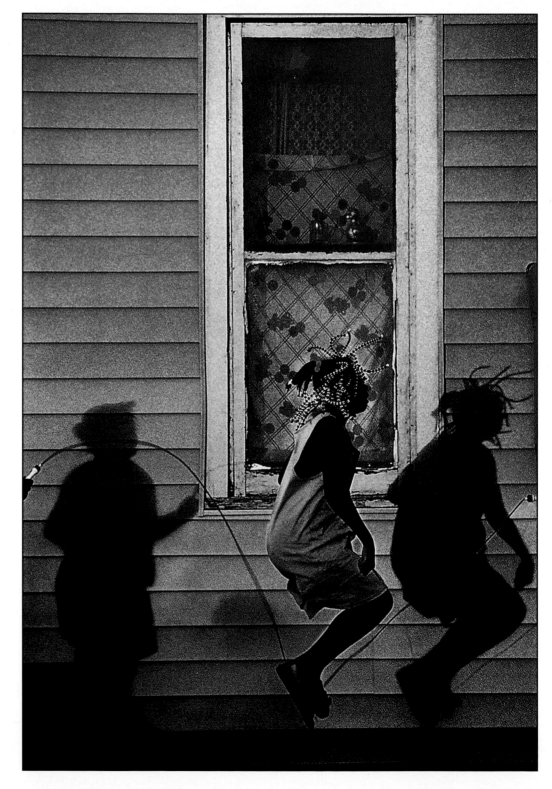

Late afternoon light leaves a crisp, distinct shadow of a girl and her friend jumping rope "double dutch." The warm glow results as the atmosphere absorbs blue wavelengths in the sky and leaves more red as the sun sets. Brian Plonka, for the *Herald News* [Joliet, Illinois]

The time of day determines the color of light striking your subject when shooting outdoors.

While working on a book about the Russian city of St. Petersburg, former *National Geographic* staffer Steve Raymer photographed Palace Square, scene of revolution and bloodshed during both the reigns of the Czars and Lenin's Bolsheviks. Searching for just the right combination of dramatic light and editorial content—in this case horses ambling across the square and suggesting a bygone era—he returned a dozen or more times until he found the ideal moment.

"This picture took compulsive attention to light and color," Raymer says.

Raymer also photographed the broad and muddy Red River as it flowed across the mountainous border between China and Vietnam. "I actually waited until after sunset . . . when the sky was filled with a reddish-pink afterglow," he explains.

In this situation, the reddish hues in the final image added to the message of tranquility he was trying to convey and also played off the river's name.

SHOOTING FROM DAWN 'TIL DUSK

While you cannot control when a peace demonstration or a car wreck will occur, you often can select the time of day for shooting an outdoor portrait or a building exterior.

Dawn

For soft shadows and monochrome colors, shoot at dawn.

Midday

Many photographers try to avoid the harshness of the midday sun. Although colors might appear bright in transparencies or prints, people photographed on a sunny afternoon often have shadows running across their faces. These unflattering shadows can turn eye-sockets into billiard pockets.

If you must shoot portraits on a bright, clear afternoon, try moving your subjects into the shade of a building or tree, or turning your subjects so that their backs face the sun. Here is where you can use fill flash to your advantage. (See Chapter 9, "Strobe.")

Late Afternoon

As the sun falls lower in the sky, its rays travel farther through the atmosphere. Molecules of water in the sky tend to scatter the short, blue wavelengths of light. The long, red wavelengths pass freely toward earth. This is why, as the sun sets, late afternoon light turns redder and redder. Also, as the sun drops, shadows stretch and lend a sculptured look to

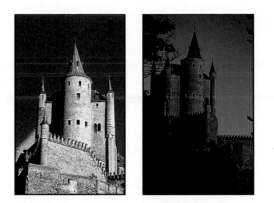

The time of day a subject is photographed—particularly a building—affects the mood of the final picture. The mood shifts from stark at noon (ABOVE, LEFT) to rich in late afternoon (ABOVE, RIGHT). © Ken Kobré

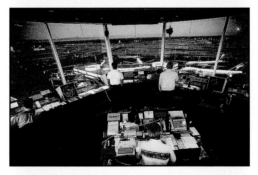

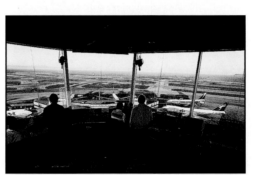

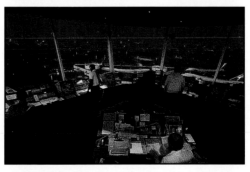

To show both the landing strip outside and the air controllers inside, the photographer waited until the waning afternoon light matched the exposure of the indoor light. Note also in this series of pictures how the color and quality of light change as the time of day changes.

© Ken Kobré, for *San Francisco Business*

Digital cameras provide internal controls for balancing color. When these are employed, a white object will look white in the final image regardless of the light source in the original situation. Once white is white, everything else, from faces to furniture, retains its appropriate color balance.

Most cameras provide several ways to correct color balance in the camera. For the most precise control use Nikon's "preset white balance" or Canon's "custom white balance."

In the same light as that striking your subject, point the camera at a known white object, such as a piece of paper, filling the frame. Be sure there is no shadow falling onto it.

Activate the white balance command. As long as you continue working in the same lighting conditions, the following pictures you take will not have a color cast. (See your manual for the details on how its white balance feature operates.)

Many cameras also provide a choice of factory-set options indicated by symbols for incandescent, fluorescent, direct sunlight, flash, clouds, and shade. Some cameras may provide choices in Kelvin degrees, a technical way of describing color.

Finally, the "auto" setting is the best choice when you are moving rapidly from one situation to another with varying lighting conditions.

Whichever method you use, test the camera and yourself by looking at the LCD monitor to see if images appear strangely blue or orange. A pronounced color cast usually indicates that you need to change the color balance setting.

Read more about white balance on pages 175–177. ∎

CAMERA'S WHITE BALANCE SETTING

LIGHTING CONDITIONS

INCANDESCENT LIGHT

DAYLIGHT

PRESET / CUSTOM

In these two situations, the photographer took a white balance reading off a sheet of white paper held in the same light as the subjects before shooting in each location. Both the art gallery and the flower market are color balanced correctly.

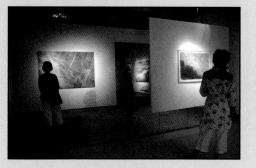
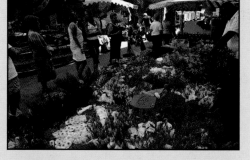

DAYLIGHT

In these two situations, the camera was set to daylight white balance. The indoor art gallery, lit by incandescent light, has a yellow cast, while the outdoor flower market, lit by daylight, looks normal.

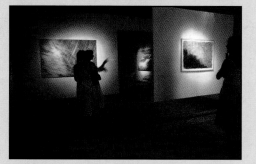
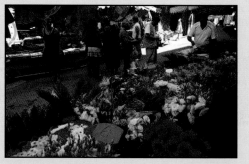

INCANDESCENT

In these two situations, the camera was set to incandescent white balance. The indoor art gallery, lit by incandescent light, looks normal. The outdoor flower market, lit by the sun, has a blue cast.

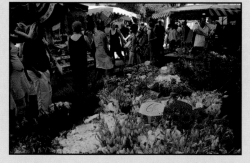

the landscape. This time of day is the choice of many photojournalists working in color.

Although the reddish light of late afternoon usually flatters a subject, you will occasionally need a more technically correct picture at this time of day. As sunset approaches, the sky takes on its most flamboyant corals and oranges, and makes a dramatic backdrop for silhouettes.

To avoid a silhouette but still use the sky's palette, try balancing your strobe with the early evening sky. In this situation, the strobe becomes the dominant light source. The ratio of strobe light to the skylight would be equal. Many photojournalists shoot portraits and fashion using this balanced-light technique. (See pages 180, 184, 186, for examples of this technique used in various circumstances.)

Evening
Lacking the warmth of the sun, evening light is cold and blue. Sometimes streets and buildings that look as bland as white bread during the day look haunting by night. Do not overlook the possibility of using flash to illumi-

nate the foreground and a long shutter speed to pick up ambient light in the background. Also, setting the camera's white balance symbol to "light bulb," incandescent, or 3200 Kelvin turns the nighttime sky a rich blue. (See opposite page and following section for more on white balance.)

CONSISTENT COLOR
The colors of different light sources—outdoor noonday sun compared to indoor tungsten light, as one example—affect the overall hue of the final image. Most digital cameras have a "white balance" feature that can compensate for different light sources (see opposite page) in each shooting situation without the hassle of filters or extravagant lighting setups.

Under many circumstances, the camera's automatic white balance feature will work fine. The camera actually detects and attempts to neutralize color shifts caused by different light sources. Auto white balance works well outdoors on sunny days but can be thrown off indoors under fluorescent or sodium-vapor lights. It's usually the preferred choice in

Incandescent light has a warm, golden yellow tone—note the lamps in the hotel room. Strobe light, which illuminates the mime and the bed, is balanced for daylight. The mime's shirt and the bedspread remain white rather than taking on the color cast by the incandescent light.

Two strobes, positioned off-camera, are bounced into umbrellas. One, to the right and out of camera view, lights the mime. A second, also out of camera view, lights the canopy bed.
© Ken Kobré, for *San Francisco Business*

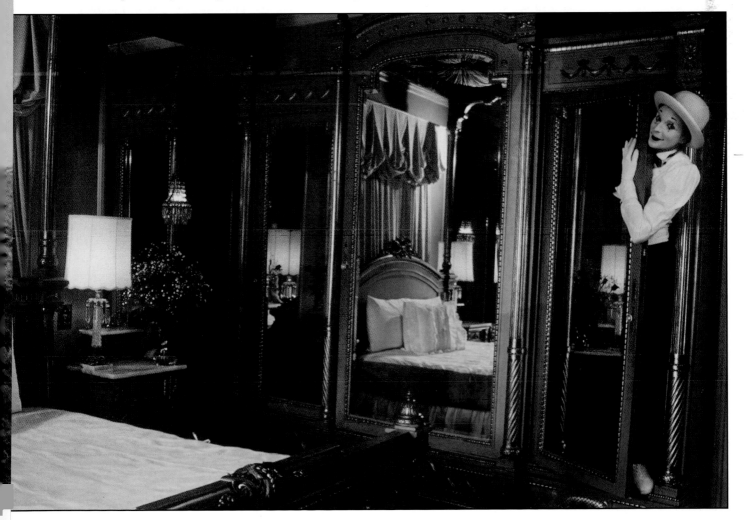

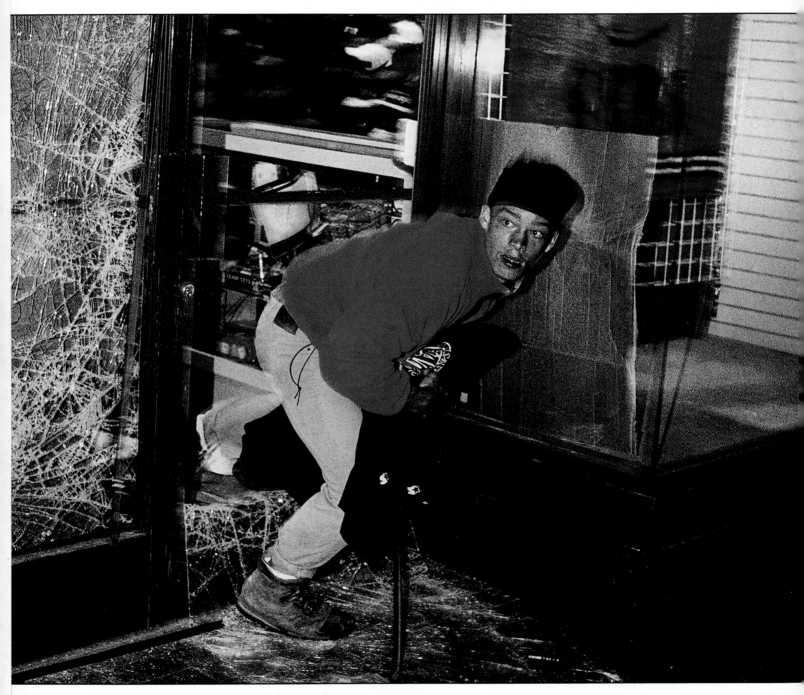

Following a not-guilty verdict in the trial of Los Angeles police officers who beat the
unarmed Rodney King, rioters in San Francisco broke into shops and hauled out stolen goods.
The photographer used a relatively slow shutter speed (1/15 sec.) to balance the strobe's light
with that coming from the store's interior. © Ken Kobré

9

Strobe

SUNSHINE AT YOUR FINGERTIPS

Originally, photographers were limited to picture taking only when the sun was out. However, not all news, happens in the light of day. From flash powder through flash bulbs to electronic flash, photojournalists have searched for a convenient light source that would enable them to take pictures under any circumstances.

Today, possessing a compact strobe is akin to having a pocketful of sunshine at your fingertips. Manufacturers sell portable light sources in the form of miniaturized, lightweight, high-powered, battery-operated, portable, built-in, and external strobes for single-lens-reflex (SLR) cameras.

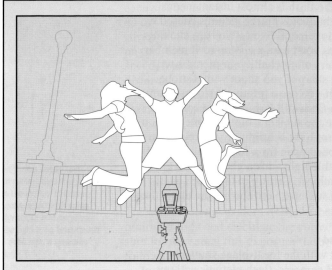

You can use flash at any shutter speed at or below your camera's flash/sync speed.

When using flash, the f-stop is determined by the amount of light emitted by the flash that reaches the subject.

In this case, strobe was set to TTL (through-the-lens metering). The f-stop on the camera remained at f/4. With the flash mounted on the camera and the camera on a tripod, the photographer varied the camera's shutter speed from 1/500 sec. to 1 sec. (Not all cameras will allow the strobe to sync at 1/500.)

To demonstrate the full range of shutter speeds and the effects of changing them, the photographer shot at dusk. He also had the subjects jump in every frame.

Study how changing the shutter speed influences the picture. The amount of time the shutter is open controls the amount of available light reaching the sensor.

As the shutter speed slows and the camera gathers in more ambient light, the background gets progressively lighter in each picture, eventually matches the light from the strobe, and then even overpowers it.

Generally, a strobe exposure about two stops brighter than the background (1/30 sec. in this example) generates a dramatic but natural-looking picture.

Photos by John Hernandez

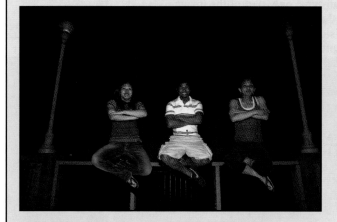

• **1/500 sec. You can see that the background is very dark. At this exposure, the scene behind the subjects is completely underexposed. The short duration of the flash freezes the subjects in mid-air.** F-STOP STAYS AT F/4.

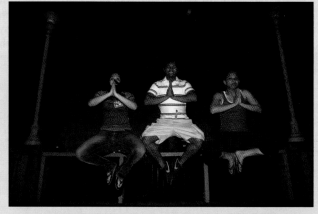

• **1/250 sec. The subjects are correctly exposed, but the background is still dark because the shutter is not open long enough to record any brightness in the sky. The flash freezes the subjects in mid-air.** F-STOP STAYS AT F/4.

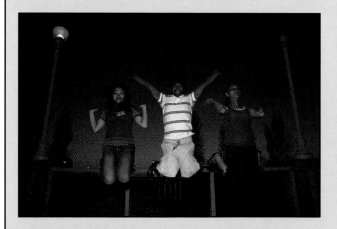

• **1/125 sec. The background lightens as the shutter speed lengthens. The subjects remain frozen.** F-STOP STAYS AT F/4.

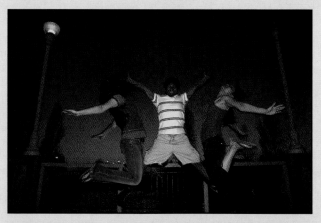

• **1/60 sec. The subjects remain correctly exposed while the background gets yet lighter. By keeping the exposure on the subject constant and varying the shutter speed, you can control the background's brightness.** F-STOP STAYS AT F/4.

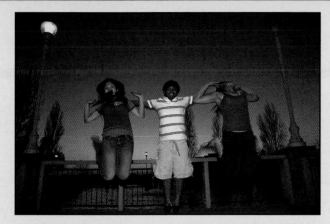

• 1/30 sec. Here, the subjects "pop" out of the background, which is about two stops darker but still readable. F-STOP STAYS AT F/4.

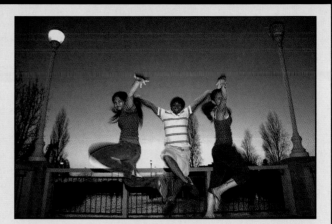

• 1/15 sec. The moving subjects produce two images, the sharp one frozen by the electronic flash, the other blurring in the available light. The strobe's light lasts but a split second, thereby freezing the subjects in mid-air, while the available light remains constant—lighting the subjects' motion—throughout the entire 1/15 sec. exposure. The slightly "ghosted" blur from the available light becomes noticeable only when a subject is moving. When a subject is stationary, the strobe and available light images exactly overlap. F-STOP STAYS AT F/4.

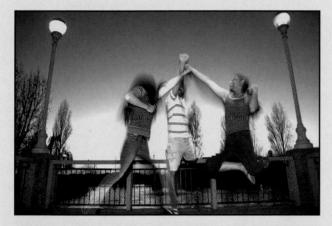

• 1/8 sec. Strobe/available light balance point for this lighting situation. As the shutter stays open longer, the available light image (the ghost) gets stronger. Here, the flash and ghost images become equal. At the point of equality, the picture is said to be balanced for flash and for available light. F-STOP STAYS AT F/4.

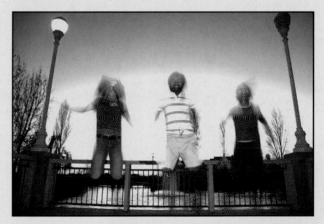

• 1/4 sec. As the shutter speed slows further, the available light begins to overpower both the background and the subjects. The available light is washing out the flash picture. F-STOP STAYS AT F/4.

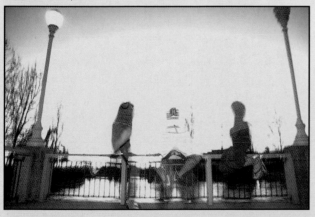

• 1/2 sec. At this exposure, the available light further overpowers the light from the strobe. The subjects are starting to disappear. F-STOP STAYS AT F/4.

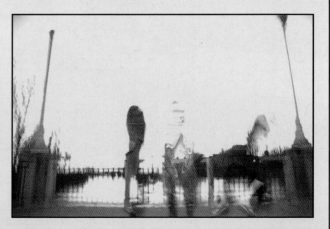

• 1 sec. The available light washes out the entire image in this exposure. The flash exposure leaves just the subjects' legs. Without the flash, they would have disappeared in motion. F-STOP STAYS AT F/4.

But because the shutter remains open for a period longer than the flash's duration, the camera has the opportunity to absorb the natural light in the scene, effectively creating a second image.

The longer the shutter remains open, the more the available light adds to the overall exposure. Thus the camera is combining both the flash exposure and the available light exposure into one final image.

With the camera set on 1/200 second, the flash will fire and light your subject for the flash exposure, but the shutter will not remain open long enough to gather much light for the second exposure.

However, if the shutter speed is set to 1/15 sec., say, the flash exposure will come out the same, but the second, available light exposure will have 1/15 sec. to absorb ambient light in the scene. This relatively long second exposure will cause the background to come out brighter. (See pages 182–183.)

Typically, you will want the background to be about two stops (two full shutter speeds) darker than the subject. You can achieve this by putting the strobe on TTL and the camera on manual. Choose a wide aperture like f/2.8 or f/4.

Adjust the shutter speed of the camera until the light meter indicates that the ambient light in the scene is two stops less (two full shutter speeds faster) than the light level needed for a correctly exposed picture without flash.

When you shoot with the strobe set to through-the-lens metering (TTL) the strobe will correctly expose the subject whether used direct or bounced. The slow shutter speed will gather in enough light in the background to illuminate the area without overpowering the main subject.

For example, the ambient reading for the looter coming out of the store in the photo on page 178 was 1/4 sec. at f/4. With his strobe on TTL but the camera on manual, the author selected a shutter speed of 1/15 sec. The strobe lit the subject and stopped his motion as he hauled the stolen goods through the broken door. The slow shutter speed simultaneously picked up ambient light from the display window. Because the exposure for the window was underexposed by two stops, it did not overwhelm the image of the thief in action.

Many professional photographers also like the effect that the combination of strobe and a slower shutter speed has on moving subjects. Although the strobe freezes the subject's movement for one instant, the long exposure also captures the subject's continuing movement, adding a ghost-like blur. The result is a sharp image combined with the

This portrait combined flash and available light. The longer the shutter remains open during an exposure, the brighter the background appears. As the shutter remains open longer—in this situation for 1/2 sec. at f/5.6 —the moving cars disappear and leave only trails of light from their head and tail lights. John Shearer, San Francisco

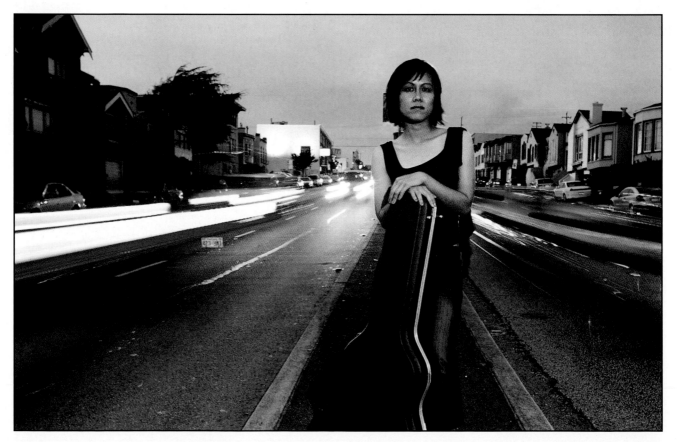

blur of motion (see pages 178 and 183. For less ghosting, simply use a faster shutter speed.

If you want the "ghost" to come from the opposite direction, use rear curtain sync. This option will fire the strobe at the end rather than the beginning of the exposure. The ghosting trail will appear to follow the subject.

Beware that some dedicated flash-camera combinations allow for limited or no variance in selecting the shutter speed. Other systems balance the strobe and available light automatically. Again, check your manual.

High Speed Sync for Special Occasions

Many modern electronic 35mm cameras and flash units have a feature called "High Speed Sync," "FP sync" or similar term. This feature allows the flash to synchronize with the focal-plane shutter at shutter speeds faster than a typical sync speed.

This feature is useful for brightly lit outdoor fill-flash situations where you want to use a wide aperture.

When using the high-speed sync option, the flash delivers a series of light bursts that coincide with the shutter's curtain as it moves in front of the sensor. The feature works by synchronizing the flash to fire repeatedly. Despite the seemingly instantaneous nature of pressing the shutter, firing the flash, and taking the picture, different parts of the same photograph are thus exposed at different moments as the moving slit in the curtain exposes the image.

This technique is limited by the strobe's recycling time. Also, the faster shutter speeds will work only at wide apertures and close ranges.

DETERMINING APERTURE

Manufacturers build their strobes in different ways, so a brief check of your instruction book will indicate how to operate your unit. Some common principles apply.

MANUAL

You can use some built-in or external strobes on manual. On manual, they can be used at

---

DIRECT FLASH

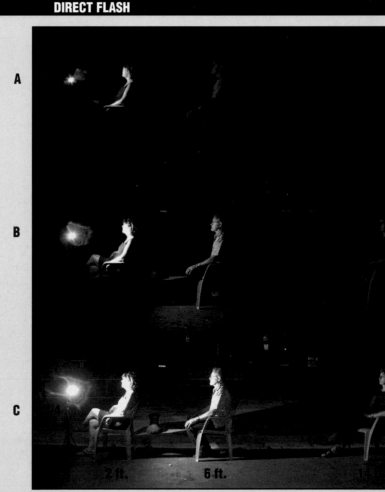

Light spreads out and decreases in brightness as it leaves the strobe. A subject near the strobe receives more light than someone farther away. In a situation where subjects are uneven distances from the flash, only one person can be properly exposed.

In these examples, exposing for the nearest person (A), who is two feet from the flash, requires stopping the lens aperture down to f/16. Because of the light fall-off, the two people who are farther away do not receive enough light and are underexposed.

Properly exposing the middle person (B), who is six feet from the flash, requires opening the lens two stops to f/8. This overexposes the first person, while the farthest person still receives too little light to be properly exposed.

In the bottom picture, the third person is positioned 14 feet from the strobe. For this person to receive enough light from the flash and be properly exposed (C), the lens aperture must be opened to f/4. The two people closer to the light source are overexposed in this frame.

Changing the brightness of the light on a subject requires changing the aperture on the camera, as in this example, or adjusting the strobe output with the compensation dial either on the strobe back or on the camera. Whichever method you use, remember: when subjects are at different distances from the strobe, only one person will receive the correct amount of light for proper exposure. (See page 187 for more on uneven lighting.)

full power, half power, quarter power, etc., or by changing the f/stop (see page 185).

For some external strobes, determine the aperture by measuring the distance from the flash to your subject, and then checking the distance scale on your strobe. Watch out. Some dials are marked in both meters and feet. Also, be careful to set the dial or read the scale for the ISO you are using.

Luckily, you can check your results on a digital camera's LCD screen and then immediately modify your exposure based on whether you think the picture is too light or dark.

THROUGH-THE-LENS METERING (TTL)

With dedicated camera-strobe systems, the flash sensor is located in the body of the camera. You can select almost any lens aperture since the sensor is located behind the lens. Tripping the shutter causes the flash to emit a pre-flash. The light returns through the aperture and strikes the camera's light meter. It calculates the correct exposure taking into consideration the f/stop, shutter speed, and the available light with certain settings. Regardless of where the flash is pointing, the internal light meter puts out the correct

amount of light for a well-exposed image almost all the time. Some strobes measure light reflected off the subject and compare this information with the subject's distance from the camera. If the reading is wildly off the mark when compared with the distance to the subject, the camera will use its preprogrammed distance exposure instead. If, for example, the subject is only a few feet away but is wearing black, the auto sensor on a standard strobe would mistakenly direct the strobe to put out a lot of light, thereby overexposing the picture. With the advanced metering systems on many cameras, the camera recognizes that, at this close distance, the light needed is much less than the reflected-light reading is reporting. The strobe, instead, would deliver the amount of light for a correct exposure at the close distance. The sensor will not be fooled by a subject's extremely light or dark clothing, or even the person's position outside the center of the viewfinder.

Many photographers find that dedicated flashes are consistently too bright or too dark, points out John Burgess of the *Santa Rosa Press Democrat*. With direct flash, he says, "My Nikons need to be powered down 2/3 of a stop for a good look; the Canons are more

With two pitchers from the College of St. Scholastica in silhouette, the photographer lit the third with a strobe coming through a softbox placed to the side and out of camera range. The photographer sought a layered look in this portrait by positioning the athletes on different planes.

Josh Meltzer, *The Roanoke Times*

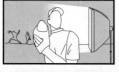

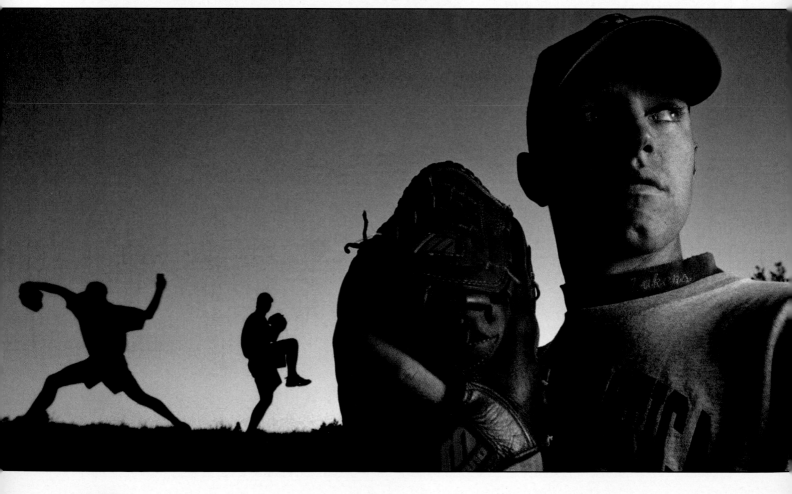

consistent." Bounce flash, on the other hand, often requires boosting the flash output by using its +/- compensation feature. Conduct your own tests to find the look you prefer.

HISTOGRAM

The good news is that you can easily check your exposure with the camera's own histogram. (Also see Chapter 8, "Camera Bag," pages 156–158.) The histogram is the most accurate way to determine whether an exposure is correct since it uses the data from the actual captured file. The good news is that if the histogram indicates you have detail in the highlights and shadows, you can rest assured that picture is exposed correctly with enough detail to extract a perfect digital image. Of course, you need to check the histogram against the image on the LCD screen to see if you are getting the effect you wanted.

PROBLEMS TO AVOID WITH DIRECT STROBE
UNEVEN LIGHTING

A fundamental principle that applies to all light is that it spreads out as it gets farther from its source. A subject nearer the light source receives more light than one farther away. The technical term for this is called the inverse square law. If one subject is five feet from the flash and another is ten feet away, the second person will only receive one-quarter the amount of strobe light as the first.

What does this mean for the photographer? When using direct strobe, if the front subject is correctly exposed, the second person will come out two stops underexposed (see page 185).

Photographers using flash have found three ways around this problem. One is to use bounce flash (see pages 188–192) so that the light is redirected to a larger surface, where it will spread, bounce back, and cover a much broader area evenly. Another is to combine the available light with the flash (see pages 182–183). A third is to use the flash off-camera and positioned so that it is equidistant from each subject.

SHADOW ON THE WALL

A strobe mounted on the top or side of a camera produces a direct light aimed at the subject. At night, outside, or in a big gymnasium, direct strobe-on-camera works satisfactorily. However, direct strobe-on-camera creates a harsh shadow behind a subject in a normal-sized, light-colored room.

If you cannot avoid using direct strobe by bouncing (see pages 188–192), you can eliminate the lurking black shadow by positioning the subject in front of a dark wall if

possible. Now the black shadow created by the strobe will blend somewhat with the dark wall and be less prominent. Or move the subject away from the wall. If you and the subject move away from the wall, keeping the same distance between the two of you, the subject will receive the same amount of light, but the wall behind will get less. The wall will darken and the obtrusive shadow will merge with the darkened wall and disappear.

Another way to eliminate unwanted shadows is to move the subject in front of a light source such as a window. The shadow will disappear into the light.

REFLECTIONS

If you face someone wearing glasses to take a picture using strobe, often you will get an annoying bright reflection off the subject's lenses. To avoid reflections of eyeglasses, or even polished metal or glass, position the strobe at an angle to the reflective surface.

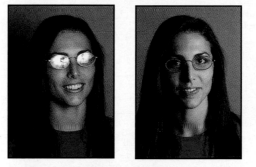

Reflections will disappear if the strobe is positioned to the side, at an angle to the glass.

INCOMPLETE COVERAGE AREA

Some strobes have automatic zoom heads that allow you to adjust the area the light covers to match the lens on the camera. These units change the light pattern to coincide with the views of a range of lenses, usually from about 16mm to 105mm.

Most strobes, though, are designed to light an area no wider than a 35mm lens. When you use a wider lens, you need to spread the light out farther. For telephoto lenses, it helps to focus the light on a more narrow area.

Therefore, some strobes have attachments that will spread the light so the scene will be evenly illuminated (down to 20mm-lens coverage), or focus the light so that it will project farther. Many camera-strobe combinations automatically sense the focal length of the lens and adjust the strobe output accordingly.

CREATING DIFFERENT EFFECTS
FILL-FLASH HANDLES HEAVY SHADOWS

At noon on a sunny day, the sun's harsh light can leave some subjects buried in shadow while others scorch in the sunlight.

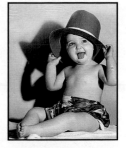

With direct strobe, avoid harsh shadows on the wall like those behind the baby, above, by moving the subject away from the wall, or placing the subject in front of a dark curtain.

Shadowed eye sockets on faces turn into raccoon-like masks. Fill-flash to the rescue. Light from the strobe opens the shadow areas of subjects who are within 10 or 15 feet of the strobe without overpowering the highlights.

If important shadow areas meter more than one or two stops darker than highlight areas, adding fill light will probably improve your picture. For fill flash using the camera's built-in flash or an external strobe aim the flash directly at the subject or into an umbrella or other reflective device.

Many portable and built-in strobes have a fill-flash setting that automatically balances the available and strobe light. In fact, some strobes allow you to dial in just the amount of fill-flash you might want to use. You can also change the "flash compensation" in many cameras and thereby control the strength of the fill light. You can adjust the fill yourself to put out one to three stops less than the available light.

It's easy enough to check your exposures on the camera's LCD screen. Try some trial shots to see how much fill the situation requires. Ideally, the fill flash should lighten but not eliminate shadows. If the flash is too strong, it will wipe out all shadows and give the picture an artificial, 1950s look.

BOUNCE STROBE FOR SOFTER LIGHT

To avoid the harsh effects of direct strobe, a photographer can bounce the strobe's light off a room's ceiling, walls, or any other light-colored surface.

The *Canton Repository*'s Scott Heckel accompanied the girls' high school swim team to witness the first time their male counterparts shaved their legs for an upcoming swim meet. Because the locker room was too dark for shooting with available light, the photographer needed the extra light provided by a strobe. Heckel stayed outside the shower to watch for a girl's reaction (see page 190).

Direct strobe on camera would have correctly lit the girl in the foreground but not the boys in the background. So Heckel bounced the light from his strobe off the ceiling, which evenly illuminated the entire scene.

Light from a strobe comes out in a bundle of rays the size of the strobe face—about three inches in diameter, depending on the size of the flash. The rays spread out as they head toward the ceiling. By the time they reach a typical ceiling, the rays cover an area about ten feet across. Because the surface of the ceiling is rough, the rays bounce off it in all directions, evenly lighting a much larger area below and leaving few shadows.

Bounce light has at least two advantages over direct strobe. Bounce light eliminates unattractive shadows, and it helps light a group of people evenly, removing the danger of burning out those in front or letting those in back go dark.

Not only can you bounce the strobe light from an external flash off the ceiling, but you can also bounce light off a wall, partition, or

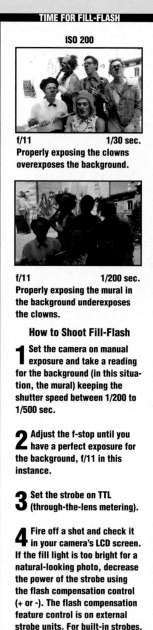

FILL-FLASH: CONTROLLING BRIGHTNESS EXTREMES

Situations of high contrast—where the background is brightly lit or includes the sky and the foreground is in shadow—are difficult to capture as we see them with our eyes. You can use flash to fill in the shadows.

TIME FOR FILL-FLASH

ISO 200

f/11   **1/30 sec.**
Properly exposing the clowns overexposes the background.

f/11   **1/200 sec.**
Properly exposing the mural in the background underexposes the clowns.

How to Shoot Fill-Flash

1 Set the camera on manual exposure and take a reading for the background (in this situation, the mural) keeping the shutter speed between 1/200 to 1/500 sec.

2 Adjust the f-stop until you have a perfect exposure for the background, f/11 in this instance.

3 Set the strobe on TTL (through-the-lens metering).

4 Fire off a shot and check it in your camera's LCD screen. If the fill light is too bright for a natural-looking photo, decrease the power of the strobe using the flash compensation control (+ or -). The flash compensation feature control is on external strobe units. For built-in strobes, the control is in the camera.

Shutter speed 1/200   ISO 200   f-stop f/11
Flash on TTL
The background mural should remain at relatively the same brightness for all the pictures. The foreground will change as more or less flash is added.

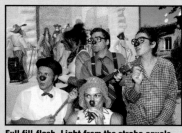
Full fill-flash. Light from the strobe equals that of the natural light on the background.

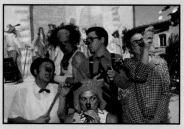
Flash reduced by one stop. Dial -1.

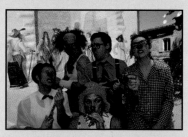
Flash reduced by two stops. Dial -2. Most natural in this example.

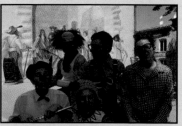
Flash reduced by three stops. Dial -3.

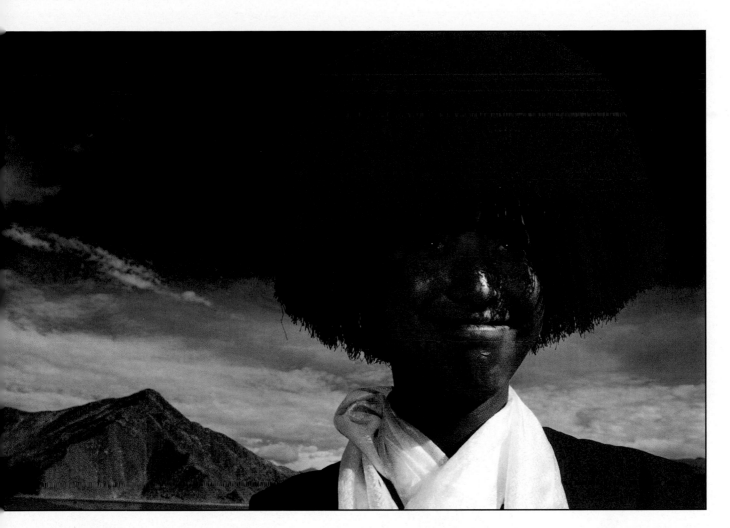

Without fill-flash adding light to the Tibetan horseman's face, the subject would be lost in a shadow from his hat. John Kaplan, Gainesville, Florida

any other large, opaque object. Light bounced off the ceiling results in a soft, relatively shadowless effect similar to that produced by fluorescent tubes found in most modern buildings. Light bounced off a wall or partition gives a more directional effect, such as light from a window. The directional effect becomes more prominent the closer the subject and the flash are to the wall.

In a pinch, you can achieve the same effect with a built-in flash by using Professor Kobré's Lightscoop (see page 194), although the built-in flash will not be an adequate solution for all lighting situations.

Because light leaving the strobe spreads out and is partially absorbed by the wall where it is aimed, you generally need to use wide apertures such as f/2.8 or f/4, and higher ISOs like 400 or 800, for an effective bounce. John Burgess offers this tip, "I typically zoom the head of my strobe to its highest setting when bouncing so I get a little more light falling back." Check your histogram and LCD screen to make sure you are getting a correct exposure.

When bouncing an external strobe, many photographers attach a small white card behind and up several inches from the top of the strobe head. The card picks up a little light when the strobe goes off and reflects the light into the subject's eye sockets. This reflected light avoids the raccoon look that often occurs with bounced light when the subject is near the camera. This kicker also will add a small "catchlight" to the subject's eyes.

When photographing a child lighting candles for Hanukkah, this author could have taken the picture by the available light from the candles. He knew, however, that the candles in relation to the boy's face were so bright that they would wash out in the final image. The rest of the picture would fall into deep shadow. Bouncing a strobe's light off a nearby wall gave the impression that the light was coming from the candles. The effect leaves both the candles and the boy in sharp relief (see page 191).

Rather than bouncing the strobe off a wall, photographers often find they have more control by bouncing the light off the inside of a white or silver-lined umbrella. They attach the portable strobe to a light stand with a special clamp, and with the same clamp, attach

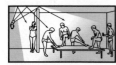

A female swimmer reacts after entering the boys' locker room to see the team shaving their bodies in preparation for the district meet. The photographer bounced the strobe off the ceiling to increase the overall illumination in the locker room and freeze movements by the subjects. Notice how the light from the bounce strobe falls off toward the back of the shower. There, the subjects are lit only by the available ceiling light.
Scott Heckel, *Canton* [Ohio] *Repository*

the umbrella to the light stand. The umbrella-strobe combination situated on a light stand is easy to move around and position. The strobe is pointed toward the inside of the white or silver-lined umbrella. You also can hard-wire the strobe to the camera with a cable, fire it with a radio slave or external infrared trigger, or, in some instances, use the camera's own on-board flash to trigger it.

In any of these cases, tripping the camera's shutter release fires the strobe, causing its light to strike the inside of the umbrella and bounce outward in a widening pattern. The light striking the subject emulates the soft light from a north window. The demarcation between shadow and highlight on the subject is gradual as opposed to the abrupt line produced from a direct strobe. The shadow on the background becomes less distinct (see page 199).

Placing the umbrella and strobe to the side of the subject will create a dramatic side-lit portrait, whereas positioning it directly in front will create a flatter light

that, for example, de-emphasizes the wrinkles in someone's face.

For optimum softness, whether positioned on the side or in front, keep the umbrella as close as possible to your subject. The closer the umbrella, the fewer shadows the light will produce. When close enough, the umbrella light almost seems to wrap around the subject. Remember, of course, to keep the light stand out of the picture.

For a soft effect offering even more control, photographers sometimes use what's called a "soft box." The box consists of nylon fabric held together with tension rods. The box contains several layers of diffusion material inside the white translucent window. The strobe is mounted inside the box facing the translucent window. The setup is mounted on a sturdy stand. You can trigger the strobe with either a PC cord hard-wired between the camera and strobe or an infrared trigger on the camera and a "slave" on the strobe. You can also use a radio and receiver combination like the PocketWizard.

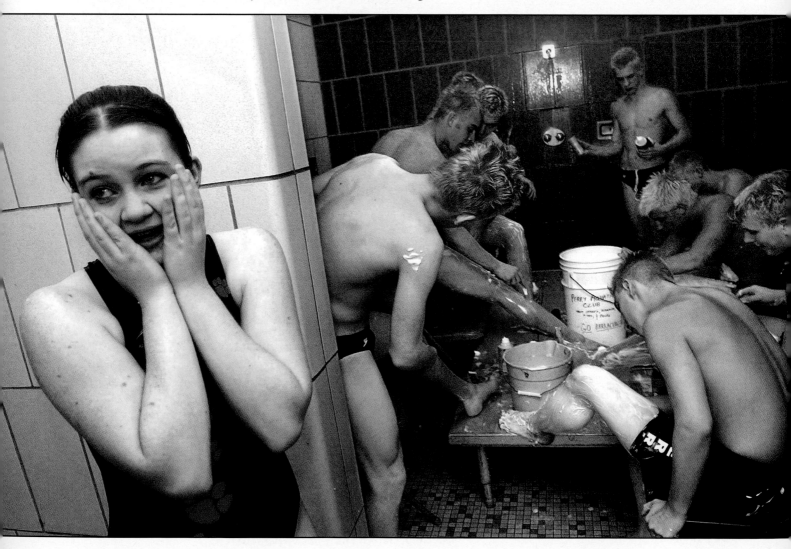

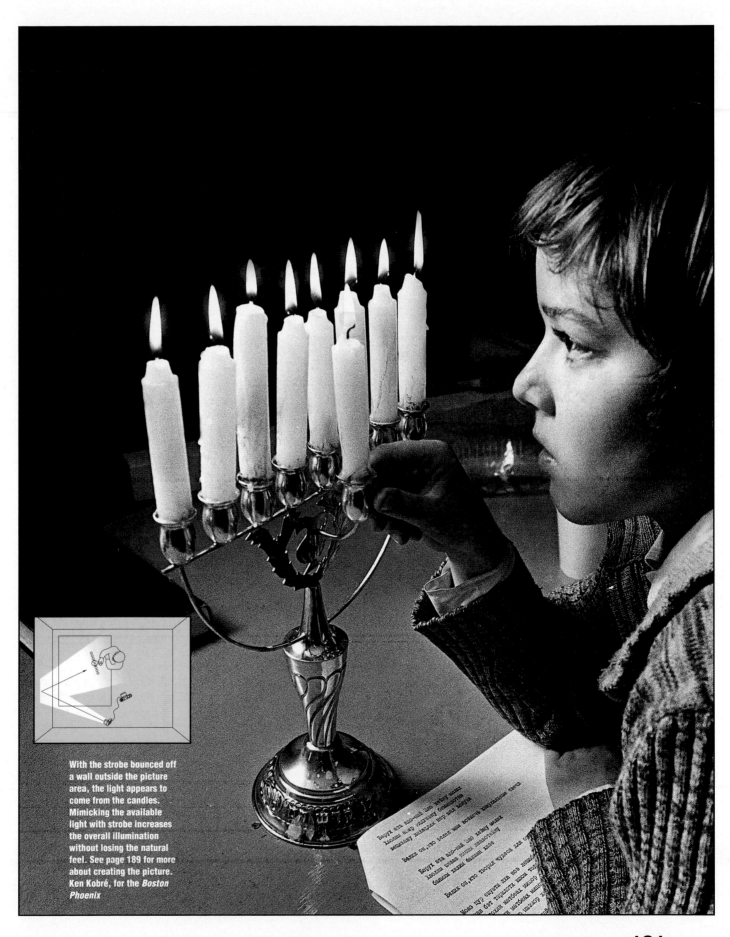

With the strobe bounced off a wall outside the picture area, the light appears to come from the candles. Mimicking the available light with strobe increases the overall illumination without losing the natural feel. See page 189 for more about creating the picture. Ken Kobré, for the *Boston Phoenix*

Attach the sender to the camera and the receiver to the strobe. The soft box gives light an effect similar to that produced by the umbrella, but allows the photographer to control fall-off at the edges of the light source more precisely.

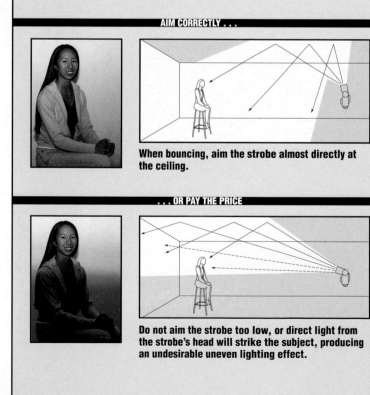
"I like soft-box light better than umbrellas," says Peter Menzel, the globetrotting photographer whose books include *Material World: A Global Family Portrait* and *Hungry Planet: What the World Eats*, "because I like to have the light as close as possible to the subject. The soft box gives a softer, more even light in these situations."

OFF-CAMERA LIGHTING FOR BOLD EFFECT

Sometimes side lighting with direct strobe can add drama to a picture. To achieve this effect, remove the flash from the top of the camera. Attach the flash to the camera with a PC-extension cord or other remote-triggering device (see pages 196, 198, and 200). Aim the flash so the light hits the side rather than the front of the subject. Moving the flash away from the camera will dramatically change the picture's light. (Also see pages 180, 186, 194, 195, 200, and 201 for pictures taken with strobe off-camera.)

For a complete exploration of off-camera use of portable strobes, visit *The Strobist: www.strobist.blogspot.com*. Created by *Baltimore Sun* photographer David Hobby, this blog and the discussions and links it has spawned provide a gold mine of information for photographers of all levels of expertise.

EXPLOITING THE BUILT-IN STROBE

Many mid-price-range SLR cameras come with a built-in, pop-up flash. These built-in flashes work in the same manner as the larger external dedicated flash units but are limited by their size, placement on top of the camera, and the strength of their output. While no substitute for a full-featured dedicated strobe, these little flashes can be used effectively for direct flash, fill flash (see page 188), and with Professor Kobré's Lightscoop (see page 194) for indoor bounce in some situations. Do be aware of built-in flash's limitations so as to avoid problems:

- Direct pop-up flash will not throw enough light at a subject at some distance from the camera.
- Direct pop-up flash used with wide-barreled or long lenses will cast an unsightly shadow in the bottom of horizontal direct-flash pictures or on the side of vertical pictures (beware in fill-flash situations, too). This combination can also produce red eye, the demon-like red color in the pupils of the eye caused by light directly reflecting off the subject's artery-rich retina.
- Direct pop-up flash emits light from the top of the camera. This is an unnatural place for light to come from since most indoor scenes are lit by a ceiling fixture or window light.

FRONT-LIGHTING
When the main light is placed near the camera, the face looks flatter and skin texture disappears.

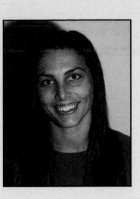

HIGH 45° LIGHTING
With the main light high and to the side of the camera, about 45°, shadows model the face, creating a more rounded shape. This is often the main light position used in commercial portrait studios.

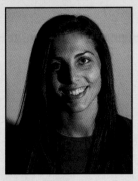

SIDE-LIGHTING
A main light that is at about a 90° angle to the camera will light the subject brightly on one side and cast long shadows across the other side.

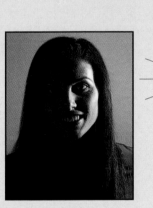

BACK-LIGHTING
Here the light is moved almost to the back of the subject. If the light were directly behind the person, her entire face would fall into shadow.

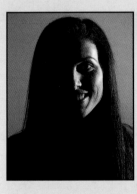

TOP-LIGHTING
The light is directly overhead and is casting dark shadows into the eye sockets and under the nose and chin. Few portrait subjects would pick this lighting arrangement.

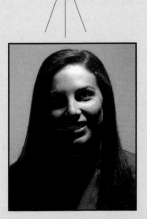

BOTTOM-LIGHTING
Lighting that comes from below looks distinctly odd in a portrait. This is because light on people outdoors or indoors almost never comes from below. This type of light casts unnatural shadows that often create a menacing effect.

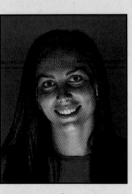

Photos by Paolo Vescia

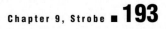

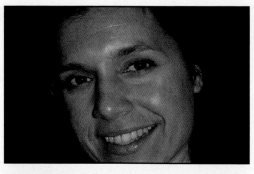

Direct pop-up flash is harsh and unflattering.

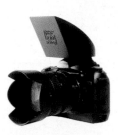

Professor Kobré's Lightscoop redirects light from a pop-up flash to bounce it off a ceiling or wall. www.lightscoop.com

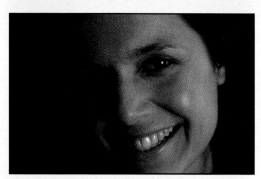

Pop-up flash bounced off a wall with Professor Kobré's Lightscoop emulates window light. A wall bounce with an external flash also improves portraits by redirecting and softening the light.

The addition of Professor Kobré's Lightscoop overcomes most of these limitations indoors by redirecting the pop-up flash to bounce off a ceiling or wall for a more natural, less "deer-caught-in-the-headlights" look. While it can also be a valuable supplemental tool for those occasions when an external flash is not functioning properly or its batteries have run low, it is not a replacement for a professional's external strobe system.

POWERING THE STROBE
BUILT-IN CAMERA STROBES

Pop-up strobes built into cameras draw on the camera's battery power. This setup is convenient but carries one danger. Using flash drains the battery more quickly than when shooting pictures in available light. A spare, recharged battery will avoid the problem of running out of battery juice at the moment you need it.

SHOE-MOUNT STROBES

Most shoe-mount strobes are powered by AA batteries. Lithium batteries last the longest but are the most expensive. Alkaline and nickel-cadmium batteries (NiCads) are easily available, but rechargeable batteries are cheaper over the long haul.

Rechargeable NiCads, which store the least amount of juice, do provide a consistent recycle time before they completely and suddenly lose their charges. Lithium and

Alkaline batteries, on the other hand, run down gradually, resulting in excessively long recycle times as they wear out. Always carry backup batteries. Nothing is more frustrating than waiting eons for dying batteries to recycle the strobe. While lithium, alkaline, and NiCad batteries designed for shoe-mounted strobes are convenient, none provides enough power for more than 100 exposures when the flash is used at full power.

MEDIUM-POWERED STROBES

The typical battery-powered strobe most photographers use has a maximum output of 50 watt-seconds of light. When working at a low ISO for high-resolution images with maximum detail, many photographers have turned to more powerful portable strobes like the Lumedyne, Norman, Broncolor, or Comet Power Pack that can generate anywhere from 200 to 1200 watt-seconds. Although heavier and more costly, these strobes provide the needed power for using umbrellas or soft boxes to produce finely detailed high-resolution images at low ISO ratings. With some of these medium-powered portable strobes, you can add on batteries for more power.

AC-POWERED STROBES

With most AC-powered strobes, a modeling light is built into the strobe head. This allows you to see where the light will fall without anxiety, or even a lot of test shots. AC-powered strobes come with tremendous light output—important when working at a low ISO.

Also, large-format cameras like the 4"x5" or 8"x10" view camera need this quantity of light for maximum depth of field. Much of the photography shot in studios requires high-output power supplies. You can buy an AC-powered strobe with 500, 1000, 2400, 4800 or more watt-seconds of light. These AC-powered units also can drive two or more strobe heads at the same time.

Many photographers regularly haul medium-sized AC units like the Dyna-Lite, Novatron, or Speedotron on assignment. These allow shooting at small apertures and provide fast, dependable recycling. High-wattage strobes with modeling lights allow photographers to light a room and see where all the shadows will fall.

While these strobes usually have more power than a portable unit, they also require AC power and are consequently less convenient than their smaller counterparts. AC units always operate on manual, so a handheld strobe meter is helpful to determine exposure although you can also confirm the quality of the exposure using the histogram in your camera.

When shooting outdoors, remember to bring along either a long extension cord or a portable generator. The strobes' fast recycling, practically limitless number of flashes, and powerful light output make them ideal for multiple-light photography.

MULTIPLE STROBES

Shooting at a low ISO requires lots of light. Suppose you are shooting a corporate president inside his high-rise office and wish to include the sun-drenched view outside his window. The eye has no trouble seeing both the wrinkles on the president's face and the sparkling bay outside. But this brightness range is probably beyond the capability of the digital camera even when shooting on RAW (see pages 158–159). You may need to set up several lights to bring the two worlds into brightness balance.

Sometimes you may simply want more control of a scene than the light from one strobe can provide. You want to produce a special effect. Perhaps you seek to add a highlight to someone's hair, or you want to feature one member of a group more than the rest, or you want to use a light on either side of a dancer to emphasize the person's form.

Multilight Setups

While you will find no two lighting situations identical, you often can use a basic lighting combination for shooting portraits: set up a main light and reflect it into an umbrella or through a soft box. Set the light about 45

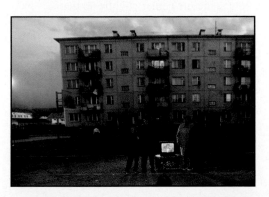

This Mongolian family had lost their home and had to move into a rented room in a concrete block apartment building. The only item they had purchased for themselves in the previous eight years had been a color television set. The photographer made a 250-foot extension cord to power the television from their apartment and also set up Dyna-Lite strobes in their apartment window, which he triggered with a radio slave. He created a strong backlight and sidelight with two additional strobe heads powered by a portable Lumadyne battery pack.
Peter Menzel
Material World: A Global Family Portrait

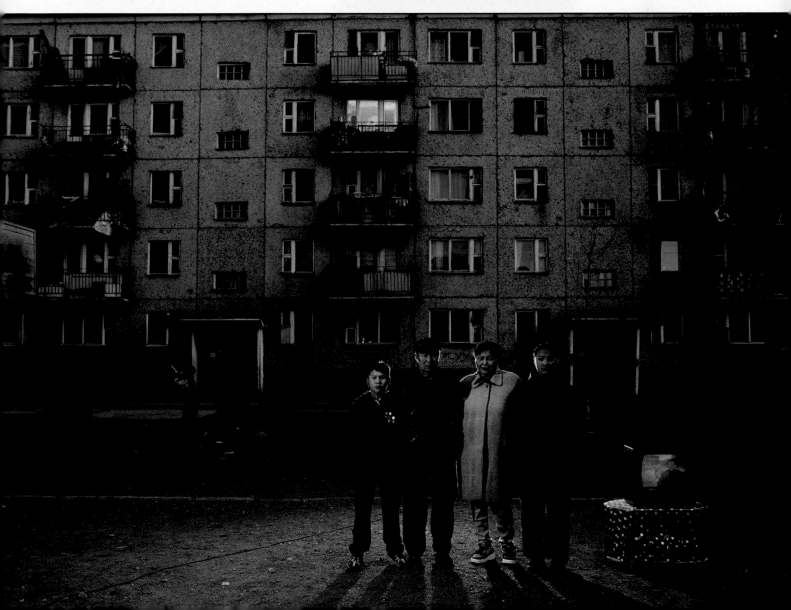

degrees to one side of the camera. Bring the light as near as possible to the subject while still evenly lighting the person. This is your main light. Next, use a large reflector card to bounce light into the shadow side of the subject's face. Attach a second strobe to a boom, a weighted arm that extends over the subject's head. Locate the strobe above and behind the subject to provide a hair light. If you do not have a boom, you can achieve a hair-light effect by placing a strobe high on a light stand off-center slightly so that it is out of the frame. Direct a third light toward the background. (See opposite page, bottom left, for a multilight setup using strobes positioned inside softboxes.)

Setting up multiple lights can result in time delays as well as accidents caused by cords running from the wall to the power supply and to the strobes. To eliminate the need for long cords between your camera and strobes, use a radio transmitter and receiver or infrared "slave." Attach the slave or radio receiver to your strobes. Put the infrared trigger or radio transmitter on your camera. Pressing the

camera's shutter release will activate the transmitter and send a signal to your strobes. The receiver on the strobes (infrared or radio wave) will pick up the signal and fire all the strobes simultaneously at the exact moment that your camera's shutter is open.

The infrared sender-and-receiver system basically works like a garage door opener setup. To function properly, it needs line-of-sight between the sender and receiver. Also, when using an infrared system, your strobes will fire if any flash in the area goes off. The infrared system does not work well at public events where numerous photographers and spectators might be using strobes.

A radio transmitter-receiver does not need a direct view between the sender and receiver. You can dial radio transmitters and receivers to different channels to avoid interference from other photographers.

Integrated Camera-Strobe Wireless Systems
Several camera manufacturers sell a line of portable strobes that include a built-in infrared sensor receiver in the strobe. Some

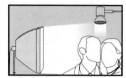

For this portrait the photographer positioned a softbox near and to the left of the couple as well as a hair light from a grid spot positioned above the duo. The grid spot is an adapter placed over the strobe head that softens and directs the light.

© Ken Kobré

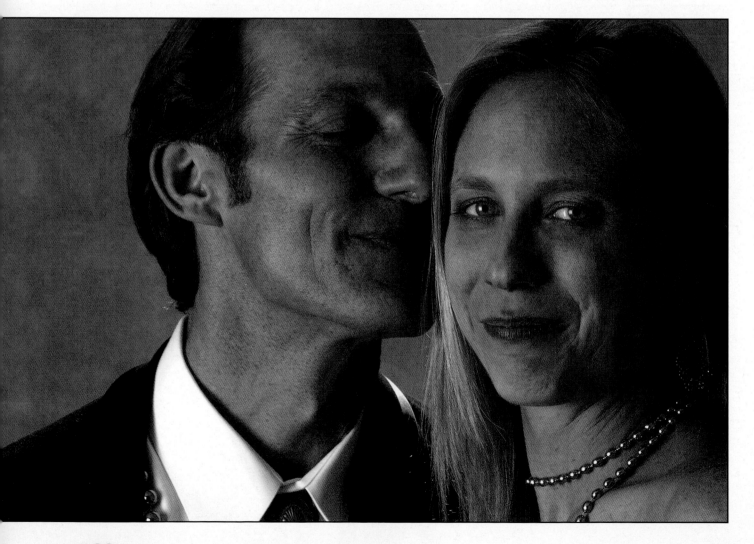

When a wall or ceiling is not available for bouncing the strobe light, photographers use a number of other techniques and devices to attempt to soften the light and reduce shadows. Umbrellas and softboxes take the concentrated bundle of light coming from the strobe's face and broaden it before the light heads toward the subject. The broader the light source, the softer the effect. (See comparisons on page 199.)

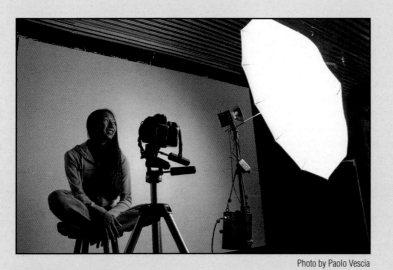

Photo by Paolo Vescia

UMBRELLA

Because direct-strobe light comes from a small light source, it produces a harsh effect. Light bounced off the ceiling is soft but produces somewhat featureless pictures. Many photographers use photographic umbrellas as softening alternatives that provide more control over position and direction of the light.

The photographic umbrella is similar to a standard rain umbrella, only the inside is covered with a white or silver material, and the handle can easily be attached to a light stand. When the photographer aims the strobe into the center of the umbrella, out comes a soft white blanket of light that wraps around the subject. Because the umbrella is on a light stand, the photographer can move it easily from side to side or up and down—allowing for total control of the light's direction. The nearer the light is to the subject, the more the rays will encircle the person. The shadows will be softer and more pleasing looking.

SOFT BOX

The strobe is attached inside a lightweight nylon box that contains diffusion panels to evenly spread the light. The result is a window-like light that is portable. Compared to reflecting light off an umbrella, the soft box gives more even light with a defined edge. In the setup below, A is the main light, B is the fill light, and C is the hair light.

Deborah Whitney Prince

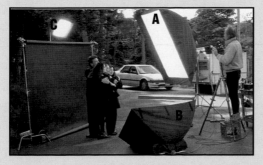

LITTLE EFFECT FROM SMALL DIFFUSERS

Small devices placed over the strobe can increase the effective light area somewhat. Some attempt to combine the characteristics of direct and bounce light. The indirect light bouncing off the ceilings and walls is supposed to help soften the direct light coming straight from the strobe. Other devices are supposed to enlarge the effective light source by reflecting light off an angled hood to scatter the rays so that they will bounce off nearby surfaces and further soften the light on the subject.

However, if you look at the comparisons on page 199, you will see that small diffusers are not at all effective outdoors. The outdoor shots were done at night to eliminate the impact of ambient light 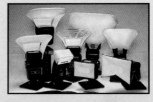 and thus show solely the effect of the strobe and the impact of the accessory. Thus, in cavernous areas such as gyms, churches, or ballrooms with tall ceilings without nearby bounce surfaces, the devices cannot improve light.

Indoors, the small diffusers typically are about as effective as bouncing the light off a ceiling or wall.

Generally, diffusers work best not in softening light but in broadening it. Light from a direct strobe aimed at a subject often does not spread evenly enough to cover an area taken in with a wide-angle lens. Diffusers help spread the light so that when you take a picture with a wide-angle lens the light will be even from corner to corner.

Small diffusers will give satisfactory results when the ceiling is low and walls are near, but keep in mind that in the same circumstances, you could just as easily bounce the light off a ceiling or wall with no accessory at all.

cameras employ a master flash or even the built-in pop-up flash to trigger the remote strobes. Others require attaching an infrared transmitter trigger to the camera in order to fire the remote flash. Check to see if your camera and strobe have the wireless-strobe feature.

Using the flash with the integrated trigger (pop-up or external) or an external "master flash" allows the photographer to control the relative power of all the flashes from the camera. Menu settings on the camera or master flash allow adjusting the power output of all the other strobes on the system. Of course, the strobes and the camera must be set to the same channel. Pressing the shutter release fires all the flashes at the same time.

This system allows you to place the remote strobes on light stands, position them with mini-clamps, or just set them on a convenient bookshelf or the floor. Their location

will depend on the effect you want to achieve. They do need to be located within a short distance and in line of sight of the trigger on the camera. The infrared trigger and slave combination sometimes performs inconsistently in bright sunlight. In these situations the more expensive radio transmitter and receiver, mentioned previously, work more reliably.

This easy-to-use wireless setup allows photographers to produce sophisticated lighting with just one camera and two external dedicated flashes. The freedom to place strobes anywhere in a room and trigger them without connecting cords provides a wealth of possibilities for improved lighting. You might want to place a strobe behind the subject to light up the background or eliminate a shadow. Position a strobe to the side of the subject to produce a more dramatic side, rim, or hair light. You can also bounce the

GET CLOSE FOR SOFT LIGHT

Bringing the flash close to the subject produces soft light—a fact that runs counter to many people's notions about using flash. This is the case regardless of whether the flash is bounced, shot through a soft box, or even used direct. The closer the light to your subject the more it creates a wrap-around effect, which softens the light and helps decrease harsh shadows.

Bring the light source as close as possible to your main subject without getting the strobe itself in the picture.

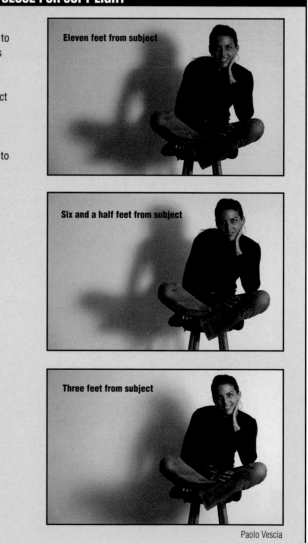

Eleven feet from subject

Six and a half feet from subject

Three feet from subject

Paolo Vescia

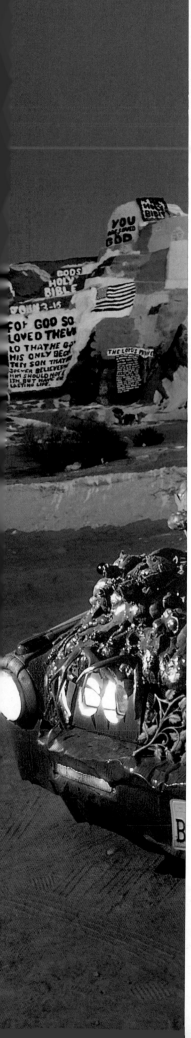

COMPARING THE EFFECTS OF STROBE ACCESSORIES: A TEST

	Indoors	Indoors	Outdoors at Night no reflective surfaces

Because the harshest light comes from a camera-mounted strobe, photographers use different accessories to soften the light and reduce dark shadows behind the subject.

The tests to the right compare some of these accessories in controlled settings. The off-camera strobe was located nine feet from the subject.

In a light-colored room, some light bounces off the ceiling, walls, and floor. This extra, scattered light helps soften the shadows when strobe accessories are used indoors.

The outdoors series was shot at night to emulate the effect of a large ballroom or gymnasium with few secondary bounce surfaces. These show strictly the effect of the strobe and the effectiveness of the accessory.

Outdoors at night, of course, there are no walls or ceilings, so all the accessories work less well at softening shadows. The scattered light rays coming from the accessories have few surfaces from which they can bounce. Notice, in the outdoor series, that the shadow behind the model is darker in almost each situation.

Bouncing a strobe off a ceiling creates a wide spot on the ceiling that is a much larger effective light source than the strobe face. The bounced light fills in shadow areas.

Because a large light source produces the softest light, light from a 3'x4' soft box is softer than the light direct from a tiny 2"x3" strobe face.

Photographic umbrellas, whether you are reflecting off them or shooting through them, provide a relatively large light source, depending on their size.

Although smaller devices such as the Omnidome, Lumiquest Bouncers, and Fong Diffusers are not as effective as the larger light sources, many of the smaller items work well indoors—but are they any more effective than a ceiling bounce?

Outdoors at night, with no secondary bounce surfaces, only the larger accessories (like the umbrella and softbox) and the larger effective light sources they create can do much to soften the shadows.

DIRECT

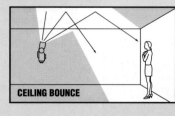 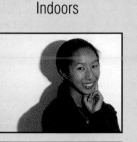 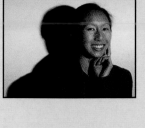

CEILING BOUNCE

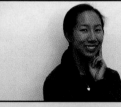

NO CEILING
OUTDOORS

FONG DIFFUSER

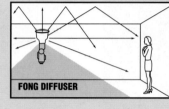 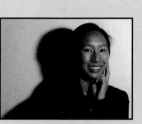

LUMIQUEST

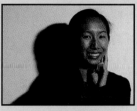

OMNIDOME

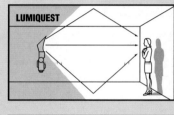 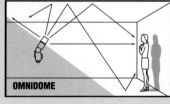 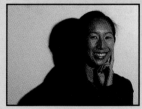

THROUGH A SOFT BOX

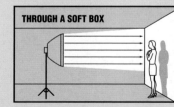 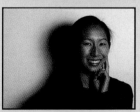

OFF AN UMBRELLA

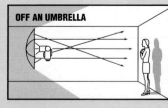 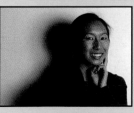

THROUGH AN UMBRELLA

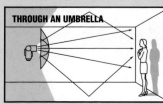 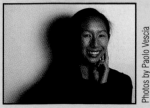

Photos by Paolo Vescia

The photographer was
assigned to illustrate a st[...]
about six athletes and ho[...]
they represented the trad[...]
tional six basic elements [...]
the world: fire, water, wo[...]
wind, metal, and earth. F[...]
the soccer star, the shoot[...]
placed a mattress about 2[...]
yards in front of the fire p[...]
at a fire academy training
facility. Above the mattre[...]
and high on a boom, he se[...]
up a large soft box. Once [...]
fire was ignited, he shot
with a medium-length lens
to compress the apparent
distance between the
flames and athlete. As a
friend fed balls to the athlete, the photographer
tripped the shutter. The
strobe light coming throug[...]
the softbox bathed the sub[...]
ject in an even, overhead
light that contrasted nicel[...]
with the raging fire in the
background.
Rob Mattson,
Sarasota Herald-Tribune

Girls brave a sandstorm in Bahai, Chad, roughly seven kilometers from the Sudan border. Thousands of Sudanese refugees have fled to Chad from persistent fighting in their country. © Lynsey Addario

A link to this piece and other online stories can be found at
http://kenkobre.blogspot.com/2007/10/multimedia.html

10

Covering the Issues

Photojournalism can bring about change. Since the turn of the century, on every continent on the globe, concerned photographers have brought to public awareness issues ranging from hunger and poverty to repression and torture. In the early 20th century, Jacob Riis (see pages 422–425) exposed slum conditions suffered by new immigrants in New York City. Lewis Hine (see pages 423–425) sneaked into American factories to document industry's abusive use of children as laborers. During America's Great Depression, Dorothea Lange (see pages 439–440) recorded bread lines and crop failures for the Farm Security Administration (FSA).

photographers often turn to grants to help underwrite their projects. Alan Berner received a grant from the National Press Photographers Association and Nikon to explore the changing face of the West (see pages 222–223). John Kaplan's powerful story on torture in Africa (see pages 220–221) was largely self-funded, but he did receive help from a University of Florida summer research grant. Kristen Ashburn began her five-year project on the impact of AIDS on families in Africa on her own time but received a grant from Getty Images to complete the work (see page 319). This author received a Freedom Forum stipend to partially underwrite a project on children born to crack-addicted mothers (see pages 216–217). The Guggenheim, the Alexia Foundation, and Fifty Crows Foundation are among other grantmakers for photojournalists.

Other photographers have undertaken projects on their own time and dime. David Guralnick flew to Bucaramanga, Colombia, in South America, at his own expense, to photograph American plastic surgeons providing free medical help to children born with harelips and other disfigurements.

Without backing or assurance of publication, Ken Light photographed the Mississippi Delta region of the United States (see page 230).

Lou Dematteis, now with Redux picture agency, documented the long-term effects on the health of the local population in a region in Ecuador where ChevronTexaco left toxic waste after drilling for oil there. Although he started the project, "Crude Reflections: Oil in the Amazon," while on assignment for Reuters, he completed the essay with six self-financed return trips (see page 205).

Andrea Hoyer funded her own five-year project documenting the remnants of Stalinist Russia. In addition to shooting, Hoyer's project involved learning several languages while living in and traveling throughout the country (see page 465) .

Some photographers work alone. The *Boston Globe*'s Stan Grossfeld, a former winner of the Pulitzer Prize, shoots his own picture stories and often writes the accompanying text. Zed Nelson worked alone on his revealing essay "Gun Nation: A Journey into American Gun Culture" (see pages 226–227).

Of course, teams also come together to investigate big topics. See pages 212–218, "Developing a Feature Beat," for how one group developed a beat to tackle a large project. Although Gary Coronado and reporter Christine Evans worked alone on "Train Jumpers," about Central American immigrants hopping trains to reach the United States, production team develop the multimedia package. The story appeared online and in print (see pages 302–304).

Some photographers like collaborating with a writer. Rick Loomis of the *Los Angeles Times* worked closely with reporter David Zucchino on "Lifeline," which chronicles the extraordinary medical care involved in treating U.S. wounded in Iraq both in the field and back in the United States (see pages 298–301).

Photographer Michael Williamson worked with writer Dale Maharidge on book projects including ***Journey to Nowhere: The Saga of the New Underclass***, which documented the effects of lost U.S. jobs.

The photographer/writer team also coauthored ***The Last Great American Hobo***, about riding the rails in America. And the team produced a book called ***And Their Children After Them***, a follow-up to the famous book from the 1930s, ***Let Us Now Praise Famous Men***, which itself was a collaboration between a writer, James Agee, and Walker Evans, an FSA photographer.

While only a few documentary photojournalism projects wind up in bookstores, many are published as special sections or multipart series in newspapers, as a series of double-truck layouts in magazines, or as online slide shows.

Erin Lubin was documenting the impact of debilitating illness on the committed relationship between two lesbian partners, one of whom was dying of ALS, Lou Gehrig's disease (see page 219). The dying partner asked the photographer to collaborate on a book. Lubin's images accompany the dying woman's essays about illness and dying in ***Falling Practice: What Illness Teaches Us***.

While some newspapers and magazines make room for these projects, others won't give up the space for photo-driven stories.

Fortunately, the Internet is providing an excellent outlet for in-depth projects. Todd Heisler and Jim Sheeler of the *Rocky Mountain News* worked on "Final Salute" for a year following Marines whose sad duty is to accompany fallen comrades home to burial and to share the grief of their families (see pages 58 and 59). The story ran in the newspaper and on the news outlet's web site.

Lynsey Addario's images documenting elements of the Darfur crisis were published by national magazines but also can be found on the web at "Crisis Guide: Darfur," produced by *MediaStorm.org* for the Council on Foreign Relations (see page 202).

MediaStorm.org has published many of the issue-related stories featured in this book as multimedia pieces. Some, like ***Kingsley's***

Crossing, by Olivier Jobard (see pages 282–285), and **Black Market**, by Patrick Brown (see pages 278–279), have been published as books, as well.

Other photographers have shared their stories with the public by exhibiting in art galleries and even cafés.

As important as how photojournalists choose to work on and share their projects is how they identify the topics to pursue. Here is where their journalistic skills come in.

ISSUE REPORTING
NURSING HOMES: A CASE STUDY
Translating Numbers Into People

In California, investigators determined that over a three-year period, poor care in state nursing homes was a factor in 126 deaths.

The *San Jose Mercury News* decided to investigate the findings. Journalists discovered that "An aide shook a 74-year-old man in Long Beach so violently, an investigator said, that his brain was slammed against his skull 'like a clapper in a bell.'" Nurses diligently charted the progression of bedsores on an 81-year-old woman until there was "black stuff oozing from her body"—but failed to act to save her life.

Photographing Statistics

The paper's graphics editor assigned Judy Griesedieck to illustrate the series.

Problem one: The subjects of the story, the abused elderly, were dead and buried.

The solution: Photograph current treatment of the elderly in nursing homes.

Problem two: Nursing home owners and managers, aware of the stories the paper had already published, did not want a *Mercury News* photographer anywhere near their nursing homes.

The solution: Griesedieck started by calling 20 nursing homes. Only two said she could come in and look around. The paper's lawyer pointed out that while the homes were private property, she could enter and photograph with an invitation from one of the residents. She could photograph the person who invited her without being evicted by the management.

Gaining Access

To meet people in the homes, Griesedieck attended meetings of Bay Area Advocates of Nursing Home Reform. Most members were relatives of people in nursing homes and were happy to introduce the photographer to their mothers, fathers, wives, and husbands who were living with inadequate care. With invitations from people she met through the Advocates, Griesedieck began to shoot.

In one home, a daughter brought Griesedieck to see her mother. The older woman had bedsores because of neglect. In another, a patient would be in bed at 9:00 A.M. and still be there—undressed, unattended, with no outside stimulation— when the photographer left at 5:00 P.M.

But Griesedieck also found evidence of love and compassion at the nursing homes. The *Mercury News* photographer watched a

continued on page 212 ▶

Judy Griesedieck bypassed nursing home officials to develop relationships with families and doctors who allowed her to photograph the conditions of neglect in the nursing homes. She balanced her hard-hitting pictures of neglect with pictures showing love and care by staffers as well as by family.
Judy Griesedieck, for the *San Jose Mercury News*

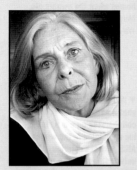

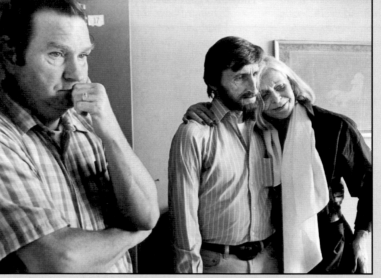

Annemarie Madison (FAR LEFT) is a volunteer hospice worker. (NEAR LEFT) Annemarie provides emotional support to the friends and relatives of Ernie, one of hundreds of "boys" to die of AIDS. (BELOW) She comforts Ernie during his dying moments.

These pictures are part of a story that was the product of a feature beat.

Sibylla Herbrich, from *Helpers in the War on AIDS*

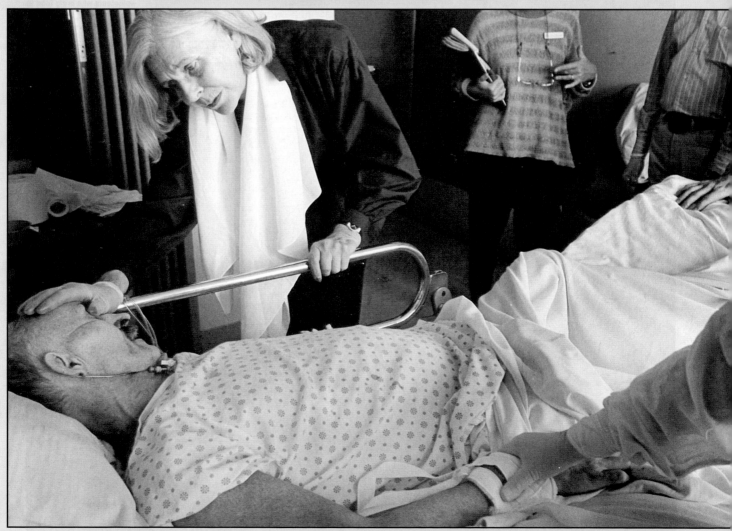

department—the seasoned police officer as well as the rookie fresh from the police academy. From these contacts and observations, beat reporters don't just react to the news; they also can interpret and anticipate it.

If the police go on strike, they can explain why. If a cop dies in the line of duty, they can write a story based on personal knowledge of the officer.

Feature photographers—whether they work on the staff of a news outlet or work independently as freelancers—can also cover a beat. Rather than choosing the police, hospital, or courts, they might select education, science, medicine, or religion.

As a freelance photographer with Sipa picture agency, Olivier Jobard had shot a series of assignments for stories about the desperate plight of African immigrants arriving in France and Spain. Immigration, in effect, became his beat. His past stories on and increasing knowledge of the topic yielded contacts in Cameroon, where he met 23-year-old Kingsley. Jobard followed the young African as he crossed the desert and braved the Atlantic Ocean in a leaking boat to reach economic opportunities in Europe (see pages 282–285).

GETTING THE IDEA

Sometimes a beat can grow out of one story. In the mid-1980s, this author happened upon volunteers assembling panels of the AIDS quilt. Each piece was a memorial to a person who had died of the disease, and the whole a testimony to the collective toll that the disease had taken.

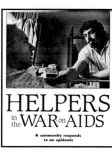

Magazine about those who helped people with AIDS.
(Cover photo by Annie Wells)

Though "The Names Project" since has been displayed in venues around the world, only its volunteers knew about it at the time. After photographing a story about the quilt and the people working on it for *People* magazine, the author did another story about an AIDS volunteer, entertainer Rita Rockett, who threw catered brunches and performed every other Sunday for AIDS patients on Ward 5A of San Francisco General Hospital. It turned out that there were many unsung volunteers at work in San Francisco to help the growing number of people afflicted with the deadly disease.

PAST STORIES ON THE TOPIC

By 1987, there had been several excellent photo stories on people with AIDS. Steve Ringman, who was with the *San Francisco Chronicle* at the time, Cheryl Nuss at the *San Jose Mercury News*, and Alon Reininger for Contact Press Images had all photographed moving stories. Each had focused on patients' battles against the agonizing deaths they faced.

A new angle would focus on the outpouring of support in the San Francisco Bay Area to provide emotional, physical, and economic help to people with the incurable disease. The resulting photo project, produced by journalism students at San Francisco State University (SFSU), was eventually called "Helpers in the War on AIDS."

While the original identification and later unraveling of the cause of AIDS provided the basis of important news stories, approaching the issue from the viewpoint of the helpers gave the story a new twist.

ORGANIZATION

One photographer could have photographed the AIDS "beat." However, in this instance, "Helpers in the War on AIDS" became a group beat at SFSU's journalism department. Each student photographer researched, developed, and photographed three stories over a 14-week period. In addition to taking pictures, all group members either worked with writers or provided the text for the project's stories themselves.

RESEARCH

Before photography began on the project, the group brought in experts in order to learn about AIDS and to get story leads. Specialists ranged from San Francisco's Health Department expert on AIDS to journalists who had been tracking the story for several years. All group members read ***And the Band Played On***, a book by gay journalist Randy Shilts that analyzed the government's delayed and inadequate response to the growing epidemic. Other leads came from classified listings in local gay newspapers. Chris Adams, a student writer in the group who has since died from the AIDS virus, provided a key link to the gay community.

Having a beat gives a focus to research, and research directs you beyond the facts to investigate a problem's causes, solutions, and, usually, stories that other journalists have not covered extensively.

INITIAL STORIES

To get a handle on such a large subject, the SFSU photographers divided the topic into

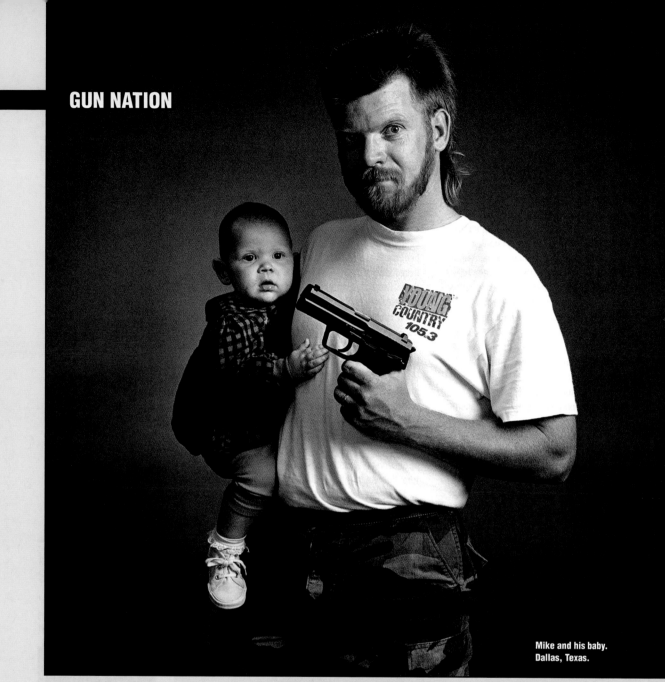

Mike and his baby.
Dallas, Texas.

A JOURNEY INTO AMERICAN GUN CULTURE

Photos by Zed Nelson

Over a period of three years, Zed Nelson documented America's gun culture. In "Gun Nation," he avoids the stereotypical groups that are often conveniently portrayed as the reason behind the "problem." There are, significantly, no images of gang-members posturing with their weapons, and no fringe-element extremists in camouflage fatigues. Instead, Nelson focused on so-called 'ordinary' law-abiding citizens, at gun shops and NRA conventions, in living rooms, emergency rooms, and school-yards. "I wanted to show how guns pervade all areas of society," says Nelson.

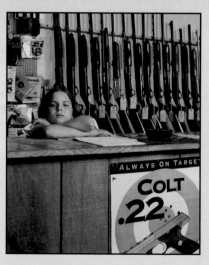

▲ Sarah Read, age 11. "I got a .410 shotgun from Santa last year." Los Angeles, California.

These images explore the paradox of why America's most potent symbol of freedom is also one of its greatest killers—resulting in an annual death toll of more than 30,000 American citizens.

"I wanted to work on a story that stripped guns of their glamour, to show what they can do to the human body, and to reveal their real impact on society."

Nelson began his study of American gun culture in the wake of a shocking and unusual British gun massacre in Dunblane, Scotland, where 16 children and their teacher were shot to death. The incident prompted a fierce back-lash against guns in the UK, and calls for a ban on privately owned firearms.

While gun-control measures were being debated in Britain, Nelson turned his focus on the United States, a nation where a centuries-old gun culture was clashing with the realities of modern life. ∎

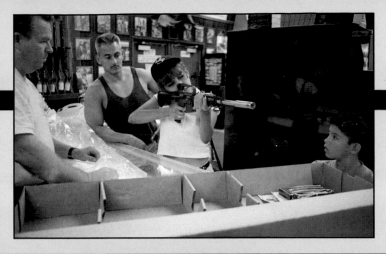

◄ A Los Angeles family purchases an AR-15 assault-style rifle "for home protection."

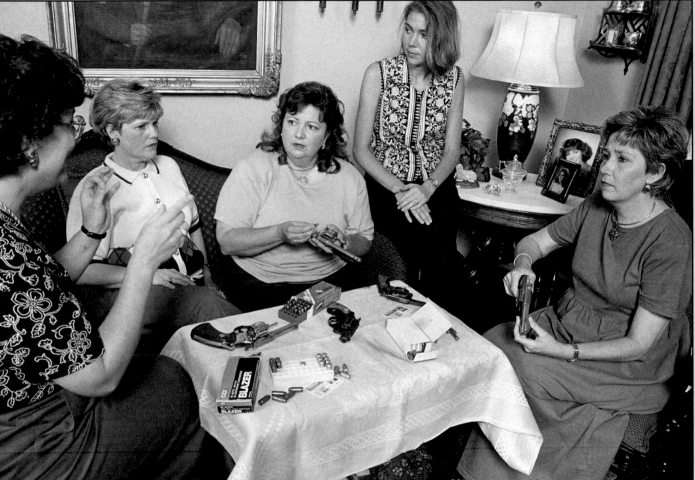

▲ Memphis housewives compare recently purchased guns.

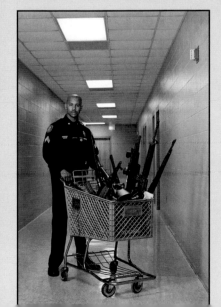

◄ Officer Rallins, Memphis police, moves weapons confiscated from the streets and from homes of Memphis residents.

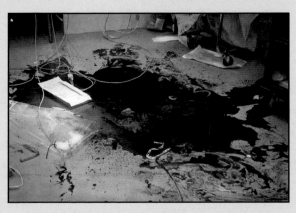

◄ Blood on the floor of a Memphis ER is from the treatment of a gunshot wound.

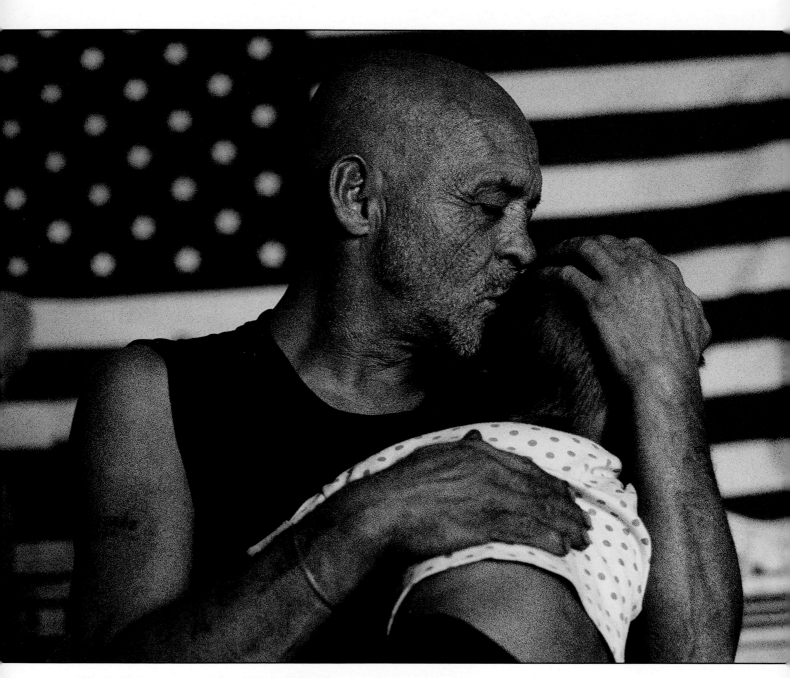

When his girlfriend was sent to jail, Henry Guiliante was left with
their four children in a single motel room. Having already abandoned
six children by three other women, would Henry find the strength to
be a real father? Kari René Hall, Los Angeles

circulation maga
of *Time* magazin
Time, Inc., edito
azine featuring p
ject. Naturally, tl
zine *People*. Thi:
steady photo die
famous and the i
but also an assor
from *Vanity Fair*
less variety of st
personalities, me
(See behind-the-
by Diana Walker
Bentley, page 40
see celebrity por
page 94, and by
Today, celebrity
of most mass-cir

LITTLE KNOWN BU
In addition to th
prints photo stor
who either do sc
it eccentric char:
   Hero or not, 1
to fascinate read
climbed the Wor
champion stacke
ples of people w
ments. The your
tographed qualif
of people living
pages 252–253)
at bounty hunter
unusual occupat

LITTLE KNOWN BU
One Person as an
Another type of
the life of a littl
example of a ne
For example, a
in the United St:
   Nancy Andre
story about sing
time, she counte
of the absent Af
page 132 for on
"Never Too Old
251) is the story
85-year-old wid
dating again. Pe
for Baby Boom
   Thousands o
try to reach Eur
one individual v
Jobard selected
from Cameroon
ments this one r
starvation, threa

Photo Story

TELLING STORIES WITH PICTURES

For many photojournalists, telling whole stories with pictures is the ultimate professional experience, regardless of whether they run in print, on the Internet, or even on television.

Sometimes stories can be built in a matter of minutes; sometimes storytelling can take years. Whereas Jim MacMillan of the *Philadelphia Daily News* photographed his story about a hostage situation in fewer than five minutes (page 30), Alan Berner shot his essay about the New West (pages 222–223) during a six-month sabbatical from the *Seattle Times*. Brian Plonka, of the *Spokane*

FACE TO FACE WITH BREAST CANCER

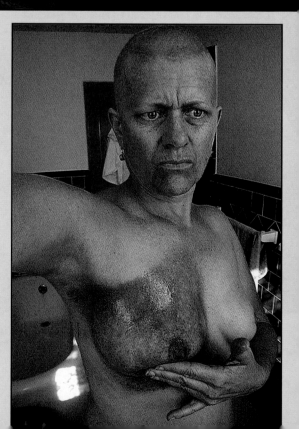

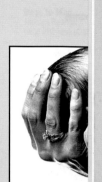

▲ Diane Long, Obste

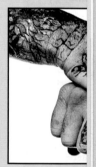

▲ Larry Wright, Tatt

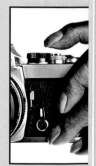

▲ Ernest Withers, Pl

(ABOVE and RIGHT) The radiation treatments were easy compared to chemotherapy. But after about a month they fatigued me. They obviously burned my breast, too. There wasn't much I could do except to apply aloe. After awhile the aloe didn't help, but since I kept fresh leaves in the refrigerator, they were at least cool.

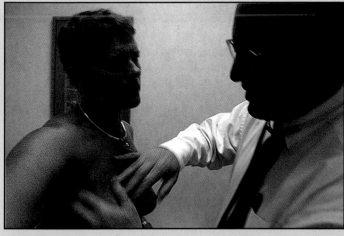

◄ My life will be punctuated by frequent visits to my oncologist. So far I'm okay. Slowly coming out of the fog of cancer treatment. My strength and stamina are returning in fits and starts. It's frustrating.

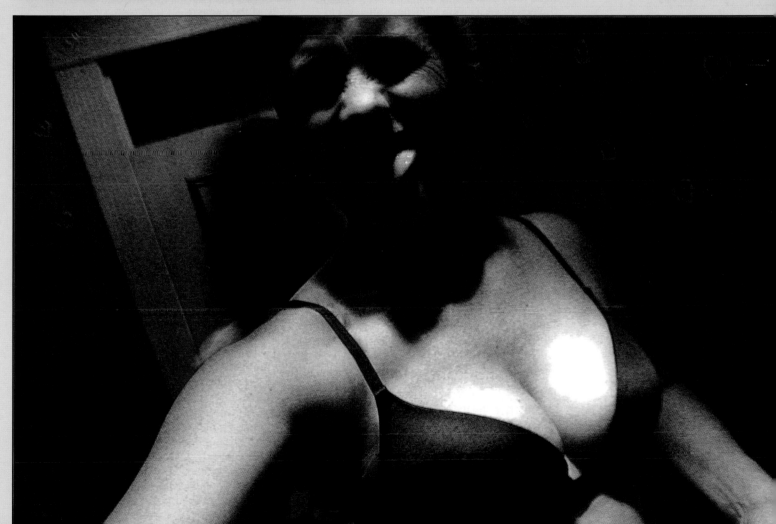

▲ For my birthday I bought a push-up bra. I've never had cleavage and figure I may as well, while I still can. My friend Amy came along to celebrate and help strap me in.

A DOG'S LIFE

PAMPERED POOCHES

Photos by Mike Stocker
South Florida Sun–Sentinel

Mike Stocker searched out the best examples he could find for this amusing photo package about over-the-top treatment of dogs. His project is a good example of "hitting the highlights" of a topic. He plowed the yellow pages, sought out newspaper assignments, called on old contacts, and pounced on pure chance to find dogs living the good life. While the individual pictures are fun, the package shows the extremes people go to in order to pamper their four-legged friends. Stocker has created an essay that carries its own punch without the need of a great deal of text. While readers don't get to know any individual dog or owner, most might envy a "dog's life." ∎

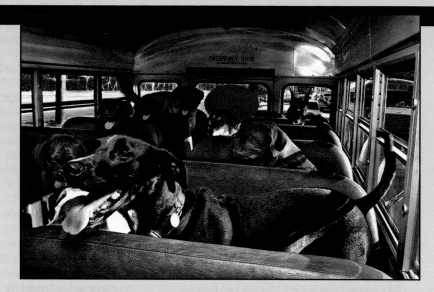

▲ A yellow school bus picks up dogs each day for **Planet Dog**, a training and day camp in Homestead, Florida. The dogs receive training in English and Spanish and also enjoy playgroups, cageless sleepovers, and swimming in a bone-shaped pool.

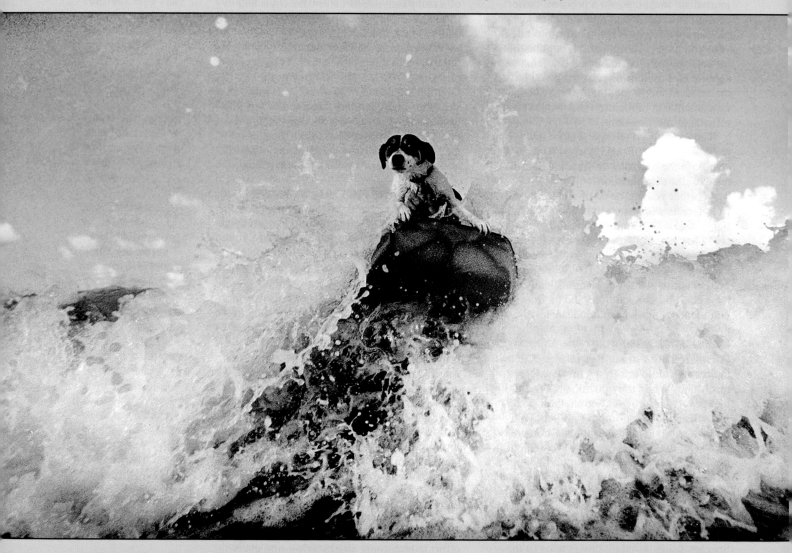

▲ Toto goes surfing on a boogie board.

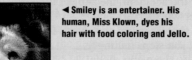

◀ Smiley is an entertainer. His human, Miss Klown, dyes his hair with food coloring and Jello.

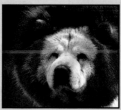

▼ Sheba and Truman await cake at Truman's second birthday party at the Three Dog Bakery. Their humans own the bakery.

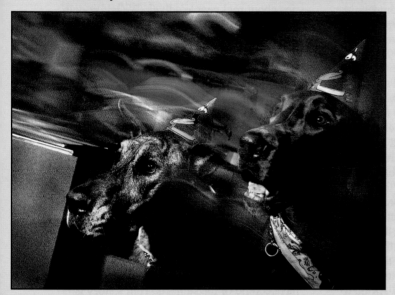

▼ Doctors perform in vitro fertilization on Champion Celtics Starstruck Sabrina, an English Mastiff.

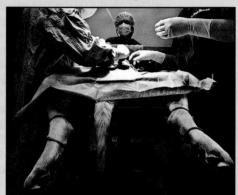

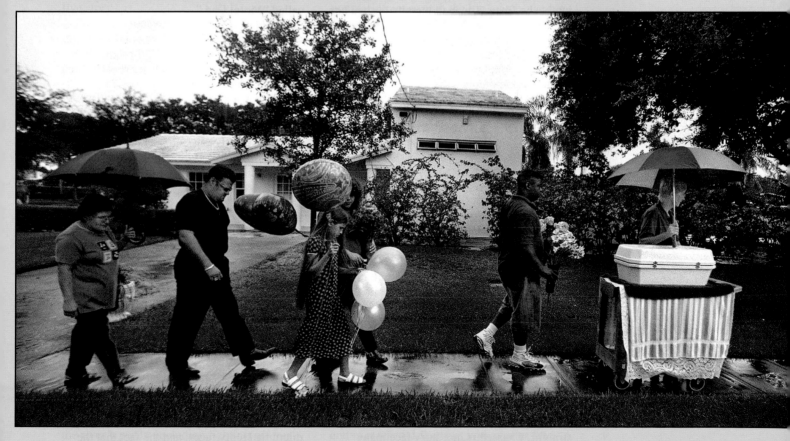

▲ At the Broward Pet Cemetery, a family holds a funeral for Nicholas Sebastian, their Shih Tzu.

CASANOVA AT 85

Photos by Mary Calvert
Washington Times

Because they live longer, women outnumber men in later life—good news for guys over 80 who are still in the game of love. An energetic elder is hot property among the femmes fatales of his generation.

Recognizing that love among the elderly was a rarely examined but increasingly relevant topic to millions of maturing baby boomers, Mary Calvert set out to do a story about dating during life's sunset years.

During a routine newspaper assignment, Calvert found her silver-haired Casanova, 85-year-old Charlie Thunell, whose wife of 60 years had died four years earlier.

By following Thunell's life and recent loves, Calvert tells the story of one man's quest for companionship while opening a window on the world of romance and dating among the elderly.

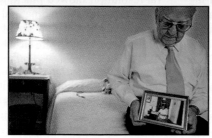

▲ Following the death of his wife of 60 years, Charlie Thunell is lonely.

Calvert's narrative story introduces the reader to Thunell's problem—his wife's death and his resulting loneliness. The opening photo of the solitary Thunell holding his wife's portrait in their bedroom sets the stage for the rest of the story.

The story continues with a set of exposition pictures laying out some of Thunell's options for finding female companionship. The pictures demonstrate that a single man, even at 85, is a desirable commodity in a world abundant with unattached women. The story comes to a temporary resolution with a tender moment between Thunell and his date for the evening.

While the story has a narrative flow, the pictures were not necessarily taken in the order that they are presented. By carefully choosing the serial position of the pictures, the photographer presents Thunell's search for happiness as a narrative story with a complication and resolution, rather than just a collection of pictures about a lovelorn man. The pictures don't document "everything you ever wanted to know" about Charlie Thunell. Instead, they explore one aspect of his life. The pictures go beyond a documentary and try to tell a story with a bigger message. They help to explain why a man might be searching for love and, perhaps, eventually finding it in some of the right places. The images help demonstrate everyone's need for love and companionship, regardless of their age. ∎

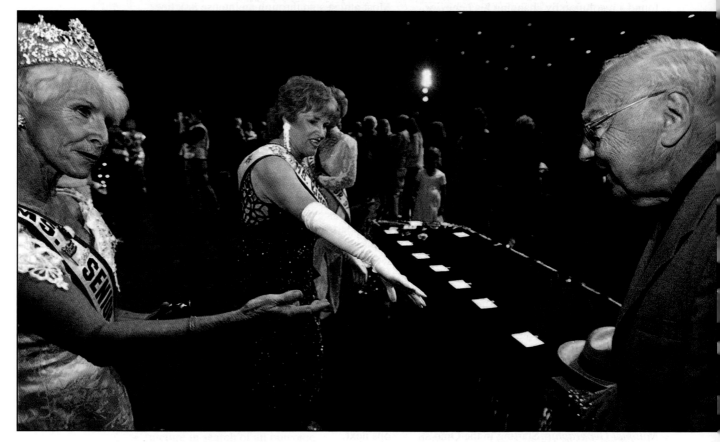

▲ Ms. Senior America 1999/2000 (left), and Ms. Virginia Senior America 1996 (right), greet Thunell backstage at the state pageant. Thunell went behind the scenes to meet the beauty queens after the competition.

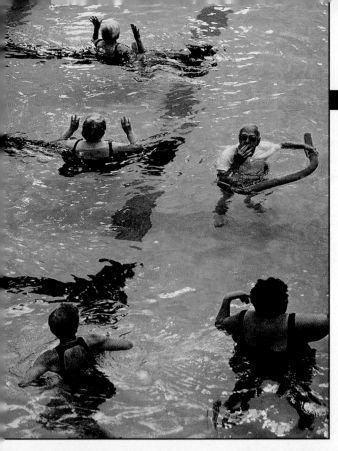

◄ Thunell is often the only man in his water aerobics class.

▼ (TOP) One of the women in the group looks to Thunell for help with her music during a Merry Makers rehearsal.

▼ (MIDDLE) Always the life of the party, Thunell, middle, flirts with two friends at a widow and widowers group that meets monthly for potluck dinner parties. He meets lots of ladies there, he says.

▼ (BOTTOM) Grabbing his coat and his hat, Thunell leaves his worries on the doorstep and prepares to step out for a night on the town with a favorite lady.

▼ Thunell, middle, performs at a nursing home with the Merry Makers, a group of seniors who do song-and-dance routines at local senior centers, nursing homes, and community centers.

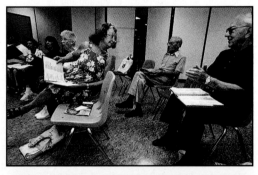

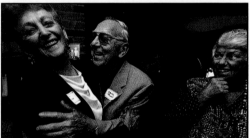

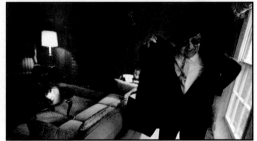

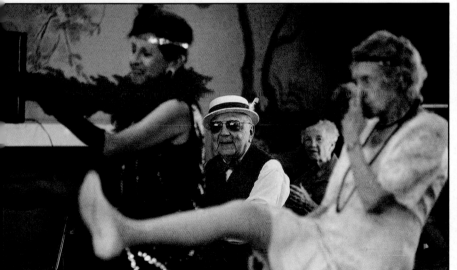

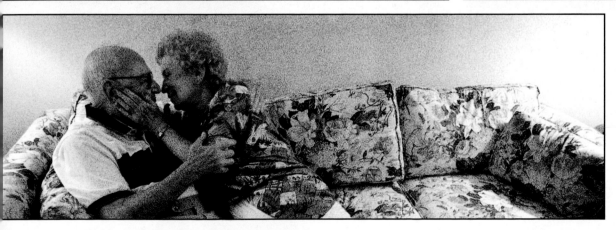

▲ Thunell shares a tender moment with his date during her visit to the townhouse he shares with his son and daughter-in-law.

Michelle Harig first became pregnant at 16. Ten years later, in 1996, she shares a soda with Cailee, the youngest of her four children. In the doorway is the children's father, Henry Guiliante, a mechanic who works only sporadically.

Though Henry is sweet with his children, Michelle is the one who handles all the family responsibilities, including looking after the children, preparing them for school, cooking, and cleaning the one room they all share at the roach-infested Ha' Penny Inn as they struggle to get by on welfare and food stamps.

Henry, who has abandoned three other women and six other children, thinks of child care and housework as woman's work. These four children know he has left the others and fear he will leave them, too.

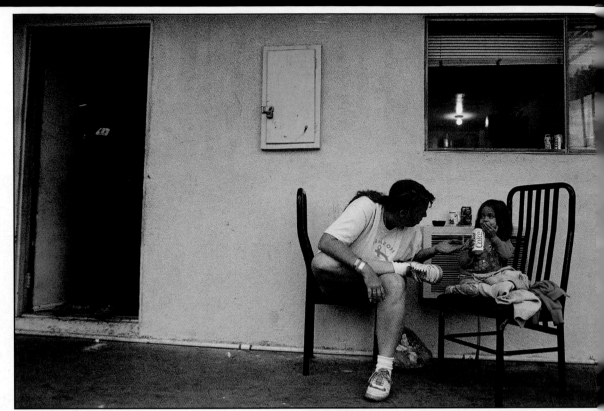

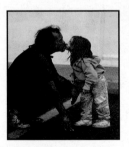

STRUGGLING WELFARE FAMILY

Photos by
Kari René Hall, Los Angeles

Kari René Hall was working for the *Los Angeles Times* when she began investigating photo projects to pursue. On her first visit to the roach-infested Ha' Penny Inn, the photographer was seeking a methamphetamine addict for a possible story. She found something quite different.

"As I was leaving, a little girl named Cailee, dressed in pink, dashes through the motel parking lot yelling 'Daddy! Daddy!' A scraggly, tattooed little man, Henry Guiliante, wearing a greasy mechanic's uniform, kneels down to kiss her. This moment seemed out of place in such a harsh environment," says Hall. "I didn't know it at the time, but the photo was the beginning of a five-year documentary project."

The original subject of Hall's project was to become Michelle Harig, the mother of the little girl in pink. Because editors at the *Times* weren't interested in pursuing the story, Hall began visiting the Guiliante family at the motel after her shift ended. The photographer anticipated that through Michelle and her family, the pictures would tell the story of the ongoing struggles of a mother who had become pregnant as a teenager. A 26-year-old former heroin addict, Michelle had given birth to the first of her four children at 16.

"I wanted to build a relationship, for them to trust me and to allow me into their life," Hall told *Photo District News* (May 2001). "I didn't come in with cameras blazing." Hall told the family she didn't want any posing, just life as normal. Michelle, Henry, and the kids discussed it and agreed.

All went smoothly until Michelle was convicted of welfare fraud and sent to jail. Henry already had fathered six other children with three other women and abandoned them all. This time, Henry himself had been abandoned with children needing care. At first Hall thought her story was gone. After all, Michelle was gone, and Henry was likely to leave, as he always had. Or would he somehow become a responsible father?

continued on page 256 ►

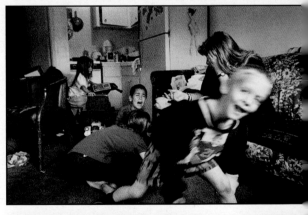

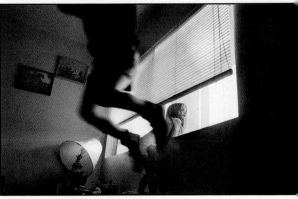

▲ (BOTH) Michelle and Henry do not allow the children to leave the motel room without supervision for fear of exposing them to the unsavory lifestyles at the Ha' Penny Inn.

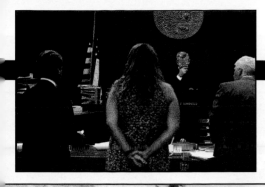

◄ Charged with welfare fraud for not disclosing that Henry lives with her, Michelle pleads "no contest" in hopes that she will get little or no jail time. Instead, the judge sentences her to six months in jail and orders her to pay $25,000 in restitution. She must surrender in one week to serve her sentence.

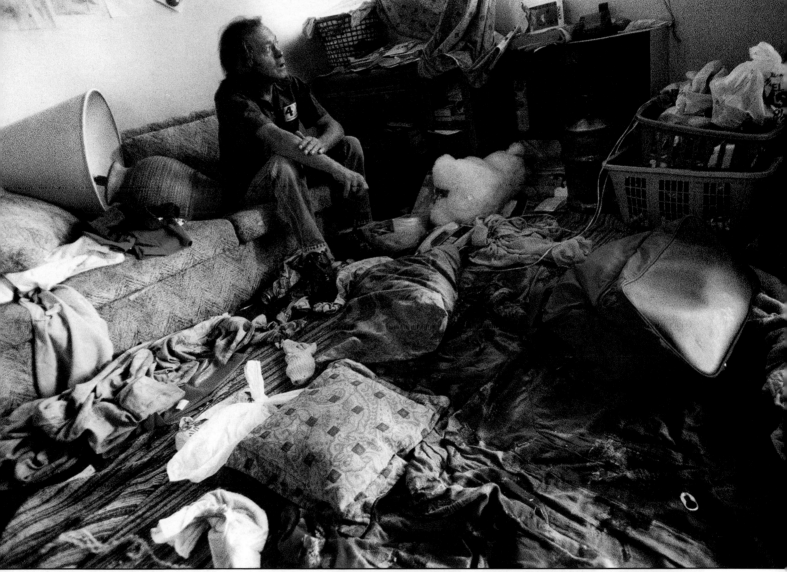

▲ Without Michelle, Henry manages to feed his kids and get them off to school, but he is overwhelmed by all his other parental duties. How long can a man who had disparaged "woman's work" put up with this? Will he leave these four children as he has left his six others?

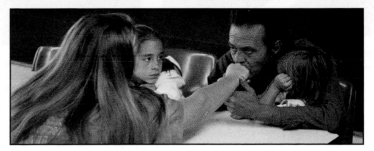

▲ "Are you going home, Mommy?" asks Cailee, seated in her father's lap. Michelle answers, "No. No, sweetie." After Michelle's release, the children's mother returns briefly but then leaves for good.

FATHER IN MORE THAN NAME

Henry even organizes his motel neighbors to protest their living conditions and to take the owners to court. He buys an $11 pin-stripe suit to go to court. Though the group loses the court case, Henry and his kids stay together as they move from that motel to another.

With his kids in school, Henry's next priority becomes finding a decent job. He joins a job program. He prepares a résumés, performs an Internet job search.

"God's gave me a second chance," he says. "He's gave me a second chance with a family. He taught me how to love and be loved."

With any great movie or book, the viewer or reader does not know the outcome at the beginning. The complication in Henry's story occurred when, alone, he faced whether or not to take responsibility for his family. In this type of saga, the photographer must keep shooting while waiting and seeing what develops.

For the reader, the story lasts beyond the final picture. The story is gripping, its final outcome unknown. The story's theme is about taking advantage of a second chance in life.

As Hall says, "This is a story of somebody realizing what it means to be a father. It is a story of somebody finding a purpose in life and possible redemption through being needed."

Hall shot the story on her own time, after work, and on weekends, often sitting in a corner waiting and watching the lives of the family unfold. She processed more than 350 rolls of film and made 4"x6" prints at her local grocery store for editing. She paid for everything out of her own pocket.

Henry's story went on to win the Canon Photo Essay award in the Pictures of the Year Contest, as well as to appear on *MSNBC.com*, *www.msnbc.com/modules/ps/henry/splash.asp*. The *Los Angeles Times Magazine* also published it.

Following the publication of Henry's story on the Web and in the *Los Angeles Times Magazine*, estranged family members, including his brother, two of his older sons, and his first wife, contacted him. Strangers have donated money, gift certificates, mechanics' tools, clothes, and food. A reader paid Henry's driver's license fees. Credit bureaus cleared his record. Job offers rolled in.

"I now have a fresh start at life," he says. ■

▼ (TOP) Henry decides to take on poor living conditions at the motel. He gathers other Ha' Penny residents to discuss their rights as outlined in sections in the *Landlord's and Tenant's Rights Book*. He also calls authorities to inspect the motel, which is cited with more than 300 infractions.

▼ (BOTTOM) The management responds with eviction notices, which spurs Henry to paint placards and lead a protest.

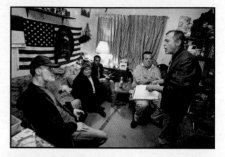

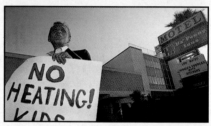

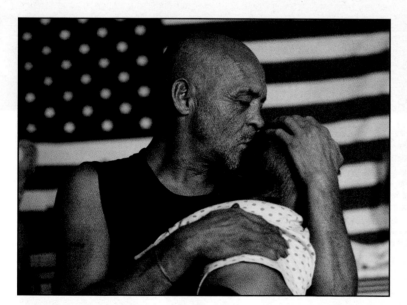

▲ Seeing the misery of his four children when their mother left makes Henry realize how much his six others had suffered. "I seen the abandonment they felt. I've left my wives with the children, and I never got to see that part of it. . . . It's really nice to be able to feel your child cuddling up to you and know that they feel safe in your arms. And if my drinking and my rowdiness kept on or I would've blew my brains out, I never would've got to know these feelings or these emotions. I would never have got to hear a child saying, "I love you, Daddy." Here, he comforts Cailee, sick with a fever.

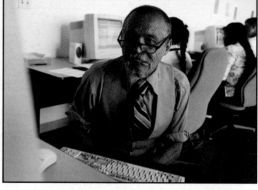

▲ After years of only sporadic work as a part-time mechanic, Henry begins to search for employment that will adequately support his children. "If I don't find a job today, I'll find one tomorrow, but I will succeed. Because I've got four little ones depending on me."

▼ Henry challenges the evictions in court, but loses the case when the management claims the evictions are necessary to renovate the building into a tourist motel. He and the children must leave the the Ha' Penny Inn, where they have lived for five years. Cailee tries to cheer up her dad by playing the saxophone when she catches him looking sad.

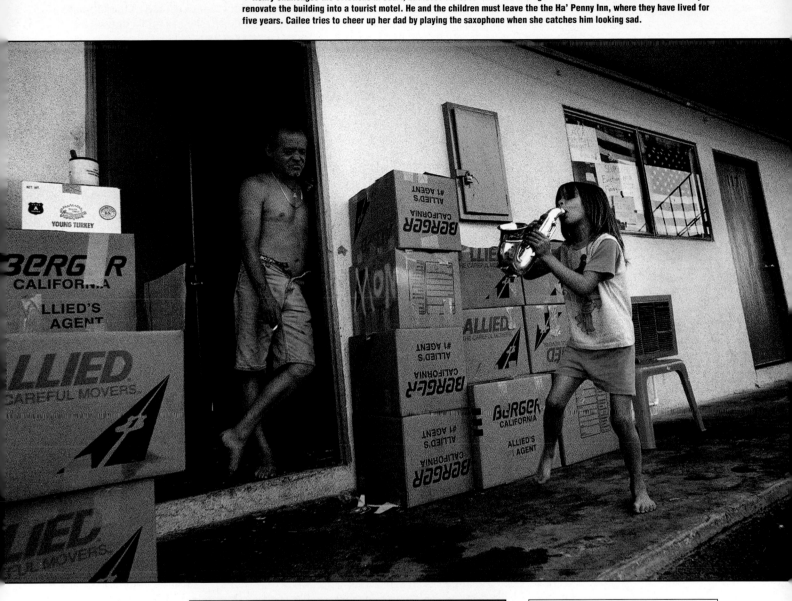

FIND MULTIMEDIA PIECES DISCUSSED IN THIS CHAPTER
http://kenkobre.blogspot.com/2007/10/multimedia.html

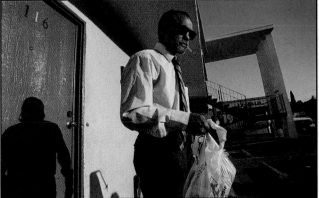

▲ On the day Henry and the children must move, Henry puts on his suit and a clean white shirt, packs a change of clothes in a plastic bag, and heads out to search for a new home for his family. The move is a setback not a failure.

the mother, and the child did not know if the boy would live or die. Everyone, including the reader, had to wait for the story to play itself out. The same can be said for the little boy blown up in Iraq. Would the fragile child live or die before having the shrapnel removed from his brain? No one knew. Great stories hold readers' attention through the tale because the reader wants to find out how the story ends. You can test whether your story is a true narrative by noting at the beginning of shooting if you already know the outcome of your piece or if the end is still in doubt.

COMPRESSING NARRATIVE TIME

Writers can reconstruct past events with an interview. For photographers, the biggest problem with shooting narrative stories is that many complications faced by potential subjects simply don't take place in the relatively short time allotted for most assignments. Sometimes, months or even years pass before a person resolves a complication. Kari René Hall followed "Motel Dad" for more than five years.

Editors sometimes allot photojournalists just a few days to work on stories. Following are various methods for compressing time in a narrative story.

Resolution near at Hand

Pick a story in which the resolution is near at hand. To shoot a story about a political newcomer running for mayor, zero in on the subject a few weeks before the primaries or before the actual election. At this time, you will be able to show how the candidate grapples with the complication of getting into office: glad-handing potential voters, strategizing, chain-smoking, meeting late at night, prepping for television interviews.

The narrative story will resolve itself on election eve or perhaps on the mayor's first day in office. Starting too early or too late, however, means you may miss the complication or resolution.

Strazzante's story about the female boxer delivers a complication and resolution, and the photographer knew from the beginning when this resolution would take place. Sports stories typically have the advantage of a built-in complication with a clear resolution that will occur at a fixed time. These kinds of projects allow advance planning for timely publication (see page 239).

A Small Resolution

Within a story, you might zero in on a small resolution to the complication rather than its ultimate resolution. Annie Wells's breast cancer journal presents a small resolution. While

the story follows her confrontation with the disease over the course of a year, an excellent prognosis—the story's end—is not a cure. Although Wells cannot yet report the ultimate victory over death, she has told a unified story (see pages 240–243).

In "Crude Reflections," Lou Dematteis has not only documented health effects of oil exploration in the Amazon but also has shown how the local population has successfully brought the oil companies to court. His pictures don't tell the final resolution of this tragic environmental pillage, but they do provide a temporary resolution (the beginning of the trial) for his story at this point in time (see page 205). The case remains in court and is expected to take years to unwind.

While Gary Coronado's story "Train Jumpers" shows the horrible injuries of some who try and fail to ride the rails through Mexico to the United States, his pictures also document a shelter in Mexico where those injured or maimed on their quest can recover (see pages 302–304).

Mary Calvert's assignment on Homeland Security agents tells the immigrant story from another point of view, that of U.S. immigration officials. The pictures do not follow the immigrants on their journey northward or explore why they left their home country, but they do show a kind of resolution—after their arrest for being in the United States illegally, the immigrants are temporarily detained and then sent back to their home countries. (See two pictures from this project on page 56.)

The endings of these stories help to give the reports a sense of completion, even if the end they show is only temporary.

Existing Pictures

Investigate photo albums or archives to show what your subject or location used to look like. If your story is about a successful banker who has overcome a poverty-stricken past, can you show the complication with photos of the person as a youngster living in a cold-water flat or a run-down shack? Without these pictures, the banker's success (resolution) may seem unearned.

If your story is about a neighborhood, can you find old pictures from the historical society or your paper's morgue that indicate whether the neighborhood used to be wealthy or poor, or perhaps even farmland or forests?

Different Developmental Stages

Photographing a narrative story about the long-term impact of crack cocaine on newborns does not require following one child from birth through preschool. To address this issue at different critical stages, this author photographed infants suffering withdrawal at San Francisco General Hospital, (complication) toddlers in a testing program (partial resolution), and then crack-affected youngsters in an early intervention program in an East Palo Alto school (partial resolution). Part of the project is reproduced on pages 216–217.

In the extensive multimedia piece "The Lifeline," Rick Loomis shows each phase of the process wounded soldiers go through, from arrival by helicopter at the field hospital, through field surgery and follow-up treatment to returning to civilian life. He does so by photographing different soldiers at each critical stage of the process. The reader can follow the arc of the narrative, but the time frame from injury to recovery has been highly compressed and played out in the lives of different subjects. (See pages 298–301.)

THE INHERENT APPEAL OF A NARRATIVE STORY

Narrative stories often require the research skills of a librarian, the patience of Job, and the planning of an air-traffic controller. Often, the end is not predictable. Yet the difficulties are worth it. Rather than presenting a collection of pictures that holds readers' attention for a few minutes, a narrative story draws the viewer into the subject's predicament.

With a narrative story, viewers start to care about the subject and want to know how he or she is going to solve the dilemma. What is going to happen? When picture stories are done well, readers want to see the last picture that reveals the story's outcome. The story has a plot line—not an invented, preplanned script typical of early picture magazines but a real story line in which people face problems and overcome them in some honest way.

Most important, the reader comes to care about the story's protagonist. Whether the story is about Annie Wells, who has cancer, or Henry, the motel dad, the subject is not shown just once but is repeated in picture after picture. The reader gets involved in the subject's life. What will happen to Annie? Will Henry abandon this set of children, too? And, perhaps, if the story has merit and is well-photographed, the reader won't just give a passing glance to the pictures and move on, but will remember the story, repeat it, and show it to others.

COMPARING THE DOCUMENTARY AND THE PHOTO ESSAY TO THE NARRATIVE STORY

Editors, photographers, writers, and readers apply the term "picture story" to just about any group of pictures. One can divide the picture story into several categories.

EDITORIAL ESSAYS: A POINT OF VIEW

Some groups of photos don't set out to tell a narrative story. Rather, like a magazine opinion piece or newspaper editorial, they seek to make a point. These editorial photo essays clearly have a point of view. For instance, Brian Plonka does not tell the tale of one alcoholic in a narrative style (pages 208–211). Rather he exposes the highs and lows of alcohol addiction. He has a clear point of view. He is certainly not an advocate of alcohol consumption. His pictures look nothing like the ones shown in beer ads. Nor is he neutral, just recording everything about the beer industry from growing hops to bottling the product. Rather, his pictures all have a clear point of view. His photo of a father trying to get his son to taste beer makes some readers want to recoil. Plonka is not making an impartial statement about drinking. He is presenting an editorial essay with a clear point of view.

Likewise, Alan Berner has some interesting observations about development in the western United States (pages 222–223). Ironic juxtapositions in his photographs force readers to think. His picture of a line of abandoned refrigerators in front of a mountain range contrasts the ugly, disposable world of modern society against the naturally beautiful vista of the West.

The line of appliances in the foreground and the mountains in the background share eerily similar silhouettes.

Berner finds another ironic contrast when he combines a city skyline and the tops of Native American tepees. He makes readers confront the old and the new. His picture of a mall opening, complete with dignitaries sitting outside in folding chairs to watch the eruption of a fake Mt. Rainier, pokes fun at the artificiality not only of this event but of development in general. Each picture in Berner's essay, to a greater or lesser extent, conveys his distinctive sensibility and point of view.

British photographer Zed Nelson's "Gun Nation: A Journey into American Gun Culture" is an essay (see pages 226–227). The photographer had a clear point of view when he started the project. Nelson's opinion of the United States's warped love affair with guns comes through in each image of the essay.

DOCUMENTARIES

Photographers don't always have a point of view about their subjects. They don't always want to tell a narrative tale with a complication and resolution. Sometimes photographers just want to show their readers

continued on page 266 ▶

OPERATION LION HEART

Photos by
Deanne Fitzmaurice
San Francisco Chronicle

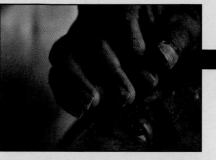

► Saleh gets headaches from
the shrapnel in his brain, and
finds comfort as his father
strokes his head.

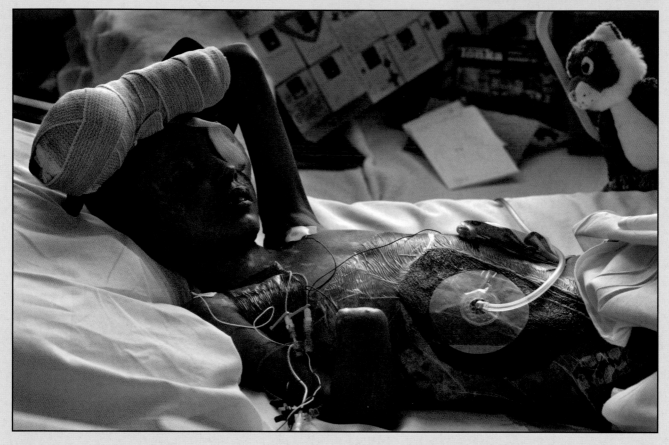

Saleh Khalaf was playing with his brother the day he picked up an explosive device near his village in southern Iraq. The resulting blast killed his brother and led to an international mercy mission to save Saleh, who lost both hands and his left eye. His stomach also had been blown open, and a piece of shrapnel lodged in his brain.

As part of an international effort to save Saleh, he and his father, Raheem, eventually were flown to California for surgery at Oakland's Children's Hospital. His sisters and pregnant mother had to stay in Iran.

Deanne Fitzmaurice of the *San Francisco Chronicle* first met him there on a routine assignment.

"We thought Saleh would be taken care of and sent back to Iraq in six weeks or so," she says. "Our idea was to follow him as long as he was here. I shot this photo of this unconscious little boy. He looked so frail; they didn't know if he would survive."

From the beginning, Fitzmaurice's captivating pictures of this little boy's recovery gripped the *Chronicle*'s readers.

Of course, no one knew how the story would turn out. Like any real story, the end is not obvious at the beginning. Fitzmaurice took the reader through a true story arc from seeing this frail and damaged child on his bed awaiting brain surgery, through his 30 operations, then by his gradual recovery, release from the hospital, and new life. The doctors nicknamed the boy Lion Heart Saleh.

"I communicated with Saleh through photography early on, about the third visit," Fitzmaurice says. "I was working digitally, so I would show him an image when I thought it would make him laugh or smile. He began to want to shoot himself. It was difficult for him to manage with the stump on his right arm, but he could fire the shutter."

continued on page 264 ►

▲ During his first few weeks in Children's Hospital, Saleh stabilizes. His injuries include a lost eye, shrapnel in the brain, both hands (except for one finger and part of another that remain on his left hand), and a blown-open abdomen held together with a wound-vac, a surgical dressing that absorbs fluid as it slowly pulls the skin together.

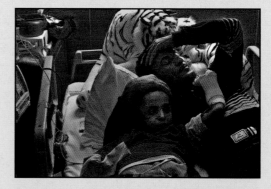

▲ Most nights, Raheem Khalaf climbs into Saleh's hospital bed. From Iraq to Oakland he spends nearly every minute with his son.

▼ Khaled Abdorabihe, a custodian at Children's Hospital in Oakland, plays soccer with a recuperating Saleh one night in the hallway until a nurse orders him back to bed. Khaled is from Yemen and sometimes translates between Arabic and English for Saleh.

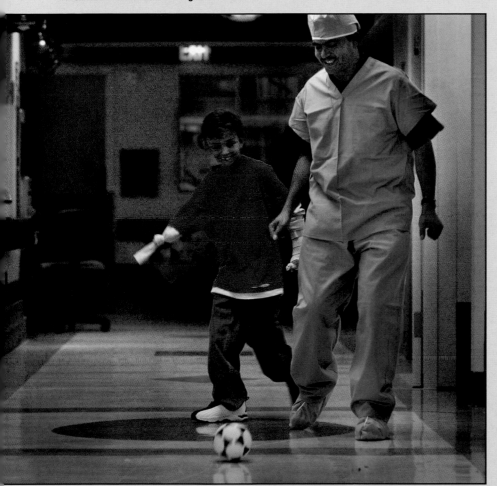

▼ Saleh jumps for joy on his new mattress as a friend of his father's assembles the bed frame inside Saleh's father's new Oakland apartment.

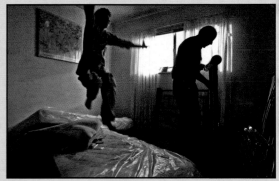

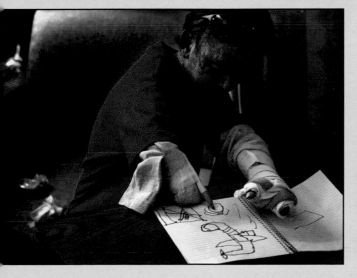

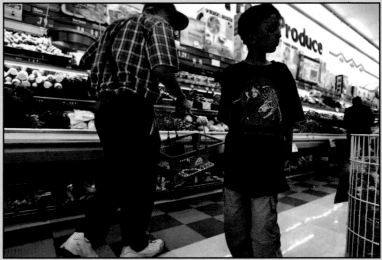

er in the day, staring children had upset Saleh. He uses a pen taped to his arm by a o draw an airplane dropping bombs.

▲Saleh becomes very upset when people stare at his missing eye. He has forgotten the sunglasses he usually wears in public. His father will have to carry him home kicking, screaming, and crying.

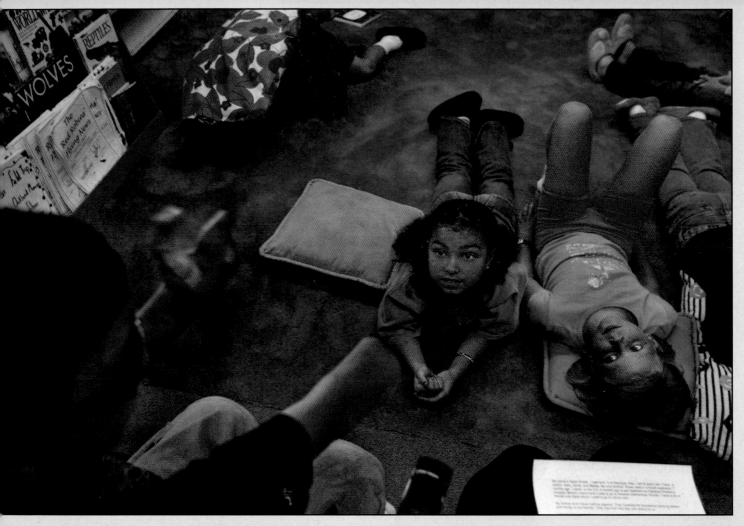

Saleh begins attending school and even talks about village life in Iraq during fourth-grade storytime at Park Day School in Oakland.

Eventually, Saleh's father was able to get a job, which allowed the boy to continue healing in the United States. Saleh learned to live in an American apartment, mastered English as part of his schooling, and learned to fit in among his classmates despite the loss of his hands and eye. Along the way there were many tearful, angry moments. Eventually, his mother and little sister were able to come from Iraq, reuniting the torn family. Saleh was ready to be a regular boy again. ∎

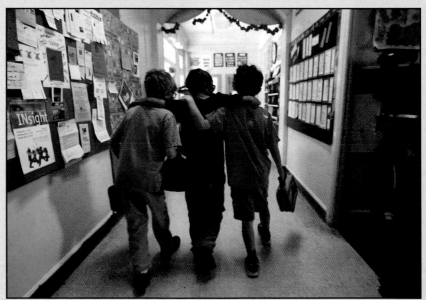

Saleh began to form friendships at the Park Day School.

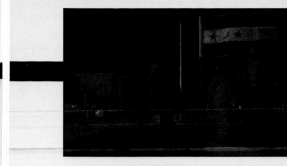

◄ Saleh's mother, Hadia, and her other children flee Iraq to come to the United States after being apart from Saleh and Raheem for more than a year.

▼ Hadia drops to her knee to embrace Saleh the moment she sees him at San Francisco International Airport. In the background Raheem rushes to embrace his daughters. Hadia is holding son Ali, 6 months old, whom Saleh and Raheem had not yet met.

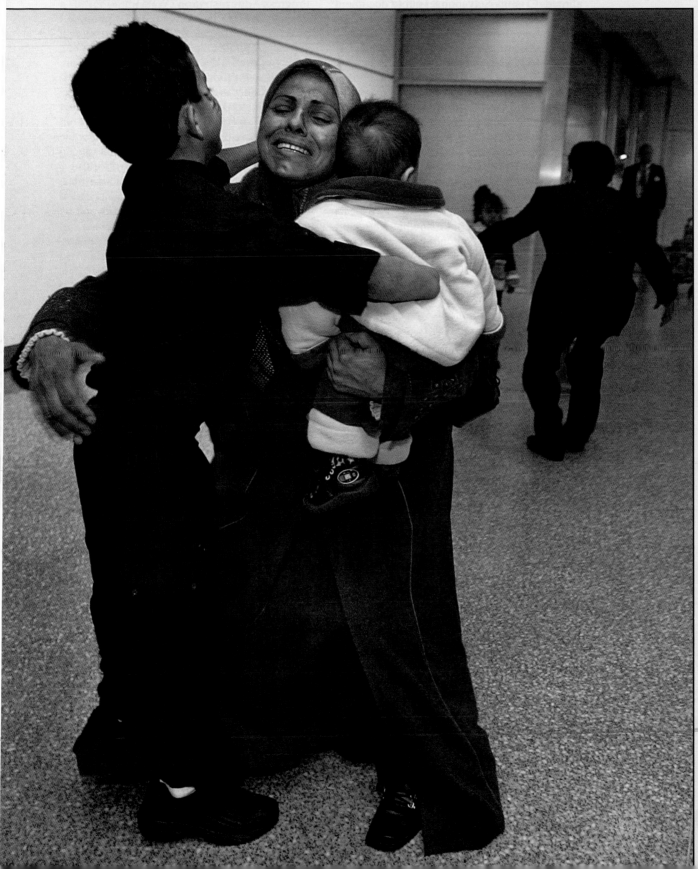

KINGSLEY'S CROSSING

Photos by Olivier Jobard
Sipa Press
Multimedia package by Brian Storm, *MediaStorm.org*

Kingsley was a 23-year-old lifeguard from the Cameroon in West Africa. As a lifeguard, Kingsley earned just enough to pay for food and the rented two-room house he shared with his parents and seven siblings. In Europe—the new El Dorado — Kingsley knew that African immigrants could vastly increase their incomes while also providing for their families back home.

Photojournalist Olivier Jobard was aware of the wave of African immigrants desperately seeking better lives and economic opportunities in Europe. He wanted to document one person making the treacherous and illegal journey from Africa to Europe. Having been on assignment in Cameroon, he already had local contacts.

Jobard's research let him to select Kingsley as his subject because the young man had attempted the crossing before and understood what he was getting into.

Jobard accompanied Kingsley as he left Cameroon for the excruciating six-month journey across half of Africa. Together, they endured the arduous trip through Nigeria, Niger, the Sahara Desert, and Algeria—including a truck breakdown in the middle of the desert.

Finally, the hopeful migrant and the determined photographer reached Morocco. They waited there for three months while Kingsley tried to make arrangements for the illegal trip before boarding a handmade skiff bound for the Canary Islands.

To reach Europe, Kingsley ultimately had to cross the Atlantic Ocean from Mauritania, a country in Africa just below Morocco, in order to reach the Canary Islands, which are owned by Spain but are about 120 kilometers off the coast of West Africa.

After paying the smugglers, Jobard and a friend who is a video journalist made the crossing with Kingsley.

FROM AN INTERVIEW WITH OLIVIER JOBARD
Question: How did you feel about the ocean crossing?

"You have paid the smugglers but you never know if they are going to get you there or not.
Question : You knew the boat was no good?

Of course. But I knew that some boats managed to cross…. Not all of them…. A little bit more than half of them.
Question: What happened when you put the boat in the water?

When the boat launched we got maybe 200 or 300 meters from the beach. We tried to pass the big wave, but the boat got on the side and capsized. At 2 A.M. there was just moonlight.

continued on page 285 ▶

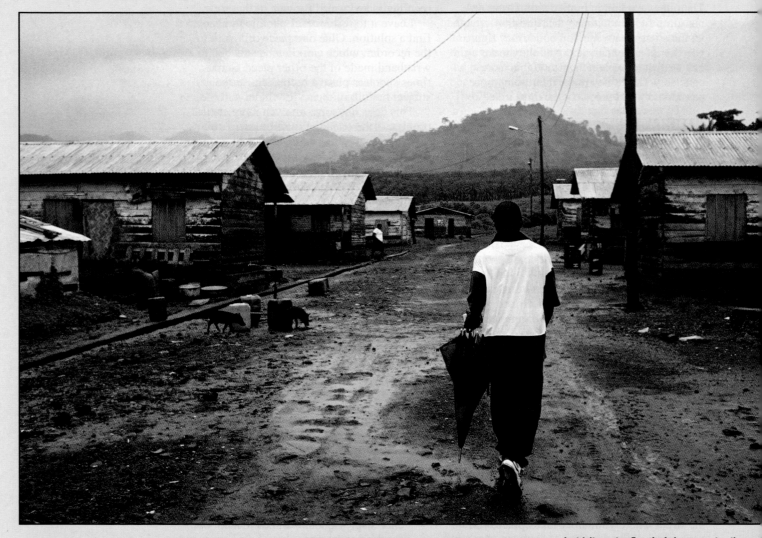

▲ "If you come from a poor family, you always stay in a poor family 'til you die. Equivalent to 50 Euro. That's all I was earning per month. All of my salary was just for feeding, hospital, clothing, paying my house rent, paying electricity, water. Everybody in my country, they are ing for a solution for their children to get to Europe helping their family behind." — *Kingsley*

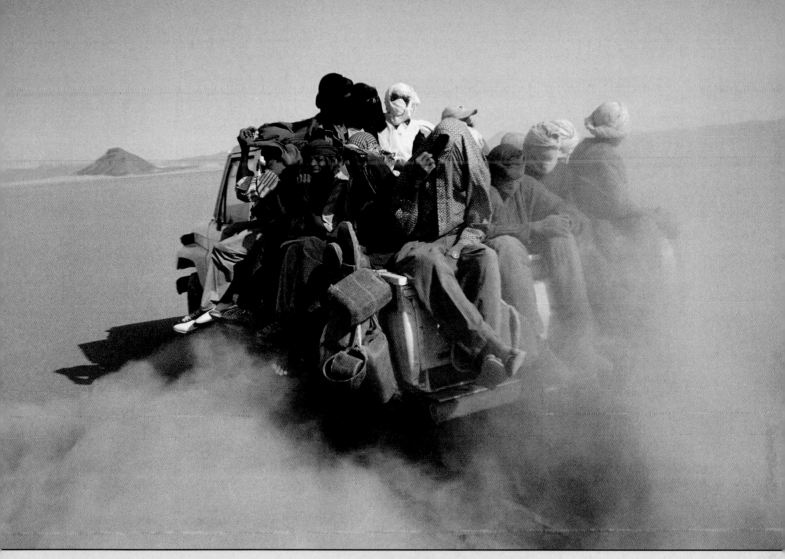

▲ "I was really scared not to fall off from the car because I was sitting just at the side at the edge of the car. And behind me there was guys fighting. 'Get off my leg, my leg, please my leg.'

So the next day we continue our journey early in the morning. We supposed to drive until about 11 or 12, and then the driver has to stop because the desert is too hot and the engine become very, very warm so we have to rest.

The more we driving, the more we suffer from heat, sun, and dust." — *Kingsley*

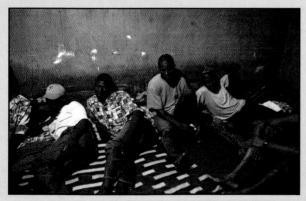

▲ "Finally I got in contact with one Senegalese who proposed for me to come to his ghetto. There were so many, many guys that came in. He tell me to wait for him to go for someone who is going to lead me to cross the ocean. He kept me there in the ghetto without calling me, without telling me anything. I spent all that full month of August in that ghetto. Sad, sad, sad. I even cry at night. It was miserable for me. I lose contact with my family. I'm going to die like this. My family would not even see my corpse. I was lost. I was really, really lost. Finally he called me. He's telling me, 'You will be traveling next week, so I will be coming for you tomorrow.'" — *Kingsley*

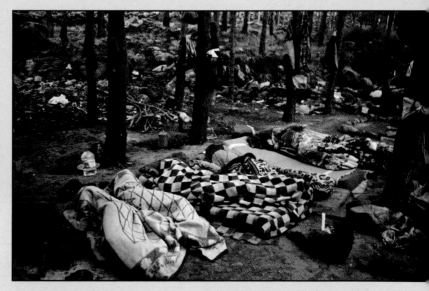

▲ "We arrive Nador. There is a forest there. There are about 3000 person living in there. They are living group by group according to their nationality. There's Cameroonian, Nigerian, Senegalese, Malian.... We spent two weeks. These guys arrive. They brought small wooden boat with holes everywhere." — *Kingsley*

KINGSLEY'S CROSSING

▶ From Tangier, Kingsley and the others can see Spain from the garbage dump. For the first time, Europe is within reach. The final leg is short, but Kingsley cannot afford the smuggler's high fee. After weeks of waiting, a smuggler takes him to a new, secret location, where he is told to wait—again—for a boat.

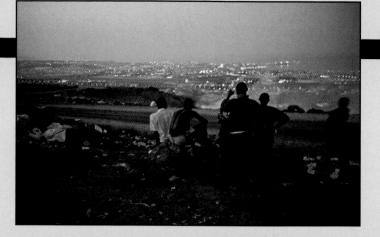

▲ "The captain was struggling to cross the waves. The fifth wave capsized the boat. The boat, it sank. I decided to turn back in to help some guys. I brought him out to the shore. Guys were crying out, my brother. People were shouting. We lost two persons. One Cameroonian and one Senegalese. They are dead. They are dead. We should leave because maybe officers might arrive here at any time. It's risky for us to stay and look for their corpses." — *Kingsley*

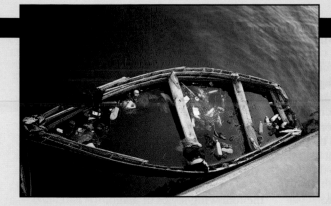

◄ "The next day they told us they are going to repair the same boat. I see nothing that guarantees me that this boat can sail and cross the Atlantic Ocean. We are all discouraged.
   [*Nonetheless, the group departs in the boat again.*]
   The captain successfully crossed the waves. Water was getting in everywhere. Rapidly. People become more and more frightened. Guys were shouting, 'Hey captain, turn back, turn back, turn back!'
   [*At this point, a Spanish Coast Guard boat comes near.*]
   They [*the Spanish Coast Guard*] told us nobody should make any move. Our boat might capsize, so they were calling us one after each. We were very, very happy. Now my life is safe."
— *Kingsley*

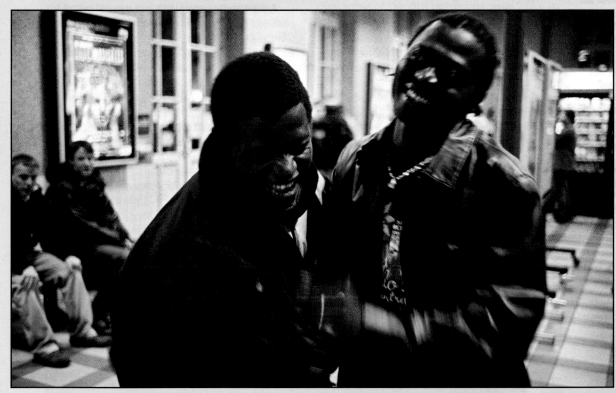

◄ "I contacted my only friend. We have grown up together. He's married to a French woman living in France. So I phone him and let him know that I've arrived.
   At the train station I was there waiting for my friend. He arrived behind me, and when he touched me it was a joy. Shouting, rejoicing. It was something marvelous.
   Later he carried me with his car to his house. Met his wife. We spent all our time talking. That day was really an exciting one.
   Crossing the ocean, the desert, that was the only way for me to make it out. And I did it."
— *Kingsley*

"Jumping into the water, you don't even know which side of the boat is toward the coast. It is a shock. When we capsized I realized that all the others in the boat didn't know how to swim. And because we are the whites in the boat, they know we knew how to swim. They wrapped themselves around us.

   "My cameras were in two or three plastic bags. I tried to shoot when I got to the beach. It was moonlight. Exposures were one or two seconds per exposure. I had to lie on the sand. I could finish my roll but I could not change film because I was wet. And also I was shaking because I was freezing like crazy. I made 10 pictures."

   A month later Kingsley, Jobard, and the videographer tried a second time. This time the Spanish Coast Guard intercepted the boat just off the coast of the Canary Islands as the boat was filling with water.

Unable to determine Kingsley's nationality, the Spanish could not deport him, which allowed him eventually to reach Spain and then France, where he lives legally today.

   The multimedia presentation of "Kingsley's Crossing" on *MediaStorm.org* combines Olivier Jobard's still images with a videotaped interview of Kingsley. The on-camera interview introduces Kingsley personally to viewers, who also hear the young man's story, in his own voice, over Jobard's images as the determined immigrant describes his desperate journey. ∎

FIND MULTIMEDIA PIECES DISCUSSED IN THIS CHAPTER
http://kenkobre.blogspot.com/2007/10/multimedia.html

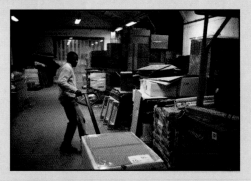

▲ "Since arriving in France, it was very, very difficult. I was even thinking going back to my country. I work on machines in a small printing press. Piling papers, busting holes in papers.
   My salary here is also not a good salary. My family, I send them money. What I think I can do on my part.
   I'm still hoping to further my electrical education here. To go for a better job. Everything is determination. I know with time things will be okay." — *Kingsley*

A DEADLY SEARCH FOR MISSING SOLDIERS

Photos and first-person account
by Michael Kamber, *The New York Times*

From captions in Kamber's transmitted files:
"Scenes from a combat patrol that ended in tragedy
today when one U.S. soldier was killed and four
wounded (3 U.S., one I.A.) when the KIA either
stepped on a pressure-activated land mine or was
killed by a command-detonated IED buried along a
dirt road where the patrol was walking."

For several years, I had avoided returning to Iraq. During my last trip, in 2004, I had several close calls: rocket propelled grenades (RPGs) that sailed just wide, an improvised explosive device (IED) that went off an instant late, mortars that missed by meters. I've covered numerous conflicts, but save for the worst days in Liberia, this violence was on a new level.

In Iraq there was often no buildup to the violence and there were few big operations to photograph. And the rebels you wanted to embed with—they wanted to cut your head off. The car bomb scenes and hospitals and morgues—in other conflicts, good sources of photographs—were off-limits. So you were largely restricted to embeds....

After looking at pictures taken of previous wars, Kamber changes his mind and returns to Iraq.

continued on page 290 ▶

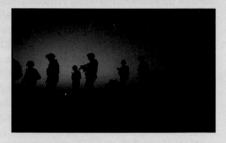

▲ Iraqi soldiers leave their vehicles and begin the walk along a dirt road toward homes to be searched. It is on this road that a U.S. soldier with them will be killed minutes later.

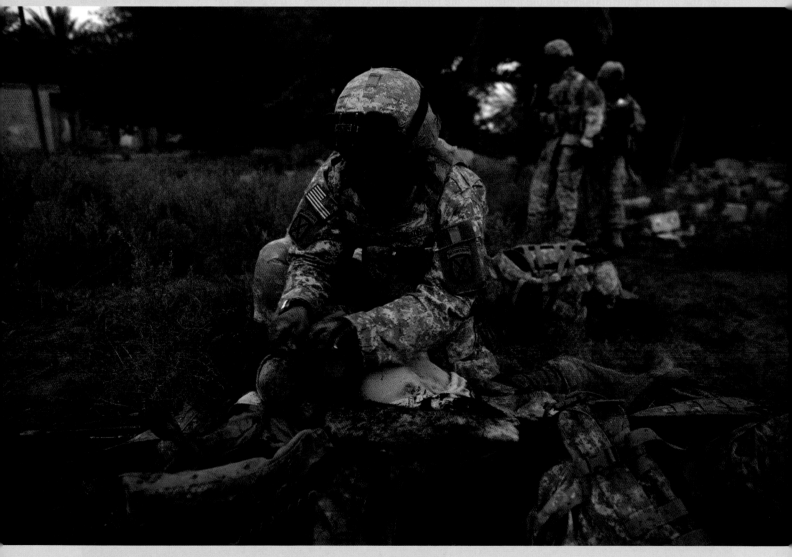

▲ Medic Sgt. Joshua Delgado of Lompoc, California, bandages the face of a wounded comrade who was hit by shrapnel. The wounded soldier was conscious and talking and was expected to survive.

► (NEAR RIGHT) Soldiers cover a wounded comrade on a stretcher to keep debris off him that is being kicked up by a medevac chopper landing nearby. (FAR RIGHT) Soldiers bear the stretcher carrying their wounded comrade to the medevac helicopter.

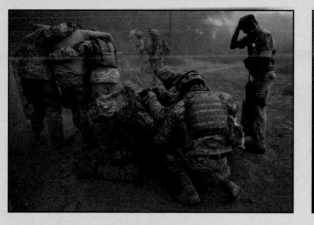

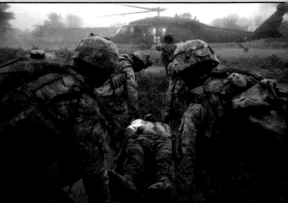

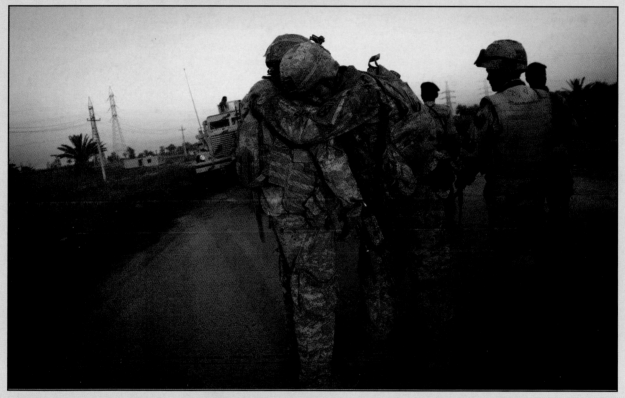

▲ Soldiers mourn the death of a comrade killed less than an hour earlier.

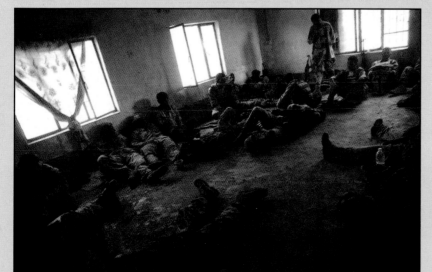

◄ The patrol for three missing U.S. soldiers continues. Exhausted Iraqi and U.S. soldiers take a break in a house after walking for hours in the plus-100-degree heat.

A FIRST-PERSON ACCOUNT

Photos and first-person account by Michael Kamber, *The New York Times*

So I left the conflicts I'd been covering in Africa—Somalia, Darfur, and Chad—and returned to the Baghdad bureau of *The New York Times* for another tour.

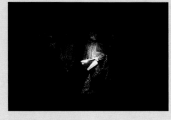

I had gotten up around 3 A.M. of May 19th to go on patrol with a platoon from the 10th Mountain Division. We were near Mahmudiya in the infamous "Triangle of Death" south of Baghdad. The platoon was leaving early to do a search in the countryside for three missing American soldiers taken hostage a few days earlier. The military has this code: you don't leave behind your missing brothers, ever.

I was sleepy and irritable from lack of sleep. There was a briefing around 5 A.M., the soldiers looking at maps and photos by flashlight. Then we put on our flak jackets, climbed into the Humvees and rolled out past the wire.

A kilometer or so away, we met a group of about 50 Iraqi soldiers. Everyone milled about for a while. As it began to get light out, we set off down a dirt road into the countryside.

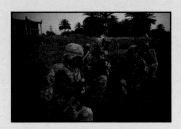

We had not gone far, 150 meters or so. There was a destroyed house by the side of the road. I stepped inside to shoot out through the broken window. As I crossed the threshold, there was a massive, horrific explosion.

I had the same fleeting thought I always have at these moments: "Why can't I turn back time, fast-forward past that one bad scene – this one bad scene – that didn't come out the way I wanted it to." But you know there will be no replay and you have to pick up the camera and go out and face it.

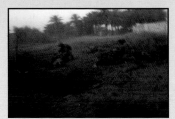

There was the possibility of an ongoing grenade or rocket attack, but I heard no small arms. That left an IED or a land mine. And if there was one land mine, there could be others. I decided to chance it—I couldn't stay in the house—and I began to run toward where I'd come from, toward the cloud of dust and explosives.

I crouched for a moment and photographed the slightly wounded Iraqi soldier. Then as the smoke cleared I saw an American soldier, clearly dead. He had died instantly, probably before he hit the ground. Sprawled about him were three other wounded Americans.

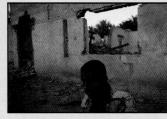

The dead soldier had landed partly on top of a badly wounded soldier, his head on the wounded man's legs. It had only been a matter of seconds, but already a medic was at his side, unzipping his medical bag.

I took a few photos as I approached, seeing things but not really processing them completely. I had taken a half-dozen frames when a captain shouted at me not to photograph. As I thought about how to respond, the medic looked up and asked me to help him.

I took the medic's shears and cut away the wounded man's flak jacket and clothes, and talked to him, asking him about where he was from. The medic's name was Delgado and the two of us tried to keep the soldier alert and distract him from the pain. He was conscious, but his face was terribly wounded. It was already swelling and covered in blood from shrapnel, and his eyes and ears were caked in dirt. When I cut away his shirt I could see that he had no serious wounds to his torso. And I thought immediately that he would survive, as bad as he looked.

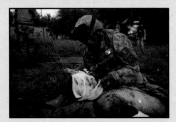

I was surprised at how quiet it was. I heard someone in the distance calling for a helicopter evac, giving Global Positioning System (GPS) coordinates. A soldier nearby, who looked to be about 19, began to curse and swear revenge. Delgado looked at him and said simply, "Not now, this isn't the time," and the soldier quieted down.

I got up and ran to the captain and told him that I had permission to be there and that I was going to do my job. I said they could seize the photos later if they wanted to. He nodded to me. I ran back and knelt by the medic and began to shoot as he checked vital signs and searched for puncture wounds.

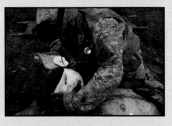

Delgado asked me to help him again as he bandaged the wounded man's arms. I was glad for the request and put down the camera. Helping bandage the soldier made me feel like less of a vulture.

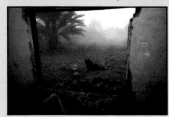

Behind me was another wounded soldier; he was on his knees, his eyes closed and blood trickling down his face. I did not know the wounded soldier had been temporarily blinded and lost much of his hearing in the blast.

As he knelt there, pitched slightly forward, he kept asking how his sergeant was. "I'm worried about my sergeant," he said. No one had yet told him the sergeant was dead. I took the wounded man's photo and moved away. I wasn't going to be the one to do it.

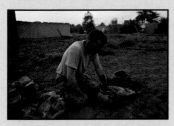

The badly wounded man had been put on a litter now and another soldier was bent over him saying, "I love you, man, I love you." Many of the soldiers I've met in Iraq are bar brawlers who tell fag jokes. But the soldier kept repeating, "I love you man," and finally the wounded soldier said, "Why are you saying you love me? Stop saying that."

The first soldier seemed hurt, "I can tell you I love you if I want to," he replied.

They had found a body bag by now, and they unzipped it and laid it next to the corpse. The Lieutenant (L.T.) began to pull some gear off the soldier's flak jacket, then thought better of it, and the four men lifted him, moved forward and gently lowered him into the bag with his helmet and gear still on. They put him down as you would lay down a sleeping baby.

We waited what seemed a long time for the medevac chopper. In reality, it took 30 minutes from the time of the attack. We heard it coming in

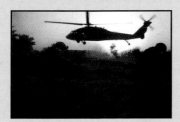

the distance and a soldier threw out red smoke to mark the [landing zone] LZ. As the chopper came in, the air filled with dirt and debris, and the soldiers huddled around the wounded man to keep his wounds clean.

Four soldiers carried the litter out to the chopper, then returned for the other two wounded and, lastly, the body bag. The slightly wounded Iraqi soldier was left to return to base with his unit.

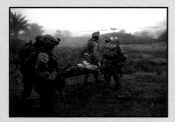

Then we walked single file through the grass back out the main road, each man trying to step in the footsteps of the man in front of him.

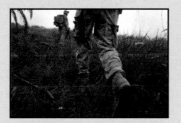

I looked back at the dirt road and wondered how they had managed to place a land mine on a traveled pathway and not kill any Iraqi villagers, or even Iraqi soldiers. An L.T. later said they didn't care who they killed, but somehow they had hit exactly whom they wanted to hit. I had seen no wires, yet I wondered if the explosion had been command detonated.

Beside the Humvees, the soldier who had earlier sworn revenge was now crying, his arms wrapped around another soldier. I shot a frame from the hip, and then as I raised the camera, he moved away.

Nearby, the soldiers were handcuffing the informant with the ringing cell phone. They believed he might have helped to set up the attack through the phone calls.

The dead soldier was 22 years old. His buddies said he had a girlfriend back home that he was going to propose to on his next leave.

I was shaken by the death, as was Damien Cave, the writer I was with. We agreed we'd had enough for the day, but then changed our minds as a new platoon came in to take the place of the one that had suffered the four casualties. The missing soldiers were still out there and the search would continue.

With the new platoon, we walked back down off the main road, this time staying to the grassy fields and away from the soft sandy areas where the explosive had been planted. The sun was fully up now and it was soon well over 100 degrees. I was carrying about 50 pounds, including my flak jacket. Within minutes, sweat had soaked through my shirt and then it began to seep down past my waist, towards my knees until my pants were wet as well.

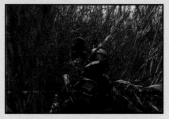

Contrary to what we had been led to expect by the Army, the soldiers from the unit that suffered the casualties came to thank us on the day of publication. One wounded soldier asked for copies of the pictures. They said we had shown the American people what they go through in Iraq, the sacrifices they make. ■

FIND MULTIMEDIA PIECES DISCUSSED IN THIS CHAPTER
http://kenkobre.blogspot.com/2007/10/multimedia.html

in Iraq as they called home to tell their families what had happened to them.

The team also recorded doctors during surgery. The natural sound of doctors, medics, and patients backed by the sounds of a busy medical setting gives the piece an authenticity that would have been missing in a formal voice-over interview.

"I cried," wrote one *Times* reader on the outlet's web site, "when I watched and listened to the words scribbled by a wounded soldier with a tube inserted into his throat that prevented him from speaking being communicated by a nurse via the phone to his family back home."

PREPARING AUDIO
TRANSCRIBE THE WORDS

One of the most tedious but necessary steps in producing a multimedia piece or a video is to transcribe interviews from audio to paper.

This step in the process is called logging. You do not have to note every word exactly, but this stage of the editing allows you to see on paper what was said and to more easily identify and edit out the unnecessary parts.

ORGANIZE THE COPY

Identify the crucial quotes. Circle your favorite three or four comments from each interview. Find the critical parts that tell the story. Save the emotional, the humorous, the powerful moments, but toss out boring or repetitive dialogue. Do not worry yet about "umms" and "ahhs." You can clip those out later when editing the sound track.

Eliminate your own questions. In most cases, your edited piece will omit your questions and contain just your subject's responses. This strategy speeds up the presentation of the material. In a piece edited in this manner, the subject appears to be speaking directly to

the listener/viewer without the interference of a correspondent. The approach puts the emphasis on the speaker not the questioner.

Save the best. Having noted the most interesting parts on paper, return to the computer to copy and paste them into a new document. You will probably have reduced an hour of interviewing into five minutes of interesting quotes.

Let the quotes tell the story. Finally, reorganize the quotes into a logical, story-telling order.

WRITE THE SCRIPT

When you sit down to edit the final piece, you will have at your disposal a set of photographs, interviews, and natural sound. You can build the story by ordering the images first and then marrying the sound to the photographs, or you can build the audio track and match the images to it.

If the story has particularly good images, you might start with those first. Typical video documentaries build the audio track first and later support it with complementary images.

Once you have selected and arranged your best storytelling quotes, you will quickly see if a voice-over script is necessary. Great interviews and natural sound accompanied by strong images may well make a narrated script unnecessary. If critical facts are missing from the interesting quotes you have chosen, a voice-over must supply them instead.

Include the five Ws and H. For either scripted narration or natural sound, include who, what, when, where, why, and how early in the piece.

Identify the dramatic arc. The difference between writing a narration for voice-over and a straight news story lies in the need to create a dramatic arc. The opener needs to grab the viewer's interest. The middle of the piece must explain the problem or show the reason for covering the story, and the end must leave the viewer feeling satisfied. (See Chapter 11, "Photo Story," pages 244, 245, 248, 249, 260, and 261 for more about complication and resolution; also see page 280, "Ask 'what it all means.'")

Write simply. Write in short sentences using simple words. The mind cannot absorb oral information as quickly as the words read on a page, observes Jesse Garnier of the AP.

Keep in mind that long parenthetical and complex sentences are difficult to read out loud. Write the way you talk. Do not use words or phrases that you would not use in normal conversation. Tell the story to your roommate, your friend, or your colleague. Then write the voice-over in the same conversational manner.

Oakland, California, faces an ever-growing homicide rate. "Not Just a Number" is a multimedia web site including rollover maps showing where the murders are taking place, interviews with surviving relatives, and ideas about how to help stop the violence.

San Francisco State University student Monica Radrigan photographed and produced "Men of Iron" for the site. Her story looks at one of the attempted interventions—a military-style after-school program designed to keep young boys off the streets.

Using a handheld digital recorder, she collected ambient sound of the young men marching in formation and doing pushups dressed in army fatigues. She also recorded interviews with the director, who by day is the County Sheriff. Radrigan then edited out unnecessary audio segments to leave a clean set of comments that, when woven together, told the story of the unusual program.
Monica Radrigan

A link to this and other pieces in this chapter can be found at http://kenkobre.blogspot.com/2007/10/multimedia.html

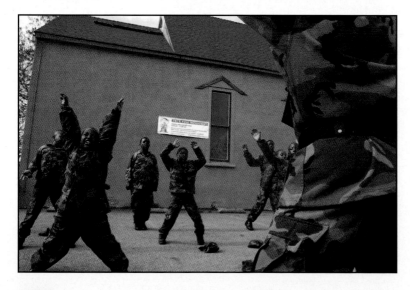

Natural Sound can Provide a Script

Documentaries often are assembled from natural sound segments alone. The same can be done with multimedia. The natural sound, if clear, often contains enough information to dispense with voice-over narration.

Natural sound segments are useful for "establishers." Many documentaries start with a segment that places viewers in the midst of action so they can experience what is happening. Steal this approach from the documentary maker to create powerful multimedia.

In an extensive documentary about White City in southern Peru, students from the University of North Carolina and the Univer-sidad Catolica de Santa Maria used the ambient sound of nuns praying to introduce "Cloistered for Christ," a multimedia story about women living apart from society. "White City Stories," a web site featuring multimedia stories about education, tradition, and industry in this city, was named one of the top web sites of the year by *Time* magazine.

Editors sometimes do find one drawback to natural sound. The information can spill out in haphazard and highly emotional bursts, sometimes requiring the addition of supporting material in a voice-over narration.

RECORDING THE NARRATION

Journalists typically write a script after the photography has been completed and then assemble the images to fit the script.

A voice-over is a narration written and usually read from the script by the reporting journalist—often the photographer these days. The narrator's voice will play over a sequence of still images or video clips that tell the story. You can record a voice-over using an audio recorder, a video camera, or, with recording software and an external microphone, even your computer.

Reading a script is an art that requires smooth, natural delivery and clearly emphasized main points. This is a very new skill for photojournalists to master. Some people reading a script sound as though they are talking to a person right in the same room. Others sound wooden, forced, and unnatural even if they wrote the script themselves.

Try voicing your script and let others tell you which category you fall into. If it is the latter, you might find someone else to handle this role.

A stand-up features the journalist appearing on camera to narrate at least part of the story.

Tip: The UC Berkeley journalism web site is a treasure trove of advice for multimedia journalists. *www.journalism.berkeley.edu/multimedia/tutorials/standups*

EDITING SOUND

There are a number of commercial and even free software programs for editing sound. These are easy to learn with tutorials, manuals, or supplementary books. Also, check out the help feature on each application.

With your final script at the ready, set up a three-column spreadsheet or other document to note down your sound bits in one column, the corresponding images next to them, and written captions beside those.

A grid like this provides a tangible, visual guide to setting up the story in the multimedia software you will be using. Referring to your three-column guide, use the sound editing software to slice out and label the important quotes and supporting ambient sound.

Your edit points are almost always at the very beginning of a word or at the end of a word. Sometimes you need to add a little pause between phrases so that an idea being expressed by your subject has time to resonate. Editing software allows you to add pauses like these easily. And if you remembered to capture ambient sound from the place where you conducted the interview, you can cover the pause with ambient sound, making the pause sound even more natural.

Although you can edit each phrase spoken by your subject to slice out those irritating and surprisingly time-consuming ums, ahs, and "you knows" that sprinkle conversations, it is important to keep the rhythm of speech natural. This is another place where the sound of silence you remembered to record earlier can be used in final editing.

SHOOTING STILLS FOR MULTIMEDIA

Although storytelling approaches are universal (see Chapter 11, "Photo Story"), the difference between shooting still images for a print layout and still images for an audio-driven slide show is not unlike the difference between writing haiku and writing a novel. Both forms use words but the latter uses a lot more of them.

An average magazine story in *Esquire* or *Rolling Stone* might use six images. A multimedia, audio-driven slide show—even a three-minute report—needs a minimum of 40 or more different images to engage a viewer to stay with the pre-timed piece.

Just adding more pictures from a routine assignment can be a photographer's trap.

David Leeson, a photojournalist whose still images have helped win Pulitzer Prizes for *The Dallas Morning News*, notes that it is challenging enough for a still photographer shooting for a typical print assignment to get 10 or 12 great storytelling images. Leeson, who now shoots video for the newspaper's

continued on page 304 ▶

Photos by Renée Byer,
Sacramento Bee / Zuma Press

No one wants to hear the words, "Your child has cancer." Many stories have chronicled the courage of patients going through this devastating disease. In this story about Cyndie French and her 11-year-old son, the photographer sheds light on a mother's struggles as her son sickens and dies.

Billions of dollars go toward cancer research but virtually nothing is given to help families through the emotional and financial realities of not only facing the disease but simply spending time with their dying child.

This year-long story chronicling a single mother's struggle shows the complex relationship between a mother and her preadolescent son as they face this tragic emotional challenge. The pictures take us beyond the doctor appointments that hold bad news to the unrelenting anger of a boy faced with neuroblastoma, a rare and aggressive childhood cancer.

Derek died at home in the arms of his mother. This is not a story about his death. It's the story of how he was guided with the unconditional love, persistence, and patience of his mother despite all odds.

Renée Byer, the photographer, met Cyndie French at an assignment to cover "Race for the Cure," a fitness run to raise cancer research funds. French was volunteering at the event. **continued on page 297 ▶**

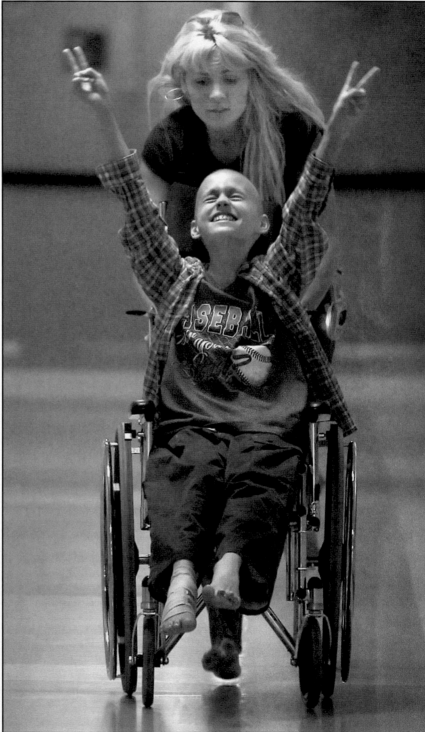

▼ Racing barefooted after kicking off her flip-flops, Cyndie French pushes her son Derek Madsen, 10, up and down hallways in the UC Davis Medical Center, successfully distracting him during the dreaded wait before his bone marrow extraction. Doctors want to determine whether he is eligible for a blood stem-cell transplant, his best hope for beating neuroblastoma, a rare childhood cancer.

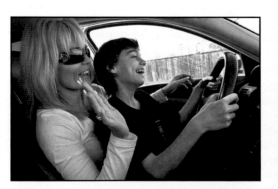

▲ Realizing her son may never have an opportunity to get his driver's license, something he's told her he is anticipating, Cyndie defies the rules and lets 11-year-old Derek drive up and down their street in West Sacramento while sitting on her lap. Cyndie is determined to give him moments of joy whenever possible. On the same day, she had met for the first time with hospice workers and learned there is little time left for Derek to live.

▼ Derek is tearful as Cyndie tries to reason with him at the UC Davis Cancer Center. She and Dr. William Hall, right, argue that Derek should have a series of radiation treatments to shrink the tumors spreading throughout his body and alleviate his pain. "Derek, you might not make it if you don't do this," Cyndie tells her son. Derek fires back: "I don't care! ...Take me home.... I'm done, Mom! Are you listening to me? I'm done!"

▼ After days of almost no sleep while caring for Derek, Cyndie confronts "grandpa" Patrick Degnan, a longtime family friend, about whether he'll be able to help with rent and funeral expenses as Derek is caught in the middle. Cyndie hopes to set up a non-profit organization so families don't have to endure the same financial struggle and chaos they have experienced. "I just wish that some of the percentage of money that goes to cancer research can be diverted to families going through this because many people will never benefit from the research," says Cyndie.

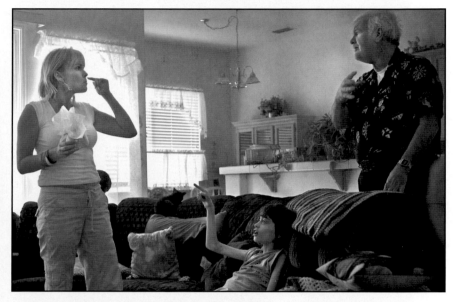

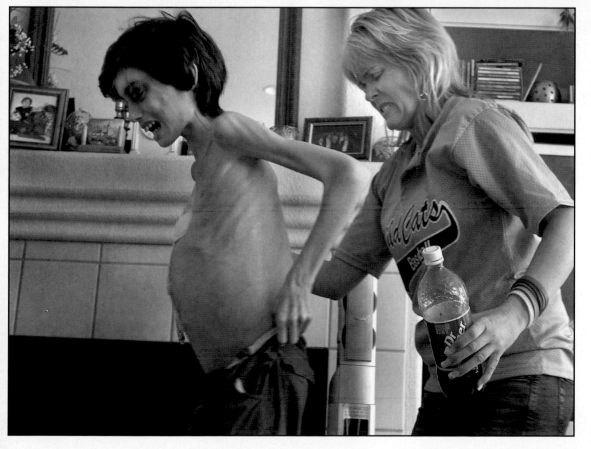

◄ As Derek has a final burst of energy after days of Cyndie keeping vigil at his bedside, she helps her anguished son walk. A cancerous tumor has distended Derek's stomach so far that his pants no longer fit, while another in his brain has impaired his eyesight, which makes it hard for him to navigate inside their rental home.

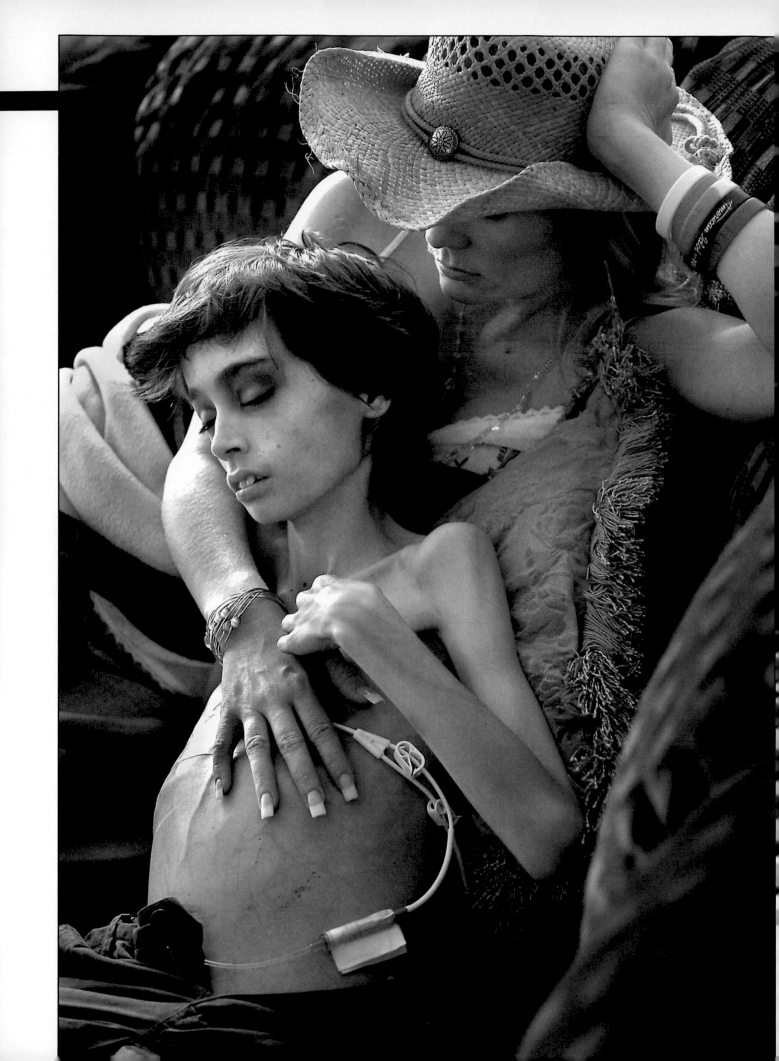

◄ Derek is on medication that hinders his speech and keeps him awake all night. Cyndie spends nearly 24 hours a day at his side, except for a few minutes while hospice nurses are with him. "I was exhausted beyond belief but I had to do this. He would call my name and always expected me to be there," Cyndie said.

▼ Cyndie French tearfully rocks her dying son as the song "Because We Believe" plays. Cyndie sings along with Andrea Bocelli in a whispery voice. "Once in every life/There comes a time/We walk out all alone/And into the light..." From left, family friends Ashley Berger, Amy Morgan, and Kelly Whysong offer comfort as Cyndie tells Derek, "It's okay, baby. I love you, little man. I love you, brave boy. I love you. I love you."

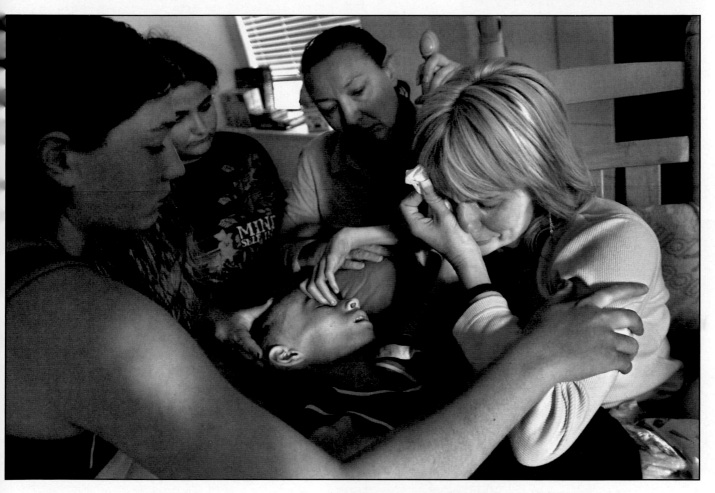

"Derek was not a happy boy when I met him. In fact, he was upset and angry, as most preadolescent boys would be after almost five month of treatment to try and cure his cancer. I didn't think I would be able to break his anger and get him to accept me, but with a lot of patience and time, I gained his trust and love," says Byer.

"My instincts were to try and help, but I knew as a journalist I had to let things unfold, and the most important thing was not to interrupt their daily pattern of life."

The response to the story was overwhelming, with more than 700 readers posting comments to the *Sacramento Bee* web site, calling and donating $4000 to "Derek's Wish," a nonprofit set up by his mother. ■

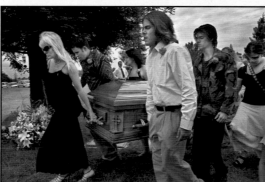

▲ Cyndie leads Derek's casket to burial with assistance from her sons Anthony Moffe, foreground; Micah Moffe, opposite him; and Vincent Morris, who is not visible; as well as several friends. "I will forever carry your memory in my heart and remind others to give of their time, energy, and support to other families like ours," Cyndie says at the funeral.

FIND MULTIMEDIA PIECES DISCUSSED IN THIS CHAPTER
http://kenkobre.blogspot.com/2007/10/multimedia.html

BRING BACK THE WOUNDED WITH HEART, SOUL, AND SURGERY

Photos by Rick Loomis, *Los Angeles Times*

Rick Loomis of the *Los Angeles Times* shot and produced a three-part series following the lives of the soldiers wounded in Iraq. The series includes Part One, "Bring Back the Wounded with Heart, Soul and Surgery"; Part Two, "The Journey Through the Trauma"; and Part Three, "New Battle on the Home Front."

After three years of war, the U.S. military has perfected a highly streamlined lifesaving process that carries the wounded quickly from the battlefield to emergency surgery in the combat zone, and on to military hospitals in Germany and the United States. More than 17,000 troops wounded since March 2003 have been helped in a medical effort unmatched in any previous war.

continued on page 300 ▶

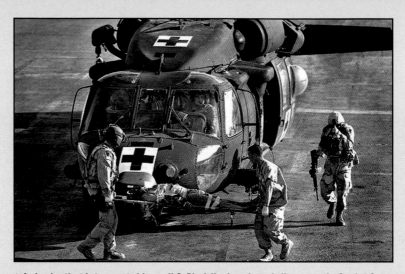

▲ An Iraqi patient is transported from a U.S. Black Hawk medevac helicopter to the Combat Support Hospital in Baghdad. U.S. medical personnel routinely treat injured Iraqis, including insurgents.

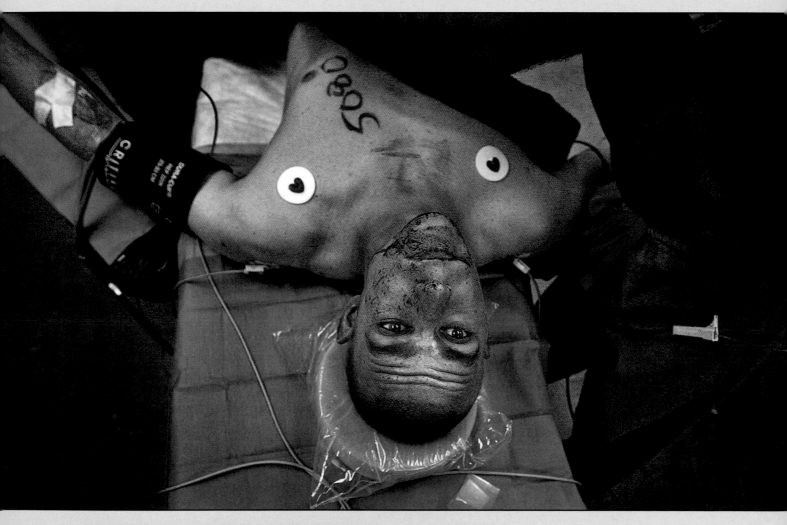

▲ U.S. Marine Corps 2nd Lt. James Michael Geiger III, 24, of Fayetteville, N.C., is prepped for an operation on his foot after he was injured by a land mine while giving out candy and radios to Iraqis south of the Haditha Dam in western Iraq. "We were out there trying to be nice," said Geiger before his surgery.

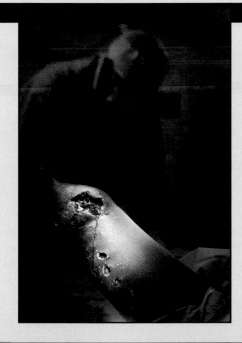

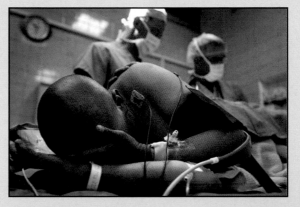

◄ U.S. Army Sgt. Colin Johnson, lying on an operating table awaiting surgery for a broken kneecap and shrapnel damage to his leg that was caused by a roadside bomb in central Iraq. The surgery took place at the Air Force Combat Support Hospital in Balad, Iraq.

◄ Baghdad, Iraq—Marine PFC Jose Alarcon holds his head in pain as doctors in Baghdad operate on him after he was injured in a grenade attack. When asked about the level of pain he was enduring Alarcon said, "I ain't gonna lie. It's bad."

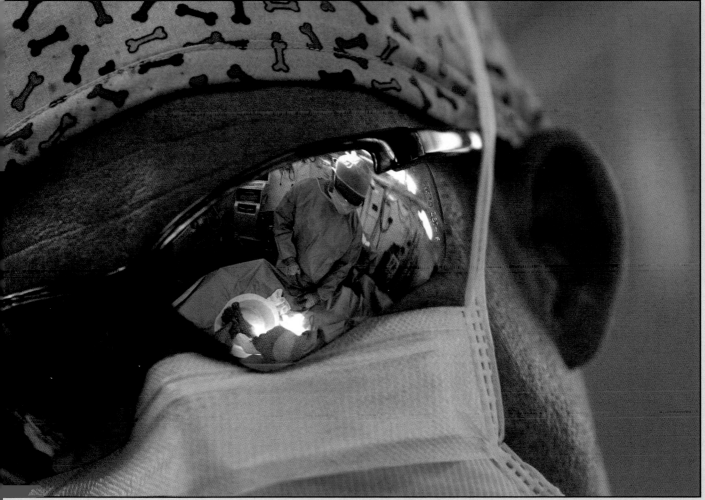

▲ Lt. Col. Jim Keeney, an orthopedic surgeon, works on a wounded U.S. soldier in the Air Force Combat Surgical Hospital in Balad, Iraq. Many of the more than 17,000 U.S. military personnel that have been wounded since the war with Iraq began in 2003 have been treated there.

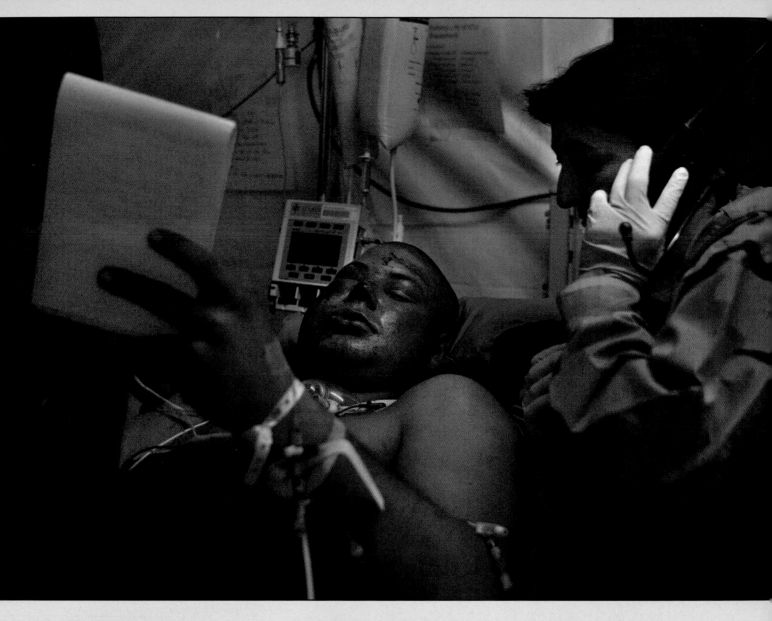

THE JOURNEY THROUGH TRAUMA

Loomis and writer David Zucchino worked as equal partners on a multimedia and print story to tell the story of this life-saving effort. The two went to Iraq to record the care wounded soldiers were receiving in military hospitals there. Loomis met the wounded soldiers as they arrived at Balad and asked to take pictures. Once he received their okay, he proceeded to photograph bloody men torn apart by bullets and shrapnel produced by improvised explosive devices (IEDs).

The images are strong and in your face—an honest reflection of the reality of the injured soldiers. Loomis seems to have censored little.

▲ Major Nancy Walter, a nurse, relays messages from Spc. Joshua Griffin to his mother back in Humble, Texas. Griffin, a patient at the Air Force Theater Hospital in Balad, Iraq, was unable to talk because a tracheotomy tube had been put down his throat. Major Walter's conversation with Griffin's mother plays over this and other images of Griffin as he writes what to say to his mother.

"The men are helpless and traumatized. Viewing the run of images is not unlike being punched in the stomach," says Marianne Fulton in her piece "Following the Thread: Rick Loomis" on *DigitalJournalist.org*.

While in Iraq, Loomis recorded audio in the field to accompany "The Lifeline." He captured atmospheric sounds, conversations, and interviews that complement his strong images.

Another significant element of the story came when the team visited the soldiers back at home to record and photograph the formerly helpless men during their recoveries.

Here is multimedia at its finest. The powerful set of images, both bold and at times even beautiful, lock viewers' attention. The riveting audio provides context to the images and drives the natural story arc from arriving at the hospital to the flight to Germany, and, finally, to partial recovery at home.

Loomis says the upshot professionally of publishing the project online was receiving comments directly from the public. This was an unusual circumstance for the photographer and writer, and one they say they appreciated. ■

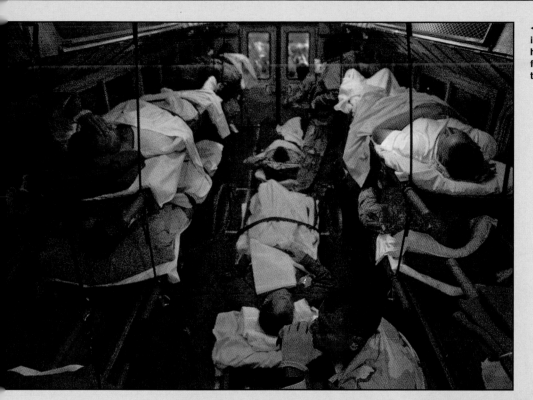

◄ Wounded troops are taken by bus to a plane in Balad, Iraq, bound for a U.S. military hospital in Germany. Most will later be flown back to the United States for further treatment.

NEW BATTLE ON THE HOMEFRONT

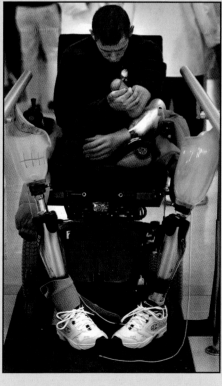

▲ U.S. Army Specialist Bryan Anderson stares at where his hand used to be before he lost it along with both legs in a roadside bombing incident that happened while he was driving a Humvee in Baghdad, Iraq, in October 2005.

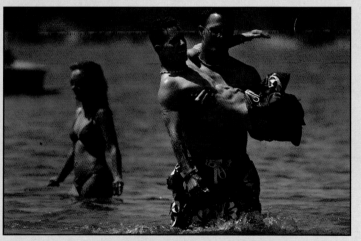

▲ U.S. Army Specialist Bryan Anderson, 25, is carried out of the water by his close friend Stephen Crenshaw after he went tubing on Belton Lake during a visit to the Fort Hood, Texas, area where he was stationed before being injured in Iraq. Though he struggled early on in his recovery, less than a year later Anderson had learned to walk again using prosthetics and can catch a ball using an attachment where his arm once was. About 30 friends came to a barbecue to show their support for Anderson.

FIND MULTIMEDIA PIECES DISCUSSED IN THIS CHAPTER
http://kenkobre.blogspot.com/2007/10/multimedia.html

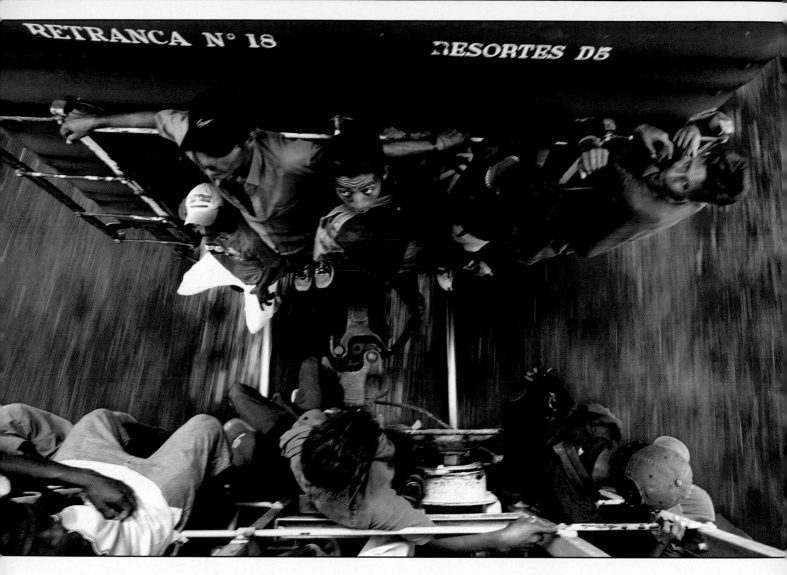

Photos by Gary Coronado, *Palm Beach Post*

Gary Coronado, who shoots for the *Palm Beach Post*, first learned about the challenges faced by immigrants coming to the United States from Mexico and Central America from an opinion piece in his newspaper. Later he saw a piece by Don Barteletti of the *Los Angeles Times*. Barteletti's "Enrique's Journey" retraced the trip of one young man who caught dangerous but free rides on trains in order to reach the "promised land" of the United States of America.

Coronado approached the story of desperate immigrants from a unique angle by concentrating on those who do not complete the journey—and the people who are there to help them. Desperate for a new life, many migrants nearly starve or die of thirst on the train trip. Ninety-six were maimed in one year as they failed to successfully leap aboard the speeding trains that lead north from a point in Mexico about 15 miles from the Honduran border. Others have died. Grupo Beta is the humanitarian branch of Mexico's immigration agency. Individual

▲ Central American migrants jump and ride a train headed northwest from Gregório Méndez, Tabasco, Mexico. The train ride is roughly three hours until the next stop. The majority of the Central Americans walk the 55.6 km from the Guatemala border to Tenosique, Mexico, where they begin their train journeys.

volunteers help the migrants as they journey north and one woman has even built a shelter for those injured and maimed along the way. ■

photos continued on page 304 ▶

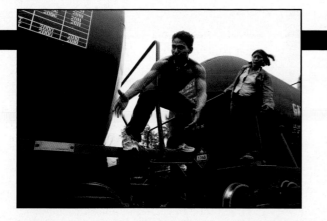

▲ A Central American migrant attempts to help a woman jump aboard a moving train at in Tenosique, Tabasco, Mexico. The woman did not make it because the train was moving too fast.

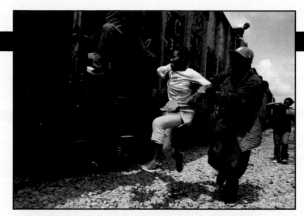

▲ A Central American migrant is helped aboard a moving train by a fellow migrant headed northwest from Tenosique, Tabasco, toward Palenque, Chiapas, Mexico.

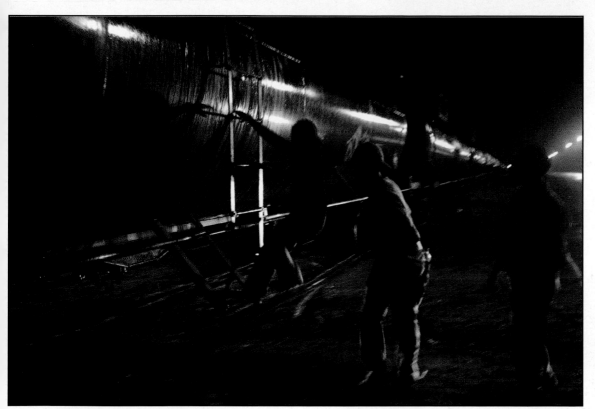

◄ Central American migrants jump a moving train near the railway station in Tenosique, Tabasco, Mexico. The poorest of the poor ride the trains to the U.S.-Mexican border in search of the American dream.

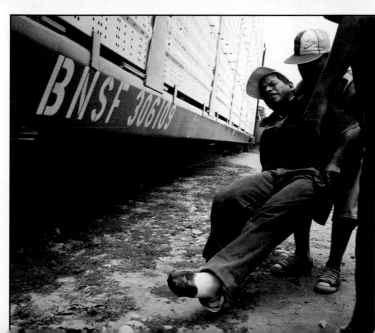

◄ Manuel Perez of Honduras is helped by another migrant after having the lower part of his left foot crushed by the train's knuckle-coupling while the train was moving forward and backward attaching cargo cars in Tenosique. He was transported to the General Hospital Tenosique by the Municipal Police. The initial diagnosis listed crushed left foot, amputation of five toes, and maybe part of his foot. Perez said he was trying to get to Miami, Florida, where his cousins live. He was transported to Hospital Rovirosa in Villahermosa, Tabasco.

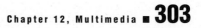

TRAIN JUMPERS

▼ Honduran Oscar Noe Ortiz Carrasco, left, is transported by a Grupo Beta truck to the hospital in Tenosique, Tabasco, Mexico. When Oscar was jumping the train, his foot caught in the train's coupling, amputating the big toe on his right foot. Grupo Beta, a branch of the Mexican Immigration Service, provides protection, rescue, and medical attention to migrants. Hermenegildo Lopez Cahum, right, accompanies Carrasco to the hospital.

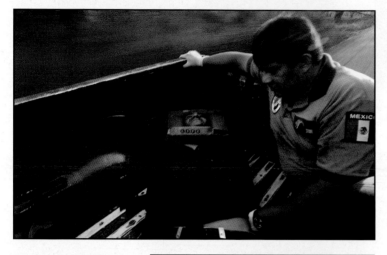

▶ Raul Ordoñez Martinez of Honduras is recovering after having both legs amputated. He had tried to jump on a moving train in Tenosique, Tabasco, Mexico. His hands were sweaty when he grabbed the stairs to a tanker, and he slipped and fell beneath the wheels of the train.

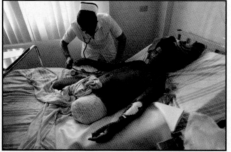

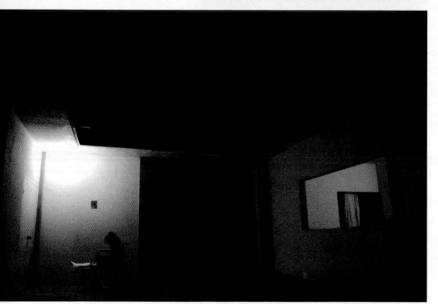

▲ Cenia Lovato of El Salvador, who broke her right ankle jumping off the train, wheels herself to her room at the Albergue Jesus el Buen Pastor del Pobre y Migrante in Tapachula, Chiapas, Mexico. Doña Olga Sanchez Martinez started the shelter more than 16 years ago for Central American migrants headed to the United States who instead were mutilated by the train headed there. Many at the shelter have lost arms and legs.

FIND MULTIMEDIA PIECES DISCUSSED IN THIS CHAPTER
http://kenkobre.blogspot.com/2007/10/multimedia.html

web site, opines that the other 28 stills in most multimedia slide shows tend to be weak. "Those are the images that would have wound up in File 13—the trash can," he says.

Sean Connelley, multimedia producer for the *Oakland Tribune*, says that slide shows need many more detail shots than a typical picture story in print. The photographer also needs to shoot images that will serve as transitions to introduce and end sequences. (For more on shooting sequences, see pages 323–327 in Chapter 13, "Video.")

Even though each shot in a slide show may be on the screen for as few as three seconds (or less), you still need quality, well-composed, and candidly shot images, just a lot more of them. Obviously, the longer the sound track runs, the more images you will need. The *Sacramento Bee*'s Renée C. Byer's story of "A Mother's Journey," which follows a mother and her dying son through the boy's final months, shows how powerful a combination of words and great images can be. The moving story won a Pulitzer Prize.

When shooting for multimedia, you must keep audio in mind. Creating a powerful multimedia piece demands that the words and images work together directly since they are presented—and absorbed by the viewer—simultaneously. In a report for the *Washington Post* titled "Cleaning Floors, Brightening Minds," photographer Lois Raimondo and audio reporter/producer/photo editor Nancy Donaldson tell the story of a school custodian who also serves as the after-school art teacher and all-around role model for the school's youngsters. The excellent images, interviews with multiple subjects, and natural sound provide an interesting, well-rounded report (see page 270).

SHOOT LIKE A FILMMAKER

See Chapter 13, "Video" pages 320–328, for a description of shots used by documentary photographers. Filmmakers use a number of shots that are sometimes overlooked by a still photographer searching for the decisive moment. Action shots of the subject are important in multimedia, but reaction shots of observers or others also help tell the story.

For a more cinematic effect, some photographers use continuous shooting mode to capture a series of images that are then edited to rapidly appear on the screen almost like a movie. Andrew Craft of *The Fayetteville Observer* used this technique to good advantage in his piece on "The National Hollerin' Contest." Although most of the images are of people at microphones, the photos of individual contestants flashing by rapidly add a film-like dimension to the report.

IMAGES AND SOUND IN A SLIDE SHOW

Once you have finished editing the sound, you will begin to combine the sound with your photos to make a multimedia slide show.

Soundslides is a simple and popular software application that photojournalists use to combine sound and images to create multimedia pieces for the Internet. The program basically digests JPEG photos and sound files and outputs them as a slideshow in Flash files ready to display on the Internet.

You should import the images into Soundslides in the order that you want them to appear. This program will then automatically make a Flash animation.

You might want to use iPhoto, Apple's Aperture, or Adobe's Photoshop Lightroom to order the images. Apple's iMovie, Final Cut Pro, Final Cut Pro Express, and Adobe's Premiere also are commonly used for combining sound and images. These programs will make a movie file instead of a Flash file.

PACING THE IMAGES

Viewers accustomed to fresh televised images flashing on a screen every few seconds tend to expect the same when watching a multimedia piece. Of course, you cannot achieve this rate of image bombardment using stills, but you do not want to bore viewers. Leaving images on the screen too long is likely to send them clicking away to another story on the Internet. On the other hand, viewers will not have sufficient time to absorb each image if they pass through too quickly. Nancy Donaldson, who produces multimedia reports for *WashingtonPost.com*, generally limits the time the image is on the screen from five to eight seconds. For a five-minute piece, she says, she includes about 40 images.

When viewing Gary Coronado's "Train Jumpers" online, watch for the effective pacing of images during a series in which a young man races for a rapidly passing train and misses.

IMAGES, SOUND, AND TEXT

While many multimedia reports include images, sound, and text, do not assume that viewers will read captions while looking at pictures and listening to audio.

Despite all the hype about multitasking, scientists have proven that the human mind can do only one thing at a time well. It can move quickly between activities, but it jumps linearly. You might say that the mind "cannot walk and chew gum" at the same time.

Plan your presentation so that viewers can concentrate on watching and listening to the slide show. Do not expect that they can or will read captions on the pictures while also listening to the sound and looking at the images.

Think about how you yourself examine a picture layout in a newspaper, magazine, or book. You cannot read the captions at the same moment you are looking at the picture. In fact, you may look at all the pictures before you return to the captions. Imagine adding narration or dialogue to the mix.

GIVE AN ATTENTION TEST

Once you have finished, ask other people to watch the piece in your presence if you have time. Watch them, not the screen. Are they alert? Do their eyes wander? Are they moved in the appropriate places?

After the piece plays, ask a few questions to see if the story they saw is the one you thought you presented. Is your story complete and accurate? If not—you really do not want to hear this, but it is true—you may need to rewrite, reorganize, or otherwise re-edit the report.

Ultimately, you do not want to lose the journalism in the sound and Flash. ∎

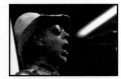
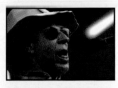
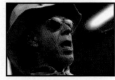
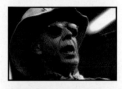
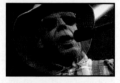
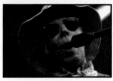

For his multimedia package on the National Hollerin' Contest, the photographer shot a burst of frames. The series, displayed rapidly in the slide show, gives the piece a cinematic feel.
Andrew Craft,
The Fayetteville Observer

A link to this piece can be found at
http://kenkobre.blogspot.com/200
7/10/multimedia.html

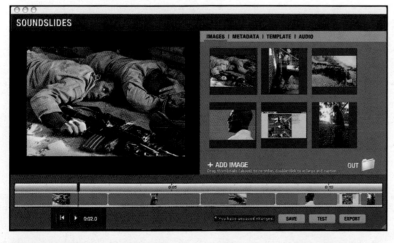

The software application Soundslides allows you to combine a series of images with an audio file to produce a slide show ready to upload to the Internet.

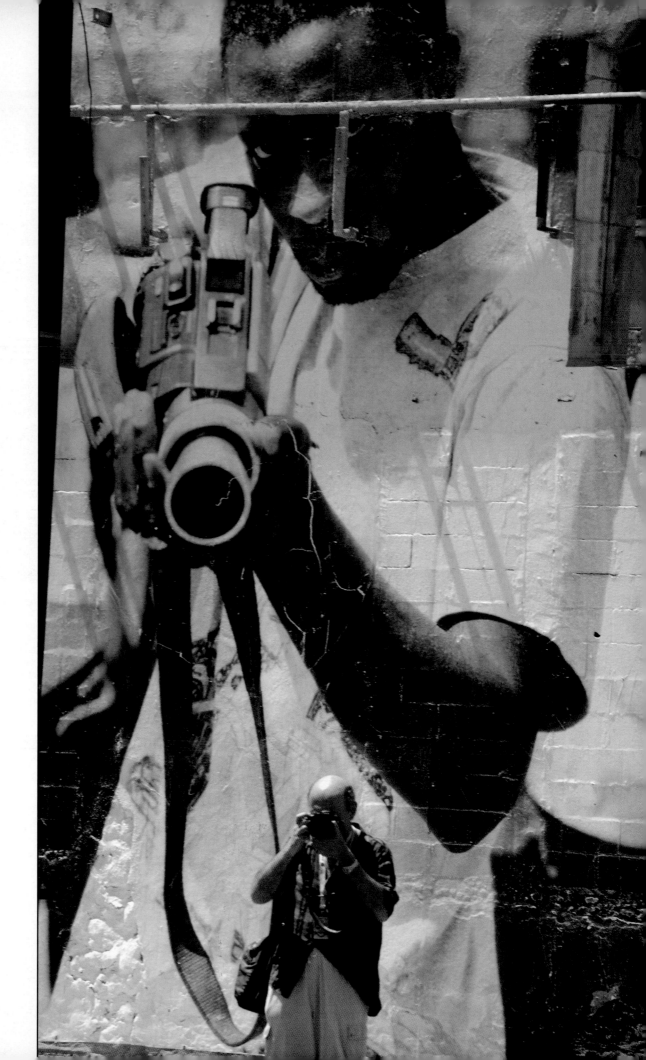

13

Video

PICTURES THAT MOVE

Kim Komenich, whose still pictures earned a Pulitzer Prize, assigned himself to master the world of video.

His subject—a man who not only looks like Santa Claus but acts the part. With a long white beard, wavy white hair, and bright blue eyes, George Goetz is often mistaken for Santa, even in July. It does not hurt that Goetz's favorite color is red.

Komenich met the Santa look-alike on a still assignment for the *San Francisco Chronicle* and, on the photographer's own time, started

The still photographer stands before a three-story-tall poster of a young man holding a video camera like a gun. The poster was part of a project by two French photographers to paper walls with outsized images.
© Ken Kobré

videotaping him for a short documentary. "You must start with a good character and not try to do *Lord of the Rings*," Komenich warns.

Goetz, who plays the role of Santa in the San Francisco Bay area every December, was a perfect choice. He had lost his own father and so decided to "be there" for other children.

Further living the role, Goetz flies every year to Barrow, Alaska, the town nearest the North Pole, to see the children there.

Komenich, whose career had centered on still photography, accompanied Goetz to Alaska to shoot video.

"Most of my first problems with shooting video were dumb things," he says. "I thought the camera switch was off when it was on and the other way around."

In Alaska, Komenich discovered a whole different set of complications with the video equipment. As he got out of the warm van in the –34 degree Fahrenheit weather to take some shots with the video camera, the cords to his headphone and microphones froze solid. That was not all. "I watched the battery indicator go from full to empty in just a few minutes as I was standing out in the cold."

In his warm hotel room each night, Komenich reviewed the day's footage, checking to see if he had shot reverse shots—new territory for a still photographer

(see pages 320–328)—and overalls to go with the close-ups.

"If you approach the story as a still photographer you are going to miss the transitional stuff," he says, "seemingly unimportant stuff that will make the story flow well."

Komenich started with a character-driven story. His subject was willing, available, colorful, and did a lot of visual things.

Komenich tackled the project on his own time and dime so that he could master the medium. He logged, transcribed, and then turned over his five tapes to be edited by KPIX-TV, the CBS local affiliate. His two-minute show on Goetz aired the following Christmas Eve at 5 P.M. and 11 P.M., with a lead-in from the anchor. Komenich now adds video and multimedia to his award-winning skills set for the *San Francisco Chronicle* and its web site, *SFGate.com*.

THE PLATYPUS IS A ONE-MAN BAND VIDEO JOURNALIST WITH A BACKPACK

Komenich is part of a growing troupe of former still photojournalists now employing the video camera to shoot, report, and even to produce their own stories. Travis Fox of *WashingtonPost.com* and David Leeson of *The Dallas Morning News* are others.

The photographer turned an assignment about a man who lives the life of Santa Claus for part of each year, into his first video project.
Kim Komenich,
San Francisco Chronicle

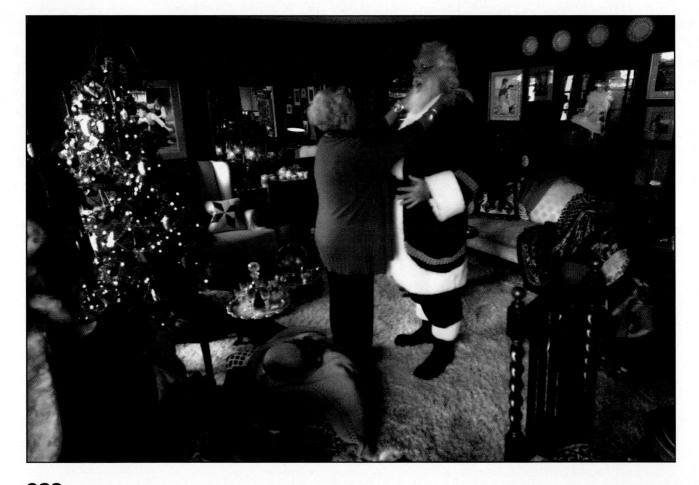

At major market TV stations like KRON-TV in San Francisco or smaller markets like WKRN-TV in Nashville, journalistic roles are shifting as reporters, editors, on-air talent, and behind-the-scenes camera operators with a digital video camera and a laptop have become the Lone Rangers of news, riding the reporting range hoping their digital video cameras will be their silver bullets.

At the newsgathering center of the storm is a new, multiarmed journalist still in search of a title. Dirck Halstead, a former *Time* shooter who early foresaw the evolution of still photojournalism into video, coined the phrase "Platypus" in the 1990s. The platypus is an egg-laying, semi-aquatic mammal—some of this and some of that—like the still shooter using a video camera to capture still and moving images. Another term that has emerged is video journalist. "One-man band" (regardless of the gender of its practitioner) is another. Travis Fox, a pioneer who is doing it all, refers to himself as a video producer. Others call themselves backpack journalists.

Whatever the name, this new breed of journalist is in many instances juggling what would have been the work of four people in the past. Traditional television crews consist of a photographer who handles the camera, a sound technician who records audio, a reporter who perhaps interviews subjects, writes a script, and then reads it on camera and, finally, an unseen and often unsung producer who makes the original contacts with the subjects and then organizes the shoot and interviews.

Each former specialist—the photographer, reporter, producer, the sound technician—now may be called upon to shoot the story, report, collect sound, conduct interviews, produce segments, and even edit the final package.

The one-man band sometimes even uploads edited video to the Internet or sends it out for broadcast.

Of all the skills necessary for the evolving journalism industry, maintains Halstead, "The number one skill that will be required to make newspaper web sites a success is the eye of the photojournalist."

Even more important is the ability of the photojournalist to recognize stories and tell them visually. See Chapter 11, "Photo Story," pages 232–267.

Technically, getting the right image is no longer enough. Photojournalists now must report accurately, avoid shooting dull footage, and, equally important, avoid technical

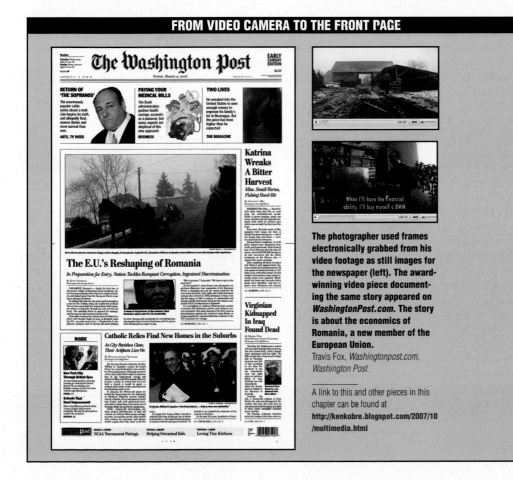

FROM VIDEO CAMERA TO THE FRONT PAGE

The photographer used frames electronically grabbed from his video footage as still images for the newspaper (left). The award-winning video piece documenting the same story appeared on *WashingtonPost.com*. The story is about the economics of Romania, a new member of the European Union.

Travis Fox, *Washingtonpost.com, Washington Post*

A link to this and other pieces in this chapter can be found at http://kenkobre.blogspot.com/2007/10 /multimedia.html

glitches that will ruin the sound track—all this in addition to editing the package on a deadline while preparing for the next day's story.

Travis Fox, perhaps the first full-time video journalist working for a newspaper's web site, prefers working alone. "I can get more intimate moments and establish a rapport with the subject," he says.

Few journalists, however, are expert in all aspects of reporting, shooting, sound gathering, and editing. Further, the four minds that helped shape the classic video story, and the eight hands that helped deliver it are all falling to a single person.

"The product often looks good, sounds good, or is written well, but seldom all three. Then again, in fairness, probably not even Edward R. Murrow could excel at three jobs at once," wrote Ron Russell in *San Francisco Weekly* in a piece about KRON's transition to one-man-band reporting. "Reporters don't necessarily make good shooters or [video] editors, and people who've worked behind the camera don't necessarily know how to convey a story," says Greg Lyon, a former KRON staffer quoted in the same article.

Even proponents of the one-man-band approach to video journalism admit

STILL FRAME GRABS FROM A VIDEO CAMERA

Photojournalists are using video cameras to photograph documentaries, but that's not all. From their captured video, many are pulling still images for web sites and even for print.

Some photojournalists are even trading in their 35mm SLRs for high-definition video cameras. David Leeson of *The Dallas Morning News* cannot quite bring himself to give back his company-issued, high-end Canon still camera, but he is shooting all his assignments with a video camera.

When he needs stills for the paper, he views the take on his computer, finds a frame he likes—and grabs it. He has found that he can pull a computer-enhanced single frame that is of sufficient quality to produce a non-pixelated five- or even six-column image for the paper.

"The first thing I did upon receiving an HDV (high definition video) camera just prior to departure to cover Hurricane Katrina in 2005 was shoot a few seconds of video, import it with iMovie, and make a frame grab," Leeson wrote in a column for *DigitalJournalist.org*. "The results were almost as magical as the first time I saw a print emerge in a tray of developer. I knew the world of photojournalism, as we knew it, would never be quite the same again."

Leeson predicts news photographers will be using high-definition video cameras exclusively.

They will be able to take four approaches to any assignment, he says, producing:

- **A video report** with sound and moving images;
- **An audio report** alone for a podcast or radio program;
- **A photo-audio report** in the form of a slide show with sound and still images;
- **Single or multiple still pictures** for a print page.

Leeson goes further than most by claiming that photojournalists using frame grabs from a video camera can make "better and impactful" still images. However, he cautions, "you can't just spray the scene with the video camera and hope you will catch a good picture."

Leeson thinks that the present quality of frame grabs is amazing, yet even that fact misses the point, he says. "When did we ever make quality the most important factor?" he asks." He argues that frame grabs from video have so many advantages that they outweigh the slight loss in fine detail.

Not all shooters who have made the transition are convinced. Travis Fox is a one-man-band photojournalist who refers to himself as a video producer.

His award-winning work for the *Washington Post* has appeared on *WashingtonPost.com*, as well as on television and in the newspaper. Frame grabs do not work well if the original video was shot in low light, he points out, or if the

subject was moving quickly. Getting shallow depth of field with video is difficult, he adds.

"You can get good screen grabs when all the planets are aligned," says Fox, "but not all the time." While frame grabs from his video have run on the front page of the *Washington Post* (see page 309), Fox took a still camera on his latest trip to Samoa to produce high quality still photos for the print version of the story.

"Because you shoot video in a different way—looking for sequences rather than moments—finding screen grabs that make good still images is difficult," he says.

If you are planning on using a frame grab from your video, remember before starting to shoot to adjust the video camera's shutter speed. If you are shooting a fast moving Formula 1 racecar, the 1/60 sec. default on most video cameras may result in good video but will not freeze the action of the speeding car for a single frame grab.

Note, however, that changing to a fast or slow shutter speed will affect the look of the video footage that you record. Also, frame grabs taken from video shot in low light tend to look muddy. Adding some external lighting to the scene during your original video shoot will help both the video footage and individual frame grabs look better.

While it is possible to use the video camera to take single

technical quality can suffer. But that does not bother WKRN news director Steve Sabato. "If it's an interesting, compelling story the audience isn't sitting back saying the lighting doesn't look very good; it doesn't seem the focus is as sharp as it is on those other cameras," he says in an article for *American Journalism Review*. "The audience doesn't react like that."

The article goes on to pose a larger concern: "Can one person, striving to shoot video that's in focus and capture sound you can clearly hear, also manage to get all the details right when working against the clock?"

That's what worries photojournalist David Carter of WFAA-TV in Dallas. "It's going to jeopardize accuracy," he says.

If one person does it all, there is a greater risk of airing mistakes, and, as Carter puts it, "wrong facts will get you sued."

The lesson here is to hone your reporting skills as finely as your camera techniques. For a review on how to do this, see page 313.

THE CHARACTER-DRIVEN STORY

Almost every video journalist interviewed for this chapter talked about finding a specific character to drive the storyline for successful

images, many photojournalists feel that the video camera itself is not as functional as a still camera for capturing moments and controlling the technical and aesthetic quality of still images. Is today's video camera the Swiss Army knife of photojournalism?

As this book goes to press, many newspaper photojournalists have made the switch to video.

Ultimately, technology will determine the outcome of this debate. ∎

Photographers are developing ways to freeze video frames and use them in print publications. This self-portrait by David Leeson, an early proponent of using frame grabs in print, was grabbed from footage shot with a high-definition video camera.
David Leeson, *The Dallas Morning News*

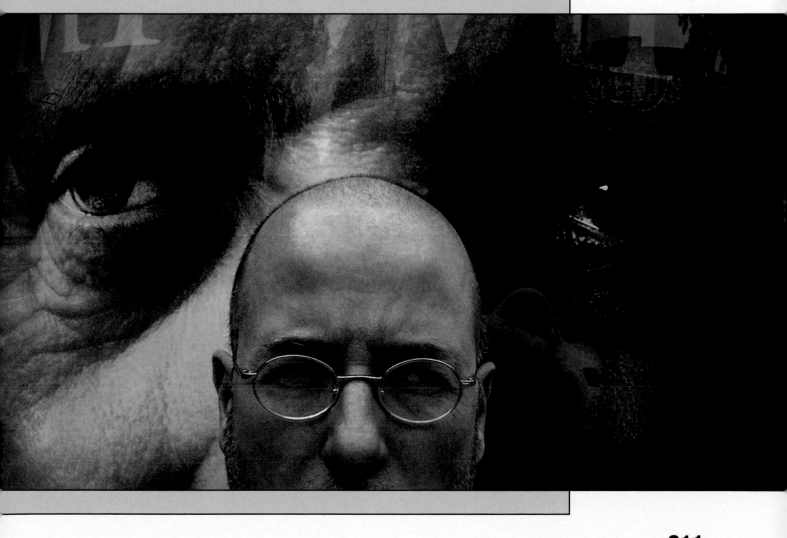

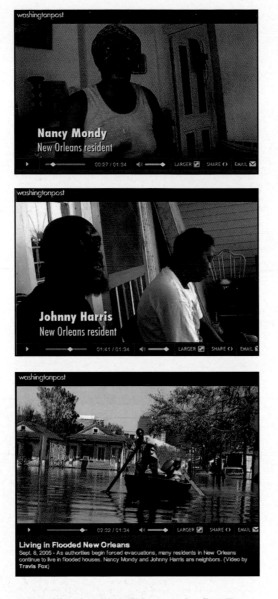

people-driven stories that have long been the mainstay of multiple-image layouts in print.

The difference between print and video or even audio-driven slide shows is that the subjects must be articulate. They must be able to speak about themselves easily, says Fox. They must have something to say on the topic. "They can pump out the good quotes," he says.

The viewer of your piece is going to spend three to thirty minutes with your subject. The viewer must find the person engaging.

Fox does not take chances on the subjects of his pieces. "I do a pre-interview before I record anything," he says. "I talk to people and ask questions. 'What do you do on a daily basis? What are you going to do tomorrow?' Then I select a character. If it doesn't work then I jump on to someone else."

In "Feeding Baby Izzedine," part of a larger package called "Crisis in Darfur Expands," Fox's main subject shares her moving story in a clear and articulate way. One of millions of refugees fleeing genocide in Darfur, she tells of her heartbreaking efforts to feed her child in a refugee camp. Interviews with aid workers provide context to the story.

Fox, who speaks Romanian, found another engaging subject through a friend of a friend. Fox builds his 10-minute piece "Romania's Hopes Lie with EU" on a series of articulate characters whose stories represent the issues facing the country's entrance into the European Union.

One is a man who with his wife struggles to survive on $260 a month from their combined salaries. They live in a dull-looking apartment house with a broken elevator. He blames his problems on government corruption. "The low standard of living in Romania is caused by the high levels of corruption," says the Romanian.

For Fox, the featured Romanian is a sympathetic character. "I wanted someone that was struggling financially and had a lot to say." Fox rounds out the facts of the story with his own narration and with interviews with analysts and local politicians involved in Romania's entry into the European Union.

A written story accompanied by a frame grab from Fox's video ran on page one of the *Washington Post* (see page 309).

David Leeson, who shoots and produces video fulltime for *The Dallas Morning News* web site, says that he looks for "subject-driven" stories—those featuring a character or characters but in which subjects tell the story in their own voices instead of using a correspondent or narrator. In a story Leeson shot and produced about animal training, for

storytelling in video. Fox won the first Emmy award for original video journalism created specifically for new media. His award-winning pieces include several character-driven, first-person stories about Hurricane Katrina and the subsequent flooding in New Orleans. "Living in Flooded New Orleans" shares with viewers, through the eyes and voice of neighbors Nancy Mondy and Johnny Harris, what life was like for those who stayed behind.

The hardest kinds of stories to produce, Fox says, are those that are cerebral—stories that are not about a place or a person.

Komenich of the *San Francisco Chronicle* started with a good character in the man who would be Santa Claus and followed that single storyline.

Good characters are key to storytelling of all kinds. Review Chapter 11, "Photo Story," pages 233, 235, and 238 for the kinds of

example, the voice of Barbara Heidenreich, who teaches zookeepers how to control their animals, alternates with voices of zookeepers explaining what they have learned.

A link to this and other pieces discussed in this book is at *http://kenkobre.blogspot.com /2007/10/video.html*.

SHOOTING VIDEO AND STILLS: A COMPARISON

Just as any amateur can take pictures with a point-and-shoot still camera, photographers can shoot video on automatic by pointing the camera at a subject and pushing the button. But mastering the equipment and the craft

that goes with it will assure consistently usable footage with interesting images and clean sound. While there are many similarities between video and still photography, "Vive la difference."

Having used a still camera, you may find the video camera a bit awkward in shape and design. With time and experience, you will find the location of all the manual and automatic controls. Here is where you must be conscious of the differences. Both have lenses, of course. But with video you see what you are recording in real time. You don't press the button and "chimp" the image on the LCD screen as you can on a still camera.

REPORTING BASICS

Without going back to Journalism 101, here are some basic reporting necessities. The following elements do not guarantee a good story—but most good stories have these elements.

Scene-setters, also called establishing shots, show the viewer the location of the story and also set the mood of the piece. Whether you shoot your scene-setter in the cool evening or in harsh midday light, whether you edit with fast cuts or slow pans, each choice you make will impact the flavor of the rest of the piece.

Basic journalistic reporting is essential. Almost all stories require that you cover the fundamentals including: who, what, where, when, why, and how. For some types of stories you need to put this information in the lead or beginning of your piece. With others, you might delay presenting this critical data until the story has caught the notice of the viewer. Regardless of where the facts are presented, you must collect them to begin with.

A vignette throws the viewer into the action of your piece and provides something concrete with which to relate. If your story is about inadequate street cleaning, you will follow for a few minutes the action of one street cleaner as he or she goes about the daily routine before you explore the more general issue of cleanliness in the neighborhood. Many magazine articles start with a vignette and then they explain the bigger meaning of the story in the "nut graf,"

A "nut graf," which in writing sometimes comes three or four paragraphs into a story, explains why the story is important. How would you describe the essence of the story you are covering to a friend or colleague? Why should the reader care? What is the bigger point or issue? How are others affected? What facts do you need pull from your subjects to provide this context and immediacy?

Numbers (statistics) can demonstrate the impact. How many people make up this trend? How big? What percent? Are the numbers changing? If so, why? What is your source for this information?

History connects the dots that complete the picture of a person's life or the background of a story. What steps brought the person or group to this point? When did it start? Stop? The beauty of video is that while the images must be shot in the present, the subjects' quotes can fill in the blank spaces of the past.

Money is often a motivating factor in stories. Who gains; who loses? How much does it cost the individual, the group, or society?

Experts provide analysis and context. Interview sociologists, psychologists, educators, etc.— people who have studied the phenomenon, the problem, or fad.

Opposing viewpoints can be as important as what your subject has to say. You are not in public relations. Ask the subject who opposes the theme of the story. Interview someone who is against the issue. Of course, talk to friends and supporters, too.

Quotes in the subject's voice as well as those by others provide the color, the flavor—the very backbone of a story in video.

Anecdotes generally are an example or vignette that makes a point. Give the general observation or point, then follow it with an action example from life that supports the generality. Your subjects may provide these during interviews, or the narration may have to provide them. (David lets nothing get in his way. For instance, David's car broke down last week, and instead of missing class, he walked five miles to school.)

Senses round out viewers' comprehension. Is music playing? Is the television blaring? Can you hear a grinding bus in the background? Are people arguing or laughing in the background? Capturing natural sound will convey the atmosphere. If relevant to the story, also ask your subjects to comment on smell, taste, and texture. "What is that awful odor? Tell me about the taste of that packaged food in the survival kit. Describe the texture of the fabric you're using."

The still photographer is like a hawk waiting for its prey. One moment. One instant. One press of the shutter and you can capture a prize-winning moment on your compact flash card. A photographer shooting with a video camera, by contrast, needs to put that amazing moment in context. What happened before and after the peak action is as significant as the moment itself. In video, you cannot edit one frame.

More important, you are recording sound and capturing movement with a video camera. Rather than taking the single decisive moment you are capturing the telling sequence, which consists of series of shots. Komenich of the *San Francisco Chronicle* calls this approach the search for the "decisive sequence."

Fox of *WashingtonPost.com* agrees. "You shoot video in a different way than stills," he says. "You are not concentrating on moments. Instead, you are concentrating on getting sequences."

The still photographer, of course, depends on written captions to go with pictures. Now, at last, through audio interviews and natural sound, you can bring the past and future to your pictures. You can give them necessary context. You can even handle abstract concepts "where one perfect word might be worth a thousand pictures," Komenich says.

What is the difference between shooting stills and shooting video? This chapter addresses that question by looking at the video camera itself—as well as some approaches to shooting video—through the eyes of a still photographer. What is familiar and what is new in video?

SHOOTING VIDEO IS LIKE COMPOSING A SYMPHONY

Komenich compares making a documentary video to writing a symphony. When Beethoven wrote the 9th Symphony, only he knew what the score would sound like. Although the master wrote each line of music separately, he knew how they would sound when played simultaneously.

The master of a different craft, the video producer shoots each shot, sequence, and scene separately—gathering materials that will be integrated in a completely unique way. Interviews will play on top of video. Natural sound will run underneath. Some parts of the final report will play with synced sound while other moments will consist of combinations of words from one interview with pictures taken at another time. Like Beethoven and his score, only the video producer knows how he or she intends to assemble the pictures, words, and sound to package the final story.

"It's previsualization on steroids," Komenich says. "Many video shots aren't blockbusters but are vital to the flow of the story."

Says Fox, "If you don't have it in the field. You don't have it. You are constantly storyboarding in your head. You need to think about what the final product will look like even though you are in the middle of shooting. Where is the story going to start? What will make a great opener?"

The video producer needs to think on the macro and micro level—keeping an eye out for the perfect character while keeping in mind the closing shot.

In Fox's opinion, the key difference between shooting stills and video is that with stills you are going for "moment after moment after moment."

With video, it is hard to capture genuine moments as you would in still photography because shooting video requires photographing all the elements that will make an editable sequence. You need wide, medium, tight, and extra-tight shots of the same action.

"I shoot a wide shot and then go in and shoot parts of the scene to show the viewer what to look at," Fox says.

Stills allow the viewer time to contemplate an entire scene from background to foreground. An individual video shot is not on screen long enough to study.

You must guide the viewer's eye with a combination of individual shots. Then you

A timeline for Apple's Final Cut Pro (FCP) video-editing program looks almost like a symphony score. Like a music composer, only the video producer knows how the piece should finally sound when all the parts are woven together.

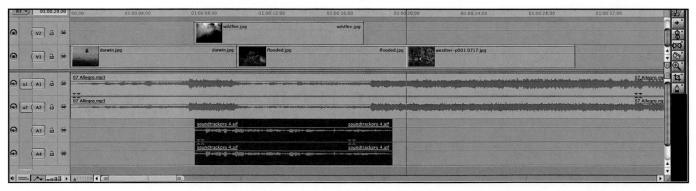

must shoot transition shots to help end the sequence and begin the next sequence.

WORKING WITH A VIDEO CAMERA
SHARPNESS

The autofocus feature in both still and video cameras is amazing. When either type of camera focuses successfully, the feature can be a godsend, but when it fails, autofocus can be horribly frustrating.

A video camera's autofocus function works in a manner similar to that of a still camera. Pressing the shutter causes the camera to adjust its internal optics until the image achieves the highest degree of edge contrast. At that point the image appears sharp.

For the still shooter moving to video, though, using autofocus requires a change in thinking. Most digital 35mm SLR cameras, for example, allow the shooter to choose a point of focus anywhere in the frame. A video camera on automatic, however, always seeks sharp focus in the middle of the frame.

Tip: If the main subject in a video is off-center, switch to manual focus.

Autofocus for street shooting. Autofocus is your best choice when you are trying to photograph a street altercation, track the mayor out of his office, or follow some other situation when you will not have time to focus, refocus, or follow focus. Autofocus is remarkably good and often better and easier than manual focus, but, as noted earlier, certainly not perfect in all situations.

Autofocus can be fooled. Situations such as the following can throw off autofocus:
- shooting through a glass spotted with water droplets;
- shooting through vertical stripes like the bars on a prison cell; or
- shooting a subject with little contrast, such as a blank wall or blue sky.

For these reasons, shooters use a combination of manual and autofocus. "I prefer autofocus, but I will switch if there is some problem," says Fox. "The autofocus of the camera is often thrown off if there is a complicated background."

Manual focus for interviews. The autofocus mechanism is particularly sensitive to high contrast subjects and responds to any slight change, even when refocusing is not necessary. This effect is especially common when someone is wearing a patterned shirt or jacket. On autofocus, the video camera constantly rechecks to see if the image in the lens is still sharp as the camera is rolling.

Fox always puts the camera on manual when shooting interviews for this reason. During a sit-down interview, the camera on autofocus will seek out a new point of focus

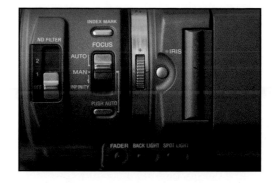

For sharpest focus many video camera operators:
1) keep the lens on manual focus
2) zoom in to the subject
3) briefly hit the temporary autofocus button (called "push auto" on the camera shown)
4) zoom out to reframe
5) leave the lens on manual focus as the camera rolls

if the subject sways even a bit. The resulting footage will contain a distracting blurring of the image as the lens seeks a new point of sharpness.

This temporary blur will occur even though the subject never left the chair.

The solution: Always focus your lens manually when shooting a fixed interview.

In either static interviews or normal coverage, the professional video shooter:
- zooms in fully on the face of the subject (or central object);
- adjusts the lens into sharp focus;
- zooms out again to reframe the shot for a well-composed picture.

The subject will remain sharp during the zooming out and reframing and will stay sharp once the camera starts recording.

Follow this routine every time you shoot, and your pictures will be consistently sharp.

In fact, many pros start the camera rolling during this set-up process so as to capture ambient sound—another technical aspect most still shooters don't have to consider.

Tip: Some cameras allow manual focus but provide access to an autofocus "momentary button" (a Sony term). With the camera set to manual, you would zoom in tight to focus on your subject's face, and then push the "momentary button." At this point, the camera switches to autofocus and the subject pops into sharp focus.

Releasing the "momentary button" returns the camera to manual and allows the photographer to zoom out and reframe. This technique permits shooting in manual mode with the option of briefly using the autofocus button when necessary to finely adjust focus.

DEPTH-OF-FIELD CHALLENGES

Because the sensor in a video camera is smaller than that of a still camera, video images have great depth of field. You may find it hard to blur the background when shooting video, even on a telephoto setting. There are ways to overcome this limitation.

Use a telephoto lens. "You need all the telephoto you've got, a long subject-to-background distance, and a wide aperture to blow the background out of focus in order to remove distracting hard edges from the background," advises Komenich.

Use a neutral-density filter. To isolate a subject quickly, you can force the aperture to widen by using the built-in neutral density (ND) filters available in some video cameras. Of course, you can purchase a separate neutral density filter if your camera does not have one built in.

Increase the shutter speed. If using the neutral density filter doesn't open the aperture to its maximum, you may be able to increase the camera's shutter speed. This will cause the aperture (known as the iris setting in video parlance) to open, causing the depth of field to fall off. Be aware that you still may not get the dramatic blurred background effect common in still photography.

Some videographers do not like the effect of a fast shutter speed in video footage because the final effect is not as smooth as that produced at the slower shutter speed typically used for video.

Tip: Keep the lens clean. The extreme depth of field in most video lenses poses a different technical problem. The slightest speck on a lens shows up in final footage as a recurring spot in every frame.

To avoid this problem, install an ultra-violet (UV) protective filter on the front of the lens; cover the lens with a lens cap when the camera is not in use; and check and recheck the lens to eliminate foreign objects that might have found their way onto its front element.

Removing dust or lint from your lens or UV filter before you shoot is far easier than attempting to fix the problem later. Correcting video footage is more complicated than doing the same repair job with a Photoshop cloning tool for still images.

EXPOSURE

Auto-exposure in a video camera has all the same advantages and disadvantages as a still camera. The camera expects to see a scene with the same brightness as 18 percent neutral gray. If the total scene is very dark or almost white, the meter will be thrown off.

Tame bright backlight. If you are photographing a scene that includes a window, for example, the video camera will respond to the brightness and underexpose your subject.

You can manually adjust the video camera's aperture or, on some cameras, press a backlight-compensation button that will let in more light and better expose the interior subject.

The auto-exposure feature of many video cameras is accurate. Travis Fox sets his camera on Iris Priority at the widest possible aperture and leaves it there. "If I have a lot of back light, rather than adjust exposure I prefer to rotate my angle and avoid the blown out background," he says.

If your subject is too dark in the viewfinder or on the LCD screen, you will see the problem and can correct it by turning off auto-exposure and opening up the iris (aperture).

Zebra patterns show overexposure. Still cameras often have a menu option that allows seeing whether an image is overexposed. Image highlights, the areas of image that are "washed out," are indicated by a flashing border. Video cameras have a special aid called "zebra" patterns for confirming overexposure.

With the zebra pattern feature turned on, a series of wavy, angled lines will indicate areas that exceed maximum exposure. These are not part of the image, just visual cues for the photographer. Maximum exposure means pure white or 100 percent. With the camera set at 100 percent zebra, areas with undulating stripes will be completely blown out.

Many photographers set their cameras for 70 percent zebra. Areas containing the pattern at this setting will appear very light in the final footage but not blown out.

If your subject's face is covered with wavy lines at this setting, however, you will know that the image is probably overexposed. Overexposed areas at this setting are pure white—and obvious in comparison to the light areas with the lines.

In either case, you can adjust the lens iris (aperture) or the camera's shutter speed to decrease the exposure. The zebra pattern will diminish as you reduce the amount of light reaching the sensor.

Tip: In your desire to avoid overexposure, do not attempt to eliminate all zebra stripes. In general, a few highlights in the brightest part of the image are just fine and often desirable.

Deal with Darkness. In a very dim situation, auto-exposure may bring the exposure to a level of acceptability, but not to your satisfaction. Some cameras provide a degree of

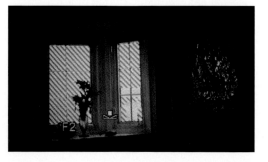

Overexposed parts of an image, like the bright windows in this picture, will show up as "zebra" stripes. This photo was taken from the LCD screen of a video camera.

photographer control through what is called db gain. Measured in some cameras from -6 to 18 db, db gain is analogous to setting the ISO on a digital still camera. Although auto-exposure also self-adjusts the gain, you can further fine-tune the electrical sensitivity at which the camera will respond to the scene or set the db gain at a particular level.

Cranking up the gain increases the sensitivity of the sensor, but it also introduces more "noise" in the image (see page 170). Sometimes, of course, a little noise will be the trade-off for capturing a good exposure in low light.

CONSISTENT COLOR
Both digital still and video cameras provide white balance adjustments to match the color temperature of light that illuminates a scene. (See Chapter 8, "Camera Bag," pages 174–176 for more on this topic.) The mechanism is a bit different for each type of camera, but the results are generally the same.

To perform a white balance correction, point your camera at a neutral-colored object like a white or gray piece of paper or cardboard. Make sure the object is in the same light at the scene you are going to photograph and that the object takes up the entire viewfinder. Now use the camera's manual white-balance setting to take a reading.

As long as you continue to shoot under the same lighting conditions, your images will have no shift in color. Of course, you must reset the white-balance setting when you move to a new location.

Alternatively, you can manually set the camera for a specific known color temperature like 5500 Kelvin when shooting under a blue sky or 3200 Kelvin when shooting under tungsten light bulbs.

Finally, you can simply allow the auto white balance to take over. Typically, auto white balance works well outdoors on sunny days but can be thrown off indoors under fluorescent or sodium vapor lights. Auto white balance also can shift during a scene, even through the camera does not move. To avoid this change of color tint when you do

not want it, switch to manual and set the white balance for the situation in which you are working.

Tip: Keep in mind that you do not always want to neutralize scenes using the white-balance setting. If you are shooting a colorful sunset, pulling out the orange is likely to destroy the beauty of the scene you are trying to capture.

KNOW WHEN TO START
AND WHEN TO HOLD ON A VIDEO CAMERA
For the still photographer, perhaps the most difficult habit to overcome when turning to video is the tendency to push the video camera's start button as if it were the shutter release on a still camera.

The first push of the button turns on the camera but the next turns it off. If the camera is already running, hitting the button at the peak action will stop the recorder and leave you with nothing to show, as a chagrined Komenich discovered when shooting the Santa Claus look-alike. "I screwed up everything from time to time, but I overshot so it didn't matter," he confides. Sometimes, old habits are hard to break.

With video, pressing the start button only warms up the camera, which subsequently— not immediately—begins to take pictures. The key for the photographer is to start shooting before the action starts and to continue until the action is complete. Pressing the button again will put the video camera on standby. The next press will activate the camera almost immediately.

When photographing a diver going off the high platform, for example, you would want to start the video camera before the athlete approaches the end of the board and continue until the last drops from his splash into the water have disappeared.

KEEP IT STEADY
Most photographers, especially still photographers, love the freedom of shooting without a tripod. In fact, today's wide-aperture lenses, many with stabilization technology that reduces the impact of camera movement, allow still photographers to shoot in low-light

The video photographer needs to start the camera and let it run as the scene plays out, even if that means moving the camera during the shoot.
© Ken Kobré

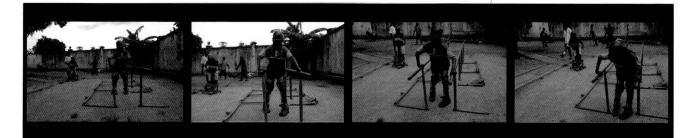

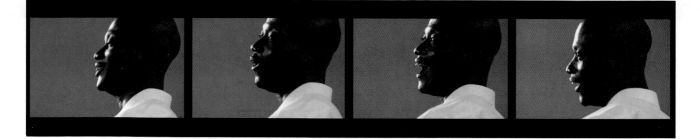

migrates seamlessly from camera to camera as you upgrade.

"In short," Komenich concludes, "learn sound from a sound guy. Video guys know a lot, but a sound specialist will help you with the global stuff you need to know for video, audio, and multimedia reports."

REAL PROS WEAR HEADPHONES
This is the only way they can listen for interruption of the audio stream as they record sound. Nothing else—not the dial, not the auto gain—will reveal if you are recording a scratchy, distracting sound track.

Earbuds do not qualify as headphones, says Halstead, founder/editor of *DigitalJournalist.org* and the Platypus Workshops that train still photojournalists transitioning to video.

EXTERNAL MIC IS A MUST
An external microphone (mic, for short) is an essential tool. Few microphones built into video cameras are adequate for capturing anything remotely professional. Built-in mics tend to pick up sound immediately around the camera, while muffling voices and music from even just a few feet in front of the lens.

The most successful professionals use at least two mics—a shotgun mic mounted to the top of the camera and a lavalier mic attached to the subject. Even during sit-down interviews, professionals often use both shotgun and lavalier mics simultaneously.

The shotgun is good for picking up ambient sound as well as providing a backup recording of the subject's voice. A wired or wireless lavalier is ideal for recording the primary subject's voice. (See Chapter 12,

"Multimedia," pages 272–273 and 276 for more on microphones.)

In general, pros keep the sound channels on manual rather than Auto Gain Control (AGC) so they can check and adjust sound levels constantly while shooting.

John Hewitt, documentary professor at San Francisco State University says, "The goal is to maintain the audio level at 12db. If the level goes higher than 0db when digitally recording sound, the sound goes off the scale, turns to noise, and loses all definition. Sound recorded digitally at this high amplitude cannot be recovered during editing." (See Chapter 12, "Multimedia," pages 274 and 276, for mic placement.)

SHOOTING WITH EDITING IN MIND
THE VIDEO JOURNALIST'S VISUAL GRAMMAR
"Photojournalists begin learning multimedia with their core competency in decisive moment-based still photography, and then apply their stills 'chops' and original point of view to video, which is hungry for the 'decisive sequence,'" Komenich wrote on *SportsShooter.com*. "Our world is full of verbs. Life is rich with the sounds and movements of the living, walking, talking paradoxes we get to meet every day."

While still and video shooters share a common visual language, still photographers coming to video will discover an expansive visual grammar and a vocabulary rich in verbs (motion!) with which to tell stories.

STILL AND VIDEO SHARED VOCABULARY
A Camera Fixed on a Scene
The following terms should be familiar to most still photographers. But while the still

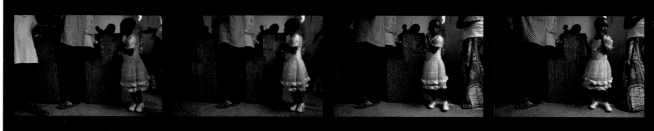

image may capture a decisive moment in any of the following shots, the video shooter is recording life as it unfolds in real time. See pages 14–18 and 321 to review the kinds of still shots you also will employ when shooting video.

- Overall / long shot / wide shot / establishing shot
- Medium shot
- Close-up
- High angle
- Low angle

Of course, still pictures throughout this book represent these kinds of shots. When shooting video, though, remember to hold each shot as long as necessary for action to play out—but never for fewer than 30 seconds (see page 324). Keep the camera stationary while subjects move within the frame and even out of it. And remember—releasing the shutter button will turn off the camera.

THE VIDEO CAMERA'S VISUAL VERBS

The still shooter turning to video will discover yet more storytelling options since they are photographing continuous action over a period of time and can move the camera as well as record the moving images.

Dolly In/Dolly Out refers to moving the camera toward or away from a subject while keeping the lens at a fixed focal length. Hollywood photographers put the camera on a sturdy wheeled cart called a dolly, which is then rolled on a track or a flat surface toward or away from the subject.

Documentary shooters and video journalists rarely have the luxury of using a dolly. Some create the same effect by putting the camera and tripod in a shopping cart, on a wheeled chair, maybe even on a skateboard or other contraption that allows the the photographer to roll the rig relatively smoothly toward the subject.

The dolly shot has more impact when "dollying" past objects. Houses, cars, or anything else flying by on the edge of the frame give the dolly shot a feel of real forward movement that is completely different from the effect of zooming the lens.

Cinematographers often use a "steadicam" for the dolly shot. This device, which attaches the camera to the photographer, absorbs sudden movements, including the up-and-down motion of walking. It allows the camera to remain level even as the photographer walks.

Some video journalists use a lightweight pseudosteadicam for the same purpose. An Internet search will turn up some of these as well as plans for making an inexpensive version yourself.

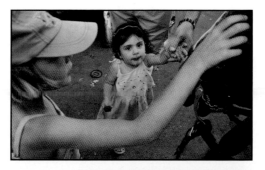

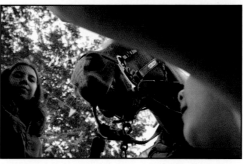

Cinematographers prefer the dolly shot to the zoom. The effect is more natural. In the real world, we can walk up and greet a person, but our eyes cannot zoom.

Truck, usually referred to by photographers as Truck Right or Truck Left, means that the camera moves with, often parallel to, the subject. Truck shots are achieved ideally with the camera on a wheeled tripod, but also by aiming the camera out a car window, hand-holding it while on a skateboard, or even while walking. The steadicam device will work in this situation also.

Effective use of the truck shot can add energy and variety to footage. For example, you might be following your subject as she strolls the Champs d'Elysée in Paris. You could track your subject, keeping the camera to her side as she saunters down the street. Allowing people and objects to cross between the video camera and the subject causes the viewer to lose the subject momentarily but then see her reemerge an instant later farther down the block.

PAN AND ZOOM — FALSE FRIENDS

The following shots may seem familiar to you as a still photographer, but don't be fooled! While still and video photographers each pan and zoom, the visual outcome is completely different. The still photographer shooting at a slow shutter speed while panning or zooming the camera produces a partially blurred image—an often striking effect in stills. The same pan or zoom shot in video, though, produces sharp continuous footage.

Pan shots result from slowly swinging the camera to follow action without changing position. As the peloton of cyclists passes during the Tour de France, for instance, the video camera pans just enough to keep the lead rider continuously on the right-hand side of the frame. A smooth pan is one in which the rider stays in the same approximate place in the frame during the entire shot.

Videographers also pan to mimic action of the human head. We turn our heads in a semi-circle to take in a wide view of a scene.

Someone seeing the Grand Canyon for the first time usually absorbs the vastness by surveying it from one end to the other in one continuous sweep of the head.

In situations like this, the pan shot is akin to a panoramic still photograph. However, the video shooter, whose tools don't include an extreme wide-angle lens, can instead pan the camera slowly to record the entire view. The pan shot can take in as much area as the photographer likes.

Tip: It is difficult to shoot pans without creating shaky images. A sturdy tripod with a "fluid" head and steady hands are a must for swinging the camera at a steady pace.

Zooming the Lens in or Out

The most overused button on a video camera is the zoom control. Yet zoom shots rarely add to any documentary. On the contrary, points out Kim Komenich, "the eye can't zoom, so a zoom instantly puts the viewer into a situation that is not real."

In his book *iMovie, the Missing Manual*, author David Pogue observes, "For the camcorder operator, zooming imparts a sense of control, power, and visual excitement. For the viewer, zooming imparts a sense of nausea. Overly zoomed and panned shots are a quick giveaway that a rank amateur has shot the footage."

Pros disdain the zoom, pan, or tilt. In fact, there is a great sentiment in the profession to remove zoom lenses from cameras. The KPIX "Photographer Standards and Practices" handbook for San Francisco's major market Channel 5 says of pans and zooms, "Don't like 'em. Don't want to see 'em. If a zoom or a pan ends up on the air, there better be a good reason, and there aren't too many good reasons."

Okay. Okay. So you just watched MTV before you read the last few paragraphs.

You saw zooms so fast you thought you were in a time-travel machine. You experienced pans executed as if they were shot from a centrifuge. You witnessed camera tilts violent enough to throw off a pinball machine. And let's not forget about the camera tipped at angles so severe that you normally experience this viewpoint only after a night of serious binge drinking. What is going on here?

MTV's shooting style provides eye-candy to accompany music. The music's driving beat powers the piece while the sometimes chaotic images add visual spice to the mix. For MTV, the fast cut, zoom-in-zoom-out style maintains a large audience and has spawned a unique visual shooting language of its own. Most documentaries, on the other hand, try to emphasize a story's content rather than support the beat to popular music or show off a photographer's shooting style.

Having said that, there are times when zooming the lens will be necessary.

Keep in mind that zoom-in actually changes the focal length of the camera lens from wide angle to telephoto. The effect is completely different from physically moving the camera closer to the subject like the dolly in previously discussed.

Consider one scene and compare the effects of zooming versus dollying in. Notice the relationship between the subject and the background. Which shot feels more natural? Generally, the camera brings us into situations as if we were there. We would walk toward something to see it more closely, not zoom with our eyes to get there.

If you must zoom, it is usually necessary to gradually tilt up or down to maintain proper framing throughout the shot. Sometimes photographers carefully zoom in during a particularly emotional moment of a painful interview and then hold on the close-up shot.

Tip: Always use the optical zoom on your camera. Avoid the "digital zoom," which is accomplished through software manipulation rather than changing the actual focal length of the lens. Digital zoom produces undesirable electronic noise in the final footage.

Zoom-in and -out changes the lens's focal length from telephoto to wide angle then back to telephoto. Professionals consider a zoom-in and then zoom-out within the same shot poor camera work. The effect for the viewer is like being on a roller coaster. Generally, only one camera move will be used for the final edit.

Rather than zooming, you should simply move the camera. "Always keep moving," says George Lang, a veteran shooter for KGO-TV in San Francisco. "Don't get bogged down in one spot."

You will understand why he says this by studying the camera work in any movie. For more than 100 years, cinematographers have been perfecting the art of camera placement.

Suppose you are shooting a sequence of a musical group performing in a plaza in a French village. You wish to create a series of shots from which you can build a sequence that will bring the viewer onto the square where musicians are playing.

You will follow the interaction between the group and its audience; you will move the camera for each shot and take overalls, mediums, and close-ups in order to assure visual variety. ■

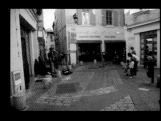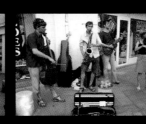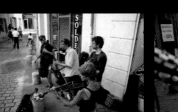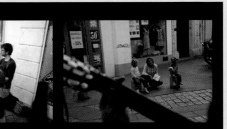

Establisher. From a small street leading into the plaza, you shoot a wide shot that shows the overall scene—the little plaza, the shops, the musicians, and the spectators. Allow time to record the passersby who may or may not stop to listen to the music play. Let the shot roll for at least ten 10 seconds.

Medium shot. Next move the camera and tripod to about 10 feet in front of the group for a medium shot. Keep the camera stationary but continue shooting.

Action. Now shoot the same group from above and to the side.

Reaction. Next move forward a little and change angles so that you can see from behind the musicians to the small group of listeners, which include a mother and her two children. From the point of view of the musicians, the viewer can observe how the audience reacts to the music.

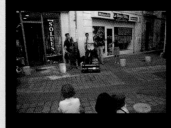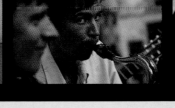

Reaction. A shot from behind the family back to the musicians shows viewers what the family sees—the audience's point of view.

Reverse shot. Come in tight on the children to see their expressions as they watch the group and listen to the music.

Close-up. A close-up on the musicians shows the source of the music.

Medium. A medium shot from a new angle provides editing variety.

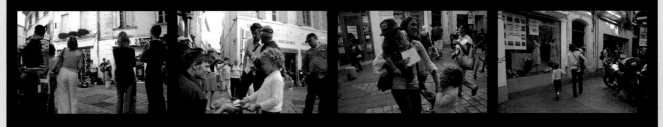

Medium. Another medium shot from a new angle shows a different audience point of view and provides more editing variety.

Action/climax. Next you will move to the side to capture the scene when the children come forward to interact with the musicians and to buy a CD.

Closing shot. Standing in one position, hold the family in the frame as the mother gathers up the children and they walk away while the music plays in the background.

For more about MAKUMBIK, the traveling musicians, see www.makumbik.de.

© Ken Kobré

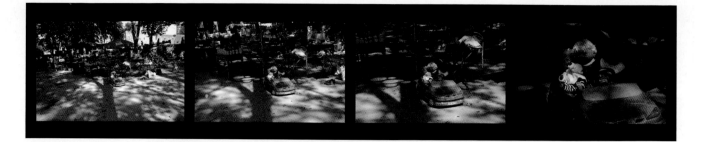

Sophisticated viewers are accustomed to a variety of camera positions and views.

Motivated Zooming and Panning

If you are going to zoom or pan, each camera action should have a logical starting place and a visual destination or payoff for the viewer at the end of the movement.

If photographing your subject at a café, for example, you might position the camera outside a building across the street. The zoom would start out wide and include the plaza in front of the café, with the wide shot lasting for at least 10 seconds. Only then would the camera slowly zoom onto the subject drinking coffee—and hold for at least 10 seconds. The subject is the prize at the end of the zoom.

Alternatively, you may want to pan from the neighborhood church and then slowly swing the lens around the plaza to show its expanse, winding up the pan with your coffee-sipping subject at a table sitting under the colorful umbrella.

In either approach, the movement would have started at a logical place and arrived at the espresso-sipper. The ending of the shot has a payoff for the viewer. This move is called a "motivated" pan or zoom. The motivation of the shot was to find the coffee connoisseur. The camera should start and stop at specific places that help to move along the story.

Tip: Keep in mind that editing a pan or zoom for the final piece is often a challenge. It is almost impossible to cut a pan in a way that makes visual sense. They really need the starting and ending points. Also, since some pans can run as long as 20 seconds, they can slow down an otherwise well-paced documentary.

TILT UP OR DOWN

You might tilt the camera up or down while shooting if you want to show the viewer the height of a building. Also you might want the viewer to discover something at the end of the tilt. Perhaps you start the shot showing a man's tennis shoes but end the tilt up to reveal him wearing a tux.

FROM SINGLE SHOT TO SEQUENCE

Sequences are the building blocks of any video story, whether it is a three-minute feature or an hour-long documentary. Thoughtful shooting will make editing the footage faster and simpler.

One Shot is Never Enough

"One shot is never enough," warns Rolf Behrens, a veteran freelance shooter from South Africa. He means that if you have only one shot of an incident, you will not have enough footage to edit. You need multiple shots of each scene in order to produce a usable sequence. Remember this mantra— "one shot is never enough"—and you will shoot more professional video footage starting with your first attempt.

The 10-second Rule

In shooting video, even if the scene is a static shot of a painting, you should shoot it for a minimum of 10 seconds. You can count to 10 or watch the clock on the screen while away the time. Fewer than 10 seconds of footage is almost impossible edit. Of course, you can shoot scenes longer than 10 seconds. If the subject is doing something of interest like kissing the bride or revealing why he embezzled money, keep the video camera rolling.

Often, you will keep the camera static and simply allow your subjects' actions to take place before the lens.

Each Shot Tells a Mini-tale

Shoot each shot as if it were telling a tiny tale. A girl drinks from a cup; a boy walks down a hall; a woman chops a tomato. A man rises from a chair and goes to the door.

Keep the camera rolling as the mini-tale unfolds. For this last situation, for example, start shooting before the man gets up. Keep the shot rolling as he crosses the room. Stop shooting after he opens the door and closes it behind him. This simple act of getting out of a chair, strolling across a living room, opening a door, and leaving a room has a beginning, middle, and end. The shot starts before the action begins and ends a few seconds after the action is over.

Especially in documentary video, the photographer's planning must precede the editor's work. Photojournalists do not have the luxury of re-creating action over and over to get lots of shots of the same action. Photojournalists record real people going about their lives—not actors playing to a script.

However, when a subject is involved in a repetitive activity—like a woman cutting tomatoes, for example—the video shooter can photograph the same action repeatedly from different angles and with various focal-length lenses.

For example, a wide shot would show the cook as she starts to cut the first tomato and tosses the first piece into a bowl.

As she cuts the next tomato, the camera comes in close and again captures the action from beginning to end.

The shooter can photograph the same action when she cuts the third tomato but from a high angle directly over her head.

During editing, these shots can be combined into a sequence that appears as if it were shot with multiple cameras: The woman in the kitchen starts to cut the tomato, the knife enters the tomato, the knife slices through it.

Each step was photographed as the woman prepared a different tomato, but editing the sequence combines the three occurrences into one continuous action.

The mini-sequence, built from parts of three different shots, tells the tiny story of how the woman cut up a tomato. The viewer has seen so much film in the cinema and on television that these shots from different angles and distances appear perfectly natural. ■

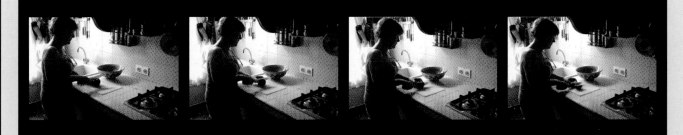

A wide shot shows the cook as she starts to cut the tomato and continues until she is finished. A sequence shot from this view only does not offer the viewer variety.

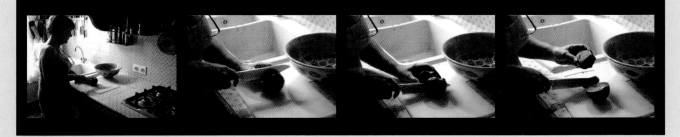

A cut to a close-up shows the cook as she starts to cut the tomato and continues until she is finished. The close-up is more dramatic than the medium shot above, but a sequence made up of close-ups is uninteresting if it goes on for more than just a few seconds.

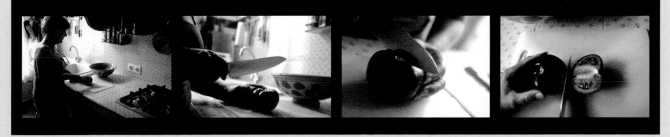

© Ken Kobré

Shooting the cook as she cuts a second and third tomato, the videographer can take pictures from different angles. These shots can then be pieced together into one continuous action.

Anticipate Natural Reactions

Good camera work means anticipating the way viewers would respond to a scene had they been present. For instance, if a person is talking, a loud bang occurs, and the person glances in the direction of the sound, the natural reaction of anyone in the room is to follow the speaker's gaze to see the nature of the distraction. That is human nature.

Likewise, the camera needs to pan from the speaker to the source of the noise. Here the pan shot has a "motivation" or reason that it takes place. The camera has a motivation to move and a motivation to stop (see page 324).

MANY SHOTS BUILD A SEQUENCE
The Sequence Establisher

This shot introduces the location of what follows in the sequence. Viewers, for example, should easily identify from the pyramids in an establishing shot that the following sequence takes place in the desert in Egypt rather than in the canyons of New York.

Fox of *WashingtonPost.com* says he might shoot the scene setter for his stories from a mountaintop. Sometimes he will use a highway sign.

An establishing shot might just be a long shot of a room that shows all the characters from a particular scene. A scene about a murder in a college lecture hall, for example, might begin with a shot that shows the entire classroom—including a lecturing professor and the students taking notes. An exterior shot of a large building on a rainy night, followed by an interior shot of a couple talking, implies that the conversation is taking place inside that building.

Interaction

For every action, there is a reaction. And this is the challenge for the video journalist seeking to tell a complete story in images. The video journalist must look for decisive actions and reactions.

Relationship shots frame the field of view to include two principal elements/subjects of a story in action—a father and son playing ball, a person looking at a computer screen.

Father and son

*   Action – A shot of a father throwing a ball to his son.
*   Reaction – A shot of the boy catching (or missing) the ball.
*   Reverse – A shot of dad jumping up and down, smiling, yelling.

Person at computer

*   Action – A shot of a person looking at a computer screen.
*   Reaction – A shot of the computer screen with an email joke.
*   Reverse – A shot of the email recipient laughing.

Closers. Ultimately, you need some kind of shot that closes the sequence. Perhaps the camera pulls back, a person walks out of the scene, or the person walks away from the

Each scene you shoot is a tiny story within the bigger narrative piece. Here, a young Congolese man paralyzed since a childhood attack of polio is being carried into a workshop where he will be fitted for braces and will walk unaided for the first time in his life.
© Ken Kobré

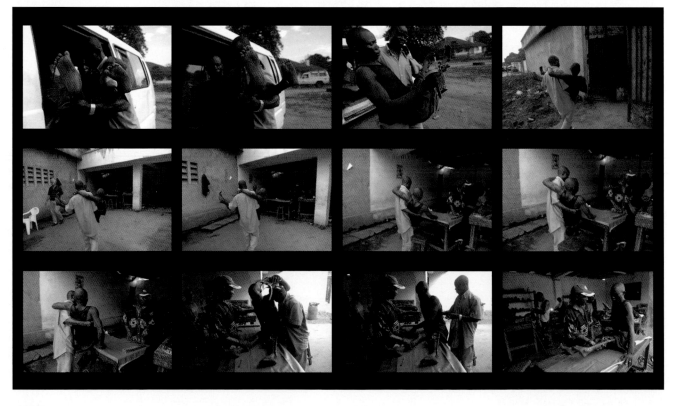

camera. "I will shoot someone walking into the sunset for the closer," says Fox. "Sometimes, a shot of someone closing a door or going to bed will help end the piece."

These shots will be edited into a sequence that looks like a fluid chain of repetitive action is unwinding—the game with the father and son; the person reading email; a woman making a salad (page 325); musicians performing (page 323); a demonstration of some type.

AVOIDING COLLIDING IMAGES ON SCREEN

Here's a new one for the still shooter. Let's say you are covering a parade. You are set up with your tripod on the south side of the street. You start the camera rolling as the marching band approaches from the left, passes in front of you, and continues to the right down the street.

What happens if you now cross to the opposite side of the street to photograph the next band? The second band is marching from the same direction, yes, but in your footage, they will appear to be coming from the right to the left on the screen.

Cutting the footage of the two bands together during editing will make it appear as if they are coming from opposite directions. One band will be going left to right on the screen when suddenly the second band will be marching from right to left. This apparent shift in direction is visually confusing.

Maintaining the same apparent screen direction avoids confusion, but the prepared shooter has plenty of options to avoid colliding footage.

Pick a Side

One solution is simply to stay on the south side of the street. The following shots will show the next band also moving from left to right. The direction for all the bands will stay apparently consistent.

Think of a line drawn down the middle of the street with an arrow going in the direction in which the band advances. Any number of shots you shoot on one side of the line will cut together with shots taken from the same side.

Shoot Visual Buffers

Sometimes you must shoot from both sides of the street. How can you reverse the cinematic direction on the screen without disturbing the viewer? This is another case where the prepared shooter must think ahead for editing the final piece.

Shoot from a Neutral Position

Try shooting a shot that with no left or right direction. For example, if you could stand on

an overpass as the band marches beneath, the action would be coming from the top of the screen to the bottom.

Another solution would be to shoot from the middle of the street as the band marches toward or around you. Now the direction becomes neutral since the band members are coming straight at you.

With either of these shots edited between the footage from the two different sides of the sidewalk, the mind accepts the sequence as natural.

Cutaways

Watch for details; watch audience reaction. Other transitional shots for these kinds of situations—called cutaways in film parlance—include close-ups, which typically have no particular left-right direction: a trumpet blower's face, for example, or the drummer's busy hands. A shot of the audience can also provide a visual buffer that will prevent the bands marching from two apparently opposite directions from appearing to collide on the screen.

Faces Can Collide, Too

Marching bands are not the only situations that present directional problems. A person's profile also implies a direction. If you are shooting from one side of a person's face and the person is looking to the right, for example, the otherwise stationary subject implies direction from left to right.

Photographing from the opposite side will cause the person to appear on screen as if looking from the right to the left.

This is an editing nightmare in the works. If you try to cut the two individual pieces together, the person's head will appear to be swinging from one direction to the other.

Neutral footage such as a detail of the hands or general footage showing what the person is talking about will provide neutral visual breathers between the two strongly directional shots.

Jumping without Direction

Neutral shots also will help avoid what's called the "jump" cut.

The jump cut typically occurs with interview footage in which the camera was locked on the subject. Taking a piece from one part of an interview and then splicing it with another selection from the same interview causes the subject's head to appear to jerk at the edit point. Naturally—the subject's head cannot possibly be in the exact same position at different points in the interview. The audio will sound perfectly normal, but the footage will convey an abnormal appearance.

B-roll. B-roll is primarily visual material without significant corresponding sound. These visuals help tell the story, but they will be covered with narration or parts of the interview. If you have ever noticed a piece of footage being replayed again and again in a news piece or documentary, it is because the photographer had not shot enough B-roll, or there wasn't sufficient existing material to cover the subject being discussed.

The documentary about "Visa Pour L'Image," the annual international photojournalism festival held in France, is built on an extensive interview with François LeRoy, the founder and director of the event. (The piece is on the DVD enclosed in this book.)

The documentary introduces LeRoy talking in his office. His voice continues on the soundtrack over B-roll that shows various scenes of the festival in progress. This allows viewers to see what LeRoy is talking about rather than simply watching a talking head.

Tip: Include only B-roll that complements what is being said on the A-roll interview. "Avoid just using B-roll that serves simply as wallpaper," warns Hewitt. "Wallpaper images are there for decoration not for information."

Narration. If a written script drives your story line, you will need to record the narration separately as a voice-over or voice track. (See page 293, Chapter 12, "Multimedia.") The narration should be written to overlay and so draw the viewer's attention to the B-roll images.

As you might expect, narration plays a crucial role in many documentaries. Turn off the sound while watching a documentary such as "NOVA," for example, on the U.S. Public Broadcasting Service (PBS). Quickly, you will lose the thread of the program.

If you are working with a reporter, correspondent or producer, he or she may write and read the script. As a video journalist, video producer, or one-man band, you may need to write and "voice" the script yourself.

Make sure to write the narration to your pictures. However, the narration should not describe each image. The viewer can see those. Rather, you should add information that might help the viewer understand the images on the screen.

If the viewer is seeing a barren refugee camp in Darfur, your narration should describe the desperate lack of food, water, and shelter, for example.

Also, your narration needs to fill the holes left by the interviews you have collected from your subjects. The script needs to set up the sound bite in an introduction and then add

Apple's Final Cut Pro and Final Cut Pro Express, Adobe's Premiere, and Avid are among software programs used by video producers to edit their stories. With an original Final Cut Pro manual more than 1400 pages long, this chapter obviously makes no attempt to teach this or similar extensive programs. There are plenty of excellent books, classes, and online tutorials for learning editing software.

Final Cut Pro has a lot of depth. Entire Hollywood movies have been edited with it. However, it is also possible to learn a few basic maneuvers that will allow you to edit your pieces relatively quickly.

The screen on the opposite page displays the Timeline of a documentary called "Bracing for the Future."

The numbered items, below, correlate to the numbers on the screen and introduce a few terms and functions of Final Cut Pro.

1 Playheads are available in the Viewer (**1a**), the Canvas (**1c**), and in the Timeline (**1b**). Dragging a Playhead is called "scrubbing" through the clips. The Viewer Playhead (**1a**) is used to move through a single clip. Either the Timeline Playhead (**1b**) or the Canvas Playhead (**1c**) can be used to move through the edited piece. The Canvas screen shows what is under those Playheads (**1b**) and (**1c**).

2 The Transport Controls perform the same kinds of functions as a DVD player: playing, rewinding, forwarding, etc.

3 In (**3a**) and Out (**3b**) points in the Viewer indicate the starting point of a selection and its ending point.

4 Editing and Marking Controls allow the editor to mark the beginning and the end of a clip.

The Final Cut Pro toolbar is similar to that in Photoshop, but with functions specific to video editing.

The razor blade, for example, is used to separate out a specific clip. You can cut a clip of audio and video at the same time or cut each track separately.

The audio meter is an indicator of how loud each track is playing. The sound is too loud and will distort when the gauge reaches the upper limits in the red zone. Moving the pink band in the Timeline (**C, D**) adjusts the level of sound in your audio track.

BROWSER

The Browser window displays all the video and audio clips, which are organized in folders and bins. You can place a clip in your documentary by dragging it from the Browser to the Timeline (BELOW).

VIEWER

The Viewer allows you to mark In (3a) and Out (3b) points, and to review individual video and audio clips. By double-clicking on the Timeline (below), you can load clips from the current Timeline into the Viewer, where you can refine edits, apply effects, create titles, and more. You can also drag a clip from the Browser (left) to this Viewer window.

CANVAS

The Canvas shows what the edited sequence looks like when played. "Scrubbing" (moving) the Timeline Playhead (1b) or the Canvas Playhead (1c) plays the piece at the rate the Playhead is moved (quickly or slowly). Hitting the keyboard space bar or using the Transport Controls (4) will also play the edited piece in the Canvas.

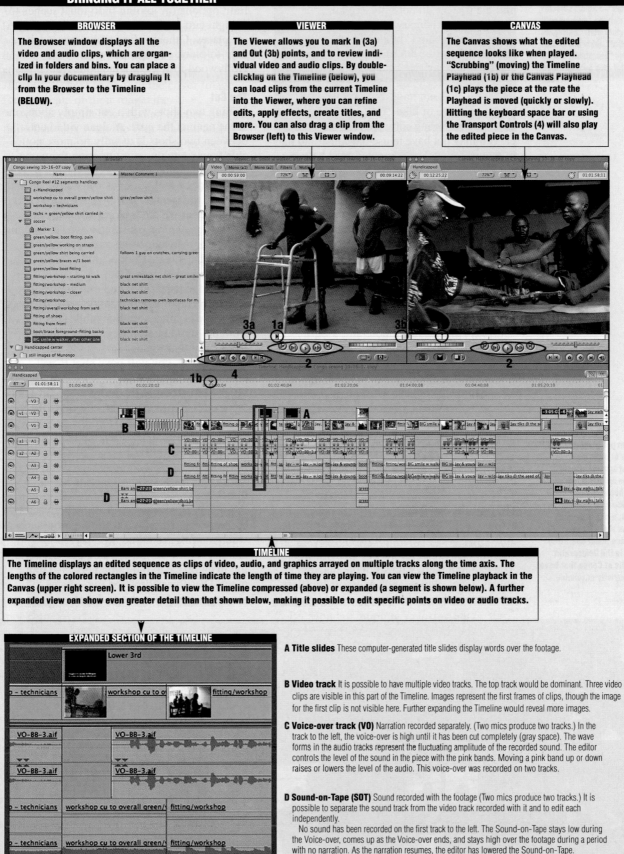

TIMELINE

The Timeline displays an edited sequence as clips of video, audio, and graphics arrayed on multiple tracks along the time axis. The lengths of the colored rectangles in the Timeline indicate the length of time they are playing. You can view the Timeline playback in the Canvas (upper right screen). It is possible to view the Timeline compressed (above) or expanded (a segment is shown below). A further expanded view can show even greater detail than that shown below, making it possible to edit specific points on video or audio tracks.

EXPANDED SECTION OF THE TIMELINE

A Title slides These computer-generated title slides display words over the footage.

B Video track It is possible to have multiple video tracks. The top track would be dominant. Three video clips are visible in this part of the Timeline. Images represent the first frames of clips, though the image for the first clip is not visible here. Further expanding the Timeline would reveal more images.

C Voice-over track (VO) Narration recorded separately. (Two mics produce two tracks.) In the track to the left, the voice-over is high until it has been cut completely (gray space). The wave forms in the audio tracks represent the fluctuating amplitude of the recorded sound. The editor controls the level of the sound in the piece with the pink bands. Moving a pink band up or down raises or lowers the level of the audio. This voice-over was recorded on two tracks.

D Sound-on-Tape (SOT) Sound recorded with the footage (Two mics produce two tracks.) It is possible to separate the sound track from the video track recorded with it and to edit each independently.

No sound has been recorded on the first track to the left. The Sound-on-Tape stays low during the Voice-over, comes up as the Voice-over ends, and stays high over the footage during a period with no narration. As the narration resumes, the editor has lowered the Sound-on-Tape.

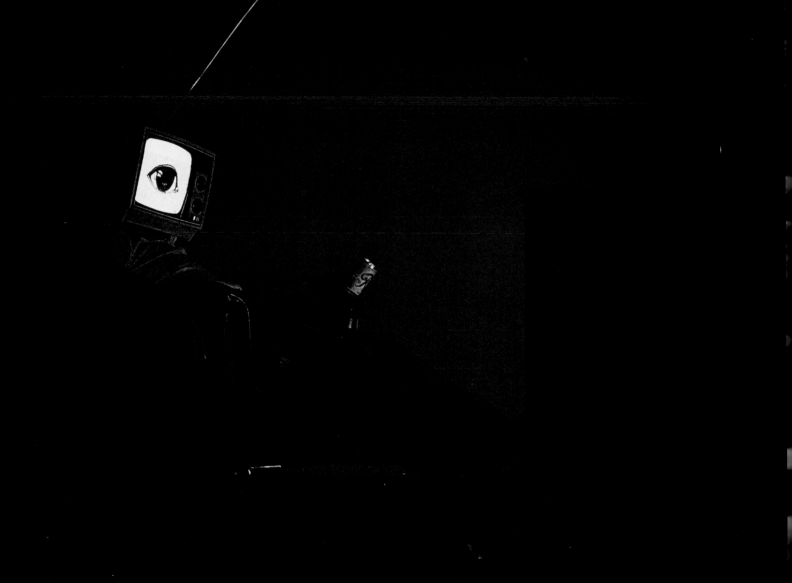

In this photo illustration—a visual metaphor—a TV set becomes the head (and brains) of a television addict. Peter Haley, *Tacoma* [Washington] *News Tribune*

14

Illustration

ILLUSTRATE THE ABSTRACT

Today's photojournalists are borrowing the techniques of the advertising photographer to illustrate stories based on issues and abstract ideas. This blend of advertising technique and photojournalism—the editorial photo illustration—came about as newspapers and magazines shifted from the "simple account of what happened yesterday" to analysis of what happened over a period of time and to evaluations of what may happen in the future. This change in journalistic emphasis from immediate reaction to longer-term interpretation of the news has led to stories about more abstract—and

A product illustration (below, top) is often an attractive still life that simply shows what an object looks like. An editorial illustration (below, bottom) depicts a concept. Here, the concept is how to protect yourself against the vapors of the odoriferous onion.
Joseph Rodriquez, *Greensboro* [North Carolina] *News & Record*

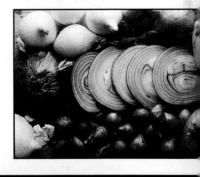

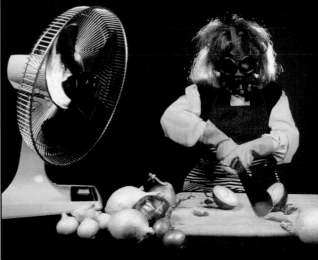

TRANSITION:
From adolescent to adult

dressed as a tooth fairy holding a large prop toothbrush. He photographed her in her costume against a seamless backdrop. A picture of a blue sky completed the original photography for the project. Then Hendricks combined the three images in Photoshop for his final picture.

Hendricks transformed what could have been a dull product shot of toothbrushes into a concept. The tooth fairy, lost in a forest of brushes, provides a more captivating image than a catalog shot of common teeth-cleaning instruments.

The subject of an editorial photo illustration may be about aging, latchkey children, or it might involve politics or food. But if you create a concept photo about onions, you will not produce a photo of the onion itself. Rather you may try to show how people defend themselves against the vegetable's vapors—perhaps with an image of a chef wearing a gas mask while cutting the odoriferous onions (see page 335).

DOCUDRAMA

The docudrama photo illustration, by contrast, actually appears to be real. The docudrama looks just like a candid but is really a complete creation or recreation. Rather than abstracting or idealizing, like the product photo or the concept illustration, the docudrama photo imitates reality; intentionally or not, it fools the reader.

Avoid the docudrama at all costs.

The docudrama approach is tempting to photographers with little time to establish contacts for a story, or to conceive and prop a concept photo. To set up a real-looking photograph may not seem so far from what an artist does to "illustrate" a story, but docudramas threaten to undermine a news outlet's credibility.

Jeff Breland's picture of a latchkey child dangling from a key chain is clearly unreal (see page 351). A docudrama photo illustration, on the other hand, depicts a lonely-looking child sitting on a doorstep. While this young model surely was not really alone or lonely, the reader's only clue to the deception was the tiny tag line "photo illustration." The reader has no way of knowing from the picture that the image was a purposely staged.

And, equally important, do latchkey children really look lonely? The one thing we

know is that they do in the imagination of a docudrama photographer.

PRODUCING EDITORIAL ILLUSTRATIONS

After a photo illustration appears, you might overhear the following conversation in the newsroom.

The writer whines, "This headline doesn't go with the gist of my insightful story."

The copy editor replies, "When I wrote that head, the story wasn't ready, and I never saw the picture."

From the photo department: "The headline type runs across the model's face."

And, from the page designer's corner of the room: "The inept photographer didn't

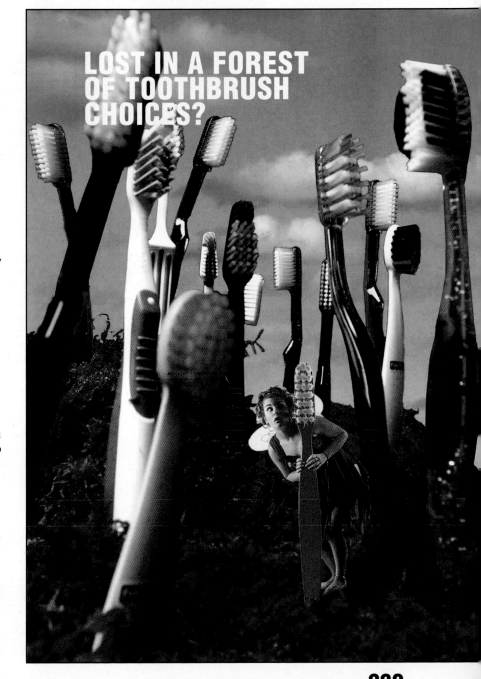

LOST IN A FOREST OF TOOTHBRUSH CHOICES?

leave room for type on the picture. And anyhow, the vertical picture didn't fit into the horizontal hole on the page left me by the copy desk." Avoid this scenario.

When producing an editorial photo illustration, get all the players together from the beginning. The advertising world calls a group like this a creative team. Businesses in Japan call it a quality circle. Regardless of what you call it, get everyone together who will participate in the creation and execution of the photo illustration. By communicating, all team members will perform their own creative tasks better; knowing what others are doing will help quell territorial battles.

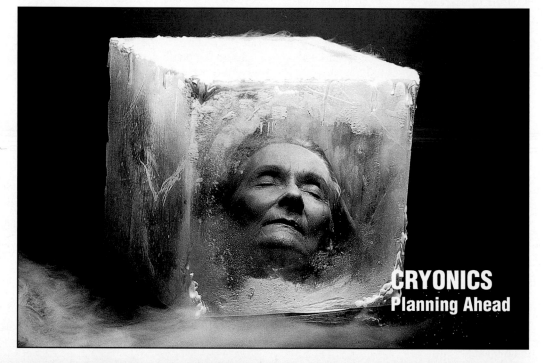

CRYONICS
Planning Ahead

▶ **This shocking photo illustrates cryonics, the practice of freezing people who have just died in hopes of reviving them with future medical advances.**
Susan Gardner, *Fort Lauderdale Sun-Sentinel*

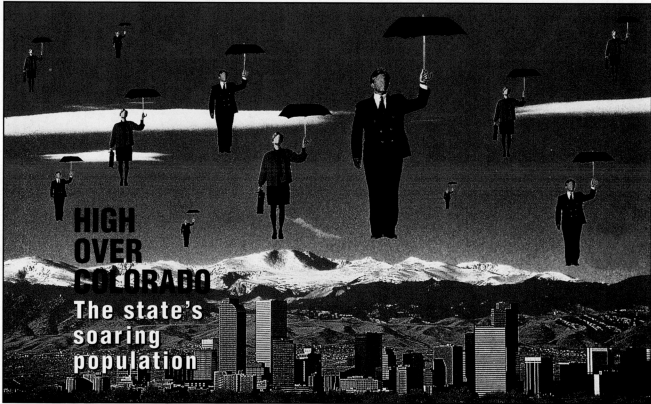

HIGH OVER COLORADO
The state's soaring population

BRAINSTORM THE CONCEPTS

Alex Osborn, a partner at Batten, Barton, Durstine, and Osborn (BBD&O), a large New York advertising firm, formulated the brainstorming method for bringing workable, productive ideas to the surface. He recommends getting a group of people in a small room where everyone can voice their ideas, no matter how foolish-sounding. Each suggestion stimulates and generates another suggestion. A brainstorming session can produce more than a thousand ideas, Osborn claims. Brainstorming works even if you just talk over your ideas with another person.

Philippe Halsman, who produced more than 100 *Life* covers, explains why he uses the brainstorming technique in his book ***Halsman on the Creation of Photographic Ideas***. "You are not alone, you face someone who serves you as a sounding board, who prods you and who expects you to answer. . . . Your system is stimulated by the challenge of the discussion. There is more adrenaline in your blood, more blood flows through your brain and, like an engine that gets more gas, your brain becomes more productive."

One cardinal rule prevails when working in a brainstorming session: never put down anyone else's ideas. Like turning on the lights at a high school dance, a negative comment will be inhibiting. By the end of the brainstorming session, surprisingly good ideas will float to the surface and poor suggestions will sink out of sight from their own weight.

WRITE A HEADLINE

After each member of your group has read the story or heard a presentation of the central theme, everyone should try to write a headline. Compared with writing headlines for a news story and documentary picture, writing headlines for a photo illustration requires the writer to take a different approach.

In a traditional news headline, the editor tries to summarize the story in a few words. The headline usually includes an active verb: "President proposes new legislation today."

A photo illustration headline might have no verb. In fact, the headline might consist of only a phrase or sentence fragment. The

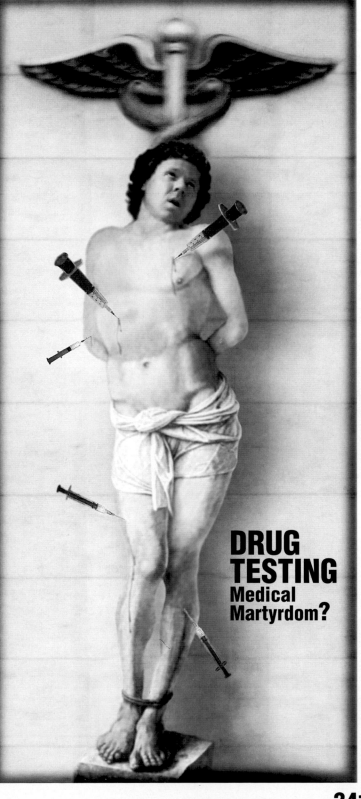

◀ To illustrate the problem of population growth in Colorado, the photographer shot an overall of downtown Denver with the mountains in the background. In the studio, keeping the light from the same direction as the overall, he photographed two models holding umbrellas. With the computer, he cloned the models, obliterating their faces so that they would become generalized figures representing all newcomers. Finally, he melded all the elements together into one image. Jay Koelzer, for the *Rocky Mountain News*

▶ St. Sebastian, who was executed with arrows, symbolizes martyrdom in this illustration for a story about college students who are paid to test new drugs. With the help of Photoshop and an out-of-copyright painting of the martyred saint, the photographer replaced the arrows with syringes and used the traditional symbol of the medical profession for a background above the figure. William Duke, for *Spy* magazine

DRUG TESTING
Medical Martyrdom?

headline might play on words, like a pun, or it might work off a movie, play, or song title. Or the words might raise a question.

- "Is There a Hare in Your Soup?" for a story about rabbit stew.
- "M-M-M Mail Order" for a story about buying food through the mail.
- "Making the First Move" for a story about women asking men on dates.

Once everyone has read the story, the group must try to write several headlines. Do not stop to analyze each one. Never reject any idea at this stage of the process. Let your thoughts flow. Then read over each one to see if the idea lends itself to a photo.

Almost always, the best idea pops out.

TRANSLATE WORDS INTO IMAGES
Symbols

Once you have the headline you must translate words into pictures. When you translate to picture language, you speak with symbols, analogies, and metaphors. You are trying to find visual ways to express amorphous, sometimes theoretical ideas and concepts.

For photography, however, concepts must become something concrete.

For example, how do you say America or American without words? You might use a generally accepted visual representation of an idea—a symbol like the Stars and Stripes. You could use an actual flag or turn something else into a flag. You might decorate a cake in red, white, and blue to symbolize America's birthday. The Statue of Liberty also serves as a symbol of the United States, as does the "Uncle Sam Wants You" recruiting poster from World War I. Grant Woods's painting, "American Gothic," which shows a farmer and his wife staring stoically out at you, also has become a symbol of the United States.

Photographs themselves can become symbols. Joe Rosenthal's photograph of the flag raising at Iwo Jima has been reproduced and transformed so many times it has become a symbol of American patriotism.

The Eiffel Tower, a baguette, or a bottle of wine might symbolize France. Balanced scales suggest justice; a dove represents peace; a gun symbolizes war. A light bulb often stands in for abstractions like thinking or ideas.

Carl Fischer, who produced many famous *Esquire* magazine covers, says that some symbols come to exist in our subconscious, like those which the psychoanalyst Carl Jung described as archetypes. Some of these symbols, although they may originate in one culture, become cross-cultural icons that people instantly recognize. The multiarmed Hindu god, Shiva, appears over and over as a symbol for handling multiple tasks.

Literature, too, can provide visual symbols. The nose of Pinocchio, which grew longer with each lie he told, turns the act of lying into a concrete object. In an illustration for *Spy*, a humor magazine, William Duke played off the image of St. Sebastian, who has come to symbolize martyrdom. The story concerned college students who earn money by participating in tests for new compounds for drug companies (see page 341).

Symbols can be reinterpreted or newly invented. As pointed out by Steven Heller and Seymour Chwast in *The Sourcebook of Visual Ideas*, smokestacks were used at one time to symbolize progress. Today, they represent pollution. Still, the skull and crossbones, an ancient symbol for poison, continues to evoke the message "hazardous to your health."

Will computers, which today convey the idea of technology, someday be associated with obsolescence?

Visual Metaphors

When you use a metaphor, you replace one image with another to suggest a likeness of some characteristic.

For instance, you might substitute an hourglass for an old person to suggest aging.

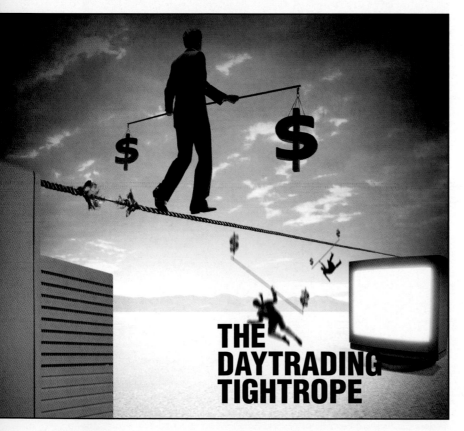

The metaphor for danger—a frayed tightrope—helps illustrate a story about risk-taking daytraders, who use the computer to bet on minute-by-minute swings in the stock market. William Duke for *Time* magazine

THE DAYTRADING TIGHTROPE

In this situation, the hourglass becomes the passing of time. The sand at the bottom of the hourglass represents age. Sand can also become power. Sand sifting through hands could become a metaphor for disappearing power.

In an illustration for *Time* magazine, William Duke used a frayed tightrope as a metaphor for danger. His picture (opposite page) shows a man in a suit walking a fraying tightrope. The man balances with a pole on the ends of which hang dollar signs. The rope is strung between two computers. Other suited men farther down the rope are falling. The story is about daytraders, who use the Internet to make quick trades betting the stock market will go up or down within a few seconds or minutes. While the practice can be lucrative, many traders have quickly gone broke with this approach to investing.

The metamorphosis from caterpillar to butterfly could represent the change from childhood to adolescence, as in the photograph created by Jay Koelzer for the *Rocky Mountain News* (see page 338). A TV screen becomes the head of a television addict (see page 334).

SELECT THE MOST WORKABLE IDEA
Simplicity and practicality come into play when you are pondering a list of headlines to illustrate. Sometimes, the least number of props, models, backgrounds, and special effects give the best chance of producing a successful photo illustration.

For example, suppose you have selected the following headline: "The Nuclear Family Crumbles."

You could illustrate this idea by breaking apart clay figures made in the form of a family. Great idea, but . . . You do not know how to work in clay, so you call a sculptor friend. She says, "Great idea, but . . . I'll need five days and $500." Your editor says, "Great idea, but . . . I need the illustration in three days, and we have a $20 prop limit."

It is time either to rethink the visual for the headline or to continue down the list to find a different headline that can be illustrated more easily. Remember, the nuclear family can unravel just as easily as it can crumble, and knitting a family portrait just might be easier than sculpting it.

PRODUCE THE PICTURE
Once you have a headline to accompany a visual and have drawn a sketch, you need to plan the location, props, and models. On a big-budget ad shoot, you might hire a stylist to find the props, call a casting director to locate models, and ask a location specialist to scout the best backgrounds. On a low-budget shoot, you probably will play all the roles yourself.

Props
Remember that precise propping can perfect the picture, whereas inappropriate props can destroy the desired illusion. For example, a photographer was assigned to illustrate a story about an English butler serving tea. The sketch called for the butler to wear a bowler hat. The photographer returned from the local theatrical prop shop with a hat that was black like a bowler but round on top like a hat worn by the Amish. No self-respecting English butler would be seen serving tea (or much else) in such a piece of headgear. While viewers of the picture might not spot the exact error, they would sense something was wrong with the high-tea scene.

On a low budget? Here are some ways to find props for a limited outlay of cash. You can find period props in antique and second-hand stores. High schools and colleges maintain costumes for their theater departments. They, too, will often lend out period clothing for photo shoots.

For his daytrading illustration, William Duke needed to show a man on a tightrope. For one piece of the composite, he photographed a frayed rope against a white background. He then had a model stand on a stack of boxes in front of a white seamless, and

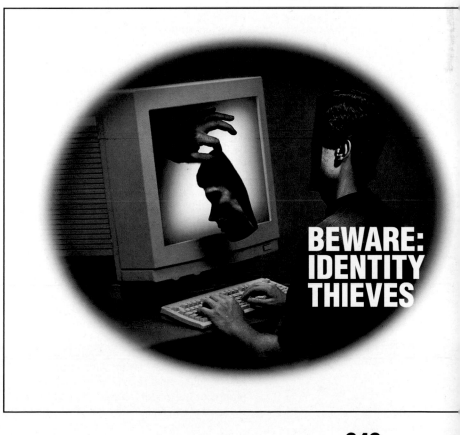

Via the Internet, thieves are stealing individuals' personal information to access financial accounts. To represent unique personal numbers and private codes like a social security number, driver's license, and birth date, the photographer selected a mask as a metaphor for individual identity.
William Duke,
for *Newsweek* magazine

BEWARE:
IDENTITY
THIEVES

photographed him from a low angle. The desert in the picture came from a snapshot Duke had taken years ago. The clouds were added from another file photo. Duke composited all the elements together with Photoshop to create the photo illustration, "The Daytrading Tightrope" (see page 342).

John Burgess based his idea for "The Face of Today's Digital Camera" (see page 337) on an Annie Leibovitz portrait of comedienne Lily Tomlin. Burgess found all the props he needed in a local camera shop.

Models

You do not need a trained Shakespearean actor to model in your photo illustration. Most illustrations do not depend on facial expressions or acting. They do, however, depend on stereotypes. You need a person who fits the part.

For an editorial photo illustration about runners hitting "the wall" at 22 miles, you may not need a world-class marathon runner, but do not pick a couch potato, either. Save your friend the couch potato for the story on the dangers of being sedentary.

William Duke often uses himself as a low-cost model in his illustrations. For example, the photographer constructed his illustration of St. Sebastian from an out-of-copyright painting of the martyr's body topped with Duke's own face.

Backgrounds

A background is a photograph's most important layer when you are creating the mood of a photo illustration. To avoid any confusion between true and manufactured pictures, photographers have shot many successful photo illustrations against seamless paper backgrounds. The seamless paper adds an abstract quality to a photo since almost nothing in the natural world is ever seen against the purity of simple black or white.

Award-winning photographer Jay Koelzer, however, says that photographers can "look at the background not as something to make disappear but rather as something to add to the image so that it will carry a stronger statement." Koelzer frequently combines realistic backgrounds shot on location with subjects photographed in the studio to produce eye-catching, intellectually challenging images. For example, he photographed Denver's skyline for an illustration about population growth in Colorado (see page 340).

In the studio, he photographed two models holding umbrellas. Using the computer to assemble the final image, he replicated the photos of his models, erased their faces, varied their sizes, and positioned them on the background. Like images from a René Magritte painting, the faceless characters appear to be gently rising and falling over Denver's cityscape with the Rocky Mountains in the background. Although the background is real, no one would mistake the final picture for a documentary photo.

The bottom line with all photo illustration, including use of the background, is that the reader should instantly know that the image is created, not recorded. Do not confuse the reader.

Time

Allow time—lots of time—to conceptualize, prop, and photograph an editorial photo illustration. Editors are accustomed to asking photographers to run down to Castro and 14th Streets to take a quick shot before the 5:00 P.M. deadline. Unfortunately, editors frequently maintain the same mindset when they request editorial photo illustrations.

Most photo illustrations, though, require much longer than two hours. Photo illustrations can take hours that stretch into days. Dreaming up concepts takes time. Rarely do the first headline and visual that come to mind result in the final photo. Propping takes shopping.

Without the right props, the picture will look amateurish. Finding the perfect model can be as difficult as finding the perfect spouse. Then comes shooting. With the patience of Job, the meticulousness of a watchmaker, and the flair of a set designer, you will build the picture. The clock ticks as you move the props one inch to the left or right. Each change requires an adjustment of the lights.

After you have taken many test shots to check each detail, the time finally arrives to click the shutter release. The moment is almost anticlimactic.

When an editor at the *Fort Lauderdale Sun-Sentinel* in Florida assigned Susan Gardner to illustrate an article on cryonics—freezing corpses in the hopes of reviving them in the future—the photographer knew to allow time for the whole production (see page 340).

First, Gardner commissioned a fake block of ice from Plexiglas. She sprayed this with fake snow, lit it with blue gels, and created a mist with dry ice. A hole in the bottom of a table allowed the model to slip her head inside the cube.

The first model, however, took one look at the set and backed out, saying it would be "detrimental" to her career. Her replacement, an elderly woman, was touched up with some white and blue makeup.

One month elapsed from the original concept to the final exposed image.

Melanie Rook D'Anna, shooting for the *Mesa* (Arizona) *Tribune*, was illustrating the return of the movie "101 Dalmatians."

She contacted the local Dalmatian kennel club and persuaded members to bring their dogs to a movie theater—all at the same time. She positioned several highly trained dogs in the front row. These dogs followed the commands of their owners to stay. The rest of the dogs were not so well-behaved, so their owners hid under the seats, their dogs resting comfortably above. The photographer filled the theater with more than 81 Dalmatians, all in their seats at the same time.

The addition of popcorn, colas, and careful lighting gave this picture its striking look.

THINKING CREATIVELY: A STRUCTURE

John Newcomb's *The Book of Graphic Problem-Solving: How to Get Visual Ideas When You Need Them* is based on the premise that visual problem-solving starts with words. He suggests that the starting point is the editor's working title for the story.

Take a story about men who are losing their hair. The editor's working title: "Are You Worried about Balding?" Start by analyzing the nature of the subject.

LIST THE FACTS

What is balding? How would you describe balding to someone from another planet? What words might you use? Round, smooth, hairless. List some of the characteristics of the subject.

Source. What is the source of the problem or item you are illustrating? In this example, where does balding come from? What causes it? Balding in men is a hereditary trait that comes from their mothers, grandmothers, and great-grandmothers.

Delivery. If the topic is about a service or object, describe how it is delivered. If the story is about a cure for balding, how would the patient get the cure—pill, surgery, or diet?

Size. How large is the object or problem—both physically and emotionally? In the

Theater distributors were bringing back the movie "101 Dalmatians." For an illustration, the photographer propped an entire movie theater with dogs from a local kennel club. The well-trained Dalmations in the front row sat unattended, but the less orderly animals in succeeding rows were firmly held in place by their owners, who were hiding under the seats.
Melanie Rook D'Anna, *Mesa [Arizona] Tribune*

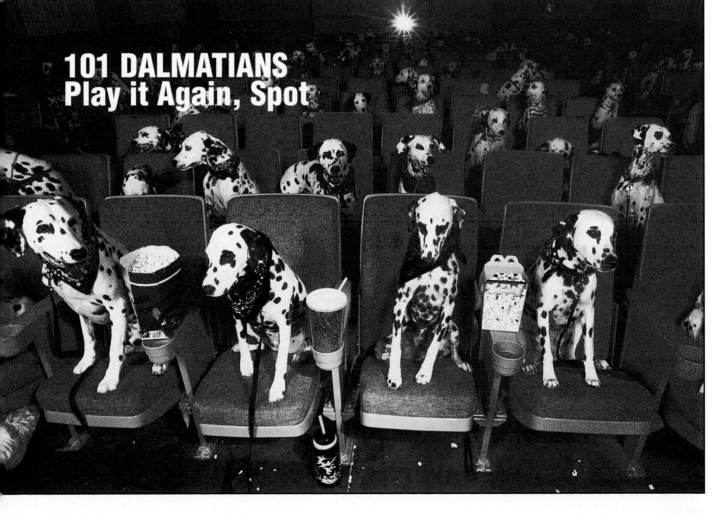

101 DALMATIANS
Play it Again, Spot

balding assignment, is the hair loss partial or complete? Does balding make men feel like jocks or like jackasses?

Weight. Is the subject of the assignment physically or emotionally heavy or light? Is it a crushing burden, or a minor irritant? Do those with just a few remaining wisps of hair feel dragged down or light-headed?

Winners or Losers. Who gains and who loses with balding? Most stories requiring illustration have a winner or loser, a survivor, or a victim in the plot. At first, you might not think anyone gains from balding. But charlatans with patent cures gain, as do pharmaceutical companies that develop cures for baldness. Doctors who perform transplants gain. Wigmakers gain. Psychiatrists gain. Who loses? When men lose hair, do they sometimes lose their wives or girlfriends, too?

First, write sample headlines for the story. Next, draw a rough sketch to go with each headline. Then select the best headline and sketch. Finally, locate the right props, costume, and background before taking the picture. Photo illustration by Marilyn Glaser; sketches by Ben Barbante

FACTS BECOME PHRASES
As you have just seen, Newcomb's method requires you to identify the facts about your topic. Write each answer down without worrying about being creative. Just start listing information.

Next, try sayings, phrases, proverbs, or any other bits of traditional wisdom. In the list of facts, we noted that the source of balding is genes inherited from the mother—not the father. Try the headline "Balding—Not Dad's Fault After All." To illustrate this idea, you could photograph a bald man holding a hairless baby.

In the fact list under weight, we noted that some bald men feel like jocks and others feel like jackasses. Think about twisting the emphasis. To suggest that bald men are not burdened by their hair loss, twist the line "Blondes Have More Fun" to "Balds Have More Fun." Now illustrate this line with a photo of a Telly Savalas-like character, bald and proud of it, surrounded by women.

Play Word Games
Now take the key words from each of the facts above and play word games with them. For instance, in describing the nature of a bald man's head, we listed the word "smooth." Smooth as a balloon, as a billiard ball, as a bowling ball. Imagine a bowling ball looking like a bald man's head. The phrase "Bowling, Anyone?" could evolve into a photo of a bald man with his head in a rack of bowling balls.

From the editor's original working title, "Are You Worried about Balding?" came first a set of facts about baldness. The facts led to plays on words and phrases. These sayings, puns, and double entendres produced visual ideas that could easily illustrate the story.

The final photograph, by the way, of the man's head lined up next to bowling balls, has since been shown to hundreds of editors, photographers, and others. The photo has never failed to bring the house down with appreciative laughter.

ELECTRONIC CUT AND PASTE
To create a surreal effect, you might want the picture's subjects to appear completely out of proportion—the mayor of New York towering over the Empire State Building, or a sailor carrying the QE II under his arm.

To do so, you might need to photograph each element separately and then combine them. If you cannot photograph all the subjects and props at the same time in the same location, remember to keep the light consistent for each image you plan on combining later.

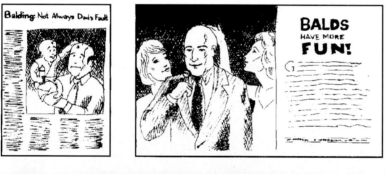

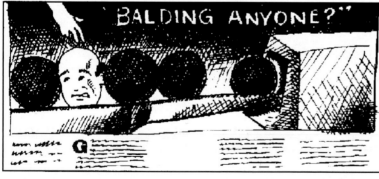

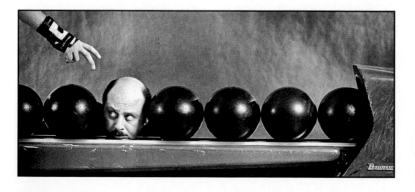

For example, if the light appears to be diffused and coming from the upper left side of the scene, keep the same effect on all subsequent studio photos. Then, when you put all the elements together, the final picture will have natural-looking light that appears to be coming from only one source.

In today's high-tech age, you can scan in old images or new ones and electronically alter them freely. Once you have scanned the

pieces, you can easily change the size, color, and left-right orientation of each separate image. You can place the subject into another setting (see pages 339–343, 347, and 348) or take the head off one subject and put it on another (see page 341). Software can bring alive almost anything you can dream up.

Having shot or gathered the individual pieces for the illustration and scanned them, you can manipulate and combine all the

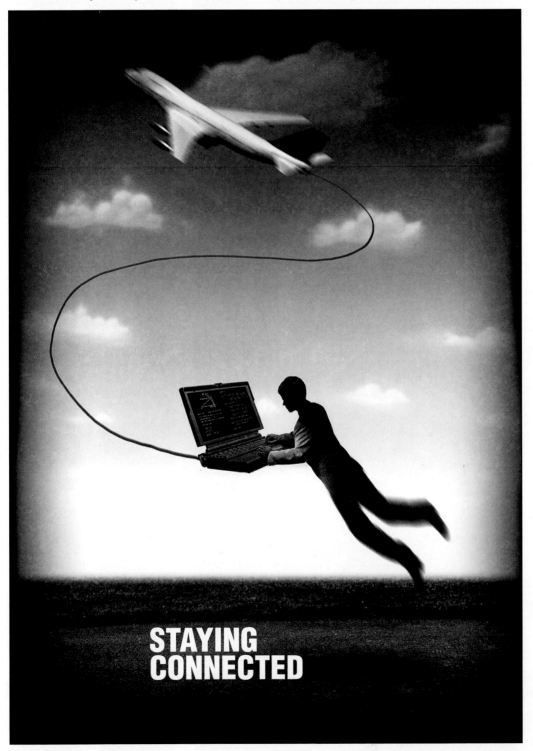

STAYING
CONNECTED

Business travelers using their laptop computers on airplanes have become ubiquitous. To illustrate a story about the trend, the photographer combined three images to create a photo of a computer user tethered to an airplane. The photographer gave both the airplane and the man's legs the effect of movement by applying a computerized blur filter to that part of the image. William Duke, for *Fortune* magazine

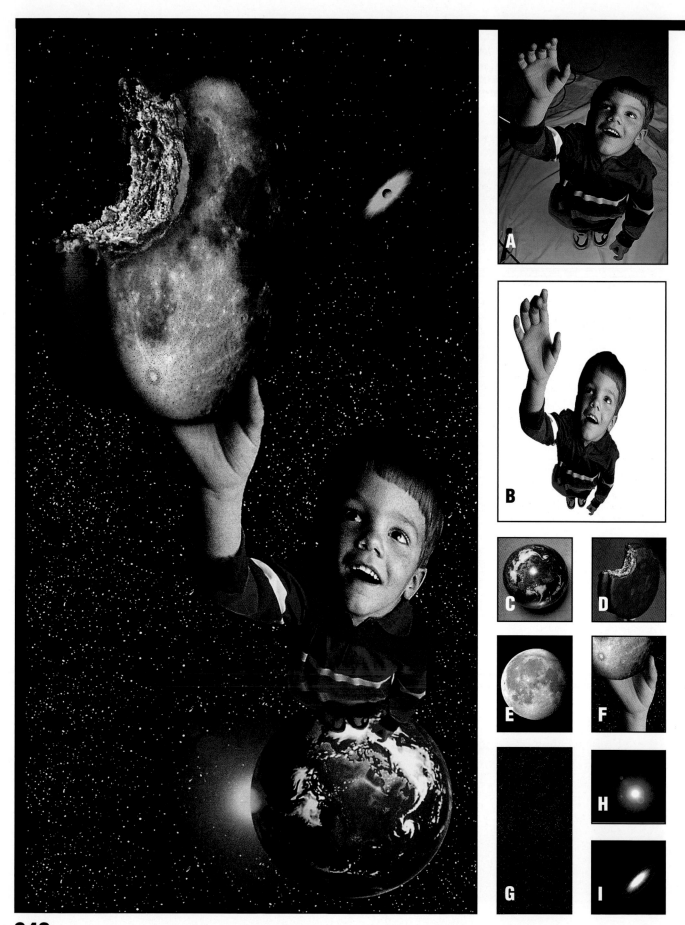

parts seamlessly. Do beware that combining pictures in Photoshop can absorb much more time than originally planned. Even powerful fast computers can take a long time to process complex images.

DO NOT INFRINGE COPYRIGHTS

One word of caution. Copyright protection extends to "found" images in magazines, newspapers, and on the Internet.

Unless the image is one you have shot or one that you have permission to use, do not be tempted by the ease of scanning it or downloading it to use someone else's image or work of art to enhance your photo illustration. Doing so is illegal—regardless of how much you change the original.

SOME WORK, SOME DO NOT

Some editorial photo illustrations cause the reader to say, "Dear, you have to see this. It's just too funny." Others fail to stop the reader at all, or, even worse, they cause the reader to ponder the strange picture, wondering why anyone would go to the trouble to publish it.

Why do some photo illustrations hit the reader like a sledgehammer and others leave no mark at all?

WEAK PHOTOS

Sometimes the photo is weak. Everyday, readers see slick ads produced by high-priced ad agencies. Consequently, readers are accustomed to illustrations that appear flawless.

Poorly planned editorial photo illustrations look unprofessional. If the models look like they were grabbed out of the newsroom, if the set looks like it was a corner of the cafeteria, and if the whole production looks like it was thrown together between assignments, then the final photo will look amateurish.

For an illustration titled "Sitters Can Be a Pet's Best Friend," the photographer had a subject pretend she was reading comics to two German shepherds. The scene, however, took place on a beat-up old couch. The run-down setting distracted from the concept.

One publication ran a photo illustration showing a man's handwriting on a chalk-board with the words "American education stumbles." The foreground contained a few books sitting vertically on a desk. The strong headline in this instance was not supported by an imaginative visual. The photographer failed to find a symbol for American education or to play off the idea of stumbling.

How might you have conceptualized the headline?

POOR HEADLINES

While editorial illustrations often fail because of poor photography, they also fail because of poor headlines. Rather than "leaving 'em laughing," an unclear headline leaves readers scratching their heads in confusion.

Sometimes, even a clear headline is not enough, if it is clear but dull. Beware of headlines that start out "Everything You Ever Wanted to Know about Pizza" or "The Entire History of Bicycles." These headlines do not suggest a theme but instead lend themselves to an encyclopedia entry on the topic.

Sometimes the writer has provided a label headline like "Potatoes." A headline like this probably came from a story that had no theme or focus. Suppose the story had focused on the role of the potato in the Irish famine or had described the many ways to prepare potatoes. Either article would lend itself to a possible editorial photo illustration. If the story has no focus, however, the photographer is left to take a product photo of the potato itself, a vegetable all too familiar to most readers.

Sometimes headlines are too news-oriented. Photo illustrations work best with ideas, not events. Avoid headlines like "Stock Market Drops for Third Straight Day."

HEADLINE AND PICTURE DO NOT MESH

Still, the headline might be great. The photo might be eye-popping. But if the two do not mesh, then the final package looks like an afterthought. Sometimes the reader gets the impression that the headline was written without the editor seeing the photo.

This headline and this picture leave the reader wondering just what the central theme of the story is. The headline, not the subhead, should tie the picture and the words together. A nicely executed photo loses its impact with a weak headline.

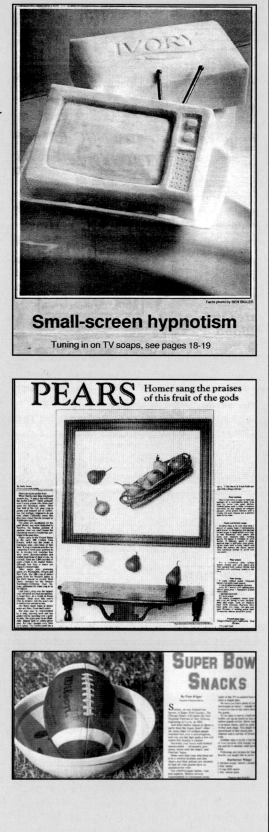

Facts photo by BEN BIGLER

Small-screen hypnotism

Tuning in on TV soaps, see pages 18-19

A good image in this example was matched with a weak headline. A better headline might read "Picture Perfect Pears."

PEARS Homer sang the praises of this fruit of the gods

This illustration combines an unimaginative headline, "Super Bowl Snacks," with a picture that is too literal. Try thinking of some alternatives for both words and pictures.

SUPER BOWL SNACKS

Or the page looks like the photographer never saw the headline or story before snapping the shutter.

One copy editor wrote this catchy headline: "When Marriage Seems Like War." The photographer produced a strong photo showing a couple having a highly stylized argument. The man's tie is blowing out behind him. Both models look like they are talking with their hands. The problem: they do not look like they are at war. The couple appears to be arguing in the wind, not battling. The words and pictures, like the married pair depicted in the photo, do not communicate.

WORDS OF CAUTION
DOCUDRAMA CONFUSION

Like editorial photo illustrations, docudramas are created situations. By mimicking reality, though, docudramas cause confusion in readers' minds. They are fake photographs that masquerade as authentic documentary images. Avoid these real-looking docudramas. Create photo illustrations that look unbelievable and cannot be confused with honest reportage.

Look at the images illustrating stories about "Latchkey Kids" on the opposite page. Is it not conceivable that a photographer could have happened upon a child sitting on the front steps of his house, as depicted in the top image? The picture looks like a candid but in fact is a docudrama. No reader, however, would mistake the bottom photo illustration, of a child dangling from a keychain, as real.

Even with the words "photo illustration" published beneath the picture, photographers should avoid docudramas. Docudramas detract from a publication's credibility. The reader should never have to ask, "Did that picture really happen that way?"

The job of the photojournalist is to show the world as it is, not as the photographer imagines it is. True editorial photo illustrations, by contrast, add to the reader's understanding and can even add a little fun. A picture should either be real or so outrageous that no reader is fooled. Do not leave the reader in the twilight zone of the docudrama.

PROBLEMS IN PLACEMENT AND IDENTIFICATION

Imagine for a moment a newspaper that sprinkles its editorials and analysis—unidentified—throughout its pages, including the front page. How would a reader, accustomed to the straight news on page one, know where fact ends and interpretation begins?

Failing to identify contrived photographs is every bit as serious as failing to properly identify written editorial comment—and playing editorial photo illustrations on the front page or alongside documentary photographs is as questionable as mingling editorials with unbiased news stories.

While newspapers prior to the Civil War did not hesitate to mix fact and opinion on the front page, most modern media outlets shy away from this practice and carefully limit opinions to a well-marked editorial page or clearly designated opinion column. The same stringent rules should be applied to editorial photo illustrations. Regardless of how unreal they may appear, they, too, should be labeled and segregated from straight photo reporting.

PRACTICAL AND ETHICAL GUIDELINES

The following are practical and ethical guidelines for using photo illustrations:

- Eliminate the docudrama. Never set up a photograph to mimic reality, even if it is labeled a photo illustration.
- Create only abstractions with photo illustration. Studio techniques, for example, can help to make situations abstract—the use of a seamless or abstract backdrop, photomontage, or exaggerated lighting. Contrast in size and content, juxtaposition of headline and photo—all can give the reader visual clues that what appears on the page is obviously not the real thing.
- Always clearly label photo illustrations as such—regardless of how obvious you may think they are.
- Never play photo illustrations on news pages. Restrict them to feature pages or to section fronts. Display them so that they are obviously distinct from news or feature pictures.
- If you lack sufficient time to do a photo illustration properly, do not do one. Suggest another solution. ■

DOCUDRAMA VERSUS CONCEPT PHOTO

Avoid docudramas such as the top one, below. They fool the reader. Instead, create a concept photo like the one at the bottom, which is so abstract that no one will mistake it for real.

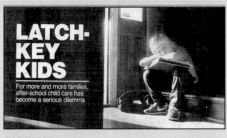

DOCUDRAMA

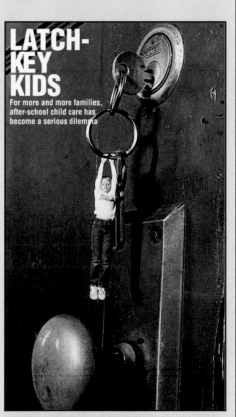

EDITORIAL PHOTO ILLUSTRATION
Photo illustration by B. Jeff Breland

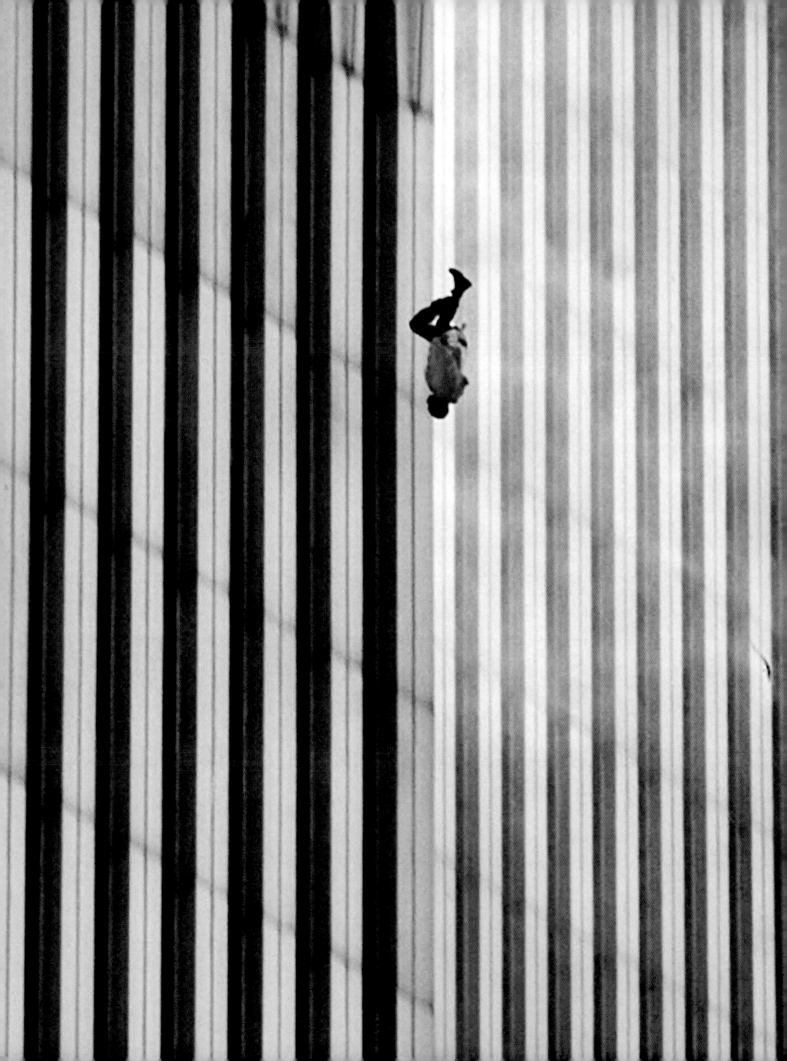

15

Ethics

Photojournalism as a profession imposes a set of responsibilities. Some are fairly routine and fall neatly into the
"daily duties" category: get to the scene, frame and
focus the shot, collect the caption info, and so forth. Beneath these
functional tasks lie broader ethical considerations. Confronting these
issues is often more challenging than the assignment itself. At times,
these ethical issues pit the photographer's professional duties against
his or her own conscience, that internal barometer that guides behavior and ultimately maintains social order. Photographers may, in the
course of completing their assignments, be forced to choose between

**Without other routes of escape, people jumped to their deaths
from the World Trade Center towers before the buildings
collapsed following terrorist attacks on September 11, 2001.
Many publications declined to run this picture. Were they
right?** Richard Drew, *Associated Press*

how they might act as individual citizens and how they feel they should act as visual journalists.

This dilemma—personal choice versus professional responsibility—is certainly not unique to photojournalism. Consider, for example, the plight of the public defender charged to represent a rapist who he knows is guilty; the doctor who has the resources and training to prolong artificially the life of a suffering patient. In these examples, the U.S. Constitution and the Hippocratic oath, respectively, are compelling codes, but what about the individual rights of the attorney, the private conscience of the physician?

Now consider the less dire but still clouded situation of a photographer shooting a story about suburban high schools. While scanning a clattering lunchroom scene, the photographer spots a trio of students exchanging $20 bills for bags of white powder.

Does the photographer, acting as a genuinely concerned citizen, try to stop or at least to disrupt the deal? Report the incident to the principal and offer a description of the players? Or, does the photographer take the picture and publish it?

Almost every day, photojournalists face decisions of morality—ranging from removing a distracting item from a photograph to taking a gruesome picture at a murder site.

But a looming deadline or the logistical challenge of a six-site assignment sheet can pressure the photographer into making snap judgments about even the most morally delicate situations.

Thus, thinking about issues ahead of time may allow photojournalists to avoid a crisis on the scene or regret after an image has run. Photojournalists use several arguments to explain their decisions to shoot or publish controversial pictures. One argument, which sometimes fails to distinguish between practices and standards, relies on the "other guy" argument: "I did it because that's the way other photojournalists do it."

These photographers are comparing their actions with a perceived industry standard. Whether the action is inherently right or wrong is irrelevant to their argument. "This is the way everyone does it." While such a decision-making strategy might reflect professional practices, it does not create a standard grounded in the norms of ethical decision-making.

FOUNDATIONS OF ETHICAL DECISION-MAKING

Many photographers, whether they realize it or not, turn to an established ethical framework to try to guide their decisions.

UTILITARIAN

This framework includes the Utilitarian principle as defined by ethicists. Here the overriding consideration is "the Greatest Good for the greatest number of people."

The Utilitarian position recognizes that photojournalism provides information critical to a democratic society. Photography can show the horrors of war, the tragedy of an accident, or the hardship of poverty. Therefore, it is right to take and publish pictures. Without a journalist's photographs, viewers are deprived of what may be critical decision-making information.

Take the case of the distraught family of a drowned child in a body bag (see opposite). From a Utilitarian point of view, publishing this picture might decrease the number of drowning accidents. In fact, that was the outcome of printing this picture in the newspaper. The picture might have been painful for the grieving family members, but it ultimately saved tens and maybe hundreds of lives by reminding parents to be more cautious when their children are swimming.

ABSOLUTIST

However, the Utilitarian principle of "the Greatest Good . . ." bumps up against a competing ethical principle that says there are certain principles that are fixed, like "Thou shalt not kill." This statement is absolute and inviolable regardless of the benefits to society.

For some, an Absolutist principle might say, "People have the right of privacy." Taking and publishing a picture of the distraught family of a drowned child may cause others to be more cautious and thus benefit society, but invading the privacy of a family's grief—regardless of the societal benefits— would be unacceptable to an absolutist who adheres to an individual's right to privacy.

THE GOLDEN RULE

Another of the ethical cornerstones is the precept, "Do unto others as you would have them do unto you." This rule, too, can conflict with the Absolutist's view on privacy and with actions that might benefit a democratic society in need of information.

In the previous example, you as a grieving parent might not want your picture taken. If you followed the Golden Rule, you would not run the photo because of how publishing the picture would have made you feel.

The boy in the body bag had just drowned. His family was grief-stricken. Might running the picture in the paper help prevent future drownings? For a discussion about the photo, see above.

John Harte, Bakersfield, California

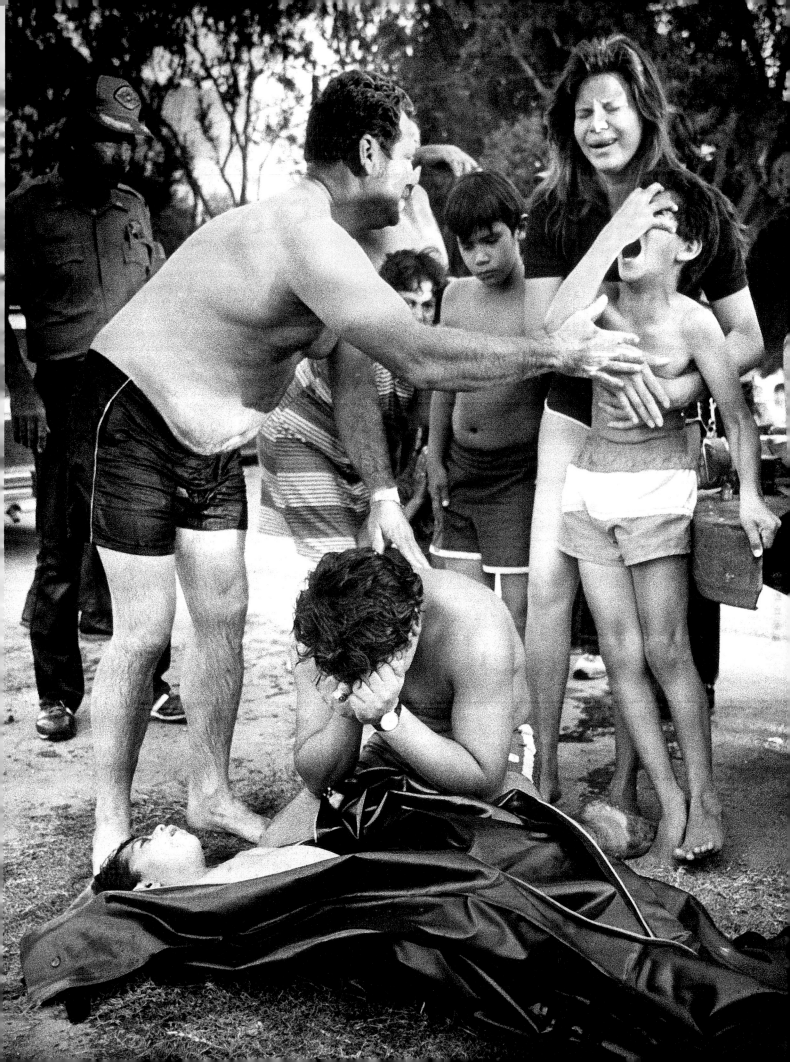

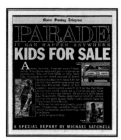

On this cover, two of the
girls are models. One is not.
How would the reader know
which is candid and which
is set up? Would a reader
have known what "photo
illustration" means had the
disclaimer been included?
© Parade.

anywhere." Three small color photos
of unidentified and unidentifiable sultry
adolescent "girls of the street" dotted
the text-dominated black cover (left),
which announced a "special report" on
child prostitution.

Anywhere, the article purported, included
New York City; Van Nuys, California; and
"placid little towns like Waterville, Maine."

A local Maine newspaper challenged the
story. Reporters discovered that the attorney
general's office in the Maine jurisdiction had
prosecuted only two cases of prostitution in
Waterville, none involving teenagers—and
that the young Waterville "prostitute" in the
photo was actually a model.

When freelance photographer Dean
Abramson was unable to find an actual street-
walking teen in Waterville, his *Parade* magazine editors told him to hire a model.
Abramson complied and eventually snapped
the posed picture.

Although *Parade* editors initially denied
the subterfuge, later they recanted, saying
that an explanatory line of type had been
omitted. In a follow-up article for *News
Photographer* magazine, they further rationalized the situation by telling writer Betsy
Brill that they routinely used models for stories involving minors.

In interviews with other photographers on
the project, however, Brill discovered that,
despite editors' claims, only two of the three
pictures had been set up with models for the
Parade cover. A third photographer captured
an actual candid moment.

Camera 5 freelancer Neal Preston verified
that his assignment from *Parade* had been to
find and photograph actual teenaged prosti-
tutes (not models). He had done so in Van
Nuys, California.

"I could have saved a lot of time and film
if I had hired a model," he said when he
learned the other photos had been set up. "I'm
proud my picture was the one that was real."

Award-winning photojournalist Eddie
Adams, who photographed the New York
City setup, told Brill that concern over the
staged photos was "a lot of bullshit." He said
that hiring models for stories involving children is done "all the time"—not just by him,
he said, and not just by *Parade*, but by all
magazines, especially for cover stories.

"There's a difference," Adams said,
"between an illustration and a straight picture." (See Chapter 14, "Illustration.") Yet, he
acknowledged, the reader has no way of
knowing the difference without words.

Adams, however, begged the ethical question and relied on the familiar "everybody
does it" argument. The question is not: "Do

Between moving an obstructing cola bottle and
hiring a model to impersonate a teenage hooker lies
a large, gray ethical chasm. This gray zone, with its
myriad shadows and shadings, can challenge
even the most clear-sighted photographer. Are all
situations alike?

Do the same rules apply to features, portraits, and
illustrations, as well as to hard news? Far from being a
fixed commodity, the photographer's level of control is
variable, logistically and ethically. A photojournalist's
weekly assignment sheet is likely to represent a continuum of control—from strictly hands-off to complete
manipulation.

Photojournalists cover subjects ranging from a war
in the Middle East to a fashion shoot in midtown. Like
the fashion shoot, some pictures require complete control. Other situations, like accidents or arrests, require
the hands-off, fly-on-the-wall approach.

Any time you take pictures, you are affecting the
scene to some degree. According to noted physicist
Werner Heisenberg, observation itself alters the object
being observed. This principle applies to photography
as surely as it does to the subatomic world.

For instance, whether a subject consciously thinks
about the photographer or not, that person's behavior
changes in the presence of a camera. Some subjects
exaggerate their behavior; others shy away from the
camera. Even thinking a camera might be present can
alter some people's behavior.

Even though photographers and their cameras have
some influence on the scene they are photographing,
the question the working pro must ask is, "When
should the photojournalist remain an observer,
removed as much as possible from the scene? When
should the photographer intervene?"

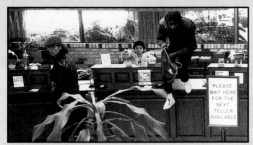

Photo courtesy Bank Security

• **Hidden cameras** represent one extreme of the continuum. The security camera at First Local Bank automatically snaps a picture at regular intervals, regardless of who is standing at the teller window. The bank camera, which simply operates, exerts no control at all. Despite its passivity, however, even the bank camera alters the scene being observed: most criminals would take different precautions if robbing a bank under constant photographic surveillance.

• **Sports photography** is near this end of the continuum. A hurdler races down the track. Even if she wanted to, the sports photographer could have little influence on the athlete. She would not tell the runner to run to the right

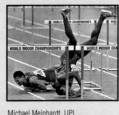

Michael Meinhardt, UPI

for a better picture. The sports photographer has virtually no control over the subject but does select the moment to release the camera's shutter.

• **Hard news.** Elsewhere along the continuum you will find the news photographer covering a riot. Most photographers would hesitate to direct a demonstrator or tell a policeman to stand aside to improve a photo-

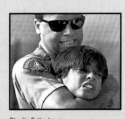

Charlie Fellenbaum, the *Hemet* [California] *News*

graph's composition. The photographer could initiate control but refrains in a true hard-news situation.

• **Features.** This is where the continuum becomes slippery. Here, photographers disagree about when to intervene and when to merely observe. The action is

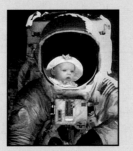

Juanito Holandez, *Long Beach* [California] *Press-Telegram*

touching, but the light is not great. Is it okay to ask the subject to move over a few feet so you could get perfect backlighting? Different photographers have determined different points where they will draw the control line when faced with a feature assignment. Some photojournalists would not hesitate to ask the subject to move. Others would never consider disturbing the moment, even if leaving the situation untouched meant sacrificing a superb picture.

• **Portraits** usually require some direction on the part of the photographer. If the assignment is to take pictures of the president of the local university, the photographer usually must tell her where to sit and what to do with her hands. The photographer might ask the president to look directly at the camera. This

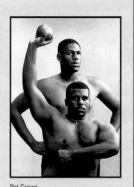

Pat Crowe, *Wilmington News Journal*

way the reader knows that the administrator was aware of the photographer and won't think the picture is a candid photo. An unwritten but probably accurate rule holds that a subject looking at the photographer (i.e., the reader) is aware of the camera.

• **Photo illustrations** represent the the other extreme, the full-control end of the continuum. Photojournalists manufacture every aspect of an illustration—including editorial concept photos, food photos, and studio and location fashion shoots. The photojournalist arranges the props, perhaps builds the set, and hires and even dresses the models. The viewer has no

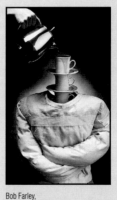

Bob Farley, *Birmingham Post-Herald*

illusions about the photo or the photographer's role. If the photographer has been careful, the created photo cannot be mistaken for real. Through the use of exaggerated size, seamless backgrounds, and other visual devices, the photojournalist can assure the reader that the picture is constructed and not a slice of real life. (See Chapter 14, "Illustration.") With photo illustrations, the photographer exercises complete control. ■

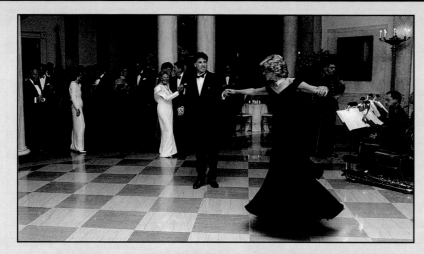

Diana, Princess of Wales, danced at the White House with actor John Travolta. The White House photographer was allowed to take this picture. Paparazzi, on the other hand, shot thousands of pictures of the princess during public as well as private moments without her permission.
Pete Souza, Reagan Library Collection

What is the difference between paparazzi, who photograph celebrities, and photojournalists, who cover the news?

Both kinds of photographers use the same cameras and strobes. They look alike, and sometimes their work is even printed in the same publications. However, the purposes of the two breeds of photographers are quite different. Photojournalists hope to inform the public. Paparazzi take pictures to entertain or titillate. (For more on paparazzi, see page 403–404, Chapter 16, "Law.")

Unfortunately, the general public often lumps paparazzi and photojournalists in the same category. That is what happened following the death of Britain's Princess Diana. She died in a horrific car crash during a high-speed chase in which her car's driver was attempting to outrun seven or more photographers. The public was outraged at the paparazzi.

After the tragic accident, photographers who had nothing to do with the accident and, in fact, had never staked out a celebrity in their lives, faced a barrage of insults on their regular assignments. Covering a routine news event, bystanders yelled, "Photographers killed Princess Diana" at Scott LaClair of the *Herald-Standard* in Pennsylvania. One man even started swinging at LaClair with his fists. During the incident, the photographer's glasses were scratched, but he wasn't injured. When Susan Watts photographed the memorial for Princess Diana outside the British Embassy in Manhattan, a passing motorist shouted "Murderer . . . paparazzo assassin . . . You killed Diana."

Photographers killing people? What is this all about?

Diana's death pushed the public's patience over the edge. Even before the tragedy, surveys indicated that the public feels the news media are too invasive. A 1996 poll by the Center for Media and Public Affairs found that 80 percent of those surveyed thought the media ignored people's privacy. After Diana's death, more than 95 percent of respondents to an informal *USA Today* online survey thought the Princess had been unfairly hounded by the news media.

Perhaps the public has a right to confuse the paparazzi and the photojournalist. Aside from the use of the same equipment, other similarities do exist between them. Sometimes both kinds of photographers cover celebrities.

Few photojournalists, however, spend their lives staking out a Hollywood star or international glamour figure in the hopes of catching a private or risqué moment.

The distinction between the two types of photographers grew narrower during the coverage of Monica Lewinsky, the intern whose affair with President Clinton nearly ended his presidency. When independent counsel Kenneth Starr focused his five-year $47 million investigation into alleged presidential misconduct concerning Clinton's relationship with the young woman, photographers of all stripes staked out her apartment and tried to get any image they could of the former intern.

Although the behavior of photojournalists in the Lewinsky situation mimicked that of paparazzi, from an ethical standpoint their purpose was different. Lewinsky was an accidental celebrity for the moment—and the subject of real news story. Though she

had not thrust herself into the public eye, her relationship with the president did culminate in an impeachment trial that could have changed the course of history.

The lives of Hollywood stars and glamour figures, the standard subject matter for paparazzi lenses, on the other hand, rarely have an effect on the nation or the world.

Of course, even when photojournalists cover a legitimate news story like alleged presidential misconduct, they should not resort to using ladders to peer over fences into the private homes or engage in high-speed car chases to grab a snap of a reclusive subject, points out David Lutman, a past president of the National Press Photographers Association.

Because photojournalists look like paparazzi, and sometimes even act like them, the public naturally confuses legitimate news gatherers with shooters who survive by selling pictures of celebrities.

The key difference, however, between these two distinct forms of photography is their intended purpose.

Photojournalists take pictures to show readers events that they cannot see for themselves. Paparazzi shoot pictures to satisfy the public's insatiable curiosity about the lives and love affairs of the famous.

Hopefully, the behavior of the paparazzi will not lead to such a backlash from the public that the work of authentic photojournalists will be further impeded. ∎

the continuum of control? At any given time, what part of the continuum should I choose? Which spot along the continuum is appropriate for this assignment?"

KEEPING UP WITH SHIFTING STANDARDS

The decision regarding control is a choice often based more on a photographer's time in history than on any established guidelines (see pages 358–360).

Photojournalism has no bible, no rabbinical college, no pope to define correct choices. And although surveys like those by Wilcox and Brink help establish current practices in the field, professional standards do not remain fixed in time. Standards change, and so do readers' expectations. Staying abreast of professional standards and evaluating decisions with an eye to the ethical foundations described at the beginning of this chapter should be helpful when faced with difficult moments.

In his book *Truth Needs No Ally*, Howard Chapnick, long-time head of Black Star Picture Agency, observed that changes in camera technology "have made it a truism that anything we can see we can photograph." He argued that now there is no excuse for the photojournalist to manipulate people in real-life situations.

JANET COOKE

What has caused this change in standards for the profession? Many observers point to one incident of outright fabrication as the pivot-point for journalists.

In 1981, Janet Cooke, a reporter for the *Washington Post*, won a Pulitzer Prize for her story "Jimmy's World," about an 8-year-old heroin addict. After the prize was awarded, investigators discovered that the child had never existed. Jimmy was a figment of Cooke's imagination—a "composite" of characters and incidents she had come upon in her research. Cooke lost the prize and gained a place of dishonor in journalism history. The journalism profession threw up its arms in outrage and began a hard, soul-searching reexamination of its ethical practices. Professional groups sponsored seminars, authors wrote books, and universities initiated classes in journalism ethics. The public's opinion of the press, its practices, and its prizes fell to a new low.

The outgrowth of this examination was an increased sensitivity, even vigilance, to how the profession performs its work. The profession began to question some of its accepted standards. The spotlight on the Cooke case also heightened sensitivity toward ethical

---

GUIDELINES FOR PHOTOGRAPHING TRAGIC MOMENTS

For an article in *News Photographer* magazine, Michael D. Sherer collected comments from photographers who had covered tragic events. Here are some of their guidelines:

ON CONDUCT

Be early, stay out of the way, and don't disrupt what's going on. Be sensitive to your subjects and the situation. Be compassionate. Do not badger or chase subjects to the point of annoyance. "How would I feel if I were the person being photographed?"
Jim Gehrz,
Worthington [Minnesota] *Daily Globe*

ON EQUIPMENT

In sensitive situations, carry as little gear as possible, leave the motor drive off, and use the longest lens possible. Don't become a spectacle.

ON SELECTIVITY

Pick your shots carefully—look for angles and subjects that will not offend subjects' and readers' sensitivities.

ON DRESS

Wear "appropriate" clothing. "Dress is an important part of the way the public perceives us and in their acceptance of us in times of stress. I think many of us can dress better day-to-day without having to wear a three-piece suit."
Mark Hertzberg,
Racine [Wisconsin] *Journal Times*

ON FOLLOW-UP

"Consider contacting the subjects sometime after publication to discuss the reason for, and reaction to, publishing the image."
Dave Nuss,
Salem [Oregon] *Statesman-Journal*

---

standards within the photojournalism community, indeed within the entire industry.

MONITORING ETHICAL STANDARDS

For the neophyte photographer or the seasoned pro, the profession does not provide a fixed yardstick, a definitive set of guidelines, or a regular measure of what other photojournalists in the trade are thinking and doing.

In fact, photojournalists disagree among themselves about the correctness of many choices. Craig Hartley, in a national survey of professionals for his thesis on photojournalistic ethics, found that of 19 hypothetical problems presented to working pros, almost half the questions resulted in a wide split among respondents.

On nine questions, at least a third of the photojournalists did not agree with their other responding colleagues. Clearly photojournalists do not think as a monolithic block when the topic turns to ethics.

Read about the Profession

Interested photographers can use the trade media and other resources to monitor the thoughts of their fellow journalists and shape their own ethical touchstones. The NPPA is the major proponent of ethical standards among photojournalists. Its publication, *News Photographer* magazine, reports on controversial issues. Read, in particular, the magazine's "Letters to the Editor" column to check

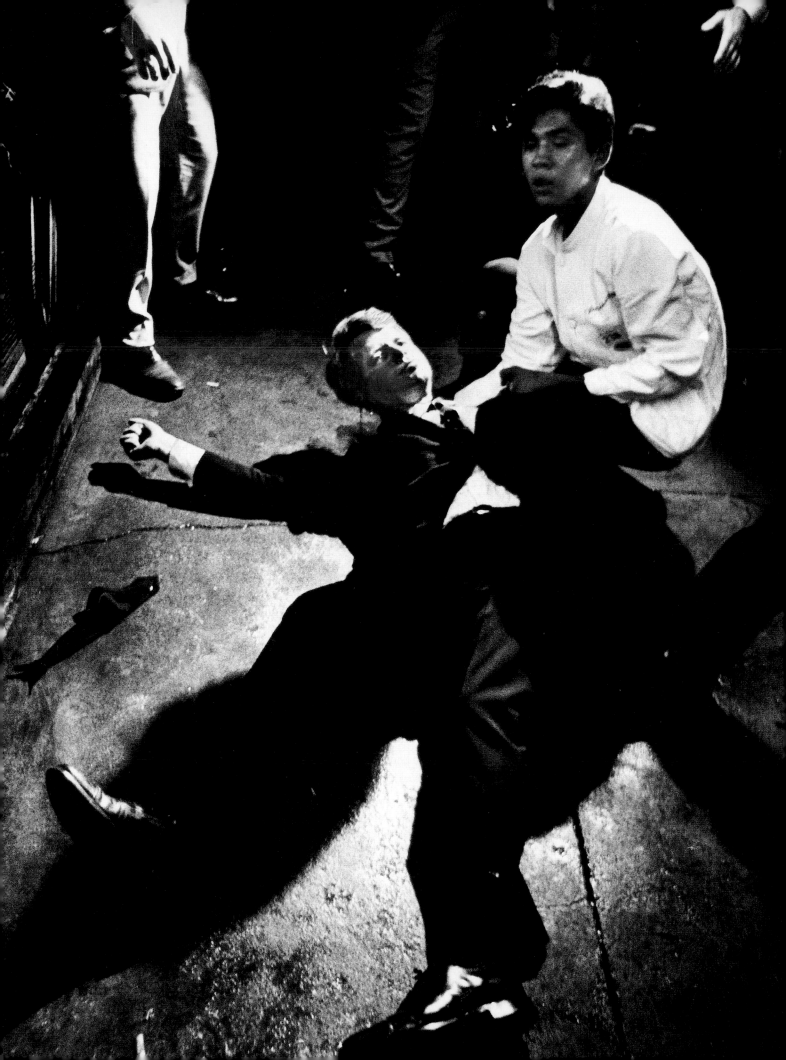

When Robert Kennedy was assassinated, a bystander blocked Boris Yaro's camera. He said to the woman, "Goddammit, lady, this is history!" and took this unforgettable picture. See page 367 for a discussion about the situation. Boris Yaro, © *Los Angeles Times*

the pulse of the working pro.

Magazines like *Columbia Journalism Review*, *American Journalism Review*, and *Photo District News* report on changing professional standards. *Journalism Quarterly* also publishes research on ethics.

In addition to magazines, workshops such as NPPA's Flying Short Course and the organization's online forum at *www.nppa.org*, provide valid insights into photojournalism's shifting standards. Other web sites where professionals discuss ethical issues are *www.DigitalJournalist.com*, *www.poynter.org*, and *www.SportsShooter.com*.

Let Your Subjects Guide You

Besides looking to other professionals, photographers also should monitor the reaction of their subjects to gauge shifting standards.

In her study "Listening to the Subjects of Routine News Photographs: A Grounded Moral Inquiry," researcher Cindy Brown surveyed individuals whose photographs had appeared in a number of Midwestern newspapers. She asked them about their experiences with the photographer when the original pictures were taken and how they felt about the published images.

Happily, Brown reports that the people she questioned generally liked the photojournalists who took their photographs and found the experience positive. Even when the news situations were anything but upbeat, the subjects felt good about the published photos and understood why their pictures were in the paper.

Considering a subject's responses and ethical concerns can help sensitize you to your news outlet's constituency.

A General Rule

What if you're not abreast of current standards, and you find yourself in a touchy situation on assignment? You might use this test of your own honesty, originally suggested by Elisabeth Biondi. Biondi has been a photo editor for *Geo*, *Vanity Fair*, and *Stern* magazines. She suggests that photographers test their ethical decisions by considering whether they would feel comfortable writing a note to the reader explaining how the picture was taken. For example, would the photographer mind explaining, "I brought these clothes for the subject to wear, and then I told him to make that crazy face?"

If the photographer is willing for the reader to know how the picture was constructed, what props were added, and what direction was given, then, Biondi says, the photo is probably ethically acceptable. However, if the photographer would feel uncomfortable revealing to the reader his or her involvement, then the picture likely falls on the unethical side of the line.

COVERING TRAGEDY AND GRIEF

When injuries occur at a car crash, a hotel fire, or a natural disaster, bystanders and relatives often block a camera reporter from taking pictures. Understandably these people are upset. In his benchmark book on media ethics, ***The Messenger's Motives***, the late John L. Hulteng wrote, "Photographers have acquired the reputation of being indifferent to the human suffering they frame in their viewfinders."

While the law gives photographers the right to take a picture, the law is an institution, not a human being who has just lost a son or daughter.

Using the Utilitarian principle of ethical decision making, on the other hand, photographers have a moral responsibility to their readers to show the world accurately, showing its tragedies as well as its triumphs. A democracy in which citizens must be informed to vote intelligently depends on accurate information. Photos help provide that information. In the long run, individuals cannot make informed decisions without a balanced and accurate picture of the world. Utilitarianism argues that people will benefit from seeing the good and bad, the happy and sad, and the joyful and tragic elements that comprise our world.

However, does this case for the "common good" supersede the rights of the grief-stricken individual? Do photographers have the right—or the obligation—to record moments of individual loss? These issues are complex, but there is one clear tenet to guide photographers' behavior in traumatic situations: photographers have a responsibility not to inflict greater suffering than necessary on survivors of a tragedy. "Than necessary" is obviously a troublesome phrase here, one defining that difficult gray zone. There is no clear measure of necessity. In the end, photographers must balance the harm to an individual caught in the jaws of tragedy with the long-range needs of society to see an unvarnished picture of the world.

John Long, past president of the NPPA and author of the organization's online guide "Ethics in the Age of Digital Photography," observes, "the rights of society are the

MAKE ARRANGEMENTS IN ADVANCE.

When you get a funeral assignment, contact the family or close friends to let them know you are coming. Express your sincere sympathy by simply saying you are sorry about their loss. If you are unable to speak with a family member or friend, the funeral director is your next best choice.

DRESS SOBERLY.

Photographers must dress as if attending the funeral—a suit or dress in dark color.

ARRIVE EARLY.

You will be situated and a part of the scene when everyone else arrives.

LIMIT CONTINUOUS FIRING.

Don't unload with rapid bursts of images. Even if the family has said okay, you'll offend those who are also grieving and who don't know you have family permission.

NO LIGHTS, PLEASE.

Avoid using strobes. Nothing is more offensive than a strobe flashing in the face of a crying person during a funeral service.

Mary Lou Foy,
Washington Post

concern of journalism, and the preponderance of the rights of the individual seen today are causing journalism headaches. I always go back to (Star Trek's Dr.) Spock when he said, 'sometimes the needs of the many outweigh the needs of the one.' As journalists, this is where we put our emphasis."

Pictures of grief personalize the news. Statistics about car accidents, spousal violence, murders, and accidental drowning distance the reader from the event. Seeing a picture of a particular person who was hit by a drunk driver gives the issue a face. No matter how large the numbers, statistics remain abstract.

From "Thousands die on the road every year" to "Katy Smith was struck by hit-and-run driver in a Honda yesterday and here is what she looked like," photographs transform an otherwise abstract issue into a personal event. The reader is more likely to care about Katy than all the thousands of other people who died last year.

Pictures can actually help victims and families. Some families understand that running the picture of a tragedy may prevent the same thing from happening to others. A published picture can give a family some rationale for a terrible calamity.

Dave LaBelle observes in his book *Lessons in Death and Life*, "Although many cry foul when photographs of grieving subjects are published, often the subjects themselves are helped to deal with their grief." He notes this story: "Two days after the *Albuquerque Tribune* published graphic pictures of burn victim Sage Volkman, it ran a letter from the girl's parents explaining why they thought the public needed to see the photos. 'We would like you to be aware of her struggle from when she was first burned and almost through death's door to her return to us as a 6-year-old girl with feelings who sees life in terms of Barbie dolls and her Brownie troop. When you come upon her unexpectedly in a store or restaurant, your first reaction may be one of sadness. But if you do run into her, we hope you will see her as we do—as a brave little girl.'" Publication of the photos helped raise more than $50,000 to aid with Sage's medical bills.

DO ALL TRAGEDIES NEED PHOTO COVERAGE?
If you are familiar with your equipment, you can usually take a few quick, available-light candid shots nearly unnoticed at any accident scene. Beyond these photos, you must weigh the short-range pain of your presence versus

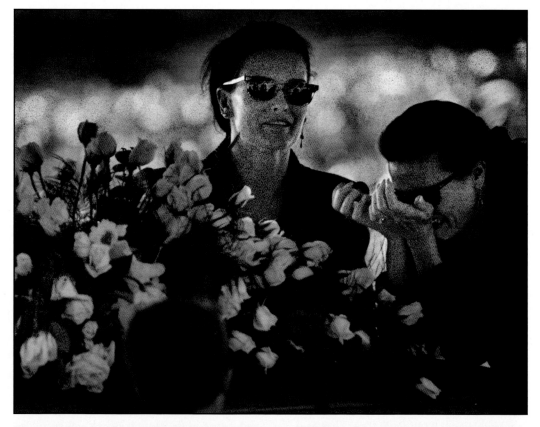

These women are crying over the coffin of their recently murdered sister, Nicole Brown. Brown was the former wife of football legend O.J. Simpson, accused but found innocent of her murder. When photographing a funeral, call ahead to express your sympathy and to let the family or friends know you are coming. At the graveside, wear appropriate clothing. Al Schaben, *Los Angeles Times*

the long-range value of your potential photos—a difficult judgment each photographer must make. Neither photographers at the scene nor editors back at the office are clairvoyant. Neither can look into a crystal ball and predict a picture's effect.

Photojournalists must maintain a belief in the overriding long-range importance of photos and the specific contribution of their particular image. Emotion-laden events lead to a cautious, continuous balancing act.

Adams, who won the Pulitzer Prize for his photograph of a Viet Cong suspect being executed in the streets of Saigon (see page 381), told this author about a photo he didn't take while covering the war:

On a hilltop in Vietnam, I was pinned down with a Marine company. Machine guns were going off. Dead bodies were lying on either side of me. Rocket fire seemed to be coming from everywhere. I was lying on the ground 5 feet away from an 18-year-old Marine. I saw fear on that kid's face like I had never seen before. I slid my Leica, with its preset 35mm lens, in front of me. I tried to push the shutter, but I couldn't. I tried twice more, but my finger just would not push the button. Later, I realized that I was just as scared to die as that kid was. I knew my face looked exactly like his, and I would not have wanted my picture seen around the world. I think his and my face said 'War!' but I still think I did the right thing by not taking that picture.

Adams chose to invoke the "do unto others . . ." Golden Rule. However, the photographer might also have considered the possible value to society from seeing the censored image. Adams's Pulitzer Prize-winning picture of the Vietnamese police chief executing a suspected Viet Cong did help to change public opinion about the Vietnam War. In the execution situation, society's greater good was served by photographing the scene.

Adams's hesitation at taking pictures on the hilltop in Vietnam was rare. Most professional photographers don't hesitate to take pictures when faced with a gut-wrenching accident or tragic murder.

In fact, many photographers say that because the critical moment is fleeting they shoot instinctively. They point out that you can always decide not to use the picture, but you can't revisit the moment. The consequences of taking someone's picture, the momentary disturbance or embarrassment, is relatively minor. Publishing the picture, which will be seen by friends, colleagues, and strangers, has a different and perhaps longer-lasting impact on the subject.

Finally, hesitating to take pictures can conflict with the professional role of the photojournalist. In most circumstances, professional standards would support the "shoot now—edit later" approach.

Boris Yaro, a *Los Angeles Times* photographer, had no trouble deciding to take pictures when he photographed Senator Robert Kennedy's assassination at the Ambassador Hotel. Later he told the story to John Faber, author of **Great News Photos**.

I was trying to focus in the dark when I heard a loud Bang! Bang! I watched in absolute horror. I thought, 'Oh my God, it's happening again! To another Kennedy!' I turned toward the senator. He was slipping to the floor. I aimed my camera, starting to focus, when someone grabbed my suit coat arm. I looked into the dim light, seeing a woman with a camera around her neck screaming at me. 'Don't take pictures! Don't take pictures! I'm a photographer and I'm not taking pictures!' she said." For a brief instant, Yaro was dumbfounded. Then he told her to let go of him. "I said, 'Goddammit, lady, this is history!'

He took the photographs (see page 364).

RESPECTING PRIVACY AT FUNERALS

Funerals are sad, stressful, and emotionally draining. They provide a context for grief and a forum for sharing sorrow among family and friends—not photographers. But sometimes they are newsworthy.

The decision to cover a funeral generally rests with an editor, but once that decision is made, it's the photographer's responsibility to complete the assignment. And it is the photographer, not the editor in the office, whom mourners notice, resent, and berate.

Photographers and the public have widely differing views about professional ethical conduct at these ceremonies.

Craig Hartley surveyed NPPA members and citizens of Austin, Texas. He wanted to compare each group's reactions to a number of ethical situations, including one that involved the funeral of a slain police officer, an event that an uninvited photographer attends and photographs even after being asked to leave.

Hartley found that although 63 percent of the news photographers he surveyed found the photojournalist's behavior at the funeral "ethical," 85 percent of the public found the behavior "unethical."

Readers, who vehemently denounced the actions of the photojournalist at the funeral, did not perceive the picture's value as meriting this intrusion into the private ceremony.

PROFESSIONAL OR GOOD SAMARITAN?

When should the photographer act as a professional photojournalist, and when should the cameraperson act as a responsible citizen? What happens when the roles conflict? Consider these scenarios:

- You are driving along the street and see a man running out of a pawnshop carrying a television set under his arm with the proprietor in hot pursuit. Do you try to stop the thief with the intent of holding him for the police, or do you take a picture of the scene as the criminal escapes around the corner?

- Later in the day, you see an accident by the side of the road. A child, stuck behind the car's dashboard, cries inconsolably. Do you take the little girl's picture, or sit and comfort her?

- A terrorist group has agreed to let you photograph their activities. They take you on a secret mission to plant a bomb. Do you take their pictures or try to stop them from activating the explosive? How would you handle the situation if you were photographing a similar raid, only this time the group was a unit of the U.S. army, not a terrorist cell?

The argument for professionalism often parallels the Utilitarian principle of ethics. The photojournalist has a role in society just as a doctor or lawyer has. That role is to inform the public. Information allows citizens to make intelligent decisions. By actually seeing what is going on—a thief in the act of stealing a television set; terrorists planting a bomb; a person committing suicide; or even the agony of a child in a car wreck—citizens can perhaps learn enough or be moved enough to create public debate. Information can lead to changes in public policy, laws, funding, or perhaps just improved behavior.

A photographer's job is to record the news, not to prevent it or to change it. Like an anthropologist observing a foreign culture, the photojournalist should look, record, but not disturb what is going on.

The Good Samaritan argument, on the other hand, is absolutist: a photojournalist is, first and foremost, a human being. A photojournalist's primary responsibility is to the person needing immediate help. Journalism comes second. No one can measure the good a photo will do later, but you can see the immediate needs of the present.

Joe Fudge, of the *Newport News* (Virginia) *Daily Press Times Herald*, had no problem making the ethical choice between being a Good Samaritan and a professional photojournalist when he saw smoke pouring from the third floor of a house.

First asking the newspaper office via two-way radio to notify the fire department, Fudge charged into the burning house and alerted residents that their attic was ablaze. "I went into the house and found three people sitting around eating. They didn't know that a fire was burning off the top of their house. The woman said, 'Oh, my God, my husband is asleep in the third-floor bedroom.' By this time, the flames were coming through the ceiling of the third floor. We went up and woke him up. Then all of us escaped."

When Fudge jumped out of his car after spotting the fire, he did not take in his cameras. He decided to save lives first. Later, he returned for his equipment and photographed the father saving the family dog.

In their book *The Race Beat*, Gene Roberts and Hank Klibankoff related an anecdote that argues strongly for the photographer's role as witness. Flip Schulke was covering the racial clashes in Selma, Alabama, for *Life* magazine when he saw Sheriff Clark's deputies shove children to the ground. He stopped shooting and began dragging the children away. Martin Luther King, who led the march, called out to Schulke, "The world doesn't know this happened because you didn't photograph it. I'm not being cold-blooded about it, but it is so much more important for you to take a picture of us getting beaten up."

SUICIDE: A SPECIAL CASE?

While working for the *Oregon Journal*, photographer William T. Murphy, Jr., faced the dilemma of taking pictures or trying to help a woman stop her husband from killing himself. He tried to do both—by taking five shots as he attempted to talk the man out of jumping 100 feet into the Columbia River and as he yelled at another motorist on the bridge to go for help. But the man soon struggled free from his wife's desperate grip and jumped to his death in the swirling river.

Few readers sympathized with Murphy's ethical dilemma. According to "Ethics of Compassion," an article by Gene Goodwin in *Quill* magazine, many readers complained about Murphy's photo of the suicide, which went out over the UPI (United Press International) wires.

"Don't the ethics of journalism insist that preservation of human life comes first, news second?" asked a reader from Philadelphia. A New York reader wrote, "He let a man die for the sake of a good photograph."

Murphy replied to the criticism, "I don't know what I could have done differently. I am a photographer, and I did what I have been trained to do. I did all I could."

SUICIDE AS A FORM OF PROTEST

No one attempted to stop a Buddhist monk in 1963 when he set himself afire to protest the Diem government in South Vietnam. The shocking picture showed readers dramatically and convincingly how serious the country's problems were. The monk was the first of many who used his own death the ultimate form of political protest (see page 448). The AP's Peter Arnett, who reported the event, said that he could have prevented that immolation by rushing at the monk and kicking the gasoline away. "As a human being I wanted to; as a reporter I couldn't."

One person's private turmoil resulted in a national issue when Pennsylvania State Treasurer R. Budd Dwyer called a press conference hours before he was to be sentenced for his conviction in a $300,000 kickback scandal. Dwyer, 47, was facing up to 55 years in prison. After 30 minutes of proclaiming his innocence to reporters and photographers, Dwyer picked up a large manila envelope and pulled out a long-barrel, blue-black handgun. He placed the gun in his mouth and pulled the trigger.

Could photographers, reporters, or TV camera crews have stopped Dwyer? The consensus was no. Once the gun was out of the envelope, only 15 seconds elapsed before Dwyer shot himself. Also, Dwyer had built a barricade of chairs and tables between himself and the press.

Should photographers have stopped Dwyer if they had the opportunity? Was Dwyer making a political statement? In any case, are the pictures so upsetting to the public that they cause the reader to look away rather than consider the underlying issues?

According to one study, almost every editor surveyed (95 percent) thought that the photo of Dwyer's body slumping after he fired the shot was too shocking for their readers to view on the front page.

Robert Kochersberger surveyed newspapers in three states to see how they used the photos. He found that most newspapers (66 percent) used the photo of Dwyer holding out his hand, but exercised restraint by not publishing either the photo of the pistol in Dwyer's mouth or the one of his body slumping to the floor.

SUICIDE AS MENTAL ILLNESS

Photographing suicide also raises the issue of documenting severe mental problems.

In Wichita Falls, Texas, a former mental patient committed suicide with a twelve-gauge shotgun. In this situation, the photographer had no chance to stop the man. Don James, executive editor of the normally conservative *Record News*, explained running the picture to readers by saying, "We felt the story leading up to the suicide illustrated a shocking failure on the part of our system."

In the United States, mental illness remains hidden behind closed doors. Yet half the deaths by gunshot are a result of suicide. Rarely does the problem of mental illness become apparent enough to be photographed. The relatively rare pictures of someone in the act of suicide might help to call attention to the failure of U.S. mental-health policies.

MORAL DILEMMAS OF A PICTURE EDITOR
GRUESOME PICTURES: SEEN OR SUPPRESSED?

Editors who deal with pictures are also on the ethical firing line. A photographer at the scene of an accident or disaster does not have the

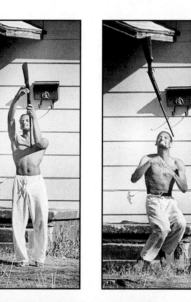

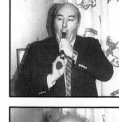

A former mental patient shot himself with a 12-gauge shotgun. Do the pictures help call attention to the problems of the mentally ill? Peter Bradt, *Wichita Falls [Texas] Time Record News*

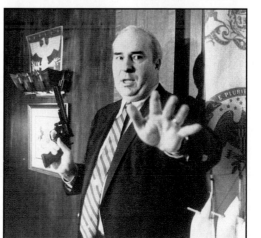

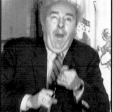

At a press conference called by R. Budd Dwyer, Pennsylvania's state treasurer, he proclaimed himself innocent of a kickback scandal and then killed himself. No photographer could have stopped him. Should these pictures have been published?
Gary Miller (LEFT); Paul Vathis (BOTH, RIGHT), Associated Press

time to determine if a particular picture is too gruesome or horrible to appear in the news.

Only when the images have been processed can the photographer and the editor study them with an impartial eye toward deciding if the photos are too indecent, obscene, or repulsive for publication.

The reader, with the morning edition of the *Republican-Democrat* neatly folded between his coffee and his oat bran, might gag on a gory front-page accident photo (ultimately tossing both the paper and his cereal). Editors sometimes refer to this as the "breakfast test" for hard-to-digest pictures.

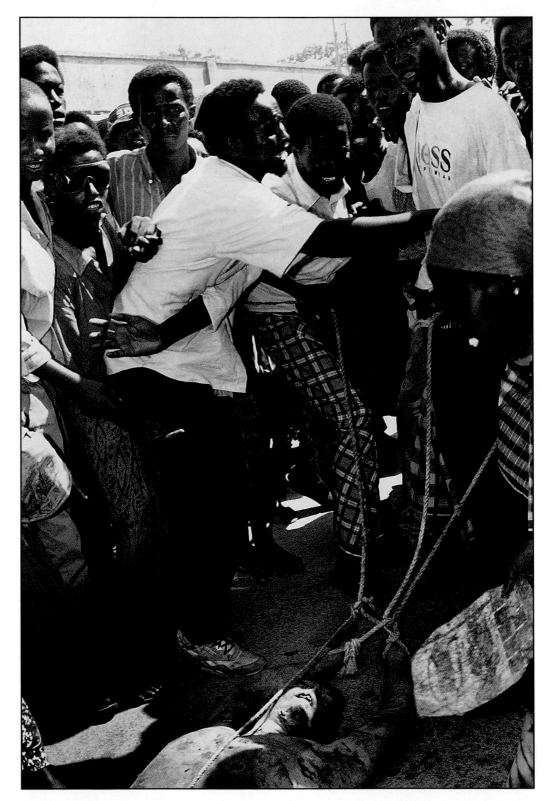

On a mission in Africa to provide food for starving Somalians, an American soldier was killed and then dragged through the streets of the city of Mogadishu. The picture was so powerful that it helped to change U.S. policy toward involvement in Somalia. Paul Watson, *Toronto Star*

Yet editors must not whitewash the world. Murders, accidents, wars, and suicides happen. Eliminating violence presents readers with a false view of their community and the world. (See Chapter 7, "Photo Editing.")

In fact, totalitarian dictators always try to muzzle the press to suppress dissent, withhold critical information, and hide truth.

Editors and producers must negotiate a fine line between informing the public about the enormous human toll of wars, bombings, terrorism, and tsunamis versus overloading sensitive viewers with horrific images and thus possibly shortchanging the human tragedies, observes researcher Carol Schwalbe, in her article "Bloody Lens."

Too much visual coverage can carry the risk of sensationalism and offending people, while too little can oversimplify complex issues and fail to inform the public about the magnitude of horrors. Questions of whether to give viewers and readers what they want, what they will accept, or what they need to know face photographers and editors on a regular basis.

EDITORIAL SELF-CENSORSHIP IN CONFLICT ZONES

Sometimes censorship comes not from governments but from editors and even from photojournalists. David Douglas Duncan, a former Marine who covered the Korean War, shot combat only in black-and-white because he thought color would be a distraction. Out of respect for the soldiers, he never showed corpses or mutilated bodies, according to Peter Howe in his book **Shooting Under Fire: The World of the War Photographer**.

Newspapers at the beginning of World War II never showed dead American soldiers, because editors wanted to keep morale high on the home front. Until *Life* magazine ran a photo showing dead American soldiers strewn on a beach, the public was sheltered visually from some of the war's impact. While George Strock's image of three maggot-infested bodies on a New Guinea beach shocked many readers, soldiers praised *Life* magazine for having the courage to print an image that gave meaning to their struggle.

Is it right or even responsible for the press to protect the public in this way? Is it possible that, by withholding these scenes, the press actually prevented Americans from developing a healthy outrage about events in Europe, a fury that perhaps could have fueled the war effort? (See pages 446–447, in Chapter 17, "History.")

The photos without corpses were not inaccurate per se. They were merely incomplete. Arbitrarily editing out death—or any other sign of violence or tragedy—gives readers a false sense of their own security and a skewed view of their world.

Sebastian Balic, an Associated Press stringer, shot a grisly set of pictures of youths stoning, then stabbing, and finally setting a man on fire in Soweto, South Africa. The *New York Daily News* ran the photograph of the stoning. Referring to these pictures in an article by Sue O'Brien, Jeff Jarvis, the newspaper's Sunday editor, said, "I don't think the breakfast test works for the nineties."

Mike Zerby, photo editor at the *Minneapolis Star Tribune*, agreed. "The standard line," he said, "is 'we don't bleed on your eggs,' but I think at this particular newspaper we've grown past that."

INVISIBLE CARNAGE

Kenneth Jarecke's photo from the end of the 1991 Gulf War (see page 372) provides a revealing case study of how the media handled a tough but thought-provoking image. Jarecke was on assignment for *Time* magazine when he photographed the blackened corpse of an Iraqi soldier incinerated at the wheel of his vehicle. American pilots had relentlessly attacked the retreating convoy of a thousand vehicles. Some of the pilots referred to the attack as a "turkey shoot," reports Colin Jacobson in his book, **Underexposed**. Estimates of this "turkey shoot" put the number of dead between 400 and 2000.

Although Jarecke was shooting for *Time*, the magazine hesitated to publish the image. The Associated Press (AP) received the photo in its New York office but did not transmit the image under the assumption that "Newspapers will tell us 'We can't present pictures like that for people to look at over breakfast.'"

Life magazine laid out a two-page spread with the photo but pulled it before publication. The managing editor cited the effect it would have on children as his reason for rejecting it. Eventually the image appeared in *Time*'s end-of-year special and ran the size of a postage stamp.

In **Underexposed**, former picture editor Jacobson writes, "The Gulf War was presented to the world as a squeaky-clean technological masterpiece and the public were not encouraged to associate computer-controlled, laser-directed weapons with subsequent human carnage."

Photographer Jarecke, in a TV interview, said, "If the U.S. is tough enough to go to war, it should be tough enough to look at the consequences."

A similar sentiment was expressed by Sydney H. Schanberg of the *Village Voice* and

David Leeson of *The Dallas Morning News* in their commentary "Not a Pretty Picture: Why don't U.S. papers show graphic (Iraqi) war photos?"

"How else can voters make informed decisions about a war their government has led them into?" the journalists asked.

DOMESTIC EDITORIAL SELF-CENSORSHIP

Curtis MacDougall, author of ***News Pictures Fit to Print . . . Or Are They?***, recalled that, when he was a reporter on the *St. Louis Star Times*, the managing editor once spent a full hour soliciting the opinions of everyone in the newsroom regarding the propriety of using a picture of a lynching. The photograph showed a corpse slumped at the base of the hanging tree.

MacDougall recalled the photo and the incident: "No facial expression was visible; nevertheless the decision was made to black out the body and substitute an artist's drawn 'X' to mark the spot."

This conservatism was typical of American editors through a century of brutal torture and murder of African-Americans. According to MacDougall, plenty of photographs were available to document this

inhuman treatment; however, when those photographs reached newsrooms, they were relegated to files rather than to news pages.

Of another lynching picture described as "shocking and unnecessary," Ernest Meyer wrote in the *Madison* (Wisconsin) *Capital Times*, "So was the crime. The grim butchery deserved a grim record. And those photographs were more eloquent than any word picture of the event."

At the time, newspaper editors argued that lynching pictures were too grisly to print. However, during that same era, editors did play up pictures of blood-soaked, maimed car-accident victims.

Editors rationalized that accident pictures served as a warning to careless drivers and thus improved highway safety. Sadly, no one thought to add that lynching pictures might also have had a positive benefit by stirring up moral outrage against racism and mob rule.

Today, the number of accident photos has decreased. Because accidents have become so common, they are less newsworthy. Accident photos, too, are often more difficult to get because the police remove bodies promptly. But the underlying moral question remains: does the sight of mutilated victims

To the reading public, the 1991 Iraqi war was almost surgical in its precision and presumed lack of bloodshed. Most Americans never saw this horrific image of a dead Iraqi soldier, incinerated while retreating in his tank at the close of that earlier conflict. Might exposure to the war's brutal realities have influenced U.S. opinion about launching the 2003 war in that country?
Kenneth Jarecke,
Contact Press Images

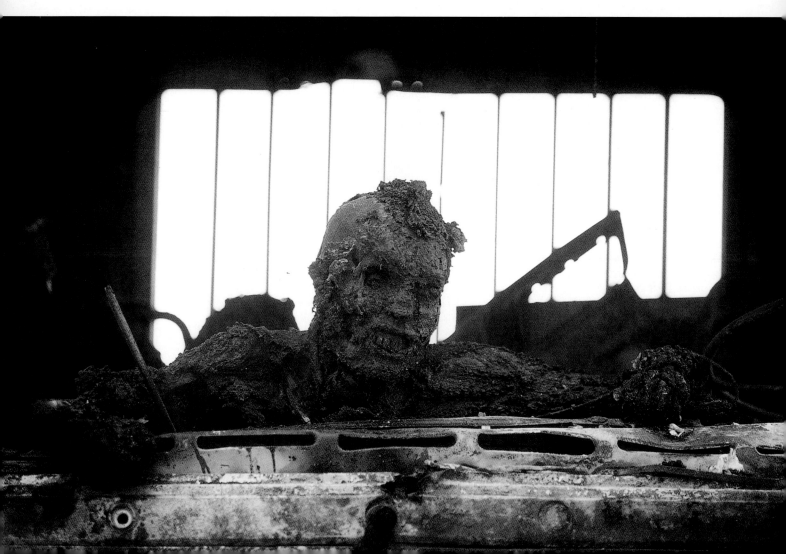

in a mangled car frighten readers into caution when they drive their cars? And should this type of picture be published?

The *Akron Beacon Journal* said in an editorial about accident coverage:

The suddenness and finality of death, the tremendous force of impact, are vividly depicted in crushed, twisted bodies, and smashed vehicles. The picture implants in the minds of all who see it a safety lesson that could not be equally well conveyed in words alone. How long the shock value of such a picture persists, varies. But one can be sure that a majority of those who see photographs of traffic accidents are more concerned with their safety than they had been before seeing the picture. 'This can happen to you!' is the unwritten message of every picture of an accident.

WEIGHING IMPACT

Do powerful photographs drive home a social message, shock readers to distraction, or have no effect at all?

The late Susan Sontag, critic and author of **On Photography**, doubted that strong, graphic pictures continue to have an impact in our super-saturated media environment. She argued that photographs of human suffering no longer actually move the public. Further, she claimed that little good comes of seeing photographic horrors when viewers have no power to change them.

She conceded that a few photographs retain their power to shock—like that of a napalm-burned Vietnamese girl fleeing a bomb attack. Images like these, she says, become moral reference points. But in general, Sontag maintained, repeated exposure to photographed atrocities habituates us to horror, leading us to view even the most grotesque images as "just pictures." Could she be right?

Would Sontag have published a picture of the journalist Daniel Pearl's severed head after his murder by Pakistani extremists? Or the beheading of the American civilian Nicolas Berg by his captors in Iraq?

The Ethics Committee of the Society of Professional Journalists wrote of the *Boston Phoenix*'s decision to publish the Daniel Pearl image, "Granted, there is a certain awful truth that the photo represents. The hatred his murderers have for Jews and Americans is crystallized in the image, but that truth does not outweigh the harmful shock to readers and to Pearl's family."

Stephen Mindich, the *Phoenix*'s publisher, told the Ethics Committee it would have been unethical not to bring the information to the attention of the American public—which had not felt the full weight of the event nor fully understood that Pearl was killed because he was Jewish.

The photo published by the *Phoenix* came from a video taken of the execution and titled "The Slaughter of the Spy-Journalist, the Jew Daniel Pearl."

Images from the Berg beheading, which took place several years after the Pearl execution, were published by four European newspapers but more importantly, they were widely available and often downloaded from the Internet. While newspapers remain hesitant to show these shocking pictures, what readers see is no longer limited by editors' tastes. They can access just about anything they want to see for themselves.

SEPTEMBER 11, 2001

When people fell to their deaths from the burning World Trade Center after terrorists crashed two planes into the towers on September 11, 2001, editors were faced with perhaps their most difficult ethical task. Several photographers, including Susan Watts of the *New York Daily News* and Richard Drew of the Associated Press, photographed the tragic sight of people falling, sometimes headfirst, from the buildings. Of all the images taken on that horrific day—and there were thousands—those of people falling to their deaths (see page 352) caused by far the most consternation and controversy for editors and readers.

James Kenney, professor at Western Kentucky University, reported for *American Editor* that most newspapers decided against front-page use of the most graphic images of people jumping to their deaths. Kenney points out that intense pictures like these can "shift readers' attention away from the event and redirect their outrage to demanding why a newspaper would run such a picture?

"But," he notes, "...predicting reader reaction is tricky."

Eric Meskauskas, picture editor of the *New York Daily News*, argued that a photo of victims jumping to their deaths "was part of the story and we shouldn't shield our readers from it." Brian Storm, who was multimedia director at *MSNBC.com* at the time, made his decision under the extreme deadline pressure that faces a web site editor. He reasoned that the picture was an "essential part of the story" but presented the material in a way that allowed readers to choose whether to view the image or not.

Since the 9/11 tragedy, world events and the almost instant global communication made by possible by the Internet are serving up horrific images that challenge editors in the traditional mass media. Conflict at one time meant dead or wounded soldiers in war zones. Today's victims are as likely to be children and mothers murdered by suicide bombers for whichever cause moves them.

Donald Winslow, editor of *News Photographer* magazine, writes, "Over the past couple of years the threshold for mainstream print editors has crept upward considerably, possibly unnoticed by the average viewer, as war and terrorism increasingly occupy more of the front page and, therefore, more of our attention."

According to Carol Schwalbe in "Bloody Lens," editors have debated whether or not to run disturbing images of the bullet-riddled bodies of Saddam Hussein's sons, the charred bodies of four slain U.S. contractors hanging from a Fallujah bridge, nude Iraqi prisoners being tortured by American GIs at Abu Ghraib prison, and the beheading of Nicolas Berg.

The moral compass, however, continues to swing. The new point on that compass has allowed many news outlets to show the hanging of Saddam Hussein and even the gruesome hanging that beheaded his brother.

Kenny Irby, visual journalism group leader of the Poynter Institute, asked pros in the field whether they would run a picture of Saddam Hussein being hanged, if available.

In his article "Displaying Death with Dignity," Irby interviewed Ricardo Ferro, a veteran staffer of the *St. Petersburg Times*. "Would you run Mussolini hanging, or Christ at the cross?" Ferro responded. "Of course I would. The question is where and how big."

News organizations are "no longer the gatekeepers of what Americans see and don't see," says Vaughn Ververs, editor of "The Hotline," the *National Journal*'s online political newsletter. As former NPPA president John Long points out, "Due to timing, everyone had seen the (Hussein) hanging pictures before we had a chance to publish them."

Today's public sees its images not only in the mass media but also on YouTube, Flickr, Memory Hole, cable stations, and a host of web sites, some run by terrorist organizations themselves. Many news consumers want to feel that they are getting the very latest uncensored material, whether that is the beheading of Berg or the hanging of Hussein.

READER COMPLAINTS

In a survey comparing photojournalists' and general readers' reactions to ethical situations, Craig Hartley found that the two groups differed widely in their reactions to shooting and transmitting gruesome pictures.

Fifty-eight percent of the professionals he surveyed considered ethical the actions of a hypothetical photojournalist who photographed the removal of a famous actress's body from an automobile crash and the editors' subsequent decision to send the pictures over the wires. However, nearly three-fourths (71 percent) of the public disapproved of the journalists' actions.

The Associated Press Managing Editors National Credibility Roundtable Project surveyed 2400 readers and 400 journalists who viewed five photographs and then decided whether the images should have been published. The images included tsunami victims, American soldiers, and violence in Iraq.

Readers and professionals consistently differed on the merits of publishing the sensitive photos. News pros recommended publishing the images on the front page of the paper while readers tended to want the images placed inside the publication.

Kelly McBride, ethics group leader at the Poynter Institute, wrote that professional journalists make their moral decisions on duty. "They believe it is their duty to inform. The public, on the other hand, tends to make moral decisions on the basis of harming the people in the photo as well as harming the audience who might view the photo."

For example, 41 percent of the journalists would run the image of a grieving mother

When Nicolas Berg, an American civilian, was beheaded by Islamic extremists in Iraq, few print media outlets showed the actual execution. Footage of the savage murder was readily available, however, on the Internet.
Front page,
Philadelphia Daily News

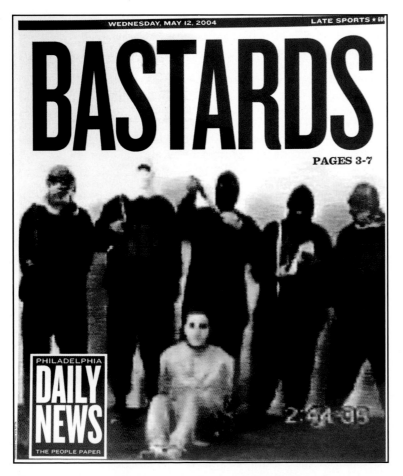

among children who had been killed in the tsunami, but only 26 percent of the readers felt comfortable with this image on the cover.

"I believe the only way to make something as vast as this tragedy understandable is to reduce it to a single, human image," said David Offer, a journalist from Augusta, Maine. Ed Roussell, a reader from Medford, Oregon, agreed but shied away from running the image on the front page.

In a unique study, researchers Abhinav Aima, Patricia Ferrier, Les Roka, Lynn Silverstein, and James Staebler tried to determine if the amount of blood shown in a picture changed a reader's reaction to the image. Their study was called "A Visual Experiment in Acceptance: Does Quantity and Location of Blood Affect Readers' Reaction to a Photograph?"

Using a car accident photo as the base image, the investigators created a set of pictures in which each one contained more blood on the ground, on the corpse, etc. The researchers showed the photos to Midwestern college students and asked them which pictures they would run if they were the editors. The college students, especially the women, found the bloody photographs too "intrusive and inappropriate" regardless of how much blood was in the photograph.

Interestingly, students' and the public's approval does not always coincide with their curiosity. Regardless of their opinion on news coverage, drivers routinely slow down to "rubberneck" at a highway accident. The distressing video of Berg's beheading continues to draw viewers on the Internet.

When editors select and publish strong, compelling, but perhaps hard-to-look-at pictures that include mangled bodies, blood, or victims' or bystanders' tearful reactions, readers often complain. From an economic point of view, editors certainly care what readers do and don't want to see on page one.

From an ethical perspective, should editors make decisions based on reader preferences? Do editors have a responsibility that supersedes the likes and dislikes of their audience?

THE "DISTANCE" RULE

For stories involving tragedy, editors sometimes make conflicting decisions regarding the play of written stories compared to photos. For written stories, geographic proximity is one of the determining criteria in assessing news value. The closer the event, the more importance and, therefore, more prominent play it is given. Yet, because readers are more likely to complain about gruesome local pictures than images from far away, editors

often will play down or suppress strong pictures that involve hometown residents but run revealing pictures of atrocities in other parts of the world.

In fact, some newspapers, like the *Tampa Tribune*, even have policies mandating this practice. Denise Costa of the *Tribune* says she wants to "protect the people involved more than she would want to run the photo." This attitude toward news photography is counter to traditional news criteria for written stories—top among them, proximity. Editors apparently don't like fielding calls from irate local readers.

Jessica Fishman confirmed in her doctoral dissertation, "Photojournalism and Spectacles of the Morbid in the Tabloid and Elite Newspaper," U.S. newspapers' reluctance to show American bodies in most all circumstances.

However, she also found that respected broadsheets like the *New York Times* or *Los Angeles Times* are more likely to publish graphic images of corpses (of non-Americans in foreign countries) than the oft-maligned tabloids. Despite their reputations for outrageous coverage, the tabloids tend to publish pictures of bombed buildings, destroyed buses or airplanes, closed caskets, or other discreet references to death.

HIDING DEAD BODIES

The question of when to run and when to hold a photo often comes up when editors must deal with a picture containing a dead body. A front-page photograph of a firefighter carrying a dead child from a house shocked readers of the *Detroit Free Press*. Locked inside, alone, seven brothers and sisters had died in a tragic blaze (see page 376). Doors and windows that had been barricaded or barred to keep out burglars trapped the children inside.

SHOCKING-PICTURE WARNING SIGNS

If five or more of the following conditions apply to a shocking picture, editors should prepare for reader reactions before the firestorm hits:

- images that show subjects overcome with grief
- pictures containing dead bodies
- pictures portraying mutilated bodies
- pictures run in color
- photos containing nudity
- photos taken for a local story
- photos taken by a staff photographer
- images printed in a morning paper
- images printed on the front page
- images with no accompanying story

Paul Lester, *Photojournalism: An Ethical Approach*

Though routine, the photo of the accident could have provided a warning to young people tempted to speed. Ultimately the top editor decided to spike the picture. During the process, Borden observed, no one from the newspaper ever contacted the family. A polite and sympathetic phone call could have determined just how distressed the family was about the photo, what it was about the image that disturbed them, and how adamant they were about keeping it out of print.

Based on the principle "do unto others as you would have them do unto you," editors often act as they presume families would want them to. Sometimes, however, relatives or friends of a victim recognize that publishing a picture may be one of the few beneficial outcomes of a tragic situation.

When a child fell through ice and drowned in a pond in Columbia, Missouri, the *Columbia Missourian*, after much discussion regarding the family's feelings, ran a photo showing rescuers recovering the child's body. The next day, the child's mother came to the office, where she picked up extra copies of the newspaper after thanking the editors for running the photograph. She said she hoped that the front-page picture of her child would help deter others from playing on the thin pond ice.

Perhaps news outlets should routinely call victims' families to warn them that an emotional photograph will run. This procedure would diminish a family's shock at seeing the image but still allow the wider public to be informed in the strongest way possible about the news event. (For more on censorship, see pages 446–447, Chapter 17, "History.")

PHOTOGRAPHY CAN MAKE A DIFFERENCE

Stanley Forman's 1975 photo of a collapsing fire escape during a blaze in Boston—a woman plunging to her death along with a falling child who miraculously survived— was printed on more than 100 front pages across the country (see page 377). Later, telephone calls and letters to newspapers charged sensationalism, invasion of privacy, insensitivity, and tasteless display of human tragedy for the purpose of selling newspapers.

Hal Buell, who was AP's assistant general manager for news photos at the time, said he received more reaction to the Forman picture than to any other news photo. Buell wagered that if the woman had survived, there would have been very little reaction. "The pictures would not have changed, but the fact of death reached into the minds and feelings of the readers," he said.

Most of the nation's editors published Forman's picture on their front pages. Yet in a survey taken by the *Orange County Daily Pilot* in Costa Mesa, California, 40 percent of its readers did not approve of publishing the photo. Wilson Sims, editor of the *Battle Creek* (Michigan) *Enquirer and News*, defended publishing the picture: "The essential purpose is not to make the reader feel pain or to bring the reader happiness. It is to help the reader understand what is happening in the world. Therefore, we ran the picture."

Forman's photograph of the falling woman and child not only won a Pulitzer Prize, but it is also a classic example of how photography can bring about change. That shocking image contributed to a change in fire-safety laws in Boston. Forman's editor, Sam Bornstein, said, "Without the picture, the word-story would have been 'page 16.' Only pictures of this magnitude would have resulted in something being done by the safety agencies."

Sometimes pictures not only can change a state's laws but can influence a country's foreign policy. In response to the starvation of Somalians in Africa, the United States sent troops to help United Nations peacekeepers quell fighting and distribute food in that country. Despite the presence of U.S. troops, warlords continued to pillage. At one point, followers of one of the warlords killed a U.S. soldier. At great personal danger, the *Toronto Star*'s Paul Watson photographed the screaming crowd as they dragged the almost nude body of the soldier through the city streets. The horrifying picture of the body of an American soldier being desecrated in the streets of a country halfway around the world was so shocking to the U.S. public that the administration quickly reversed policy and pulled U.S. troops out of Somalia (see page 370).

While a single picture alone did not change American foreign policy, this image, which generated immediate reaction from the public, commentators, and legislators, certainly played a significant role in hastening the withdrawal of U.S. troops.

MATTERS OF TASTE
NUDITY

Nudity in pictures generates more disagreement among editors than even the most gruesome picture. An editor's judgment about nudity in pictures generally reflects his or her understanding of readers' attitudes and of mores in the host community. In most cases, the standards for pictorial nudity are more a matter of taste than a question of ethics. With the advent of Hustler and other "skin" magazines, almost no part of the human anatomy is reserved for the imagination.

Yet most American newspapers and magazines refrain from printing nudity on their pages. AP's Hal Buell says that the wire service won't carry frontal views of nude men or women, except in extreme cases. "Such a story has yet to occur," he observes.

Professionals and the public again disagreed in Hartley's ethics survey when he turned to the question of nudity. Here is the hypothetical situation: two women athletes collide in a volleyball game, with one falling in such a way that her shorts are pulled down and her bare buttocks are exposed.

While a majority of professionals surveyed endorsed sending out a photo of the athlete's derriere, a whopping 75 percent of the public turned thumbs-down on the bottoms-up picture.

Robert Wahls, who was a photo editor for the *New York Daily News*, avoided running nudes except under unusual circumstances. Despite the *Daily News*'s reputation as a genuine tabloid, Wahls felt that, although nudity is acceptable in film and theater, "it is inappropriate when you can sit and study it." The photo editor made an exception when there was an overriding news value to a picture. The photos from the original Woodstock, a massive outdoor rock concert in 1969, showed members of the audience frolicking in the muddy field without their clothes on. The sheer size of the audience—300,000— gave the activities news value.

Wahls, however, pointed out that, even if nude pictures help push up the circulation of a newspaper, the gain might be useless if advertisers start to consider the paper pornographic. "A newspaper's job is to inform, not to titillate," Wahls said.

Twenty-five years later, the *Washington Times*'s Ken Lambert photographed Woodstock's silver anniversary, which, like the original, gave kids an excuse to party, wear tie-dye, and "get naked." Although only a few got naked this time around, Lambert took a picture of a young woman glancing disapprovingly at a long-haired "hippie" wearing only his birthday suit—a true testament to the difference between the eras. The picture was too dicey for the *Washington Times*, whose editor, Josette Shiner, called the *Times* "a family newspaper."

The photo, however, was not too spicy for judges of the White House News Photographers Association (WHNPA) photo contest, who awarded it a first place for features.

Judges for the Best of Photojournalism competition, conducted by the National Press Photographers Association (NPPA), faced an ethical decision about a sexually

explicit news picture. The judges awarded a first place for domestic news to an unpublished picture that showed a half-naked woman being sexually assaulted while attempting to struggle free from a crowd of out-of-control men at a Mardi Gras event in Seattle. Her face, as were those of her attackers, was clearly visible. The judges decided that the photo, taken by Mike Urban of the *Seattle Post-Intelligencer*, should be published in the contest's book and on the web site. But the image was so disturbing that even the organization that

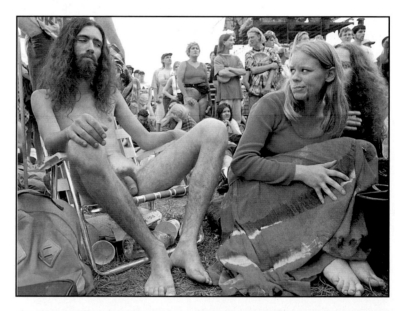

Taken by their staffer at the 25th anniversary of the Woodstock music festival, this photo was too risqué for *Washington Times* editors, who refused to run it. Trade magazines *News Photographer* and *Editor & Publisher* did publish it, uncensored, with stories about the controversy it generated as a contest winner. *E&P*'s headline: "No Nudes is Good Nudes." Kenneth Lambert, *Washington Times*. (For publication in this book, the following special credit note was required by the editor-in-chief of the *Washington Times*: "This photograph did not run in the *Washington Times* due to reasons of taste.")

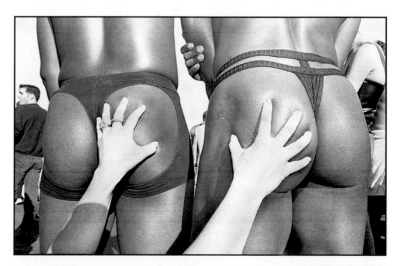

At a gay street festival in San Francisco, bystanders check out the local talent. While thousands of people from around the country attend this festival each year, local newspapers downplay the event by running few if any photos. (For more on coverage of the gay community, see page 133, Chapter 7, "Photo Editing," and page 381 in this chapter.) Alain McLaughlin, Impact Visuals

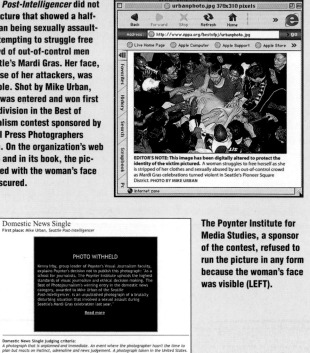

The Poynter Institute for Media Studies, a sponsor of the contest, refused to run the picture in any form because the woman's face was visible (LEFT).

www.poynterextra.org/centerpiece/photo/DomNews.htm

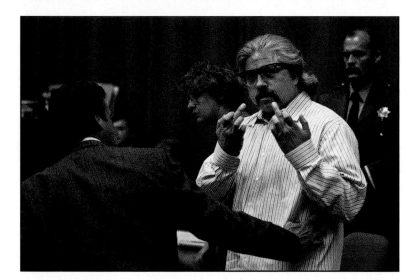

Publication of the photo of this defiant act by convicted child-murderer Richard Allen Davis upon hearing the jury's guilty verdict generated a firestorm of negative response for newspaper editors in the San Francisco Bay Area. The shocking picture, however, provided a revealing insight into the man's character. Previously, he had remained quiet and subdued. John Burgess, *Santa Rosa Press Democrat*

represents photojournalists, the NPPA, censored the photo by putting a digital mask over the woman's face.

After a highly unusual and hotly contested debate, the judges' decision was not unanimous.

They weighed the woman's privacy and potential embarrassment against the need for readers to fully comprehend the violence and brutality that erupted during this public event. Urban had not obtained the victim's name, so no one could solicit her opinion.

Neither Urban's own newspaper, the *Post-Intelligencer*, nor The Poynter Institute for Media Studies web site, which published other contest-winning pictures, ran the photo at all—with or without the digitized face.

Maria Mann, director of photography for Agence France-Presse and one of the contest judges, wrote, "The commission of any act of hate is not easy to take—whether in the form of crimes against humanity in war, or in every day life. But the truth cannot be a convenience; it needs to be a constant. We have a mission—to document the truth. If this mission has given way to politics or queasy stomachs then we have yet another important mission—to defend the very essence of our profession."

OBSCENE GESTURES

In an instance that enraged many readers, editors in the San Francisco Bay Area published John Burgess's picture of convicted murderer Richard Allen Davis gesturing with upraised middle fingers following the jury's guilty verdict in his trial. Davis's abduction and murder of 12-year-old Polly Klaas had horrified Bay Area citizens.

Burgess, who shoots for the *Santa Rosa Press Democrat*, was the pool photographer in the emotionally charged case. Bay Area papers all ran the photo on their front pages. Executive editor Jerry Ceppos, of the *Mercury News* in San Jose said his newspaper logged 1,284 messages from readers, overwhelming voice mail, email, fax, and online systems. Ceppos said 817 readers agreed with publishing the photo, while 481 did not.

At the *San Francisco Chronicle*, said editorial-page editor John Diaz, "the overwhelming majority" of callers and writers objected to the picture's page-one play. Diaz defended running the picture. "The moment captured by Burgess's Nikon added new dimension to the story. It may well have an impact on jurors as they decide whether to sentence the defendant to death or life in prison. It certainly says something about the murderer. . . . The Davis verdict story would have been incomplete without the photo."

FAIR AND BALANCED REPORTING

The experienced professional reporter continues to dig up the facts of a news story until he or she feels prepared to write an unbiased, balanced report of the event. News reporters take several paragraphs to explain the position of each conflicting party. Many stories have no clear heroes or villains; hence, the reporter simply extends copy to explain the complexities of the situation.

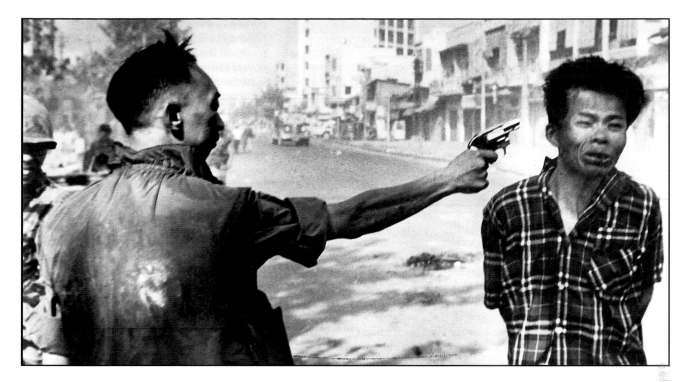

The writer has not only the advantage of several paragraphs, but the subtlety and precision of language, with its great store of adjectives and adverbs. These modifiers enable the writer to emphasize an idea or soften a phrase. Think of the difference between the words "the suspect stared at me" and "the criminal glared at me."

The photographer has no adjectives or adverbs, no pictorial thesaurus to refine an image. A single picture captures only one moment in time, one set of circumstances, one expression or action. If the newspaper's managing editor has allotted space for just one picture to illustrate a complex story, then the photo editor is faced with a task as difficult as if the writer had to tell a multifaceted tale in one sentence. Of the 200 or so exposed frames shot on an assignment, which single image tells the whole story?

The Vietnam War presented a constant challenge for photo editors. Each day they had to sum up a complicated, tragic event in a few pictures. Adams won a Pulitzer Prize for a shocking photo of a South Vietnamese Brigadier General, the police chief of Saigon, executing a suspected Viet Cong on a Saigon street (see above).

During this war, the South Vietnamese were our allies. The overwhelming message of the picture, however, spoke of the cruelty of the South Vietnamese officer.

To balance this view of the war, many editors chose to run, on the same day, another picture portraying the terrorism of our enemies, the Viet Cong. Although not as

dramatic as Adams's picture, the photo showed a soldier leaving a civilian house recently bombed by the Viet Cong.

Do the two photos really explain both sides of the conflict? Can any two pictures be balanced?

The question of balance also arises in local stories. Many groups point out they receive scant if any media coverage, and when they do, they see stereotypes of themselves. Nancy Andrews, deputy managing editor at the *Detroit Free Press*, has won numerous awards, including Photographer of the Year.

"I believe a lot of stereotypes are visual stereotypes," she says. "In my own community, as a gay person, [I see how] photographers have often looked for the most arresting pictures. The most arresting are valid—it's valid to show people dying [of AIDS] or dressed in drag at a gay pride parade—but if these are the only pictures used to represent the gay community, then it's an inaccurate picture of the whole community.

"Being aware of how visual images are used to show my own community," she says, "has made me aware of how important it is to show the average people in other communities." (See one image from Andrews's picture story about an African-American single father on page 132.)

LOOKING FOR A YARDSTICK
Not all pictures showing dying and death help readers or society. A picture of a man dying at home of natural causes does not

Brigadier General Nguyen Ngoc Loan, police chief of Saigon, executes a Viet Cong suspect. Because the South Vietnamese were U.S. allies, this picture disturbed the American public and is among those credited with changing sentiment about U.S. involvement in Vietnam.
Eddie Adams, Wide World Photos

With the former athlete on trial for his ex-wife's murder, the *Enquirer* doctored the photo to "illustrate" how the victim would have appeared following an earlier instance of alleged abuse by her ex-husband. Labeled as a computer manipulation, the image nonetheless stunned shoppers in grocery stores everywhere. How many people, do you suppose, knew what the *Enquirer* meant by computer manipulation?

HOW FAR WILL MAGAZINE EDITORS GO?

Curiously, while newspaper editors have erred in the past and been called to task for it, some magazine editors show little hesitation in altering cover photographs. "Magazines, I think, can get away with a little more," said Rocco Alberico of *Sports Illustrated for Kids*. "I mean, they can fool around a little bit more than newspapers."

"The practice of airbrushing cellulite and stretch marks or tweaking an errant nipple is standard procedure at most magazines that count on their flawless cover shots to woo readers," according to Lia Haberman in E! Online (*www.eonline.com*).

In her study "Digital Alteration of Photographs in Magazines: An Examination of the Ethics," Shiela Reaves found that all thirteen magazine editors and art directors she interviewed said emphatically they would never digitally manipulate a news photo. However, most had no problem in "cleaning up" an image by removing indistinguishable blobs or extending the sky or a background tone so a news photo could fit the layout.

Michele Stephenson, *Time* picture editor, likened it to cropping people out of a picture. "You crop a picture, there's a corner of an elbow, and somebody says, 'We'd better take that out. It looks funny.' We do that sort of thing . . . everybody does that."

Newsweek went a bit further when it became the digital dentist for Bobbi McCaughey, the new mother of septuplets. The smiling mom on *Newsweek*'s cover enjoyed straighter and whiter teeth thanks to careful computer manipulation.

Surprisingly, readers approved of this digital dental work, according to a survey by researcher Edgar Huang. Sixty-seven percent of surveyed readers approved the editor's digital dentistry in a feature photo or as a photographic illustration because they liked the new mother and did not want her to be presented with crooked teeth.

Perhaps emboldened by that success, editors at *Newsweek* used digital subterfuge to boost homemaking diva Martha Stewart out of jail before her sentence was up. Right on the cover, there was Stewart advancing from behind a curtain—while she was still serving time instead of dinner.

Careful readers who searched inside the magazine's table of contents noticed that the picture credit for the headshot went to Marc Bryan-Brown but the photo "illustration" credit went to Michael Elins. The seamless but fake photo showed Stewart's head digitally pasted onto a model's body.

Readers had no way of knowing the image had been sewn together unless they inspected the tiny credits on page three. *Newsweek* hid its indiscretion behind the words "photo illustration," but most of the public has no idea what this technical term really means even if they bother to read the fine print.

Texas Monthly pulled a similar stunt when it depicted then-governor of Texas Ann Richards in a white, leather-fringed outfit atop a Harley Davidson motorcycle. Although Richards did ride a motorcycle, the picture actually showed the governor's face melded onto a professional model's body. (Richards retorted that she was happy the model had good thighs.)

The hallmark of good photo illustrations is that they don't look "real." (see Chapter 14, "Illustration"). The Martha Stewart and Ann Richards covers look perfectly real. The *Newsweek* cover of Stewart caused an uproar among journalism professionals, but the finger pointing will not stop other magazines from following the same bad recipe.

As part of her survey, Reaves asked Bob Furstenau, director of magazine production for Meredith Corporation (publisher of *Better Homes and Gardens* and other magazines) what things he would change in a picture.

"Anything," he said, "that interferes with the ultimate aesthetic of the picture—spots, telephone wires, people, whatever." He estimated that 45 of the 48 covers he had worked on at the time had been digitally manipulated.

STANDARDS DIFFERENT FOR DAILY JOURNALISM VERSUS MAGAZINE JOURNALISM?

Reaves found that newspaper picture editors were significantly less tolerant of digital manipulation. She also discovered that only 22 percent of the magazine editors had a photojournalism background, whereas 85 percent of those at newspapers had previous professional photojournalism experience. Perhaps this difference in professional background accounts for the stricter standards regarding digital manipulation held by daily newspaper photo editors.

DOES ANYONE CARE?

What happens as the public discovers that news outlets alter images electronically? Will the profession lose credibility? Do people believe photographs if they know that editors and photographers can easily alter images?

ACADEMIC STUDIES SHOW
READERS ARE APATHETIC

In part, the credibility of the photograph depends on the reputation of the photographer and the publication that produces it, observes Paula Habas in her thesis, "The Ethics of Photojournalistic Alteration: An Integrated Schema of Determinants."

In another study, James Kelly and Diona Nace compared how much subjects believe a photograph before and after being shown a video demonstrating the techniques of computer manipulation. After watching the video, the subjects actually maintained their trust in photos. Seeing the computer's wizardry does not automatically destroy the believability of a photographic image.

In a similarly conducted study, researcher Mara Vernon discovered no significant effect on the group's faith in photojournalism after seeing a video of digital manipulation.

Based on a survey of 350 college students, Tom Wheeler found that respondents held newspapers to a higher standard than general interest magazines like *Cosmopolitan*, *Esquire*, *MacWorld*, and *National Geographic*.

They found digital manipulation more unacceptable when carried out by newspapers than by general interest magazines. The researcher also discovered that while some types of manipulation—like removing a distracting tree from the background—were not offensive to the majority of subjects, more extensive photo manipulation like retouching a model's facial blemishes, increasing her cleavage, or enhancing her nipples, was unacceptable. Finally, Wheeler discovered, women were consistently more critical of photo manipulation than were men.

In a follow-up study, Jennifer Greer and Joseph Gosen found women continued to be less tolerant than men of major technical manipulation. Women, however, were found to be more tolerant than men of minor technical alterations like dodging and burning.

Researcher Edgar Huang found that 57 percent of surveyed residents of Bloomington, Indiana, thought that digital retouching of cover photos on *Time* magazine and the ***Day in the Life of America*** was acceptable. Only 31 percent objected.

Huang reported that readers found that removing a cola can from a picture was fine if journalists erased it for editorial purposes. Not surprisingly, study participants found digital alteration of photos like photo illustration more acceptable than for hard news photos.

In general, researchers have not found the public to be overly upset by minor digital manipulation to some types of journalistic pictures. At the time of these studies, the public still generally trusted journalistic images.

A NEWSSTAND TEST
BRINGS READER CONDEMNATION

When readers saw a real-life comparison of altered and unaltered photos on newsstands, however, they reacted strongly and loudly. *Time* magazine electronically altered a police mug shot of O.J. Simpson, who had been arrested for the alleged murder of his former wife. Labeling the image a "Photo Illustration," *Time* ran it on the cover the same week that *Newsweek* published the untainted original. The American public joined a loud debate about the use and misuse of digital alteration.

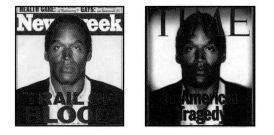

On every newsstand across the country, the two covers sat side-by-side—each with the same police mug shot. Yet the covers were dramatically different. *Time* hired an illustrator who darkened the image and reduced the police identification numbers. *Time* editors thought they had covered themselves by using the label "Photo-Illustration for *Time*" in the table of contents.

Shocked at public outrage—including 70,000 messages on *America Online* as well as articles in *The New York Times* and Associated Press—a *Time* editor pondered, "but we do illustrations all the time. Why is this different?"

While Kelly and Nace demonstrated that just knowing about digital manipulation does not cause readers to disbelieve photos, Wheeler has shown that readers object to certain kinds of manipulation. The reaction to the *Time* cover confirms that when people care about the event or the person, and when they can see both the altered and unaltered photos, they will respond—loudly.

Except for the rare case of two magazines covers showing identical pictures, viewers do not realize photographers or, more likely, editors have manipulated some of the photos that appear in magazines and newspapers.

The studies mentioned above show that when told, some viewers find certain kinds of manipulation of pictures objectionable. However, that does not mean that viewers doubt pictures they see in publications.

Photography critic Andy Grundberg has predicted, "In the future, readers of newspapers and magazines will probably view news pictures more as illustrations than as reportage, since they can no longer distinguish between a genuine image and one that has been manipulated." No evidence to date demonstrates that this depressing forecast is coming true.

DON'T GET FIRED

With the ability to edit their own images in the field before submitting them to editors, some photographers have used editing software to radically change their work. Some changes have been so profound as to literally alter content and meaning. Other photographers have used what they consider conventional darkroom techniques to improve the aesthetics of a picture or even to reproduce what they think they saw versus what the camera captured. These actions have cost photographers their jobs and their reputations—and represent a cautionary tale for all.

ALTERING HISTORY

Adnan Hajj. Far from his editors' desks at Reuters, Lebanese freelancer Adnan Hajj altered and transmitted two photographs from Beirut to make Israeli attacks there appear more widespread and damaging—cloning and intensifying plumes of smoke from smoldering debris. His digital deception was spotted by bloggers who are constantly scrutinizing controversial images from politically sensitive hot spots around the world.

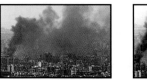 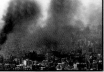

The international news agency Reuters had to recall this photo of an Israeli bomb attack on Beirut after bloggers fingered the picture as a manipulated image. Notice the clear evidence of Photoshop cloning used to alter the image.
Adnan Hajj, Reuters

According to Daryl Lang in a story for *Photo District News*, the alteration was so obvious that bloggers spotted it almost immediately and located others that had been changed.

Reuters fired Hajj, investigated his other work, withdrew more than 900 of his photos from its archives as a precaution, and even stopped using freelancers. Hajj's deception

cost the photographer his job, tarnished Reuters's reputation, and closed doors to other freelancers who probably would never have considered altering a picture.

Brian Walski. A well-respected staffer for the *Los Angeles Times*, Brian Walski combined parts of two already strong pictures from the war in Iraq to create one with a better composition. The photo was shared primarily with news outlets owned by Tribune Company, which owns the *Los Angeles Times*, and the *Hartford Courant*, where it ran across six columns on the first page. A *Courant* employee spotted duplication in the image and reported it to the copy desk.

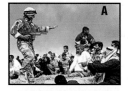 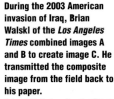

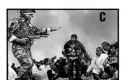

During the 2003 American invasion of Iraq, Brian Walski of the *Los Angeles Times* combined images A and B to create image C. He transmitted the composite image from the field back to his paper.
Brian Walski, *Los Angeles Times*

The revelation spilled forward and shocked editors and journalists around the country. Colin Crawford, director of photography for the *Los Angeles Times*, was stunned but fired Walski, who acknowledged the manipulation. Award-winning reporter Don Barteletti, also in Iraq at the time, described what he saw as a judgment-impaired Walski being sunburned, not having eaten in days, and not having slept for 36 hours.

"Fatigue and horrific conditions are only part of why crazy things can happen in war zones," wrote Kenny Irby on Poynter Online, "and Crawford admits that he 'really worried about him [Walski], but was confident that he was stable after several conversations (via sat phone).' He contends the firing was 'the right thing.'

"What Brian did is totally unacceptable, and he violated our trust with our readers," Crawford told Irby. "We do not for a moment underestimate what he has witnessed and experienced. We don't feel good about doing this, but the integrity of our organization is essential. If our readers can't count on honesty from us, I don't know what we have left."

THE QUEST FOR THE PERFECT IMAGE
From Cleaning Up to Faking It
Allan Detrich. Formerly an award-winning photographer for the *Toledo Blade*, Allan Detrich's decisions to manipulate images cannot be ascribed to battle fatigue. Instead the already talented photographer succumbed to digital manipulation's tempting ability to create seamlessly clean and perfect images.

What brought him down was a front-page photograph in which he removed what he saw as distracting legs behind a banner. A nearly identical image that ran in a competing newspaper showed the scene as it actually was in all its inconvenient reality.

At first, Detrich claimed that the submission of the image to the paper had been a mistake—that he had cleaned up the image for himself, as he liked to "make pictures beautiful."

Sadly, when the *Blade*'s editors scrutinized images submitted by the photographer over the prior year, they found 79 that had been altered, including 27 that the newspaper had unwittingly published in print and online, plus another 31 that had been published only online. Twenty-one of the altered images had not been published. Detrich resigned.

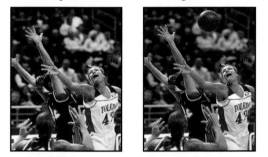

After photographers from a competing newspaper challenged an image in the *Toledo Blade*, *Blade* editors searched their photographer's back files. Among dozens of others that had been altered, editors found the picture to the left, along with the one to its right, to which the photographer digitally added the basketball. The photographer had submitted the altered image for publication, but it had not run.
Photo by Allan Detrich, *Toledo Blade*

In a column to the *Blade*'s readers, executive editor Ron Royhab wrote, "The changes Mr. Detrich made included erasing people, tree limbs, utility poles, electrical wires, electrical outlets, and other background elements from photographs. In other cases, he added elements such as tree branches and shrubbery.

"Mr. Detrich also submitted two sports photographs in which items were inserted. In one he added a hockey puck and in the other he added a basketball, each hanging in mid-air. Neither was published."

Royhab continued, "When a *Blade* reporter or photographer covers a news event, the newspaper and its readers expect an accurate record of the event. Reporters and editors are not allowed to change quotes or alter events to make them more dramatic. Photographers and photo editors cannot digitally alter the content in the frame of a photograph to make the image more powerful or artistic."

DO PICTURES REPRODUCE WHAT YOU SEE?
HOW FAR IS TOO FAR?
Patrick Schneider. Award-winning photographer Patrick Schneider covered a fireman's funeral for the *Charlotte Observer*. He then darkened the background behind two grieving firefighters in Photoshop. When the image won an award in the North Carolina Press Photogra-phers Association (NCPPA) contest, two unidentified photographers challenged the prize saying the image had been manipulated by excessive burning in of the background (see page 388).

The contest judges took their concerns to the *Observer*, which performed an audit of the photographer's work. Editor Jennie Buckner concluded that Schneider did not intend to deceive readers or contest judges, but that "he went over the line in the use of some techniques, which altered the backgrounds in ways that left us uncomfortable."

The NCPPA board voted 4-0, with one abstention, to strip Schneider's awards. The *Observer* suspended Schneider for three days, and the newspaper's management laid down guidelines for handling pictures.

Three years later, Schneider photographed a firefighter silhouetted against the sun and a vivid red sky. It ran in color on the front of the paper's local news section (see page 388).

After the image was published, *Observer* editors investigated the picture. Editor Rick Thames published a note to the readers saying, "In the original photo, the sky in the photo was brownish-gray. Enhanced with photo editing software, the sky became a deep red, and the sun took on a more distinct halo."

Schneider defended the picture in an article in *Photo District News*, saying he had not intended to mislead readers, only to restore the actual color of the sky. The color had been lost, he said, when he underexposed the photo to offset the glare of the sun.

"In two of the pictures," Schneider explained, "I used a darkening technique that photographers throughout the profession have used for decades, and continue to use at many reputable newspapers today," said Schneider. "Unfortunately, the rules for how much a background can be darkened in order to improve a picture's visual impact have never been clear."

Schneider was fired. The basic argument against his actions was that he had altered the

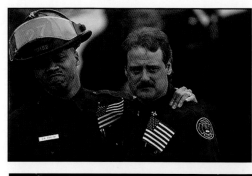

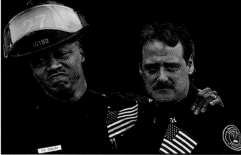

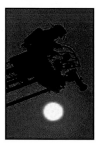

original content of the picture by the way he had toned it, according to Chuck Liddy, president of NCPPA at the time and a photographer at the *Raleigh News and Observer*.

Irby of the Visual Journalism Group for the Poynter Institute pointed out that dodging and burning is an accepted professional technique. Pedro Meyer, editor of *Zone Zero* (*www.zonezero.com*), said, "The changes introduced by Mr. Patrick Schneider did not alter the fundamental information in the photographs."

Schneider's story is not an isolated case of one photographer who bumped up against his employer's notions of right and wrong when it comes to digital darkroom technique. The story reveals a widespread ethical dilemma. The sad tale raises questions of what practices are acceptable by the industry and what actions are unethical in the slippery realm of the pixel puzzle.

PICTURES DO NOT DUPLICATE REALITY

While cases of combining images, putting basketballs within reach of athletes' hands, and multiplying the damage of a bomb attack are straightforward and obvious, the unspoken implications of the Schneider case are that photographs reproduce reality and that a negative or original digital file contains the most accurate rendition of that reality.

Select a picture, print it out on your color printer, and return to the original scene where you shot the image. Hold it up and compare it to the original subject. Is it identical in color, tone, brightness, contrast, etc.?

Not surprisingly, your truthful answer will be no.

The differences may be greater or smaller depending on whether you shot the original in black-and-white or in color, whether you used a strobe or available light, the brightness range of your camera's sensor, the camera's software, the software used to open the picture on your computer, your own memory of the scene, and certainly the profile of your monitor, printer, etc. These variables always affect the way a picture looks even if you don't dodge, burn, or adjust its saturation.

Do all these intervening variables that occur between the moment you took the picture and the instant a viewer sees your image mean that the viewer has been deceived?

Let's just investigate one variable: adding strobe light to a picture. Direct strobe used at sync speed may expose the subject correctly, but indoors or in low light, the background is likely to go dark. (See Chapter 9, "Strobe" for more on the effects of using different flash techniques.)

Does this technique deceive the reader? Should this technique be outlawed even though the final image does not look like what the human eye saw at the original scene?

How is the use of strobe different than dodging and burning?

The camera does not see the way the human eye sees. Photography represents but does not reproduce reality. So the argument that the final image is "true" even if no human hand adjusted it does not hold up. Rules that govern the use of modern tools like Photoshop must take that fact into consideration.

WHO BENEFITS?

How should the profession resolve this dilemma? Perhaps photojournalists should consider turning to the Utilitarian foundation of ethical decision-making.

Ask the question "Who benefits and who loses?" by altering photos.

The photographer?
The editor?
The reader?

Consider this. In the situation where *National Geographic* moved the pyramids editors and designers sought to fit a horizontal picture onto a vertical cover format. Could another picture have sufficed? Could the cover design have been changed to fit the shape of the image? Who benefited? Editors and designers benefited. Was the reader any better off? Not really. Removing a cola can from a picture cleaned up an image for an editor. But did the reader gain anything from this move? In these instances, electronic manipulation eased the jobs of editors, designers, or publishers. Not one was carried out to benefit readers.

When a photographer darkens or lightens the print in the computer, on the other hand, the reader might benefit by seeing more clearly items in the picture that might have been missed with an unaltered picture. Did the reader benefit when Schneider burned down the background in his picture of the grieving firemen?

TOOLS FOR THE FUTURE?

The development of sophisticated photo editing software has introduced new tools for the profession. The ability to digitally blur the background or change the direction of the primary light source of an already photographed scene cannot be ignored. Software developers will continue to create more advances in the future.

Although the industry can hark back to ancient darkroom techniques to find its ethical standards for digital manipulation, doing so does not address these new techniques that were impossibly difficult before the computer age.

While technology can impact ethical choices, ethics is not about technology. Technology has advanced and will continue doing so over time. "We have a whole panoply of techniques that will be ethically okay once they develop the same level of universal acceptance as we have for traditional burning and dodging, etc.," observes former NPPA President John Long, also the organization's Ethics co-chair.

Instead of using old darkroom practices as the ethical guide, the profession ultimately must return to the foundations of ethical decision-making—the Utilitarian principle, the Absolutist principle, or the Golden Rule.

NATIONAL PRESS PHOTOGRAPHERS ASSOCIATION DIGITAL CODE OF ETHICS

1991. As journalists we believe the guiding principle of our profession is accuracy; therefore, we believe it is wrong to alter the content of a photograph in any way that deceives the public.

As photojournalists, we have the responsibility to document society and to preserve its images as a matter of historical record. It is clear that the emerging electronic technologies provide new challenges to the integrity of photographic images ... In light of this, we the National Press Photographers Association, reaffirm the basis of our ethics: Accurate representation is the benchmark of our profession. We believe photojournalistic guidelines for fair and accurate reporting should be the criteria for judging what may be done electronically to a photograph. Altering the editorial content ... is a breach of the ethical standards recognized by the NPPA.

"Who benefits?" is the Utilitarian principle that usually underlies journalistic decisions. Does this choice we are about to make achieve the Greatest Good for the greatest number of people?

If a new tool helps the reader see the content of a picture more clearly or understand what occurred in the picture more completely, perhaps the software should be used.

If, however, no one can make a clear case that the reader is, in fact, better informed by deploying the latest tool, then the picture should remain in as pure a state as possible.

Individual photojournalists make these decisions at their own risk. The industry ultimately must find its bearings and provide clear and unambiguous guidelines.

AVOIDING ETHICAL LANDMINES

For photographers new to the field as well as for veterans, there is only one sure thing. Digital editing of images is an ethical minefield. Although the NPPA's Digital Code of Ethics (below) admonishes photographers not to alter the content of an image, the Schneider case shows that even what defines content can be debatable.

The best way to prepare for potential problems is to understand from the beginning where the lines at your news outlet are drawn—whether you are on staff or a freelancer. If there are no written guidelines, develop your own by talking to fellow photographers, and by discussing the issue with photo editors and editors. Review your guidelines with all the editors so that you won't lose your job because an editor was "uncomfortable" with how you adjusted an image—even if you think your choice of editing tools would better inform readers.

At the crux of any guideline is this: "Electronically alter pictures only when doing so clearly benefits the reader. Avoid altering pictures when doing so fools the reader in any way."

Finally, inform your editors of your editing choices lest your decision be questioned later. ∎

the New York, New Jersey, Washington, and San Francisco subways despite the attempts of some transit authority police and city councils to ban photography in these places.

City officials and police are on high alert in part due to elevated security after the September 11, 2001, terrorist attacks in the United States. The Patriot Act and Homeland Security Act, however, do not prevent photography in public places or around public buildings. Structures such as bridges, industrial facilities, and trains remain perfectly legal to photograph.

You can photograph on the campus of a publicly owned institution of higher education like Florida State University or the University of Michigan. The law does not forbid taking pictures in a lab, a classroom, or a gym. However, without the teacher's permission, you can't take pictures of Mr. Weintraub's physics class or Mr. Knowlton's journalism class while they are in session.

Photographing in the university's dorm sets up a different situation even if a public university owns the dorm. Dorm management has the right to restrict entry into the building for security reasons. Students' dorm rooms as well as common bathrooms are considered private, which means you need the permission of the student renter to take pictures in these locations.

Your rights to take pictures in the dorm's dining hall are less clear. Is the dining space open to all students on campus and therefore to the press—or is it more like a dining room in someone's home in which case the residents would have the expectation of privacy?

In any event, when you take pictures in a dorm, even if you live there, you should announce yourself as a journalist so other students know you are not taking pictures just for your own pleasure and that the pictures you snap might be published. Telling everyone that you are a working photojournalist warns those who don't wish to be photographed to stay beyond the reach of your lens in order to preserve their privacy.

TAKING PICTURES IN PUBLIC PLACES

Although a public grade school or high school is publicly owned, it falls under its principal's jurisdiction. While there is no law against photographing inside public schools, the principal has the authority to determine who comes and goes on school grounds, effectively granting or denying access to photojournalists. Typically, you can gain access to these buildings with permission from someone in authority who works in the principal's office.

You may take pictures of elected officials or private citizens in public places, such as on the street or in the park. They may be the center of interest in your photo, or just part of the crowd. If a news event occurs on public property, you may cover that event as long as you do not interfere with police or the flow of traffic.

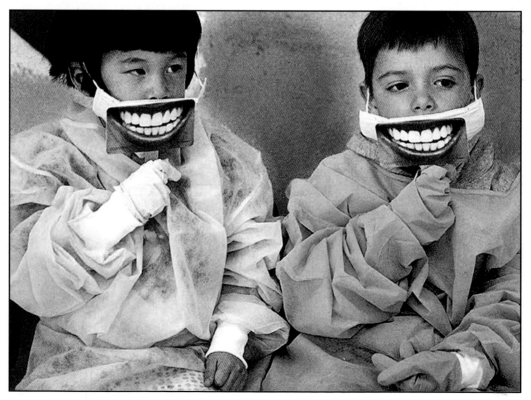

You can take pictures of children in public places, such as at the community center where these children were photographed. At a school, you would need permission of the principal to enter the school grounds.
Chris Riley, *Gilroy* [California] *Dispatch*

There are times when bystanders try to physically prevent photographers from taking pictures. In such instances, the courts have generally protected photographers shooting in public places, according to George Chernoff and Hershel Sarbin in their book *Photography and the Law*. They note that, some years ago, the state of New York even made it illegal to damage the equipment of news photographers engaged in their occupation in public places.

Difficulties arise when police authorities try to stop photographers from shooting on public property. In many situations, an overeager police officer may block a photographer's lens.

In Iowa, highway patrol officers and the National Guard once prevented photographers from taking close-ups at the scene of a civilian airline crash. Once airline officials arrived, photographers were given a free hand. In Philadelphia, police forcibly prevented photographers from taking pictures as officials bounced a heckler from a political rally. Philadelphia's city solicitor issued a formal opinion in which he told the police commissioner, "Meaningful freedom of the press includes the right to photograph and disseminate pictures of public events occurring in public places."

Police and fire officials have the right to restrict any activity of a photographer that might interfere with the officials' actions. In ordinary circumstances, taking pictures and asking questions do not constitute interference. However, police and fire officials are permitted to restrict newsgathering conduct if the photographer disrupts the pending investigation or activity.

Unfortunately, if an insistent police officer stops you at the scene of a breaking-news event, you might find it hard to argue a fine point of law. Photographers who disregard police directives—even if the shooters have the right to be where they are—can be arrested for disorderly conduct or for interfering with the performance of a police officer's duty. Continuing to take pictures or failing to move after a policeman gives you a direct order could constitute a possible felony.

The National Press Photographers Association (NPPA) and some of its chapters have for years worked with fire and police academies to improve the graduates' understanding of the role of the news media in society. NPPA members have written police/press guidelines designed to reduce the conflict between working photojournalists and law enforcement officers. The result has been improved cooperation between photographers and fire and police personnel.

WHERE AND WHEN A PHOTOJOURNALIST CAN SHOOT

	ANYTIME	IF NO ONE OBJECTS	WITH RESTRICTIONS	ONLY WITH PERMISSION
PUBLIC AREA				
Street	X			
Sidewalk	X			
Airport			X	
Beach	X			
Park	X			
Zoo	X			
Train Station	X			
Bus Station	X			
IN PUBLIC SCHOOL				
Preschool			X	
Grade School			X	
High School			X	
University Campus	X			
Class in Session				X
IN PUBLIC AREA— WITH RESTRICTIONS				
Police Headquarters			X	
Government Buildings			X	
Courtroom				X
Prisons				X
Military Bases				X
Legislative Chambers				X
IN MEDICAL FACILITIES				
Hospital				X
Rehab Center				X
Emergency Van				X
Mental Health Center				X
Doctor's Office				X
Clinic				X
PRIVATE BUT OPEN TO THE PUBLIC				
Movie Theater Lobby		X		
Business Office		X		
Hotel Lobby		X		
Restaurant		X		
Casino				X
Museum			X	
Shopping Mall				X
Store in Mall				X
PRIVATE AREAS VISIBLE TO THE PUBLIC				
Window of Home	X			
Porch	X			
Lawn	X			
IN PRIVATE				
Home		X		
Porch		X		
Lawn		X		
Apartment		X		
Hotel Room		X		
Car		X		

GOVERNMENT BUILDINGS: PUBLIC BUT UNDER SPECIAL RULES

Although facilities may be publicly owned, a photographer does not have unlimited access to government buildings, such as the U.S. Senate and House of Representatives, the state legislature, or the chambers of the city council. The mayor's office and city hospital also fall under the special-rules category. Military bases and jails also are strictly controlled, especially in the aftermath of the 2001 terrorist attacks in the United States.

A college football stadium or a downtown baseball park might be publicly owned, but access to these venues is completely controlled. At a college football game, sideline access is legally restricted by the school's athletic department. The athletic director or designee wants to control the number of photographers covering a game. The athletic office usually issues press passes to both the working and the credentialed student press. However, the National Collegiate Athletic Association (NCAA) restricts photographers from shooting any video of the "March Madness" basketball playoffs. The NCCA has sold the rights to televise these games and they don't want unauthorized footage available. Likewise, NASCAR controls access and usage of all stills and video shot at their races, even if they are using a publicly owned track.

Hospitals, even if they are publicly owned, publicly supported, and publicly operated, occupy a special place under the law. The admission list to hospitals is usually public information, but that's about all. You might be allowed to photograph scenes in a hospital for, say, a feature story. But check your pictures. Are there people in the pictures? Yes. Are some of them patients? Yes. Are they identifiable? Yes. Do you have a release? No. You say the people in the photo are "incidental?" For instance, a picture taken of a corridor or waiting room shows several people sitting and reading magazines. Don't even think about it. You must either get a release or not run the picture.

PRISONS AND JAILS

Your rights to photograph in a city, county, or state jail are subject to the discretion of the warden, who may or may not permit you to enter and who then may determine everything you may or may not shoot once you are inside. Even if a riot is taking place inside, the warden still controls all access. Unfortunately, the Supreme Court in *KQED vs Houchins* ruled that the press has no more rights than the general public when it comes to photographing prisoners.

MILITARY BASES

Like prisons, military bases are controlled by a government agency. You may enter at the invitation of the officer in charge. In the 1991 Iraq War, the military carefully controlled all combat photos. This attitude changed for the 2003 invasion of Iraq, when the Pentagon allowed a number of photojournalists to "embed" with military units fighting their way to Baghdad. While the military reserved the right to censor images taken by the embedded photojournalists, photographers reported that local commanders did not block images as long as they did not show a dead American solder. Commanders asked the journalists to hold the images until the next of kin had been notified.

The Pentagon, however, did impose a policy prohibiting photography of the caskets of slain American soldiers arriving at Dover Air Force Base in Delaware.

OTHER GOVERNMENTAL INSTITUTIONS

Not surprisingly, public institutions such as the Central Intelligence Agency (CIA) and the National Security Administration (NSA) are off limits without permission. Even the meetings of the Securities and Exchange Commission and the Nuclear Regulatory Commission require advance approval. Presidential libraries require permission for photos intended for publication.

Photographers often have been hassled in recent years at such places as public airports, train stations, and subway terminals. Few of these public places have formal regulations restricting photography, according to Ebert Krages in his book *Legal Handbook for Photographers*.

LAWMAKING VENUES

The halls of the U.S. Congress are certainly public places, as are meeting rooms of state legislatures and city councils. But such places are generally run by their own unique rules. Even though the House of Representatives does allow television cameras limited access to debates, this legislative body will not allow photographers to take still pictures at a regular session of Congress. Photojournalists can photograph legislators in committee meetings, elected officials in the halls of Congress, or legislators in their offices.

However, certain buildings — the Capitol and its grounds, all House and Senate office buildings, the Library of Congress, and the General Accounting Office — are controlled entirely by rules passed by Congress. The Constitution grants Congress the right to formulate the rules for operating these buildings. These rules are not subject to judicial review.

Senators and congressmen are afraid that the photographers' uncensored images will catch one of the members of this august body taking a nap, reading the newspaper, or, as is more often the situation, absent from his or her seat. Photographers are usually allowed in the U.S. House or Senate chambers only during ceremonial sessions, such as the opening day of Congress.

TRIBAL LANDS

Tribal lands are considered separate nations. Native American tribes can impose any restrictions they like, including fees on photography or outright bans on photographing homes and ceremonies.

THE COURTROOM: ANOTHER SPECIAL SITUATION

The U.S. Supreme Court does forbid the presence of photographers in federal but not in state courtrooms.

The effort of photojournalists to obtain access rights to both federal and state courtrooms has had a turbulent history. A low-water mark in photographing in the courtroom occurred during the trial of Bruno Richard Hauptmann for the kidnapping and murder of Charles Lindbergh's baby. Lindbergh had captured the world's imagination and admiration for his nonstop solo, transatlantic flight. The kidnapping and murder of his child attracted international interest, and an estimated 700 reporters, including 129 photographers, came to the old courthouse in Flemington, New Jersey, to cover the trial. Photographers were allowed to take pictures in the courtroom only three times each day: before court convened, at noon recess, and after court adjourned. Early in the trial, however, a photographer took unauthorized pictures of Lindbergh on the stand. The photographer claimed that he was "new on the job, having been sent as a relief man, and he did not know the rulings."

Another illegal picture was taken at the end of the trial. Dick Sarno of the *New York Mirror* concealed a 35mm Contax camera when he entered the courtroom on February 13, 1935, the day the verdict and sentence were announced.

At the key moment of the proceedings, Sarno, who had wrapped his camera in a muffler to conceal the noise, took a one-second exposure of the courtroom. Sarno later related, "As Hauptmann stood up and faced

During Bruno Richard Hauptmann's trial for kidnapping and killing Charles Lindbergh's baby, the judge prohibited photographers from taking pictures while court was in session. On January 3, 1935, Lindbergh himself took the stand. Despite the judge's orders, a photographer snapped this picture during the trial. Following this incident, with only a few exceptions, cameras were barred from the courtrooms until the 1970s.

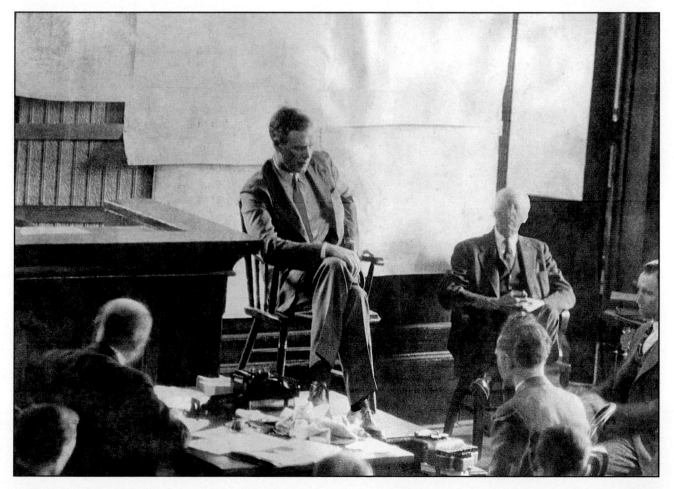

the jury, you could hear a pin drop. I tilted the camera, which I had braced on the balcony rail. The judge was directly in front and below me. If he looked up, I was sure he could see me."

As the foreman of the jury stood to recite the verdict, Sarno recorded the instant.

Prejudicial press reports, contemptuous statements by trial attorneys and police, the rowdy behavior of the 150 spectators and numerous reporters added to the holiday atmosphere of the proceeding, according to extensive research by Sherry Alexander in her report, "Curious History: The ABA Code of Judicial Ethics Canon 35." The raucous atmosphere created by journalists covering the trial outside the courtroom as they mobbed each witness, as well as indiscretions by still and newsreel cameramen inside the courtroom, shocked a committee of the American Bar Association (ABA) that reviewed the legal proceedings in 1936.

Nevertheless, Alexander found, the original ABA Committee did not recommend a total exclusion of photography and broadcasting in the courtroom. Instead, it was the 1937 convention of the group that adopted a flat ban on cameras in court as the 35th Canon of Professional and Judicial Ethics. Many states, but not all, adopted these canons, effectively slamming the courtroom door shut on photojournalists for 40 years.

COURTROOM RESTRICTIONS EASING

Florida's judicial system and legal code are viewed as the model to follow by many states. In the late 1970s, when the Florida Supreme Court opened the courtroom to photographers and television equipment on a limited basis for a one-year period, the event was significant. The Florida test allowed nationwide broadcast of the trial of 15-year-old Ronnie Zamora, who was charged with killing his 82-year-old neighbor.

Zamora's attorneys tried to blame television for the murder committed by their client. Noting that he avidly watched Kojak, a popular detective program, defense attorneys claimed the boy was under "involuntary subliminal television intoxication."

While the defense proved unsuccessful, the experiment allowing photographers to cover the trial worked well. With modern fast films and compact electronic television cameras, photographers did not require excessive lighting, and their behavior did not interfere with the trial's progress. Florida permanently opened its courts to the camera.

In 1980, the U.S. Supreme Court upheld the constitutionality of Florida's open courts law.

In *Chandler vs Florida*, two police officers convicted of burglarizing a restaurant claimed that the presence of TV cameras denied them a right to a fair trial because local stations broadcast only highlights of the

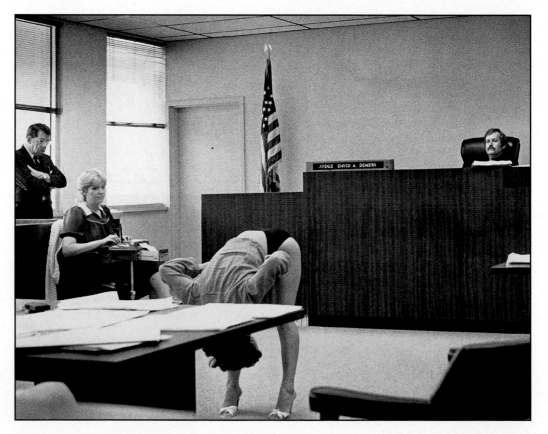

Accused of bending over to bare it all during their show, exotic dancers demonstrated for the judge that their underwear covered up anything "illegal." Pictures are now possible in most courtrooms. The photographer in this instance got a tip that an interesting performance might take place in court. Jim Damaske

prosecution's case. But when the Supreme Court considered the officers' appeal, the justices ruled unanimously that states are not prohibited from allowing still and television cameras in their courts. The decision was a major victory for photojournalists' First Amendment rights.

In spite of research indicating that most state Supreme Court justices dislike cameras in the courtroom, almost all states have opened their trials to camera coverage. There is even a cable television channel devoted to covering trials.

Each state, however, continues to have unique and individual restrictions. Some states permit only coverage of criminal trials and then only with the defendant's permission. Other states prohibit coverage of sex-crime trials or divorce proceedings. Some states allow coverage of first trials but not appeals. Verify your state's regulations before shooting. Phone cameras and other new technologies will undoubtedly result in fluctuation of these rules. In some cases they may be tightened; in others, the rules might be significantly relaxed.

At a minimum, every state will place a restriction on photographing jurors in the courtroom so as to protect their privacy.

Check with the presiding judge before taking pictures in a given courtroom. The presiding judge usually has a court clerk who will be able to share with you the local rules governing a given jurisdiction or courtroom.

While cameras are still banned in federal trial courts and in the U.S. Supreme Court, you can shoot on the sidewalk or street outside a courtroom, city hall, or jail.

Keep in mind that the police or other officials cannot restrict photojournalists from taking pictures while allowing other members of the public to continue doing so. "Thus, when a government official attempts to remove media personnel from a public sidewalk, the media personnel should (politely) inquire whether the ban extends to the general public as well. If not, the government's actions probably violate the First Amendment," according to a report by Covington and Burling law firm for the National Press Photographers Association.

Also note that the police do not have the right to discriminate against you if you work for an alternative paper or a web site and not a major daily. Police at the scene of a plane crash, for example, cannot bar a photographer from the *Boston Phoenix* while admitting the photographer from the *Boston Globe*.

TAKING JOURNALISTIC PICTURES IN PRIVATELY OWNED PLACES

Without going onto a person's property, you may, from the street, photograph someone in her yard, on her porch, or even inside her house if you can see the person. You don't need the subject's permission. For instance, the courts consider people sitting on their verandas, mowing their lawns, or standing behind a picture window in their living rooms to be in "public view" and therefore legitimate subjects for photography.

The photographer, however, still should be somewhat cautious when shooting onto private property and should not step onto the grounds to get the picture. Nor should the photographer use an extremely long telephoto lens, which would capture more than the naked eye could see.

In fact, the court says you shouldn't go to any extra trouble to get this porch-sitting, lawn-mowing, or window-standing shot. You shouldn't even climb a tree to gain a better view. Although not all photographers follow these guidelines, all are limited essentially to the view of an average passerby, according to the courts.

ACCESS VERSUS TRESPASS

Cindy Fletcher, 14 years old, died in a house fire in Jacksonville, Florida. Her mother, away at the time, learned about the tragedy in the next day's edition of the *Times-Union*. Alongside the story appeared a picture that showed where her daughter's burned body had left a silhouette scorched on the floor. Newspaper photographer Bill Cranford had entered the Fletcher home to take the photo. Mrs. Fletcher sued the Florida Publishing Company, owner of the *Times-Union*, on grounds that the photographer had invaded her home, hence her privacy.

This actual court case serves to illustrate the problem of access for the working photographer.

• Did the photographer, as a representative of the news media, have the right to enter the house?

• Could the fire chief invite the photographer to enter private property to take a news photo?

• Which right comes first: the right of Mrs. Fletcher not to have someone trespass in her house, or the right of the public to know what happened in that house?

This is a classic test of the strength of opposing rights: private property and personal privacy rights versus the First Amendment freedom of the press.

Would you have entered the Fletchers' home if you were the photographer?

Cindy Fletcher's burned body left a silhouette on the floor of her home. The girl's mother, who wasn't home when the picture was taken, sued for trespass when she saw the published photo. At the time, the courts said that it was common custom to allow photographers to cover news on private property if the owner does not object. Over the years, that interpretation has changed. Bill Cranford, [Jacksonville] *Florida Times-Union*

In *Florida Publishing Co. (Times-Union) vs Fletcher*, the court found in favor of the photographer. He had the right to enter the house and take the pictures.

Trespass generally means entering someone's home, apartment, hotel, motel, or car without permission. This right of private ownership prohibits someone from walking in and taking pictures inside a house, without the permission of the resident. The court holds that a person, in his or her home or apartment, has a reasonable expectation of privacy.

Why, then, did the court find that the *Times-Union* photographer had the right to enter the Fletcher house and take pictures of the silhouette left from Cindy Fletcher's burned body?

Why was this not a case of trespass?

In the Fletcher case, the police and the fire marshal had invited the news photographer into the home, and no one objected to the cameraman's presence. In fact, the authorities had asked the photographer to take pictures because they needed photos for their investigation, and the fire marshal's camera was out of film.

Mrs. Fletcher's suit was dismissed because it was "common custom" for the fire department or police department to permit the press onto private premises for the purposes of covering such newsworthy events.

First, the court found that a government official had the authority to invite a press photographer to enter someone's home without the owner's permission. The fire department office had invited the *Times-Union* photographer into the house to take the pictures of the burned body.

Note, however, the Fletcher case turns out to be an exception. According to Bert Krages's *Legal Handbook for Photographers,* "most if not all other courts that have faced this issue have ruled the other way."

In other words, the general rule of law is that government officials do not have the authority to allow the media to enter private property without the owner's permission. The Fletcher case would appear to be an exception to this general rule. Such exceptions may typically be relied upon only when the later situation is virtually identical.

UNREASONABLE SEARCH AND SEIZURE

Take the case of a CBS documentary called "Street Stories."

The facts: a CBS camera crew was shooting an episode for "Street Stories," a reality cop show, when police invited the news team to "ride along" for a raid on a suspect's home to look for evidence of credit-card fraud.

However, the suspect was not at home when the raid occurred. Only his wife, Tawa Ayeni, and her small child were there when the police officers pushed their way into the apartment—with the CBS video crew right behind them. The woman, clad only in her nightgown, implored the all-male crew, "Please don't take my picture."

She cowered, covered her face with a magazine, and directed her preschool-aged son not to look at the camera. "Why do you want to take a picture?" she asked. When the raid was over, law enforcement officials found nothing they had sought, but the CBS crew had footage of the raid, including shots of personal letters and paycheck stubs.

Tawa Ayeni sued CBS and won at both the trial level and in the U.S. Court of Appeals. Judge Jack Weinstein wrote, "Allowing a camera crew into a private home to film a search-and-seizure operation is the equivalent of a rogue policeman using his official position to break into a home in order to steal objects for his own profit or that of another."

Although law enforcement officials generally have a right to enter private property to conduct a reasonable search, Judge Weinstein maintained that this privilege does not extend to photojournalists invited along for the ride. Judge Weinstein wrote that inviting a camera crew into a private home is a violation of the Fourth Amendment, which protects citizens against "unreasonable searches and seizures."

Note that this finding runs counter to the "common custom and practice" concept that was established in the Fletcher case, where fire officials had invited the photojournalist into a private home to shoot the aftermath of a fatal fire. In the ruling against CBS, Judge Weinstein's views are more in line with contemporary court opinions that generally find little support for a police officer's right to invite photojournalists and reporters onto private property.

Supreme Court: Ride-alongs Violate Fourth Amendment with Illegal Search and Seizure

The question of ride-alongs finally reached the Supreme Court. In the early morning hours of April 16, 1992, a special team of U.S. Marshals called the "Gunsmoke Team" had invited a reporter and photographer from the *Washington Post* to accompany them as part of a Marshals Service ride-along policy.

At around 6:45 A.M. with media representatives in tow, the officers broke into Charles and Geraldine Wilson's home while the couple was still in bed. The Marshals were looking for Charles Wilson's son, who was not at home. The father, dressed only in a pair of briefs, ran into his living room to investigate the noise. Discovering at least five men in street clothes with guns in his living room, he angrily demanded that they state their business and repeatedly cursed the officers. Believing he was the subject of the warrant, the officers quickly subdued Wilson on the floor. Geraldine Wilson next entered the living room to investigate, wearing only her nightgown.

When the protective sweep was completed, the officers learned that Dominic Wilson, the couple's son, was not in the house. They left. During the time that the officers were in the home, the *Washington Post* photographer took pictures, although the newspaper never published those photographs.

Mr. and Mrs. Wilson sued the law enforcement officials (*Wilson vs Layne*). They contended that the officers' actions in bringing members of the media to observe and record the attempted execution of the arrest warrant violated their Fourth Amendment rights.

The case wound its way to the Supreme Court, which came to unanimous agreement in 1999. "While executing an arrest warrant in a private home, police officers invited representatives of the media to accompany them," wrote Chief Justice William Rehnquist. "We hold that such a 'media ride-along' does violate the Fourth Amendment."

In all probability, this Supreme Court finding will have a discouraging effect on opportunities for photographers and other members of the media to accompany police when they enter a house to execute a search warrant. Most police will not want to violate the Fourth Amendment, or have their cases thrown out of court in the future, because they invited or allowed photographers to go along on a drug bust or police raid inside someone's home.

However, the ruling does not stop the police from allowing photographers to cover their activities on public property such as streets and sidewalks.

NON-POLICE AUTHORITY

Can you photograph a newsworthy event in a person's home if the owners are not there to object and the police have not yet arrived?

If you were riding down the street, for instance, and heard a gunshot followed by a scream coming from a house, could you park your car, enter the house, and begin photographing the victim and the assailant?

If you walk into a private home, you will have trespassed on private property even if your purpose is to cover a crime under way.

If the homeowner walked in and objected to your taking pictures, the owner could ask you to leave. You would have to obey or be arrested for trespassing. Even if the police were there, you would have to leave if the homeowner objected to your presence. In a real situation, most likely, the homeowner would be more worried about the gunshots than your presence.

PRIVATE PROPERTY OPEN TO THE PUBLIC

Do you have the right to take pictures on private property that is open to the public, such as a restaurant or grocery store? This area of

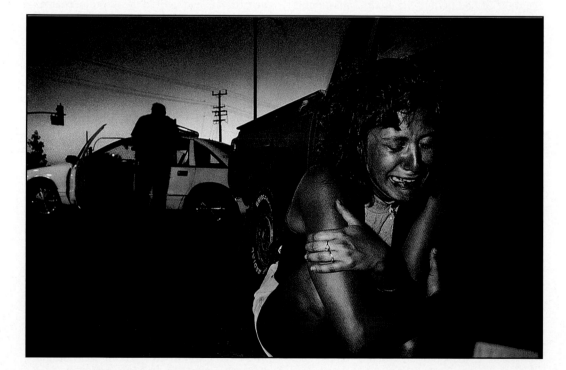

A photographer has the legal right to take this picture because the accident occurred on a public street.
Carolyn Cole, for the
Sacramento Bee

the law is murky. Some authorities hold that you can take pictures unless the management has posted signs prohibiting photography or unless the owners object and ask you to stop.

However, CBS was sued when its photographer entered Le Mistral restaurant in New York, with cameras rolling, to illustrate a story about the sanitation violations of the establishment. The management objected, but CBS kept filming.

Although no signs prohibiting photography were posted, CBS lost the suit on the grounds that the photographer had entered without the intention of purchasing food and was therefore trespassing. Although CBS was covering a legitimate news story in a private establishment open to the public, the network was found guilty of trespassing.

In a 1972 case (*Lloyd Corp., Ltd. vs Tanner*) the court ruled that "the public's license to enter a private business establishment is limited to engaging in activities directly related to that business and does not normally extend to the pursuit of unrelated business, e.g., news gathering."

Camera journalists have no right to enter a property, even in a spot-news situation, if the owners of the establishment prohibit them from doing so. Photographers must take their pictures from the public street, or they can be arrested for trespass.

This means that even if a fire is raging inside a business the management can exclude photographers. If the management asks you to leave, you must comply with the request or risk arrest for trespass.

In some, but not all states, large shopping malls are considered traditional public forums if they have long-established common areas that invite the public onto the property for purposes other than shopping. Many malls have a Santa at Christmas time. Choirs and bands sometimes perform. Photographers in many states can photograph these public events without special permission from the mall owners.

Casinos and restaurants are located on private property. Some establishments object to photography while others allow it.

You may always publish any pictures you have already taken. The owner can stop you from taking more pictures but can't prevent publication of the ones you already have.

Retired California Appeals Court Justice John Racanelli points out that penalties for trespass are usually "nominal" if there is no intent to "do actual harm or injury."

Sometimes the owner or manager of a store will demand that you turn over film or erase a memory card to eliminate images you have taken inside a shop.

On this point the law is clear. You do not have to do either. The owner or manager can ask you to stop taking pictures but can't take away personal property. Touching you or your camera to take away your property may constitute battery against you.

PRIVACY: WHEN DOES A JOURNALIST'S CAMERA ILLEGALLY INFRINGE?

When people talk about "privacy," they usually mean the "right to be left alone." But privacy is simply not a broad constitutional right basic to American citizens.

The U.S. Constitution does not explicitly grant us any explicit right of privacy—this general right to be left alone. In fact, most analysts believe that there never will be an explicit, expressed constitutional right of privacy similar to the rights outlined in the First Amendment that protects and guarantees free speech and a free press

Over the years, however, some commonly recognized legal principles of privacy have evolved, based on federal and state laws and court cases. As applied to photography, these principles protect individuals from anyone:

• intruding by taking pictures where privacy could be reasonably expected. In legal

TIPS FOR AVOIDING JAIL

The following suggestions come from Lucy A. Dalglish, executive director of the Reporters Committee for Freedom of the Press, a nonprofit organization dedicated to protecting journalists' First Amendment rights.

• Carry your credentials at all times.
• Do not trespass onto property that is clearly private or marked with a police line.
• Do not take anything from the crime scene—you will be charged with theft.
• Do whatever a police officer orders you to do, even if it seems unreasonable or ridiculous or interferes with your job, unless you're willing to live with the consequences of being arrested.
• Do not call the arresting officer names or get into a shoving match.
• If covering a demonstration or other event likely to result in arrests, keep $50–$100 cash in your pocket to purchase a bail bond.
• Give your memory card, if possible, to another journalist who can get it to your newsroom promptly.
• Keep a government-issued photo ID (in addition to a press pass) in your pocket at all times. It may speed up your release from custody.
• Know the name and phone number of a criminal lawyer, bail bondsman, and the police department spokesperson.

must get a model release signed, even if the subject is unknown.

UNFAIRLY CAUSING SOMEONE TO LOOK BAD

The law holds that people have the right not to be placed in a "false light." In other words, photos can't make a person look bad without cause. For example, a photographer took a picture of a child who had been struck by a car, and the photo appeared in a newspaper. No problem so far. Two years later, the *Saturday Evening Post* ran the same picture under the title, "They Ask To Be Killed," with a story about child safety. The original use of the picture was a legitimate publication of a newsworthy event. But when the *Saturday Evening Post* used the headline with the picture and placed the subhead "Do You Invite Massacre with Your Own Carelessness?" next to the photo, the parents claimed that the words and photo implied carelessness on their part. The words and photo gave the impression that the child had willingly run out in front of the car. The court decreed that the photo/headline combination placed the parents in a "false light." The parents won the lawsuit.

Saturday Evening Post editors used an old picture from their photo file to accompany this new story. They used the old picture as an illustration of a general, ongoing problem. Often, this use of file photos provides the grounds for later lawsuits.

In another such incident, even a legally obtained photograph was found defamatory. John Raible signed a model release allowing *Newsweek* magazine to publish his picture

with a story about "Middle Americans." The editors, however, chose the headline "Troubled American—A Special Report on the Silent Majority," and printed Raible's picture below the headline. Raible felt that the headline, associated with his picture, implied he was troubled, thus putting him in a false light. He sued and collected damages. Both the *Saturday Evening Post* and the *Newsweek* cases show a picture's meaning can be affected drastically by the words associated with it. Although the picture itself might have been legal when it was taken, after captioning or headlining, the photo-plus-word combination when published can be considered illegal. Robert Cavallo and Stuart Kahan, in their book ***Photography: What's the Law?***, say that "Pictures, standing alone, without captions or stories with them, generally pose little danger of defamation. However, an illustration is usually accompanied by text, and it is almost always that combination of pictures and prose which carries the damaging impact."

The *Newsweek* case points up a second legal danger for the photographer. The model release signed by Raible did not protect the photographer. The model release is not a carte blanche; it is a limited authorization given by the subject to the photographer, warning the photographer to use the picture in an understood and agreed-upon manner. A model release does not necessarily give photographers or picture editors the right to use a picture in any way they see fit.

TRUTHFUL BUT EMBARRASSING PHOTOS

The right of privacy does include some restrictions on printing truthful but private or embarrassing information about a subject. Generally, the media may publish newsworthy information in the public interest. The courts have liberally interpreted "public interest" to mean anything interesting to the public—and there are few things that won't interest at least some people.

PUBLIC BUT EMBARRASSING

The courts, however, have put certain limitations on the right of the public to know and see true but confidential facts about a person. Photographs, even if taken in a public place, should not ridicule or embarrass a private person unless the situation is patently newsworthy. The photos should not be highly offensive to a reasonable person and must be of legitimate concern to the public.

A Ms. Graham went to the Cullman, Alabama, county fair. After several rides, she entered a sideshow fun house. In the fun house, she walked across a grate that blew up

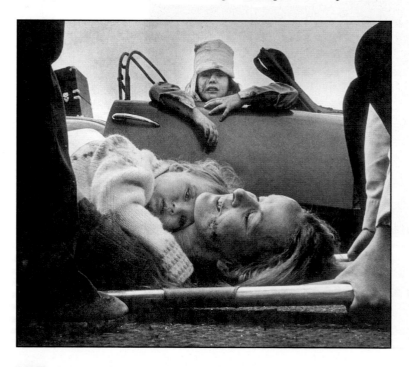

It is legal to take pictures at accident scenes in public places because accident victims have what is called a "public medical condition." Below, once the woman on the stretcher was moved into an ambulance, her medical condition became private. The photographer would have needed her permission to continue taking photos.
Dan Poush, *Statesman-Journal* [Salem, Oregon]

her dress. At that unlucky moment, a photographer from the *Daily Times Democrat*, Bill McClure, was on his first photo assignment for the paper—looking for "typical" features at the fair. With his Speed Graphic camera, he snapped Graham's picture just as her skirt blew up around her hips, exposing her underwear. After the picture was published, Graham called and complained. Getting no satisfaction from the photographer with an apology or retraction, Graham hired an out-of-town lawyer and successfully sued the *Democrat* for damages. The picture was truthful, but the jury found that the photo was embarrassing and contained no information of legitimate concern to the public.

Media lawyer Bo Bogatin of Bogatin, Corman and Gold cautions that a kind of libel known as trade libel can arise with truthful images that subject a company's logo or trademark to disparagement.

PHOTOGRAPHING CHILDREN
There are no legal restrictions that prohibit you from photographing children. Although unauthorized photography of youngsters can arouse suspicions of a nearby parent or guardian, the photojournalist does have the legal right to photograph little ones playing in a public park.

A school principal has the authority to block a photojournalist's access to the school's building and grounds, but administrators actually don't need a parent's permission to allow photography of the students. Although many administrators do say they need parents' permission, the courts do not require parental permission to take pictures of children in schools.

While you can take and publish pictures of children in schools and public parks, you are open to suit only if the photo might be considered embarrassing or derogatory. Because of concern over kidnapping and sexual molestation, however, be cautious when photographing children you do not know. Always try to explain to a parent or other responsible adult at the scene who you are and what you are doing. While you might have the legal right to take and publish the picture, dealing with an irate parent can distract you from your original assignment.

Special Children
Photographing children in special education classes is another story. The parents of these children may consider that photo truthful but embarrassing. They could successfully sue you and your news organization. Getting a teacher's permission is not sufficient. To publish a picture of a mentally or physically disabled child, you must have the consent of the parent or legal guardian.

MEDICAL SITUATIONS
In 1942, an International News Photo photographer entered the hospital room of Dorothy Barber, who was in the hospital for a problem with an eating disorder.

Without Barber's consent, the photographer took a picture of her, which *Time* magazine bought and ran under the headline "Starving Glutton." Barber sued the

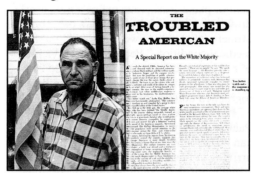

Even though John Raible had signed a consent form, he sued *Newsweek* and won because he felt the headline and this picture put him in a "false light." Reprinted from *Newsweek*

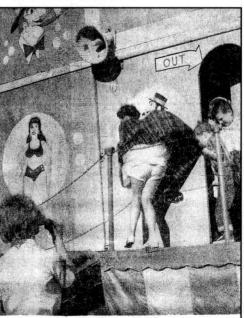

All's Fair in Fair Fun

Ms. Graham was in a public place and her face wasn't even visible when she was photographed at the Cullman County Fair. She said her children were recognizable, and the courts agreed with her that this picture, though truthful, was embarrassing, and therefore, she could collect damages. Reprinted from the [Alabama] *Daily Times Democrat*

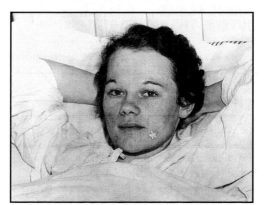

Without Dorothy Barber's permission, a photographer took her picture in her hospital room. When the photo ran in *Time* magazine, Barber sued for invasion of privacy and won. International News Pictures

The agency or publication has first rights to use the image, but you can resell the photo to other outlets the first publication.

COPYRIGHTING YOUR OWN PHOTOS

If you don't work full-time for a news organization, how do you protect yourself from someone reprinting your photos and not giving you credit or paying you? How do you prove the printed photo is yours if it does not carry your credit line? These questions are addressed in the U.S. Copyright Act.

If you are a freelance photographer you have copyright protection of your work as soon as you take a picture and develop the film or save it to a digital file.

To protect your rights, put your copyright notice on the back of each print with either of the following notations: © or the word Copyright, with the year you shot it followed by your name. Although not required, it is a common practice to include a statement that reflects the concept of "all rights reserved" or "permission required for use."

After you've placed the copyright notice, you can register the image with the U.S.

Copyright Office in Washington, D.C. Do this by completing the form you will find online and sending your images, along with the stated fee. The fee covers all the material you are sending, not just one image (see *www.copyright.gov*).

Although technically your photograph is protected at the moment you press the shutter, collecting damages is far easier if you have legally registered it.

Media attorney Bogatin suggests doing this every quarter for all your published work. You can also register your work in bulk—a body of work, tear-sheets, videotapes of your slides, contact sheets, etc.

"Visual artists are at the eye of a perfect storm, and copyright is at ground zero," says Eugene Mopsik, executive director of the American Society of Media Photographers (ASMP).

"Both Congress and the public need to know that you value your intellectual property, and the best way to do that is to register your work... Don't wait until you are infringed and then possibly lose the available remedies," Mopsik says.

On assignment for *People*, the photographer took this picture of buff brothers who made the career transition from hog farming in Nebraska to modeling for a New York talent agency. The magazine has the right to use the picture one time but the photographer retains the copyright. Three months after the picture first appeared, the photographer could sell the picture to other publications. Keith Philpott, for *People*

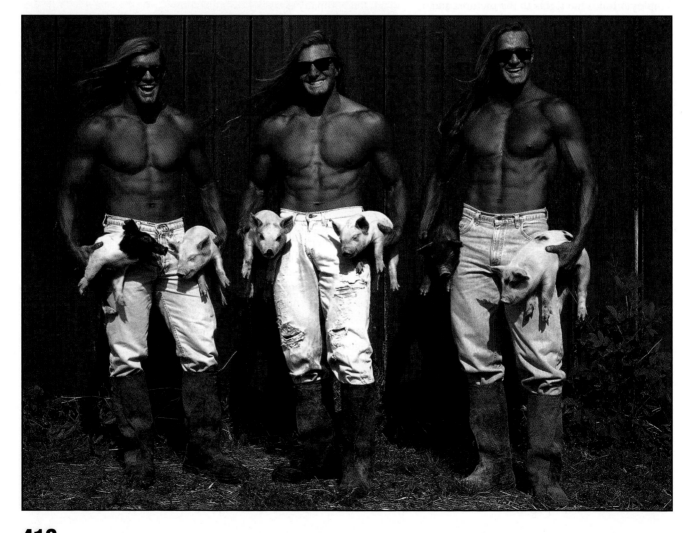

ASMP has posted a thorough step-by-step tutorial on how to register both published and unpublished works: *www.asmp.org/commerce/legal/copyright/*

Keep in mind that if someone publishes your image without permission, and you have not registered your copyright within three months of your publication of the image, or before the infringement, you will still be required to register before the courts will let you proceed with an action. If you have a preregistration infringement action, you are likely to win the fee you would have charged for the picture as well as compensatory damages (the infringer's profits, if any). For example, if *Train Lovers* magazine published your photo of a train wreck without your permission, you may have lost sales from other magazines that would have purchased the image. With the image registered, you can sue for the money the publication should have paid you, as well as the money you can prove you lost from possible future sales.

You can also sue to stop *Train Lovers* magazine from using the picture again or featuring it in their upcoming calendar.

However, if you have a preinfringement registration before *Train Lovers* magazine publishes your photo, you can elect to pursue a judgment of up to $150,000 if you can prove the magazine willfully published the image without your consent. The additional statutory benefit under the Copyright Act is that you can possibly recover legal fees. However, if you have not registered your copyright within three month of publication or before the infringement occurs, you cannot recover your fees and costs, and will likely lose the prospect of retaining legal counsel on a contingency-fee basis, which otherwise is often available.

RESPECTING THE COPYRIGHTS OF OTHERS

The ease of taking images off the Internet or scanning photos and incorporating them into photo illustrations makes it easy to forget that other photographers or artists enjoy the same copyright protection you do. Remember not to use "found" images from newspapers, magazines, or the web without express permission to do so, or unless you have established with confidence that the underlying image as well as the photograph of it are in the public domain.

Just as no one can legally make a painting or sculpture from your photograph, you may not photograph someone else's copyrighted painting or sculpture. Your photo becomes a derivative work, which only the copyright owner—usually the creator of the work—can create or license to be created. ∎

LAW REFERENCES

Barber vs *Time*, 1 Med. L. Rep. 1779 or 159 S.W. 2d 291 (Mo. 1942)

Branzburg vs Hayes, 408 U.S. 665 (1972)

Burton vs Crowell Publishing Co., 81 Fed. 154 (2d Cir. 1936)

Chandler vs Florida, 449 U.S. 560 (1981)

Daily Times Democrat vs Graham, 276 Ala. 380 162S. 2d 474 (1964)

Deteresa vs American Broadcasting Co., 121 F.3d 460 (1997)

Dietemann vs *Time* 449 F. 2d 245

Estes vs Texas, 381 U.S. 532, 536

Florida Publishing Co. vs Fletcher, 340 So. 2d 914

Food Lion, Inc. vs Capital Cities/ABC, Inc., 964 F. Supp. 956, 959 n.2 (M.D.N.C. 1997)

Galella vs Onassis, 487 F. 2d 986

Le Mistral vs Columbia Broadcasting System, N.Y. Sup. Ct., N.Y. L.J. (1976)

Leverton vs Curtis Publishing Co., 192 F. 2d 974 (3d Cir. 1951)

Lloyd Corp. Ltd. vs Tanner, 407 U.S. 551, 92 S. Ct. 2219, 33 L. Ed. 2d 131 (1972)

People vs Berliner, 3 Med. L. Rep. (1942)

People vs Zamora, 361 So. 2d 776

Raible vs *Newsweek*, Inc., 341 F. Supp. 804 (1972)

Saunders vs American Broadcasting Co., 20 Cal. 4th 907 (1999)

Sbyszko vs *New York American*, 1930: 239 NYS, 411

Tawa Ayeni vs CBS Inc., 848 F. Supp. 362 (E.D. N.Y. 1994)

United States of America vs Anthony Sanusi et al., 813 F. Supp. 149 (E.D. N.Y. 1992)

Wilson vs Layne, 27 M.L.R. 1705 (1999)

OPPOSITION TO PHOTOS

In 1893, four years after the demise of *The Daily Graphic*, Horgan, who helped introduce the halftone to New York, was working as art editor for the *New York Herald* when he recommended the use of halftones to James Gordon Bennett, the paper's owner. After a brief consultation with his pressmen, Bennett pronounced the idea unfeasible.

Similarly, Joseph Pulitzer, who had been publisher of the *New York World* since 1883, initially expressed reluctance to print halftones. In fact, Pulitzer feared that widespread use of any pictures, including line drawings, would lower the paper's dignity, so he tried to cut down on the extensive use of woodcuts, which already had made his paper famous. When circulation fell as a result, Pulitzer reconsidered his decision and reinstated the drawings.

As Pulitzer recognized the paper-selling potential of such illustrations, he began to increase their size from the original one-column to four- and five-column spreads. When the halftone was finally perfected, the *World* was one of the first newspapers to make liberal use of the new process. The daily's circulation rose rapidly. Other publishers and editors soon jumped onto the pictorial bandwagon. One such newsman, Melville Stone, investigated the potential of newspaper illustrations for the *Chicago Daily News*. He ultimately concluded, "Newspaper pictures are just a temporary fad, but we're going to get the benefit of the fad while it lasts."

Today we know that newspaper pictures were neither temporary nor faddish, but, in the closing years of the 19th century, the halftone continued to struggle for legitimacy in newspapers despite its outstanding showcase in magazines of the period.

By the late 1890s, the process had yet to achieve daily use, although *The New York Times* did print halftones in its illustrated Sunday magazine, begun in 1896. Skeptical newspaper publishers still feared that their readers would lament the substitution of mechanically produced photographs for the artistry of hand-drawn pictures; also, artists and engravers were well-established members of the newspaper staff.

Thus, long after the halftone was perfected, carefully drawn copies of photos continued to appear in many papers. Gradually, however, papers joined magazines and adopted the halftone process. By 1910, hand

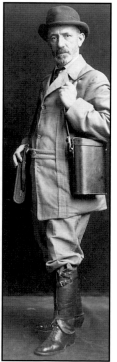

Jimmy Hare (BELOW), with his two folding cameras carried in their leather cases, covered the globe for *Collier's Weekly*. He photographed everything from the Spanish-American War (RIGHT) to the closing days of World War I in Europe.
Jimmy Hare Collection, Humanities Research Center, University of Texas at Austin

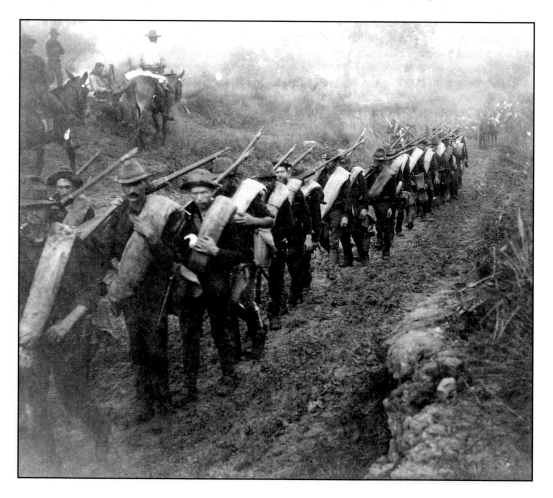

engraving was becoming obsolete and the halftone, in turn, had become a staple of the newspaper's front page.

THE MAINE BLEW UP, AND JIMMY HARE BLEW IN

While these technological strides were taking place in the latter part of the nineteenth century, several photographers were setting photojournalistic precedents. Jimmy Hare, one of the most colorful of the pioneer photojournalists, wrote the handbook for future photographer-reporters.

During his career, Hare covered nearly every major world event, from the wreckage of the U.S. battleship Maine in Havana harbor during the Spanish-American War in 1898 to the closing days of World War I in Europe. His ingenuity and his no-holds-barred attitude when it came to getting the picture set a standard for the new profession of photojournalism.

London-born Hare, whose father crafted handmade cameras for a living, came to the United States in 1889. One magazine, *Illustrated American*, committed itself to using halftone photographs. From 1896 to 1898, Hare worked as a freelance photographer, supplying the magazine with photos of events ranging from presidential inaugurations to sporting matches.

A month after he left *Illustrated American*, the battleship Maine exploded, thus signaling the start of the Spanish-American War. The ever-enterprising photographer promptly presented himself to the editors of *Collier's Weekly*, and offered to take pictures of the wreckage.

Twenty years after the Maine episode, then-editor Robert J. Collier was to recall, "The Maine blew up and Jimmy blew in! Both were major explosions!" Jimmy continued "blowing in" to important world events for the next several decades.

So successful were his pictures of the Maine and of Cuba, where American soldiers were fighting in the Spanish-American War, that the publisher named Hare special photographer for *Collier's*, thus beginning a long and productive association.

Whether trekking over the Cuban countryside, touring battlefields with Stephen Crane, author of ***Red Badge of Courage***, or following Teddy Roosevelt's Rough Riders, Hare remained intrepid and resourceful in his coverage of the Spanish-American War. Hare made use of the new folding cameras (with lenses as fast as f/6.8) and of roll film (with 12 exposures per roll). His lightweight equipment gave him more mobility than his competitors, who were shooting with fragile glass plates and awkward 5"x7" Graflexes, the popular news cameras of the day.

Regardless of his folding camera's light weight, Hare still had to get to the middle of the action to take a picture. In one battle during the Spanish-American conflict, a soldier spotted Hare snapping away as wounded bodies dropped all around him. "You must be a congenital damn fool to be up here! I wouldn't be unless I had to!" the soldier shouted. Hare's even-handed reply: "Neither would I, but you can't get real pictures unless you take some risks."

In addition to his exploits in the Spanish-American War, Hare's photographic escapades brought him to the combat lines of the Russo-Japanese War, the Mexican Revolution, the First Balkan War, and World War I. Hare described these experiences as "one-sided adventures in which it was always my privilege to be shot at but never to shoot." But shoot he did—with his camera, that is—and his pictures contributed greatly to the rapidly rising circulation and national prominence of *Collier's*.

HARE COVERS FIRST FLIGHT

Not all of Hare's exploits took place on the battlefield. The story of how Hare managed to record on film the experiments of the Wright brothers in 1908 is indicative of his tenacity and his skill. The Wrights' first successful flight had taken place in 1903, but five years later, the public remained unconvinced that men had actually flown. Rumors abounded, but no one had documented and published proof of any flight. The brothers refused to allow reporters to witness their experiments at Kitty Hawk.

Hare was determined to check out the rumor for *Collier's*, however, and, along with four reporters from various newspapers, he secretly went to the Wright brothers' testing area. The five intrepid men spent two days hiking over the sands of Kitty Hawk, North Carolina. Approaching the site of the rumored flights, the newsmen took cover in a clump of bushes and anxiously waited for something to happen.

Covered with mosquito bites and tired of lugging his camera, Hare was tempted to dismiss the rumors as false and head back home. But suddenly an engine noise was heard, and, as the reporters watched in disbelief, an odd-looking machine glided across the sand and gradually rose into the air. Hare ran out of the bushes and managed to snap two photographs of the airborne machine. The party of reporters then sneaked back to their base and prepared to reveal their booty to the world.

Because Hare was far away from the plane, the image in his photo was small and indistinct. But *Collier's* was proud to publish the picture in its May 30, 1908, issue. The photo proved at last that man could indeed fly. Hare had the distinction of taking the first news photograph of a plane in flight.

Hare began chronicling his world during photojournalism's infancy. When *Collier's* first published his photos, editors considered pictures mere embellishments of the text. But through his dogged efforts to capture with his camera a sense of immediacy and excitement, Hare served as a catalyst in the evolution of the photographer into a full-fledged "reporter with a camera."

WOMEN ENTER THE FIELD

Since 1900, female photojournalists have made their mark in the newsroom. Frances Benjamin Johnston, an indomitably spirited photographer, managed to transcend the constraints usually imposed on Victorian women. She documented early educational methods in white, African-American, and Native-American schools. She shot a series of photographs on the activities in the White House and on the visits of foreign dignitaries. Then Johnston sold her pictures to the newly formed Bain News Service (see pages 450–451) and became its photo representative in Washington. Johnston was considered the unofficial White House photographer, according to historian C. Zoe Smith's article "Great Women in Photojournalism." D.C. Bain, the agency's owner, suggested that Johnston photograph Admiral George Dewey

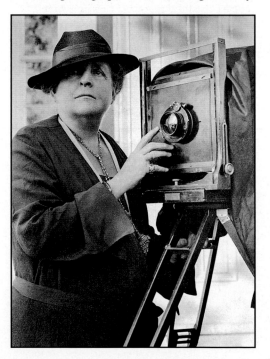

Frances Benjamin Johnston, an early photojournalist around 1900, represented the Bain News Service in Washington, D.C.
Library of Congress.

aboard his battleship after his successful takeover of the Philippines. With great ingenuity she made her way to Italy, where Dewey's ship first docked. She managed to endear herself to the crew and, when it came time to fill out an enlistment record, she earned five out of five possible points for everything from seamanship to marksmanship, but only a "4.9" for sobriety.

Jessie Tarbox Beals was another photojournalistic pioneer. She started out as a schoolteacher but soon discovered the lure of photography. In 1902 the *Buffalo* (New York) *Inquirer and Courier* hired her as a press photographer. Early on, she exhibited an important skill of the photojournalist—the "ability to hustle," as she once put it. Before her career ended, Beals sneaked photographs through a transom at a murder trial, rode the gondola of a balloon above the St. Louis World's Fair for a photo, and photographed Mark Twain.

THE CAMERA AS A REFORMER'S TOOL

Social-documentary photographers, notably Jacob Riis and Lewis Hine, demonstrated that the camera could not only provide a record of events but could also serve as a potent tool for social change. Hine once summarized his goals as a concerned photographer: "There were two things I wanted to do. I wanted to show the things that had to be corrected. I wanted to show the things that had to be appreciated." As America moved into the new century, crusading photographers chose to concentrate on Hine's goal to correct social injustice. Riis and Hine were among the first to press the camera into service as an agent for social awareness.

Their photographic pleas for reform placed them in the ranks of such late 19th-century and early 20th-century social muckrakers as Upton Sinclair, Lincoln Steffens, and Ida Tarbell. Together with these writer-reformers, the camera journalists probed the underside of city life, exposed the unimaginable, and brought into the open what had previously been shielded from view.

RIIS EXPOSES SLUM CONDITIONS

Neither Riis nor Hine, in fact, began as a photographer. The Danish-born Riis started out in the 1870s as a carpenter and then got a job as a reporter for the *New York Sun*. He wrote firsthand accounts of the indignities and inequities of immigrant life. When he was accused of exaggerating his written descriptions of life in the city slums, he turned to photographs as a means of documenting the human suffering he saw.

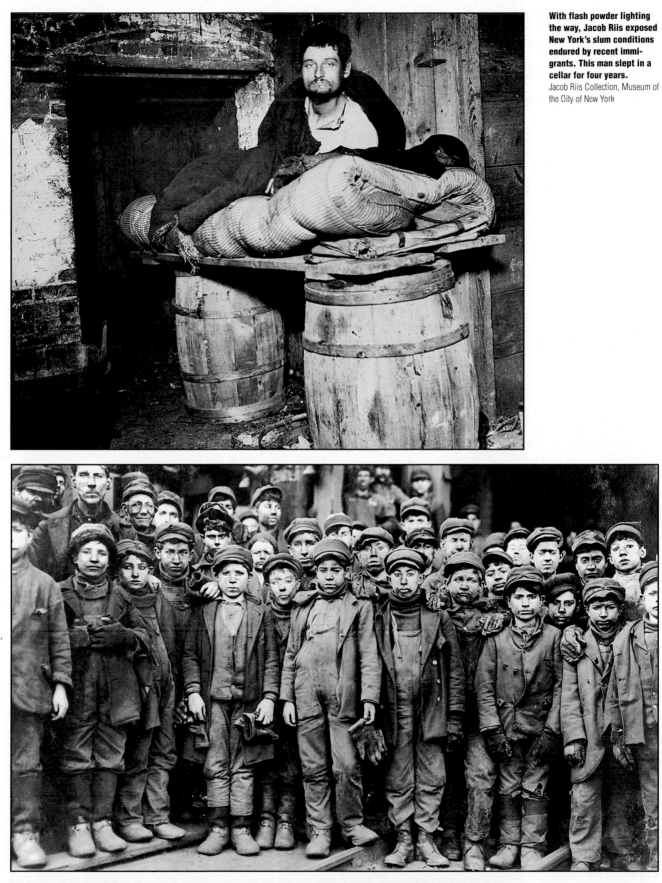

Lewis Hine photographed the soot-blackened children who worked in the coal mines. In part because of Hine's photos, Congress passed protective child-labor laws. Lewis Hine, Library of Congress

For Riis, the photograph had only one purpose: to aid in the implementation of social reform. Pictures were weapons of persuasion that surpassed the power of words and the absolute veracity of the photographic image made it an indispensable tool. As Riis stated, "The power of fact is the mightiest lever of this or any other day."

But Riis was up against many obstacles as a photographer. The crowded tenements were shrouded in darkness and shadows. To show the perpetual nighttime existence in the slums, Riis pioneered the use of German Blitzlichtpulver—flashlight powder—which, although dangerous and uncontrollable, did sufficiently illuminate the scene. Lugging a 4"x5" wooden box camera, tripod, glass-plate holders, and a flash pan, Riis ventured into the New York slums with evangelical zeal. With a blinding flash and a torrent of smoke, he got his pictures. The scenes he recorded of immigrant poverty shocked and goaded the public into action for reform.

The Riis pictures are poignant glimpses of ghetto life. Grim-faced families stare at the camera with empty eyes. Shabbily clothed children sleep amid the garbage of a tenement stoop. A grown man stands in the middle of the street and begs for someone to buy one of his pencils. An immigrant sits on his bed of straw. In a coal bin, a newly arrived American citizen prepares for the Sabbath.

Unfortunately, when Riis was photographing, the halftone had yet to achieve widespread use. Consequently, his actual pictures were not directly reproduced in printed sources and so were seen by only limited numbers of people, such as those attending his lantern slide shows. At these talks, he used his pictures to buttress his plea for attention and reform.

When Riis' first book, ***How the Other Half Lives***, was finally published in 1890, it consisted of 17 halftones and 19 drawings modeled on his photographs. The halftones were technically poor—somewhat fuzzy and indistinct—but the pictures exerted a powerful influence that drew attention to slum conditions. They remain moving documents of human suffering.

HINE'S PHOTOS HELP INSTITUTE CHILD LABOR LAWS

Lewis Hine began as an educator and, like Riis, turned to photography as a means of exposing "the things that had to be corrected." In turn-of-the-century urban America, many conditions begged to be noticed and changed. The influx of immigrants into the cities and the simultaneous growth of industrialism were important characteristics of the new century. With the reformer's commitment, Hine set out to catalogue how people survived in this new way of life.

HAPPY ACCIDENT AT *NATIONAL GEOGRAPHIC*

IMMEDIATE RIGHT
On deadline at *National Geographic* and faced with 11 open pages, editor Gilbert Grosvenor used free pictures from Lhasa, Tibet, to fill the space for the magazine's first extensive photo layout. Courtesy of *National Geographic*

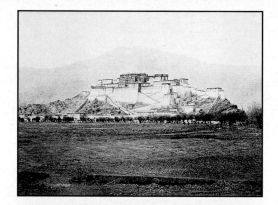

IMMEDIATE RIGHT
George Shiras III took the first night nature photos for *National Geographic*.

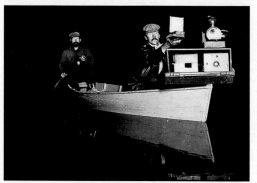

FAR RIGHT
Readers were so delighted with the magazine's first picture layout that editor Grosvenor ran 32 pages of pictures about the Philippines in the next issue.

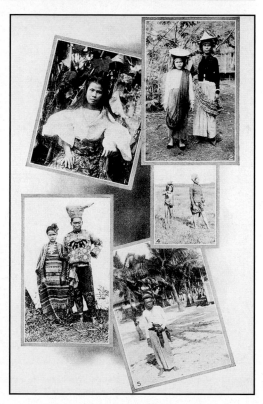

In 1908, the magazine *Charities and the Commons* published a series of his pictures of immigrant life. The series included some of Hine's most famous pictures: portraits of newly arrived immigrants at Ellis Island. The power and eloquence of these pictures attracted much attention. With the further refinement of the halftone, Hine published his work in books and magazines, and gained a good deal of public exposure for the social issues that concerned him.

That same year, Hine began to work as an investigator and reporter for the National Child Labor Committee. His work took him everywhere, from St. Louis slums to California canneries. To get through the doors of offending factories and mines, Hine posed as every type of worker, from a fire inspector to a bible salesman. One time he packed his camera in a lunch pail, filed with the workers into a clothing factory, and surreptitiously snapped pictures of sweatshop conditions. Hine juxtaposed diminutive children against huge machines. The weary stares of young knitting mill operators and seamstresses spoke more eloquently than words. The impact of his photos, including those of the soot-blackened faces of child coal-miners, helped facilitate the passage of Child Labor Laws restricting exploitation of youth.

PHOTOGRAPHY FILLS MAGAZINES AND "ROTO" SECTIONS
PHOTOS COME IN HANDY AT *NATIONAL GEOGRAPHIC*

National Geographic did not start out as a picture magazine. In fact, its first issue in 1888 contained no photos. It was not until 1903 that the magazine ran its first halftone, a photo of a Filipina at work in the rice fields.

Not until 1905 did the magazine try a photo spread unbroken by text. As it happened, the photo display was unintended.

On the day the magazine was scheduled to go to the printer, the editor, Gilbert Grosvenor, was faced with 11 open pages and no material whatsoever to fill the space. By coincidence, he had received that same day a package of photographs from the Imperial Russian Geographic Society.

These pictures of the previously unphotographed Tibetan city of Lhasa had been taken by two Russian explorers and were being offered to the Geographic for publication. Grosvenor, fascinated by the photographs, decided to take a risk. He laid them out as an 11-page spread—all pictures and almost no text—and sent them to the printer.

Grosvenor was sure he would be fired for having made this unprecedented and expensive editorial decision. Instead, readers stopped him in the street to congratulate him.

Although Grosvenor had run the Lhasa pictures primarily to fill up empty pages, he repeated the experiment after seeing the stir they created. In April 1905, he ran 32 consecutive pages of 138 photographs of the Philippines—a turning point in the magazine's history.

National Geographic contributed many photographic firsts, including the first nighttime nature pictures ever published, shot by George Shiras III, in 1906.

The magazine's first color photos, in 1910, were not color photos at all. In fact, they were hand-painted black-and-white pictures from Korea and China by William C. Chapin. Coloring black-and-white pictures continued until 1916, when Autochromes Lumières, real color photos, made their debut in the magazine's pages.

The first series of Autochromes had no particular theme other than that they were all natural-color photographs. In fact, the magazine invited amateurs to submit photos and ran them alongside pictures made by scientists, writers, and professional photographers. Since those early Autochromes, the magazine has published color photos from every part of the world, as well as from the bottom of the sea and from outer space.

ROTOGRAVURE AND THE PICTURE PAGE APPEAR

In 1914, *The New York Times* began publishing the first Sunday rotogravure section. Several other newspapers followed. The rotogravure process, which usually used dark sepia ink, offered a cheap printing process that could print 16 pages simultaneously— and an unlimited number of screened photos.

That same year, *The Times* also started the *Mid-Week Pictorial War Extra* to absorb the flow of World War I pictures pouring in from Europe. Printed on a superior grade of paper that yielded reproductions of higher quality, the supplement was sold separately at newsstands. Before the United States entered the war, restrictions were so severe that civilian photographers were not allowed at the Western front under threat of arrest or even death. Even after the United States entered the war in late 1917, pictures of American dead and severely wounded soldiers were censored.

Despite this severe U.S. censorship, picture agencies managed to obtain photos of trench warfare, the effects of poison gas, and the wholesale destruction of small towns taking place in Europe. The *Mid-Week Pictorial* occasionally ran portraits of men who had been killed in battle. Late in the war photographers added a new dimension for the reader back home by taking pictures from airplanes.

human struggle evocatively in text and images and continues to remain an important work in documentary studies.

The FSA photo project not only helped at the time by providing images to newspapers, magazines, and books, but it has left us with one of the greatest photographic records of any period of the American past.

Hyunju Choi's dissertation reviewed how the media actually used the FSA photos. Books and art exhibits tended to showcase portraits to call attention to rural migration.

Although newspapers and magazines ran photos showing the migrants' poor living conditions and ragged clothing, they neither investigated the fundamentals of the human migration nor examined its historical background or cause.

Photos in government-sponsored exhibits and pamphlets contrasted poor living conditions before government intervention with better circumstances resulting from federal aid to local projects.

Documentary books, by contrast, showcased the work of the FSA photographers.

Dorothea Lange's portrait of Florence Owens Thompson and one of her children is one the most iconic images taken during the Great Depression in 1930s America. The photo was one of a series of photographs that Lange made of Thompson and her children. Thompson said that they had been living on frozen vegetables from the surrounding fields and birds that the children killed. She had just sold the tires from her car to buy food.
Dorothea Lange,
Farm Security Administration

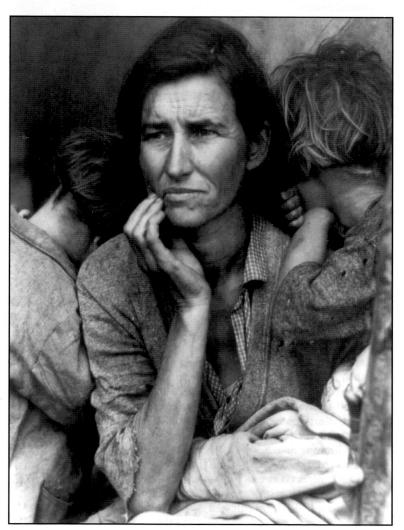

Gordon Parks

During his first month in Washington in 1942, Parks photographed a black government cleaning woman named Ella Watson. He chronicled her life at home, at work, and at church, creating a masterful photographic essay about her life. Offended by the discriminatory practices in the nation's capital, Parks wanted to show the evils of racism. He was quoted in Martin Bush's book, *The Photographs of Gordon Parks*:

The photograph of the black cleaning woman standing in front of the American flag with a broom and a mop expressed more than any other photograph I have taken. It was the first one I took in Washington. D.C. I thought then, and Roy Stryker eventually proved to me, that you could not photograph a person who turns you away from the motion picture ticket window, or someone who refuses to feed you, or someone who refuses to wait on you in a store. You could not photograph him and say, "This is a bigot." Because bigots have a way of looking like everybody else.

MAGNUM: THE LEGENDARY PHOTO AGENCY

Magnum, like Black Star, was another picture agency formed by European émigrés.

While the three former photo editors who started Black Star secured assignments for photographers and kept a percentage of their fees, Magnum was formed in 1947 as a cooperative that shared its profits among its photographer-members.

Magnum was founded by Henri Cartier-Bresson, a wealthy French photojournalist; George Rodger, an English photographer who worked for *Life* magazine; David Seymour, known to everyone as Chim; and André Friedmann, a Polish photographer who immigrated to the States and changed his name to Robert Capa. (Friedmann supposedly took the American name so editors would think of him as a successful American photographer rather than a struggling young émigré.)

The agency actually was born as a way for its founders to have a political impact. Cartier-Bresson, Rodger, and Chim spent many hours at the Café du Dome in Paris discussing liberal politics rather than photography. They were interested in how they could use their cameras to examine the social and political problems of the day. For a long time Capa had been toying with the idea of a cooperative picture agency, so that photographers could hold on to more of their earnings and retain rights to their images. During World War II, Capa met Rodger in Naples when both were taking pictures for *Life*.

CAPA: THE GREATEST WAR PHOTOGRAPHER

By the time he and his friends founded Magnum, Capa was already a legendary war photographer who had covered both the Spanish Civil War and World War II. He took perhaps the most famous war photograph of all time—a Spanish Republican militiaman, arms flung wide, dropping backward at the instant he was killed by a bullet (see page 442).

During World War II, Capa photographed the landing at Normandy on D-Day and produced classic photographs that people still associate with that battle. Two thousand men lost their lives that day. Capa landed with the first wave of soldiers.

"The water was very cold and the beach was still more than a hundred yards away. The bullets tore holes in the water around me, and I made for the nearest steel obstacle," Capa later wrote.

Using two cameras, he took 106 pictures of the bloody battle on the beach before rushing back through the surf to clamber onto a landing craft returning to the invasion fleet offshore. A messenger delivered the undeveloped film to *Life*'s London office, where the deadline to send the pictures to New York was rapidly approaching. John Morris, picture editor for *Life*, took the four rolls of 35mm film and gave it to an assistant to develop. In his book ***Get the Picture***, Morris recounts the story of when his darkroom assistant ran into the office, sobbing, "They're ruined! Capa's films are all ruined!"

Recalls Morris:

Incredulous, I rushed down to the darkroom with him, where he explained that he had hung the films, as usual, in the wooden locker that served as a drying cabinet, heated by a coil on the floor. Because of my order to rush, he had closed the doors. Without ventilation the emulsion had melted.

I held up the four rolls, one at a time. Three were hopeless: nothing to see. But on the fourth roll there were eleven frames with distinct images . . . their grainy imperfection —perhaps enhanced by the lab accident— contributed to making them among the most dramatic battlefield photos ever taken. D-Day would forever be known by these pictures.

Capa went on to cover the liberation of Paris, the Battle of the Bulge, and the war between Israel and the Arabs. Later he photographed the war in Vietnam, always taking his own advice, recorded by his biographer, Richard Whelan: "If your pictures aren't good enough, you're not close enough."

HENRI CARTIER-BRESSON: PHOTOJOURNALIST OF THE DECISIVE MOMENT

After joining Magnum, Henri Cartier-Bresson, who during his career shot more than 500 pictures and stories for magazines, sailed for Bombay in the summer of 1947 to cover the partition of India. The political and religious animosities there had turned into a bitter and violent struggle. At least 10 million Hindus, Muslims, and Sikhs were abandoning their homes and fleeing in both directions across the new border between India and Pakistan. At least one million Indians were slain, and hundreds of thousands were made refugees during the exodus.

In January 1948, Cartier-Bresson photographed the Indian independence leader Mohandas Karamchand Gandhi on the day he broke his 15th fast. Margaret Bourke-White was also in India to cover Gandhi and the breakup of India for *Life* magazine.

The same day that Cartier-Bresson photographed Gandhi, the world leader was shot and killed by a Hindu opposed to Gandhi's defense of Muslims. When Margaret Bourke-White took a flash picture of the slain Gandhi

Gordon Parks, an African-American photographer shooting for the Farm Security Administration, photographed this cleaning woman in Washington, D.C. Parks later remarked that discrimination and bigotry were worse in D.C. than any other place he had seen.

Gordon Parks, Farm Security Administration

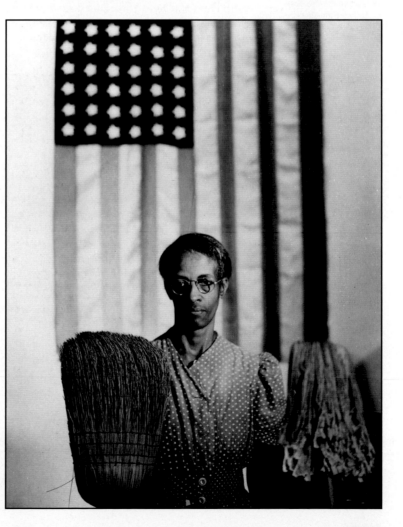

lying in state, Gandhi's entourage felt that the flash was disrespectful and took the film from Bourke-White. She tried to slip in again but was blocked. She left empty-handed, reports historian Claude Cookman in his dissertation, "The Photographic Reportage of Henri Cartier-Bresson."

Hearing that Gandhi had been shot, Cartier-Bresson, meanwhile, returned to the compound on his bicycle. With his Leica and available light, he succeeded in taking and keeping several photographs of the deathbed scene. "All night the crowds rushed into the garden of Birla House and pressed forward to try and see him," Cartier-Bresson recalled in his book *The Decisive Moment*. "I managed to reach one window, greasy from the pressure of many foreheads, and polished with my elbow a place big enough for the lens of my camera." *Life* magazine eventually paid Magnum a handsome price for the exclusive photos of an event that Bourke-White, their own staffer, had been unable to photograph.

AGENCY ADDS NEW RECRUITS

Magnum, which eventually had offices in both Paris and New York, added several more photographers to its stable. Werner Bishof, an abstract still-life photographer associated with Black Star, joined the agency.

Austrian photographer Ernst Haas left *Life* magazine to become a Magnum photographer. Despite the limitations of slow color films of the day, Haas was a color specialist. "I am not interested in shooting new things," he later wrote. "I am interested to see things new. In this way I am a photographer with the problems of a painter; the desire to find the limitations of a camera so I can overcome them."

Aspiring photographers found joining Magnum in the early days a casual, non-bureaucratic experience. Marc Riboud showed his pictures to Robert Capa while the famed war photographer was playing pinball in the café below Magnum's Paris office. Without a vote, without consulting anyone, Capa took one look at Riboud's portfolio and said, "OK, come with us. Allez!"

Eve Arnold showed up at the New York office with a portfolio containing just two stories—a fashion show in Harlem and an opening night at the Met. She was immediately invited to become a stringer—a freelance contributor. After Dennis Stock won a *Life* competition for young photographers, Capa invited him to join the agency.

Today applicants undergo a lengthy process that includes a trial period and a vote by all member photographers.

Robert Capa's famous "falling soldier" picture was taken in 1936 just as the man was struck by a bullet at the battle of Cerra Muriano on the Cordoba Front during the Spanish Civil War. Robert Capa © 1996, Magnum Photos, courtesy of Magnum Photos

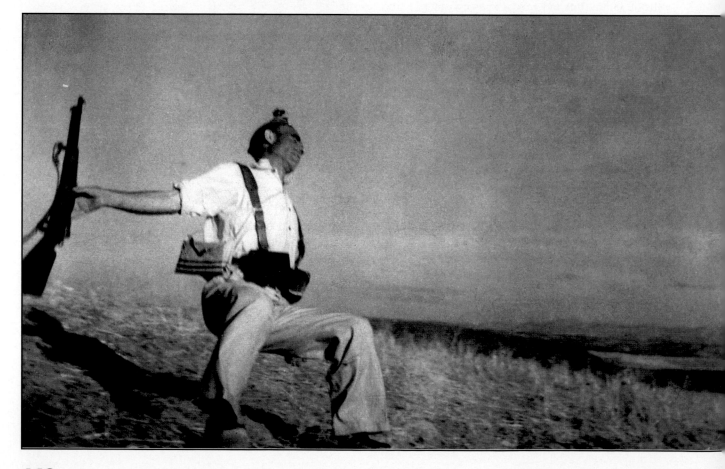

AGENCY SURVIVES DEATHS IN THE "FAMILY"

Magnum suffered a tremendous setback in 1954 when, within days of one another, Capa was killed by a land mine in Vietnam and Werner Bishof died in an accident in Peru. Two years later, Chim was killed while covering the aftermath of the Suez crisis between Egypt and Israel. After the death of two of its original founders and one of its members, Magnum lost direction, observes Russell Miller in *Magnum: Fifty Years at the Front Line of History*. Robert's brother Cornell then joined the agency and, according to Miller, helped steer it back on course. Magnum went on to attract some of the most outstanding photojournalists in the world.

Burt Glinn covered Fidel Castro's triumphant entrance into Havana after the overthrow of the Batista regime in Cuba. Philip Jones Griffiths produced a soul-searching book from his coverage of Vietnam that shattered many American myths about the country. He showed that everything happening in Vietnam was being done against the will of the people. Marc Riboud was one of the few outsiders to get into North Vietnam during the war.

In 1968 Magnum produced the book *America in Crisis*, which included its photographers' coverage of the assassinations of Martin Luther King and Bobby Kennedy, the rise of black power, and riots at the Democratic Convention in Chicago.

As big picture magazines like *Look*, *The Saturday Evening Post*, and, eventually, even *Life* folded, Magnum photographers survived by shooting corporate annual reports and advertisements in addition to editorial work.

THE COMPLICATED CAREER OF W. EUGENE SMITH

Perhaps the most influential, controversial, and well-remembered photographer ever to work for *Life* was W. Eugene Smith, who also was associated at different times with both Black Star and Magnum. He signed a contract with *Life* magazine in 1939, and subsequently shot many photos and photo essays for the magazine. He quit the magazine not once but twice. Smith resigned first in 1941 because he felt he was in an assignment rut at *Life*. He referred to his pictures at this time as having "a lot of depth-of-field but not much depth-of-meaning." He covered World War II first for Ziff-Davis Publishing Company and then was rehired by *Life*.

Obsessed with the gap between the reality of war and the comfortable headlines about war seen by the people back home, the 24-year-old correspondent hurled himself

Working with an unobtrusive Leica camera, Henri Cartier-Bresson roamed the streets of Seville looking for the combination of the perfect instant within the ideal composition. He called the combination the "decisive moment." Besides shooting for himself, Cartier-Bresson took on many magazine assignments around the world. Henri Cartier-Bresson © 1933, Magnum Photos, courtesy of Magnum Photos

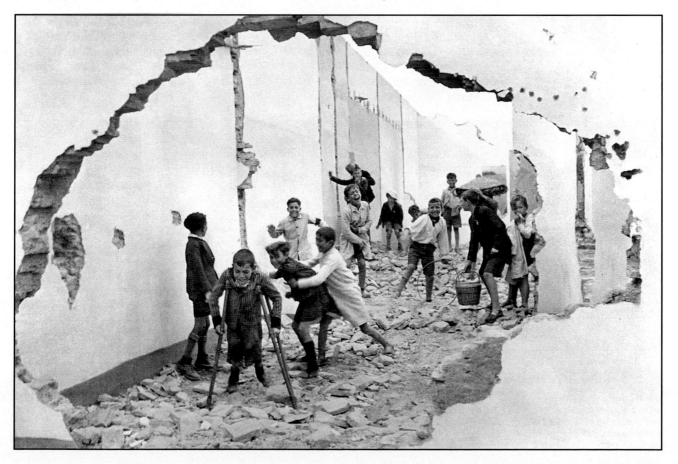

into the front lines, trying to catch on film the horror of killing. Smith followed 13 invasions, taking memorable pictures of the war—a tiny, fly-covered, half-dead baby held up by a soldier after being rescued from a cave in Saipan; a wounded soldier, bandaged, stretched out in Leyte Cathedral; a decaying Japanese body on an Iwo Jima beach.

Then, while shooting a story on a day in the life of a soldier, Smith was hit by a shell fragment that ripped through his left hand, his face, and his mouth—critically wounding him. Two years of painful convalescence followed.

In 1947, Smith resumed his work for *Life* magazine. During the next seven years, he produced his best-known set of photo essays: the exhausting dedication of a country doctor; the poverty and faith in a Spanish village; the pain of birth, life, and death being eased by a nurse midwife, Smith's own favorite essay. "In many ways, shooting these photos was the most rewarding experience photography has allowed me," said Smith of the midwife essay.

According to Jim Hughes's extensive biography, ***Shadow and Substance***, Smith himself was not an easy photographer to work with. While most *Life* staffers shot their assignments and shipped the film back to New York, Smith developed his own negatives and then held on to them. With control of his negatives, Smith could threaten to withdraw a story if he felt the editors were not going to play the photos accurately.

In 1954 Smith photographed the essay "Man of Mercy," about Dr. Albert Schweitzer and his leper colony in Africa. After carrying the Schweitzer essay back to America, Smith quarreled with *Life*'s editors about it. In a futile attempt to affect the use of pictures and captions, and to expand the Schweitzer layout, Smith resigned from *Life* a second time.

With the help of his wife, Eileen, Smith later photographed a moving story about the effects of mercury poisoning in Minamata, Japan, which was published first in *Life* and eventually appeared as a book, ***Minamata***.

PHOTOGRAPHERS COMPETE
RIVALRY AMONG AMERICAN NEWSPAPER PHOTOGRAPHERS

The success and style of the picture magazines had some important effects on newspaper photojournalism. The photo essay layout influenced many newspapers to adopt a similarly simple and direct arrangement of pictures about one subject. Likewise, newspapers began running more feature stories and using larger pictures.

Philadelphia boasted 20 daily newspapers during the 1920s and more than 200 press photographers. Their photos, however, ran without byline credit. During the Depression, however, many papers died. While newspapers competed for readers, press photographers competed for scoops. Photographers were not above sabotaging one another. Joe Costa, who worked for the *New York Morning World* and later the *Daily News*, recalled that photographers never let their camera bags out of their sight. He called it a "dog-eat-dog" business. A competitor might expose the film in a fellow photographer's

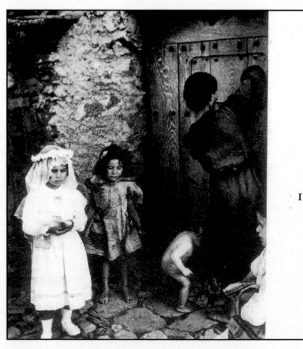

W. Eugene Smith's landmark essay "Spanish Village," for *Life* magazine, opens with a young girl preparing for confirmation and closes with a wake for a dead villager.
Life, April 9, 1951

holders or simply switch holders: the exclusive picture would be in the opposition's newspaper the next day!

On the other hand, photographers sometimes helped each other. A B-25 bomber, lost in the fog, crashed into the 79th floor of the Empire State Building. Glenn Lowry describes staffer Ernie Sisto's photographic heroics on behalf of the *Times* as well as his competitors in *Pictures of the Times: A Century of Photography from The New York Times*.

Sisto asked his competitors to hold him by the belt as he leaned perilously from the 81st floor to photograph the disaster. In return for the favor, he continued to dangle there while making an exposure for each of them.

Using the basic 4"x5" Speed Graphic, photographers of this period covered gangland slayings and bootlegged booze all without the aid of an exposure meter. Photographers determined most exposures by "guesstimations." The effective film index at this time was around ISO 25.

Guessing lighting exposures was just one of the shooting techniques photographers learned from one another, because few went to school to learn photojournalism. In fact, almost no universities prior to the 1940s offered photojournalism as a major. News photographers often got started as copyboys or copygirls on newspapers. If they expressed a leaning toward pictures, they could start an apprentice program in which they mixed chemicals and loaded film holders in the darkroom—progressing then to developing film and printing. They also carried equipment for photographers in the field. Moving from printing in the lab to covering news in the street was a major hurdle that took some photographers five years or more to leap, according to Sam Psoras, who started with International News Photos (INP) before joining the *Philadelphia Daily News*.

Photographers were held in low regard on some newspapers. Frank Gannett opined that "with the proper technology anyone could take pictures, even 'girls.'" The emphasis on some papers in the Gannett chain was on saving money, not taking great images.

One newspaper that maintained a large photographic staff was the *Milwaukee Journal*. Historically, the *Journal* staff worked under a unique setup. They were a part of the engraving department rather than the editorial department. Because they were part of the production team, large capital expenses for photo equipment did not shock them. As a result, the photo department instigated many technological advances, including the early use of the 35mm camera.

Staff photographer Brownie Rowland brought back a Leica from Germany, and Frank Scherschel was interested enough to borrow the little camera and try it out. History books credit Bob Dumke with inventing a synchronizing switch for his Speed Graphic that allowed him to shoot flash pictures in daylight. Ed Farber developed the portable electronic strobe for covering news events. The *Journal* continued to experiment with color pictures throughout the paper during the Depression.

The *Des Moines Register and Tribune* also was noted for outstanding use of pictures. In 1928, the paper bought an airplane and hired a pilot to transport film from rural areas of Iowa. In the latter half of the 1930s, the trade journal *Quill and Scroll* ranked this paper first in the number of pictures published.

The New York Times began hiring a staff of full-time photographers to cover local events in the early 1920s, and by 1927 sent photographers to cover Lindbergh's arrival in Paris following his solo flight across the Atlantic. It took more than a week for the pictures to return to New York by boat from Europe. Luckily for *The Times*, someone had taken a head shot of Lindbergh before he launched his historic flight.

A plane crashed into the Empire State Building and tore a hole between the 78th and 79th floors. With the help of his fellow press photographers, Ernie Sisto of *The New York Times* leaned out a window above the crash to take this picture. He then took pictures for everyone else who helped. Ernie Sisto, *New York Times*

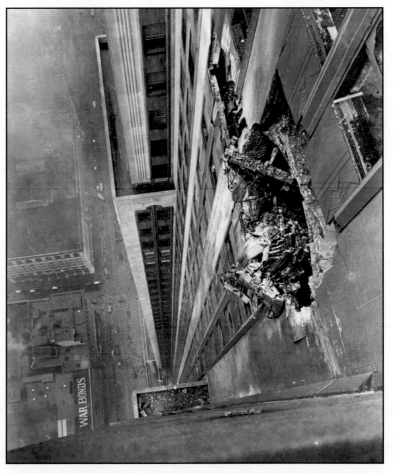

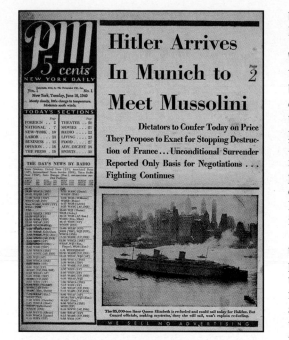

A PROGRESSIVE VISUAL NEWSPAPER

PM, a short-lived, liberal tabloid, exhibited the most progressive and modern use of pictures by a newspaper. Founded in 1940 by Ralph Ingersoll, who previously had helped edit *Time* and *Life*, the paper combined the textual approach of the newsweekly with the visual approach of the picture magazine in a daily, tabloid newspaper. The tabloid hired the best photographers of the day, including Weegee and Margaret Bourke-White. The paper was beautifully printed with special ink and stapled so that the pages would not fly apart. Its sections, with eight consecutive pages of full-page pictures, constituted an approach that was unheard of in its day and, in fact, has been rarely if ever seen since.

The crusading paper used photographs to document its exposés, including one series on the unsanitary conditions in the New York poultry market.

Researcher Cindy M. Brown, in "*PM*: Just Another Picture Paper?" reports that *PM* not only ran more pictures than its New York rivals—including the *Post*, *Sun*, and *Mirror*—but that it ran them larger and grouped them in a more storytelling way. In fact, the paper approached a 50-50 picture-text split, unheard of in today's newspapers. Brown wrote that *PM* not only ran more visually interesting pictures, but the pictures had stronger compositional elements than did its rivals. *PM's Weekly*, the paper's Sunday edition, featured a gallery of full-page photographs. The paper crusaded against racism and the excesses of big business. Unfortunately, relying on newsstand sales and subscriptions alone, *PM* eventually died, because it contained no advertising and thus lacked sufficient revenues to survive.

WAR CENSORSHIP

World War II produced corpses in abundance, but American citizens saw few dead soldiers during the war. When they did, it was thanks to the U.S. government's attempt to influence public opinion. This censorship was not new. During the entire 19 months of American involvement in World War I, the government prohibited publication of any photographs of dead American soldiers. A similar prohibition lasted for the first 21 months of American involvement in World War II.

However, unlike World War I, in which the government tried to completely restrict photographers' access to the front lines, photojournalists during World War II could move freely on battlefields and accompany naval assaults. Photographers could shoot where, when, and what they wanted, but all exposed film was screened by two layers of censors—one in the field and another in Washington. Early in the war, censors placed all photographs of dead and badly wounded Americans in a secret Pentagon file known to officials as the "Chamber of Horrors."

Initially, censors were worried that if the population saw pictures of dead American soldiers they would press for a compromise settlement with Germany and Japan. Later, as government leaders became concerned about public complacency brought on by Allied victories, they released some of these photographs of war's brutality. For example, published George Strock's photograph of three American soldiers lying dead on Buna Beach in New Guinea. After almost two years of American involvement in the war, this photo was the first released to show dead American soldiers. The *Washington Post* said it was time that the government treated Americans as adults, and that photographs "can help us to understand something of what has been sacrificed for the victories we have won." Yet even the Post went on to say "an overdose of such photographs would be unhealthy."

But until the war's end and after, the government continued to censor photographs of mutilated or emotionally distressed American soldiers, even though more than a million soldiers suffered psychiatric symptoms serious enough to debilitate them for some period. The censors held back any pictures showing racial conflicts at American bases, and other visual evidence of disunity or disorder. In ***The Censored War***, George Roeder tells how American opinions about World War II were manipulated both by wartime images that citizens were allowed to see and by the images that were suppressed.

Until the Normandy invasion of Europe, photographs had to be passed through the long chain of official headquarters and censors. The photographs taken by W. Eugene Smith on Guam appeared in *Life* some three or four months after the event. It was only with the invasion of Europe that pictures were processed on the spot and made immediately available for publication. By then, the Allies were winning, observes Jorge Lewinski in his book, ***The Camera at War***.

Following the war, photojournalists recorded the result of some of the most horrible crimes the world had ever seen. Photographers were present when the Allied forces opened the gates of German concentration camps and found stacks of emaciated corpses waiting for the crematorium. The written accounts were incredible and, in fact, were often not believed, according to Vicky Goldberg and Robert Silberman, authors of ***American Photography, A Century of Images***. The photographs, however, provided indisputable evidence of Hitler's attempted genocide of Jews, homosexuals, and gypsies. "The pictures had confirmed a degree of evil the world has yet to come to terms with," they wrote.

KOREAN WAR

At the beginning of the Korean War, photographers operated under a system of voluntary censorship. However, on November 2, 1950, American troops came into direct contact with Chinese forces as the Chinese Communist army entered the war in full strength.

What followed was a long and difficult retreat covered by the media. Embarrassed personally, General Douglas MacArthur ended the voluntary censorship system and imposed full military censorship on news media. Before the general clamped down, photographers had covered all aspects of the Korean War. Despite relatively free access, and limited only by self-censorship, fewer than five percent of the photos published by *Life*, *Newsweek*, and *Time* were actual combat photos.

VIETNAM WAR

The same reticence about showing soldiers under fire did not hold true for America's next war. During at least part of the Vietnam War, 40 percent of the published pictures run by *Life*, *Newsweek*, and *Time* portrayed soldiers in the heat of battle, according to a study by Michael Sherer. The American public saw more of the brutal side of combat during the Tet offensive alone in Vietnam than during all the major battles in Korea.

During the Vietnam War, images of dead and wounded, plus photographs of people in immediate, life-threatening situations, were offered to the public on a regular basis.

Did Photography End the Vietnam War?
Certainly no one claims that pictures stopped World War I or II or even the Korean War. How could pictures have caused the U.S. government to pull out of Vietnam?

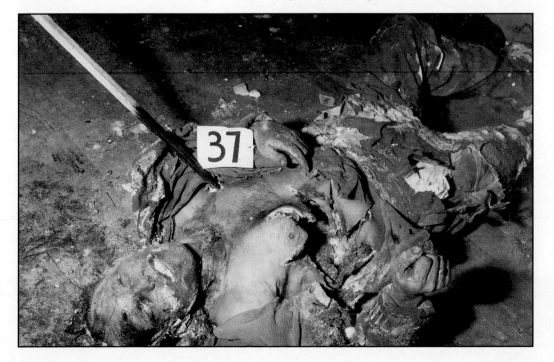

This World War II photo of a frozen American soldier with a stake driven through his body was censored by the U.S. government for fear of discouraging citizens on the home front. Courtesy of the National Archives

People who lived through the Vietnam War era, its controversies, and its termination as adults often mention several images that remain anchored in their minds.

The first is of the Buddhist monk who set himself afire—after notifying the news media—to protest the Diem regime's treatment of Buddhists in South Vietnam in 1963 (below). Although the country was primarily Buddhist, the Diems were Catholic. The monks felt that the Diem regime, a puppet government of the United States, repressed the Buddhists. The shocking picture showed readers dramatically and convincingly how serious the country's problems were. The monk used his death as the ultimate form of political expression. Although *The New York Times* originally refused to publish Malcolm Browne's photograph for the Associated Press, many other newspapers across the United States did run the image.

Another powerful image often cited from the Vietnam War was taken by photojournalist Eddie Adams. On February 1, 1968, a South Vietnamese chief of national police, General Nguyen Ngoc Loan, summarily executed a suspected Viet Cong guerrilla prisoner in the street in front of Adams' camera (see page 381). The photo captured the brutality of the war and demonstrated the lack of democracy in the country America was defending.

The third iconic image from the Vietnam War was taken in June 1972. Nine-year-old Phan Thi Kim Phuc was seeking refuge from a battle when napalm-loaded explosives dropped by American bombers scorched her tiny body. Nick Ut captured her agony in one of history's most memorable images. *Life* editors said that this photo more than any other exposed the American conscience to the full horror of the Vietnam War.

Other images from the Vietnam War include those of the My Lai Massacre. While the press had published a story about Lt. William Calley, who was charged with murdering South Vietnamese civilians, the nation only took note after they saw the images of the bodies of women and children taken by Ron Haeberle, an army photographer who had gone into My Lai with the troops.

Taken by college student John Filo, the photo of an anguished young woman grieving over the body of a slain Kent State

This picture of a monk's self-immolation protesting the Diem regime's treatment of Buddhists in South Vietnam has been credited as a factor that helped to change American opinion about the Vietnam War.
Malcolm Browne, Associated Press

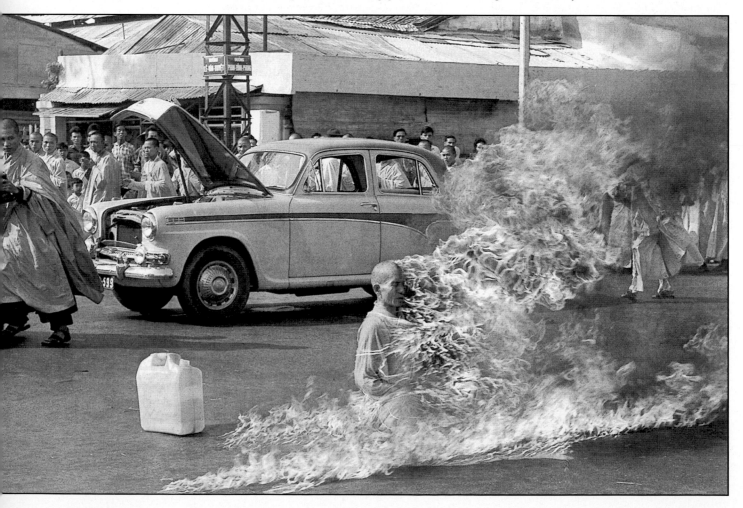

student, one of four killed by Ohio National Guardsmen on May 4, 1970, showed Americans killing Americans in their own country because of a war halfway around the world. The photo fueled campus strikes and student activism. Huge marches on Washington followed the Kent State killings.

Did these images change public opinion toward the Vietnam War? Did they cause the nation to change its political course and withdraw from the conflict?

The images appeared over a long span of time ranging from 1963 to 1972. Unlike the more recent images of the Iraqi prison debacle at Abu Ghraib that have saturated today's media, the iconic images from Vietnam were seen only sparingly at the time they were taken and published.

Unlike the prison images from Abu Ghraib, the Vietnam images did not appear on the cover of nearly every news magazine in the world almost simultaneously. They did not dominate the airwaves every night and the front pages every morning. Rather, the images from Vietnam provided a slow drip, drip, drip effect on the American conscience.

Perhaps the reason we now associate that war was these images is that they have been seen repeatedly since 1972. For more than 30 years, one of those iconic images accompanies any story or broadcast about the Vietnam War. Perhaps because of their constant repetition, the images have been drummed into the minds of readers and viewers. The question remains whether the pictures of the executions in the streets of Saigon by Eddie Adams or the napalmed child taken by Nick Ut caused the Vietnam War to end.

James Nachtwey, the renowned contemporary combat photographer, has considered the question of whether his images can stop war. He says that it would be unlikely that an image could stop a war, but that he hoped the images over time added up to change people's thinking about the conflicts he covered.

THE RISE OF PROFESSIONALISM
PHOTOGRAPHERS ORGANIZE

As the public began to recognize such names as Margaret Bourke-White and Alfred Eisenstaedt, photographers began to achieve parity with writers.

Originally, the photographer was a second-class citizen in the newsroom. According to one common story, when a news photographer's job opened up, the editor would find the nearest janitor and hand him a camera, telling him to set the lens at f/8 and shoot.

Frank Luther Mott, former dean of journalism at the University of Missouri, wrote that news photographers had long been "looked upon as queer fellows—half artist and more than half roughneck, and his product was referred to as 'embellishment of a story or a feature.'" In a *Library Journal* book review, Michael Rogers describes photographers of the period as "whiskey-breathed news hacks and cigar-chomping shutterbugs leering out from behind weathered and monstrous 4"x5" Speed Graphics."

Attached to their Speed Graphics were light saber flashes and no. 2 press bulbs. Because the range of the flash was only about 10 to 12 feet, the photographers needed to be close to their subjects.

They carried PRESS cards tucked into the bands of sweat-stained fedoras. News photographers were thought of as the people who chased fires and took cheesecake pictures. Taking cheesecake pictures involved meeting incoming passenger ships to take snaps of pretty women with "lots of leg showing."

And when the press photographers were not firing their hot flash bulbs in the face of criminal suspects or movie starlets, they often tried to show life as they hoped it might be: comic, slapstick moments, real or otherwise—innocent children playing, puppy dogs, flowers, curvy beauty queens. Their daily assignments often included crime scenes, setup public relations photo opportunities, gag pictures, sports, handshakes among businessmen, and check-passing ceremonies.

In the newsroom, photographers were not equals of their pen-toting brethren. Editors often referred to photographers as "reporters with their brains knocked out."

In their article "Sixty Years of NPPA," Marianne Fulton and Donald R. Winslow report, "Movies were the popular new entertainment of the day, and in just one postwar year, six major movies portrayed press photographers as unsophisticated slugs, slippery double-dealers, rough and tumble denizens of the lower classes. Cigar smokers. Bums."

After experiencing the respect and responsibility that came with wearing the nation's uniform during World War II, press photographers came back to a life where they were not even allowed to enter the front doors of hotels or lobbies, but were instead required to use the "service entrance" around back, Fulton and Winslow note.

In part to gain respect in the newsroom and as well as from the public, Burt Williams, a photographer with the *Pittsburgh Sun-Telegraph*, started organizing a professional association for photographers in 1945—The National Press Photographers Association.

Photographers were even being attacked at this time. Williams thought that an organization should be established to "protect the working press photographer on the job." He began talking about it with Charles J. Mack of MGM News of the Day (Metrotone News) in Washington, D.C., and with Joe Costa of the *New York Daily News* in Manhattan.

According to Claude Cookman's history of the organization, *A Voice Is Born*, Williams obtained financial backing for the organization from the Cigar Institute of America and began the groundwork with a 10-city coast-to-coast telephone conference in which leaders in press photography took part. At a meeting in New York City on February 23 and 24, 1946, the group adopted a constitution and elected officers: Joseph Costa, *New York Daily News*, president; Burt Williams, *Pittsburgh Sun-Telegraph*, secretary; and Charles Mack, Hearst Metrotone News, treasurer.

The organization started a magazine, *National Press Photographer*, edited by Costa, and created the annual Flying Short Course, an intense one-day professional development workshop held in different cities across the country during the same week. The goal of the ambitious effort was to raise standards of photojournalism across the country. U.S. Air Force Colonel Bill Lookadoo arranged for a transport plane and pilot to take the photo faculty from city to city as long as they also made a stop or two at Air Force bases along the way to conduct the same workshops for military photographers.

Of the 700 members in the organization by its second year, only six were women. At the second convention of NPPA, held in Atlantic City, the organization put on its own Miss NPPA beauty contest.

NPPA started running contests even before it formalized its own charter. The first contest was run for the Cigar Institute of America, perhaps the reason many cameramen of the day smoked stogies. In 1948 they started "The Best Picture of My Life" competition. It was won by AP photographer Murray Becker for his picture of the airship Hindenburg exploding in Lakehurst, New Jersey.

Today the organization still hosts an annual conference, continues to operate the annual Flying Short Course and other educational seminars, publishes an attractive, well-written magazine, *News Photographer*, and maintains an informative web site, where it hosts a lively discussion forum. With more than 10,000 members including pros and students, the association also administers a major photojournalism contest and sponsors professional development workshops in video photojournalism and electronics.

FORMAL EDUCATION SPREADS

The first college grad to work on the picture side of a newspaper was Paul Thompson, who graduated from Yale in 1902.

In 1943, the University of Missouri hired Cliff Edom to teach news photography. Edom had never been a newspaper or magazine photographer and had never taught journalism. At the time the school had no major in

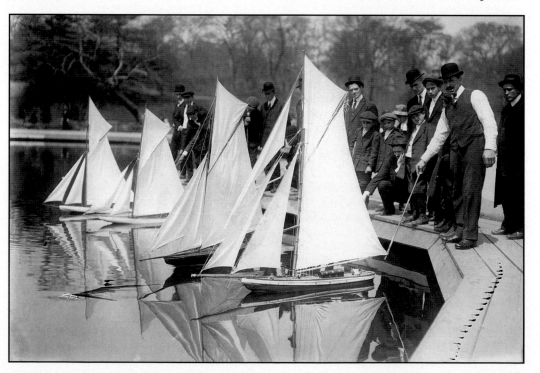

Bain News Photographic Service provided a steady supply of photos, including light feature pictures like this one, to member papers around the country. Bain Collection, Library of Congress

the subject. In fact, the word photojournalism had yet to be coined.

Despite his inexperience, Edom had a vision. Along with his teaching duties, Edom sought a way to bring to the isolated Midwest college town the work of the finest professionals. He created a contest, which came to be known as the "Pictures of the Year Contest." Thus, his students had the opportunity to view the contest entries and then to meet the professionals who came to collect their awards. The contest served to further professionalize the field by recognizing the work of America's best image-makers. Edom also created the week-long Missouri Photo Workshop, to which he recruited well-known picture editors to coach young or mid-career photojournalists seeking more hands-on training in the field.

Today many schools offer courses and even degrees in photojournalism. More than 90 colleges and universities offer at least one class in news photography. Some universities even grant a PhD. in journalism or communications with an emphasis in photojournalism.

DISTRIBUTING PICTURES ACROSS THE LAND
BAIN CREATES A PICTURE SERVICE

In 1895, a newspaper writer and photographer, George Grantham Bain, started the Bain News Photographic Service in New York City. As manager of the Washington, D.C., United Press office in the 1890s, Bain realized that he could accumulate pictures on his own and sell them to subscribers.

After leaving United Press, he began his own photo service. He catalogued and cross-indexed photographs he had bought from correspondents or newspapers that subscribed to his service. From newspapers throughout the country, he received pictures, copied them, and sent the copies to his list of subscribing newspapers. Bain's business expanded rapidly and, by 1905, he had acquired a million news photographs. Many of his pictures were the first of their kind, including the first federal courtroom pictures, the first photos of the Senate in session, and the first automobile race. Although a massive fire in 1908 completely destroyed Bain's archives, he immediately set about rebuilding his collection.

OTHER PHOTO SERVICES ENTER THE PICTURE

Other picture services developed, including Underwood & Underwood (1896), which started out making stereoscopic pictures. Newspaper editors would call on the Underwoods for pictures to illustrate stories about remote countries where they had operators. Two brothers, the Browns, circulation managers on *Harper's Weekly*, also decided to exploit the possibilities of selling news pictures to publications.

Soon the Underwood, Brown, and Bain photographers were all competing for scoops.

In 1907 United Press (UP) was founded. Originally called United Press Associations, it was a creation of E.W. Scripps. The much older Associated Press (1848) had refused to sell its news stories to several of Scripps' papers. Scripps believed that news should be available to anyone, including his competitors, according to Gary Haynes in his history of United Press International, ***Picture This: The Inside Story and Classic Photos of UPI***.

By 1919 the Hearst organization formed International News Photos (INP). Wide World Photos, which was started by *The New York Times*, followed. In 1923 Acme News Pictures appeared. The Associated Press News Photo service began in 1927. By 1933, some 50 photographic news services were operating in New York.

According to Haynes, a former UPI editor, photo news agencies often got their images from Paramount Pictures' newsreels by making prints directly from the film. This frame-grab technique would be reincarnated 75 years later as photojournalists began taking frame grabs from high definition video to publish in newspapers and on web sites.

These services sent their pictures by train, giving a tip to the porter to hand-deliver the package of photos for extra-quick service. Local event photos were no longer limited to the immediate area. If the picture had enough sensational interest or sex appeal, it could be sent around the world.

For pictures from Europe or the Far East, photographs were sent by ship to the United States. In New York harbor, speedboats hired by the various picture services like Wide World Photos or INP retrieved packets of

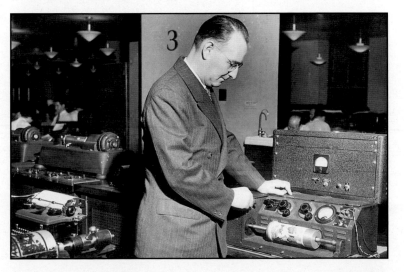

Transmitters like this Associated Press machine did for photographers in the 1930s what the telegraph had done for writers prior to the Civil War. The device allowed photographers to send pictures by wire across the country and eventually around the world. Courtesy of the Associated Press

photos dropped from the incoming ships. Acme and INP later combined into United Press International (UPI), and Wide World Photos became part of the Associated Press (AP).

AGENCE FRANCE-PRESSE

Agence Havas, the predecessor to Agence France-Press, was created in 1835 and actually pre-dated U.S. news services. Its photo service was created in the 1930s and until 1985 focused primarily on France and French-speaking Africa. The agency worked out agreements with AP and UPI to provide images from other parts of the world. Agence Havas, which had continued operating during World War II, was nationalized following the war and renamed Agence France-Presse.

INSTANT PICTURE TRANSMISSION

Ever since newspapers began publishing pictures, the search was on for a way to transport the images quickly over long distances. As early as 1907, Professor Alfred Korn of the University of Munich, Germany, had demonstrated an electrical system using a photocell that would transmit and receive a picture over a telegraph wire. A "Photographic Fac-Simile Telegraph"—a picture of the German Crown Prince—illustrated the new technology on the cover of *Scientific American*.

In the same year, *L'Illustration* of Paris and the *London Daily Mirror* inaugurated a cross-channel service that later included other capitals of Europe.

In 1924 Dr. Herbert Ives of Bell Labs demonstrated an experimental "telephotography" machine that a year later, the American Telephone and Telegraph Co. (AT&T) used to send a photo of Calvin Coolidge being sworn in as president to newspapers in three cities simultaneously.

In 1925 the first permanent transmission line was set up in the United States when AT&T opened a commercial wire linking New York, Chicago, and San Francisco. It was first come, first served, and cost $60 to send a picture coast-to-coast.

On May 1, 1926, the first commercial radio photograph, using technology created by Radio Corporation of America (RCA), was transmitted from London and appeared on page one of *The New York Times*. The picture of the Viceroy of India, Sir W. Mitchell Thompson, had been made three days earlier. Due to bad weather, the transmission took two hours. The transmitted image is shown below.

The original transmitted photos were often of such poor quality as to be almost unrecognizable. Often they had to be resent due to lightning, static, and other troubles. After spending $2.8 million, AT&T abandoned its first system.

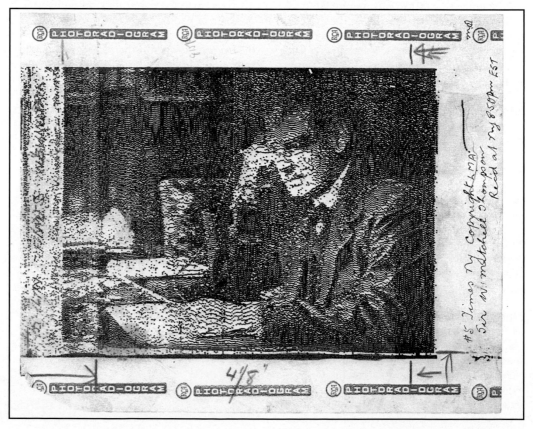

This picture isn't pixelated. It is called a photoradiogram. This portrait of Sir W. Mitchell Thompson was sent wirelessly by transoceanic radio "Fac-Simile" (the forerunner of the fax machine) from England to New York. Because of bad weather, the transmission took two hours.

AT&T sold its second wire transmission service to the Associated Press in 1934. Many AP subscriber newspapers tried to block the sale because of the $5 million cost, a major expense during the Depression. Besides the steep cost, Frank Knox of the *Chicago Daily News* claimed that there would only be two pictures a day worth sending by wire. In the end, though, the AP bought the Bell Lab equipment, leased AT&T wire, and set up 25 stations. On January 1, 1935, the AP transmitted an aerial picture of a plane wreck in the Adirondack Mountains, and the age of rapid photo transmission began in the United States.

Soon other picture services, including International News Photos and Acme, started their own wire transmission networks. For a long time, such uncontrollable factors as poor weather wrecked the quality of pictures sent on long-distance transmission lines. Even worse, pictures sent across the Atlantic by radiophoto were often fuzzy and indistinct.

Even so, newspapers and magazines used the transmitted pictures because they could accompany the immediate story rather than appear days after the news had broken, according to Jonathan Coopersmith in his paper "From Lemons to Lemonade: The Development of AP Wirephoto."

By 1936, only the tabloid *New York Daily News* subscribed to AP's pricey service, which charged $150,000 per year.

By the same year, Acme Newsphotos (owned by Scripps) had developed its own machines called "Telephoto," which were more sophisticated and reliable than AP's, and capable of better quality, according to Gary Haynes in *Picture This: The Inside Story and Classic Photos of UPI*. Acme scored a scoop by securing exclusive rights to all photographs taken of the first quintuplets to survive, the Dionne quintuplets, who were born in 1934. With their hair carefully curled and wearing identical dresses, the five little girls grabbed the attention of newspaper readers—and forced papers to subscribe to the Acme photo service.

Smaller wire services like Acme had to outsmart the competition from the AP. For example, Acme located its darkroom and transmitter inside the 1948 Democratic National Convention in Philadelphia, thus sending images to its clients in fewer than 30 minutes. AP and INP had off-site darkrooms requiring more turn-around time.

United Press (UP), which had no photo service of its own until 1952, absorbed Scripps' Acme Newsphotos and introduced in 1954 the Unifax, a revolutionary machine that required no operator. Pictures could be viewed as they came in on a continuous roll of inexpensive electrolytic paper. Now the UP's pictures were within reach of the country's smallest newspapers. In 1958 United Press absorbed the International News Service and became UPI.

In 1960 the Associated Press sent a picture of President Eisenhower from Cedar Rapids, Iowa, to Dallas, Texas. The clear, crisp image was the first to be relayed by satellite, which eliminated interference from bad weather or the poor condition of long-distance land lines.

Sending pictures from the road could be arduous. When President Lyndon Johnson was traveling to Australia in 1968 he stopped in Pago Pago, American Samoa, for a few hours to give a speech while his plane refueled. UPI's staffer transmitted from Pago Pago the first images ever wired from that country using the 700 pounds of extra equipment he had lugged along, a feat hard to imagine in the digital age.

While the technology for taking and sending images has steadily improved, the market for still images has shifted. By 1960 the number of households that took a daily newspaper began a steady decline. This resulted in newspapers closing across the country. Afternoon papers were often the first to fold. While before World War II most cities had at least two daily papers and some as many as eight, few American cities today still have competing dailies.

After a long struggle for economic survival, including periods where their freelancers were not paid, UPI was absorbed into Reuters' picture operation. The agency's 11.5-million picture library was sold to the Bettman Archive, later to become part of Corbis, which houses them for protection in a cave in Pennsylvania.

Instead of cheesecake photos taken with flash-on-camera, today's photojournalist can produce creative and expressive photographs and even videos. These story-telling pictures, taken with available light or light from portable strobes, can capture candid moments that were impossible in those days of *The Daily Graphic*. And from laptop computers, satellite transmissions, and even cell phones, today's candid moments are being transmitted around the world within minutes of when photographers shoot them. ■

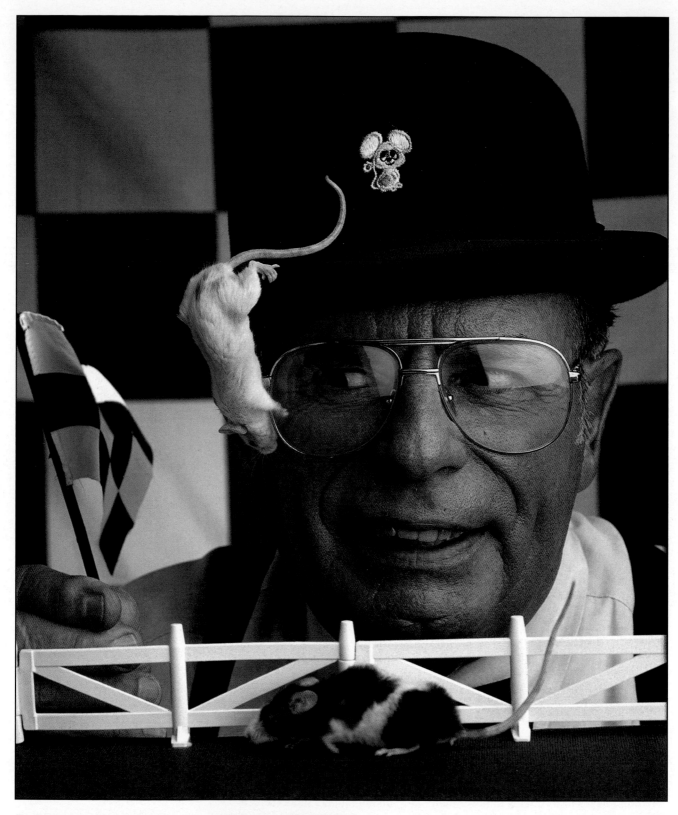

The photographer received an assignment from *People* magazine to take a picture of this retired aerospace engineer, who began racing mice after he stopped designing fighter jets. The magazine paid a day rate for the assignment but would have upped the fee had the picture run on the cover. The copyright belongs to the photographer, not to the magazine. Keith Philpott, for *People* magazine

Turning Pro

MAKING A LIVING IN PHOTOJOURNALISM

Breaking into photojournalism is hard to do, says Jim McNay, a former newspaper photographer, photo editor, professor of photojournalism at San Jose State University and Brooks Institute of Photography, and contributor to this chapter. You will find here advice from him and two other professionals who have "been there" and beyond. McNay takes on internships, workshops, and contests. David Weintraub, a freelance photographer and book author, spells out the how-to's of the business of freelance photojournalism. Pulitzer Prize-winner John Kaplan, now a professor at the University of Florida, outlines the essentials of a journalistic portfolio.

SO YOU WANT TO FREELANCE

by David Weintraub

Can you make a living in photojournalism? Most photographers who do follow one of two routes: staff or freelance. There are about 1500 daily newspapers in the United States, and most of these use staff photographers. There are also many weekly and alternative newspapers that use staffers. Some large magazines employ staff photographers, but these positions are few and hard to get; most magazines rely on freelancers. If you are a staff photographer, you are usually an employee of the publication. This means you are paid a salary, have taxes withheld from your paycheck, and are generally provided with equipment, supplies, and benefits such as health insurance and a pension plan. In return, you give up your copyright to the photographs made under the terms of your employment—the publication owns the pictures you create for it. Depending on the terms of your employment, you may or may not receive a share of any income the publication receives from reselling your work.

If you choose the freelance route, you will join the ranks of the self-employed. Being self-employed is a dream many people share. You strike out on your own, set your own schedule, and earn your living by your wits and talent. But there are some hard realities to consider.

First, you have to be a damn good photographer, because you probably will be competing for each and every job, at least until you build up a steady clientele.

Second, you need to have substantial savings, or be gainfully employed, to finance your venture. And third, you have to be skilled in all aspects of running a business, including marketing, self-promotion, negotiating, sales, bookkeeping, financial planning,

---

PORTFOLIO: CONTENT FIRST

by John Kaplan, University of Florida

A strong photojournalism portfolio needs to demonstrate versatility. For newspaper work, this means a command of news, sports, features, and picture stories. A portfolio does not have to include every category, but to work at better publications and compete in portfolio competitions, picture stories are absolutely essential. Magazine photojournalism portfolios may instead be highly specialized, but those first breaking into the business almost always get their start at a paper.

The best portfolios are intimate and filled with emotion. They have a point of view and a fresh vision that goes beyond a merely literal interpretation of a scene. However, to fall back on a cliché, "Do not put the cart before the horse." Look first to tell any story well through photography, with technically solid pictures that can be understood and appreciated by any reader. Quit trying so hard to be deep or subtle, or to impart secondary meaning in your work. Be sure that your pictures communicate on a primary, visceral level. Let your style and strengths evolve naturally rather than forcing yourself into a formula.

Virtually all photojournalism portfolios are now submitted to editors electronically on disk. Often, photojournalists send links to their web sites, too. But don't include links to personal, conversational blogs, or MySpace pages. Instead, let your pictures do the talking. Recent trends in packaging include submitting the portfolio in HTML or PDF formats; both are universally readable in both Mac and Windows. With today's growing emphasis on multimedia storytelling, consider sending at least one tightly edited Soundslides picture story, too.

Consistently ranked as one of the finest small newspapers in the nation, the *Concord* (New Hampshire) *Monitor* is able to hire many of the brightest young photojournalists. It does not pay as well as some larger papers, but photographers clamor to work or intern there because it uses pictures superbly and can be a stepping-stone to other opportunities. Its director of photography, Dan Habib, started at a newspaper and later became an award-winning freelancer doing assignments for *People*, *Time*, and *Fortune*. Habib returned to newspapers because "I missed having some control over my work and how it gets published. I also like having a close connection with a community."

Known for his thoughtful feedback, Habib sends a letter to each job or intern candidate that gets at the crux of what most editors want to see. Here's an excerpt:

"Those who reached the final round had a few things in common. They had at least one strong photo story, which showed an ability to obtain access to intimate and difficult situations. Original ideas are a big bonus. Stories are often the best forum for a photographer to convey a sensibility for subtle moments and strong journalistic instincts.

"Stories were complemented by diverse singles, a range of sports, spot news, general news and features. They demonstrated technical proficiency, ideally in color and black-and-white, as well as the use of flash. The top contenders had unusual, complex compositions as well as tight, high-impact moments. All of the photographs were thoughtfully composed and cropped, and led the viewer's eye through the frame."

In terms of editing and packaging, Habib likes to see one picture story and eight to twelve singles for an internship application. From an experienced photographer seeking a job, he expects two strong stories and ten to fifteen single images. Badly toned or poorly printed images hurt the package, he says. "Most editors agree that if photographers can't create well-toned images for their portfolio, they may not make technically excellent photos every day."

Habib receives stacks of portfolios in many forms. Whatever the packaging, he says, "what really sets a portfolio apart is good emotion with socially relevant subject matter. Photographers get so caught up in their vision they forget that editors want to see sports, too, particularly shot with long lenses."

Excerpted from *Photo Portfolio Success*, Writers Digest Books, 2003
www.photoportfoliosuccess.com

and time management. Of course, as your business grows, you may be able to outsource some or all of these tasks. But initially, they all rest on your shoulders.

Ask yourself if this sounds like a challenge you look forward to meeting, and answer honestly. The best time to find out you are not suited for self-employment is before you dive in.

Peter Howe, who served as director of photography at *Life* and as picture editor for the *New York Times Magazine*, spent 13 years as a freelance photojournalist. He says a newspaper staff job, an internship with a publication (see pages 458–459), stringing for a wire service, or assisting an established photographer are all great training for a career as a freelance photojournalist. When you are ready to freelance, having a great portfolio and lots of persistence is essential. Howe also advises finding a project to work on, something that will create a solid body of work. He cites the example of Lauren Greenfield, whose books **Fast Forward** and **Girl Culture** have kicked off a successful career in freelancing (see page 461).

Greenfield initially began photographing young girls growing up in Los Angeles, a world she understood and that was literally in her backyard. "Coming of age" has interest and relevance, says Howe, and Greenfield made a valuable contribution by documenting its many aspects in her books. The power of those personal projects has established her as a leading editorial photographer.

Be prepared to live on a tight budget, Howe cautions, because very few photojournalists get rich. In fact, he compares the profession to teaching or acting, which rely on passion rather than on financial rewards to attract practitioners. According to the Bureau of Labor Statistics' most recent data [May 2004] the top 10 percent of photographers earned no more than about $54,000 per year with the median income around $26,000.

AGENCIES

Are there other alternatives besides running the whole show yourself? Many leading photojournalists are members of agencies that handle many, if not all, of the business aspects, leaving the photographer to do what he or she does best—shoot pictures. Some agencies work with photographers with different shooting styles to appeal to a wide range of potential clients.

Agencies such as Corbis, Getty Images, Magnum, Black Star, Contact, VII, and Zuma circulate portfolios, pitch story ideas (either proposed by a photographer or by someone within the agency), get assignments, negoti-

ate rates and rights, maintain picture files, and explore resale possibilities for their photographers.

In return, an agency takes a percentage of the assignment and resale fees and, in some cases, controls the copyrights to their photographers' images. With international sales, both the rep in the other country and the agency take a cut of the proceeds.

In addition to copyright ownership, agency contracts may address questions of duration—how many years a photographer is signing up for—and exclusivity. Some photographers find the larger agencies to be impersonal and imperial, with a "take it or leave it" approach to percentages and rights.

Tip: If you have a unique picture of an important news event, you can approach an agency to handle the sale of that image even if you are not a member.

Jason Grow has looked at photography from all sides—as a newspaper staffer, an agency photographer, and a freelancer. He says agencies perform many valuable functions, especially for two groups of photographers. Up-and-coming photographers benefit from the stamp of approval and instant credibility that agency affiliation can bring. Established photographers who need help running their business affairs benefit from the agency's organizational and managerial skills. In return, Grow says, agencies take from 30 to 50 percent of assignment and reuse fees.

Agencies may also help with production, such as making travel arrangements and getting assistants in far-flung locations. Sometimes an agency will help pay for travel and materials so a photographer can shoot a story on his or her own. In that case, the agency will pursue publication outlets for the story to recoup its investment.

For many photographers, whether or not to sign with an agency is a purely economic decision. A photographer billing several hundred thousand dollars a year in fees might find an agency relationship worthwhile, whereas a photographer making $50,000 per year might prefer to continue solo, Grow says.

CONTRACT PHOTOGRAPHERS

Another option is to become a contract photographer for a magazine. Contract photographers are not staffers, but like staffers they enjoy some measure of financial stability. How does this work? Only elite publications like *National Geographic*, *Sports Illustrated*, and *Time* use contract photographers, and these plum positions are awarded to a select few. A contract photographer agrees to be available—in other words, to drop everything

By Jim McNay

Professional editors like to know a new hire can meet a deadline—regularly. They like to know a new staffer can produce pictures at an acceptable level—regularly. They like to see if someone has the inventiveness and passion to go beyond the ordinary picture or project—regularly.

And this is true whether the publication is in Scapoose, Oregon; Scooba, Mississippi; or Sacramento, California. Students who demonstrate these skills while in school—probably through internships—have the edge when it comes to landing a job.

Spending 10 to 12 weeks shooting two to five assignments a day lets you show you can come to grips with a new town, a new part of the country, perhaps a new regional culture, and still deliver solid storytelling pictures made in an unfamiliar landscape. Your resourcefulness to learn an unfamiliar town and get to know people in the community will be tested.

The resulting glowing reports from your bosses or supervisors will circulate among other editors with lightning speed. Other pros will be lining up to look at your portfolio, waiting for the chance to offer bigger challenges with the next internship or even your first job. Nothing beats a "win" at a publication. Any editor who happily nurtured a hard-working intern is going to be in that photographer's corner for a long time.

INTERNSHIP SEASON

Summer break is the traditional internship window. This is when publications across the nation expect to have interns and the budget to pay them. The traditional time to apply for summer internships is in January after the holiday break. Sometimes the internship hunt continues right up until June 1, when the only option left may be that night manager's job at Pup and Taco.

Many students start with internships at small publications and move up to larger ones in succeeding years.

Part of the good news is that an increasing number of excellent internships are offered year around.

RÉSUMÉ

Résumés should be standard. Include your contact information at the top: name, address, telephone, email address, cell phone and web site address.

Address the following:

*   **Educational background**, such your degrees, your current educational path. You need not review your high school career. Start with your current school first, the one immediately before that, and so forth.
*   **Employment history**, including your current job, followed by one or two before.
*   **Special skills, interests, or certifications**. Part of the aim of a résumé is to say something about yourself that separates you from the pack of other aspiring photographers out there. This is the place for scuba and water-safety certification and pilot's licenses. Foreign languages or overseas study experience are important to point out.

While no one wants to stifle creativity, your résumé is not where to get cutesy. Day-glow paper, angels flying across the page, glitter sprinkled on the paper will irritate, not endear you to, potential employers.

The creative challenge is to fit all this information on one page. For students just completing a degree (any degree, first or fourth) the bias is toward a one-page résumé, unless you have had a distinguished career in some other field.

This should leave room for about three references on the page. Listing references—with telephone numbers and email addresses—accelerates the process.

COVER LETTERS

The challenge is to write in an interesting way without slipping into silliness or bragging. A cover letter should briefly introduce you and explain why you are writing.

Touch on a couple of your college career highlights, such as work on the student or local newspaper, or a previous internship. Even if these are in the résumé, these are worth repeating since a potential employer may miss them at first glance. Explain what you did and what you learned from these different experiences.

Why do you want to intern for that news organization in that town? It helps to have looked at the publication or researched what happens in that part of the country. Avoid

saying you "like people" and your goal is to become "a photojournalist." These points are obvious and will not differentiate you from other applicants. Do, however, include aspects of your life that make you stand out such as experiences in which you have taken a leadership role, handled dangerous situations, or worked under pressure.

Wrap up the letter with a thank you. That's it. Oh, yes. As you address the letter ask yourself, how does the editor spell her name? Sarah or Sara? Or is his name John Smith or Jon Smyth?

Ya wanna know.

AFTER THE INTERNSHIP

No, it is not time to send flowers. But do maintain regular contact with your former editor. The best place to start is with a thank-you note. Make this a hand-written item on good paper found at a local stationary store. Like your portfolio, the stationary should be simple, clean, and professional. Thank the pro for his or her time. Say something about what you learned. Be brief, polite, and appreciative.

Follow up every couple of months with some examples of recent work. Editors like to see what you have done lately. A simple note with three or four recent pictures will keep you on an editor's radar screen. Class assignments printed on a basic printer are another fine opportunity for sharing work.

Emailed images may work, too, but only if you have asked if your editor is willing to accept them. Professionals are so flooded with excessive email that they may just hit delete before ever opening your file.

The idea is to keep your name in front of someone for whom you would like to work—either in the next internship, the one after, or perhaps for a job opening—without being an obnoxious pest. Most editors will appreciate your effort to stay in touch.

Bottom line: Follow up. Few students make the effort, so yours will make you easier to remember .

Krista Niles had recently begun a photojournalism internship at *The New York Times* when terrorists attacked the World Trade Center on September 11, 2001. Her friends' first news of her safety was when they saw a photo she had taken, right, in *The Times*. Her pictures, including the one to the right and the first one below it, were part of the coverage that won the *The New York Times* a Pulitzer Prize in news photography.

Part of Krista's first email to her friends after the attack is reproduced below with her permission. All photos by Krista Niles, © *The New York Times*

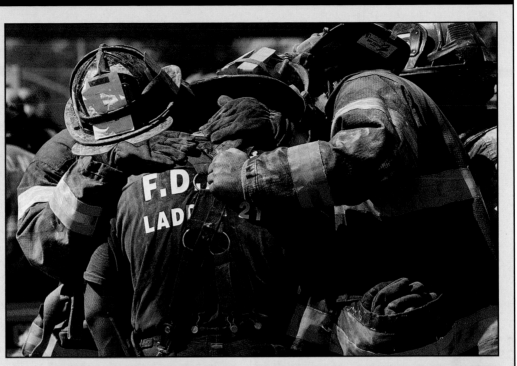

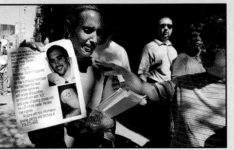

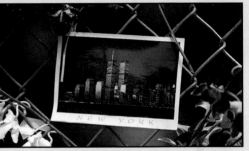

Subject:
i cannot even comprehend
Date:
Thu, 13 Sep 2001 19:26:07

hey gang. i am indeed alive, but not all that well.

i wish i could describe what i've seen these last three days, but my mind isn't functioning all that well... from physical and mental/emotional exhaustion.

i got on scene about 20 minutes after the towers fell... the last photos i shot as i was heading into the subway from brooklyn was of people watching the towers burning. when i finally got out from underground after train delays, i kept searching for the towers to orient myself...no towers to be found...thinking they were just blocked from view by the buildings in front of me it took a good while for me to realize that they had collapsed. i could see how the first may be fallen, but surely not both. and as i ran past thousands of people running the opposite way i wondered what the hell i was getting myself into. the thing i keep grappling with is this...in any accident, fire, disaster scene there are injured people running, being carried and being helped.

THERE WERE NO INJURED PEOPLE. NONE. not one person bleeding. not one person limping. not one person crying for help. nothing. it was quiet, except for explosions and shifting debris and shouting from police and firefighters trying to figure out how to rescue people.

i did not see a single injured civilian in the six hours i was at "ground zero"...and i was literally at the base less than 100 yards to my right and portions of the top about 200 yards to my left. i only saw one firefighter pulled from the debris.

the debris was amazing. a fine dust, inches thick, coated the entire area. breathing was impossible. thankfully i ran into co-nyt photographer angel franco who gave me a mask. my eyes are still recovering from all the dust.

angel and i were talking today about what we saw...and about the fine dust. as troubling as this is for me to put into words... that dust is the ash of people...mixed with cement and everything imaginable.

that thought kept running through my head as i kept walking. i just wanted to see one person...all i saw were helpless firefighters who were in such a state of shock they didn't know what to do, or how to start.

having been to the WTC observation deck (86/7th floor of tower 2) one month ago with my mother and sister at that same time of day, this was even more bizarre. i knew there had to be thousands of people in those buildings.

i'm still in shell-shock, especially after the last two days. yesterday and today i was photographing people looking for missing people. i cried today standing in front of a wall that was plastered with pictures of missing people. seeing their faces and names made it so real to me... especially since i know most of these people will never be found. i cried again when i had to ask people for caption information. some photos i have to force myself to take... the one that you all have seen is one of them. that firefighter in the center couldn't locate his brother, who was also a firefighter at the base of WTC1 when it collapsed. i keep telling myself that i have to document this horrible event. i just can't make much sense of it all.

I apologize for my stream of consciousness. thanks to all of you for your emails and concern. i send my best and i'll send some photos soon...
krista

and run—for a certain number of days each year to work for a particular publication. In return, the publication guarantees to pay the photographer an annual fee, which is determined by the number of days multiplied by the magazine's day rate. Both parties benefit, because the photographer receives a stable income and the publication gets the services of a top photographer. At the end of the year, the contract can be renewed, altered, or cancelled. Unlike staffers, contract photographers generally own the rights to their photographs. Some publications may demand ownership of published images, and there may also be restrictions when and where contract photographers can resell work originally made for their publications.

FREELANCE

In order to be a successful freelancer, you have to answer three questions. What do I do? Who buys what I do? How do I reach them and get work?

If you answered "I'm a photographer; I make pictures" to the first questions, take a deep breath and find a pad and pencil. Now write down all the things that photographers and photographs do: record events, capture decisive moments, communicate ideas, illustrate a story, grab the viewer's attention, and solve a client's visual-communication problems. Now get up close and personal. What do you love to photograph? What do you bring to the party? Every photographer has a set of life experiences, interests, and skills that inform his or her images. Successful photographers use these to develop a personal style—a way of seeing the world and expressing it visually. Ultimately, your personal style is what will help you develop a career.

On to question number two. Who buys what I do? Here is where your research skills come to the fore. Get that pad and pencil. Spend a couple of hours browsing the newspaper and magazine rack at your local library or bookstore. After a while, you should begin to get a sense of the types of pictures that get published, day after day, week after week.

See any that look like yours? See any that look better? Be honest. Or worse? Make a list of the publications you could shoot for today based on your skill level and expertise. Be brutally honest. Make another list of "dream" publications, ones you would love to work for someday, when your talents develop.

Magazines are particularly easy to research, because most have a masthead that shows the address and phone number of the editorial office, and the name of the art director, photo editor, or director of photography. Write these down.

Repeat this process whenever you find yourself near a collection of publications—this is a productive way to use the hour or so waiting at an airport for your flight.

Now you have got a basic list of newsstand, or consumer, publications, but this is just the tip of the iceberg. And it is the same list most photojournalists have. But there are many more publications out there besides *National Geographic*, *Time*, and *Newsweek*. These are the specialty, or trade, magazines that cater to a specific audience, group, profession, or industry. We are talking here about publications like *Construction Site News*, *Diagnostic Imaging*, *Information Week*, *Motorcycle Product News*, and *Poultry International*. You will not find trade publications on most newsstands, but many are listed in books such as **Photographer's Market**, and they also can be found on the web at *www.tradepub.com*. Researching trade publications involves making lots of phone calls to find out who assigns photography. This is boring, frustrating work, but it does pay off.
Tip: Do not just concentrate on publications located where you live. Newspapers and magazines that rely on freelancers need them to be where the stories are.

Also, do not forget the lucrative international market, with magazines such as *Paris Match* (France); *Airone*, *Focus*, and *Oggi* (Italy); and *Stern* and German *Geo* (Germany). Some of these have offices in the United States, usually in New York. As in the United States, many Sunday newspapers overseas have photography-rich magazines.

According to Peter Menzel, whose pictures routinely appear in publications around the world, there are three ways to work with overseas clients. The first is to deal with the publication directly and be assigned to cover a story. The second is to have agencies in various countries representing your stock photography. And the third is to resell stories that have appeared in U.S. publications. If you are interested in pursuing resale options, Menzel says, it is important not to sign away your rights when you take a magazine assignment. Menzel keeps in touch with editors via email, and supplies his 11 overseas agents with pictures and brief story descriptions.

REACH YOUR PROSPECTIVE CLIENTS

Now you are ready to answer question three: how to reach your prospective clients and get assignments. Do you have a killer portfolio? What about eye-grabbing mailers? Even with an Internet-based portfolio, these are essential if you are going to break into the competitive world of freelance photojournalism. A portfolio should represent your best work.

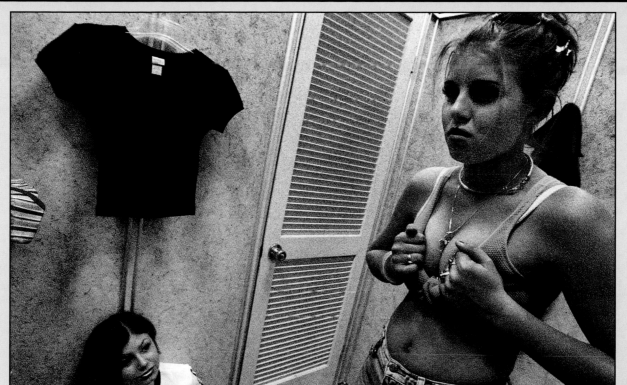

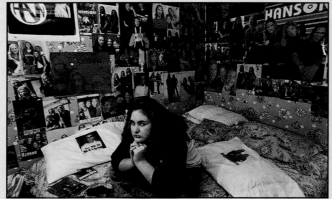

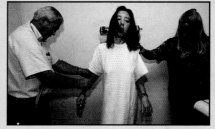

Sheena tries on clothes with her friend Amber, 14, in a department store dressing room in San Jose, California.

Lisa, 13, in her room, Edina, Minnesota.

Erin, 24, is blind-weighed at an eating disorder clinic in Coconut Creek, Florida. She has asked to mount the scale backward so as not to see her weight gain.

by Lauren Greenfield

Girl Culture has been my journey as a photographer, as an observer of culture, as part of the media, as a media critic, as a woman, as a girl.

These photographs are both very personal and very public. ...They are about the girls I photographed. They are also about me. I was enmeshed in girl culture before I was a photographer, and I was photographing girl culture before I realized I was working on Girl Culture.

In this work, I have been drawn to the pathological in the everyday. I am interested in the tyranny of the popular and thin girls over the ones who don't fit that mold. I am interested in the competition suffered by the popular girls, and their sense that being popular is not as satisfying as it appears. I am interested in the costly and time-consuming beauty rituals that are an integral part of daily life. I am interested in the fact that to fall outside the ideal body type is to be a modern-day pariah...

These interests, my own memories, and a genuine love for girls, gossip, female bonding, and the idiosyncratic rituals of girl culture, have motivated this five-year photographic journey.

... The body has become the primary canvas on which girls express their identities, insecurities, ambitions, and struggles. It has become a palimpsest on which many of our culture's conflicting messages about femininity are written and rewritten.

Photography is an ideal medium with which to explore the role of image in our culture. The camera renders an illusion of objective representation, just like a mirror. But as every woman knows, a mirror provides data that, filtered through a mind and moods, is subject to wildly differing interpretations. This project has been my mirror and my attempt to deconstruct the illusions that make up our reality.

© Lauren Greenfield/VII. From the book **Girl Culture**, Chronicle Books, 2002

Each photograph should stand on its own merits, but the entire portfolio should have a rhythm and a flow that leads the viewer from beginning to end. Your portfolio should contain from 12 to 20 pages presented in a visually pleasing way. Each portfolio page should consist of one or more photographs and your name printed in a simple font. This repeated conjunction of name and photographs helps create your visual identity, or brand, in the viewer's mind. Remember: You often ship or drop off your portfolio, so it represents you in your absence. It gets only one chance to make a great first impression.

PORTFOLIO

As a collection of your best work, your portfolio represents the past—what you have done. But many photographers create images for their portfolios that look to the future—what they want to do. Photographers often refer to this as personal work, as opposed to assigned work. Some create a separate portfolio for their personal work, and it is often these images that propel their careers forward. You also want to consider whether you see yourself as a generalist or a specialist.

Generalists shoot everything—spot news, environmental portraits, sports, food, and fashion. Specialists carve out a niche—such as underwater photography or wildlife—and become well known for that type of work.

Do you want to compete with all the other generalists for a wide range of assignments? Or do you want to focus on the subjects (and therefore the markets) that you feel passionate about? Only you can decide.

Clients are sometimes frustratingly literal: if the assignment is to shoot red lawnmowers, you had better have red (not green) lawnmowers in your portfolio. Yet art directors and photo editors are often artists too, and they will appreciate the artistic, adventurous images that push the envelope of your creativity.

Get help editing your work and be ruthless. A picture that needs explaining does not belong (you often are not there to explain). Just because a picture was tough to get does not make it portfolio material. Make sure the subject matter is appropriate for the client; avoid pictures that may offend. If you are not well versed in typography and layout, seek professional assistance. Although once quite costly, portfolios are now more affordable thanks to computers. Many photographers are turning to scanners and ink-jet printers to create their own portfolios and mailers.

Tip: Although most newspapers accept digital portfolios, it is important to do your research in other industries to see if editors and art directors are willing to review CDs or other electronic portfolios. See opposite page for information on preparing electronic portfolios. Resist the temptation to show tear sheets—samples of your published work—unless the printing, layout, and design are all first-rate. Most of the people viewing your portfolio will immediately recognize flaws in these areas, and the value of your photographs, by association, will be diminished.

SHOWING YOUR WORK TO MAGAZINES

Many magazines are based in New York City, so photographers often find it productive to visit there at least once a year. Before you book your flight, do some planning. First, have a clear goal in mind, such as a dozen portfolio showings and four personal visits. Then draw up a list of target publications that use the type of pictures you shoot. Call each in advance to find out its policy regarding portfolios. Most publications accept only drop-offs, meaning that you leave your portfolio for a few hours or overnight (this is a good reason to have multiple portfolios).

In some cases, you may be able to schedule personal meetings, but these may also happen on the spur of the moment, for example when you come to pick up your portfolio. If you are lucky enough to meet face to face with an art director or photo editor, use your (limited) time wisely. Make sure you are intimately familiar with the publication.

Ask questions. What are the current and future needs for photography? What problems does the publication face in getting consistently great pictures? Which topics or geographic regions are particularly tough to cover? If the editor or art director could change just one thing about the photographs submitted each week or month, what would it be?

The most important part of a personal visit comes when you are ready to say goodbye. Take this opportunity to agree on the next step—remember, you are trying to build a relationship, not just entertain someone for a few minutes with your pictures. Did you discuss ideas for stories? Then you should agree to send a list of 10 story ideas within the next few weeks (and do it). Ask your contact how you should stay in touch: through regular mailers, monthly phone calls, email? Try to use questions—how, what—that cannot be answered with a simple yes or no. These are called open questions, and are very helpful in continuing the dialogue and getting the information you need. In most cases, the editor or art director will not have an immediate need for your services, so do not be disappointed if you leave without an assignment. Remember,

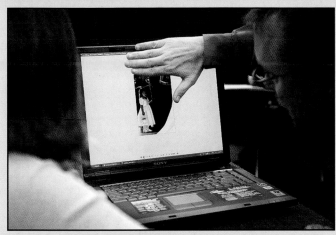

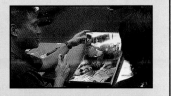

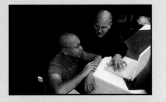

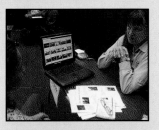

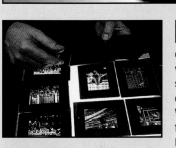

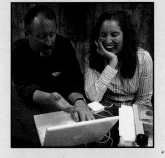

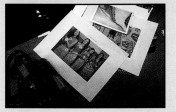

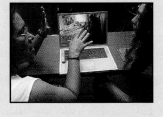

Most publications are set up to review digital portfolios. Call or email first to see if the people you will see prefer to look at CDs or web sites. It also helps to know if their computers are Macintosh or Windows-based. Just in case, configure the portfolio for both Macintosh and Windows-based computers. You would hate to have the perfect portfolio incapable of being seen!

Test your digital portfolio on a couple of computers—other than your own—before visiting a pro in the newsroom. It is embarrassing to make a long journey only to watch an editor trying unsuccessfully to open a disk.

For slide-show programs that run when the disk is opened, include buttons on each screen that allow reviewers to either hold an image to view for longer reflection or to click through the slides one at a time. These options allow editors to move through portfolios at their own pace. A stop or hold feature also allows them to call someone over to the screen to see a particularly interesting image.

Music? An editor's taste may differ from yours. Include a "music off" button prominently on the opening page, if not every page. Editors have little time to devote to student work. For digital portfolios, always use JPEGs. They open quickly.

Do not give busy professionals an excuse to bail out early.

by Jim McNay

most publications depend on having a network of freelancers they can call on to provide pictures for each issue, rain or shine. You perform a valuable service by staying in touch and coming up with leads and story ideas. Eventually, your persistence will be rewarded.

Tip: You also can pitch your story ideas and proposals to someone on the publication's editorial side (as opposed to the art or photography side). Look on the masthead to find the names of various editors. Look for someone several rungs down from the top, such as an associate editor. If the editors have specific beats, such as travel or technology, find the appropriate one.

THE INTERNET

Don't forget the Internet as a marketing tool. If you have a well-designed site and appropriately selected keywords, picture editors and researchers can more easily find the photographer who has a specialized collection of images, say, of rickshaws in Bangladesh, or women working in Asian countries. When a researcher turns to the web to find sites on a topic like rickshaws or women working, the photographer's page appears. Then the researcher can write or call for a high-quality image. At this point, the buyer and seller would determine a price and rights for using the image. For more on copyright, see Chapter 16, "Law."

Internet-based archive and web presentation services for photographers further simplify the web presentation capability for photojournalists. See *www.digitalrailroad.net* as well as *www.PhotoShelter.com*.

SELLING A BREAKING NEWS PICTURE

If a story has significant national or international appeal, a news magazine like *Time*, *Newsweek*, or *U.S. News & World Report* might buy a freelancer's photo, especially if it is in color. These magazines maintain very small full-time photo staffs, so they also buy outside photos. Good editors do not mind a quick telephone call on a spot-news story because they cannot afford to ignore you and possibly miss the chance of publishing a Pulitzer Prize-winning picture.

RATES

As a freelancer you do not get paid a salary, the way staff photographers do. Instead, you earn a fee for your photography and you get reimbursed for your expenses. The fee-plus-expenses model is one of the keys to understanding the economics of freelance photojournalism. Consider fees first. Newspapers and magazines generally pay their freelancers what is called a "day rate." This is a misleading term, because it implies you are being paid for your time—a "day" equals eight hours, for example—rather than for your skills as a photographer. Your assignment might take two hours or ten, it might be simple or complex, it might draw on all your creativity or simply involve recording an event such as a press conference—no matter, the pay is fixed. Of course, that doesn't mean you shouldn't negotiate for a higher fee.

In fact, the day rate is just part of the equation. Magazines and newspapers also have what is called a space rate—how much they pay for pictures based on the size and placement of the image. In other words, a quarter-page photo run inside may be worth $300, whereas a cover may command $1500 or even $5000. The day rate is meant to be a guarantee against the space rate. In other words, you are guaranteed the day rate, let's say $800, no matter how your picture is used. Even if it is used as a quarter-page photo, you still get $800. But if it runs on the cover, you instead get paid the cover rate, which could be twice to six or seven times the day rate, depending on the publication.

FEE PLUS EXPENSES

What about your expenses, such as equipment rental, mileage, an assistant, meals, etc? These are called billable expenses. This means they are billed to the publication and itemized separately from your fee. When you talk to a potential client about price, make sure you understand whether or not the amount quoted includes expenses. For example, a magazine photo editor calls and says she has an assignment, and her magazine usually pays $800 per day.

Your first question should be, "Does that include my expenses?" It is common to have at least half the total cost of an assignment be for expenses, especially when an assistant and travel are involved. Magazine freelancer Brian Smith says it's not uncommon to have expenses of least six times the actual creative fee.

In any case, for the purposes of our hypothetical assignment, if the $800 also must cover your expenses, which at their minimum are likely to be half what you are being paid, you are going to take home only $400 or less. If the expenses are more, well, you're not going to be making much at all.

If the $800 is just your fee, you will probably end up billing the magazine at least $1500 to $1600 for the assignment.

Check with Editorial Photographers, *www.editorialphotographers.com*, a web site and professional group that helps independent photojournalists gain fair pricing.

RIGHTS

What exactly is the publication getting for its money? First of all, photojournalists rarely sell photographs.

Instead, they license the use of their images for specific uses. Licensing photographs is based on the copyright law, which says that ownership in a freelance situation belongs to the creator, NOT to the party commissioning the work.

This means that you, as a freelance photographer, own all your photographs from the moment they are made. You (and only you) have the right to license their use however you see fit.

CONTESTS CAN OPEN DOORS

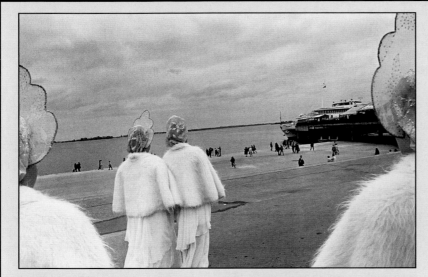

Andrea Hoyer was an unknown young photographer when she submitted 12 images to be considered for Leica's Oskar Barnack Prize. The photographs were from her self-funded, five-year effort to document the vestiges of the former Soviet Union in Russia. She joined the ranks of well-established photographers like Sebastião Salgado and Magnum photographer Larry Towell to win the prestigious international award. Photo by Andrea Hoyer

Are you ready to compete with the pros? If you can say yes honestly, you may want to make the effort and investment to enter other contests aimed for professionals. The same caveats apply. Use contests as a way to review the power of your work and then to put it out there if you feel it may meet the challenge.

Atlanta Photojournalism Seminar
www.photojournalism.org

Best of Photojournalism
www.nppa.org/bestofpj

International Photography Awards
www.photoawards.com/

Leica's Oskar Barnack Prize
www.leica-camera.com

Pictures of the Year International
www.poy.org

World Press Photo
www.worldpressphoto.nl

A frequent question from young talent is, "How do I get recognized, get noticed?" One way—though not the only way—is to participate in photojournalism competitions, especially those available to students. One of these, the prestigious College Photographer of the Year (CPOY) competition, has a fall deadline, usually early October.

You can do well in this competition either by excelling in the overall portfolio category or by earning recognition in one of the individual picture categories. Such a performance signals potential employers that coming out of school you are ready to produce advanced work. Names of portfolio finalists spread quickly among editors and photographers throughout the country.

One of the beauties of the competition is that entries need not have been published, just created within the last year. This allows you to enter pictures you think will represent your best work.

There are also many individual picture categories—sports, features, portraits, stories—

if you are not yet ready to take on the full portfolio competition. There is room to participate in the CPOY competition for students at all levels.

And compete you should. Review your work for the past year and enter at least one picture in one category. Being a part of the competition is a sign of being "engaged" in the process of serious journalism, of striving to improve, to get in the game, to grow and to be recognized.

At the same time, keep a clear head about contests. Yes, they are useful. Recognition is important in the job search. But contest results are unpredictable. Excellent work is often overlooked. And, sometimes, good journalism may be lost in the flurry of images that speed by judges' weary eyes. Contests should not be what a photographer is about or why one takes pictures. Your pictures should be about your audience, about your community.

Let contests provide you the opportunity to review your year's work—a crucial

endeavor for pushing yourself toward improvement. And if you win? Winning can bring recognition that ignites the afterburners of a young career.

College Photographer of the Year
www.cpoy.org

OTHER CONTESTS FOR STUDENTS

Student members of the National Press Photographers Association (NPPA) may enter published as well as unpublished work in the Quarterly Student Clip Contest.
www.nppa.org

The Society for Photographic Education (SPE) gives awards to its student members. Its largest is the $5000 Crystal Apple Award, which recognizes work in traditional black-and-white imaging.
www.spenational.org

by Jim McNay

Historically, magazines and newspapers asked for one-time rights for assignment pictures generated by freelancers. Subsequent reuse and/or use in another edition (foreign language, for example) were negotiated and paid for separately. This was true, despite the fact that the publication paid the photographer to create the image and paid for the expenses.

With the consolidation of the publishing industry and the advent of the Internet, however, this is changing. Photography contracts now routinely ask for electronic rights (for a publication's web site), or even outright ownership, forever. In return, the photographer may get an increased fee (best case) or perhaps be told to "take it or leave it" (worst case). Before accepting an assignment, ask to see a copy of the news outlet's contract.

Pay particular attention to the words "work made for hire." If you sign a work-for-hire contract, you lose your copyright and ownership of all photographs made under that contract. Avoid at all costs signing Work for Hire contracts or any other agreement in which you

WORKSHOPS ARE A PLACE TO NETWORK AS WELL AS TO LEARN

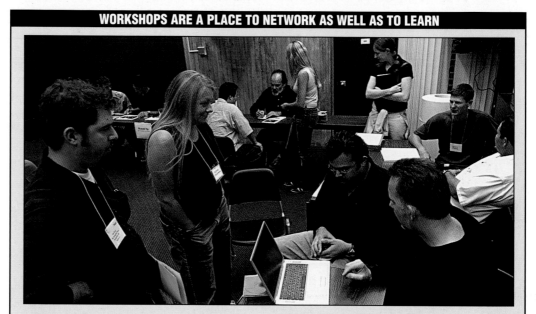

Workshops are terrific for hands-on portfolio critiques and for getting to know editors and other shooters. Many of the best—and least expensive—in photojournalism are sponsored by NPPA (National Press Photographers Association).

These include one-day seminars like the Flying Short Course, shown above, and weekend workshops including the Northern Short Course, Southern Short Course, and Atlanta Seminar.

The Mountain Workshop, sponsored by Western Kentucky University, and the Missouri Workshop, sponsored by the University of Missouri, are excellent for learning to shoot photo stories. Young professionals and students interested in freelancing learn from top shooters and New York picture editors at the Eddie Adams Workshop. The photo agency VII offers workshops featuring their top-notch shooters as speakers.

To make the jump to international photojournalism and editorial freelance photography, Visa Pour L'Image, held each September in Perpignan, France, is perhaps the most influential in the world. (See the documentary video "Visa Pour L'Image" on the DVD included with this book.)

Good technical workshops abound, including the Maine Photographic Workshops and the Palm Beach Photographic Workshops. The Sports Photography Workshop is a great place to learn from *Sports Illustrated* shooters and Allsport photo agency editors, and *SportsShooter.com* also hosts workshops.

The Platypus Workshops organized by Dirck Halstead are the place to get hands-on training in digital video, and NPPA sponsors workshops on digital video and video storytelling, as well.

FINDING WORKSHOPS

Among the best of the best (in alphabetical order)
Eddie Adams Workshop: *www.eddieadamsworkshop.com*
FotoFusion: *www.fotofusion.org*
Julia Dean Photo Workshops: *www.juliadean.com*
Maine Photo Workshops: *www.theworkshops.com*
Missouri Photo Workshop: *www.mophotoworkshop.org*
Mountain Workshop: *www.mountainworkshops.org*
NPPA educational programs: *http://www.nppa.org*
Palm Beach Photographic Workshops: *http://www.workshop.org/*
Photo Agency VII: *www.viiphoto.com*
Platypus workshop: *www.DigitalJournalist.org*
Rich Clarkson Sports Workshops: *www.photographyatthesummit.com*
Santa Fe Workshops: *www.sfworkshop.com*
Sports Shooter workshops: *www.SportsShooter.com*
Toscana: *www.tpw.it*
Visa Pour L'Image: *www.visapourlimage.com*
White Cloud Workshop: *www.whitecloudworkshop.com*

by Jim McNay

sign over the copyright to your images. Editorial Photographers' web site has copies of contracts used by many publications. Prepare yourself by studying these. Remember, all contracts can be negotiated; that's what lawyers are for. (For more on copyright see Chapter 16, "Law," pages 411–413.)

More on Why "Work for Hire" is a Bad Deal for Photographers

"Work for hire" (or "work made for hire" or "WFH") is a contract term meaning that all work being done under the contract becomes the property of the person paying for it, not of the photographer. Under a contract like this the photographer becomes an "employee-for-a-day." But as Editorial Photographers points out, this relationship "almost always fails to adequately compensate freelancers for the usual expenses of being self-employed: employment taxes, liability coverage, equipment and automobile depreciation and insurance, office overhead, computers and software, health and disability insurance, retirement plans, non-billable time such as marketing, accounting, and image management, etc., as well as for all the potential lost revenue from secondary licensing."

Many contracts simply state the job is a "work for hire" without offering additional compensation at all. Editorial Photographers recommends avoiding work-for-hire contracts in editorial work in all but the most rare circumstances and for the most extraordinary compensation.

Tip: Check the sources under "More Information" on this page and talk to other photographers to get the scoop on standard business practices—particularly on their experiences with bad contracts.

FIXED COSTS

Billable expenses are those you can bill to your client. But there are other expenses that are part of the cost of doing business, such as camera and computer equipment, repairs, software, office supplies, telephone, insurance, and utilities. These are called fixed costs. You pay them day in and day out, whether you are busy shooting assignments or waiting for clients to call.

Who pays for these costs? You do—they come out of your fee. The only way to know if a fee is reasonable or not is to figure out your fixed costs. Find out how much you spend each month to be in business. Let's say it is $2000. Now let's go back to our hypothetical assignment.

In the first example, your fee after expenses was $400 (best case), so you must have five similarly priced assignments just to break even.

In the second example, your fee was $800, so you would break even and make a little profit with your third such assignment.

PROFIT

Did you notice that word profit? It is not a dirty word. In fact, you need to make a profit if you are going to survive as a freelancer. Profit is what enables you to pay yourself a salary and thus pay the rent, put food on the table, pay your taxes and insurance, and contribute to a retirement fund. Profit also enables you to put money back into your business to make it grow.

Where does profit come from? It is what's left over after you have paid your fixed costs and the cost of your billable expenses such as film, processing, assistants, and travel expenses. There are only a few ways to increase profit: do more assignments, charge higher fees, charge more for billable expenses (called a "markup"), reduce fixed costs, and/or reduce the cost of billable items. If you pay close attention to these details, you just may survive in today's tough freelance market. ■

MORE INFORMATION

BOOKS AND MAGAZINES
ASMP Professional Business Practices in Photography
Photography: Focus on Profit
   by Tom Zimberoff
Business and Legal Forms for Photographers
   by Tad Crawford
Pricing Photography
   by Michal Heron and David MacTavish
The Photographer's Guide to Marketing and Self-Promotion
   by Maria Piscopo
The Photojournalist's Guide to Making Money
   by Michael Sedge and Ron Engh
Photo District News (PDN), www.pdn-pix.com

ORGANIZATIONS AND WEB SITES
American Society of Media Photographers (ASMP)
   www.asmp.org
The Digital Journalist
   www.DigitalJournalist.org
Editorial Photographers (EP)
   www.editorialphotographers.com
National Press Photographers Association (NPPA)
   www.nppa.org
Sports Shooter
   www.SportsShooter.com

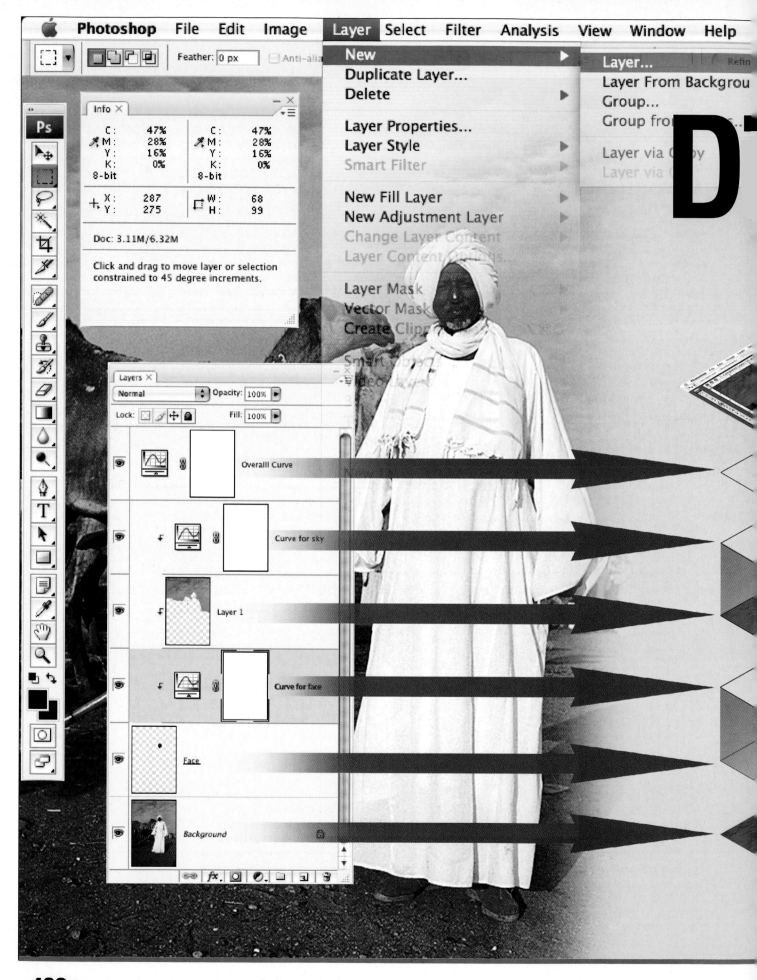

gital Darkroom

After you take a picture with a digital camera , you will need to use the computer to save, adjust, transmit, or print the image. Most photojournalists have adopted Adobe's Photoshop software to edit images for publication, whether for print or for the web. You can transform images in literally millions of ways with this software.

However, photojournalists typically follow a restricted set of operations for assignments other than photo illustrations. These basic darkroom adjustments include correcting contrast, brightness, and color balance, as well as cropping, digitally sharpening, and setting the appropriate size and resolution for an image's ultimate use. Photographers have devised seemingly limitless ways to accomplish these tasks. Photoshop itself is so robust and multifaceted that you can attack each problem with a choice of solutions. Some approaches take more time. Others might degrade an image if not carried out properly. The choices can be dizzying.

This special section features one straight-forward method to handle the majority of your images in Photoshop. The method uses numbers to establish blacks and whites with details as well as to neutralize color casts. The "Curve" command recommended in this section is only one place where you can establish numerical tonal values, but working in Curves offers the most flexibility as you become more proficient in Photoshop. You also will learn a simple technique to select one part of a picture in order to darken or lighten it without obvious "burning" or "dodging" effects. Finally, you will learn to work in "Layers," a technique that will provide ultimate flexibility without permanently altering the original image.

Use the method shown in the following step-by-step procedure, and feel free to modify the steps as you become more comfortable with Photoshop. Keep in mind the ethical limitations placed on all photojournalistic pictures except photo illustrations. See Chapter 15, "Ethics."

Getting started	**470**
Set up a Workspace	
Layers Palette	
Info Palette	
Blacks, Whites & Neutral Gray	
Balancing Color with Curves	**471**
Curves Overview	
Color Balance by the Numbers	
Set white, black, and neutral points	
Brightness and Contrast	**472**
How Curves Work	
Step-by-Step Guide	**472**
Selections with the Lasso Tools	**474**
Working with the Layers Palette	**475**
Layers: The Power Tool	**476**
Sharpening an Image	**477**
Sizing the Photograph	**478**
Resolution, File Size, and Image Size	
Image Size Dialog Box	
Cropping an Image	**480**
Saving for the web	**480**
Archiving with File Info	**481**
File Formats	**481**

With film-based photography, a few numbers were important: film ISO, shutter speed, and lens f/stops. The photographic vocabulary of digital photography requires a few more relevant numbers. In fact, a digital image is nothing but numbers, thousands of them, even for the smallest photograph. Those numbers, from bits to bytes to pixels and beyond, make up the foundation of the digital photograph.

As with traditional photography, the aim with digital technology is to produce the highest quality image possible for any of the lives a photograph may have—whether on the web or in a newspaper or magazine. Manipulating the numbers that make up a digital image allows precise quality control—from tonal scale to color balance to sharpness. Whether you are scanning negatives or slides or importing files from a digital camera, preparing photographs by the numbers will almost always yield the best results.

Numbers are particularly useful for color adjustments. Color gamut, the range of colors you can see or that can be printed, varies drastically from digital cameras and scanners to computer monitors to the printing press. Without sophisticated color management equipment and software it can be difficult to know if what you see while editing will be what appears in print.

The adaptive nature of the human eye and our own expectations affect how we perceive color. Even your eyes can't be trusted. Someone standing in a room lit by fluorescent light looks fine to the eye, but an uncorrected photo will probably have a decidedly green cast.

Luckily, while equipment may mislead you, and your eyes may deceive you, numbers don't lie. Neutral tones—black, white, or any shade of gray—are not subjective. A neutral tone in a digital color image has equal amounts of Red, Green, and Blue (RGB). The three colors cancel out one another and produce neutrality, whether it's black,

white, or any shade of gray in between. Pure black (0) has no Red, Green, or Blue. A black with no colors prints as black with no detail. Pure white has the maximum tonal level of each color (255). At the maximum value of 255, the three colors cancel out one another to create a white that uses NO ink and thus has no detail. Middle Gray is 128 of each color—halfway between 0 and 255. Any other tone without a color cast has equal amounts of each primary color. As long as the three colors are in balance, an RGB tone is neutral, so the photograph will be cast-free.

Do note that there are some pictures where the color of the light itself may be important. You may not want to fully neutralize, for example, photos of situations where the flamboyant shades cast by a setting sun are important.

Set up a Workspace

Open the toolbox

Open the layers palette

Open the info palette

Before adjustment/After adjustment

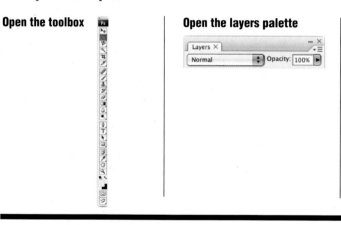

When the cursor or an eyedropper tool is positioned over a point in a photograph, the numbers that appear in the Info palette indicate the different color values on that exact point (notice the X-Y coordinates below the numbers outlined in red).

You can tell that the numbers here are for an unedited image because those to the left of the slash are the same as those on the right. After editing, the numbers on the right side will reflect their adjusted values.

Exact coordinates of where you have placed the eyedropper.

Black, White, and Neutral

1. Open Photoshop. Open any picture.

2. With the Toolbox open (Window>Tools), open the Toolbox Options Bar (Window>Options).

3. Highlight the Eyedropper Tool, select an eyedropper, and in the option bar at the top of the screen, define the sample size as 3x3 average (3 pixels x 3 pixels). 1x1 selects just one pixel. Selecting only one pixel may throw off the average.

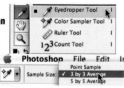

4. Open the Curves dialog box by choosing Image>Adjust>Curves.

5. Locate the three eyedroppers.

6. Click twice on the black eyedropper to open the Color Picker box (below). Look for the RGB settings (circled).

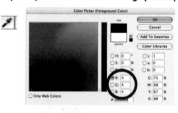

ALERT: The publication where you are working will have numbers that produce the best file for its press. Ask before you prepare images for reproduction.

7. Set the Red, Green, and Blue values at 4 to define the darkest black with some detail. (Zero in each color would produce a pure black with no detail at all.) Click OK.

R: 4
G: 4
B: 4

8. Click twice on the white eyedropper to reopen the Color Picker box. Set Red, Green, and Blue values at 244 each for the brightest white with detail. (The number 255 in each color would produce a white without any ink at all, with no detail. This is sometimes called paper white because the paper shows without any dots of ink.) Click OK.

R: 244
G: 244
B: 244

9. When prompted, allow these settings to become the new default. Quit Photoshop to save the settings.

ALERT: The middle eyedropper represents neutral gray. Clicking on a nearly neutral point in a photograph will bring the RGB settings into neutrality and help eliminate remaining color casts. Do not set any numbers here.

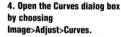

Curves Overview

The Curves command is the ideal tonal and color correction tool for photojournalists. Here, you can use eyedropper tools to quickly establish whites and blacks with detail. You also can precisely adjust as many as sixteen points on the Curve to change specific highlight or shadow areas, for example, or just the mid-tones. See the following two pages for how to change the curve. **ALERT:** Although the Curves command is available at Image>Adjust> Curves, go instead to Layers>New Adjustment Layer>Curves. See pages 472–475 for a full exploration of Layers.

The diagonal line in the Curves dialog box represents the potential tonal values of ANY image—from 0 (pure black) to 255 (paper white). Every "curve" starts as a straight line, regardless of what the image looks like! Black is at the bottom left, white is at the top right. The middle point, 128, is middle gray. Changes to the line become the curve.

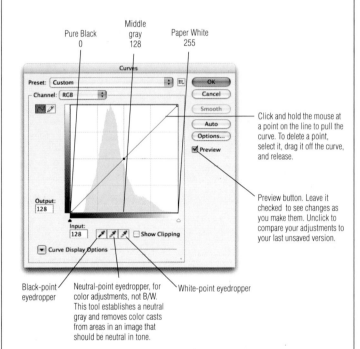

Pure Black 0

Middle gray 128

Paper White 255

Click and hold the mouse at a point on the line to pull the curve. To delete a point, select it, drag it off the curve, and release.

Preview button. Leave it checked to see changes as you make them. Unclick to compare your adjustments to your last unsaved version.

Black-point eyedropper

Neutral-point eyedropper, for color adjustments, not B/W. This tool establishes a neutral gray and removes color casts from areas in an image that should be neutral in tone.

White-point eyedropper

ALERT: If the publication you work for requires you to prepare files in CYMK, you will receive specifications on how to best to prepare them for your press.
  The basic concepts are the same. Equal numbers create neutrality.

Color Balance by the Numbers

With the Info palette available (Menu>Window>Info), open an Adjustment Layer Curve. At this stage, you will only use the eyedroppers.

First, set a clean white in the highlights and a good black with detail in the shadows. This will go a long way toward cleaning up color casts.

The neutral-point eyedropper is a powerful color-correction tool. Make sure the Info palette is open. Identify a neutral area in the image. Without a gray card in your photo, pinpointing an area that "should" be neutral is always subjective. Because equal amounts of color neutralize one another, a point at which the color values are very close is probably an area that should be neutral.

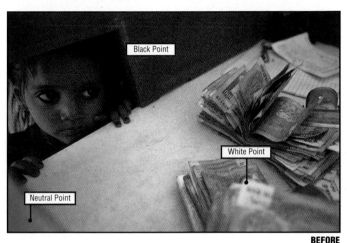

Black Point

White Point

Neutral Point

BEFORE

 Set the white point. With the info box open, move the white-point eyedropper over the image to find the brightest area in which you want detail. Clicking with the eyedropper creates a white with detail and no color cast.

 Set the black point. With the info box open, move the black-point eyedropper over the image to find the blackest area in which you want detail. Clicking with the eyedropper creates a black with detail and no color cast.

 Set the neutral point. With the info box open, move the neutral-point eyedropper over the image to find an area you know or expect to be neutral. A spot where the color values are near one another is a likely choice if you don't know for sure. Clicking with the eyedropper brings the color values into balance and thereby removes any color cast for the whole image.

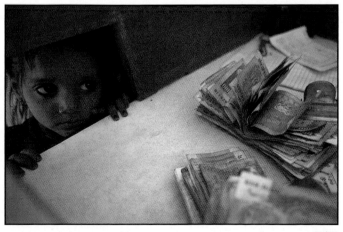

AFTER

How Curves Work

The Curve dialog box for every image opens with a diagonal line. Clicking on the midpoint of the line identifies 128 as middle gray. 0, at the bottom left, is pure black; 255, at the top right, is pure white. Pure white prints with no ink at all.

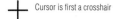 Cursor is first a crosshair

and becomes a grab tool once a point is selected.

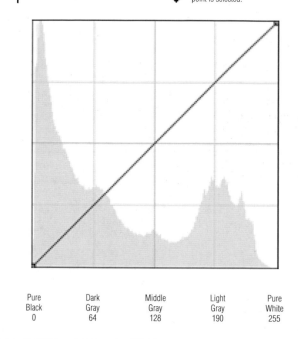

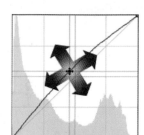

Click and hold the mouse at a point on the line to pull the curve.

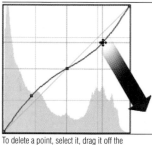

To delete a point, select it, drag it off the curve, and release.

Pure Black	Dark Gray	Middle Gray	Light Gray	Pure White
0	64	128	190	255

The terms to the left are among those used to describe darkness and lightness values in an image.

PUTTING IT ALL TOGETHER: A PRACTICAL STEP-BY-STEP GUIDE

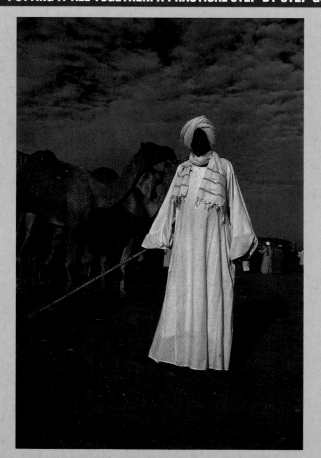

THE UNCORRECTED IMAGE.

1. Make a New Adjustment Layer.
Make an Adjustment Curve Layer (Layers>Make New Adjustment Layer>Curve). This is the layer on which to set the white point, black point, neutral point and make basic lighten or darken decisions.

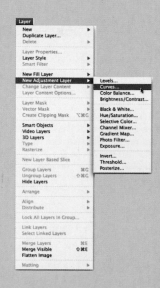

2. Name the layer.

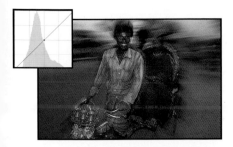

Original photo.

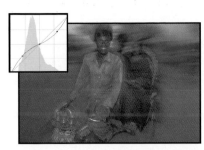

A downward pull in the highlights and an upward pull in the shadows flattens contrast. Here, the mid-point happens to be locked at middle gray, but it can be moved, too.

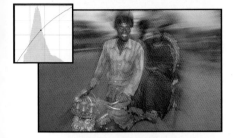

Click on the middle of the line and drag the curve up to lighten the image overall. See how all the points on the line except black and white have changed?

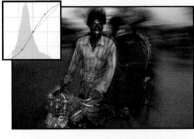

Pulling the shadows down and the highlights up increases contrast. Again, the mid-point happens to be locked here but does not have to be.

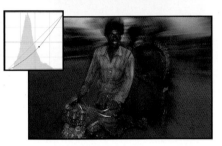

Moving the mid-point down darkens the image overall. Again, all the points on the line have changed, yet the black and white points remain fixed.

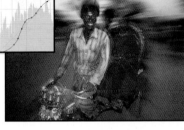

You can lock down many points on a curve to make fine adjustments between the points.

3. Select the white-point eyedropper.

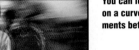

6. Click on the part of the image that should be the blackest with detail.

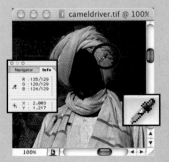

4. Click on the part of the image that should be the whitest with detail.

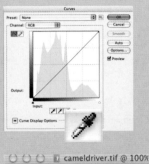

7. Select the middle, neutral-point eyedropper, and click on an area that should be neutral yet still has a color cast.

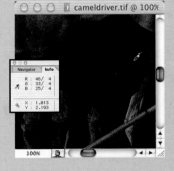

5. Select the black-point eyedropper.

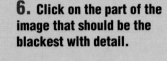

8. If the image is still too light or too dark, bend the curve accordingly. Dragging the curve downward lightens the entire image.

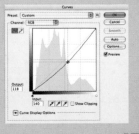

CLICK-DRAG LASSO TOOLS TO OUTLINE ITEMS AND DRAW SHAPES

FREEHAND. Once the regular Lasso has been clicked on a starting point, drag it around, but continue to hold it until you have returned to the original point point. The area inside will be selected. The Polygonal Lasso lets you click on multiple points before returning to the start. This provides more precision when outlining irregular shapes. The Magnetic Lasso snaps to the edges of an area being outlined. A Lasso set to feather edges at a minimum of 30 pixels creates an inconspicuous blend between the adjusted and unadjusted edges. For the purposes of "burning" and "dodging," which is essentially what is happening here, a loose selection with the regular lasso, set to feather at 30 pixels or more, will give excellent results even without the precision offered by the other lassos.

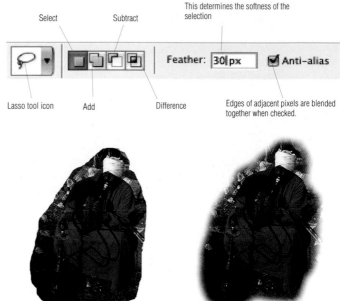

This determines the softness of the selection

Select Subtract

Lasso tool icon Add Difference

Feather: 30 px ☑ Anti-alias

Edges of adjacent pixels are blended together when checked.

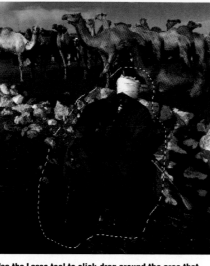

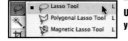

Use the Lasso tool to click-drag around the area that you want to select.

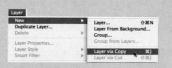

Hard-edged selection
This selection was made with Feather set to 0 pixels.

Feathered selection
A soft transition is created by setting Feather to a minimum of 30 pixels.

---

9. Lasso tools.

To adjust part of an image, do the following.

Feather: 30 px ☑ Anti-alias

Set the lasso to feather edges at 30 or more pixels to create an inconspicuous blend between the adjusted and unadjusted edges.

10. Select the face with the Lasso tool.

With the background layer highlighted, use a selection tool to outline the part of the image to be adjusted.

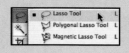

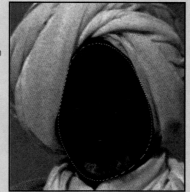

NOTE: It is possible to make tonal adjustments directly on a selection (for example, this face). However, doing so permanently alters the pixels in the file. If you find it necessary to make another change to the face later—to compensate for a different printing press, for example—you will be further altering the pixels. Working in layers protects the integrity of your original image and allows limitless changes as long as you always save the merged file with a new name.

11. Copy the selection.

Keyboard command Command-J (PC, use Control-J) copies the selection and creates a new layer for it simultaneously. This layer contains only the pixels selected from the background layer.

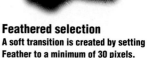

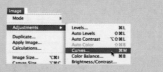

12. Apply a Curve adjustment to the new layer.

Create a new adjustment layer curve. Important: when the naming box appears, check "Group With Previous Layer" to confine the changes to the layer immediately below it.

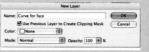

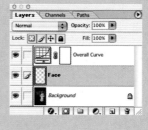

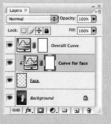

13. Raise or lower the curve to adjust just the selection on the linked layer. Here, lowering the curve lightens the face.

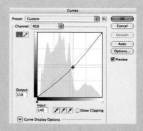

LAYERS (MENU>LAYERS) ARE THE ULTIMATE "OOPS" COMMAND.
The concept underlying all types of layers is the same. Layers protect the original photograph and its pixels during editing and compositing tasks. This results in ultimate flexibility for working with the image today and into the future.

What is a layer? Think of it as a glass plate that sits on top of your photograph. The glass plate is where you darken, lighten, or otherwise edit the image without ever actually touching it. Because the glass is clear, you can see the effects of the changes, but the original photo (A) remains unaltered. It is possible to have many pieces of glass stacked above a photograph, each with different effects. The cumulative changes are applied from the top plate to the bottom, with each plate changeable and interchangeable.

Here, for example, the first adjustments on the top layer (B), Overall, apply to everything below that layer.

You also can copy part of the original photo onto a different glass plate (C). Here, the pipe-smoking man was too dark after the overall adjustment that made the rest of the image just right. He was selected with a lasso tool feathered at 30 pixels, copied from the original layer (A) and pasted onto a new, separate layer (C). Another adjustment layer (D) was added and linked to (C) the man. [Note: Layers (C) and (D) have been linked to restrict the adjustments only to (C) the man. These changes don't penetrate to the rest of the image, or to any other layers that might come later.]

Regardless of how many plates are in use, you can save the file with all its layers and corrections preserved, and return later if you change your mind. You can eliminate a plate and its changes altogether or return to a plate to fine-tune the corrections made there.

Adjustment Layers (Menu>Layers>Adjustment Layers) are ideal for making even basic changes to photographs. Because each correction is performed and saved on a separate layer, you can easily try out different approaches and then compare results by clicking on or off the eyeball to the left of each layer.

Most experienced photographers work in layers when applying Curves or other adjustment commands.

Photo illustrators have long used Layers for complex image combinations like many in Chapter 14, "Illustration." To make composites, you can open a completely new picture, adjust its size to equal the one currently open, and, using the Move tool, simply slide the new photo into the current file. Photoshop automatically creates a layer for the second photo. This new layer can be manipulated and eventually merged with the others in the file. (See Chapter 14, "Illustration," for examples of illustrations composited in Photoshop.)

Once you are satisfied, flatten the layers into a single image (Menu>Layers>Flatten Image OR access the command from the Layers Palette). At this point, all the changes are applied and cannot be undone. **ALERT:** Before merging, give the file a new name so you don't mistakenly save over the layered file, which would prevent returning later to alter the layers for other purposes. Merged files are much smaller and so take up less storage space than files with all their layers.

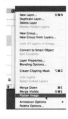

14. Select the sky with the Lasso tool.
With the background layer highlighted, use a selection tool to outline the part of the image to be adjusted. For this picture, the sky was still flat.

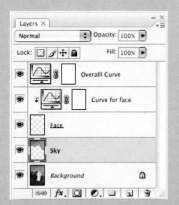

15. Copy the selection.
Keyboard command Command-J (PC, use Control-J) copies the selection and creates a new layer for it simultaneously. This layer contains only the pixels selected from the background layer.

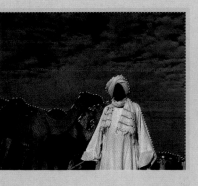

16. Apply a Curve adjustment layer to the new layer.
Create a new adjustment layer curve. Don't forget: when the naming box appears, check "Group With Previous Layer" to confine the changes to the selected area below it.

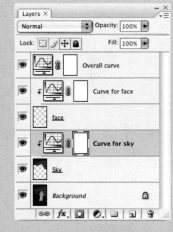

17. With the curve for sky layer selected, adjust the curve as necessary.

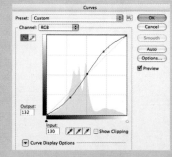

Blend mode: "Normal" Is the default. Leave here initially; explore other effects later.

Preserve transparency & lock pixels. Use this default while learning.

The eye is an icon indicating that changes made on that layer are visible on the monitor. Click the eye off to see how the photo looks without the changes applied. Here, the cumulative effects are visible.

The arrow pointing down indicates that adjustments on this layer apply only to the layer directly beneath it, here the pixels that make up the man smoking his pipe.

Just pixels selected and copied from the Background Layer are visible. Adjustments to a layer like this affect these specific pixels. It is not possible to make changes to other areas in the photo from this layer.

Shortcuts to choices also available under the Menu>Layers Command.

An icon, here a curve, identifies the type of adjustment layer.

The white box is the "glass plate" (in reality a mask) where the adjustment to the left is being applied. The icon is white —or blank—because it contains no pixels.

The opacity of each layer can be controlled. When working with more than one image, decreasing the opacity of the active layer makes the layer below it visible. For basic adjustments, leave at 100%.

Shortcuts to choices available under the Menu>Layers Command.

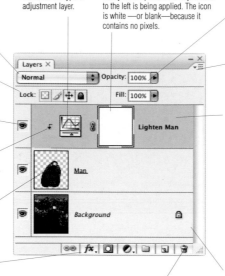

A highlighted layer is the ONLY active layer. Only one layer can be active at a time.

ALERT: Except when the Background layer is invisible (eye off), you will always see the entire image along with changes made on other visible layers (eye on). If it seems no changes are occurring where you are altering the picture, you have not highlighted the layer where you want to make changes.

For example, it is impossible to adjust anything else in this photo except what is on the active layer —here, the man and his pipe. What you would see on the monitor is the entire image with the changes being applied to the selection

Confusion might arise if you decide to select, copy, and adjust the sky, for example, while on the active layer holding just the man. No sky pixels are on the active layer. Those pixels are on the original Background Layer.

"Background" is the layer with the original image and where all its pixels reside. You should never change this layer.

Because the Background layer is where the pixels are, it must be active (highlighted) when copying the photo or selecting and copying part of it onto another layer. For example, the Background layer above was highlighted when the lasso tool selected the man in order to copy and paste him onto a new layer.

Deletes the active (highlighted) layer.

ALERT: Deleting a layer eliminates only the changes made on it. The original (background) image and all the changes on other layers remain untouched.

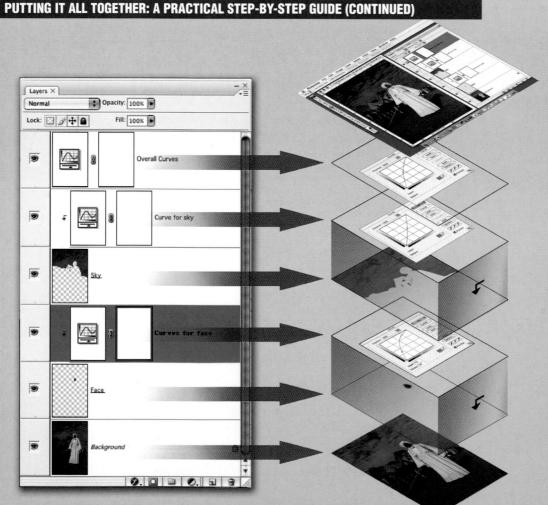

What You See on the Screen
A composite image showing the cumulative adjustments is visible in the Photoshop window, along with the Photoshop tools and palettes on your desktop.

What is Actually Happening
Steps 1–8. An Adjustment Layer/Curve was applied to the image. It affects overall contrast and lightness. Even with a good overall exposure, parts of an image may need lightening or darkening.

Steps 14–17. For example, the sky remained too flat, so it was selected with the Lasso tool and copied to a new layer.

An Adjustment Curve applied only to layer with the sky brightened it while leaving the rest of the image intact.

Steps 9–13. Just the man's face was selected with the Lasso tool and copied to a new layer. An Adjustment Curve restricted to the layer with the face left the rest of the image intact.

The original image remains the same until the layers are compressed. The compression (see opposite) will apply all the changes at the same time.

SHARPENING AN IMAGE

Don't be confused by the name. Unsharp Mask sharpens a digital image. By emphasizing the edges between different tones, the mask corrects softening of detail that occurs in images captured by digital cameras as well as scanned or resampled images (pages 394–395). You may need to experiment with the settings to determine the best results for your images. Remember, sharpening cannot correct a technically blurry or out-of-focus photo.

Choose Filter>Sharpen>Unsharp Mask.

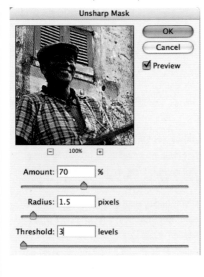

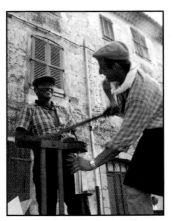

Before sharpening

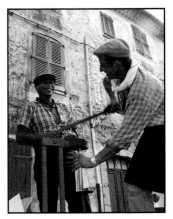

After sharpening

Photographers have different preferences for sharpening. You are likely to hear a different "recipe" from every other professional you meet. Also, different images will require different amounts of sharpening. To start, try setting the amount to 70 percent. Use the radius and threshold figures here. One to 1.5 pixels usually works. A threshold of 0 affects all pixels; a higher threshold minimizes noise because it affects only those edges with a high tonal difference. Compare effects by placing the hand pointer on the preview image and then releasing it. Some photographers apply Unsharp Mask more than once in a series of small percentages.

---

18. Finished? Save the file with a new name, flatten the image to a single layer. Save it in the appropriate format (page 481).

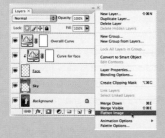

19. Use the Unsharp Mask filter to sharpen the flattened file.

Note that is possible to select certain areas, paste them into a layer, and sharpen them there. For example, you might want to sharpen everything BUT the sky. You will want to experiment for the best results with your images.

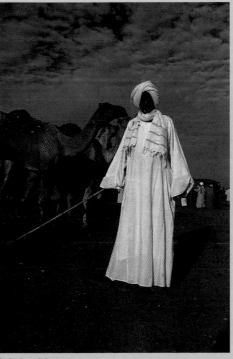

Original Image

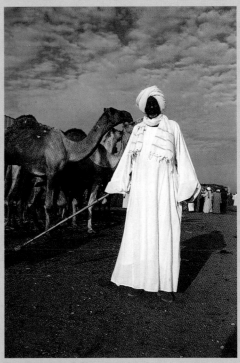

Image after Adjustments

Whether you plan to work on a photograph taken with a digital camera or on a traditional print or negative scanned into digital form, you will find it valuable to think about the size of your final image before you ever begin. Understanding the impact of file size and resolution on your final image is crucial when technical quality is important.

Think of a digital image file as a set of virtual tiles with all the colors necessary to create a realistic scene in a mosaic. The more tiles in the mosaic, the more detail in the scene. Each pixel in a file is one tile in the mosaic. The total number of tiles is the image file size.

Image size (the physical size of a photograph, or the document size in Photoshop's dialog box, right) is like the surface where the mosaic is being installed—a 3'x5' bathroom, for example.

Resolution is the number of tiles per foot you have to work with in your bathroom—the number of pixels per inch in a photo. You can see the problem if there are enough tiles to create a image on a 3'x5' bathroom floor, but you decide to install the same image in an 8'x10' kitchen instead. When you spread the same number of tiles meant for a small bathroom over a large area like the kitchen floor, the image will break up.

You can actually view the interrelationships among image size, file size and resolution using Photoshop's Image Size command. In Photoshop, open File>Image Size to see the dialog box to the right.

Do not check "Resample." Observe what happens as you change the dimensions in "Document Size" (final print size) box. Notice that the resolution changes. Now vary the number in the "Resolution" box. The document size changes. The file size (the number of tiles) never changes. Resolution and image size work in tandem. Changing the picture size changes the resolution; changing the resolution changes the picture size.

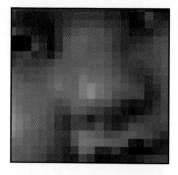

Until they are viewed on a monitor or as a print, pixels are just a set of ones and zeros indicating color, position, and brightness. When magnified (above) each can be seen as a tiny square.

The Image Size command cannot add new tiles, but it can "stretch" them to cover the kitchen floor. The larger the floor, the more coarse the image will appear as the tiles grow larger. The command can also shrink the tiles should you prefer a mosaic for a small panel on the wall instead of a large one on the bathroom floor. The total number of tiles remains constant.

Now, check Resample. It appears possible to change the number of tiles along with the resolution and image size! This isn't the same as going out and buying the correct number, color, and size of tiles necessary for the mosaic to be as pleasing to view in the kitchen as it would have been in the bathroom. Resampling, also called interpolation, evaluates existing tiles and makes duplicates next to them of approximately the same color, brightness, etc. The detail possible with the correct number of original tiles is missing, but a fair rendition is possible. To create a little wall panel instead of a bathroom floor, for example, the software discards unnecessary tiles for a reduced version that keeps its detail.

To open the Image Size dialog box in Photoshop, first open an image file (File>Open). Then open the dialog box (Image>Image Size).

Decisions about file size and resolution depend on the intended use for the photograph. Are you preparing a one-column headshot for the newspaper or an 8.5"x11" magazine cover? Do you want to have an image that will load quickly on a web site?

If there is ever a possibility that you might want a large image—a two-page spread in a magazine, for example—your best bet is to start with the largest file size your camera or scanner is capable of producing. Edit the largest size possible, save it, and then save it with a new name, size, and resolution as appropriate for the web, a newspaper, or magazine. (Buy enough tile now because you will not be able to buy more later!)

INTENDED USE	RESOLUTION
Internet	72 dpi
Newspaper	150–200 dpi
Photographic-quality print	
Inkjet or dye-sublimation printer	200 dpi
Glossy magazine, book	300 dpi

Resampling discards or adds pixels to decrease or increase file size and resolution. Discarding pixels is not a problem. Adding them results in less-than-ideal quality. Recapturing them is impossible.

Why throw away pixels? A small file for viewing on the web does not require all the tiles necessary for the kitchen floor—or for a magazine cover. The software analyzes the pixels and discards unnecessary ones. The file will upload faster but still have enough resolution (tiles per square foot) for a good image on a monitor. A smaller file size is almost always best for transmitting images or viewing them online.

What about going larger? To add pixels when a file is too small—or to create tiles for a larger floor—the software analyzes the color and brightness of each pixel and tries to create similar new ones to surround it. Like making do with tiles of approximate color and brightness, resampling to make a picture that ran two columns in a newspaper for a glorious new life as magazine cover can smooth out the differences but cannot supply missing detail (see opposite page).

ALERT: Photoshop and software like Genuine Fractals resample digital files with increasingly good results. However, for the best technical quality, it's better to shoot large files or to rescan a photo or negative to the correct size and resolution than to resample. Knowing the maximum final size and use for your digital image will protect against disappointment later.

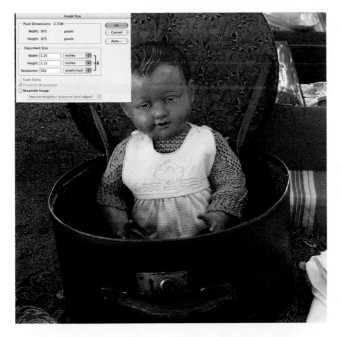

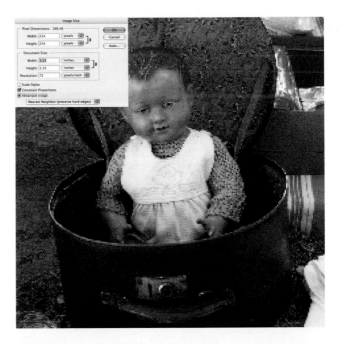

IMAGE #1, above, was digitized at 300 ppi at 3.25 inches by 3.25 inches. A resolution of 300 ppi is ideal for book and magazine reproduction and for subtly detailed inkjet and dye-sublimation prints. Compare this quality to that of the resampled image below, #3. Note that the image above would look good on a web site, but it would take a long time to download on the viewer's screen because of its large file size.

IMAGE #2 would look as fine on a computer monitor as #1, left! A monitor cannot display more than 72 pixels per inch—regardless of how much resolution an image has. This image's small file size allows it to transmit easily over the Internet and load quickly on a web site. But its quality as a printed image is poor. It also would print poorly on an inkjet or dye-sublimation printer.

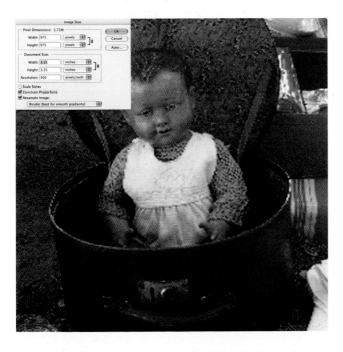

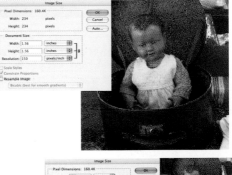

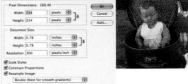

IMAGE #3, directly above, began life as the 72 ppi Image #2 (above, right), but has been artificially pumped up (resampled) to the same resolution and file size as #1. It's smoother-looking than #2, but can't compare to #1.

Three sizes and resolutions from the same file.
Note that the number of pixels in each of these images is the same, but that the resolution increases as the physical size of the images diminishes. The quality of each image also improves as its physical size decreases. Why? Because the same number of pixels has less surface to cover, more detail becomes visible in the image as it grows smaller.

ALERT: The quality of these images would have appeared identical when viewed at 100 percent on a computer monitor.

CROPPING AN IMAGE

You can crop any digital image, whether it was scanned or imported from a digital camera.

 The Cropping Tool is available whenever Photoshop is open, so you can always crop later. These and the examples on upcoming pages assume you are working on an image that is open in Photoshop.

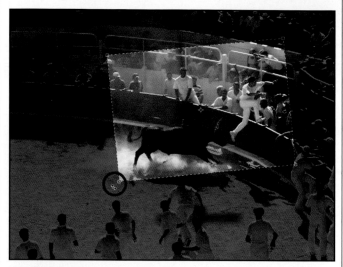

Setting the Tool Option Bar to display a semi-opaque screen (Opacity 75%) will darken the part of the image that is being deleted, as below.

Select the Crop tool.

Click at one corner of the picture, and then drag the tool diagonally across the image until you have selected the area you want. Releasing the tool outlines the selection.

Prepare the angle change. With the Crop tool still highlighted, move the cursor slightly away from the edge of the photo until a bent arrow (circled above) appears. This tool lets you change the angle of the cropped area to match that of the scan.

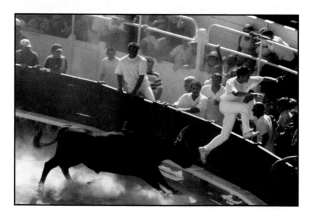

SAVING FOR THE WEB

Saving images for web display is another exercise in trade-offs among resolution, file size, and quality. Typically, you need to keep file sizes small (no more than 30 kilobytes per picture). The larger the file, the longer it takes to appear on a web site, and viewers may not be willing to wait several minutes for a photograph to download.

Photoshop (File>Save for Web) allows you to preview quality and resolution choices before making a final decision.

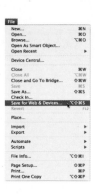

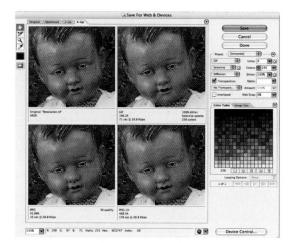

Take advantage of Photoshop's File Info to include your name and caption information for each picture. Some archiving software calls on information you enter here. So do some image browsers and web browsers. A little up-front preparation can save lots more work later.

Shooting session strategy: download the images into a folder, then open one photo, enter the general data, enter the session name in "job name." Save, then move through the other menus and save. For every subsequent photo from that session, you can load the saved information and, if necessary, add or edit caption information individually. **ALERT:** Learn about Batch Actions in Photoshop and how to fully automate this process. (Set it in motion and then go do your laundry.)

General: Lets you enter the caption, your name and copyright information, etc. To display a copyright symbol in the title bar of the image window, choose Copyrighted Work in the Copyright Status menu.

Categories: Defaults are 3-digit Associated Press codes.

Keywords: Provide a way for some image browsers and archiving software to categorize and search for an image.

Origin: Enter date taken, location, etc.

EXIF: Displays information imported from a digital camera, such as the date and time a picture was taken, resolution, ISO rating, f/stop, compression, and exposure time. For more about EXIF annotations, see the manual for your digital camera.

When you save a file from a digital camera or scanner, or after working on it in Photoshop, you can save it in a variety of formats. Some options are more versatile, allowing the image to be used in different applications or across computer platforms, in print or on the web. Some will work only with the program in which they were created. Following are common options for photographers.

JPEG (.jpg)	compresses photos by discarding those pixels the software determines to be redundant. JPEG was designed for compressing full-color or grayscale images like photographs. A 24-bit image saved as a JPEG file can be reduced to about 1/20th its original size. JPEGs, with their smaller file sizes and faster transmission time, are the preferred means of displaying continuous-tone photos on the Internet. Digital cameras offer this format as a file option. It's possible to save JPEGs at various quality levels. See pages 479–480 to compare the quality and size trade-offs when making this choice. **ALERT:** Opening and closing a JPEG image without manipulating it will not change its quality but multiple changes to and resaves of a JPEG file will degrade its look. After you have opened an image from a digital camera and changed it, save it as a TIFF file (see below). With TIFF, you can open, change, and close a picture without losing quality. You can always save the picture later in JPEG if you need to save space or transmit the image on the Internet.
GIF (.gif)	produces small web files and is best for flat-color images with type or line drawings, not for photos.
TIFF (.tif)	is a common format for bringing an image into a page-layout program and for exchanging files between computer platforms. Almost all desktop scanners can produce TIFF images.
EPS (.eps)	is also commonly used for bringing images into page-layout programs but is less flexible between PCs and Macintosh.
PNG (.png)	is a format used for web-based photos. It is a lossless compression format, can interlace images, is viewable in browser windows and uses up to 256 colors. PNG might replace .gif format web display, but not all browsers can use the new format.
PICT (.pct)	is useful when images are designed for presentations, screen displays, and video work.
PSD (.psd)	can only be opened and edited in Photoshop. However, you can still re-save the file in a variety of other formats that are readable on both Macintosh and PCs without affecting image quality. **ALERT:** A layered photo saved as a PSD file is a truly multi-purpose file because you can activate or deactivate the layers for different uses. Saving in most other formats means having to permanently combine the layers. For example, you might want to include your copyright information on a text layer for an image to be displayed on the Internet, but then deactivate the text layer to make a file for a magazine. For the Internet file, you would compress the necessary layers, save the file as a JPEG, and send the picture on its way. For the magazine, you could deactivate the text layer, compress the layers, save the file as a TIFF, and send it to the art director. There would be no need in either case to keep copies of the JPEG or the TIFF file because all your work remains stored in layers and preserved in the PSD format.

In addition to listings from previous editions of *Photojournalism: The Professionals' Approach*, this bibliography includes articles and books derived from searches of a number of different electronic databases.

A

"Backstory, Photographer Reneé C. Byer," Interview with Byer. *Doubletruck Magazine*, Volume 4, Issue 7 (Spring 2007): 14-17.

"A Public Suicide: Papers Differ on Editing Graphic Images." Associated Press Managing Editors (APME) *Report: Photo and Graphics*. New York, 1987.

"A Question of Ethics." *News Photographer* (July 1983). (multiple-article anthology).

"Eyes Wide Shut," *The Wall Street Journal*, (story about French protesters torching cars), (November 9, 2005).

"Eyewitness. A Century of Great Photojournalism." *Life* 22, no. 11 (Oct. 2001): 16.

"Future Stock: Predictions on the Fate of Photojournalism." *American Photo* (Sept./Oct. 1996): 78–80.

"Handling the horrible: Dealing with shocking images." *Poynteronline*. Retrieved July 16, 2004, from *http://www.newsu.org/articles/view.aspx?id=260*.

"Life's Work: The Photojournalism of Earl Dotter." *Columbia Journalism Review* 35, no. 5 (1997): 40.

"News Views: Edward Farber, Portable Strobe Inventor, Dead." *News Photographer* (Apr. 1982): 3.

"News Views: Milwaukee Sentinel Photographer Helps Firemen in Rescue." *News Photographer* (Mar. 1988): 4.

"Photo Essays." *Nieman Reports* 52(2) (Summer 1998): 8–27.

"Photojournalism—Journalists Learn How to Protect Themselves in War a Panel of Instructors." *Nieman Reports* 54, no. 3 (2000): 59.

"Photojournalism. A Touching Moment from the Heart of the Jungle." *American Photo* 11, no. 6 (Nov. 2001): 82.

"Photojournalism." *Nieman Reports* 54, no. 3 (2000): 45.

"Suicide." (multiple-article anthology). *News Photographer* (May 1987): 20–32, 34–43, 62.

"The Golden Age of the Picture Magazine." *Photographic Journal* 126 (Mar. 1986): 104–8.

"The Process of Recording Conflict" *Aperture* 97 (Winter 1984): 6–77. (five-article anthology).

"To Publish? Pro and Con." *News Photographer* (May 1993): 12–17.

"U.S. Supreme Court to Review Two 'Ride-Along' Cases." *News Photographer* (Dec. 1998): 32.

"Why Do They React? Readers Assail Publication of Funeral, Accident Photos." *News Photographer* (Mar. 1981): 20, 22–23.

"Women in Photojournalism." *News Photographer* (Dec. 1984): 16–17; (Feb. 1985): 25–29; (Apr. 1985): 22, 24.

20 Years with AP Wirephoto. New York: Associated Press, 1955.

Abel, Jessica, and Glass, Ira. *Radio: an Illustrated Guide*. WBEZ Alliance, 1999.

Abhinav Aima, Patricia Ferrier, Les Roka, Lynn Silverstein and James Staebler. "A Visual Experiment in Acceptance: Does Quantity and Location of Blood Affect Readers' Reaction to a Photograph?" AEJMC Convention, August 2001.

Abramson, Howard S. *National Geographic: Behind America's Lens on the World*. New York: Crown Publishers, 1987.

Adams, Jonathan. " . . . They Should Have Published It." *4Sight* (Nov./Dec. 1993): 17.

Adams, R. C., Copeland, Gary A., Fish, Marjorie J., and Hughes, Melissa. "Effect of Framing on Selection of Photographs of Men and Women." *Journalism Quarterly* 57 (1980): 463–67.

Agence France-Presse. *Facing the World: Great Moments in Photojournalism*. New York: Harry N. Abrams, 2001.

Alabiso, Vincent J. "Prospects for Photojournalism at a Time When Readers Are Bombarded by Information," *Media Studies Journal* 13, no. 2 (Spring 1999): 58.

Alabiso, Vincent, Tunney, Kelly Smith and Zoeller, Chuck, eds. *Flash! The Associated Press Covers the World*. New York: Associated Press in association with Harry N. Abrams, 1998.

Alabiso, Vincent. "Changing with the Times." *Nieman Reports* 52 (Summer 1998): 5–7.

Alexander, S. L. "Curious History: The ABA Code of Judicial Ethics Canon 35." Paper presented at the Annual Meeting of the Association for Education in Journalism and Mass Communication, Portland, Oregon, 1988. ERIC, ED296422.

Alland, Alexander. *Jacob A. Riis*. Millerton, New York: *Aperture*, 1974.

American Photo. May/June 1994. Special issue on the future of photojournalism.

Ang, Tom. *Picture Editing: An Introduction.* Oxford, Boston: Focal Press, 1996.

Anonymous. "Ethics committee criticizes Pearl photos publications." *Quill* 90, no. 7: S2.

The Art of Seeing: The Best of Reuters Photography. Ulli, Michel, editor. London, New York: Pearson Education, 2000.

Artusa, Marina. "Did You Run This Photo?" *Columbia Journalism Review* 41, no. 2 (July/Aug. 2002): 47–Back Cover.

ASMP: 1944–1994 50th Anniversary Bulletin 13 (Dec. 1994). Princeton: The American Society of Media Photographers, 1994.

Associated Press News and Photo Staff, eds. *One Day in Our World*. New York: Avon Books, 1986.

Auer, Michel. *The Illustrated History of the Camera: From 1839 to the Present*. Translated & adapted by D.B. Tubbs. Boston: New York Graphic Society, 1975.

B

Baker, Robert L. "Portraits of a Public Suicide: Photo Treatment by Selected Pennsylvania Dailies." *Newspaper Research Journal* 9 (Summer 1988): 13–23.

Barney, Ralph D., and Black, Jay. "Toward Professional Ethical Journalism." *Mass Communications Review* 17 (1/2) (1990): 2–13.

Barnhurst, Kevin G. *Seeing the Newspaper*. New York: St. Martin's Press, 1994.

Barnhurst, Kevin, and John Nerone. "Civic Picturing Vs. Realist Photojournalism. The Regime of Illustrated News, 1856–1901." *Design Issues* 16, no 1 (2000): 59–79.

Barrett, Wayne M. "Margaret Bourke-White: New Vistas in Photojournalism." *USA Today* 118 (Sept. 1989): 55–63.

Barry, Ann Marie. "Digital Manipulation of Public Images: Local Issues and Global Consequences." Paper presented at the Annual Meeting of the International Communication Association. Montreal, May 1997.

Baxter, William S., Quarles, Rebecca, and Kosak, Herman. "The Effects of Photographs and Their Size on Reading and Recall of News Stories." Paper presented at the Annual Meeting of the Association for Education in Journalism. Seattle, Washington, 1978. ERIC, ED159722.

Baynes, Ken. *Scoop, Scandal and Strife*. New York: Hastings House, 1971.

Benson, Harry. Harry Benson: *Fifty Years in Pictures*. New York: Harry N. Abrams, 2001.

Benson, Harry. *Harry Benson on Photojournalism*. New York: Harmony Books, 1982.

Bentley, P.F. "It's All in the Eyes." *Columbia Journalism Review* (May/June 1996): 45–47.

Bergeman, Rich. "Photo Editing: A Neglected Art." *Community College Journalist* 15 (Winter 1987): 18–20.

Bergin, David P. *Photojournalism Manual: How to Plan, Shoot, Edit and Sell*. New York: Morgan & Morgan, 1967.

Bernt, Joseph P. and Greenwald, Marilyn S. "Senior Newspaper Editors and Daily Newspaper Coverage of the Gay and Lesbian Community: A Summary of Past Findings and Discussion of New Findings on Reporting Sexual Orientation." Paper presented at the National Conference of Lesbians and Gays in Mainstream Media. San Francisco, California, June 25–27, 1992. ERIC, ED347599.

Bessie, Simon Michael. *Jazz Journalism: The Story of the Tabloid Newspapers.* New York: E.P. Dutton, 1938.

Best of Photojournalism. Annual, 1977–present. Publisher varies.

Bethune, Beverly, ed. *Women in Photojournalism*. Durham, NC: National Press Photographers Association, 1986.

Bethune, Beverly. "Under the Microscope: A Nationwide Survey Looks at the Professional Concerns and Job Satisfaction of the Daily Newspaper Photographer." *News Photographer* (Nov. 1983): R1–R8.

Bezner, Lili Corbus, and F. Jack Hurley. "Photography and Politics in America: From the New Deal into the Cold War." *Journal of American History* 87, no. 4 (2000): 1546–1547.

Bissland, James H. "The News Photographer's Career Ladder." An NPPA Special Report (also appears in the Oct. 1984 issue of *News Photographer*).

Bissland, James H. and Kielmeyer, David. "Bypassed by the Revolution? Photojournalism in a Decade of Change." Paper presented at the Annual Meeting of the Association for Education in Journalism and Mass Communication. Montreal, Aug. 5–8, 1992. ERIC, ED349623.

Blackman, Victor. *Naff off! Confessions of a Fleet Street Photographer*. London: BFP, 1987.

Blackwood, Roy E. "International News Photos in U.S. and Canadian Papers." *Journalism Quarterly* 64 (1987): 195–99.

Blackwood, Roy E. "The Content of News Photos: Roles Portrayed by Men and Women." *Journalism Quarterly* 60 (1983): 710–14.

Borden, Sandra L. "Choice Processes in a Newspaper Ethics Case." *Communication Monographs* 64, no. 1 (Mar 1997): 65–81.

Bourke-White, Margaret, and Sean Callahan. *Margaret Bourke-White: Photographer*. 1st ed. Boston: Little Brown, 1998.

Bourke-White, Margaret. *Portrait of Myself*. New York: Simon & Schuster, 1963.

Bowden, Charles, and Eugene Richards. *Eugene Richards*. London; New York: Phaidon, 2001.

Bowden, Robert. *Get That Picture*. Garden City, New York: Amphoto, 1978.

Bowers, Matthew. "Following the Yellow Brick Road or how this newspaper in Norfolk won the McDougall." *News Photographer* (May 1997): 14–20.

Bowie, Jennifer. "Out of Their Hands: Framing and its Impact on Newsmagazine Coverage of Indians and Indian Activism, 1968–79." Paper presented at the Proceedings of the Annual Meeting of the Association for Education in Journalism and Mass Communication, New Orleans, Louisiana, Aug. 3–8, 1999 1999.

Boylan, James. "Underexposed." *Columbia Journalism Review* 38, no. 6: 71.

Brauchli, Marcus. "Prize Under Glass . . . Chance, Ingenuity, Violence Often Cited as Key Factors in Pulitzer Winners." *News Photographer* (June–July 1981): 20–23.

Brecheen-Kirkton, Kent. "Visual Silences: What Photography Chooses Not to Show Us." *American Journalism* 8 (Winter 1991): 27–34.

Brecher, Ellie. "Reporter-Photographer Relationships and How to Improve Them." *4Sight* (Nov./Dec. 1993): 12–13.

Brennen, Bonnie, and Hanno Hardt. *Picturing the Past: Media, History, and Photography, The History of Communication*. Urbana: University of Illinois Press, 1999.

Brennen, Bonnie. "Strategic Competition and the Value of Photographers' Work: Photojournalism in Gannett Newspapers, 1937–1947." *American Journalism* 15, no. 2 (1998): 59–77.

Brill, Betsy. "Pictures Don't Lie . . . or Do They?" Master's thesis, University of Missouri, 1988.

Brill, Betsy. "Town Protests Staged Photo, Hooker Image." *News Photographer* (Sept. 1986): 4–8.

Brill, Charles. "The Early History of the Associated Press Wire Photo: 1926–1935." Paper presented at the Annual Meeting of the Association for Education in Journalism. Madison, Wisconsin, 1977.

Brink, Ben. "Question of Ethics: Where Does Honesty in Photojournalism Begin? 'The Foundation Is Basic, Simple Honesty,' an Editor Says." *News Photographer* (June 1988): 21–22, 23–33.

Brock, Oliver Eugene. "Digital Imaging in Photojournalism: Technological and Ethical Impact." Master's thesis, University of Mississippi, 1993.

Brower, Kenneth. "Photography in the Age of Falsification." *Atlantic Monthly* (May 1998): 92–111.

Brown, Cindy M. "How the Use of Color Affects the Content of Newspaper Photographs." Paper presented at the Annual Meeting of the Association for Education in Journalism and Mass Communication, Washington, DC, 1989. ERIC, ED308525.

Brown, Cindy M. "Listening to Subjects' Concerns about News Photographs: A Grounded Ethical Inquiry." Ph.D. diss., Indiana University, 1998.

Brown, Cindy M. "PM: Just Another Picture Paper?" Paper presented at the Annual Meeting of the Association for Education in Journalism and Mass Communication, Visual Communication Division, Aug. 12, 1994.

Brown, Cindy M. "The Use of Search Warrants in Canada and the United States to Obtain Photographic Evidence from Journalists." Paper presented at the Annual Meeting of the Association for Education in Journalism and Mass Communication. Kansas City, Missouri, Aug. 11–14, 1993. ERIC, ED362918.

Brown, Jennifer E. "*News Photographer* and the Pornography of Grief." *Journal of Mass Media Ethics* 2 (Spring/Summer 1987): 75–81.

Brown, Theodore M. Margaret Bourke-White, Photojournalist. Ithaca, New York: Andrew Dickson White Museum of Art, Cornell University, 1972.

Brumbaugh, L. P. "Shadow catchers or shadow snatchers? Ethical issues for photographers of contemporary Native Americans." *American Indian Culture and Research Journal* 20, no. 3 (1996): 33–49.

Brust, James S. "Photojournalism, 1877: John H. Fouch, Fort Keogh's First Post Photographer." *Montana* 50, no. 4 (2000): 32–39.

Bryant, Michael. "The Problem with Illustrations." *News Photographer* (July 1987): 36.

Buckland, Gail. *Shots in the Dark: True Crime Pictures*. Boston, Mass. London: Bulfinch, 2001.

Buell, Hal, and Pett, Saul. *The Instant It Happened*. New York: Associated Press, 1975.

Bush, Martin H., *The Photographs of Gordon Parks* (Wichita, Kansas: Ulrich Museum of Art, Wichita State University, 1983).

C

Callahan, Sean, and Astor, Gerald. *Photographing Sports: John Zimmerman, Mark Kauffman and Neil Leifer.* Los Angeles: Alskog, 1975.

Callahan, Sean, ed. *The Photographs of Margaret Bourke-White*. Boston: New York Graphic Society, 1972.

Callahan, Sean. "The Last Days of a Legend (Margaret Bourke-White)." *American Photo* 9 (Sept./Oct. 1998): 33–4, 95, 97.

Campbell, Gregory D. "A Study of Photo Editing Duties at the Small American Daily Newspaper 1994." Master's thesis, Memphis State University, 1994.

Campbell, W. Joseph. "Not likely sent: The Remington-Hearst 'telegrams.'" Paper presented at the Annual Meeting of the Association for Education in Journalism and Mass Communication. New Orleans, Louisiana, Aug. 4–7, 1999.

Cannon, Brian Douglas. "Photographs as Icons: Toward a Theory of Iconicity of Still Images in Photojournalism." *DAI* 61, no. 12A (2001): 345.

Cannon, Brian. "Discourse on Philosophical Methods for Determining Ethics in Photojournalism: Analysis of a Pulitzer Prize Winning Photograph." Paper presented to the Association for Education in Journalism and Mass Communication, Washington, DC, Aug., 1995.

Cannon, Brian. "Icon of the Oklahoma City Bombing: Revealing Connotative Meaning in a News Photograph of Tragedy and Heroism." Paper presented at the Annual Meeting of the Association for Education in Journalism and Mass Communication, Visual Communication Division, Anaheim, California, Aug.,1996.

Capa, Cornell. *The Concerned Photographer*. New York: Grossman Publishers, 1968.

Capa, Robert, and Richard Whelan. *Robert Capa: The Definitive Collection*. London: Phaidon, 2001.

Capa, Robert. *Robert Capa, Photographs.* New York: *Aperture*, 1996.

Capa, Robert. Slightly Out of Focus. New York: Modern Library, 1999.

Capture the Moment: the Pulitzer Prize Photographs. Cyma Rubin and Eric Newton, editors. New York: Norton, 2001.

Caputo, Philip. "Photojournalism—Do Images of War Need Justification?" *Nieman Reports* 54, no. 3 (2000): 51.

Carlebach, Michael L. *American Photojournalism Comes of Age.* Washington, DC: Smithsonian Institution Press, 1997.

Carlebach, Michael Lloyd. "The Origins of Photojournalism in America, 1839–1880." Ph.D. diss., Brown University, 1988.

Carnes, Cecil. *Jimmy Hare News Photographer: Half a Century with a Camera.* New York: Macmillan, 1940.

Carrigan, Michael Andrew. "The Media Print Pool and Censorship as a Department of Defense Public Relations Tool during the Persian Gulf War." Master's thesis, University of Nevada Reno, 1997.

Carroll, Darren, Cox, Stephanie, Dwyer, Jonathan J., Kenig, Nick, Layton, John and Wind, Andrew. "Sports Photography: Getting Pictures of Action." *Communication: Journalism Education Today* 31 (Summer 1998): 2–7.

Cartier-Bresson, Henri. *Europeans*. London: Thames & Hudson, 1998.

Cartier-Bresson, Henri. *The Decisive Moment*. New York: Simon & Schuster, 1952.

Cartier-Bresson, Henri. *The World of Henri Cartier-Bresson*. New York: Viking Press, 1968.

Case, Tony. "Photo Illustration on Page One Story." *Editor & Publisher* (Aug. 31, 1996): 3.

Cavallo, Robert M., and Kahan, Stuart. *Photography: What's the Law?* 2nd ed. New York: Crown Publishers, 1979.

Cavouras, Krissa Corbett. "See It Now: Photojournalism, Not Art, at the Perpignan Festival in France." *American Photo* 13, no. 5 (Sept./Oct. 2002): 10.

Chapnick, Howard. "Looking for Bang Bang: Photojournalists are Flocking to Trouble Spots Like El Salvador, and Too Many Are Not Returning Alive. Are the Results of War Photography Today Really Worth the Risks?" *Popular Photography* (July 1982): 65–67, 99, 101–102.

Chapnick, Howard. "Markets and Careers: American vs. European Picture Editing." *Popular Photography* (Dec. 1986): 38–39.

Chapnick, Howard. "Markets and Careers: Changing Views on Picture Editing." *Popular Photography* (Dec. 1986): 38–39.

Chapnick, Howard. "Markets and Careers: Getting the Pictures is Only the First Worry for Photojournalists; How it Affects Subjects is the Other." *Popular Photography* (Aug. 1983): 40, 93.

Chapnick, Howard. "Markets and Careers: Keeping News Pictures Meaningful." *Popular Photography* (Mar. 1983): 18, 130.

Chapnick, Howard. "Markets and Careers: Photographic Captions." *Popular Photography* (Feb. 1979): 42, 64, 127, 143.

Chapnick, Howard. "Markets and Careers: Words Tell the Reader What Pictures Can't: They Make a Photographer a Photojournalist." *Popular Photography* (Feb. 1979): 40, 64, 127, 143.

Chapnick, Howard. "Photojournalism Should Work On More Than One Level—and Its Images Should Be Clear, Simple, and Spontaneous." *Popular Photography* (Sept. 1984): 36–37.

Chapnick, Howard. *Truth Needs No Ally: Inside Photojournalism.* Columbia, Missouri: University of Columbia Press, 1994.

Chernoff, George, and Sarbin, Hershel B. *Photography and the Law*. 5th ed. Garden City, New York: Amphoto, 1975.

Choi, Hyunju. "The Politics of Representations in Four Genres—Documentary Photography, Photojournalism, Government Public Relations and Art Photography: A Comparative Analysis of FSA Photographs of the 1930s," PhD, Dissertation, Temple University, 2001.

Cichy, Rose M. "Seeing America: Women Photographers Between the Wars." *Library Journal* 124, no. 19: 81.

Clarke, Lois E. "Features—Community Service—Another Aspect of Photojournalism." *PSA Journal* 66, no. 6 (2000): 26.

Cockerham, Michael. "Colin Jacobson's Belief in Reportage. Interview." *RPS Journal* 139, no. 9 (Nov. 1999): 404–7.

Cohen, Lester. *The New York Graphic. The World's Zaniest Newspaper.* Philadelphia: Chilton, 1964.

Cohen, Stuart. "Focusing on Humanity: The Life of W. Eugene Smith." *Boston Phoenix* (Oct. 31, 1978).

Coleman, A. D. "Documentary, Photojournalism, and Press Photography Now: Notes and Questions." In Coleman, A. D. (Allan D.). Depth of Field University of N.M. Press, 35–52, 1998.

Coleman, A. D. "New York exposed: Photographs from the *Daily News*." *Artnews* 101, no. 2 (2002): 94–+.

Coleman, Renita. "Civic Journalism on the Right Side of the Brain: How Photographers and Graphic Designers Visually Communicate the Principles of Civic Journalism." Paper presented at the Proceedings of the Annual Meeting of the Association for Education in Journalism and Mass Communication (83rd, Phoenix, Arizona, Aug. 9–12, 2000). Civic Journalism Interest Group, Phoenix, Arizona, Aug. 9–12, 2000

Coleman, Renita. "Design Characteristics of Public Journalism: Integrating Visual and Verbal Meaning." Paper presented at the Annual Meeting of the Association for Education in Journalism and Mass Communication. Baltimore, Maryland, Aug. 5–8, 1998. ERIC, ED423576.

Coles, Robert. "A place for words and images to call home." *Nieman Reports* 55, no. 3: 37.

Collins, K. "Get the picture: A personal history of photojournalism." *Library Journal* 123, no. 16 (1998): 84–84.

Converse, Gordon N. *All Mankind: Photographs*. Boston: Christian Science Publ. Society, 1983.

Converse, Gordon N. *Reflections in Light: The Work of a Photojournalist*. Boston: Christian Science Monitor, 1989.

Cookman, Claude. "Compelled to Witness: The Social Realism of Henri Cartier-Bresson." *Communication Abstracts* 21, no. 6 (1998).

Cookman, Claude. *The People's America*. Indiana University Art Museum, 1997.

Cookman, Claude. "The Photographic Reportage of Henri Cartier-Bresson, 1993–1973, Volume I." Ph.D. diss., Princeton University, 1994.

Cookman, Claude. *A Voice is Born: The Founding and Early Years of the National Press Photographers Association Under the Leadership of Joseph Costa*. Durham, NC: National Press Photographers Association, 1985.

Coontz, S., and M. Parson. "*Life*'s America: Family and nation in postwar photojournalism" *Signs* 22, no. 2 (1997): 440–452.

Cooper, Guy. "Stock Photography: A Biased View from the Trenches." *News Photographer* (Aug. 1998): mgr 3, 6.

Coopersmith, Jonathan. "From Lemons to Lemonade: The Development of AP Wirephoto." *American Journalism* 17, no. 4 (2000): 55–72.

Corrigan, Don. "Future of newspapers belongs to visual artists." *St. Louis Journalism Review* 28, no. 206 (1998): 1+.

Costa, Joseph, ed. *The Complete Book of Press Photography*. New York: National Press Photographers Association, 1950.

Costa, Joseph. "Does press freedom include photography?" *Nieman Reports* 53/54, no. 4/1: 174.

Costa, Joseph. "Cameras in Court: A Position Paper." Muncie, Indiana: Journalism/Public Relations Research Center, Ball State University, 1980.

Costa, Joseph. Collected Papers. George Arents Research Library. Syracuse University: Syracuse, New York.

Cotter, Holland 'Unkown Weegee', on (sic) Photographer Who Made the Night Noir, *The New York Times*, June 9, 2006 online *www.nytimes.com/2006/06/09/arts/design/09weeg.html*

Coupland, K. "A focus on the Web: @tlas, a showcase for serious photojournalism and multimedia." *Graphis* 53, no. 307 (1997): 32–32.

Covert, D. C. "American photojournalism comes of age." *Journalism & Mass Communication Quarterly* 75, no. 2 (1998): 429–431.

Covert, Douglas C. "Color Preference Conflicts in Visual Compositions." *Newspaper Research Journal* 9 (Fall 1987): 49–59.

Crager, Jack. "See It Now: Photojournalism Thrives at Perpignan." *American Photo* 12, no. 5 (Sept./Oct. 2001): 9.

Craig, R. Stephen. "Cameras in Courtrooms in Florida." *Journalism Quarterly* 56 (1979): 703–10.

Culver, Kathleen B. "An Open Door with a Big Spring: Cameras in Federal Courts." *VCQ* (Spring 1994): 17–18.

Cunningham, Brent. "David Pierini: Stopping time." *Columbia Journalism Review* 41, no. 2: 57.

Cunningham, Brent. "The Photographer: 'to Come up with a Different Image No Matter What It Takes'." *Columbia Journalism Review* 38, no. 5 (Jan./Feb. 2000): 40–1+.

Cunningham, Brent. "What's wrong with this picture?" *Columbia Journalism Review* 41, no. 4:11.

D

Daniel, Pete, and Smock, Raymond. *A Talent for Detail: Frances Benjamin Johnston*. New York: Harmony Books, 1974.

David, Prabu. "News Concreteness and Visual-Verbal Association: Do News Pictures Narrow the Recall Gap between Concrete and Abstract News?" *Human Communication Research* 25, no. 2 (Dec 1998): 180–201.

Davis, M. "Lee Miller—Bathing with the Enemy (World War II Photojournalism, Hitler)." *History of Photography* 21, no. 4 (1997): 314–318.

Davis, S. E. "Digital Photo Illustration." *Graphis*, no. 296 (1995): 20.

Denton, Craig L. "Supercharged Color: Its Arresting Place in Visual Communication." Paper presented at the Annual Meeting of the Association for Education in Journalism and Mass Communication, Gainesville, Florida, 1984. ERIC, ED244292.

Desbarats, Peter. *Canadian Illustrated News 1869–1883*. Toronto: McClelland and Stewart Limited, 1970.

Deschin, Jacob. "W. Eugene Smith Recalls Brutal Beating While Documenting a Poison Scandal." *Popular Photography* (Oct. 1973): 14, 20, 212.

Devine, Heather Catherine. "Controlling Digital Manipulation in Photojournalism: An Aggressive Solution to a Contentious Problem." Master's thesis, Carleton University (Canada), 1996.

Dewitz, Bobo von, and Robert ed Lebeck. *Kiosk: A History of Photojournalism 1839–1973*. Boston: Dap, 2002.

Dick, David B. "'What Did Mr. Dwyer Do, Daddy?' 'Well, As You Could See, He Committed Suicide, Darling.'" *Quill* (Mar. 1987): 18–20.

Domke, David, David D. Perlmutter, and Meg Spratt. "The Primes of Our Times? An Examination of the 'Power' of Visual Images." *Journalism* 3, no. 2 (2002): 131–59.

Dorfman, John. "Digital Dangers." *Columbia Journalism Review* 41, no. 2 (July/Aug. 2002): 60–3.

Dorfman, John. "Photojournalism on the Web: Three Models." *Columbia Journalism Review* 41, no. 2 (July/Aug. 2002): 62–3.

Drapkin, Arnold. "Journalism's idea man, John Durniak, transformed news, picture magazines." *News Photographer* (Jan. 1998): 28, 32.

duCille, Michel. "The Use of Front-Page Photography in the *Washington Post*." Master's thesis, Ohio University, 1994.

Duggan, Dennis. "Louis Liotta: He was one from the 'glory days.'" *News Photographer* (Aug. 1997): 19–20.

Duncan, David Douglas. *Self Portrait: U.S.A.* New York: Abrams, 1969.

Dunn, Philip. *Press Photography*. Sparkford, UK: Oxford Illustrated, 1988.

Durham, Michael S. *Powerful Days: The Civil Rights Photography of Charles Moore*. New York: Stewart, Tabori & Chang, 1991.

Durniak, John. "10 Stories Around You." *Popular Photography* (June 1959): 72.

Durniak, John. "Focus on Wilson Hicks." *Popular Photography* (Apr. 1965): 59.

Dykhouse, Caroline Dow. "Prior Restraint on Photojournalists." *Journalism Quarterly* 64 (1987): 88–93, 118.

Dykhouse, Caroline Dow. "Privacy Law and Print Photojournalism." Paper presented at the Annual Meeting of the Association for Education in Journalism, Seattle, Washington, 1978. ERIC, ED1655144.

Dykhouse, Caroline Dow. "Privacy Law as It Affected Journalism, 1890–1978: Privacy Is a Visual Tort." Paper presented at the Annual Meeting of the Association for Education in Journalism and Mass Communication, Memphis, Tennessee, 1985. ERIC, ED262399.

Dykhouse, Caroline Dow. "Public Policy's Differential Effects on *News Photographer*s." Paper presented at the meeting of the Association for Education in Journalism, Photojournalism Division, Seattle, Washington, 1978.

Dykhouse, Caroline Dow. "Shuttered Shutters: The Photographic Statutes and Their Faithful Companion, 18 USC 1382—An Examination of Photographic Access to Military Areas." Paper presented at the Annual Meeting of the Association for Education in Journalism, Athens, Ohio, 1982. ERIC, ED218678.

Dykhouse, Caroline Dow. "The Detroit Workshop, 1949–1951: Robert Drew and the *Life* Photojournalism Essay Formula." Master's thesis, Michigan State University, 1980.

Dykhouse, Caroline Dow. "The Response of the Law to Visual Journalism, 1839–1978." Ph.D. diss., Michigan State University, 1985.

E

Edey, Maitland. *Great Photographic Essays From Life*. Boston: New York Graphic Society, 1978.

Edgerton, Harold E. *Electronic Flash/Strobe*. 3rd ed. Cambridge, Massachusetts: M.I.T. Press, 1987.

Edgerton, Harold E., and Killian, James R., Jr. *Moments of Vision: The Stroboscopic Revolution in Photography*. Cambridge. Massachusetts: M.I.T. Press, 1979.

Edom, Clifton Cedric. *Photojournalism: Principles and Practices*. 2nd ed. Dubuque, Iowa: W. C. Brown Co., 1980.

Edwards, Owen. "A Mover Among the Shakers: Arnold Newman's Photographs Are a Tribute to the Staying Power of a Good Idea." *American Photo*grapher (Nov. 1985): 68–73.

Eisenstaedt, Alfred. *Eisenstaedt on Eisenstaedt: A Self-Portrait*. New York: Abbeville Press, 1985.

Eisenstaedt, Alfred. *Eisenstaedt: Remembrances*. Expanded rev. ed. Boston: Little, Brown, 1999.

Eisenstaedt, Alfred. *Eisenstaedt—Germany*. Edited by Gregory A. Vitiello. New York: Abrams, 1981.

Eisenstaedt. Alfred. *People*. New York: Viking Press, 1973.

Eisenstaedt. Alfred. *The Age of Eisenstaedt*. New York: Viking Press, 1969.

Eisenstaedt. Alfred. *Witness to Our Time*. New York: Viking Press, 1966.

Elbies, Jeffrey. "The Eyewitness." *American Photo* 12, no. 5 (Sept./Oct. 2001): 20–2, 88.

Eskin, Blake. "Features—Getting the Big Picture—the Power of Photojournalism Is Increasingly Resonating in the Mainstream Press as Well as in the Art World, with Images Finding a Prominent Place in Museum Holdings and Private Collections." *Artnews* 101, no. 2 (2002): 100.

Evans, Harold, and Edwin Taylor. *Pictures on a Page: Photo-Journalism, Graphics and Picture Editing*. rev. ed. London: PIMLICO, 1997.

Evans, Harold. *Front Page History: Events of Our Century that Shook the World*. London: Quiller Press in association with Photo Source, 1984.

Evans, Harold. *Eyewitness 2: 3 Decades through World Press Photos*. Updated ed. London: Quiller Press, 1985.

Evans, Harold. *Eyewitness: 25 Years through World Press Photos*. London: Quiller Press, 1981.

F

Faas, Horst and Page, Tim, eds. *Requiem, by the Photographers Who Died in Vietnam and Indochina*. New York: Random House, 1997.

Faber, John. "On the Record: Birth of *Life* Magazine." *National Press Photographer* (Aug. 1958).

Faber, John. "On the Record: Development of the Electronic Flash." *National Press Photographer* (Mar. 1959).

Faber, John. "On the Record: Development of the Halftone." *National Press Photographer* (Feb. 1957).

Faber, John. "On the Record: History of the Photo Syndicates." *National Press Photographer* (Dec. 1958).

Faber, John. "On the Record: Sacrificial Protest of Quang Duck." *News Photographer* (July 1983): 10.

Faber, John. "On the Record: The Atomic Bomb, Hiroshima." *News Photographer* (July 1980): 30.

Faber, John. "On the Record: Wire Transmission of Photos." *National Press Photographer* (Apr. 1958).

Faber, John. "This is How NPPA Came into Being." *National Press Photographer* (June 1960).

Faber, John. *Great News Photos and the Stories Behind Them*. 2nd ed. New York: Dover Publications, 1978.

Faber, John. Telephone interview with author. Sept., 1988.

Falk, Jon. *Jon Falk Presents Adventures in Location Lighting*. Rochester, New York: Eastman Kodak, 1988.

Farsai, Gretchen Jeanette. "A Review of Moral Standards Used to Select News Photographs." Master's thesis, California State University, Long Beach, 1985.

Fears, Lillie M. "Colorism of Black Women in News Editorial Photos." *Western Journal of Black Studies* 22 (Spring 1998): 30–36.

Fedler, Fred, Counts, Tim, and Hightower, Paul. "Changes in Wording of Cutlines Fail to Reduce Photographs' Offensiveness." *Journalism Quarterly* 59 (1982): 633–37.

Feinberg, Milton. *Techniques of Photojournalism*. New York: John Wiley & Sons, 1970.

Ferrato, Donna. "The eye behind the lens: photojournalists discuss their art." *WHY* magazine, no. 30 (1998): 26–30.

Fesperman, Dan. "'You're writing with light'." *Columbia Journalism Review* 38, no. 4: 44.

Finberg, Howard I., and Itule, Bruce D. *Visual Editing: A Graphic Guide for Journalists*. Belmont, California: Wadsworth Publishing Co., 1990.

Finberg, Howard I., ed. *Through Our Eyes: The 20th Century as Seen by the San Francisco Chronicle*. San Francisco: Chronicle Publishing Co., 1987.

Fincher, Terry. *Creative Techniques in Photo-journalism*. London: Batsford, 1980.

Fishman, Jessica Morgan. "Documenting Death: Photojournalism and Spectacles of the Morbid in the Tabloid and Elite Newspaper." *DAI* 62, no. 02A (2001): 345.

Fitzgerald, Mark. "Final exposure: Should newspapers publish graphic execution photos?" *Editor & Publisher* 133, no. 17: 26.

Flamiano, Dolores Louise. "Larger than Life: Collective Memory and Gender in *Life* Magazine's Photographic Essay, Photographic Pin-up, and Commemorative Photojournalism." *DAI* 61, no. 4 (2000): 1208.

Flamiano, Dolores. "The Naked Truth: Gender, Race, and Nudity in Life, 1937." Paper presented at the Annual Meeting of the Association for Education in Journalism and Mass Communication, New Orleans, Louisiana, Aug. 4–7, 1999.

Flash, The Associated Press Covers the World. Introduction by Peter Arnett. New York: Abrams, 1998.

Floren, Leola. "The Camera Comes to Court." Columbia, Missouri: Freedom of Information Center, 1978. ERIC, ED163559.

Flowers, Jackie Walker. "'Life' in Vietnam: The Presentation of the Vietnam War in 'Life' Magazine, 1962–1972." Ph.D. diss., University of South Carolina, 1996.

Fosdick, James A., and Shoemaker, Pamela J. "How Varying Reproduction Methods Affect Response to Photographs." *Journalism Quarterly* (Spring 1982): 13–20.

Fosdick, James A., and Tannenbaum, Percy H. "The Encoder's Intent and Use of Stylistic Elements in Photographs." *Journalism Quarterly* 41 (1964): 175–182.

Fosdick. James A. "Stylistic Correlates of Prescribed Intent in a Photographic Encoding Task." Ph.D. diss., University of Wisconsin, 1962.

Foster, D.Z. "Photos of Horror in Cambodia: Fake or Real?" *Columbia Journalism Review* (Mar. 1978): 46–47.

Fox, Rodney, and Kerns, Robert. *Creative News Photography*. Ames, Iowa: Iowa State University Press, 1961.

Foy, Mary Lou. "Feminine Touch." *Nieman Reports* 52 (Summer 1998): 42–3.

Foy, Mary Lou. "Photojournalism: Covering the Worst and Best." *News Photographer* (May 1993): 14–15.

Franklin, Tom. "The After-Life of a Photo That Touched a Nation." *Columbia Journalism Review* 40, no. 6 (Mar./Apr. 2002): 64–5.

Frascella, Larry. "The Searchers: Four of Today's Most Committed Picture Editors Talk about How They Hunt Out the Best Photographs, Where Visual Style Is Headed, and Why Photographers Need to be More Original." *American Photographer* (Dec. 1989): 48–51.

Freeman, John. "Are Journalism Schools Teaching the Right Skills?" *News Photographer* (Mar. 1994): 23–24.

Freeman, John. "Job Satisfaction among Photojournalists Past 40: A National Survey Looks at 'The Lifers.'" Paper presented at the Annual Meeting of the Association for Education in Journalism and Mass Communication, Washington, DC, Aug. 9–12 1995. ERIC, ED392085.

Friend, David. "The world of photo-journalism." *Columbia Journalism Review* 41, no. 2: 40.

Fulton, Marianne, ed. *Eyes of Time: Photojournalism in America.* Boston: Little, Brown, 1988.

Fulton, Marianne. "Following the Thread: Rick Loomis," *Digital Journalist, http://digital-journalist.org/issue0605/following-the-thread-rick-loomis.html)* (May 2006).

Fulton, Marianne. *Picture This, The Inside Story and Classic Photos of UPI Newspictures* (book review), (Nov. 2006) *www.digitaljournalist.org/issue0611/fulton.html*

G

Galassi, Peter and Kismaric, Susan. *Pictures of the Times: A Century of Photography from The New York Times*. New York: Museum of Modern Art, 1996.

Galella, Ron. *Jacqueline*. New York: Sheed and Ward, 1974.

Gans, Herbert J. *Deciding What's News: A Study of CBS Evening News, NBC Nightly News, Newsweek and Time*. New York: Pantheon, 1979.

Garcia, Mario R., and Fry, Don. *Color in American Newspapers*. St. Petersburg, Florida: The Poynter Institute for Media Studies, 1986.

Garcia, Mario R., and Stark, Pegie. *Eyes on the News*. St. Petersburg, Florida: The Poynter Institute for Media Studies, 1991.

Garrett, W. E., ed. *Photojournalism '76*. Boston: Godine, 1977.

Gatewood, Worth. *Fifty Years in Pictures: The New York Daily News*. Garden City, New York: Doubleday, 1979.

Geraci, Philip C. *Photojournalism: Making Pictures for Publication*. Dubuque, Iowa: Kendall/Hunt, 1976.

Geraci, Phillip C. *Photojournalism: New Images in Visual Communication*. 3rd ed. Dubuque, Iowa: Kendall/Hunt, 1984.

Gibson, Rhonda, and Zillman, Dolf. "Reading Between the Photographs: The Influence of Incidental Pictorial Information on Issue Perception." Paper presented to the Association for Education in Journalism and Mass Communication, New Orleans, Louisiana, Aug. 4–9, 1999.

Gidal, Tim N. *Modern Photojournalism: Origin and Evolution, 1910–1933*. New York: Macmillan, 1973.

Gilbert, Kathy, and Schleuder, Joan. "Effects of Color Complexity in Still Photographs on Mental Effort and Memory." Paper presented at the Annual Meeting of the Association for Education in Journalism and Mass Communication. Portland, Oregon, 1988. ERIC, ED298579.

Gleason, Timothy Roy. "The Development of a Photojournalism Historiography: An Analysis of Journalism History Approaches." DAI 61, no. 07A (2000): 181.

Gleason, Timothy Roy. "The Development of Standard and Alternative Forms of Photojournalism." Paper presented at the Annual Meeting of the Association for Education in Journalism and Mass Communication. Baltimore, Maryland, Aug. 5–8 1998. ERIC, ED423576.

Goldberg, Vicki and Silberman, Robert Bruce. *American Photography: A Century of Images*. San Francisco, California: Chronicle Books, 1999.

Goldberg, Vicki. *Margaret Bourke-White: A Biography*. New York: Harper & Row, 1986.

Goldberg, Vicki. *The Power of Photography: How Photographs Changed Our Lives*. New York: Abbeville Press, 1991.

Golden, Anthony R. "The Effect of Quality and Clarity on the Recall of Photographic Illustrations." Paper presented at the Association for Education in Journalism and Mass Communication, San Antonio, Texas, 1987. ERIC, ED287162.

Goldsmith, Arthur. "A Lesson in Portraiture from a Master: A Look Over Arnold Newman's Shoulder as He Photographs Dr. Francis Crick for His Notable 'Great British Series.'" *Popular Photography* (Dec. 1979): 100–107, 123–25.

Goodwin, James. "There It Is: New Journalism, Photojournalism, and the American War in Vietnam." *Genre* 31 (Summer 1998): 159.

Gordon, Jim. "Death of a Photograph: Assaults on Credibility or Much Ado about Nothing?" *News Photographer* (Apr. 1994): 4.

Gordon, Jim. "Here we go—again. A little photo manipulation goes a far piece." *News Photographer* (Feb. 1998): 4–5.

Gordon, Jim. "Judgement Days for Words and Pictures: To Print or Not to Print." *News Photographer* (July 1980): 25–29.

Gordon, Jim. "Nothing But the Real Thing: No Playing with Pixels—Including the Front Cover." *News Photographer* (Mar. 1994): 4.

Gordon, Jim. "Zeisloft Incident: Foot Artwork Ends Career." *News Photographer* (Nov. 1981): 32–36.

Gosen, Joseph Dorcy. "Digitally Altered News Photographs: How Much Manipulation Will the Public Tolerate before Credibility Is Lost?" *MAI* 38, no. 06 (2000): 76.

Gould, Lewis L., and Greffe, Richard. *Photojournalist: The Career of Jimmy Hare*. Austin: University of Texas Press, 1977.

Grace, Arthur. *Choose Me: Portraits of a Presidential Race*. Waltham, Massachusetts: University Press of New England/ Brandeis, 1989.

Gramling, Oliver. *AP, the Story of News*. New York: Farrar and Rinehart, 1940.

Greenwald, Marilyn, and Bernt, Joseph. "Newspaper Coverage of Gays and Lesbians: Editors' Views of its Longterm Effects." Paper presented at the Annual Meeting of the Association for Education in Journalism and Mass Communication. Montreal: Aug. 5–8 1992. ERIC, ED349621.

Grevstad-Nordbrock, Anne. "A Stolen Kiss: Robert Doisneau's Photographic Icon." *Visual Resources* 13, no. 2 ('97): 189–97.

Griffin, Michael, and Lee, Jongsoo. "Picturing the Gulf War: Constructing an Image of War in *Time, Newsweek, and U.S. News & World Report*." *Journalism and Mass Communication Quarterly* 72 (Winter 1995): 813–25.

Griffiths, Philip Jones. "The Book That Lost a War, Interview with Colin Jacobson." *Creative Review* 22, no. 2 (Feb. 2002): 68–9.

Grigsby, Bryan. "Can't stand stand-alone art? For and against discussed." *News Photographer* (Feb. 1996): 10–11.

Grigsby, Bryan. "Diana's death and public perception." *News Photographer* (Nov. 1997): 16, 18.

Grigsby, Bryan. "Disappointment at funeral dress." *News Photographer* (Oct. 1995): 16–17.

Grigsby, Bryan. "Is it dying or just a bit sick? Photojournalism special issue sparks string of 'net postings." *News Photographer* (Nov. 1996) 10–12.

Grigsby, Bryan. "The wider, the better." *News Photographer* (Dec. 1998): 14–15.

Grigsby, Bryan. "Damned if you do—and if you don't. Reflections upon relationships between photographers and editors." *News Photographer*. (Aug. 1998): 10–11.

Grigsby, Bryan. "Helping Police or a Blind Eye?" *News Photographer* (Feb. 1999): 16–17.

Grigsby, Bryan. "It's Posed?" *News Photographer* (June 1997): 12–13.

Grigsby, Bryan. "Just Photographers or Photojournalists?" *News Photographer* (Nov. 1998): 10–12.

Grigsby, Bryan. "People Photos Require Trust, Responsibility." *News Photographer* (July 1996): 10.

Gross, Deborah M. "Visual Design for the World Wide Web: What Does the User Want?" Paper presented at the Annual Meeting of the Association for Education in Journalism and Mass Communication, Baltimore, Maryland, Aug. 5–8, 1998. ERIC, ED423576.

Grossfeld, Stan. *The Whisper of Stars: A Siberian Journey.* Chester, Connecticut: Globe Pequot Press, 1988.

Grossfeld, Stan. "Restricting a photojournalist's access." *Nieman Reports* 53, no. 3: 45.

Grossfeld, Stan. "Photo Opportunities: Local Photographers Go Global." *Washington Journalism Review* (May 1986): 39–41.

Grossfeld, Stan. "Trials with Editors." *Nieman Reports* 52 (Summer 1998): 30–31.

Grossfeld, Stan. *The Eyes of the Globe: Twenty-Five Years of Photography from the Boston Globe.* Chester, Connecticut: Globe Pequot Press, 1985.

Gutman, Judith Mare. *Lewis W. Hine: Two Perspectives.* New York: Viking Press, 1974.

Guzy, C. "First-person shooter." *Media Studies Journal* 14, no. 3 (2000): 94.

H

Habas, Paula J. "The Ethics of Photojournalistic Alteration: An Integrated Schema of Determinants." Master's thesis, University Of Windsor (Canada), 1996.

Haberman, Irving. *Eyes on an Era: Four Decades of Photojournalism.* New York: Rizzoli, 1995.

Hagaman, Dianne. *How I Learned Not to Be a Photojournalist.* Lexington, KY: University Press of Kentucky, 1996.

Hagaman, Dianne. "'The Joy of Victory, The Agony of Defeat:' Stereotypes in Newspaper Sports Feature Photographs." *Visual Sociology* 8 (1993): 48–66.

Hagen, Charles. "Robert Doisneau Dies at 81; Photos Captured Gallic Spirit." *New York Times* (2 Apr. 1994): 9.

Hale, Donna, and Church, Janet. "Helping hands. News photographer's save of Dole in continuing tradition." *News Photographer* (Dec. 1996): 22–23.

Hale, Donna. "Anatomy lesson: Louisville's cover-up caper; much ado about nothing?" *News Photographer* (Dec. 1996): 16, 18.

Hale, Donna. "Photo Editor Reprimands Photographer for Helping Firefighter at Barn Fire." *News Photographer* (Jan. 1999): 29, 32.

Hale, Donna. "Trapped by riptide, swimmer saved by news photographer." *News Photographer.* (Jan. 1998): 26.

Hale, F. Dennis. "Cameras in Courtrooms: Dimensions of Attitude of State Supreme Court Justices." Paper presented at the Annual Meeting of the Association for Education in Journalism and Mass Communication. Chicago, Illinois, 1997. ERIC, ED415547.

Halliday-Levy, Tereza. "The Connotation Dimension of News Photographs." Paper presented at the Annual Meeting of the Association for Education in Journalism, Athens, Ohio, 1982. ERIC, ED217475.

Halsman, Phillipe. *Halsman on the Creation of Photographic Ideas.* New York: Ziff-Davis, 1961.

Halstead, Dirck. "One Year Later." *American Photo* 13, no. 5 (Sept./Oct. 2002): 25–6.

Halstead, Dirck. "The Platypus Papers Part One." *The Digital Journalist,* www.digitaljournalist. org/platypus/platypus2.html.

Halter, Peter. "Werner Bischof: A Portrait of the Artist as Photo-Journalist." *History of Photography* 22, no. 3 (Autumn 1998): 237–46.

Hamblin, Dora Jane. *That Was the Life.* New York: W.W. Norton, 1977.

Hamilton, John Maxwell, David D Perlmutter, and Emily Arnette Vines. "Graphics and journalism." *Nieman Reports* 56, no. 3: 47.

Hamilton, Peter, and Marc Riboud. "Witness of Our Time, Witness of Reality." The *Photographic Journal*138, no. 10 (Dec. 1998): 465–70.

Hanka, Harold. *Positive Images: Photographs.* Willimantic, Connecticut: Chronicle Print, 1982.

Hannigan, William. *New York Noir: Crime Photos from the Daily News Archive.* New York, N.Y.: Rizzoli, 1999.

Hansen, Mark Alan. "Fundamental Philosophy of Photojournalism Ethics: An Exploration of the Philosophical Underpinnings of Ethical Behavior in Photojournalism." Master's thesis, University of Nebraska, Lincoln, 1996.

Hanson, Art. "A Comparison of Documentary Approaches: Margaret Bourke-White and Erskine Caldwell, Authors of You Have Seen Their Faces" and Dorothea Lange and Paul S. Taylor, Authors of An American Exodus. Paper presented at the Annual Meeting of the Association for Education in Journalism. Boston, Massachusetts, Aug. 9–13, 1980. ERIC, ED191075.

Harris, C., and Lester, P. *Visual Journalism.* Boston: Allyn and Bacon, 2002.

Harris, John. *A Century of New England in News Photos.* Chester, Connecticut: Globe Pequot Press, 1979.

Harry Benson: Fifty Years in Pictures. New York: Harry N. Abrams, 2001.

Hart, Russell, and Zwingle, Erla. William Albert Allard: *The Photographic Essay.* Boston: Little, Brown,1989.

Hart, Russell. "9/11 in Detail." *American Photo* 13, no. 3 (May/June 2002): 18–19, 73.

Hart, Russell. "The Digital Photojournalist." *American Photo* 9 (Sept./Oct. 1998): 30–1.

Hartley, Craig H. "Ethical Newsgathering Values of the Public and Press Photographers." *Journalism Quarterly* 60 (1983): 301–4.

Hartley, Craig, and Hillard, B.J. "The Reactions of Photojournalists and the Public to Hypothetical Ethical Dilemmas Confronting Press Photographers." Master's thesis, University of Texas, Austin, 1981.

Harwood, Philip J., and Lain, Lawrence B. "Mug Shots and Reader Attitudes toward People in the News." *Journalism Quarterly* 69 (Summer 1992): 293–300.

Haworth-Booth, Mark. *Donald McCullin.* London: Collins, 1983.

Haynes, Gary. *Picture This: The Inside Story and Classic Photos of UPI Newspictures.* New York: Bulfinch Press, 2006.

Hazard, William R. "Responses to News Pictures: A Study in Perceptual Unity." *Journalism Quarterly* 37 (1960): 515–524.

Heartfield, John. *Photomontages of the Nazi Period.* New York: Universe Books, 1977.

Heller, Robert. "Photojournalism Education: Contradictions for the Nineties." *Journalism Educator* 46 (Spring 1991): 29–31.

Heller, Steven, and Chwast, Seymour, eds. *Sourcebook of Visual Ideas.* New York: Van Nostrand Reinhold, 1989.

Heller, Steven. "Photojournalism's Golden Age (Through the Great Picture Magazines of the '20s and '30s)." *Print* 38 (Sept./Oct. 1984): 68–79, 116, 118.

Herde, Tom. "Editorial Illustration." *News Photographer* (July 1979): 28–29.

Hersh, S. M. "Torture at Abu Ghraib: American Soldiers Brutalized Iraqis; How far up does the responsibility go?" *The New Yorker*, (May 10, 2004): 42.

Heyman, Ken, and Durniak, John. *The Right Picture: A Photographer and a Picture Editor Demonstrate How to Choose.* New York: Amphoto, 1986.

Hickey, Neil. "Magnum at 50." *Columbia Journalism Review* 39, no. 2 (July/Aug. 2000): 43.

Hicks, Wilson. *Words and Pictures: An Introduction to Photo-Journalism.* 1952. Reprint. New York: Arno Press, 1973.

Hightower, Paul Dudley. "The Influence of Training on Taking and Judging Photos." *Journalism Quarterly* 61 (1984): 682–86.

Hine, Lewis. *America and Lewis Hine: Photographs 1904–1940.* Millerton, New York: Aperture, 1977.

Hobsbawm, Eric, and Weitzmann, Marc, Eds. *1968: Magnum Throughout the World.* Paris: Editions Hazan, dist. by D.A.P., 1998.

Hockman-Wert, Cathleen. "Images of African Famine in U.S. Newsmagazines, 1968–1993: A Content Analysis and Exploration of Ethics." Master's thesis, University of Oregon, 1997.

Hope, Terry. *Photo-Journalism: Developing Style in Creative Photography.* Hove: RotoVision SA, 2001.

Horenstein, Henry. *Color Photography: A Working Manual.* Boston: Little, Brown, 1995.

Horton, Brian. *Associated Press Guide to Photojournalism.* 2nd ed, The Associated Press Series. New York: McGraw-Hill, 2001.

Horton, Brian. *The Associated Press Photo-Journalism Stylebook.* Reading, Massachusetts: Addison-Wesley, 1990.

Horton, Brian. *The Picture: An Associated Press Guide to Good News Photography.* New York: Associated Press, 1989.

Hovde, Ellen, Muffie Meyer, Ronald Blumer, Harris Yulin, Vicki Goldberg, Robert Bruce Silberman, KTCA-TV (Television station: Saint Paul Minn.), MiddleMar. Films, and PBS Home Video. "American Photography a Century of Images." Alexandria, Va.: PBS Home Video, 1999. Videorecording.

Howard, Caroline. "Picking Shots." *Columbia Journalism Review* 41, no. 2 (July/Aug. 2002): 45–6.

Howe, Peter. "A Passion in Search of a Market." *Columbia Journalism Review* 41, no. 2 (July/ 2002): 23–6.

Howe, Peter. "Exposure to light." *Columbia Journalism Review* 41, no. 2: 22.

Howe, Peter. "Photojournalism at a crossroads." *Nieman Reports* 55, no. 3: 25.

Howe, Peter. "The Documentary and Journalism—Photography and the Written Word— Photojournalism at a Crossroads." *Nieman Reports* 55, no. 3 (2001): 25.

Howe, Peter. "Wake Me After the Revolution." *The Digital Journalist,* www.digitaljournalist.org.

Howe, Peter. *Shooting Under Fire: The World of the War Photographer.* Artisan (a division of Workman Publishing Inc.) New York New York, 2002.

Hoy, Frank P. *Photojournalism: The Visual Approach.* Englewood Cliffs, New Jersey: Prentice-Hall, 1986.

Hoyt, James L. "Cameras in the Courtroom: From Hauptmann to Wisconsin." Paper presented at the Annual Meeting of the Association for Education in Journalism, Seattle, Washington, 1978. ERIC, ED158307.

Huang, Edgar Shaohua. "Readers' Perception of Digital Alteration and Truth-Value in Documentary Photographs." Ph.D. diss., Indiana University, 1999.

Huang, Edgar Shaohua. "Afterthoughts on the Representational Strategies of the FSA Documentary." Paper presented at the Annual Meeting of the Association for Education in Journalism and Mass Communication. Baltimore, Maryland, Aug. 5–8, 1998. ERIC, ED423576.

Hughes, Jim. "The Nine Lives of W. Eugene Smith." *Popular Photography* (Apr. 1979): 116–117, 135–141.

Hughes, Jim. W. Eugene Smith, *Shadow & Substance: The Life and Work of an American Photographer.* New York: McGraw-Hill, 1989.

Huh, Hyun-Joo Lee. "The Effect of Newspaper Picture Size on Readers' Attention, Recall and Comprehension of Stories." Paper presented at the Annual Meeting of the Association for Education in Journalism and Mass Communication. Kansas City, Missouri, Aug. 11–14, 1993. ERIC, ED361672.

Hulteng, John L. *The Messenger's Motives: Ethical Problems of the News Media*. 2nd ed. Englewood Cliffs, New Jersey: Prentice-Hall, 1985.

Hurley, Forrest Jack. *Portrait of a Decade: Roy Stryker and the Development of Documentary Photography in the Thirties*. 1972. Reprint. New York: Da Capo, 1977.

Hurley, Gerald D., and McDougall, Angus. *Visual Impact in Print: How to Make Pictures Communicate; A Guide for the Photographer, the Editor, the Designer*. Chicago: American Publishers Press, 1971.

Israel: 50 Years, As Seen by Magnum Photographers. New York: *Aperture*, 1998.

Ianzito, Christina. "Photojournalism: A Life's Work—Earl Dotter." *Columbia Journalism Review* (Jan./Feb. 1997): 40–43.

Ianzito, Christina. "Photojournalism: Tobacco Road—Rob Amberg." *Columbia Journalism Review* (Nov./Dec. 1996): 39–41.

Images of Our Times: Sixty Years of Photography from the Los Angeles Times. New York: Abrams, 1987.

Irby, K. F. "Beyond taste: Editing truth." *Poynteronline*. (2004, March 30). *http://www.poynter.org /content/content_print.asp? id=63131&custom=*.

Irby, K.F., "Displaying Death with Dignity," posted Dec. 31, *Poynteronline*.

Irby, Kenny. "L.A. Times Photographer Fired Over Altered Image" *PoynterOnline.org*. (April 2, 2003) www.poynteronline.org/ content/content_view.asp?id=28082.

Irby, Kenny. "Preserving the old while adapting to what's new." *Nieman Reports* 54, no. 4: 23.

J

Jacobs, Rita D. "James Nachtwey." *Graphis* 50 (Nov. 1994): 48.

Jacobson, Colin. "Class Action." *British Journal of Photography*, no. 7150 (Nov. 1997): 22–3.

Jacobson, Colin. "The Last Picture Show: The State of Photojournalism and Its Publication." *Creative Review* 15 (Apr. 1995): 39–40.

Jacobson, Colin, ed.. *Underexposed: Censored Pictures and Hidden History*. Vision On Publishing, London: 2002.

James, Simon. "Vietnam: The Truth Was as We See It." *RPS Journal* 141, no. 8 (Oct. 2001): 344–7.

Jaubert, Alain. *Making People Disappear: An Amazing Chronicle of Photographic Deception*. Washington: Pergamon-Brassey's International Defense Publishers, 1989.

Jett, Anne. "Diversity and a Local Newspaper: When Photojournalism Becomes Public Relations." Paper presented at the Annual Conference of the Association for Education in Journalism and Mass Communication. Atlanta, Georgia, Aug. 10–13, 1994. ERIC, ED376531.

Jobey, Liz. "In the Age of Celebrity Journalism, Newspapers No Longer Want Pictures of Disaster and Starvation; but Some People Will Buy Them for the Living Room Reissue of Book *Pictures on a Page*." *New Statesman* (London, England: 1996) 126 (May 1997): 42–3.

John, Alun. *Newspaper Photography: A Professional View of Photojournalism Today*. Marlborough: Crowood, 1988.

Johns, David. "All about Boo-Boos: Is It Ethical to Photograph Embarrassing Moments? Is Prominence Enough Justification?" *News Photographer* (July 1984): 8.

Johnson, Mark E., "Front Page Photographs: A Q Methodology Look at Types of Images That Attract College Students." Syracuse University, 2005.

Jones, Barbara Sue Hemby. "The Photojournalism of Mary Ellen Mark." Master's thesis, East Texas State University, 1994.

Josephson, Sheree. "The Readability, Recall, and Reaction to Online Newspaper Pages with Visuals and Those Without." Paper Presented at SCA. San Diego, California, Nov. 24, 1996.

Josephson, Sheree. "Questioning the Power of Color." *News Photographer* (Jan. 1996): VCQ 4–7, 12.

Juergens, George. *Joseph Pulitzer and the New York World*. Princeton, New Jersey: Princeton University Press, 1966.

Junas, Lil. "Ethics and Photojournalism: Photographer Qualities and Picture Selection." *News Photographer* (June 1984): 24.

Junas, Lil. "Ethics and Photojournalism: Posed, Set Up, Faked, Controlled or Candid?" *News Photographer* (Mar. 1982): 19–20.

Junas, Lil. "Ethics and Photojournalism: Techniques and 'Bring Back Something.'" *News Photographer* (June 1982): 26–27.

K

Kahan, Robert Sidney. "The Antecedents of American Photojournalism." Ph.D. diss., The University of Wisconsin, Madison, 1969.

Kalish, Stanley E., and Edom, Clifton C. *Picture Editing*. New York: Rinehart, 1951.

Kaplan, Daile. *Lewis Hine in Europe: The Lost Photographs*. New York: Abbeville Press, 1988.

Kaplan, John. "The *Life* Magazine Civil Rights Photography of Charles Moore (1958–1965)." *Journalism History* 1999–2000 25(4): 126–139.

Kaplan, John. *Photo Portfolio Success*. Cincinnati: Writers Digest Books, 2003.

Karsh, Yousuf. *Portraits of Greatness*. New York: Thomas Nelson & Sons, 1959.

Keaton, Diane. *Local News: Tabloid Pictures from the Los Angeles Herald Express, 1936–1961*. New York, N.Y.: DAP, 1999.

Keaton, Diane, Ed. Afterward Heiferman, Marvin and Kismaric, Carole. *Tabloid Pictures from the Los Angeles Herald Express 1936-1961*. D.A.P. Distributed Art Publisher, Inc., 1999

Keene, Martin. *Practical Photojournalism; A Professional Guide*. 2nd ed. Oxford, Boston: Focal Press, 1995.

Keim, Denise. "Exploring the relationship between photographer and subject." *Nieman Reports* 55, no. 3: 22.

Kelly, James D. "Going Digital at College Newspapers: The Impact of Photo Credibility and Work Routines." Paper presented at the Annual Meeting of the Association for Education in Journalism and Mass Communication. Anaheim, California, Aug. 10–13, 1996. ERIC, ED401533.

Kelly, James D. "The Adoption of Digital Imaging Technology at Daily College Student Newspapers and the Credibility of News Photos." Paper presented at the Annual Meeting of the Association for Education in Journalism and Mass Communication, Atlanta, Georgia, Aug. 10–13, 1994. ERIC, ED374494.

Kelly, James D., and Nace, Diona. "Digital Imaging and Believing Photos." *VCQ* (Winter 1994): 4–5, 18.

Kelly, James D., and Nace, Diona. "The Effects of Specific Knowledge of Digital Image Manipulation Capabilities and Newspaper Context on the Believability of News Photographs." Paper presented at the Annual Conference of the Association for Education in Journalism and Mass Communication. Kansas City, Missouri, Aug. 11–14, 1993. ERIC, ED362917.

Kendall, Robert. "Photo 1978: Some Provisions of the 1976 Copyright Act for the Photojournalist." Paper presented at the meeting of the Photojournalism Division, Association for Education in Journalism, Madison, Wisconsin, 1977.

Kendall, Russ. "Photographers' personal pages." *News Photographer* (Mar. 1997): 15–16.

Kennedy, Thomas. "Content and Style: How Do Limited Expectations Affect the Creative Process?" MGR (insert in *News Photographer*) (Jan. 1989): 1–3.

Kennerly, David Hume. *Photo Du Jour: A Picture-a-Day Journey through the First Year of the New Millennium*. 1st ed, Focus on American History Series. Austin: University of Texas Press, 2002.

Kennerly, David. *PhotoOp: A Pulitzer Prize-Winning Photographer Covers Events That Shaped our Times*. Austin, Texas: University of Texas Press, 1995.

Kenney, Keith R., and Unger, Brent W. "The *Mid-Week Pictorial*: Forerunner of American News-Picture Magazines." *American Journalism* 11 (Summer 1994): 201–216.

Kenney, Keith Raymond. "Newspaper Photography in China." Ph.D. diss., Michigan State University, 1991.

Kenney, Keith. "Building Alliances: PhotoJournalism Educators and Members of NPPA." Paper presented at the Annual Meeting of the Association for Education in Journalism and Mass Communication, Washington, DC, Aug. 9–12, 1995. ERIC, ED388974.

Kenney, Keith. "Effects of Still Photographs." *News Photographer* (May 1992): 41–42.

Kenney, Keith. "Ethical Attitudes." *News Photographer* (Nov. 1991): 12–14.

Kenney, Keith. "Follow-Up: Ombudsmen under Glass." *News Photographer* (Oct. 1993): 40–41.

Kenney, Keith. "Forces Affecting Selection of Photos and TV Stories." *News Photographer* (Feb. 1992): 51–52.

Kenney, Keith. "Fund-Raising Pictures: Do 'Starving Baby' Photos Really Work?" *News Photographer* (Apr. 1993): 46–47.

Kenney, Keith. "How Groups of People are Portrayed." *News Photographer* (Jan. 1992): 43–46.

Kenney, Keith. "Memory and Comprehension of TV News Visuals." *News Photographer* (Aug. 1992): 52–53.

Kenney, Keith. "Mid-Week Pictorial: Pioneer American Photojournalism Magazine." Paper presented at the Annual Meeting of the Association for Education in Journalism and Mass Communication, Norman, OK, 1986. ERIC, ED271767.

Kenney, Keith. "Photojournalism Research: Computer-Altered Photos: Do Readers Know Them When They See Them?" *News Photographer* (Jan. 1993): 26–27.

Kerns, Robert. *Photojournalism: Photography with a Purpose.* Englewood Cliffs, New Jersey: Prentice-Hall, 1980.

Kerrick, Jean S. "Influence of Captions on Picture Interpretation." *Journalism Quarterly* 32 (1955): 177–184.

Kerrick, Jean S. "News Pictures, Captions and the Point of Resolution." *Journalism Quarterly* 36 (1959): 183–188.

Kessel, Dmitri. *On Assignment: Dmitri Kessel, LIFE Photographer*. New York: Abrams, 1985.

Kielbowiez, Richard B. "The Making of Canon 35: A Blow to Press-Bar Cooperation." Paper presented at the Annual Meeting of the Association for Education in Journalism, Photojournalism Division, Houston, Texas, 1979.

Kifner, John. "Pictures from Hell: James Nachtwey's Photojournalism." *Columbia Journalism Review* 39, no. 2 (July/Aug. 2000): 44–5.

Kim, Connie. "A Single Day, a Thousand Images." *The Quill* (Chicago, Ill.) 89, no. 9 (Nov. 2001): 22–3.

King, John Mark. "Political Endorsements in Daily Newspapers and Photographic Coverage of Candidates in the 1995 Louisiana Gubernatorial Campaign." Paper presented at the Annual Meeting of the Association for Education in Journalism and Mass Communication, Chicago, Illinois, July 30–Aug. 2, 1997. ERIC, ED415547.

King, John Mark. "Visual Communication and Newspaper Reader Satisfaction." Ph.D. diss., The University of Tennessee, 1995.

King, John Mark. "Who Gets Named?: Nationality, Race and Gender in *New York Times'* Photograph Cutlines." Paper presented at the Annual Meeting of the Association for Education in Journalism and Mass Communication, Baltimore, Maryland, Aug. 5–8, 1998. ERIC, ED423576.

Kobré, Ken. "Last Interview with W. Eugene Smith on the Photo Essay." Paper presented at the Annual Meeting of the Association for Education in Journalism, Houston, Texas, 1979. ERIC, ED178948.

Kobré, Ken. "Something Different for the News Photographer: Illustrations Solve Problems." *News Photographer* (July 1979): 28–30.

Kobré, Ken. "Critiques." *News Photographer* (January 1994): *VCQ* 18.

Kobré, Ken. "Picturing Assisted Suicide." *News Photographer* (April 1994): *VCQ* 20–21.

Kobré, Ken. "Unearthing Outtakes." *News Photographer* (July 1994): *VCQ* 13–16.

Kobré, Ken. "Rwanda: Witnessing a Holocaust." *News Photographer* (October 1994): *VCQ* 12–16.

Kobré, Ken. " 'The *New York Times*' is Not What She Used to Be." *News Photographer* (January 1995): *VCQ* 15.

Kobré, Ken. "The Long Tradition of Doctoring Photos." *News Photographer* (April 1995): *VCQ* 14–16.

Kobré, Ken. "Good Things Do Come in Small Packages." *News Photographer* (July 1995): *VCQ* 20–23.

Kobré, Ken. "Where Have All the Great Portraits Gone?" *News Photographer* (October 1995): *VCQ* 13–17.

Kobré, Ken. "Slicing Into the World of Photo Non-Realism." *News Photographer* (January 1996): *VCQ* 14.

Kobré, Ken. "Comparison Photos— There's No Comparison." *News Photographer* (April 1996): *VCQ* 21–22.

Kobré, Ken. "Progress In Style Does Not Always Accompany Improvement in Substance." *News Photographer* (July 1996): *VCQ* 13–16.

Kobré, Ken. "Is the Feature Disappearing?" *News Photographer* (October 1996): *VCQ* 13.

Kobré, Ken. " 'The London Independent' Breaks Rules for Refreshing Change." *News Photographer* (January 1997): *VCQ* 13.

Kobré, Ken. "Nudity and News: How Would You Play It?" *News Photographer* (April 1997): *VCQ* 13–14.

Kobré, Ken. "Help Now or Possibly Change the World Later?" *News Photographer* (July 1997): *VCQ* 20–23.

Kobré, Ken. "The Sex Industry From A Woman's Point of View." *News Photographer* (October 1997): *VCQ* 8-12.

Kobré, Ken. "Changing the Market for a Princess' Image." *News Photographer* (January 1998): *VCQ* 14.

Kobré, Ken. "What Can We Learn From the British Press?" *News Photographer* (April 1998): *VCQ* 13–15.

Kobré, Ken. "Should Still Photographers Fear New Video Technology?" *News Photographer* (October 1998): *VCQ* 11–15.

Kobré, Ken. "When Words and Pictures Complement Each Other." *News Photographer* (January 1999): *VCQ* 16.

Kobré, Ken. "Editing for Intimacy." *News Photographer* (April 1999): *VCQ* 18–20.

Kobré, Ken. "Shedding Light on Posed Portraits." *News Photographer* (July 1999): *VCQ* 12–15.

Kobré, Ken. "Looking for Candid Moments in Posed Portraits." *News Photographer* (October 1999): *VCQ* 12–16.

Kobré, Ken. "Narrative Storytelling." *News Photographer* (January 2000): *VCQ* 12.

Kobré, Ken. "Covering Politicians In and Out of Office." *News Photographer* (April 2000): *VCQ* 14–16.

Kobré, Ken. "Finding Fun Features." *News Photographer* (July 2000): *VCQ* 14–17.

Kobré, Ken. "Discovering Pictures That Can Effect Change." *News Photographer* (October 2000): *VCQ* 14–18

Kobré, Ken. "Weegee Lives." *News Photographer* (January 2001): *VCQ* 14.

Kobré, Ken. "Freelancing Your Work." *News Photographer* (April 2001): *VCQ* 13–14

Kobré, Ken. "The Picture Story Finds a Friendly Home." *News Photographer* (July 2001): *VCQ* 14–17.

Kobré, Ken. "Visa: An International Festival and Marketplace for Photojournalism." *News Photographer* (October 2001): *VCQ* 12.

Kobré, Ken. "What's Up Down Under: Australian Photojournalism." *News Photographer* (January 2002): *VCQ* 14.

Kobré, Ken. "Ready for a Job (Ex)Change;" "Talented...AND a Nice Guy." *News Photographer* (April 2002): *VCQ* 12–13.

Kobré, Ken. "Survival on the French Riviera OR Shooting Stars at Cannes." *News Photographer* (July 2002): *VCQ* 14–17.

Kobré, Ken. " 'Life' May Be Dead, but Photojournalism Isn't." *News Photographer* (October 2002): *VCQ* 16–20.

Kobré, Ken. "Photojournalism Thrives On-Line." *News Photographer* (January 2003): *VCQ* 14.

Kobré, Ken. "How PR Pros Became a Photographer's Best Friends." *News Photographer* (April 2003): *VCQ* 12–13.

Kobré, Ken. "How to Invent a Photo Illustration." *News Photographer* (July 2003): *VCQ* 18–21.

Kobré, Kenneth. *Photojournalism: The Professionals' Approach*. 4th ed. Boston: Focal Press, 2000.

Kobre, Sidney. *Behind Shocking Crime Headlines*. Tallahassee, Florida: Florida State University, 1957.

Kobre, Sidney. *Development of American Journalism.* Dubuque, Iowa: Wm. C. Brown, 1969.

Kobre, Sidney. *Modern American Journalism*. Tallahassee, Florida: Florida State University, 1959.

Kobre, Sidney. *News Behind the Headlines: Background Reporting of Significant Social Problems*. Tallahassee, Florida: Florida State University, 1955.

Kobre, Sidney. *Press and Contemporary Affairs*. Tallahassee, Florida: Florida State University, 1957.

Kobre, Sidney. *The Yellow Press and Gilded Age Journalism*. Tallahassee, Florida: Florida State University, 1964.

Kochersberger, Robert C. "Survey of Suicide Photos Use in Newspapers in Three States." *Newspaper Research Journal* 9 (Summer 1988): 1–12.

Kodak Milestones: 1880–1980. Rochester, New York: Eastman Kodak, 1980.

Koenig, T. "Taro Gerta— Photojournalist During the Spanish Civil War: A Biography." *History of Photography* 19, no. 4 (1995): 375–376.

Kostyu, Paul E. "Picturing the Past, Media, History & Photography." *Journalism and Mass Communication Quarterly* 77, no. 2: 434.

Kostyu, Paul E. "The Burden of Visual Truth: The Role of Photojournalism in Mediating Reality." *Journalism and Mass Communication Quarterly* 78, no. 1: 195.

Kowalski, Shelley Kara. "A Poor Picture: The Failure of Concerned Photography to Arouse Social Change." Paper presented at the Society for the Study of Social Problems (SSSP), 1997.

Kozol, Wendy. "Documenting the Public and Private in '*Life*': Cultural Politics in Postwar Photojournalism." Ph.D. diss., University of Minnesota, 1990.

Kratochvil, Antonin, and Michael Persson. "The Documentary and Journalism—Photography and the Written Word—Photojournalism and Documentary Photography." *Nieman Reports* 55, no. 3 (2001): 27.

Kunhardt, Phillip B., Jr. *The Joy of Life*. Boston: Little, Brown, 1989.

Kuykendall, Bill. "Inner Eye." *Nieman Reports* 52 (Summer 1998): 46–49.

LaBelle, David. *Lessons in Life and Death*. Durham, NC: NPPA Bookshelf, 1993.

LaBelle, Dave. *The Great Picture Hunt 2: The Art and Ethics of Feature Picture Hunting*. Lexington, Kentucky: Kernel Press, University of Kentucky.

LaBelle, David. *The Great Picture Hunt*. Bowling Green Kentucky: Western Kentucky University, 1989.

Lacayo, Richard. *Eyewitness: 150 Years of Photojournalism*. 2nd ed. New York: Time Books, 1995.

LaClair, Scott. "Attacks, gibes, jeers after Diana." *News Photographer* (Nov. 1997): 14.

Lain, Laurence B. "How Readers View Mug Shots." *Newspaper Research Journal* 8 (Spring 1987): 43–52.

Lange, George. "Feature: Riding Shotgun with Annie (Leibovitz)." *American Photographer* (Jan. 1984): 56, 59.

Lasica, J. D. "Photographs That Lie: The Ethical Dilemma of Digital Retouching." *Washington Journalism Review* (June 1989): 22–25.

Lauterer, Jock. "Wrestling with the bear, Photojournalism ethics in your face." *News Photographer* (Apr. 1998): 46–47.

Lee, T. "Body horror: Photojournalism, catastrophe, and war." *Harvard International Journal of Press-Politics* 4, no. 2 (1999): 113–113.

Leekley, Sheryle, and Leekley, John. *Moments: The Pulitzer Prize Photographs*. Updated ed. 1942–1982. New York: Crown, 1982.

Leggett, Dawn, and Wanta, Wayne. "Gender Stereotypes in Wire Service Sports." *Newspaper Research Journal* 10 (Spring 1989): 105–114.

Leibovitz, Annie. *Annie Leibovitz: Photographs*. New York: Rolling Stone Press, 1983.

Leifer, Neil. *Sports!* Text by George Plimpton. New York: Abrams, 1983.

Leslie, L. Z. "Newspaper Photo Coverage of Censure of McCarthy." *Journalism Quarterly* 63 (1986): 850–53.

Lester, Paul Martin and Miller, Randy. "African American Pictorial Coverage in Four U.S. Newspapers." Paper presented at the Annual Meeting of the Association for Education in Journalism and Mass Communication. Anaheim, California, Aug. 10–13, 1996. ERIC, ED401571.

Lester, Paul Martin. "Front Page Mug Shots: A Content Analysis of Five U.S. Newspapers in 1986. *Newspaper Research Journal* 9 (Spring 1988): 1–9.

Lester, Paul Martin, ed. *Images that Injure: Pictorial Stereotypes in the Media*. Westport, Connecticut: Praeger, 1996.

Lester, Paul Martin. "Pedagogical Discussion on Pictorial Stereotypes." *Journalism and Mass Communication Educator* 52 (2) (1997): 49–54.

Lester, Paul Martin. "Pictorial Stereotypes in the Media: A Pedagogical Discussion." Paper presented at the Annual Meeting of the Association for Education in Journalism and Mass Communication, Anaheim, California, Aug. 10–13, 1996. ERIC, ED401571.

Lester, Paul Martin. "The Ethics of Photojournalism: Toward a Professional Philosophy for Photographers, Editors and Educators." Ph.D. diss., Indiana University, 1989.

Lester, Paul, and Smith, Ron. "African-American Picture Coverage in Life, Newsweek, and Time, 1937–1988." Paper presented at the Annual Meeting of the Association for Education in Journalism and Mass Communication, Washington, DC, 1989. ERIC, ED310460.

Lester, Paul. "African-*American Photo* Coverage in Four U.S. Newspapers, 1937–1990." *Journalism Quarterly* 72 (Summer 1994): 380–394.

Lester, Paul. "Computer Aids Instruction in Photojournalism Ethics." *Journalism Educator* 44 (Summer 1989): 13–17.

Lester, Paul. "Use of Visual Elements on Newspaper Front Pages." *Journalism Quarterly* 65 (1988): 760–63.

Lester, Paul. *Photojournalism: an Ethical Approach*. Hillsdale, New Jersey: Lawrence Erlbaum Associates, 1991.

Lewinski, Jorge, comp. *The Camera at War: A History of War Photography from 1848 to the Present Day*. London: W.H. Allen, 1978.

Lewis, Charles W. "From Brady to Bourke-White: An Examination of the Foundations of American Picture Magazine Photojournalism, 1860–1940." Master's thesis, Mankato State University, MN, 1986.

Lewis, David M. "Electronic Cameras and Photojournalism: Impact and Implications." MS study, Ohio University, Athens, 1983.

Lewis, Greg. "A Tribute to W. Eugene Smith." *The Rangefinder* (Dec. 1978): 35.

Lewis, Greg. *Photojournalism: Content and Technique*. 2nd ed. Boston: McGraw Hill, 1995.

Lewis, Vickie. "The Impact of Technology on Ethical Decision-Making in Photojournalism." Master's thesis, Ohio University, 1997.

Li, Xigen. "Web Page Design and Graphic Use of Three U.S. Newspapers." *Journalism and Mass Communication Quarterly* 75(2) (1998): 353–365.

Li-An. "Picture Selection: An Editorial Game." *Journalism Quarterly* 40 (1963): 230–232.

Li-An. *Editorial Predictions of Magazine Picture Appeals*. Iowa City, Iowa: School of Journalism, University of Iowa, 1965.

Life 50, 1936–1986: The First Fifty Years. Boston: Little, Brown, 1986.

Life, the First Decade, 1936–1945. London: Thames & Hudson, 1979.

Life, the Second Decade, 1946–1955. Boston: Little, Brown, 1984.

Life, Through the Sixties: An Exhibition and Catalogue. New York: Time, Inc. 1989.

Life Sixty Years: A 60th anniversary celebration, 1936-1996. Editors of Life. New York: Life Books, Time, Inc. Brown, 1996.

Light, Ken. *Witness in Our Time: Working Lives of Documentary Photographers*. Washington D.C.: Smithsonian Institution Press, 2000.

Linderman, Eric. "Kiosk: A History of Photojournalism 1839–1973." *Library Journal* 127, no. 10: 142.

Liotta, Louie, and Wadler, Joyce. "Candid Cameraman: After 50 Years of Shooting for the Front Page, *News Photographer* Louie Liotta Spills." *Time* (11 Dec. 1989): 171.

Lipton, Joshua. "A visual record of a violent year." *Columbia Journalism Review* 40, no. 4: 65.

Lipton, Joshua. "Ron Haviv: Shooting War." *Columbia Journalism Review* 41, no. 2: 48.

Livingston, Jane. Odyssey: *The Art of Photography at National Geographic*. Charlottesville, Virginia: Thomasson-Grant, 1988.

Loengard, John. "The Role of the Picture Editor." *Nieman Reports* 52 (Summer 1998): 44–45.

Loengard, John. *Life Classic Photographs: A Personal Interpretation*. Boston: New York Graphic Society Books, 1988.

Loengard, John. *Life Photographers What They Saw*. Boston: Little Brown, 1998.

Loengard, John. *Pictures Under Discussion*. New York: Amphoto, 1987.

Logan, Richard, III. Elements of Photo Reporting. Garden City, New York: Amphoto, 1971.

Lowrance, G. Newman. *Digital Sports Photography*, Boston: Thomson, 2005.

Lowrey, Wilson. "Altered Plates: Photo Manipulation and the Search for News Value in the Early and Late Twentieth Century." Paper presented at the Annual Meeting of the Association for Education in Journalism and Mass Communication, Baltimore, Maryland, Aug. 5–8, 1998. ERIC, ED423576.

Lowrey, Wilson. "Routine News: The Power of the Organization in Visual Journalism." *News Photographer* (Apr. 1999): VCQ 10–15.

Luebke, Barbara F. "Out of Focus: Images of Women and Men in Newspaper Photographs." *Sex Roles* 20 (1989): 121–33.

Lukas, Anthony J. "The White House Press 'Club.'" *New York Times Magazine* (15 May 1977): 22, 64–68, 70–72.

Lutman, David R. "An invasion of privacy?" *News Photographer* (Mar. 1998) 8.

M

MacAdam, B. A. "Focus on Capa (War photographer Robert Capa)." *Artnews* 99, no. 7 (2000): 36–36.

MacDougall, Curtis D. *News Pictures Fit to Print . . . Or Are They?* Stillwater, OK: Journalistic Services, 1971.

MacDougall, Kent A. "*Geographic*: From Upbeat to Realism." *Los Angeles Times* (Aug. 5, 1977): 1, 8–10.

MacLean, Malcolm S., Jr. "Communication Strategy, Editing Games and Q." In Science, Psychology and Communication. Edited by Steven R. Brown and Donald J. Brenner, 327–44. New York: Teachers College Press, 1972.

MacLean, Malcolm S., Jr., and Hazard, William R. "Women's Interest in Pictures; The Badger Village Study." *Journalism Quarterly* 30 (1953): 139–162.

Maddow, Ben. *Let Truth Be the Prejudice: W. Eugene Smith, His Life and Photographs*. Millerton, New York: Aperture, 1985.

Magistad, Mary Kay. "Photojournalism—Dying to Get the Story." *Nieman Reports* 54, no. 3 (2000): 58.

Magmer, James, and Falconer, David. *Photograph + Printed Word*. Birmingham, MI: Midwest Publications, 1969.

Magna Brava: Magnum's Women Photographers — Eve Arnold, Martine Franck, Susan Meisalas, Inge Morath, Marilyn Silverstone. Munich, London: Prestel, 1999.

Malcolm, Janet. "The View from Plato's Cave." *Aperture*, 67–76, 1997.

Mallen, Frank. *Sauce for the Gander. [The New York Evening Graphic.]* White Plains, New York: Baldwin Books, 1954.

Mallette, Malcolm F. "Ethics in News Pictures: Where Judgement Counts." Paper presented at Rochester Photo Conference, George Eastman House, Rochester, New York, 1975.

Mallette, Malcolm F. "Should These News Pictures Have Been Printed? Ethical Decisions Are Often Hard but Seldom Right." *Popular Photography* (Mar. 1976): 73–75, 118–120.

Manchester, William Raymond. *In Our Time: The World as Seen by Magnum Photographers*. New York: American Federation of the Arts with Norton, 1989.

Manion, B.C. "Faking It! Omaha Daily Fabricates Photo." *News Photographer* (June/July 1981): 30–31.

Marable, Darwin. "Carl Mydans: An Interview." *History of Photography* 26, no. 1 (Spring 2002): 47–52.

Marckx, Hilary F., and Graduate Theological Union. "Reformer/Photographer Jacob A. Riis within the Context of U.S. Religious History." Ph.D. diss., Graduate Theological Union 1999.

Marcus, Adrianne. *The Photojournalist: Mary Ellen Mark and Annie Leibovitz*. Los Angeles: Seskog with Crowell, 1974.

Margolick, David. "*PM*'s Impossible Dream." *Vanity Fair* (Jan. 1999): 116–132.

Mark, Mary Ellen. "An Interview with Mary Ellen Mark." Rockport, ME: Maine Photographic Workshops, 1989. (Recording).

Mark, Mary Ellen. *The Photo Essay*. Washington, DC: Smithsonian Institution, 1990.

Marks, Naomi. "Journalists debate the limits of horror." *British Medical Journal*, 326 (7393), (2003, April 12): 828.

Martin, Peter. "Gene Smith as 'The Kid Who Lived Photography.'" *Popular Photography* (Apr. 1979): 130,149–150.

Martin, Rupert, ed. *Floods of Light: Flash Photography, 1851–1981*. London: Photographers Gallery, 1982.

Marwil, Jonathan. "Photography at War." *History Today* 50, no. 6 (2000): 30–37.

Matthews, Mary L., and Reuss, Carol. "The Minimal Image of Women in *Time* and *Newsweek*, 1940–1980." Paper presented at the Annual Meeting of the Association for Education in Journalism and Mass Communication, Memphis, Tennessee, 1985. ERIC, ED260405.

Mauro, Tony. "Paparazzi and the Press." *Quill* (Chicago, Ill.) 86, no. 6 (July/Aug. 1998): 26 8.

Mauro, Tony. "The Camera-Shy Federal Courts: Why are Cameras Accepted in State Courts but Dreaded in Federal Courts?" *Media Studies Journal* 12(1) (1998): 60–5.

Mayes, Stephen. *This Critical Mirror: 40 Years of World Press Photo*. London: Thames & Hudson, 1996.

McCullin, Don, Harold Evans, and Susan Sontag. *Don McCullin*. London: Jonathan Cape, 2001.

McCullin, Don. *Hearts of Darkness*. London: Secker & Warburg, 1980.

McCullin, Don. *Sleeping with Ghosts: A Life's Work in Photography*. London: Vintage, 1995.

McCullin, Don. *Unreasonable Behaviour: An Autobiography*. New York: Knopf, 1990.

McDonald, Michele. "Photojournalism —the Unbearable Weight of Witness." *Nieman Reports* 54, no. 3 (2000): 48.

McMasters, Paul. "Public's Rights Must Be Protected Excerpt from Testimony before the House Judiciary Committee." *The Quill* (Chicago, Ill.) 86, no. 6 (July/Aug. 1998): 30–1.

McNay, Jim. "The Importance of Content, Content, Content." *VCQ* 2 (Fall 1995): 3.

Mellon, Steve. "Carefully choosing the images of poverty." *Nieman Reports* 55, no. 1: 33.

Meltzer, Milton. *Dorothea Lange: A Photographer's Life*. New York: Farrar, Strauss, Giroux, 1978.

Mendelson, A. "Effects of novelty in news photographs on attention and memory." *Media Psychology* 3, no. 2 (2001): 119–157.

Meredith, Roy. *Mr. Lincoln's Camera Man Mathew B. Brady*. 2nd rev. ed. New York: Dover, 1974.

Metz, Holly. "Interview: Susan Meiselas." *The Progressive* 62 (Apr. 1, 1998): 36.

Mich, Daniel D., and Eberman, Edwin. *The Technique of the Picture Story*. New York: McGraw-Hill, 1945.

Michel, Ulli, and Reuters ltd. *The Art of Seeing: The Best of Reuters Photography*. London: Pearson Education, 2000.

Middlebrooks, Donald M., Jones, Clarence, and Shrader, Howard. "Access: Scope of Privilege in Gathering News Is Vague and Narrow, Scope of Liability Is Far More Certain." *News Photographer* (Dec. 1981): 10–11, 13–16, 18–19.

Mili, Gjon. *Gjon Mili: Photographs and Recollections*. Boston: New York Graphic Society, 1980.

Miller, Russell. "A Vanishing Vision." *Columbia Journalism Review* 39, no. 2 (July/Aug. 2000): 36–42.

Miller, Russell. *MAGNUM: Fifty Years at the Front Line of History*. New York: Grove Atlantic, 1998.

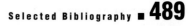

Moments in Time: 50 Years of Associated Press News Photos. Rev. ed. North Ryde, Australia: Angus & Robertson, 1984.

Mora, Gilles, and Hill, John T. W., eds. *Eugene Smith: Photographs 1934–1975*. New York: Abrams, 1998.

Morgan, Willard D. *Graphic Graflex Photography for Prize Winning Pictures*. 11th ed. New York: Morgan and Morgan, 1958.

Moriarty, Sandra, and Shaw, David. "An Antiseptic War: Were News Magazine Images of the Gulf War Too Soft?" *News Photographer* (Apr. 1995): VCQ 4–8.

Morris, Desmond. *Manwatching: A Field Guide to Human Behavior*. New York: Abrams, 1977.

Morris, John G. *Get the Picture: A Personal History of Photojournalism*. New York: Random House, 1998.

Morton, Robert, ed. *Images of Our Times: Sixty Years of Photography from the Los Angeles Times*. New York: Harry N. Abrams, 1987.

Moss, Bryan. *Photosynthesis: A simple guide to the magic of photography*.

Mullen, Lawrence J. "The President's Visual Image from 1945 to 1974: An Analysis of Spatial Configuration in News Magazine Photographs." *Presidential Studies Quarterly* 27 (Fall 1997): 819–34.

Mundt, Whitney R., and Broussard, E. Joseph. "The Prying Eye: Ethics of Photojournalism." Paper presented at the Annual Meeting of the Association for Education in Journalism, Houston, Texas, 1979. ERIC, ED173863.

Murphy-Racey, Patrick. "Pictures of the Month—January: A Case of Situation Ethics." *News Photographer* (May 1988): 30–31.

Mydans, Carl. *Carl Mydans, Photojournalist*. New York: Abrams, 1985.

N

Nachtwey, James, Christian Frei, Christian Frei Filmproductions, Schweizer Fernsehen DRS, Suissimage, and First Run/Icarus Films. "War Photographer." Brooklyn, NY: First Run/Icarus Films, 2001. Videorecording.

Nachtwey, James. "Photojournalism—Photographs." *Nieman Reports* 54, no. 3 (2000): 46.

Nachtwey, James. *Inferno*. London: Phaidon, 1999.

Nachtwey, James. *Deeds of War: Photographs*. New York: Thames and Hudson, 1989.

Natanson, Barbara Orbach. "Spot the Hyphen? Representations of Immigrants and Members of Ethnic Groups in Illustrated Newspaper and Magazine Stories, 1880–1925 (periodicals, illustrations, immigration, photojournalism)." Ph.D. diss., University of Maryland College Park, 1999.

Neubauer, Hendrik, and Black Star Picture Agency. *Black Star: 60 Years of Photojournalism*. Köln: Könemann, 1997.

Newcomb, John. *The Book of Problem Solving: How to Get Visual Ideas When You Need Them*. New York: R.R. Bowker, 1984.

Newhall, Beaumont. *The History of Photography from 1839 to the Present Day*. Rev. & enlgd. ed. New York: Museum of Modern Art, 1964.

Newman, Arnold. *Arnold Newman, Five Decades*. San Diego: Harcourt Brace Jovanovich, 1986.

Newman, Arnold. *Artists: Portraits from Four Decades*. London: Weidenfeld and Nicolson, 1980.

Newman, Arnold. *One Mind's Eye*. Boston: New York Graphic Society, 1974.

Newman, Arnold. *The Great British*. London: Weidenfeld and Nicolson, 1979.

Newton, Julianne H. "The Burden of Visual Truth: The Role of Photojournalism in Mediating Reality." *News Photographer* (Oct. 1998): VCQ 4–9.

Newton, Julianne Hickerson. "In Front of the Camera: Exploring Ethical Issues of Subject Response in Photography." Ph.D. diss., The University of Texas at Austin, 1991.

Newton, Julianne Hickerson. *The Burden of Visual Truth: The Role of Photojournalism in Mediating Reality*. Mahwah, NJ: Lawrence Erlbaum Associates, 2000.

Nicol, Mike. *The Invisible Line: The Life and Photography of Ken Oosterbroek, 1962–1994*. Cape Town: Kwela: Random House South Africa, 1999.

Niederpruem, Kyle E. "We Better Step to the Plate on Paparazzi Issue." *Quill* (Chicago, Ill.) 86, no. 5 (June 1998): 42.

Norback, Craig T., and Gray, Melvin, eds. *The World's Great News Photos, 1840–1980*. New York: Crown Publishers, 1980.

Northup, Steve. "Photojournalism—Photographers Can't Hide Behind Their Cameras." *Nieman Reports* 54, no. 3 (2000): 49.

Northup, Steve. "Words on pictures." *Nieman Reports* 53/54, no. 4/1: 177.

Nottingham, Mary Emily. "From Both Sides of the Lens: Street Photojournalism and Personal Space." Ph.D. diss., Indiana University, 1978.

Nowak, Jeffrey R. "Riot Images: Comparing Photographic Coverage of the 1965 and 1992 Los Angeles Riots in Weekly News Magazines." Master's thesis, Marquette University, 1995.

O

O'Brien, Sue. "Eye on Soweto: A Study of Factors in News Photo Use." Paper presented at the Annual Meeting of the Association for Education in Journalism and Mass Communication. Boston, Massachusetts, Aug. 7–10, 1991. ERIC, ED336795.

Olson, Cal. "Fifty Years & Counting ..." *News Photographer* 49 (Aug. 1994): SS1+.

O'Neil, R. M. "Privacy and press freedom: Paparazzi and other intruders." *University of Illinois Law Review*, no. 2 (1999): 703–716.

Oppel, Richard A. "Photography is at the heart of good journalism." *American Editor*, no. 809: 2.

Outing, Steve, and Ruel, Laura. "The Best of Eyetrack III: What We Saw When We Looked Through Their Eyes," *http://www.poynterextra.org/eyetrack2004/about.htm*

P

Packer, Lori. "Illiterate Morons and Pretty Pictures: Uses and Criticisms of Early Photojournalism in New York's Jazz Age Tabloids." Master's thesis, University of Washington, 1997.

Padgett, G. E. "Let Grief Be a Private Affair." *Quill* 76 (Feb. 1988): 13, 27.

Paine, Richard P. *The All American Cameras: A Review of Graflex*. Houston: Alpha Publishing, 1981.

Panchak, Patricia L. "Issues in Photojournalism Ethics: An Historical Analysis 1865–1987." Master's thesis, Ohio University, 1988.

Paolucci, Christina I. "Visions From Both Sides of the Camera: The Surfacing of Feminism and Photojournalism." Master's thesis, Mankato State University, MN, 1995.

Parrish, Fred S. *Photojournalism: An Introduction*. Belmont, California: Wadsworth/Thomson Learning, 2002.

Pasternack, Steve, and Martin, Don R. "Daily Newspaper Photojournalism in the Rocky Mountain West." *Journalism Quarterly* 62 (1985): 132–35, 222.

Pasternack, Steve, and Utt, Sandra H. "A Study of America's Front Pages: A 10-Year Update." Paper presented at the Annual Meeting of the Association for Education in Journalism and Mass Communication. Atlanta, Georgia, Aug. 10–13, 1994. ERIC, ED376533.

Pasternak, Steve, and Utt, Sandra H. "A Study of America's Front Pages: How They Look." Paper presented at the Annual Meeting of the Association for Education in Journalism and Mass Communication, Corvallis, Oregon, Aug. 6–9, 1983. ERIC, ED232150.

Perlmutter, David D. *Photojournalism and Foreign Policy: Icons of Outrage in International Crises*. Praeger Series in Political Communication. Westport, Conn.: Praeger, 1998.

Peters, Greg. "Ethics: Covering the Klan: Are the Sensational Photos Accurately Portraying the Event?" *4Sight* (Nov–Dec 1993): 10–11.

Peterson, John C. "Toward a Theory of Picture Editing and Use in Printed Publication." Paper presented at the Annual Meeting of the Association for Education in Journalism and Mass Communication. Boston, Massachusetts, Aug. 7–10, 1991. ERIC, ED336791.

Peterson, John Charles. "Reader Acceptance of Complexity and Picture Use in Contemporary Newspaper Design." Ph.D. diss., Ohio University, 1991.

Photojournalism. Rev. ed. Alexandria, Virginia: Time-Life, 1983.

Pictures of the Times: A Century of Photography from the New York Times. New York: Museum of Modern Art distributed by H.N. Abrams, 1996.

Pierce, Bill. "W. Eugene Smith Teaches Photographic Responsibility." *Popular Photography* (Nov. 1961): 80–84.

Pitts, R. "Readers, journalists struggle with same issues in publishing graphic photos." (2005, January 20) Retrieved March 30, 2005, from *http://www.spokesmanreview.com/survey/apme/graphicimages/* Poynter Institute. (2004, May 11).

Pollack, Peter. *The Picture History of Photography*. New York: Abrams, 1969.

Poppy, John. *The Persuasive Image: Art Kane*. New York: Crowell, 1975.

Poynor, R. "The new visual journalism." *Graphis*, no. 325 (2000): 12.

Pozner & Pomeyrol. *Leica Story*. Publisher and date of publication unknown.

Pride, Mike. "Monitor photographers and paparazzi worlds apart." *News Photographer* (June 1998): 21–22.

Professional Photographic Illustration. Rochester, New York: Eastman Kodak, 1989.

R

Rabinowitz, Allen. "Marlene Karas: In a League of Her Own." *News Photographer* (Apr. 1993): 12–16.

Ramos, Betty J. "Digital Imaging, the News Media and the Law: A Look at Libel, Privacy, Copyright and Evidence in a Digital Age." Paper presented to the Association for Education in Journalism and Mass Communication, Atlanta, Georgia, 1994.

Ranck, R. "Get the picture: A personal history of photojournalism." *New York Times Book Review* (1998): 16.

Rayfield, Stanley. *How Life Gets the Story: Behind the Scenes in Photojournalism*. Garden City, New York: Doubleday, 1955.

Reaves, Shiela. "Digital Alteration of Photographs in Magazines: An Examination of the Ethics." Paper presented at the Annual Meeting of the Association for Education in Journalism and Mass Communication, Washington, DC, 1989. ERIC, ED310444.

Reaves, Shiela. "Digital Retouching: Is There a Place for It in Newspaper Photography?" *Journal of Mass Media Ethics* 2 (Spring/Summer 1987): 40–48.

Reaves, Shiela. "Magazines vs. Newspapers: Editors Have Different Ethical Standards on the Digital Manipulation of Photographs." *News Photographer* 50 (1) (1995): VCQ 4.

Reaves, Shiela. "Photography, Pixels and New Technology: Is There a 'Paradigm Shift'?" Paper presented at the Annual Meeting of the Association for Education in Journalism and Mass Communication, Washington, DC, 1989. ERIC, ED310388.

Reaves, Shiela. "Re-Examining the Ethics of Photographic Posing: Insights from the Rank-and-File Members of ASMP." Madison, Wisconsin: University of Wisconsin, 1993. Paper presented at the Annual Meeting of the Association for Education in Journalism and Mass Communication, Visual Communication Division, Kansas City, Missouri, July 1993.

Reaves, Shiela. "The Vulnerable Image: a Hierarchy of Codes Among Newspaper Editors Toward Digital Manipulation of Photographs." Paper presented at the Annual Meeting of the Association for Education in Journalism and Mass Communication. Montreal, Aug. 7, 1992.

Reaves, Shiela. "What's Wrong with this Picture? Daily Newspaper Photo Editors' Attitudes and Their Tolerance Toward Digital Manipulation." *Newspaper Research Journal* Vol. 13/14 (Fall/Winter 1993): 131–155.

Reed, Eli. "Being receptive to the unexpected." *Nieman Reports* 55, no. 3: 32.

Reed, Eli. *Eli Reed: Black in America*. New York: Norton, 1997.

Reed, Pat. "Paparazzo, Meet Ron Galella. Nemesis of Jackie O., Brando, etc." *Houston Chronicle Texas Magazine* (Apr. 15, 1979): 20.

Reese, David. "Photo-Driven Columns." *News Photographer* Oct. 2000: 40.

Reid, Calvin. "Price is no obstacle." *Publishers Weekly* 247, no. 31: 22.

Remole, Mary K., and Brown, James W. "Ethical Issues for Photojournalists: A Comparative Study of the Perspectives of Journalism Students and Law Students." Paper presented at the Annual Meeting of the Association for Education in Journalism, Boston, Massachusetts, 1980. ERIC, ED191022.

Rhode, Robert B., and McCall, Floyd H. *Press Photography: Reporting with a Camera*. New York: Macmillan, 1961.

Riboud, Marc. *Marc Riboud: Photographs at Home and Abroad*. Translated by I. Mark Paris. New York: Abrams, 1988.

Ricchiardi, Sherry. "Photographer on small Indiana daily restores luster to Pictures of the Year." *News Photographer* (Nov. 1996): 32, 34.

Ricchiardi, Sherry. "Getting the Picture: Women are Coming to the Fore in the Long Male-Dominated Field of Photojournalism." *American Journalism Review* 20(1) (1998): 26–33.

Rich, Kathy. "Contact Sheet: Responses of Leading Picture Editors to a Survey to Determine How They Choose Pictures." *Camera 35* (Apr. 1979): 34.

Richards, Eugene. *50 Hours*. Text by Dorothea Lynch. Long Island City, New York: Many Voices Press, 1983.

Richardson, Jim. *High School: U.S.A.* New York: St. Martin's Press, 1979.

Rigger, Robert. *Man in Sport*. Baltimore, Maryland: Baltimore Museum of Art, 1967.

Riis, Jacob. *How the Other Half Lives*. New York: Scribner, 1904.

Ritchin, Fred. "The Web Waits for Photographers, Too." *Nieman Reports* 52 (Summer 1998): 38–39.

Ritchin, Fred. *In Our Own Image: The Coming Revolution in Photography: How Computer Technology Is Changing Our View of the World*. 2nd ed, Writers and Artists on Photography. New York: Aperture, 1999.

Ritchin, Fred. *In Our Own Image: the Coming Revolution in Photography*. New York: Aperture Foundation, 1990.

Roark, Virginia, and Wanta, Wayne. "Response to Photographs." *VCQ* (Spring 1994): 12–13.

Robaton, John, and Smith, Harris. *Photojournalism Basics: An Introduction to Photography for Publication.* Ipswich, Massachusetts: Upper River Press, 1994.

Roberts, Gene and Klibankoff, Hank. *The Race Beat*. New York: Alfred a Knopf, Inc., 2006.

Robin, Marie-Monique, and Sue Rose. *The Photos of the Century: 100 Historic Moments.* Köln: Evergreen, 1999.

Robins, Wayne. "Not picture-perfect." *Editor & Publisher* 135, no. 15: 26.

Robinson, G. "Interview: Donna Ferrato—Photojournalist." *Media Studies Journal* 10 (Fall 1996): 135–136.

Roche, James M. "Newspaper Subscribers' Response to Accident Photographs: The Acceptance Level Compared to Demographics, Death Anxiety, Fear of Death, and State Anxiety." Paper presented at the Annual Meeting of the Association for Education in Journalism and Mass Communication, Corvallis, Oregon, 1983. ERIC, ED234386.

Rodger, George. *Magnum Opus: Fifty Years in Photojournalism*. London: Nishen, 1987.

Roeder, George, Jr. *The Censored War: American Visual Experience During World War II*. New Haven, Connecticut: Yale University Press, 1993.

Rogers, Madeline. "The Picture Snatchers." *American Heritage* 45 (Oct. 1994): 66–73.

Rogers, Michael. "Local News: Tabloid Pictures From the *Los Angeles Herald Express* 1936–1961." *Library Journal* 124, no. 20: 122.

Rogers, Michael. "New York Exposed: Photographs from the Daily News." *Library Journal* 126, no. 20: 117.

Rolling Stone, the Photographs. New York: Simon & Schuster, 1989.

Rose, Bleys W. "Hundreds of readers object to race photos." *News Photographer* (Jan. 1995): 54–55.

Rosett, Jane M. "Photojournalists: Visionaries Who Have Changed Our Vision." *Media Studies Journal* 11 (1997): 39–57.

Rotella, Mark, Charlotte Abbott, and Sarah Gold. "Shutterbabe: Adventures in Love and War." *Publishers Weekly* 247, no. 44: 54.

Rothstein, Arthur. *Words and Pictures*. New York: Amphoto, 1979.

Rotkin, Charles E. *Professional Photographer's Survival Guide*. New York: *American Photographic Book Publishing*, 1982.

Rowland, Jack. "Please don't call me paparazzo." *News Photographer* (Nov. 1997): 10.

Rubin, Steven. "A photographer unites generations with his camera." *Nieman Reports* 53, no. 1: 79.

Rubin, Susan Goldman. *Margaret Bourke-White: Her Pictures Were Her Life*. New York: Abrams, 1999.

Rudd, James O'Malley. "Picture Possibilities: An Ethnographic Study of Newspaper Photojournalism." Master's thesis, University of Washington, 1994.

Russial, John, and Upshaw, Jim. "See No Evil? Differing Responses to an Awful Picture." *Columbia Journalism Review* (Jan./Feb. 1994): 9–11.

Russial, John, and Wanta, Wayne. "Digital Imaging Skills and the Hiring and Training of Photojournalists." *Journalism and Mass Communication Quarterly* 75 (Autumn 1998): 593–605.

Russial, John. "Digital Imaging and the Photojournalist: Work and Workload Issues." Paper presented at the Annual Meeting of the Association for Education in Journalism and Mass Communication. Baltimore, Maryland, Aug. 5–8, 1998. ERIC, ED423562.

S

Sajn, Nikolina; Heo, Kwangjun; and Merritt, Sarah. "Framing a War: Photographic Coverage of the Kosovo War in *Newsweek, Time,* and *U.S. News & World Report*." Paper presented at the Proceedings of the Annual Meeting of the Association for Education in Journalism and Mass Communication, Phoenix, Arizona, Aug. 9–12, 2000.

Salgado, Sebastião. *Migrations: Humanity in Transition.* New York: Aperture, 2000.

Salgado, S., and Nepomuceno, E. *Workers: An archaeology of the Industrial Age*. New York: Aperture, 1993.

Salgado, Sebastião. *Other Americas*. New York: Pantheon, 1986.

Salomon, Erich. *Portrait of an Age*. New York: Macmillan, 1967.

Santana, Maria Cristina. "Traditional or Digital Photojournalism Education? A Survey of Four-Year Photo Programs and Small Dailies' Photo Needs." *Journal of Educational Technology Systems* 25, no. 4 (1997): 351.

Schanberg, Sydney H., and Leeson, David. "Not a pretty picture: Why don't U.S. papers show graphic war photos?" *News Photographer* (June 2005)

Schlagheck, Carol. "Handling Critics and Controversy: How Some Editors and Ombudsmen Have Dealt with Negative Reader Response." *News Photographer* (July 1993): 17–25.

Schuneman, R. Smith, ed. Photographic Communication: Principles, Problems and Challenges of Photojournalism. New York: Hastings House, 1972.

Schuneman, R. Smith. "The Photograph in Print: An Examination of New York Daily Newspapers, 1890–1937." Ph.D. diss., University of Minnesota, 1966.

Schwartz, Donna. "To Tell the Truth: Codes of Objectivity in Photojournalism." Communication 13 (1992): 95–109.

Sedge, Michael H. *The Photojournalist's Guide to Making Money*. New York: Allworth Press, 2000.

Seelig, Michelle Ivy. "The Social Construction of News Photos: A Case Study of the Photo Editorial-Decision Process at the "Philadelphia Inquirer"." *DAI* 62, no. 02A (2001): 271.

Sentman, Mary Alice. "Black and White: Disparity in Coverage by *Life* Magazine from 1937 to 1972." *Journalism Quarterly* 60 (1983): 501–508.

Shames, Laurence. "Profile: On the Road with Annie Leibovitz, The Queen of Celebrity Photographers Is Quite a Character Herself." *American Photographer* (Jan. 1984): 38–55.

Sharkey, Jacqueline. "The Diana Aftermath." *American Journalism Review* (Nov. 1997): 19–25.

Sherer, Michael D. "A Survey of Photojournalists and Their Encounters with the Law." *Journalism Quarterly* 64 (1987): 499–502, 575.

Sherer, Michael D. "Comparing Magazine Photos of Vietnam and Korean Wars." *Journalism Quarterly* 65 (1988): 752–56.

Sherer, Michael D. "Invasion of Poland Photos in Four American Newspapers." *Journalism Quarterly* 61 (1984): 422–26.

Sherer, Michael D. "Photographic Invasion of Privacy: An Old Concept with New Meaning." Paper presented at the Annual Meeting of the International Communication Association, Dallas, Texas, 1983. ERIC, ED236626.

Sherer, Michael D. "Photojournalism and the Infliction of Emotional Distress." *Communications and the Law* 8 (Apr. 1986): 27–37.

Sherer, Michael D. "Photojournalists and the Law: A Survey of NPPA Members." *News Photographer* (Jan. 1988): 16, 18.

Sherer, Michael D. "Subpoenas Alive: Know Protection." *News Photographer* (Jan. 1999): 22, 29.

Sherer, Michael D. "The Photojournalist and the Law: The Right to Gather News Through Photography." Ph.D. diss., Southern Illinois University at Carbondale, 1982.

Sherer, Michael D. "The Problem of Libel for Photojournalists." *Journalism Quarterly* 63 (1986): 618–23.

Sherer, Michael D. "The Problem of Trespass for Photojournalists." *Journalism Quarterly* 62 (1985): 154–56, 222.

Sherer, Michael D. "Your Photos or Mine: An Examination of the Laws Governing Warranted Searches and Subpoenas for the Photojournalist's Work Product." Paper presented at the Annual Meeting of the Association for Education in Journalism and Mass Communication, Corvallis, Oregon, 1983. ERIC, ED236610.

Sherer, Michael D. *No Pictures Please: It's the Law*. Durham, NC: *National Press Photographers* Association, 1987.

Sherer, Michael D. *Photojournalism and the Law: A Practical Guide to Legal Issues in News Photography*. Durham, NC: *National Press Photographers* Association, 1996.

Sherer, Michael D. "The Photojournalist and the Law: The Right to Gather News through Photography." *DAI* 43, no. 07A (1982): 303.

Sherer, Michael D. "Fake-photo charge, filing of libel suit involve NPPA and its magazine." *News Photographer* (Oct. 1997): 27.

Shiras, George, 3rd. "Photographing Wild Game with Flashlight and Camera." *National Geographic* (July 1906).

Shoemaker, Pamela J., and Fosdick, James A. "How Varying Reproduction Methods Affects Response to Photographs." *Journalism Quarterly* 59 (1982): 13–20, 65.

Simon, Peter. *I and Eye: Pictures of My Generation*. Boston: Bulfinch Press, 2001.

Singletary, M. W. "Newspaper Photographs: A Content Analysis, 1936–76." *Journalism Quarterly* 55 (1978): 585–89.

Six Decades: The News in Pictures: A Collection of 250 News and Feature Photographs Taken from 1912 to 1975 by the Milwaukee Journal Co. Staff Photographers. Milwaukee, MN: Milwaukee Journal Co., 1976.

Skow, Lisa M., and George N. Dionisopoulos. "A Struggle to Contextualize Photographic Images: American Print Media and the 'Burning Monk.'" *Communication Quarterly* 45, no. 4 (Fall 1997): 393–409.

Smith W. Eugene. "W. Eugene Smith Talks About Lighting." *Popular Photography* (Nov. 1956): 48.

Smith, C. Zoe, and Anne-Marie Woodward. "Photo-Elicitation Method Gives Voice and Reactions of Subjects." *Journalism and Mass Communication Educator* 53, no. 4 (Win 1999): 31–41.

Smith, C. Zoe, and Mendelson, Andrew. "The Health of Photojournalism and Visual Communication Education in the Nineties: Cause for Concern or a Bright Future?" Paper presented at the Annual Meeting of the Association for Education in Journalism and Mass Communication, Washington, DC, Aug. 9–12, 1995. ERIC, ED392085.

Smith, C. Zoe, and Mendelson, Andrew. "Visual Communication Education: Cause for Concern or Bright Future?" *Journalism and Mass Communication Educator* 51 (Autumn 1996): 66–73.

Smith, C. Zoe, and Michael Winokur. "Up close and personal." *News Photographer* (Sept. 1996): 42–48.

Smith, C. Zoe, and Woodward, Anne-Marie. "Photo-Elicitation Method Gives Voice and Reactions of Subjects." *Journalism and Mass Communication Educator* 53(4) (1999): 31–41.

Smith, C. Zoe. "An Alternative View of the Thirties: The Industrial Photographs of Lewis Wickes Hine and Margaret Bourke-White." Paper presented at the Annual Meeting of the Association for Education in Journalism. East Lansing, MI, Aug. 8–11, 1981. ERIC, ED204770.

Smith, C. Zoe. "Black Star Picture Agency: *Life*'s European Connection." *Journalism History* 13 (Spring 1986): 19–25.

Smith, C. Zoe. "Dickey Chapelle." *VCQ* (Spring 1994): 4–9.

Smith, C. Zoe. "Emigré Photography in America: Contributions of German Photojournalism From Black Star Picture Agency to *Life* Magazine, 1933–1938." Ph.D. diss., The University of Iowa, 1983.

Smith, C. Zoe. "Great Women in Photojournalism." Parts 1–3. *News Photographer* (Jan. 1985): 20–21; (Feb. 1985): 26, 28–29; (Apr. 1985): 22–24.

Smith, Ron F. "How Design and Color Affect Reader Judgement of Newspapers." *Newspaper Research Journal* 10 (Winter 1989): 75–85.

Smith, W. Eugene, and Smith, Aileen M. *Minamata*. New York: Holt, Rinehart and Winston, 1975.

Smith, W. Eugene, Gilles Mora, John T. Hill, and Gabriel Bauret. *W. Eugene Smith: Photographs 1934–1975*. New York: Harry N. Abrams, 1998.

Smith, W. Eugene. "A Man of Mercy." *Life* (Nov. 15, 1954): 161–172.

Smith, W. Eugene. "Country Doctor." *Life* (Sept. 20, 1948): 115–126.

Smith, W. Eugene. "Nurse Midwife." *Life* (Dec. 3, 1951): 134–145.

Smith, W. Eugene. "Pittsburgh." 1959 *Photography Annual* (1958): 96–133.

Smith, W. Eugene. "Saipan." *Life* (Aug. 28, 1944): 75–83.

Smith, W. Eugene. "Spanish Village." *Life*.

Smith, W. Eugene. *W. Eugene Smith, Master of the Photographic Essay*. Millerton, New York: Aperture, 1981.

Smith, W. Eugene. *W. Eugene Smith: His Photographs and Notes*. Millerton, New York: Aperture, 1969.

Sobieszek, Robert A. *Arnold Newman*. Englewood Cliffs, New Jersey: Prentice-Hall, 1982.

Solomon, Deborah. "Newman at Work." *American Photographer* (Feb. 1988): 44–55.

Souza, Pete. "Kent Kobersteen: The New Director of Photography at *National Geographic*." *News Photographer* (Summer 1998): *VCQ* 3–8.

Souza, Pete. "White House top photo sparks pro, con on publishing." *News Photographer* (Feb. 1995): 26–27.

Souza, Pete. Unguarded Moments: Behind-the-Scenes Photographs of President Ronald Reagan. Fort Worth, Texas: Summit Group, 1992.

Sparks, Glenn G., and Fehlner, Christine L. "Faces in the News: Gender Comparisons of Magazine Photographs." *Journal of Communication* (Autumn 1986): 70–79.

Spencer, Otha Cleo. "Twenty Years of '*Life*': A Study of Time, Inc.'s Picture Magazine and Its Contributions to Photojournalism." Ph.D. diss., University of Missouri, Columbia, 1958.

Spigel, L. "*Life*'s America: Family and nation in postwar photojournalism." *American Historical Review* 101, no. 4 (1996): 1309–1310.

Spina, Tony. *On Assignment, Projects in Photojournalism*. New York: Amphoto, 1982.

Spina, Tony. *Press Photographer*. Cranbury, New Jersey: A.S. Barnes, 1968.

Spremo, Boris. *Twenty Years of Photojournalism*. Toronto: McClelland and Stewart, 1983.

Spruill, Larry Hawthorne. "Southern Exposure: Photography and the Civil Rights Movement, 1955–1968." Ph.D. diss., State University of New York at Stony Brook, 1983.

Squiers, Carol. "Photojournalism." *American Photo* 9, no. 6 (Nov./Dec. 1998): 64–6+.

Squiers, Carol. "Seeing History As It Happened: A Century and a Half in Life of the World, As Recorded by Its Most Daring Witness." *American Photographer* (Oct. 1988): 33–44.

Squiers, Carol. "The House of News." *American Photo* 9 (Sept./Oct. 1998): 20.

Squires, Carol. "Diana and the Paparazzi." *American Photo* 8 (Nov./Dec. 1997): 15–16.

Srihari, Rohini K. "Use of Captions and Other Collateral Text in Understanding Photographs." *Artificial Intelligence Review* 8 (Oct–Dec 1994): 409–430.

Staples, Brent. "Photojournalism—the Perils of Growing Comfortable with Evil." *Nieman Reports* 54, no. 3 (2000): 52.

Steele, Bob. "Protocols for Ethical Decision-Making in the Digital Age." *Protocol* 1991: 13–17.

Steichen, Edward. *The Family of Man*. New York: Simon & Schuster, 1955.

Stein, Barney. *Spot News Photography*. New York: Verlan Books, 1960.

Stepan, Peter, and Claus Biegert. *Photos That Changed the World.* Munich; London: Prestel, 2000.

Stepno, Bob. "Staged, faked, and mostly naked: Photographic innovations at the *Evening Graphic* (1924–1932). Paper presented at the Annual Meeting of the Association for Education in Journalism and Mass Communication. Baltimore, Maryland, Aug. 5–8, 1998.

Stern, Bert. *Photo Illustration: Bert Stern*. New York: Crowell, 1974.

Stettner, Louis, and Zanutto, James M. "Weegee." *Popular Photography* (Apr. 1961): 101–102.

Stettner, Louis. *Weegee*. New York: Alfred A. Knopf, 1977.

Stoll, D. C. "Necessary truths: Jean-François Leroy and the Perpignan Festival of Photojournalism." *Aperture*, no. 160 (2000): 2–13.

Stott, William. *Documentary Expression and Thirties America*. New York: Oxford Press, 1973.

Strauss, David Levi. "James Nachtwey: International Center of Photography, New York." *Artforum International* 39, no. 1 (Sept. 2000): 180.

Streitmatter, R. "The Rise and Triumph of the White House Photo Opportunity." *Journalism Quarterly* 65 (1988): 981–85.

Strother, Tracy. "Are We Only Wrong if Someone Gets Caught: A Study of the Credibility of Digitally Altered Photography." Master's thesis, Marquette University, 1994.

Sutton, Ronald E. "Image Manipulation: Then and Now." Paper presented at the Symposium of the International Visual Literacy Association. Delphi, Greece, June 25–29, 1993.

Swanson, Charles. "What They Read in 130 Daily Newspapers." *Journalism Quarterly* 32 (1955): 411–21.

Sweers, George, ed. *A White Paper on Newspaper Color: A Special Report*. Durham, North Carolina: National Press Photographers Association, 1985.

Szarkowski, John. *From the Picture Press*. New York: The Museum of Modern Art, 1973.

Szarkowski, John. *Photography Until Now*. New York: Museum of Modern Art, 1989.

Szarkowski, John. *The Photographer's Eye*. New York: The Museum of Modern Art, 1966.

T

Tames, George. *Eye on Washington: The Presidents Who've Known Me*. New York: Harper & Row, 1990.

Tannenbaum, Percy H., and Fosdick, James A. "The Effect of Lighting Angle on Judgment on Photographed Subjects." *Audio Visual Communication Review* 8 (1960): 253–262.

Taylor, John. "War, photography, evidence." *Oxford Art Journal* 22, no. 1 (1999): 158–65.

Taylor, John. *Body Horror: Photojournalism, Catastrophe and War.* Manchester, New York: Manchester University Press, 1998.

Terkeurst, James Varnum. "Presenting America: Photojournalism, Day-in-the-Life Books and the Western View (Visual Theory)." *DAI* 60, no. 08A (1999): 266.

Terkeurst, Jim. "A Day in Whose Life? Photojournalism, Culture and Imperialism." Paper presented at the Annual Meeting of the Association for Education in Journalism and Mass Communication, Anaheim, California, Aug. 1996.

Terrazas, Beatriz. "Using the Camera to Peer Inside." *Nieman Reports* 53 (Summer 1999).

The Associated Press Stylebook and Libel Manual: With Appendixes on Photo Captions, Filing the Wire. 34th ed. New York: Associated Press, 1999.

The Digital Journalist, www.digitaljournalist.org. (Online magazine for photojournalism).

Timacheff, Serge and Karlins, David. *Digital Sports Photography: Take Winning Shots Every Time.* Hoboken, N.J.: Wiley Publishing, 2005.

"Time: 150 Years in Photojournalism." New York: *Time,* 1989.

Tsang, Kuo-Jen. "News Photos in *Time* and *Newsweek.*" *Journalism Quarterly* 61 (1984): 578–84, 723.

Turnley, David C., and Cowell, Alan. *Why Are They Weeping? South Africans Under Apartheid.* New York: Stewart, Tabori and Chang, 1988.

Turnley, David C., Peter Turnley, Chiara Mariani, Grazia Neri, International Center of Photography, and Scavi Scaligeri (Verona Italy). *In Times of War and Peace.* New York: Abbeville Press, 1997.

U

An Uncertain Grace: Photographs by Sebastião Salgado. Essays by Eduardo Galeano and Fred Ritchin. New York: Aperture, 1990.

Ungero, Joseph M. "How Readers and Editors Judge Newspaper Photos." *APME Photo Report* (15 Oct. 1977).

Unity '94. *News Watch: A Critical Look at Coverage of People of Color.* San Francisco: SFSU Center for the Integration and Improvement of Journalism, 1994.

V

Van Riper, Frank. "Perils of the Digital Camera Age." *Nieman Reports* 51 (Winter 1997): 85–86.

Vernon, Mara Evonne. "The Credibility of News Photography in the Digital Age." Master's thesis, University Of Nevada, Las Vegas, 1997.

Vitray, Laura, Mills, John Jr., and Ellard, Roscoe. *Pictorial Journalism.* New York: McGraw Hill, 1939.

Viviano, Frank. "Time lapse: a decade of social change through the eyes of award-winning [*Mother Jones*] photographers." *Mother Jones* 23, no. 4 (1998): 53–59.

W

Waldman, Paul, and Devitt, James. "Newspaper Photographs and the 1996 Presidential Election: The Question of Bias." *Journalism and Mass Communication Quarterly* 75 (Summer 1998): 302–11.

Walker, David. "News photos you didn't see." *Editor & Publisher* 133, no. 30: 20.

Walter, Paulette H. "A History of Women in Print Photojournalism." Master's thesis, University of Ohio, Athens, 1987.

Wanta, W. "The Effects of Dominant Photographs: An Agenda-Setting Experiment." *Journalism Quarterly* 65 (1988): 107–11.

Wanta, Wayne, and Leggett, Dawn. "Gender Stereotypes in Wire Service Sports Photos." *Newspaper Research Journal* 10 (Spring 1989): 105–14.

Warburton, Nigel. "Ethical Photojournalism in the Age of the Electronic Darkroom." In Kieran, Matthew, ed., *Media Ethics.*

Ward, N. "New York's bravest: Eight decades of photographs from the *Daily News.*" *Library Journal* 127, no. 14 (2002): 191.

Warlaumont, Hazel G. "Blurring the Lines of Distinction: Photo-Documentary Advertising and Editorial Integrity." Ph.D. diss., University of Washington, 1993.

Watkins, Patsy G. "The Power of Editorial and Historical Context: A Photo History Interprets WW II for Americans." Paper presented at the Annual Meeting of the Association for Education in Journalism and Mass Communication. Kansas City, Kansas, Aug. 11–14, 1993. ERIC, ED362913.

Webb, Alex. *Hot Light/Half-Made Worlds: Photographs from the Tropics.* New York: Thames and Hudson, 1986.

Webb, Alex. *Under a Grudging Sun: Photographs from Haiti Libere 1986–1988.* New York: Thames and Hudson, 1989.

Weegee, and John Coplans. *Weegee: Naked New York.* New York: te Neues Pub. Co., 1997.

Weegee, Miles Barth, and International Center of Photography. *Weegee's World.* Boston: Little Brown in association with the International Center of Photography New York, 1997.

Weegee. *Naked City.* New York: Essential Books, 1945.

Weegee. *Weegee by Weegee: An Autobiography.* New York: Ziff-Davis, 1961.

Weegee. *Weegee: Naked New York.* Schirmer, 1997.

Weegee. *Weegee's People.* 1946. Reprint. New York: Da Capo Press, 1975.

Weill, Susan. "African Americans and the White-Owned Mississippi Press: An Analysis of Photographic Coverage from 1944 to 1984." Paper presented at the *American Journalism* Historians' Association Conference. Roanoke, Virginia, Oct. 6–8, 1994. ERIC, ED379669.

Weinberg, Adam D. *On the Line: The New Color Photojournalism.* Minneapolis: Walker Art Center, 1986.

Welch, Bill. "Fragile moments." *Nieman Reports* 53/54, no. 4/1: 180.

Welling, William. *Photography in America: The Formative Years 1839–1900, A Documentary History.* New York: Crowell, 1978.

Wells, Annie. "Worth the trouble?" *News Photographer* (July 1996): 82–83.

Welsch, Ulrike. *Faces of New England: Special Moments from Everyday Life.* 2nd ed. Chester, Connecticut: Globe Pequot Press, 1981.

Welsch, Ulrike. *The World I Love to See.* Boston: *Boston Globe*/Houghton Mifflin, 1977.

Whalen, Erin. "Shot with his own gun." *Editor & Publisher* 133, no. 33: 25.

Wheeler, Thomas H. *Phototruth or Photofiction: Ethics and Media Imagery in the Digital Age.* Mahwah, NJ: Lawrence Erlbaum Associates, 2002.

Wheeler, Tom, and Gleason, Tim. "Photography or Photofiction: An Ethical Protocol for the Digital Age." *VCQ* 2 (Jan. 1995): S8–12.

Wheeler, Tom. "Public Perceptions of Photographic Credibility in the Age of Digital Manipulation." Paper presented at the Annual Meeting of the Association for Education in Journalism and Mass Communication, Washington, DC, Aug. 9–12, 1995. ERIC, ED392085.

Whelan, Richard. *Robert Capa: A Biography.* New York: Alfred A. Knof, 1985.

White, Frank William. "Cameras in the Courtroom: A U.S. Survey." *Journalism Monographs* 60 (Apr. 1979).

Whiting, John R. *Photography Is a Language.* New York: Ziff-Davis, 1946.

Wilcox, Walter. "Staged News Photographs and Professional Ethics." *Journalism Quarterly* 38 (1961): 497–504.

Willem, Jack M. "Reader Interest in News Pictures." In *Graphic Graflex Photography,* edited by Morgan and Lester. New York: Morgan & Lester, 1946.

Williams, M. Michael. "News Photographs in Stories Related to Vietnam: A Content Analysis of Photographs Relating to the Vietnam War Appearing in *Life* Magazine from Jan. 1, 1966 through Feb. 28, 1970." ERIC, ED311505.

Williamson, Lenora. "Page 1 Fire Photos Draw Reader Protests." *Editor & Publisher* (30 Aug. 1975): 14–15.

Willis, Deborah. *Reflections in Black: A History of Black Photographers 1840 to the present.* New York: Norton, 2000.

Willumson, Glenn G. W. *Eugene Smith and the Photographic Essay.* Cambridge [England], New York: Cambridge University Press, 1992.

Wimmer, Kurt. "Supreme Court Ruling in 'Ride-Along' Case May Spell Doom for Practice." *News Photographer* (July 1999): 12, 17.

Winslow, Donald. "Unabridged War and History," *News Photographer,* May 2004, page 9.

Wischmann, Lesley. "Dying on the Front Page: Kent State and the Pulitzer Prize." *Journal of Mass Media Ethics* 2 (Spring/Summer 1987): 67–74.

Wolf, Henry. *Visual Thinking: Methods for Making Images Memorable.* New York: American Showcase, 1988.

Wolf, Rita, and Giotta, Gerald L. "Images: A Question of Readership." *Newspaper Research Journal* 6 (Winter 1985): 30–36.

Wolk, Art. "The Law in Plain English for Photographers." *Library Journal* 126, no. 10: 109.

Woo, Jisuk. "Journalism Objectivity in News Magazine Photography." *VCQ* (Summer 1994): 9.

Woodburn, Bert W. "Reader Interest in Newspaper Pictures." *Journalism Quarterly* 24 (1947): 197–201.

Wooley, Al E. *Camera Journalism.* South Brunswick, New Jersey: A. S. Barnes, 1966.

The World in Photographs 2001. New York: Harry N. Abrams, 2002.

Y

Yang, Daqing. "Image—War's Most Innocent Victim." *Media Studies Journal* 13 (Winter 1999): 18–19.

Yates, Carl. "What to Do When the Law Says, 'No Pictures, Please!'," *News Photographer* (Nov. 1993): 19.

Yu, Yong-Hoon. "Visual Silences in the American News Media: A Content Analysis of News Photos in *Time* and *Newsweek.*" Master's thesis, California State University, Northridge, 1994.

Z

Zarnowski, Myra. "Telling Lewis Hine's Story: Russell Freedman's Kids at Work." Paper presented at the 1997 Annual conference of the National Council of Teachers of English. Detroit, Michigan, 1997. ERIC, ED414574.

Zavoina, S., and T. Reichert. "Media convergence/management change: The evolving workflow for visual journalists." *Journal of Media Economics* 13, no. 2 (2000): 143–151.

Zavoina, S., and Davidson, J. *Digital Photojournalism.* Boston: Allyn and Bacon, 2002.

Zibluk, Jack. "Evaluating Photographs." *Communication: Journalism Education Today* 32, no. 4 (Summer 1999): 22–29.

Zillmann, D., S. Knobloch, and H. S. Yu. "Effects of photographs on the selective reading of news reports." *Media Psychology* 3, no. 4 (2001): 301–324.

Zillmann, Dolf, Rhonda Gibson, and Stephanie L. Sargent. "Effects of photographs in news-magazine reports on issue perception." *Media Psychology* 1, no. 3 (1999): 207–228.

Zimbel, George S, and Maggie Drucker. "Who owns this photograph?" *Columbia Journalism Review* 40, no. 1: 60.

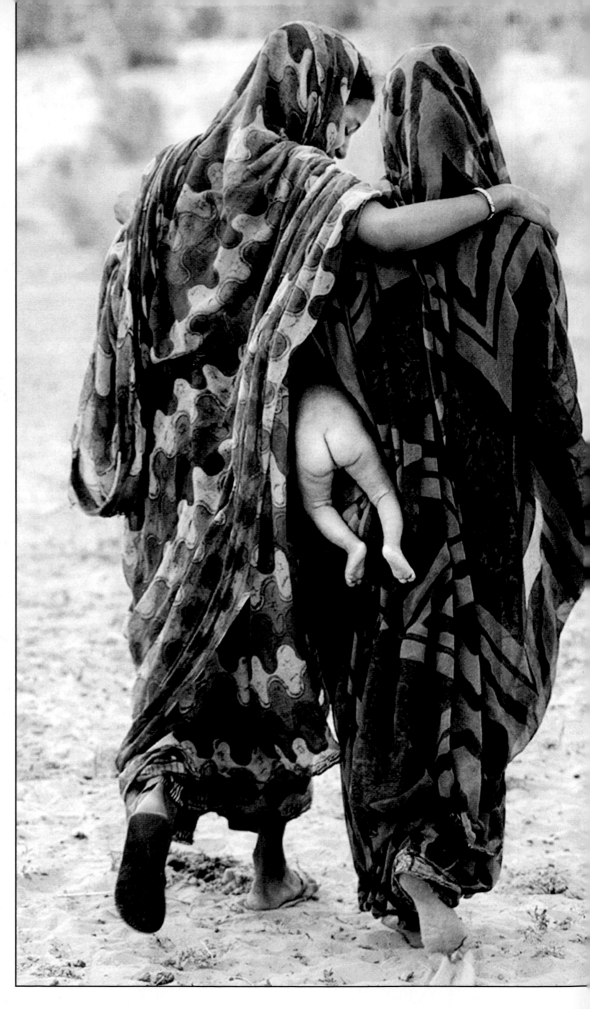

Desert wanderers, the Nomadic Tuareg people of Mali live isolated lives. They roam the Saharan desert by camel with their meager belongings. Two friends walk from their tent with a child.
Carol Guzy, *Washington Post*

A

A Voice is Born (Cookman), 450
Abaca Press, *48–49*, *60*, 146, *268*
Abilene Reporter-News, 99
Abrahamson, Rich, *15*, *163*, *171*
Abramson, Dean, 358
Absolutist, ethical framework, 354
Accidents, photography guidelines, 41–43, 408
Acme News Photos, 451
Adams, Chris, 215
Adams, Eddie, 358, 367, *381*, 448–449
Addario, Lynsey, *202*, 206, *266*
Agee, James, 206
Agence France-Presse (AFP), 25, 128, 380, 452
AIDS, 213–216, 218
Aima, Abhinav, 375
Airone, 460
Akron Beacon Journal, 373
Alberico, Rocco, 384
Albuquerque Tribune, 366
Alexander, Laurence, 409
Alexander, Sherry, 396
Alexia Foundation, 206
Alfred, K.C., *15*
America in Crisis (Magnum), 443
"American Buddhist" (Saito), 145
American Editor, 373
American Exodus, An (Lange and Taylor), 439
American Journalism Review, 311, 365
American Newspaper Reporter, The, 419
American Photography: A Century of Images (Goldberg and Silberman), 434, 447
American Photojournalism Comes of Age (Carlebach), 429
American Psychological Association, 46
American Telephone and Telegraph Co. (AT&T), 452–453
American Society of Media Photographers (ASMP), 361, 412, 467
Amsterdam News, 438
Anchorage Daily News, *127*
And the Band Played On (Shilts), 215
Anderson, Cara, vii
Anderson, Cornell, 409
Andrews, Nancy, *132*, 232, 235, 381
And Their Children After Them (Maharidge and Williamson), 206
Anecdote, story element, 313
Ang, Tom, 144, 357
Animals, features, 70
Anonymity, agreement by photographer, 409–410
Anticipation, candid shots, 22
Aperture determination
histogram, 187
manual, 185–186
through-the-lens metering, 186–187
Architectural Digest, 172
Argo Merchant, 44–45
Arnett, Peter, 369
Arnold, Edmond, 140
Arnold, Eve, 20, 442
Ashburn, Kristen, 206, 232, 266, *319*
Assignment
creation, 12
international assignment, 12–14
Associated Press (AP), *13*, 18, 25, 41, 98, 102, 110, 114, *115*, 119, 121, 122, 136, 151, 153, *176*, *177*, 280, *352*, 353, 360, *369*, 371, 373, 374, 378, 385, 448, 451–452, 453
Associated Press Managing Editors, 136, 374
Atherton, James K.W., *55*
Audio, see Sound
Autochrome, 419, 425, 426
Autotype, 419

Autofocus
applications, 158, 160
continuous for candid shots, 21
personalization of controls, 160
sports shooting and sharp images, 106–108
video camera, 315
Awards, story behind the, 63
Ayemi, Tawa, 399

B

Backgrounding the News, 203, 212
Backgrounds, portraits, 87
Bain, George Grantham, 451
Bain News Service, 422, *450*, 451
Bakersfield Californian, *355*, 376
Balanced reporting, ethics, 380–382
Balic, Sebastian, 371
Baltimore Sun, 71, 192
Barbante, Ben, 346
Barber, Dorothy, 407
Barnack, Oskar, 434, 465
Barner, Terry, 72
Bartelleti, Don, 386
Baseball, see Sports
Basketball, see Sports
Battle Creek Enquirer and News, 378
Baumann, Bruce, 126
Baxter, William, 143
BBC, 6
Beals, Jessie Tarbox, 422
Beat
feature beat development, 212–213, 215, 218
reporters and news monitoring, 9
Beck, Robert, 105
Beckman, Rich, vii
Behrens, Rolf, 324
Benchley, Robert, 437
Bengiveno, Nicole, *82–84*, 87, 90
Bentley, P.F., 51–53, 137, 235, *404*
Berliner Illustrirte Zeitung, 436–437
Berner, Alan, 71, 206, *222–223*, 229, 261, 267
Bernt, Joseph, 133
Bettman Archive, 453
Binks, Porter, vii
Biondi, Elisabeth, 365
Birmingham Post-Herald, 359
Birmingham, Keith, vii, *113*, 115–*116*, *119*
Bishof, Werner, 442–443
"Black Market" (Brown), *278–279*
Black Market, Inside the Endangered Species Trade (Davies, Goodall, and Brown), 278
Black Star, 50, 128, 150, 363, 438–440, 442, 443, 457
Black Star Picture Agency: Life's European Connection (Smith), 439
Blackwood, Roy, 133
"Bloodline: AIDS and Family" (Ashburn), *319*
Bogatin, Bo, vii, 407, 409–411
Bohle, Robert, 137
Book of Graphic Problem-Solving, The: How to Get Visual Ideas When You Need Them (Newcomb), 346
Borden, Sandra, 376, 377
Bornstein, Sam, 378
Boston Globe, 38, 40, *42*, 69, 76, 98, 206
Boston Herald, 32
Boston Phoenix, *44*, *66*, 67, *144*, 191, 281, 373
Bounce strobe, 188–190, 192
"Bounty Hunters" (Yoder), *236–237*
Bourke-White, Margaret, 14, *437*–438, 441, 442, 445, 446, 449
Boyd, Robert, 434
Bradt, Peter, 369
Branburg vs Hayes, 410
Brando, Marlon, 403
Brecher, Ellie, 9–10
Breland, Jeff, 337, 339, *351*

"Brighthaven" (Burgess), *148–149*
Brill, Betsy, vii, 336, 358
Brill, Daria, vii
Brink, Ben, 356–357
Brooks, Dudley M., *131*
Brooks Institute of Photography, 455
Brown, Cindy, 365, 446
Brown, Milbert, 7
Brown, Patrick, 207, 232, 245, *278–279*, 287
Brown, Paul, *26*, 33
Browne, Malcolm, 204, *448*
Brustein, Joshua, 286
Bryan-Brown, Marc, 384
Buckner, Jennie, 387
Budget meeting, picture editor role, 11–12
Buell, Hal, 136, 153, 378–379
Buffalo Inquirer and Courier, 422
Burgess, John, *iv*, vii, 90, 147, *148–149*, 180, 186, 232, 238, 266, *337*, 344, *380*
Burrows, Alex, 60
Burton, Tom, 76
Bush, George W., 49–50, 151, 268
Bush, Martin, 440
Byer, Renée, 233, 238, *294–297*, 304
Byrd, Joan, 376

C

Calvert, Mary, *56*, *146*, 213, 216, 233, 238, *250–251*, 260
Camera
auto-exposure, 156
autofocus, 158, 160
digital camera purchasing considerations, 167
historical perspective, 432–434
LCD monitor, 161–162
lenses, see Lenses
noise, 170
rain protection, 164
RAW files and exposure advantage, 158–159
sensor contamination, 170
shutter speed, 160–161
video, see Video camera
Camera 5 (agency), 358
Camera at War, The (Lewinski)
Canadian Association of Journalists, 71
Canadian Illustrated News, 419
Candid shots
approaches
big game hunter, 23–24
click and run, 23
introduce yourself, 24
out in the open, 22–23
features discovery, 71–72, 74
technical strategies, 21–22
Canton Repository, 188, *190*
Capa, Cornell, 443
Capa, Robert, 20, 440–443
Capitol, shooting restriction guidelines, 394–395
Captions
clarity, 150–151
picture meaning, 147, 150
sports photos, 100–101
what, who, when, where, why, and how, 151–153
writing styles, 153
Carlebach, Michael, 429
Carter, David, 311
Cartier-Bresson, Henri, 20, 23, 71–72, 74, 93, 95, 164, 408, 440–*443*
Cater, Karen, 153
Cavallo, Robert, 406
Cedar Rapids Gazette, 138
Censored War, The (Roeder), 446
Ceppos, Jerry, 380
Ceriani, Ernest, 231
Chambers, Bruce, 6, 9, *17*, 19, 28, 44, 77
Chandler vs Florida, 396
Chanute Tribune, 152
Chapelle, Dickey, 434

Chapman, Gerald, 429
Chapnick, Howard, 150, 363
Charlotte Observer, 387–388
Chernoff, George, 393
ChevronTexaco, 205
Chicago Daily News, 420, 453
Chicago Herald-Examiner, 431
Chicago Tribune, 6–7, 15, *51*, *57*, 105, *286*, 428, 431
Child labor law, historical perspective, 424–425
Children
features, 69–70
shooting restriction guidelines, 407
Chinn, Paul, *153*
Choi, Hyunju, 439–440
Christian Science Monitor, 13, 67, *204*, 266
Chwast, Seymour, 342
CIRT, see Critical Incident Response Team
Clark, Jason, *133*
Clark, Shirley, 230
Clarkson, Rich, 382
Click, 231, 438
Click, J.W., 137
Click-and-run, candid shots, 23
"Cloistered for Christ," 293
Close-up shot
dramatics, 16–17
portraits, 87
Closing shot, video, 323, 326–327
CNN, 6
Cocaine True, Cocaine Blue, 18
Cohen, Robert, 22, 23, 43, 61–62, *69*, *234*, 244
Cole Carolyn, 400
Collier's Weekly, 421–422, 436
Collier, Robert J., 421
Collins, Bill, 53
Color balance
Digital still camera, 173–177
Digital video camera, 317
Photoshop, 470–471
Coloradoan, *15*, *163*, *171*
Color
consistency, 175–177
language, 170
photo editing, 137, 139
time of day considerations, 170, 172–173, 175
video consistency, 317
Colton, James, vii, 123, 333
Columbia Journalism Review, 128, 356, 365
Columbia Missourian, 337, 378
Columbus Ledger-Enquirer, 62, 67
Condor Monitor, 456
Converse, Gordon, 67
Comedians, The, 83
Composograph, historical perspective, 382–383, 428–429
Compression, image files, 169–170
Condenser microphone, 272
Confidentiality, agreement by photographer, 409–410
Connelly, Sean, vii, 304
Contact Press Images, 215, *372*, 457
Contests, 465
Continuous shooting mode, sports, 106
Contra Costa Times, 5
Contrast
features, 79, 88
photo size in layout, 145
Converse, Gordon, 67
Cooke, Janet, 360, 363
Cookman, Claude, 20, 442, 450
Cooley, John, 111
Coppola, Dean, 5, 6
Copyright
employers, 411
freelancers, 411–412, 465–467
registration, 412–413
respect, 413
Corbis, 128, 453, 457

Coronado, Gary, 204, 206, 232, 233, 260, 287, 302–305
Cosmopolitan, 385, 436
Costa, Denise, 375
Costa, Joe, 444, 450
Costanza, Sam, 4–6, 28, *31–32*, 46
Cotter, Holland, 430
Counts, Tim, 150
Courtroom, shooting restriction guidelines, 395–397
Cowles, Gardner, 438
"Crack: The Next Generation" (Kobré), *216–217*
Craft, Andrew, 24, *305*
Crane, Stephen, 421
Cranford, Bill, 398
Crawford, Colin, vii, 386
Crime scene, perimeters, 30, 32
Critical Incident Response Team (CIRT), 46
Cropping
 photo editing, 138–142
 Photoshop, 480
Crowe, Pat, *359*
"Crude Reflections" (Dematteis), *205*
Curves, Photoshop, 469, 471–472

D
D'Addario, Vincent S., *95*
Daily Graphic, The, 415–420, 453
Daily Mirror, 430
Daily News (Hays, Kansas), 67
Daily News (New York) *45*, *135*, 427–428, 430, 444
Daily Press Times Herald, 368
Daily Times Democrat, 407
Dalglish, Lucy A., 401
Dallas Morning News, The, 82, 90, 293, 308, 310–312, 318, 332, 372
Damaske, Jim, *396*
D'Anna, Melanie Rook, *345*
Dart Center for Journalism & Trauma, 46–47
Davies, Ben, 278
Davis, Richard Allen, 380
Day in the Life of America, 385
Dead bodies, photo ethics, 375–376, 378
de Beauvoir, Simone, 95
Decisive Moment, The (Cartier-Bresson), 20, 442
"Delta Time" (Light), *230*
Delta Time (Light), *230*, 266
Dematteis, Lou, *205–206*, 232, 260
Depth of field, video camera challenges, 315–316
Des Moines Register and Tribune, 445
Detrich, Allan, *387*
Detroit Free Press, 375–376, 381
Detroit News, 101, 102, 109, 111, 116, 118, 121, 122, 160, 170, 176
DeVigal, Andrew, 145
Diana, Princess of Wales, 362
Diaz, Alan, *176*
Diaz, John, 380
Die Hamburger Woche, 426
Dietemann, Antone, 402
Digital Sports Photography (Lowrance), 110, 116, 121
DigitalJournalist.org, 271, 300, 310, 320, 365
digitalrailroad.net, 128, 464
Dissolve, video, 332
Documentary
 highlights of topic, 266–267
 issues, 266
 lifestyles, 266
 overview, 261, 266
 places, 266
 video editing, 333
"Dog's Life, A" (Stocker), *246–247*
Dolly in, video, 321
Dolly out, video, 321
Dominis, John, 150, 238
Donaldson, Nancy, 270, 304–305
Dotson, Bob, 281
Douliery, Oliver, *48–50*, *60*, *146*, *268*
Dowd, Shawn, 356
Draut, Joel, 156–*157*

Drew, Richard, *352*, 353, 373
Duke, William, *341*, *342*, *343*, 344, *347*
Dumke, Bob, 445
Duncan, David Douglas, 164, 371
Duran, Doug, 113
Durniak, John, 129
Dynamic microphone, 272

E
Ebony, 438
Economopoulos, Aristide, *71*, *100*
Eddins, J.M., Jr., *68*
Edelstein's Newsletter, 99
Edey, Maitland, 233
Edgerton, Harold, 431–432
Editing, see Photo editing; Photo editor
Editor and Publisher, 429
Editorial essay, 261
Editorial Photographers, 464, 467
Edom, Clifton, 130, 450–451
Edwards, Greg, 145
Eisenstaedt, Alfred, 82, 92, 438, 449
Eisner, Bill, *376*
El Pais, 140
Elbert, Joe, 130, 132–133
Elins, Michael, 384
Ellard, Roscoe, 130
Embarrassing photos, shooting restriction guidelines, 406–407
Entertainment Weekly, 95
eonline.com, 384
Equipment, see also specific equipment
 fires, 40–41
 political issue framing, 56–57
 sports shooting lenses, 104–105, 109–110, 112, 117–118
 spot news
  day, 28
  night, 28
  strobe, see Strobe
 tripod versus monopod, 167
Erickson, Pete, *104*
Ermanox, historical perspective, 434
Erwitt, Elliott, *21*
Erwitt, Ellen, vii
Esquire, 235, 293, *336*, 337, 342, 385
Establishing shot, video, 323, 326
Ethics
 alteration of photos
  examples, 386–388
  historical perspective, 382–383
  magazine editors, 384
  newspaper editors, 383–384
  prospects, 389
  standards for daily journalism versus magazine journalism, 384
 changing standards, 356–357, 363, 365
 continuum of photographer control, 359
 dead bodies, 375–376, 378
 editorial self-censorship, 371–373
 fair and balanced reporting, 380–382
 frameworks
  Absolutist, 354
  Golden Rule, 354, 356
  Utilitarian, 354
 funeral coverage, 366–367
 geographic distance considerations, 375
 Good Samaritan conflict, 368
 gruesome photos, 369–371, 374–375
 National Press Photographers Association
  Code of Ethics, 357
  Digital Code of Ethics, 389
 paparazzi versus photojournalists, 362
 photo illustrations, 351, 359
 photo impact considerations, 373–376, 378
 policy impact of photos, 378
 reader concerns, 385–386
 reality versus photos, 388

roles and responsibilities, 357
 scandals, 356–358, 360, 386–388
 shocking picture warning signs, 375
 suicide coverage, 368–369
 taste considerations
  nudity, 378–380
  obscene gestures, 380
  tragedy coverage, 363, 365–368
  war photos, 371–372
Evans, Christine, 206, 286
Evans, Walker, 206, 439
Evening Graphic, 428–429
"Every Day is Father's Day" (Andrews), 132
"Eyes on the News," 145
Examiner (San Francisco), 72, 74, 142
Experts, story element, 313
Exposure
 auto-exposure, 156
 RAW files and advantages, 158–159
 video, 316–317
Eye-Trac Research Systems, 125, 135–136, 142–144
Eyes of Time (Fulton), 431

F
Faber, John, 356, 367, 431, 433
"Face to Face with Breast Cancer" (Wells), 240–243
Falling Practice: What Illness Teaches Us, 206, 219
Farber, Edward, 414–415, 432, 445
Farkas, Ray, 328
Farley, Bob, *359*
Farm Security Administration (FSA), 90, 129, 203, 206, 222, 266, 439–440
Fast Forward (Greenfield), 457
Fayetteville Observer, The, 24, 305
Features
 beat development, 212–213, 215, 218
 discovery, 70–72, 74–76, 78–79
 news comparison, 67–68
 photo-driven column, 76, 78
 research for informative features, 218
 sports, 101–102
 subjects, 68–70
 universal emotions, 68
Fedler, Fred, 150
Feininger, Andreas, 439
Feinstein, Anthony, 46
Feldman, Rhoda, vii
Fellenbaum, Charlie, *359*
Fellig, Arthur, 429–431
Ferazzi, Gina, *275*, 287
Ferrier, Patricia, 375
Ferro, Ricardo, 374
Fifty Crows Foundation, 206
Fill-flash, 187–188
Filo, John, 448
Final Cut Pro, editing, 330–331
Fine, Steve, vii, 333
"Fire! Photojournalist" (DVD), 177
Fires
 economic angle, 39
 escape route, 38
 fact collection, 39–40
 feature photos, 39
 finding, 34, 38
 night fire shooting, 40–41
 overall shot, 38
 rationale for photography, 34
 safety, 38
Fischer, Carl, 336–337, 342
Fishburne, Laurence, 85, 91
Fisher, Ian, 286
Fishman, Jessica, 375
Fitzmaurice, Deanne, 160, 233, 238, 262–265
Flamiano, Dolores, 438
Flanner, Janet, 20
Flash, 438
Flash, see Strobe

Flash bulb, 431
Flash lamps
 Caywood, 431
 Imp, 431
 Victor, 431
Flash powder, 424, 431
Fletcher, Cindy, 397–399
Florida Publishing Co. vs Fletcher, 399
Focus, 460
Food Lion vs Capital Cities-ABC, 404
Football, see Sports
Forman, Stanley, *32*, *36–37*, 44, 233, 248, 249, 376–378
Forscher, Marty, 164
Fort Collins Coloradoan, 15
Fort Lauderdale Sun-Sentinel, 340, 344
Fort Morgan Times, 38
Fort Wayne News-Sentinel, 3
Fort Worth Star-Telegram, 29
Fortune, 347, 437, 456
4Sight, 9
Forst, Liz, vii
Fox, Travis, vii, 308, *309*, 310, *312*, 314–316, 318, 326–327, 328
Foy, Mary Lou, 366
Framing
 candid shots, 21
 photo editing, 138
Franklin, Jon, 245
Freedom Forum, 206
Freelancing
 agencies, 457
 breaking-news picture selling, 464
 contract photography, 457, 460
 copyright ownership, 411–412, 465–467
 fees plus expenses, 464–465
 fixed costs, 467
 Internet marketing, 464
 magazines, 462, 464
 portfolio guidelines, 456, 462–463
 profit, 467
 rates, 464
 tips, 456–457, 460
 work for hire, 411, 464, 467, 468
Freeman, Melanie Stetson, *204*, 266
Frezzolini, James, 433
Friedmann, André, see Capa, Robert
Frier, Scott, vii
Frontlines, 14
Fudge, Joe, 368
Fulton, Marianne, 300, 431, 449
Funeral, coverage, 366–367
Furstenau Bob, 384
Fusco, Paul

G
Galassi, Peter, 419
Galbraith, Rob, 106, 168–170
Galella, Ron, *403*
Gallup Applied Science Partnership, 136, 140, 142
Gallup, George, 438
Gandhi M., 441–442
Gannett, Frank, 445
Gaps, John, III, 34
Garcia, Mario, 137, 145
Gardner, Susan, *340*, 344
Garnier, Jesse, vii, 273, 280, 292
Garvin, Robert, 78
Gavreau, Emile, 428
Gear, see Equipment
Gehrz, Jim, 363
"Generations Under the Influence" (Plonka), *208–211*
Geo, 365, 460
Gerbich, Kim, 216
Get the Picture (Morris), 441
Getty Images, 128, 206, 457
Gilbert, Bruce, vii
Gilka, Bob, 434
Gilpin, John, *139*
Gilroy Dispatch, *70*, 392
Girl Culture (Greenfield), 457, 461
Give Us a Little Smile, Baby (Coleman), 427

Glaser, Marilyn, *346*
Glass, Ira, 274, 280
"Glimpsing the Goths" (Hsu), *252–253*
Glinn, Burt, 443
Goebel, Rob, 87–*88*
Goldberg, Vicki, 204, 434
Golden Rule, ethical framework, 354, 356
Goldsmith, Arthur, 78
Golon, Mary Ann, 128
Good Samaritan, ethics, 368
Goodall, Jane, *278*
Goodwin, Gene, 368
Gordon, Jim, 360
Goro, Fritz, 439
Gosen, Joseph, 385
Government buildings, shooting restriction guidelines
    courtroom, 395–397
    legislative buildings, 394–395
    military bases, 394
    overview, 394
    prisons, 394
    tribal lands, 395
Grace, Arthur, 83
Graflex, historical perspective, 421, 432, 433
Gralish, Tom, *8*, 76, *162*, 233, 244
Gravenor, Kristian, 408
Great News Photos (Faber), 367
Great Picture Hunt 2, The (LaBelle), 70
Green River Community College, 271
Green, Walter, 18
Greenfield, Lauren, 457, *461*
Greensboro News & Record, 335, *348*, 349
Greenwald, Marilyn, 133
Greer, Jennifer, 385
Griesedieck, Judy, *207*, 212, 232
Griffiths, Philip Jones, 443
Grigsby, Bryan, 62
Grogin, Harry, 382, 428–429
Grossfeld, Stan, 206
Grosvenor, Gilbert, 425
Grow, Jason, 457
Group portraits, 94–95
Gruber, Jack, *154*, 166
Gruesome photos, ethics, 369–371, 374–375
Grundberg, Andy, 386
Guerrero, Pablo Torres, 140
Guigou, Elisabeth, 408
Guimond, James, 439
Guggenheim, 206
"Gun Nation" (Nelson), *226–227*
Guralnick, David, vii, 111, 116, 118, 121, 160, 170, 176, 206
Guzy, Carol, 14, 137, 204, *224–225*, 232, *494*

H

Haas, Ernst, 19–20, 442
Habas, Paula, 385
Haberman, Lia, 384
Habib, Dan, 456
"Haitian Street Justice," (Guzy), *224–225*
Hajj, Adnan, 386
Haley, Peter, 334
Halftone screen, historical perspective, 418–419
Hall, Kari René, 228, 231, 233, 235, 248–249, *254–259*, 260
Halsman on the Creation of Photographic Ideas (Halsman), 341
Halsman, Philippe, 341, 439
Halstead, Dirck, 271, 309, 320
Hare, Jimmy, 420–422
Harper's Weekly, 419, 436, 451
Harte, John, 354, *355*, 376
Hartford Courant, 13, *141*, 386
Hartley, Craig, *40*, 363, 367, 374, 379
Hauptmann, Bruno Richard, 395–396
Hayes, Woody, 118
Haynes, Frank J., 436
Haynes, Gary, 451, 453

Hayt, Andy, 121
Headphones, 273, 320
Hearst, William Randolph, 435
Heckel, Scott, 188, *190*
Heiferman, Marvin, 429
Heisler, Todd, *58–59*, 206, 232, 233
Heller, Steven, 342
Hemet News, 359
Hendricks, Robert, 337, *339*
Heppner, Diane, vii
Heralnd-Examiner (Los Angeles), *153*
Herald News (Joliet, Illinois), *172*, *239*
Herbrich, Sibylla, 83, *214*, 218, 233
Hernandez, John, *182–183*
Hernandez, Richard Koci, 82, 84, 91, 156–*157*
Hertzberg, Mark, 67, 363
Hewitt, John, vii, 320, 328, 330
Hicks, Wilson, 129, 146, 436
Hidden camera, privacy, 404
High-angle shot, perspective, 17–18
Hightower, Paul, 150
Hine, Lewis, 203, 422, *423–426*, 439
History, story element, 313
Hobby, David, 192
Holandez, Juanito, *359*
Horgan, Stephen H., 419–420
"Hostage Hero" (MacMillan), *30*
Hostage situation, case study, 29–30
Houston Chronicle, 82, 99, 100
Houston Post, 40, 156–157
Houston, Luci S., 75–76
How the Other Half Lives (Riis), 424
Howard, Caroline, 128
Howard, Thomas, *427*, 428
Howe, Peter, 25, 128, 371, 457
Hoyer, Andrea, 206, 465
Hsu, Warren, 232, 235, 244, *252–253*
Huang, Edgar, 384
Hughes, Jim, 444
Huh, Hyun-Joo Lee, 142–143
Hulteng, John L., 365
Hungry Planet: What the World Eats (Menzel), 192
Huntsville Times (Alabama), 76
Hussein, Saddam, 374

Iacono, John, 110
Illustrated American, 421
Illustrated London News, 436
Illustrations, see Photo illustrations
iMovie, the Missing Manual (Pogue), 322
Incongruity, features, 69–70
Independence Examiner, 72, 117
Indiana University, 81
Indianapolis Star, 88
Ingersoll, Ralph, 437, 446
Inland Valley Daily Bulletin, 33
Inside *Sports Illustrated* (DVD), vii, 11, 123, 286, 328, 329, 333
International assignment, 12–14
International News Photos (INP), 432, 445, 451–453
International Society for Traumatic Stress Studies, 46
Internet
    journalism, vii, 269, 270, 231, 309
    marketing for freelancers, 464
    photo editing considerations, 145–146
Internship
    contacts, 457
    example, 458
    résumé and cover letter, 458
    timing, 458
Interview
    audio recording, 270–274, 276
    field interviews, 274
    microphone placement, 274, 276
    model radio interviews,
        National Public Radio (NPR)
            "All Things Considered," 281
            "This American Life," 274, 280, 281

natural sound, 281, 286, 313, 314
place, 274
questions
    follow-up questions, 280
    open-ended questions, 280
    pairing, 280
    pauses, 281
    repeating by subject, 280–281
shooting while recording audio, 281, 286
storytelling with audio, 286–287, 292
timing, 271, 274
video camera manual focus, 315
Irby, Kenny, 140, 374, 386, 388
Ives, Herbert, 452

J

Jacobson, Colin, 371
Jails, see Prisons
James, Don, 369
James, Ken, *72*, *73*, 74, *142-143*
Jarecke, Kenneth, 371–372
Jarvis, Jeff, 371
Jasper Herald, *100*
Jimenez Martin, 79
Jobard, Olivier, 207, 215, 233, 235, *282–285*, 287
Johnston, Frances Benjamin, 422
Johnson, Kim, *4*
Johnson, Mark, 67
Jorgensen, Karen, 219
Journal Times, 67
Journalism Quarterly, 78, 136, 142, 365
Journey to Nowhere: The Saga of the New Underclass (Maharidge and Williamson), 206
Junco, Victor, 150
Jung, Carl, 342

K

Kackovic, Michele, vii
Kahan, Stuart, 406
Kalish, Stanley, 130
Kamber, Michael, 233, 249, 287, *288-291*
Kansas City Times, 54
Kao, Anne Li-An, 134, 136
Kaplan, John, *134*, *189*, 206, 220–221, 233, 266, 455–456
Kapustin, Doug, 71, *126*
"Karen and Karen: Life, Love, and Loss" (Lubin), *219*
Kastner, Joseph, 153
Kauffman, Mark, 106
Keating, Edward, 356
Kelly, James, 385
Kennedy, Robert, 364, 367
Kennedy, Tom, vii
Kennerly, David Hume, 52–53
Kenney, James, 373
Kenney, Keith R., 426
Kerrick, Jean, 147
Kertesz, André, 244
Kettering, Dave, 87
KGO-TV, 322
Khalaf, Saleh, 262–265
King, Martin Luther, 368
King, Rodney, 34, 178
"Kingsley's Crossing" (Jobard), *284–285*
Kismaric, Carole, 428
Kismaric, Susan, 419
Klibankoff, Hank, 368
Knife and Gun Club, The, 18
Knowlton, John, vii, 271
Knox, Frank, 453
Kobré, Ken, 14, 44, *66*, 67, *70*, *87*, *128*, *144*, *173*, *175*, 178, *189*, *191*–192, 194, *196*, *216–217*, 232, *307*, 308, *317*, *320–321*, *324*, *326*, *328–329*, 330, *331*, *332*
Kobre, Sidney, iii, vii, 212, 446
Kobre, Reva, iii, vii
Kochersberger, Robert, 369
Kodas, Michael, 13
Koelzer, Jay, 336, *338*, 339, *340*, 343–344

Komenich, Kim, vii, 12, 307–*308*, 312, 314, 316–318, 320, 322, 328
Korean War, photo censorship, 447
Korff, Kurt, 437
Korn, Alfred, 452
Kosak, Hermann, 143
KPIX, 322
KQED vs Houchins, 394
Krages, Bert, 399
Kreiter, Susan, 76
KRON-TV, 309, 310

L

LaBelle, Dave, 70, 75–76, 366
LaClair, Scott, 362
Lambert, Ken, *379*
Lang, Angela, 78
Lang, Daryl, 386
Lang, George, 322
Lange, Dorothea, 203, 439–440
Larocque, Paula, 153
Larsen, Don, 114
Larsen, Kaia, 129
Larsen, Roy, 438
Larson, Frederic, *11*–12
Lassiter, Dan, *38*
Lasso tool, Photoshop, 474–475
Last Great American Hobo, The (Maharidge and Williamson), 206
Laszlo, Larry, vii
Lavalier microphone, 273
Lavrakas, Jim, *127*
Layering, images, 18
Layers, Photoshop, 475–477
LCD monitor, digital camera, 161–162
"Leap for Life" (Forman), *36–37*
Lederhandler, Marty, *41*
Leeson, David, vii, 82, 90, 293, 308, 310, *311*, 312, 318, 332, 372
Legal Handbook for Photographers (Krages), 399
Leggo, William, 419
Legislative buildings, shooting restriction guidelines, 394–395
Leibovitz, Annie, 93–*94*, 235, 337, 344
Leica, historical perspective, 434, 445
Leitz, 434
Lenses
    packing, 165
    sports shooting lenses, 104–105, 109–110, 112, 117–118
    zoom lens versatility, 162–163
Leslie's Weekly, 419
Leslie's Illustrated Newspaper, 436
Lessons in Life and Death (LaBelle), 366
Lester, Paul, 133, 375
Let Us Now Praise Famous Men (Agee and Evans), 206
Lewenstein, Marion, 145, 238
Lewinski, Jorje, 447
Levy, Tom, 501
Libel, 406, 408–409
Library Journal, 449
Liddy, Chuck, 388
Life, 14, 25, 82, 106, 128–129, 133, 153, 204, 231, 233, 238, 341, 244, 356, 360, 368, 371, 371, 402, 431, 437–444, 446, 448, 457
    historical perspective, 437–438
"Lifeline The" (Loomis), *298–301*
Light, Ken, 206, *230*, 232, 266
Lighting
    flash combining with available light, 181–185
    sports shooting, 106, 112
    storytelling element in portraits, 84, 87
    strobe, see Strobe
    time of day considerations, 170, 172–173, 175
Lightscoop, 192, 194
L'Illustration, 452
Lim, Stan, *33*
Lindbergh, Charles, 395
Linsenmayer, Steve, *2-4*
Liotta, Louie, 431

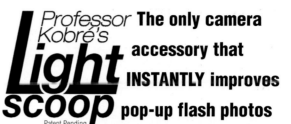
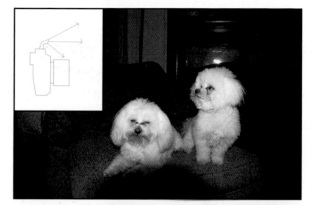
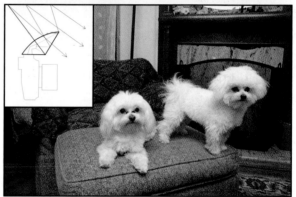

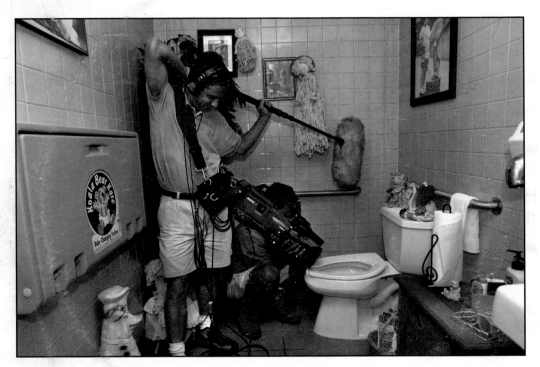

A television news crew goes right to the source—a public restroon rated by travelers as one of the cleanest in the area.
P. Kevin Morley, *Richmond Times-Dispatch*